W9-ACG-960

XERXES'
INVASION OF GREECE

DF225
H5

JUN 15 1972

163415

XERXES' INVASION OF GREECE

BY

C. HIGNETT

FORMERLY FELLOW OF
HERTFORD COLLEGE
OXFORD

OXFORD
AT THE CLARENDON PRESS
1963

Oxford University Press, Amen House, London E.C.4

GLASGOW NEW YORK TORONTO MELBOURNE WELLINGTON
BOMBAY CALCUTTA MADRAS KARACHI LAHORE DACCA
CAPE TOWN SALISBURY NAIROBI IBADAN ACCRA
KUALA LUMPUR HONG KONG

© *Oxford University Press 1963*

PRINTED IN GREAT BRITAIN
AT THE UNIVERSITY PRESS, OXFORD
BY VIVIAN RIDLER
PRINTER TO THE UNIVERSITY

PREFACE

THE origins of this book go back to the autumn of 1919, when as an undergraduate in my seventh term at Oxford I attended a course of lectures given by Mr. Norman Whatley, then Fellow and Lecturer of Hertford College. From him I learnt that the reconstructions of the Graeco-Persian War proposed by J. A. R. Munro and my own tutor G. B. Grundy, reconstructions which had been largely followed by R. W. Macan and had received a quasi-official sanction in the standard commentary by How and Wells, were open to damaging criticism. About the time of my return to Oxford as Mr. Whatley's successor at Hertford College in the spring of 1924, Kromayer published the first part of the fourth volume of his *Antike Schlachtfelder* (supplemented in a later part of the volume by the additions on pages 581–3); in this work I found further objections to the theories about the war of 480–479 still prevalent in Oxford, and also a close approximation to the views which I had already accepted from Mr. Whatley. I therefore decided to deliver a course of lectures on 'Herodotus and the Persian Wars' in the autumn of 1925, and as it proved popular I repeated the course in the autumn of every year (except 1938 and 1947) until my retirement in 1959. Although my views changed on points of detail, I never found in the numerous works that I read on the subject during that period any reason to question the truth of the fundamental principles laid down by Whatley and Kromayer, principles which I have fully discussed in Part I of this book.

There had always been some scholars, even in the late nineteenth century, who reacted vigorously against the excesses of the sceptics. Among them an honourable place must be given to Amédée Hauvette, who devoted the first part of his *Hérodote* to a thorough examination of all the ancient sources and rightly concluded that, except on points of detail, no author who wrote later than the end of the fifth century B.C. could safely be used to supplement (much less to correct) the narrative of Xerxes' invasion contained in the pages of Herodotus'

last three books. This truth is often forgotten or even flatly
denied, and in the past few years there has been an alarming
revival of attempts to extract valuable information from the so-
called 'secondary sources'. That must be my justification for
producing yet another history of the Graeco-Persian War,
although I can make no claim to be regarded as a military
historian in the narrower sense. Perhaps after all this is not
a serious disqualification; it is arguable that Herodotus has
suffered undeservedly from the criticisms of professional
military historians such as Delbrück, who were more concerned
to show how Greeks and Persians ought to have fought than to
discover how they actually did fight. My main concern has
been to establish, as far as it is possible to do so, what actually
happened in 480 and 479 B.C., and I believe that an indispensable means to that end is to re-examine the ancient sources.

In his published lecture, cited in the Bibliography at the end
of this book, Mr. Whatley has given brief but clear expression
to an important problem. He says: 'of course his [Herodotus']
account of Marathon contains, as accounts in Herodotus always
contain, absurdities, incongruities, and supernatural inter-
ruptions of human affairs. But it is the only account of Marathon which is worth anything at all.' These words call attention to the second and more difficult task which confronts the
modern historian of Xerxes' invasion. Having established the
pre-eminence of Herodotus' *History* over all the later sources, he
must then endeavour to separate the gold in Herodotus' narrative from the dross. It is in this respect that historians diverge
most from one another. Hauvette went too far in his anxiety to
defend the historical accuracy of Herodotus against all criticism,
while Delbrück and Munro fell into the opposite error in their
rejection of everything in Herodotus that could not be reconciled with their over-bold reconstructions. I believe that there
is a safe way between these two extremes, although it is not
always easy to find it. Some of my Oxford friends argue that it is
impossible to reconstruct the course of any campaign in the
ancient world unless it has been narrated by an ancient writer
still extant who was himself a military historian, such as a
Thucydides, a Hieronymus, a Polybius, a Caesar, but such
scepticism seems to me to be unjustifiable and to imply an excessive depreciation of Herodotus' qualifications as an historian.

Although in the sphere of military history he cannot compare with Thucydides, he has preserved enough of the authentic oral tradition of the Persian War to make possible a credible reconstruction of its campaigns.

Having criticized some of my predecessors, I admit with gratitude that I have learnt valuable lessons from all of them. Delbrück was fully justified in calling attention to the impossibilities of fact contained in Herodotus, notably in the estimates of numbers, even if his use of *Sachkritik* was often reckless. Grundy rendered an inestimable service to students by his thorough researches into the topography of Plataia and Thermopylai; in this and in other respects his book, *The Great Persian War*, remains an outstanding achievement of English scholarship. Munro in his numerous writings on the Persian Wars was often led astray by his own ingenuity, but he was too good an historian to put any trust in the secondary sources, his searching criticisms of Herodotus, if sometimes perverse, brought to light many real difficulties, and the clarity and brilliance of his style make everything that he wrote a pleasure to read. Macan in his great edition utilized the labours of his predecessors but added much of his own; I cannot do better than quote J. E. Powell's verdict (*The History of Herodotus*, p. 80, n. 2) that 'excepting van Herwerden no other editor has faced the textual and historical difficulties of Herodotus with so much courage and candour'.

To Kromayer I have already acknowledged my debt, but on the whole the first part of his fourth volume, in spite of its undoubted merits, is disappointing, partly because Kromayer left most of the work to collaborators of unequal capacity, did not deal at all in it with the fighting at Artemision, and gave a very perfunctory account of the campaign of Mykale; his treatment of Mykale, with no reference to its remoter antecedents, shows clearly how impossible it is to get a comprehensive idea of an ancient war from isolated discussions of the engagements that occurred in its course. I have tried in my footnotes to acknowledge my great obligations to more recent writers, but I must here emphasize my special indebtedness to the papers published during the past few years by Mr. Pritchett in *The American Journal of Archaeology*, in which he has done much to clarify the topography of the Persian Wars (I regret that I have been unsuccessful in my endeavours to obtain a copy of his monograph on *Marathon*, but a fairly detailed account of its contents has been given by Mr. Hammond in *C.R.* lxxv, 1961, 262–3). Topography is however only valuable as providing additional confirmation of Herodotus' narrative and cannot be safely used to contradict it on any important point.

Among my obligations to my precursors I must also mention the eight maps included in this volume. I hope that the professional historian will judge them leniently; they have been put in not for him but for 'the general reader' (including the lazy undergraduate) and under very strong pressure from my friends. As I am not a skilled cartographer I have had to make use of the labours of others in the preparation of these maps. The maps of the pass of Thermopylai and the battlefield of Plataia, like most of those published since 1901, are based on Grundy's personal surveys embodied in the two relevant maps in his book, *The Great Persian War*, and those of Northern and Central Greece, in their general plan and in the prominence given to communications, follow closely the maps opposite pages 189 and 412 in the second volume of Macan's commentary on the last three books of Herodotus. I gratefully acknowledge my indebtedness to the publishers concerned for their generous permission to make use of these maps in the preparation of this book, to the firm of John Murray for the first two, and to Macmillan & Co. for the last two, and also to the Clarendon Press for leave to base my maps of Salamis on that opposite page 249 in the second volume of the commentary on Herodotus by How and Wells. I have throughout borrowed details from other maps, notably Grundy's maps of Greece in the series of *Handy Classical Maps* (John Murray) and those contained in the first part of the fourth volume of the *Schlachten-Atlas* by Kromayer and Veith, published by Wagner & Debes (Leipzig, 1926); both publications should be consulted by all students who have more than a superficial interest in topographical questions.

I take this opportunity to put on record my grateful thanks to those who have helped me in various ways while I have been working on this book. I have already recalled what I owe to Mr. Whatley's teaching; to his personal friendship I am further obliged for the gift in 1927 of a copy of his unpublished paper, *On the possibility of reconstructing Marathon and other ancient battles* (read to the Oxford Philological Society in 1920), which has been constantly in my hands ever since, and for a recent loan of the volume containing his printed lecture on *Marathon* (delivered to the Hellenic Travellers' Club in 1929). During the time that has elapsed since my retirement from Oxford I have enjoyed the pleasure of working in the excellent library of the University College of North Wales, Bangor, thanks to the kindness of the Librarian, Mr. E. Gwynne Jones. Throughout the same period I have been greatly helped by the unfailing assistance of Mr. G. L. Cawkwell, Fellow of University College, Oxford, who has spared no trouble in verifying obscure references on my behalf. Mr. J. P. V. D. Balsdon, Fellow of Exeter College, Oxford, who read the proofs of my first book, has performed the same arduous service for this one, and has again detected many errors and obscurities; as I have not always agreed with his criticisms I must accept full responsibility for any blemishes that may still be found.

Finally, I consider myself fortunate in the fact that this book, like its predecessor, has had the advantage of being published by the Oxford University Press, and it is my pleasant duty to express here my thanks to the Delegates of the Press for undertaking the publication of the work and to all the members of the Press who have been concerned in any way with its appearance in print; in this connexion I must remark that my attitude to the last letter of the English alphabet remains unchanged, and that its frequent occurrence in the following pages reflects the practice of the Press, not my own.

C. HIGNETT

Penmaenmawr
June 1962

CONTENTS

LIST OF MAPS

SPECIAL ABBREVIATIONS

In addition to the current abbreviations I have made use of the following, mainly in the footnotes, to save space. For the same reason, when only one work by a particular author is listed in the Bibliography, it is cited by the name of its author; for example, 'Busolt, 708' refers to page 708 of the second volume of Busolt's *Griechische Geschichte*². Passages in Herodotus are for the most part cited without the author's name; the chapter and section numbers in these citations are those given in the Oxford text of Herodotus by Hude.

A.P.	= The *Athenaion Politeia* attributed to Aristotle.
A.S.	= Kromayer, *Antike Schlachtfelder* (vol. iv unless otherwise stated).
F.G.H.	= Jacoby, *Die Fragmente der griechischen Historiker*.
F.H.G.	= C. and T. Müller, *Fragmenta Historicorum Graecorum*.
Grundy	= Grundy, *The Great Persian War*.
HW	= How and Wells, *A Commentary on Herodotus*, vol. ii (unless explicitly cited as vol. i and except in references to notes on particular passages in Books I–IV of Herodotus).
HW²	= The second impression of the above (Oxford, 1928); passages so cited are mostly not to be found in the first edition.
KV	= Kromayer and Veith, *Heerwesen* (see Bibliography).
Legrand	= Legrand, *Hérodote, Histoires*, vii, viii, ix.
Macan	= Macan, *Herodotus vii–ix* (vol. ii unless otherwise cited).
Meyer	= Meyer, *Geschichte des Altertums*, iii (cited by the pages of the first edition, 1901).
Plut. *H.M.*	= Plutarch's essay *De Herodoti Malignitate*.
S.I.G.	= Dittenberger, *Sylloge Inscriptionum Graecorum* (unless otherwise stated, the reference is to the 3rd edition, Leipzig, 1915–24).
Stählin	= Stählin, article on 'Thermopylen' in *R.-E.* v A. 2.

PART I

PROLEGOMENA

PROLEGOMENA

Some modern postulates

HERODOTUS' narrative of the Persian Wars has frequently
been roughly handled by modern historians ever since
the writers of antiquity (including those preserved in the
Jewish scriptures) began to be subjected to the new type of criticism which developed in the course of the nineteenth century A.D.
This criticism was legitimate in itself and sprang from a more
intelligent appreciation of the ancient classics than the unques-
tioning admiration of earlier scholars, but it was carried by the
more sceptical of its exponents to extravagant lengths. Reconstruction of ancient wars and battles had a special attraction for
the more extreme critics, partly perhaps because military history is a subject in which many believe themselves to be experts,
partly also because the military history of the ancient world offers
a wide field for modern conjectures. In this process the ancient
historians received little mercy; the critics attacked not only such
writers as Herodotus and Tacitus (condemned by Mommsen[1] as
'this most unmilitary of all authors') but also those with practical experience of warfare and unrivalled opportunities for discovering the truth about the events which they described, for
example Thucydides. Even Caesar's vivid record of the campaigns
conducted by himself in person or by his generals did not escape
censure.

It is essential to disentangle the presuppositions on which the
sceptical critic bases his reconstructions of military operations in
the ancient world; these presuppositions are seldom expressed in
a definite form, but arguments are used which take their validity
for granted and have no cogency if the presuppositions are un-
sound. The most important of these postulates is that the ancient
writer who is the primary authority for a particular war or battle
is not to be trusted. Various reasons may be alleged to justify this
verdict; the author in question may be regarded as unworthy
of credit because he lacked understanding of or interest in military affairs, because (when not personally present at the events

---

[1] *Provinces of the Roman Empire* (E.T.[2]), i. 181, n. 1.

described by him) he misunderstood or was misled by the reports received from his informants, or because, though in full possession of the facts, he chose to falsify them for his own purposes.[1] Herodotus has been attacked on all these grounds, but principally for his supposed ignorance of ancient warfare.

Gomme, criticizing a modern reconstruction of the Persian Wars, pointed out[2] that the author's method 'consists in postulating (as is correct) that Herodotus knew little of military (as of constitutional) matters, rejecting anything in his narrative that seems "unlikely", and substituting much that is different and often the contrary of what he tells us'. He objected to this procedure on the ground that a critic who rejected the Herodotean narrative could have practically no other ancient evidence and would therefore be trying to make bricks without straw. Some sceptics have evaded this dilemma by the hypothesis that the truth is preserved in later writers, whose accounts they prefer to that of the primary source, but others remain undaunted by the results of their speculations, and after destroying the available ancient evidence settle down happily amid the ruins to write what can only be called historical fiction. This technique has indeed infinite possibilities. When Woodhouse claimed to have demonstrated that the battle of First Mantineia was won, in spite of what Thucydides had said, by the tactical genius of the Spartan king Agis, Gomme showed that by the same method the Athenian general Nikostratos could be proved to have been the real master mind of the campaign.[3]

The second postulate is that generals never made mistakes, and that any movements of fleets or armies recorded by an ancient writer which seem at first sight irrational must be explicable in terms of a coherent strategy. This postulate is so obviously false that it is never stated nakedly, but it none the less forms the major premiss in many arguments adduced by modern writers, with the result that their reconstructions are too logical to be convincing.

---

[1] This last is the ground on which the credibility of Caesar's historical works has been attacked; for a refutation of his critics cf. Rice Holmes, *Caesar's Conquest of Gaul*[2], 211–56.

[2] *C.R.* xli, 1927, 65.

[3] Gomme, *Essays*, c. 8. On p. 155 he notes 'a curious similarity in some details between the battles of Mantineia and Plataia', and holds that Woodhouse's reconstructions of both campaigns are vitiated by the erroneous assumption that 'the accounts of both Herodotus and Thucydides are deeply tinged by Athenian malice'.

When Munro in the fourth volume of the *Cambridge Ancient History* published his last thoughts on the history of the Persian Wars, this was the point singled out by one of the reviewers,[1] who observed that Munro's version was 'perhaps a little too perfect', that 'all concerned on both sides acted with consistent foresight', and that 'no mistakes were made'; the reviewer added that 'somehow, like Sherlock Holmes's more astonishing efforts, it seems too good and logical a story for real life'.

In view of such reconstructions as Munro's it is not superfluous to insist that generals do make mistakes, and have made mistakes even in modern wars, when they have had advantages denied to ancient generals, such as maps, telephones, air-scouts, and so on. It would therefore be very surprising if no mistakes were made by the generals on either side in the Great War of 480–479.[2] The Greek leaders in particular, not excepting Themistokles, had had no previous experience of war on such a scale. According to Thucydides,[3] the genius of Themistokles was such as to offset the gaps in his experience, and he was probably the ablest commander on either side, but after the expedition to Thessaly he played no further part in the land operations. These were directed during the campaign of Plataia by the Spartan Pausanias, who is assumed by some scholars[4] to have been a general of outstanding ability, apparently on no other ground than that the pitched battle in which he finally became entangled resulted in a decisive victory for the Greeks. There is greater probability in the view of Wells, who doubted[5] 'whether Pausanias had any real plan except somehow to get at the Persians and to beat them'. Modern narratives of the Persian Wars are too often vitiated by the fallacy *post hoc propter hoc*; their authors assume too readily that because certain results followed from certain actions, the results must have been foreseen and designed by the general who had given the orders for the performance of the actions. But, as Kipling's soldier knew,[6] there are times in modern warfare when nothing could be farther from the truth.

[1] In *The Manchester Guardian* (as it then was) for 8 June, 1926, in the course of a review of *C.A.H.* iv; the review was signed with the initials W. R. H.

[2] *All dates given are* B.C. (unless otherwise stated).   [3] i. 138. 3.

[4] For example by Wright (see his book cited in the bibliography). Even Eduard Meyer (*Forschungen*, ii. 209) thinks the military genius of Pausanias comparable to that shown by Blücher and Gneisenau at the battle of the Katzbach.

[5] *Studies*, 162.   [6] Terence in *Many Inventions*, 274 (Macmillan, 1914).

The third postulate is that the armies on both sides were well trained and well disciplined. There are some wars in antiquity for which this can be safely maintained, but the Great Persian War is not one of them. The modern hypothesis that the force brought by Xerxes to Greece from Asia was composed entirely of professional soldiers is demonstrably false;[1] it may have contained a professional nucleus, but the rest were mainly half-trained levies from the subject peoples of the empire. In the Greek army, composed almost entirely of citizen militias, the full citizens of Sparta, the Spartiatai, were professional soldiers, but even they had their limitations. The story told by Herodotus[2] about the Spartan brigadier Amompharetos has been condemned as an evident fabrication, a mere camp tale. Whether it is or not, the story cannot be rejected on the ground alleged by one critic,[3] that 'the whole scene here described is opposed to the high repute of Spartan discipline'. Spartan discipline did not always ensure obedience to orders, even at the start of a battle, as is proved by Thucydides' account of First Mantineia.[4] Moreover, the difficulties of the Spartan commanders-in-chief on land and on sea were increased by the character of their forces, drawn as they were from a large number of independent states. Nevertheless, modern writers on this war often assume the execution by both sides of complicated manœuvres which would have done credit to a highly-trained Prussian army. They tend to forget that on land the mountains of the Greek peninsula and the absence of good roads would have rendered impossible the rapid movement of large bodies of men, and that on sea the fleets were composed of triremes, which were hampered by various disabilities and were not capable of a high rate of speed.[5]

Finally, there is the postulate, already mentioned, that the narrative of Herodotus can be corrected by statements in authors who lived in the fourth century and even later. It is not denied that these authors, in view of their later date, can only rank as 'secondary sources', but the postulate takes for granted that they consulted valuable fifth-century sources which have since been lost. Arrian might be cited as a parallel; although the latest in

---

[1] See below, p. 41. [2] ix. 53 and 55–57; see below, p. 328.
[3] HW 311. [4] Thuc. v. 71. 3 and 72. 1.
[5] See below, p. 168.

time of the literary sources for the reign of Alexander the Great, he is beyond dispute the best, because he had the insight to base his *Anabasis* on two well-informed primary sources, Ptolemy and Aristoboulos. The parallel is imperfect, for the primary sources on Alexander have survived only in scanty fragments, whereas we have a valuable primary source for the Persian War surviving entire in the pages of Herodotus, and it is a mere assumption that later writers had access to sources superior to his. Yet this assumption, though rejected by some eminent scholars,[1] continues to be made. It cannot be conclusively disproved, but its inherent improbability can be established by a detailed examination of the 'secondary sources',[2] and particularly of those 'new items' in them which have been used to correct or supplement the account of the Persian Wars given by Herodotus.

The Secondary Sources

The fullest ancient description of Xerxes' invasion of Greece is that given by Herodotus in the last three books of his *History*.[3] There is not much that can be used to supplement his account in our extant evidence from the fifth century, with the possible exception of the *Persai* of Aeschylus; we have only a few references in Thucydides, a few inscriptions, and some epigrams and poems preserved by later writers. The historical content of the *Persai* must be examined later,[4] when it will be argued (in opposition to the view held by many critics) that on the battle of Salamis and the events immediately preceding it the testimony of Aeschylus is not in conflict with that of Herodotus. Thucydides, who criticized Herodotus severely,[5] might have been expected to throw fresh light, incidentally, on the Great Persian War, but though he supplements Herodotus on two minor points[6] he normally accepts

[1] Especially by Wells, *Studies*, c. 8; cf. also the remarks of Munro quoted below, p. 221.

[2] This is the method used by Rice Holmes (op. cit. 215–17) to prove that the 'secondary sources' for Caesar's campaigns in Gaul have no independent value.

[3] The division into books (for which see Diod. xi. 37. 6 and Plut., *H.M.*, *passim*) was not due to Hdt. himself; cf. Macan, ii. 77, n. 6.

[4] See below p. 222.

[5] Without mentioning him by name; cf. Thuc. i. 20. 3 (also 22).

[6] i. 89. 2 and 3 (both closely connected with Athenian history in 479); see below, pp. 261 and 291. Cf. also the passages cited in Macan, ii. 19, n. 3.

his history of the war without question.[1] His digression about the
construction of warships in the early fifth century[2] may have been
directed obliquely against Herodotus, and his famous tribute to
the genius of Themistokles[3] was certainly provoked by the anti-
Themistokles traditions which had been accepted too readily by
Herodotus, but on the whole there is surprisingly little in Thucydides which can be used to correct or even to supplement Herodotus. The same conclusion is valid for the poetic and epigraphic
evidence; often interesting and sometimes important, it does not
bear directly on the course of the war.

Herodotus was near enough in time to the invasion to be able
to question people from all over the Greek world who had taken
part in the war on either the Greek or the Persian side, and
even Thucydides might have talked with some of the survivors.
Whether Ktesias could have done so is doubtful, as the date of
his birth is uncertain,[4] but the extant summary of his *Persika*
does not suggest that it was founded on the reports of truthful
eyewitnesses. Other fourth-century historians, such as Ephoros,
came too late to draw on the living tradition of the Persian
Wars, and though they could have used the evidence of monuments and inscriptions (and even poetry) still surviving in their
day, it is not likely that these threw much light on the military
history of the war; for this they would have to turn to earlier
prose writers who had dealt with this subject. It is a problem of
crucial importance whether Ephoros and later historians (most
of whom were in various degrees dependent on Ephoros[5]) had
or had not access to trustworthy fifth-century sources now lost,
in addition to those which have been preserved to us; are the
statements in Ephoros and his successors which supplement or
contradict the Herodotean narrative traceable to a well-informed
tradition, or are they merely the product of a critical reconstruction of Herodotus in which Ephoros made some use of Aeschylus,
Thucydides, and Ktesias?

---

[1] So Thuc. follows the testimony of Hdt. even where it has been challenged by
modern critics; cf. i. 137. 4 (message said to have been sent to Xerxes by Themistokles after Salamis) and i. 73. 5 (on which see below, p. 267).

[2] i. 14. 2–3; see below, p. 52, n. 1.   [3] i. 138. 3.

[4] Cf. the article on him by Jacoby in *R.-E.* xi. 2032 ff. (especially 2033 f. and
2036). Jacoby has published the fragments in *F.G.H.* iiic, no. 688 (pp. 416–517).
There is also a convenient edition, with a translation in French, by R. Henry
(Brussels, 1947).

[5] Macan, ii. 28, also nn. 4 and 5.

Ktesias of Knidos was court-physician to Artaxerxes II of Persia near the end of the fifth century, and was in attendance on him at the battle of Kunaxa in 401.[1] A few years later he returned to the Aegean and wrote his *Persika* in twenty-three books;[2] they have not survived, but the epitome of them made by Photios is detailed enough to give a fair idea of their character. Diodoros reports[3] that Ktesias claimed to have consulted Persian 'royal parchments', but the context seems to connect this claim with Ktesias' version of the early history of Persia, and Hauvette suggested[4] that the parchments may have been epic poems of no historical value. Certainly Ktesias' account of Xerxes' invasion, as summarized by Photios, gives no support to the view that it was based on official Persian records of the war. It is not at all like the ingenious reconstruction of such records which was invented later by Dion Chrysostom;[5] on the contrary it has a marked pro-Spartan tendency, explicable by the political conditions in the Aegean area at the time of its composition. Ktesias does all in his power to magnify the achievement of Leonidas' force at Thermopylai, from which he passes on without a break to the campaign of Plataia, brought to a triumphant conclusion by the Spartan Pausanias with an army of only 7,300 men.[6]

It is possible that Ktesias was not guilty of the most glaring error laid to his charge, the transposition of Salamis and Plataia; Blakesley conjectured that the battle of Salamis was not chronologically displaced by Ktesias, but 'was related in an insulated manner after the completion of the land operations'.[7] If he narrated the naval operations as a mere appendix to the land operations and with no reference to the fighting at Artemision, the explanation may be that he wished to belittle their effect on the result of the war; the figures he gives for the Greek fleet at Salamis, 700 ships in all, including only 110 from Athens, seem

[1] Xen., *Anabasis* i. 8. 26–27.

[2] Cf. the first sentence of c. 60 of Photios' epitome. Diod. xiv. 46. 6 says that Ktesias ended his *Persika* with the events of 398–397.

[3] ii. 32. 4.

[4] *Hérodote*, 82. On p. 83 Hauvette points out that Ktesias seems to have maintained that his account of the historical period was based on Persian oral traditions (*Persika* 1).

[5] xi. 147–9; cf. Hauvette, 84 and the citation in Macan ii. 102, n. 8.

[6] *Persika* 23–25; for Ktesias as φιλολάκων cf. Plut., *Artaxerxes* 13 (ad fin.).

[7] *Persika* 25–26; cf. Blakesley, ii. 502.

designed to minimize the greatness of the Greek victory and the
contribution made to it by the Athenians.

Photios says[1] that Ktesias throughout his work frequently
attacked Herodotus' accuracy and good faith, but Ktesias'
criticisms against Herodotus cannot be taken seriously in view
of his own circumstantial (and quite unfounded) story[2] that the
shrine of Delphi was plundered by the eunuch Matakas, sent
purposely on this errand by Xerxes himself after his return to
Sardis from Greece. The Persian fleet at Salamis is said to have
been under the supreme command of 'Onophas', a figure who
bears even less relation to reality than the 'Ariamenes' of the
later tradition;[3] this tends to discredit other proper names
mentioned by Ktesias which are not mentioned elsewhere.
Clearly the old aristocratic ideal of the pursuit of historical truth
for its own sake, an ideal which was followed by Herodotus,
Thucydides, and Xenophon in their different ways, had been
discarded by Ktesias for the exciting possibilities of historical
fiction. His estimates for the Persian land forces, more reasonable
than those of Herodotus but still too high, seem to have influenced
Ephoros,[4] but though he may have been a valuable source for
Persian history during the second half of the fifth century, his
version of the events of 480–479 was too extravagant to be much
used by later writers.

A passage in Dionysios of Halikarnassos[5] has been cited as
evidence that there were numerous fifth-century historians whose
works, now lost, may have supplied later writers with valuable
information not contained in the pages of Herodotus. Dionysios
gives the name of eight 'ancient historians' from eight different
cities who lived before the Peloponnesian War; they are all little
more than names, except Hekataios of Miletos, Akousilaos of
Argos, and Charon of Lampsakos. There follows a list of those
who flourished 'just before the Peloponnesian War', Hellanikos
of Lesbos, Damastes of Sigeion, Xenomedes of Chios, Xanthos

---

[1] c. 1 of his epitome of the *Persika* (*F.G.H.* no. 688 T 8).

[2] Op. cit. 27.

[3] Onophas in *Persika* 26; cf. Henry, op. cit. 92, n. 75. Ariamenes (Plut. *Them.*
14. 3) seems to represent a blend of two genuine admirals, Ariabignes (who really
was killed at Salamis; cf. Hdt. viii. 89. 1) and Achaimenes (mentioned with
Ariabignes in Hdt. vii. 97). In the story told by Plut., *Moralia* 488 D–F, 'Ariamenes'
has taken the place of the historical Artobarzanes (Hdt. vii. 2).

[4] See below, p. 15, n. 4.

[5] *De Thucydide*, c. 5 (cited by Hammond, in *J.H.S.* lxxvi, 1956, 39).

of Lydia, 'and many others'. After these two lists Dionysios describes the common purpose of the authors mentioned in them as the examination of the ancient records preserved by the local inhabitants in sacred or secular buildings and their publication for the general public without any alteration or addition,[1] and later in the chapter he contrasts their circumscribed themes with the wider scope of Herodotus. This strongly suggests that they were compilers of local histories,[2] and it is known that one of them, Euagon of Samos, wrote a chronicle of the Samians which was cited as evidence in a boundary dispute between Samos and Priene at the beginning of the second century.[3] These chroniclers may have dealt with the Persian Wars if they carried their chronicles down to the fifth century. The Naxian chroniclers, however, who gave particulars of the history of Naxos in the early fifth century,[4] must have been later in time than those mentioned by Dionysios, and what Plutarch says of them indicates that in their accounts of the Persian invasion of Naxos in 490 they altered the facts to praise their own citizens; the same may be true of other late chronicles whose authors sought to make a place for their cities in the glorious annals of the Persian Wars.[5] Probably the fifth-century chroniclers were more scrupulous, but it is not likely that they could add anything of value to the Herodotean narrative.

The existence of fifth-century chroniclers who took the Great War of 480–479 as their subject seems at first sight to be proved by Thucydides, who in speaking of his predecessors states[6] that all except Hellanikos had written nothing about the fifty years which followed the end of the war but had confined themselves either to Greek history before the war or to the war itself. This, however, does not prove that there were several historians in the second category; as Thucydides of set purpose never mentions

---

[1] μήτε προστιθέντες αὐταῖς τι μήτ' ἀφαιροῦντες.

[2] Not necessarily only the history of their own cities; the Lesbian Hellanikos wrote the first local history of Athens (Atthis or Ἀττικὴ ξυγγραφή; cf. Thuc. i. 97. 2).

[3] Cf. Jacoby in R.-E. vi. 819 f. for Euagon's ὧροι Σαμίων and the epigraphic reference. His name is corrupted in the literary tradition (D. H. calls him Εὐγέων).

[4] οἱ Ναξίων ὡρογράφοι in Plut. H.M. 36. The text is corrupt in the crucial passage; for a valuable discussion cf. Jacoby, F.G.H. iii B, 55 f. (on Hellanikos fr. 28 = fr. 183 in Jacoby, vol. i and 81 in Müller, F.H.G.).

[5] Hauvette, 106 is good on this; cf. also what Jacoby says about the temple chronicle of Lindos in his Herodotus article, 506 f. (see below, p. 25, n. 3).

[6] i. 97. 2.

Herodotus by name, it is possible that Herodotus was the only historian of the Great War known to him.[1] There is no evidence to support the view that Hekataios, famous for his pioneer work in geography and genealogy, also wrote a history of the Ionian Revolt,[2] and it is even less likely that he went on to describe the invasion of Xerxes. Charon of Lampsakos is credited with *Persika*, but the only extant fragment[3] relates to Mardonios' expedition in 492; it is an observation that white doves were then seen in Greece for the first time. Two citations in Plutarch from an unspecified work by Charon[4] deal with events in the earlier history of Ionia, the revolt of Paktyas in 540 and the burning of Sardis in 498; both citations give the impression of a jejune summary which dealt so briefly with the events that its silences cannot be used to refute the fuller narrative provided by Herodotus.

An hypothesis which has found many advocates in Germany[5] is that Ephoros (and probably his successors) had drawn largely on an excellent source for the Persian Wars, Dionysios of Miletos, who lived so early in the fifth century that his writings may even have been consulted by Herodotus himself. The Byzantine compilation which used to go by the name of 'Suidas'[6] makes him the author of *Persika* and also of a work in five books on 'The things after Darius', which presumably started with Darius' death in 486. But as Suidas also makes Dionysios a contemporary of Hekataios, active in the 65th Olympiad (520–516), some have identified his second work with the *Persika* and have emended its title to 'The things before Darius', making it end with Darius' accession in 522.[7] This emendation might be supported by the one historical item from Dionysios which has survived,[8] for it has reference to an event of Persian history in 522. Jacoby, however,

---

[1] Perhaps Charon also, but the date of his literary activity is uncertain.

[2] For this view cf. Bury, *The Ancient Greek Historians* (London, 1909), 12; against it Jacoby in *R.-E.* vii. 2668 f., also Blamire in *C.Q.* liii, 1959, 148, n. 1.

[3] Fr. 1 in Jacoby, *F.G.H.* iii c, 687b.

[4] Plut. *H.M.* 20 and 24 = Jacoby (loc. cit.) frr. 4 and 5.

[5] Cf. the writers cited by Obst, *Der Feldzug des Xerxes*, 29, also Macan ii. 5 and n. 4. The evidence for Dionysios of Miletos is in Jacoby, *F.G.H.* iii c, 410 f. (no. 687).

[6] Σοῦδα is a title meaning *vallum* or stronghold; cf. the review in *Gnomon*, xiii, 1937, 575 f.

[7] Cf. Macan, loc. cit. (with reference to *F.H.G.* iv. 653); also Hauvette, 163.

[8] Fr. 2 in Jacoby no. 687, in a scholiast on Hdt. iii. 61. Hdt. had said that the brother of the false Smerdis was called Patizeithes; Dionysios gave the name as Panxouthes.

keeps the traditional title for the work, which he identifies with the *Persika*, and presumably dates the literary activity of Dionysios to a time later than Xerxes' invasion.

It has been well said[1] that 'a writer of whom hardly anything is known is a writer of whom almost anything may be assumed'. This freedom has been exploited to the utmost limit by Obst; after postulating that the history of Dionysios was used by Herodotus he concludes that everything in Herodotus which seems to him reasonable was derived from Dionysios and that the rest was the result of Herodotus' rejection of the authentic tradition, which can fortunately be recovered from Ephoros, for Obst believes that Ephoros used Dionysios in those passages where Herodotus strayed from the true paths.[2] Such hypotheses refute themselves. If Dionysios' work was so important, why has it disappeared almost without a trace? Why is it never quoted by Plutarch and others when they are trying to undermine the authority of Herodotus? The date in Suidas may be based on nothing more than Dionysios' choice of the Ionic dialect and an archaic style;[3] if this is correct, he may have lived a long time after the end of the fifth century. It is noteworthy that the Milesian Dionysios is not included in the long roll of fifth-century historians listed by his Halikarnassian namesake,[4] who if he had known of an authentic fifth-century Persian History of the scope and authority of that attributed by some moderns to Dionysios of Miletos could hardly have failed to mention it.

There are two good reasons for denying that the fifth-century historians whose works have disappeared had anything of importance to add to the account of Xerxes' invasion given by Herodotus. The first is that the items in the later authors, from Ephoros onwards, that contradict or supplement Herodotus are not such as to be explicable only on the assumption that they were derived from sources more accurate than his; the second is that Plutarch, when he consulted the ancient authors to obtain support for his attacks on Herodotus in the *De Malignitate*, could

---

[1] By E. M. Walker (referring to Kratippos) in *New Chapters in the History of Greek Literature* (Powell & Barber) i, 1921, 129. Cf. Jacoby (article on Hdt.) 405.

[2] Obst, op. cit. 27–30 and *passim*.

[3] Cf. Schwarz on Dionysios (no. 112) in *R.-E.* v. 933 f.

[4] Dion. Hal. *de Thucydide* 5. Some work by the Milesian was undoubtedly known to Apollodoros (Jacoby, *F.G.H.*, no. 244, fr. 165), but he cited it only for a view on the origins of the Greek alphabet.

find nothing relevant to his purpose in fifth-century historians.[1]
As Thucydides had been able to amplify Herodotus on two
points connected with the history of Athens during the Great
War,[2] his contemporary Hellanikos might have been expected
to find more when he wrote the first *Atthis*, but the only item for
which he is cited by Plutarch[3] is the number of ships brought
over to the Greek side before Salamis by the Naxians. Herodotus
gives the number as four, Hellanikos as six, Ephoros (possibly
splitting the difference) as five. There is no need to reject Herodotus here in favour of Hellanikos,[4] who perhaps misunderstood
the epigram, quoted in full by Plutarch, on the Naxian leader
Demokritos.

The Atthidographers of the fourth century, starting with Kleidemos, were too far from the Great War to do more than supplement Herodotus' narrative with some unimportant details, in
many of which the tribe Aiantis has a suspicious prominence.
Wilamowitz conjectured[5] that this prominence was due to
Kleidemos and that the Aiantis was his tribe. It was believed in
the fourth century that the decision to march the Athenian
army out to Marathon was made by a decree of the people, but
although the decree is probably authentic, the statement that
the Aiantis was the presiding tribe when it was carried cannot be
regarded as above suspicion.[6] Some particulars on the battle of
Marathon[7] may have been accessible to the Atthidographers,
but it is not likely that they gave an account of the campaign
different from that in Herodotus, on whom they certainly drew
very largely for the history of Athens in the sixth century.[8]

On the other fourth-century writers who dealt with the Great
Persian War the most important was Ephoros. The description
of it which was included in his universal history has not survived, but modern scholars agree that it was followed closely by
Diodoros of Sicily in the relevant chapters of his eleventh book,[9]

---

[1] He never cites Charon for anything in the war of 480–479.
[2] See above, p. 7, n. 6.
[3] *H.M.* 36; cf. Hdt. viii. 46. 3 (also HW ad loc.).
[4] See the discussion by Jacoby cited above, p. 11, n. 4.
[5] *Aristoteles und Athen*, i. 286, n. 36; cf. fr. 22 of Kleidemos in Jacoby, *F.G.H.*
iii B, no. 323 (14 in Müller, *F.H.G.*).
[6] Plut. *Quaest. Conv.* i. 10. 3 (*Moralia* 628 E); cf. Macan, *Herodotus iv–vi*, ii. 219.
[7] Such as the order of the tribes in the battle-line; cf. Plut. *Aristeides*, 5. 4.
[8] If the Ἀθηναίων πολιτεία attributed to Aristotle may be regarded as typical.
[9] cc. 1–19, 27–37.

and from this epitome it can be seen that writers later than Ephoros were in the main content to reproduce the version of the war which they found in him. There are some items in Diodoros which supplement Herodotus, but they are citations from poetical literature[1] (including epigrams on stone) still accessible in the fourth century, and naturally they are of only slight historical importance. Of the many statements in Diodoros which contradict Herodotus, not one is such as to prove that in making it Ephoros was relying on the testimony of a well-informed primary source. That Ephoros used Herodotus is proved not only by the explicit reference to his history which Diodoros inserts at the end of his account of the campaign of 479,[2] but also from frequent parallelism in detail; the most striking example of this, because in such marked contrast to the prevailing rationalism of Ephoros, is the statement[3] that the losses inflicted on the Persian fleet by storms seemed to have been sent by Providence to help the Greek cause. Whenever Ephoros either contradicts or merely supplements the Herodotean narrative, his novelties, so far as they are not derived from Aeschylus or Ktesias,[4] can all be explained by the characteristic features of his historical technique.

'Ephoros probably did as much as any one man ever did to corrupt history in the name of history', says Macan,[5] and this verdict is not too severe. In adapting the story of the Great War to the taste of his own age Ephoros, himself a pupil of Isokrates and a professional historian, was led astray by the combined influences of rhetoric and rationalism; as neither the rationalism nor the rhetoric was of the best quality,[6] the intrusion of both at this stage could have inflicted irreparable damage on the tradition of the war if the text of Herodotus had not survived to refute the inventions grafted on the authentic record by Ephoros. As a specimen of his rhetoric it will be enough here to mention his version of Thermopylai,[7] embellished with the absurd fiction

---

[1] e.g. xi. 11. 6 (encomium by Simonides on those who died at Thermopylai; see below, p. 148, n. 3) and 33. 2 (couplet on the war-memorial at Delphi).

[2] xi. 37. 6.   [3] xi. 13. 1; cf. Hdt. viii. 13 (both refer to τὸ θεῖον).

[4] From whom Ephoros may have got his estimate for the Persian land forces; on the figures in Isokrates cf. Macan, ii. 31, n. 9.

[5] Macan, ii. 27f.   [6] Macan, loc. cit.

[7] Diod. xi. 4 and 5. 4–11. 6 (the night attack is 9. 4–10. 4). The alleged peace-offer of Xerxes before the fighting began and Leonidas' proud reply are typical Ephorean inventions.

that Leonidas during the night before the final struggle made
a desperate attack on the Persian camp which took the enemy
by surprise and penetrated to the royal tent; unfortunately,
Xerxes had already escaped. A superficial rationalism is invoked by Ephoros to resolve many of the difficulties in the
Herodotean narrative,[1] especially the supernatural element.
Herodotus had told how in 479 the Greek forces under Leotychidas off the coast of Asia Minor, just before the battle of
Mykale, had been encouraged by a mysterious rumour that the
Greek army in Boiotia had won a great victory; as Herodotus
believed that the battle in Boiotia had been fought earlier in the
same day he concluded that the rumour must have been of
divine origin.[2] Ephoros, accepting as a fact the precise synchronism of the two battles, argues that as Leotychidas could
not possibly have heard the news from Boiotia he must have invented the report as a 'stratagem' to encourage his men.[3]

Not all examples of Ephorean rationalism are as shallow as
this one; in some he showed that he was by no means deficient
in critical insight. He cut down the absurd estimates given by
Herodotus for the Persian land forces, and though his own figures
are still too high and have no independent value, they 'attest a
legitimate incredulity.'[4] He also saw that the complete disappearance of Themistokles from the stage throughout the year
479 called for some explanation, and the one which he suggested,[5] based on indications in Herodotus, may possibly be
correct in the main. But even when he merely supplements
Herodotus, his additions to the story of the war cannot be
treated as genuine tradition; at best they are no more than the
products of 'constructive inference'[6] and at worst they are pure
fiction. The frequent appearances of his native city, the Asiatic Kyme, in his narrative[7] are probably to be ascribed to an
excessive local patriotism rather than an authoritative local

---

[1] Its superficiality is proved by Ephoros' failure to detect many real problems in
the history of the war. Cf. Macan, ii. 76, where he speaks of the 'pseudo-science'
of Ephoros, and points out that he inconsistently 'leaves the supernatural a sort of
supernumerary role in the action'.

[2] ix. 100.   [3] Diod. xi. 35. 2–3.   [4] Macan, ii. 77.

[5] Diod. xi. 27. 3; HW 276 on Hdt. viii. 125. 1, and see below, pp. 275–6.

[6] This convenient phrase is borrowed from Macan (e.g. ii. 86).

[7] Cf. Diod. xi. 2. 3, also 8. 5 (on the alleged Kymaian deserter Tyrrhastiadas;
on him cf. Macan, ii. 68, n. 3). The reference to Kyme in 27. 1 may be derived
from Hdt. viii. 130. 1.

chronicle.[1] Even when a 'new item' in Ephoros seems plausible, it cannot be regarded as having a stronger claim to acceptance than the hypothesis of a modern scholar. It will be argued later[2] that his account of Salamis is not derived from fifth-century sources other than those which we still have, but is simply a reconstruction based on his interpretation of the *Persai* of Aeschylus, and therefore is no more traditional than Goodwin's version of the battle. To prove this conclusion for all the new items in Diodoros would be as tedious as it is unnecessary, but two of them are important enough to need careful consideration.

Herodotus, after reporting the tradition current in Old Greece about the negotiations of a Greek embassy with Gelon the tyrant of Syracuse and their breakdown on the question of the supreme command, appends to it an account which he had received from Greeks in Sicily.[3] They asserted that even after the breakdown Gelon would have gone with a force to fight for the Greeks and would have submitted to the hegemony of Sparta if he had not been prevented by a Carthaginian invasion of Sicily, provoked by Terillos the tyrant of Himera, who had been driven out of his city by Gelon's ally Theron of Akragas. Both traditions presuppose that Gelon at the time of the embassy did not know that Carthage was planning a fresh offensive in Sicily; this need cause no difficulty if the embassy was sent in the autumn of 481.[4] The Sikeliot tradition added that the battle of Himera, in which the Carthaginians were routed, occurred on the same day as the naval defeat of the Persians at Salamis. Herodotus regards this synchronism as accidental,[5] and Aristotle cites it in the *Poetics* as an example of a purely fortuitous coincidence. Ephoros, whose own account survives here in a fragment,[6] denied this, and claimed that the synchronism of the

---

[1] The latter view is that of Tarn in *J.H.S.* xxviii. 1908, 233, n. 117. For ancient criticism of Ephoros' local patriotism cf. Strabo, xiii. 623.

[2] See below, p. 221.

[3] vii. 165–6. Lines 1–3 of c. 165 prove that the Sikeliot tradition accepted the story of the Greek embassy to Gelon as historical.

[4] vii. 145. 2. An early date for the embassy is also implied by viii. 3. 1. Hackforth (in *C.A.H.* iv. 377) makes his case more difficult by dating the embassy to March 480.

[5] συνέβη in vii. 166; cf. Arist. *Poetics* c. 23 (1459[a]24–27).

[6] Jacoby, *F.G.H.*, no. 70, fr. 186 (fr. 111 in *F.H.G.* i. 264); cf. Grundy, 254 ff. No importance need be attached to the statement of Diodoros (xi. 1. 5) that the Carthaginians spent three years in preparing for their invasion; these three years are the obvious pendant to the four years of Persian preparations in Hdt. vii. 20. 1.

two attacks was the result of Persian planning; Persian and
Phoenician envoys had gone together to Carthage to order the
Carthaginians to invade Sicily at the appropriate time. An
historian later than Ephoros, perhaps Timaios, must have
realized that Persia was in no position to issue orders to Carthage, and so Diodoros says[1] that the purpose of the Persian
embassy to Carthage was to make an agreement for concerted
action. Many moderns have been tempted to accept this story,
the finest flower produced by the rhetoric and rationalism of
Ephoros; it has even been suggested that it may go back to the
fifth-century Sicilian historian Antiochos of Syracuse,[2] or that
Ephoros divined the truth even if his story was based only on
probability, not on independent evidence.[3] But in fact the story,
as Macan pointed out,[4] is irreconcilable with the independent
chain of causation for the Carthaginian invasion of Sicily provided by the Sikeliot tradition in Herodotus. Ephoros could not
allow any alternative cause to throw doubt on his beautiful
hypothesis, so he dropped out all mention of Terillos' appeal,
and both the presence of Theron in Himera and the Carthaginian attack on it had to be left unexplained.

Ephoros also attempted to rationalize the list of medizing
states given by Herodotus,[5] a list which includes the Lokrians,
Thebans, and all the other Boiotian states except Thespiai and
Plataia. Herodotus declares that tokens of submission from all
these states, as well as those farther north, were brought by
Persian envoys to Xerxes at Therma, just before the invasion
began, perhaps as late as August 480.[6] By then the Thessalians
had submitted to Xerxes with all the other states north of
Mount Oite, but it is unlikely that the Central Greek states had
finally committed themselves to the Persian side at this stage.
Ephoros, knowing that Lokrians and Thebans fought in the
Greek army at Thermopylai and that Thessaly had earlier applied to the patriotic Greeks for support, proceeded to rationalize Herodotus' list by the hypothesis that all the peoples
north of Oite, except the Thessalians and Northern Achaians,
medized while the Greek army was still at Tempe (April or

---

[1] xi. 1. 4–5.
[2] By Freeman, *History of Sicily*, ii. 511; see below, p. 96, n. 1.
[3] So Meyer, 356 n.   [4] ii. 71, n. 5 (also ii. 186 f.).
[5] vii. 132. 1; cf. HW ad loc.
[6] On the chronology see below, Appendix XIV.

early May 480) whereas the Thessalians and Achaians and also
the Lokrians and Boiotians medized after the army left Tempe.[1]
Ephoros, however, has failed to grapple with the real crux in the
Herodotean list, for he too has antedated the Medism of the
Central Greeks, and is later reduced to the absurd supposition
that on the approach of Leonidas the Lokrians and Malians
changed sides again and joined the Greeks;[2] as for the Boiotians, the Theban contingent in Leonidas' army is said to have
been composed of men opposed to the pro-Persian party which
was now dominant in their city, and disappears from the story
of the last day's fighting at Thermopylai. Such novelties in
Ephoros are due simply to his reconstruction of the narrative
of Herodotus; he detected some real problems in it, but his
solutions of them, rarely convincing, are always the product
of his own critical faculty, not the relics of an authentic tradition.

There are some late authors whose evidence on points of detail is usable, such as the antiquarian Pausanias, who describes
the monuments of the war and has some valuable topographical
notices; the geographers also, especially Strabo, can sometimes
be pressed into service on the assumption that the natural features described by them had not changed since the wars. But
the historical traditions of the wars had been fatally corrupted
by the activities of Ephoros, who dominated all subsequent
writers on this theme. Wherever their accounts differ from
those of the fifth-century sources still extant they can never be
trusted; all the novelties in them seem to be traceable to one of
three causes, the influence of rhetoric, pure fiction, or sheer
blunders due to misreading of the earlier sources. It is hardly
credible what mistakes could be made by historians who had not
taken the trouble to read Herodotus carefully; so the war of
Athens with Aigina in the period just before Xerxes' invasion is
turned by Cornelius Nepos[3] into a war with Corcyra.

Pure fiction was the speciality of such authors as Phanias of
Eresos and Idomeneus of Lampsakos, whose works were largely

---

[1] Diod. xi. 3. 1–2 (accepted by Grundy in his long n. on pp. 228 ff.). The
exclusion of the Northern Achaians was perhaps suggested by the fact (Hdt.
vii. 173. 1) that the Greek expeditionary force to Tempe landed in their territory,
at Halos.

[2] Diod. xi. 4. 6–7; cf. 9. 2 (for criticisms cf. Meyer, *Forsch.* ii. 211).

[3] *Themistocles* 2. 1 and 2. 3.

used by Plutarch; untroubled by any respect for truth, they padded out the narrative of the Great War with tasteless episodes of their own invention. The fictions of Phanias are so gross that they need no refutation; it is enough to recall his story[1] that Themistokles, when sacrificing before Salamis, was prevailed on by the seer Euphrantidas to add to the victims three Persian captives who had just been brought in. A few of the stories told by Idomeneus are more plausible and have imposed on some modern scholars; as Herodotus had failed to say which of the Greek states won the reward for bravery at the battle of Plataia, Idomeneus explained that, as both Spartans and Athenians claimed the prize, the deadlock had to be resolved by a Corinthian proposal to assign it to the Plataians.[2]

The perversion of the true traditions by rhetoric, begun by Ephoros, was carried much further by later writers who threw off all restraint. Aristeides of Miletos, taking over from Ephoros the alleged night attack of Leonidas on the Persian camp, added that Leonidas, though wounded by many spears, forced his way to Xerxes and pulled the diadem from his head;[3] as Macan observes, it is hardly surprising to read after this exploit that when Leonidas' body was cut open after death, his heart was found to be covered with hair. Pompeius Trogus (or his epitomator Justin) found in Herodotus the story of Kynegeiros, brother of the poet Aeschylus, who after the rout of the Persians at Marathon, when getting hold of a Persian ship, had his hand cut off by an axe and fell. This version was not exciting enough for Justin or his source, according to which[4] Kynegeiros, having lost his right hand, seized the ship with his left hand, and when that too was severed held on with his teeth.

Plutarch alone of the post-Ephorean writers on the Persian Wars merits a closer examination. For his biographies of Themistokles and Aristeides he consulted a wide variety of sources, and in so doing preserved some interesting scraps of information which dated back to the wars, such as fragments of the contemporary poet Timokreon of Rhodes or a notice of an Athenian

---

[1] Plut. *Them.* 13. 2–5 (citing Phanias in 5); cf. also 7. 6–7.

[2] Plut. *Aristeides* 20. 1–3.

[3] In [Plutarch], *Parallels* 4 (*Moralia* 306 D). But the citations in this work (on which see Ziegler, *R.-E.* xxi. 867 f.) are not to be trusted; cf. Kraack in *R.-E.* Suppl. i (1903), 132.

[4] Justin, ii. 9. 18 (cf. Hdt. vi. 114).

decree relating to an embassy to Sparta.[1] He was thus able to supplement the narrative of Herodotus here and there in detail, but many of his new items were derived from secondary sources of doubtful value, and where they contradict Herodotus are demonstrably unhistorical. So the morning wind at Salamis is a reality, but Plutarch's reconstruction[2] of its effect on the course of the battle is a myth. His statement[3] that each Athenian ship at Salamis had eighteen marines on board (fourteen hoplites and four archers) is incredible, because the Athenian navy at Salamis, being untrained, relied on boarding tactics, which required at least thirty marines to each ship; it is possible that Plutarch wrongly referred back to 480 a piece of evidence relating to the Athenian navy at a later period. Plutarch's contributions to the topography of the Plataian campaign, although taken seriously by some scholars, have no independent value,[4] and his figures for the Greek losses at Plataia appear to be no more than a calculation based on the incomplete items in Herodotus,[5] while the new items in the appendix to his account of the battle are probably derived from the untrustworthy Idomeneus.[6] Macan has noted that in both biographies the credit for various actions attributed by Herodotus to the Athenians is ascribed by Plutarch to either Themistokles or Aristeides, and he rightly concludes[7] that such ascriptions may be due merely to constructive inference, however plausible some of them may be. They explain why in Plutarch's version of the Plataian campaign the name of Aristeides is prominent throughout, whereas in the ninth book of Herodotus he is mentioned only once, and then simply as the general commanding the Athenian contingent.[8]

The miscellaneous writings of Plutarch contain numerous references to the Persian Wars[9] and one long essay, *On the Spitefulness of Herodotus*, which is a detailed attack on Herodotus'

[1] *Them.* 21. 4–7 and *Arist.* 10. 10; on the latter see below, p. 283.
[2] *Them.* 14. 3; see below, p. 233.
[3] *Them.* 14. 2.
[4] See below, Appendix X.
[5] See below, p. 340.
[6] Who is probably also the inventor of the alleged conspiracy (Plut. *Arist.* 13) of some Athenian aristocrats before the battle of Plataia; see below, pp. 320f.
[7] ii. 86.   [8] ix. 28. 6.
[9] Cf. Macan, ii. 89–91; he concludes that these 'contribute practically nothing from the objective order of events to the history of the Persian war'.

history. Its criticisms are often inept, and on this ground it was
once maintained that the essay could not have been written by
Plutarch, or, if genuine, must have been a youthful indiscretion,
but the arguments for Plutarch's authorship are overwhelming,
and it is now believed that the *De Malignitate*, as it is usually
called, is a product of his maturity.[1] Its underlying thesis is preposterous[2] and does more credit to Plutarch's heart than his
head. He refuses to believe any evil of those who took part in the
national struggle against Persia; for him any historian of the war
is right whenever he praises the courage, wisdom, and unselfish-
ness of the Greek states and their leaders, but wrong when he
suggests any suspicion of their weakness and egoism. In spite
of the falsity of this fundamental principle Plutarch sometimes
scores a point against Herodotus, but only when he bases his
criticism on materials supplied by Herodotus himself.[3] Although
he ransacked the earlier literature to find support for his strictures on Herodotus he discovered nothing adequate to his purpose in fifth-century writers, while the testimony of the later
chroniclers whom he cites is untrustworthy, for they were
naturally concerned to put the best face on the part played by
their states during the Great War;[4] this is especially true of his
chief witness, Aristophanes of Boiotia.

Although Plutarch was himself a Boiotian he was not more
concerned to defend the behaviour of the Boiotians than that of
the Spartans or the Argives. His apologia for the Boiotians is
more elaborate partly because Herodotus seemed to him to have
been unduly unfair to them, partly because he believed that
Herodotus' account could be disproved by the evidence in
Aristophanes. He failed to realize that, though the traditions
collected by Herodotus had an anti-Theban bias, the Boiotian
historian was more concerned with patriotism than with truth.
As Aristophanes alleged that Leonidas had had a dream in the
temple of Herakles at Thebes in which he foresaw the future
greatness and sudden decline of Thebes,[5] he must have written
his history after the collapse of the Theban hegemony. His

---

[1] Cf. Ziegler in *R.-E.* xxi. 872 (also Hauvette 98 ff.) as against Macan, ii. 91.
[2] As is well shown by Hauvette, 101 ff.
[3] Hauvette, 103 f. and 109 f.
[4] Hauvette, 106 f.; see above, p. 11 and n. 5.
[5] Plutarch, *H.M.* 31 (ad fin.); the words εἶτ' ἐξαίφνης ἀφανῆ γενέσθαι are important for the date (cf. Hauvette, 106).

tendency is sufficiently indicated by his assertion[1] that Herodotus hated the Thebans because they had refused to give him money when he asked for it and because their magistrates had prevented him from talking to the young men in Thebes.

Aristophanes claimed that the Thebans 'had sent five hundred men to Tempe under Mnamias, and as many men to Thermopylai as Leonidas had asked for'.[2] The second half of this sentence is certainly false, and its falsity throws doubt on the accuracy of the first half. Theban participation in the Tempe expedition cannot be accepted on such evidence alone. Aristophanes may easily have invented both the contingent and the commander; who could prove a negative? Proper names are not sufficient to guarantee the truth of such statements; so Herodotus' story of the bribing of Themistokles by the Euboians is not made any the more credible by a later writer's addition that the Euboian who paid over the money was called Pelagon.[3] Nor is there any reason to believe that Aristophanes had epigraphic evidence for his assertion[4] that the commander of the Thebans at Thermopylai was not Leontiades, as Herodotus had said, but Anaxandros; it is clear that his object was to discredit the testimony of Herodotus by any means, fair or foul.

It has sometimes been held that the defence of Theban policy during the war put forward by Aristophanes and by Plutarch after him is confirmed by the passage in which Thucydides says[5] that as Thebes was ruled by a close oligarchy at the time of the invasion the city at large could not fairly be blamed for actions over which she had no control. Actually this defence is put by Thucydides in the mouth of a Theban speaker and need not represent his own belief; he may have given it merely as a plausible argument likely to be used by a Theban orator in 427 to answer the Plataian attack on the unpatriotic attitude of Thebes in 480. It was perhaps a favourite Theban technique to shift responsibility for inconvenient acts from the citizens in

[1] *H.M.* 31 (first paragraph).

[2] *H.M.* 31, rejected as improbable by Hauvette, 340 f.

[3] Plut. *Them.* 7. 5; cf. HW 236 f. (on Hdt. viii. 4. 2) and Busolt, 682, n. 1. (he thinks the name Pelagon was supplied by Ephoros).

[4] *H.M.* 33 (ἐκ τῶν κατὰ ἄρχοντας ὑπομνημάτων, whatever that may mean); contrast Hdt. vii. 233. 2. Meyer (*Forsch.* ii. 211, also 210, n. 1) assumes without proof the superior credibility of Aristophanes' version.

[5] Thuc. iii. 62. 3–4.

general to their leaders; Xenophon shows[1] that it could be used even when Thebes was governed by the hoplite class. Thebes was indeed ruled by a close oligarchy in 480, but according to Herodotus[2] one of the oligarchs urged that their pro-Persian policy was backed by the masses, and this contention is probably sound; the Thebans in general were not likely to favour the anti-Persian coalition when one of its two leaders was their hated enemy Athens, and Theban democrats in the fourth century[3] were not ashamed to claim credit with the Great King for the part their city had played during Xerxes' invasion. Hence on this point also the substantial accuracy of Herodotus' account is not invalidated by later criticism.

This long survey of the secondary sources will have served its purpose if it has convinced the reader that statements in them cannot safely be used to correct or even to supplement the narrative of Herodotus on any important point, and that all the novelties in these sources, except the passages in which they are quoting fifth-century writers or inscriptions still accessible in their time, are the products of one of three causes, misunderstanding, rhetoric, or constructive inference. The truth of this conclusion was firmly grasped by many earlier scholars, for example Hauvette and Wells,[4] but in some recent writings, especially those of Labarbe,[5] there has been an alarming tendency to re-examine the secondary sources, even the least trustworthy of them, for fresh illumination. Particular examples of this practice will be discussed later, but its unsoundness may be illustrated here by Labarbe's attempt[6] to make use of Ktesias' estimate for the Athenian ships at Salamis; he never considers from what well-informed source Ktesias could have obtained this precious figure 110 (which is supposed to prove that the Athenians had had seventy ships sunk or disabled at Artemision) or why it should be entitled to more respect than Ktesias' absurd total of 700 for the combined Greek fleet.

---

[1] *Hell.* iii. 5. 8.
[2] ix. 87. 2.
[3] Pelopidas in Xen. *Hell.* vii. 1. 34.
[4] Cf. Wells, *Studies,* c. 8, especially pp. 163 ff.
[5] See below, pp. 413 f. and 451 for Labarbe's use of Lykourgos and Polyainos.
[6] *B.C.H.* lxxvi, 1952, 406 ff. (citing Ktesias, *Persika* 26). On p. 426 he observes that the 700 in Ktesias is roughly the sum of the two totals given by Hdt. for the Greek fleet at Artemision and at Salamis (324 + 380 = 704).

The attempt to treat all the items in the ancient evidence, whatever their date, as complementary parts of a single whole has been vigorously attacked by Pritchett;[1] as he rightly observes, this complementary method 'is equivalent to saying that all our sources are equally valid, a statement which is demonstrably false', and he insists that any modern account of, for example, the battle of Salamis must be based on a careful evaluation of the various ancient writers who described it. There is one safe course to follow in reconstructing the history of Xerxes' invasion, and that is to rely throughout on the fifth-century sources still extant, supplemented only by geographical and topographical notices from Strabo and Pausanias or by those passages in the secondary sources which are quoted directly from fifth-century writers or from inscriptions contemporary with the Persian Wars.[2] In practice this principle means that our reconstruction must be based almost entirely on the text of Herodotus.

Herodotus[3]

When Xerxes invaded Greece Herodotus was still a boy, not more than ten years old and perhaps less.[4] The date usually given for his birth, 484, has been plausibly explained as a deduction from the colonization of Thouria in 444–443;[5] as Herodotus was one of the colonists it was assumed that this important event in his life coincided with its prime, his fortieth year. His migration to Thouria could be inferred from the introduction to his history, in which he described himself as 'Herodotus the Thourian'; such at least was the reading in some manuscripts

---

[1] *A.J.A.* lxiii. 259 ff. (especially 260 A) referring to the view of Hammond in *J.H.S.* lxxvi, 1956, 39.

[2] Contemporary epigrams are not always truthful (cf. Hauvette, 108 and Wells, 155 and see below, p. 39) and even official inscriptions may be misleading (e.g. Tod, no. 19).

[3] References to Jacoby in this section (unless otherwise stated) are to his long article on Herodotus in *R.-E.* Suppl. ii (1913), 205 ff.

[4] Stein, relying on a notice in Eusebius that Hdt. was already known as an historian in 468–467, dated his birth about 500, but Hauvette, 13 argued that it cannot have been before 490 (so too Jacoby, 237).

[5] The deduction was probably made by Apollodoros; cf. Jacoby, 229 f. and HW i. 2 and n. 1. For the form Thouria cf. Wade-Gery in *J.H.S.* lii, 1932, 217, n. 48.

current in the Hellenistic Age,[1] and if all those now extant read instead 'Herodotus the Halikarnassian', this reading is probably a correction made by Alexandrian scholars[2] on the basis of the data which they possessed about Herodotus' life and which they embodied in the biographical notice which has come down to us. According to this outline[3] Herodotus was a native of Halikarnassos whose parents were both of noble birth; when he grew up he became involved in the political struggle against the tyrant Lygdamis and had to retire to Samos. It is not clear why he did not settle again in Halikarnassos after the overthrow of Lygdamis, or why after a long period of residence in Old Greece, mainly spent in Athens, he decided to make his home in Thouria. It has been supposed[4] that he must have left Thouria when dissensions there ended in the triumph of the party opposed to Athens, but it is merely a modern hypothesis that he must have returned to Athens for good by 432 or 431, an hypothesis which is not proved by the few references to the Peloponnesian War contained in his later books. The account given by the biographers is more likely, that he died at Thouria and was buried there.[5]

Scholars have tried to supplement this scanty information by a microscopic examination of the text of the History, from which they claim to have discovered the sequence and approximate dates of the journeys made by Herodotus and also the order in which he composed the first drafts of the different parts of his book. He must at one stage in his life have resided for some years in Old Greece, and it is usually supposed that this period immediately preceded his migration to Thouria, but though this seems the most likely view, the statement of the chronographers

---

[1] Plut. *de exsilio* 13 (*Moralia* 604 F); cf. the temple-chronicle of Lindos, l. 29, and HW i. 53. The reading may have been known in Aristotle's time (cf. his *Rhetoric* 1409ª29); Powell (*The History of Herodotus*, 63 f.) regards the five relevant words in this passage as an interpolation, but thinks they must have originated in a text reading Θουρίου. See also the discussion in Legrand, i (*Introduction*), 13–15.

[2] So HW ad loc.; Jacoby, 209 dislikes this explanation but suggests no other.

[3] 'Suidas' s.v. Ἡρόδοτος, cited in full by Hauvette, 7, n. 1; cf. HW i. 1.

[4] By E. Meyer (*Forsch.* ii. 197 and 222, criticized by Jacoby, 244). On the troubles in Thouria cf. Diodoros xii. 35. 1–3; there is no suggestion there that they resulted in the expulsion of any of the citizens.

[5] Hauvette, 11 and HW i. 3, also Jacoby, 246 (where he reads Ὀλόρου for Ἡροδότου in Marcellinus' life of Thucydides, § 17; so Hauvette, 61 and n. 4). For the view that Hdt. was at Athens in 430 and fell a victim to the plague, cf. Wilamowitz in *Hermes*, xii, 1877, 359, followed by Powell, op. cit. 79.

that he received a reward for his history from the Council at Athens in 446 or 445 is not to be trusted,[1] nor is it probable that particular portions of the work were composed by Herodotus as independent showpieces for recitation in public.[2] His travels in the lands round the eastern Mediterranean may reasonably be dated before his long sojourn in Old Greece; they are not likely to have been undertaken after his departure to South Italy.

Attempts to deduce from internal evidence alone the order in which an ancient historian composed particular sections of his work are always inconclusive, as is shown by the lack of agreement between those scholars who have tried to establish by this method the order of composition in the text of Thucydides or in that of Polybius. It is quite possible that Herodotus wrote his history continuously in its present form, but the arguments of Kirchhoff and his followers[3] designed to establish this conclusion are only valid for the final draft; when they go beyond this and try to prove that the early books (or most of their contents) were written before 443, when Herodotus left Old Greece for the West, the evidence on which they rely is insufficient to justify their conclusions.[4] Hence the view of Jacoby and others, based on the supposed priority of the earlier books, that Herodotus started as a geographer and ethnographer and did not become an historian till later[5] is no more capable of proof than the suggestion of Myres[6] that Herodotus first showed an interest in historical causation at the age of four.

Some of those who take the priority of the early books for granted believe that Herodotus began by writing *Persika*, a

---

[1] Though often accepted, e.g. by Hauvette, 36 ff., also HW i. 6–7 and 7, n. 1; cf. the discussion in Jacoby, 226 ff.

[2] Many still believe that Herodotus gave public recitations, but the ancient evidence for this belief is convincingly refuted by Powell (op. cit. 31–34).

[3] Notably Powell (op. cit.), whose results differ only slightly from those of Kirchhoff.

[4] Kirchhoff and Powell attach much importance to Sophocles, *Antigone* 904–20, lines which were rightly rejected by Jebb as an interpolation, cf. HW i. 294 f. (on Hdt. iii. 119. 6).

[5] Jacoby, 468 and 471. Powell (op. cit. 45) has sufficiently refuted this view by his observation that Herodotus' standpoint in his 'Persian History' (the supposed original draft of Bks. I–IV) was 'fundamentally a historical one, however much ethnography or geography the book may contain'. Cf. de Sanctis, *Studi di storia*, 28.

[6] In his *Herodotus*, 1.

history of the rise of Persia to the early years of Darius, and
only afterwards decided to prolong it by the inclusion of the
wars waged by Darius and Xerxes against the Greeks,[1] but the
alleged *Persika*, apparently stopping short at Darius' conquests in
the first decade of his reign and lacking any unity other than that
provided by the purely external concept of Persian expansion,
is not likely to have appealed to Herodotus at any period of his
life. The rise of Cyrus would form a suitable starting-point for a
history of the Graeco-Persian Wars, and even if Herodotus' account of it originally preceded his version of the reign and fall
of Croesus, with which his history now opens,[2] the later transposition of these two sections could be sufficiently explained by
artistic reasons alone. It is necessary to bear in mind that Herodotus' idea of the subject-matter of history was always far wider
than that of Thucydides; hence it is conceivable that when he
made his extensive travels his object was from the first to gather
information for an historical work on a grand scale which he had
already planned.

On the composition of his work the common-sense view of
Hauvette[3] is as probable as any, that Herodotus took with him
to Thouria the notes which he had previously made on his
travels and in his historical inquiries, that he there proceeded to
write his history as we now have it (adding after the outbreak
of the Peloponnesian War four footnotes on recent events),[4]
and that though he had completed it[5] he had not given it his
final revision when he died somewhere between 428 and 426.
The essential point, on which most scholars would agree, is that

---

[1] This is the view of Powell, c. 2. De Sanctis in *Riv. fil.* liv, 1926, 289 ff. (reprinted in *Studi*, c. 2) had also maintained the priority of the supposed *Persika*, but
hedged his hypothesis about with so many qualifications that his real meaning is
hard to grasp.

[2] As argued by de Sanctis, *Studi*, c. 3 ; cf. Powell, 9–16. But Hdt. may always have
intended to begin with the story of Croesus, which so well illustrated his main
theme, the impermanence of human prosperity, harmonizing it as best he could
with his introduction to Book I and with the Delphic legend that explained
Croesus' fall as delayed retribution for the sin of Gyges (whereby Hdt. was forced
to start with Gyges).

[3] Op. cit. 47 and 54 ff.

[4] Listed in HW i. 9, n. 1 ; cf. Hauvette, 52 ff. (he notes on p. 54 that all four
references have a religious implication).

[5] Kirchhoff's view that Hdt. intended to carry on his history beyond the end of
479 is rejected by most scholars (Hauvette, 55 ff., also Meyer, *Forsch.* ii. 217 f.
Cf. HW i. 15 f. and Powell, 43, n. 1 and 79 f.).

Herodotus must have collected the materials for his history of Xerxes' invasion before he settled in Thouria. Even though much of this material was probably obtained by Herodotus during his long sojourn in Old Greece in the years immediately before 443, this does not exclude the possibility that he had previously decided to write a history of the Persian Wars, and that before he came to Old Greece he had already accumulated a mass of notes on this subject. Even in Asia Minor he could have learnt much about the war of 480–479 from Greeks who had fought on the Persian side, and Jacoby admits[1] that Herodotus probably knew a lot about the war when he first settled in Old Greece, though naturally not as much as he knew later. Anyhow, it seems certain that he investigated the oral traditions of the Great War before 443, and so within forty years of the events.

It is unlikely that these oral traditions had already been committed to writing by a previous historian;[2] Jacoby has ridiculed the hypothesis that all the spade-work had been done before Herodotus began to write and that he merely recast with greater art the materials brought together by a predecessor's labour. Literary sources were certainly consulted by Herodotus, but they were not primarily historical, and the information he derived from them was of secondary importance. They included works on genealogy[3] and geography, but these would be of little help to him in the last three books; there is no need to assume[4] that large parts of his account of Xerxes' march were simply adapted from a geographical handbook. Herodotus had probably read the *Persai* of Aeschylus,[5] but in his description of the battle of Salamis he supplemented Aeschylus' outline with much information derived from oral sources. He also used collections of oracles, either delivered from shrines of the gods or published by soothsayers; of the former the most important was a collection made at Delphi of the responses uttered by the priestess of Apollo.[6] The oracles quoted by him, whether of

---

[1] Op. cit. 371.

[2] In spite of Macan, i, introd., p. lxxv; see above, pp. 10 ff., and cf. Jacoby, 393 f.

[3] Hdt. vi. 55 (with Macan's note).

[4] As Jacoby apparently does (op. cit. 446 ff., also *R.-E.* vii. 2713 ff.).

[5] Cf. Macan, i. 112A (on Hdt. vii. 89. 1), also Jacoby, op. cit. 406.

[6] HW i. 31.

divine or of human origin, cannot always be regarded as authentic contemporary pronouncements, as some had probably
been rewritten after the event. Herodotus had seen many of
the memorials of the war and had studied the scanty epigraphic record, including the famous inscription on the serpent-
column at Delphi.[1] Although he must have been familiar with
the numerous epigrams commemorating the deeds of those
who fought in the war, he mentions only three, all in the chapter[2] which closes his account of the last struggle at Thermopylai.

When describing foreign countries which he had not himself
visited, Herodotus always tried to obtain reports from eyewitnesses.[3] He doubtless did the same when he was investigating
the history of the Great War, questioning survivors whenever
possible on their memories of the events in which they had taken
part, though he mentions only one of these informants by name,
Thersandros of Orchomenos.[4] Thucydides worked on the same
principle, and though he preferred to describe events contemporary with his own maturity, he did not deny the possibility
of finding out the truth about those of an earlier date. His
complaint that most people will not take the trouble to find
out the facts and his claim that he himself was not content
with the first report that came his way may both have been
directed against Herodotus,[5] but if so they are not fully justified.
Herodotus' examination of the oral traditions of the Great War
was perhaps not thorough enough to satisfy Thucydides' high
standards, but he probably consulted the best informants available. The statement in the biography that he was of noble
birth is confirmed by an anecdote in which he pokes fun at
Hekataios; he there implies[6] that if he had thought fit he could
have repeated to the Egyptian priests his own family tree for
many generations. He must not be pictured as a rather seedy
commercial traveller reconstructing naval operations from the

---

[1] The column is mentioned in ix. 81. 1, the inscription in viii. 82. 1.

[2] vii. 228. On Hdt.'s use of inscriptions see the interesting essay by Volkmann
cited in the Bibliography.

[3] iv. 16. 1; cf. iii. 115. 2.

[4] ix. 16. 1. Thersandros is described as 'a man of very high repute in Orchomenos'
(Macaulay's tr.).

[5] Thuc. i. 20. 3 and 22. 2; cf. Jacoby, 474 f.

[6] ii. 143. 1. Hdt.'s interest in Olympic victories is aristocratic; cf. Jacoby, 219.

gossip of Piraeus wineshops,[1] but as a great noble who in each city he visited would naturally consort with the aristocrats, the only trustworthy repositories of local tradition. There was indeed a serious time-lag between their participation in the events and their conversations with Herodotus, but it need not have impaired the accuracy of their recollections, in an age when the original strength of memory had not been weakened by undue dependence on the printed word; how far their accounts were distorted by local patriotism or party prejudice is another matter.[2]

It is not surprising that the traditions collected by Herodotus in Athens and Sparta should be traceable at many points in his narrative, for these two states had played the leading part in the resistance to Xerxes. But if he owed much to his sojourn in Athens and Sparta, he had investigated the oral tradition in many other states of Old Greece, including some which had sided with Persia during the invasion; moreover the information he acquired in Old Greece could be supplemented by what he had previously gathered in Asia Minor. At some stage he had learnt much from the family of the exiled Spartan king Demaratos, who had perhaps been high in Xerxes' favour at the time of the invasion.[3] Much of Herodotus' information about the history and organization of the Persian Empire is so accurate and detailed as to suggest that he must have acquired it, directly or indirectly, from leading members of the Persian nobility.[4] Artabazos, one of the Persian generals who took part in Xerxes' invasion, was later appointed to the governorship of Hellespontine Phrygia (the north-western part of Asia Minor), a position which became hereditary in his family, and Herodotus' references to him are so full and so favourable that they have been attributed to traditions preserved by his descendants,

---

[1] He is interested in trade and commerce (HW. i. 17) because he is interested in so many things. Jacoby, 248 notes that he was weak on arithmetic (for examples cf. HW, notes on i. 33. 3 and vii. 187. 2).

[2] Cf. Thuc. i. 22. 3 for the distortion of oral tradition by εὔνοια.

[3] On the Demaratos-source cf. Jacoby, 476 and 404; there is no evidence that it was anything but an oral source. Trautwein's view that it had been committed to writing by Demaratos' friend Dikaios (Hdt. viii. 65) is to be rejected; cf. Hauvette, 176 ff.

[4] This is more likely than the hypothesis that he got it from an earlier written source (Jacoby, 405 is cautious in his attitude to the view that this source was Dionysios of Miletos); see above, p. 10.

who may have supplied Herodotus with his special knowledge of the Persian Empire.[1] Another possible source of his knowledge is Zopyros, great-grandson of the Megabyzos who was one of the Seven, the conspirators who were responsible for the accession of Darius; the flight of this Zopyros to Athens is mentioned by Herodotus in a reference of tantalizing brevity,[2] and the fuller account of Ktesias is not sufficiently precise in chronology to show whether Herodotus could or could not have met Zopyros.

Herodotus claims to have been guided throughout his history by the principle that he must record what people said, but adds a caution that he is not thereby committed to belief in the truth of their accounts.[3] There must however have been diverse and often contradictory versions of particular incidents, and if Herodotus had included them all, the mass of oral tradition would have become unmanageable. He does sometimes give several conflicting traditions side by side,[4] but this procedure is exceptional, and its adoption seems to be due to one of two opposite motives, either genuine inability to choose between the variants or a desire to stress the superiority of the tradition he has accepted over its rivals, especially when he was anxious to discredit a popular tradition of which he disapproved.[5] Elsewhere he says of the death of Cyrus that though there are many accounts of it he has reported only the one which seems to him the most convincing,[6] and this must have been his normal practice. Its obvious danger is that his judgement on the relative credibility of the reports before him may be mistaken; sometimes his preference for a particular version is evidently dictated by considerations irrelevant to its historical truth.[7] If Herodotus

---

[1] On the Artabazos-source cf. Macan, i, introd. lxxv, n. 8 and HW ii. 276 f.; also see below, p. 270 and n. 1.

[2] iii. 160 (last sentence); cf. Ktesias, *Persika* 43. Bauer suggested that Hdt. met Zopyros in Athens (cf. Jacoby, 431). Wells (*Studies*, c. 5) dates the meeting to 440, but Hdt. had surely left for Thouria in 443, though he may have revisited Athens later. Cf. also Powell, op. cit. 30 f. and 31, n. 1.

[3] vii. 152. 3; cf. ii. 123. 1.

[4] Notably in vii. 148–52.

[5] Cf. Jacoby, 473 f. for a valuable discussion; he cites Thuc. ii. 5. 6 and i. 20. 2 as parallels for the two types, and Hdt. vi. 121–4 as the outstanding example of the second.

[6] i. 214. 5; cf. i. 95. 1, where he admits that three other traditions about the rise of Cyrus are known to him.

[7] e.g. on the catastrophe at Thermopylai; see below, Appendix IV.

had always repeated all the available traditions, his book might
have been less readable but it would certainly have been more
valuable to the modern historian. Nevertheless, his scrupulous
respect for truth caused him to reproduce faithfully those traditions which seemed to him worthy of preservation, and his
empirical method has great value; he has often included items
which he disbelieved or failed to estimate at their true value,
items which enable us to correct or criticize other parts of his
narrative.

It is easy to dilate on the weaknesses of Herodotus as an
historian, but more important to call attention to his un-
deniable merits. He was a pioneer whose achievement alone
made it possible for Thucydides to go further.[1] As Momigliano
has observed,[2] Herodotus on a basis of sightseeing and oral
tradition produced a very respectable history. His last three
books, describing Xerxes' invasion and its failure, are the most
successful from the historical point of view, and all subsequent
accounts are necessarily based on them. He was here dealing
with events which were within the memory of his informants, but
his success was not due merely to his careful regard for accuracy
in his record of their stories. He took the trouble to check their
evidence to the best of his ability and to supplement it by personal inspection of the ground; he was certainly familiar with
the topography of Northern and Central Greece, and it should
never have been doubted that he had visited the battlefields of
Thermopylai and Plataia. He has sometimes been accused of
bias in favour of or against particular Greek states, a charge
which must be examined later, but though he valued highly
the Greek way of life he was free from national prejudice;
with his broad sympathies he could appreciate the good quali-
ties of enemy peoples, including the Phoenicians and even the
Persians,[3] and his readiness to call attention to them was as
irritating to Plutarch as his frank recognition of the selfishness displayed by many Greek states before and during the invasion.

Herodotus has often been attacked on grounds irrelevant to
the present inquiry. Weakness in chronology is more characteristic of the earlier part of his Greek history, and it has been

---

[1] Cf. Jacoby, 472.   [2] In *History*, xliii, 1958, 3.
[3] Jacoby, 469 and HW i. 37 f.

pointed out[1] that, at the time when he was writing, official lists
of Athenian archons and Olympic victors were not yet available to provide a chronological framework for the archaic
period. When he came to describe the events of 481–479 he was
helped by the lucky accident that an Olympic festival occurred
in 480, in the middle of the triennium, and by a diary of the
Persian fleet which dated its movements from day to day at a
crucial stage in the operations;[2] even so it is surprising that with
the rudimentary means at his disposal he was able to establish
with fair accuracy and precision the most important dates of the
Great War.

As a born story-teller Herodotus delighted to give artistic
expression to popular tales current in Greece about famous
personages such as Periandros, Solon, and Polykrates;[3] they
were useful to him as supplements to his scanty evidence for the
seventh and sixth centuries, and if they illustrated character or
taught a moral lesson he was content to accept them without
too close a scrutiny of their historical truth. It is, however, unfair to single out those parts of his work in which this 'novelistic' element preponderates;[4] Herodotus reduces it where the
stream of genuine historical tradition flowed more copiously,
though even in the last three books he can never resist a good
story which appears relevant to his main theme, whether it
serves to illustrate the character of Xerxes, the nature of his
despotism, or the value attached by Greeks to athletic fame.[5]

In addition to such tales there are two other types of non-
historical material present in the last three books. The many
speeches put into the mouths of real persons do not claim to
reproduce faithfully the purport of what the speaker said, if
indeed he delivered a speech at all on the particular occasion;
they are invented to reveal character, to explain the grounds of
a policy, or to elucidate the strategical considerations by which
the two sides were guided. If their function is clearly understood
they serve a useful purpose, and the practice of Thucydides in
this respect does not differ much from that of Herodotus, in
spite of his claim to have kept closely to the general sense of

[1] Jacoby, 405 and 468.   [2] See below, Appendixes V and XIV.
[3] Cf. HW i. 35 (2) and Jacoby, 483; Germans call such tales *Novellen*.
[4] This point is made by Jacoby, 472.
[5] vii. 38 f. (a similar tale is told of Darius in iv. 84), viii. 118 f. (a tale rejected by
Hdt. himself on historical grounds), and viii. 26.

what was actually said.[1] Quite different, because harder to
detect, are the fictitious elements which early permeated the
authentic oral tradition and owed their origin to a variety of
causes, panegyric, spite, or simple error; obvious examples are
the tales that have grown up round the name of Themistokles.
Herodotus was not cautious enough in dealing with mere legend
and gossip, and repeats such a story as the alleged bribery of
Themistokles by the Euboians without any consciousness of its
inherent improbabilities.[2]

The credulity of Herodotus is especially manifested in the
sphere of religion. Although his maturity coincided with the
rise to importance of the Sophists, he remained faithful, like his
friend Sophokles, to the orthodoxy of his youth, and it cannot
be denied that his religious beliefs were a serious handicap to
him when he began to write history.[3] It was not merely that his
philosophy of history, so far as he had one, was purely theological, for an historian may hold that the march of events is
ultimately controlled by an overruling Providence. Herodotus
went further, and believed in the continuous interference of the
divine in the lives of men. In consequence of this belief, which
Thucydides wisely rejected, Herodotus took it for granted that
the gods proclaimed their will or their foreknowledge to men in
dreams or omens, and above all through the mouths of seers or
the responses of oracles. When in his researches he hears any
tale of the supernatural he accepts it without criticism, whether
it tells of the miraculous deliverance of Apollo's temple at
Delphi from Persian attack or the mysterious rumour about the
Greek victory at Plataia which reached the fleet off Asia Minor
on the same day as the battle was fought;[4] it is dangerous to
rationalize such stories, which may be pure fiction invented for
the edification of the faithful. Herodotus' orthodoxy sometimes
influences in a subtler way his presentation of events. Jacoby
has observed[5] that he does not trouble to look for historical

---

[1] Thuc. i. 22. 1; cf. Jacoby, 494. Jacoby has an admirable account (492 ff.) of
the speeches in Hdt., distinguishing the 'novelistic' speeches (usually short) from
what he calls the 'political-historical' speeches.

[2] viii. 4. 2–5. 3; cf. HW ii. 236 f.

[3] Cf. Jacoby, 479 ff. (especially 481 f.), also HW i. 41 and 48 f., and on the theo-
logy of Hdt. see de Sanctis, Studi, 53 ff.

[4] viii. 37–39 and ix. 100; see below, pp. 445 f. and 258 f.

[5] Op. cit. 482.

motives and explanations when a theological answer is available, and that although he knew all the factors responsible for Xerxes' invasion of Greece he preferred to believe that Xerxes was convinced against his better judgement by a vision of divine origin. When he described the last stand of Leonidas and his men at Thermopylai he not only preferred the version which made their deaths an act of self-sacrifice in obedience to an oracle, but dismissed the alternative tradition so briefly that the truth can no longer be discovered.[1]

A modern historian can make allowances in his reconstruction for the weaknesses in Herodotus already described, which are generally admitted by scholars. But Herodotus has often been accused of a more serious fault, the systematic distortion of the real facts by his prejudices in favour of some states and against others. It has been argued[2] that he wrote his history as a panegyric on Athens, and that his attitude to other states was influenced by their relations with Athens, so that he showed excessive tolerance towards her allies and friends, such as Thessaly, Phokis, and Argos, and excessive hostility to her enemies, Aigina, Corinth, and Thebes; this hypothesis is sometimes combined with the view[3] that his history was hastily rewritten in its present form on the eve of the Peloponnesian War as an apologia for Athens. Jacoby, usually cautious, goes so far as to say[4] that Herodotus' work is strongly subjective because both *ira* and *studium* were present as godparents at its birth; he thinks[5] that if Herodotus avoided gross unfairness to Sparta it was because he could not forget his old admiration for Sparta and the Dorian way of life, and his appreciation of Sparta's contribution to the final victory, especially on land.

There are undeniably traces of bias in Herodotus, but their extent has been greatly exaggerated, and so far as they exist they were already in the traditions as he received them, not superimposed by him on an authentic record; if blame attaches to him

---

[1] vii. 220; see below, Appendix IV.
[2] By E. Meyer, *Forsch.* ii. 202 ff. (followed by HW i. 39 ff.).
[3] Meyer, ii. 229; cf. Powell, *The History of Herodotus*, especially 78 f. and 85 f.
[4] Op. cit. 485, where Jacoby argues that Hdt. wished to inculcate the lesson that the Greek world could only stand up to the Persian Empire if headed by a strong Athens; if this was Hdt.'s message he did not succeed in conveying it very plainly. Cf. also Jacoby, 358 ff. (on p. 360 Hdt. is described as 'an Athenian by adoption'; cf. Powell, 86).   [5] Op. cit. 478.

it can only be on the ground that he was not sufficiently on his guard against possible prejudice in his informants. Particular examples of his alleged bias will be examined later as they occur; in general it must be remembered, as Hauvette pointed out,[1] that Herodotus is not necessarily prejudiced in favour of Athens because he praises her for the initiative shown by her leaders and the self-sacrifice of her citizens, as even the most impartial of historians would be bound to stress the outstanding part played by the Athenians in the Great War.

In the political sphere Herodotus' attempts to explain the behaviour of states and statesmen during the war are frequently inadequate. This was not always his fault; his failure to estimate correctly the difficulties of Sparta in this period may be partly due to the traditional secrecy of her government.[2] Whatever may be the reason, he was too severe in his strictures on the policy followed by the Spartans in 479, and never understood the political or military grounds for their reluctance to take the offensive in Central Greece, though they can be deduced easily enough by a careful analysis of the facts recorded in his narrative. But he was always more at home with details than with general principles, and tended to prefer the personal explanation, as in his account of the motives which prompted the invasion of Xerxes. He was also hampered by the deficiencies of the oral traditions on which he had to depend. His failure to appreciate the true greatness of Themistokles simply reflects the prejudices of his Athenian sources; it is unnecessary to suppose[3] that these were exclusively Alkmeonid, for all parties in Athens were ready to blacken Themistokles' memory after his fall.

As a military historian Herodotus has been roughly handled by his critics, but his ignorance of military matters has been much exaggerated. Obviously he cannot in this respect bear comparison with Thucydides, but we cannot be sure that he had had no practical experience of army life; his military service,

---

[1] *Hérodote*, 43; a grudging admission to this effect is also made by Meyer, *Forsch.* ii. 202. For a valuable protest against the hypothesis of Hdt.'s alleged bias in favour of Athens see the essay by Strasburger cited in the Bibliography.

[2] Thuc. v. 68. 2. See below, p. 280.

[3] As Jacoby, 413 f. tends to do (cf. Meyer, *Forsch.* ii. 223 f.). The fall of Themistokles may have been largely brought about by Kimon; cf. Stesimbrotos in Plut. *Them.* 24. 6.

for all that we know, might bear comparison with that of
Gibbon in the Hampshire Grenadiers. His imperfect grasp of
strategical principles must be admitted, but it is absurd to
maintain that he is as ignorant of tactics as of strategy.[1] Naturally
he does not trouble to describe Greek tactics,[2] but he has some
valuable references to Persian methods of fighting on land, the
tactics employed by their infantry and cavalry, and the technique by which a Greek phalanx could deal with an attack of
Persian cavalry on an open plain.[3] His descriptions of naval
engagements are less successful than his land battles, but this
may be due not to ignorance of naval affairs but to the greater
difficulty of reconstructing a sea-fight from the recollections of
those whose knowledge of its course was confined to a small
part of the whole.[4]

An historian like Herodotus, dependent on the oral traditions
of survivors and lacking a clear understanding of strategy, is
likely to be more trustworthy in his descriptions of the movements of armies than in his attempts to explain them. If he says
that an army moved from point A to point B he is probably
right, but when he tries to give a reason for the movement he
may easily be wrong. When he began to write, the generals and
admirals who had taken part in the war were all dead, and
though many of the survivors whom he met must have been of
the officer class, they were not necessarily in the secrets of the
high command. Yet Herodotus sometimes has an illuminating
observation on strategy. His discussions of strategical questions
are mainly to be found in the speeches; so on one occasion[5] he
makes a Persian admiral emphasize the Persian strategy,
followed by Darius as well as by Xerxes, of maintaining the
closest possible connexion between the movements of the land
and the sea forces, though he fails to realize fully that this interdependence of the fleet and army conditioned the Persian plans
throughout the campaign of 480 and thereby imposed a corresponding limitation on the strategy of the Greeks.

---

[1] There is an amusing picture (from the Persian point of view) of the strategy
normally adopted by Greek states in their wars with each other in Hdt. vii. 9.
β 1; cf. Grundy, *Thucydides*, 250 ff.

[2] Cf. Grundy, op. cit. 240 ff.   [3] ix. 62. 3, 49. 2, 18. 1.

[4] Cf. the remarks of Tarn quoted below, p. 231.

[5] vii. 236. 2 (Achaimenes). For the reaction of this on the Greek strategy cf.
Macan, ii. 262 f.

What has done more than anything else to ruin the credit of Herodotus as a military historian is undoubtedly what Macan has called[1] his 'arithmetical irresponsibility', his absurd over-estimates for the land forces which accompanied Xerxes in his invasion of Greece. It is true that the Persian numbers lost nothing in the telling, and that soon after the invasion the poet Simonides could give three millions as the number of Xerxes' fighting men at Thermopylai. Nevertheless, Herodotus cannot escape censure for his failure to criticize these inflated estimates; he seems to have made no attempt to picture to himself what problems of time, space, and, supply[2] would be created for the Persian high command by an army of nearly two million men, exclusive of the non-combatants in its train. Nor is he merely passive in face of the exaggerations which he found in the oral traditions; having obtained from some source the figure 1,800,000 for Xerxes' Asiatic troops, he proceeds to add 300,000 for the European allies of Persia, and by a process of calculation as ridiculous as it is elaborate finally reaches[3] a total of 5,283,220 for the men who took part in the invasion by land and sea. For this grotesque result he alone must bear the blame, as for the equally grotesque supposition that the Persian fleet after its heavy losses in the great storm was restored to its original strength by the contingents of a few small islands.[4] His figures for the army which Xerxes later left with Mardonios are less fantastic but are not necessarily more credible.

In spite of all these weaknesses, the history of Herodotus, based on the reports of eyewitnesses of the events, provides the only sure basis for a modern reconstruction of the Persian War, as no reliance can be placed on the other ancient accounts where they differ from his. This does not mean that we need do no more than reproduce uncritically the substance of his last three books; there is a middle course between blind acceptance of his narrative and a radical scepticism which destroys the foundations on which alone we can safely build. The modern historian in his version of the war must make the necessary allowances for all Herodotus' failings. It is fairly easy to cut out

[1] Op. cit., vol. i, introd., p. lxxxii. See below, Appendix I, p. 350.
[2] He does not draw the consequences from his own calculation (vii. 187. 2) of the supplies that would be needed by a force of this size.
[3] In vii. 186. 2; on the European troops cf. 185. 2.
[4] viii. 66; see below, p. 345.

all the fictions introduced into the tradition by gossip and
legend, to correct the distortions produced by the intrusion of
the supernatural, and to reduce the swollen estimates of the
enemy forces (though critics may disagree on the figures to be
substituted for them). Fortunately, the oral tradition preserved
by Herodotus often provides the corrective to his own statements where they are in error.[1] What is more difficult is to
detect and eliminate those items in the military history of the
war as recorded by him which are unacceptable because impossible or highly improbable. However much conservative
critics may dislike this procedure, it cannot be shirked; the
critic must, however, make sure to the best of his ability that
any statement or report in Herodotus really is untenable before
he rejects it, and must not allow himself to be led astray by false
criteria. Hence the indispensable preliminary to a reconstruction of the Persian Wars is a survey of the available information
about the military organization and methods of fighting on both
sides; this alone can provide the necessary safeguard against
misleading analogies derived from modern warfare.

The Persian and the Greek forces[2]

Xerxes is assumed by Herodotus to have been accompanied
in his invasion of Greece by contingents from all the peoples of
his empire,[3] and Herodotus later gives a catalogue of them,
forty-six in the army (including eight who provided cavalry as
well as infantry[4]) and eight who served only in the fleet. The
nucleus of the imperial army was composed of the Persians of
the homeland, by whom the conquest of the empire had been
achieved, but it is disputed to what extent, if at all, they were

---

[1] Cf. Macan, ii. 262, first sentence of section (c).

[2] On this section cf. especially the article by How in *J.H.S.* xliii, 1923, 117 ff.
(reprinted in HW², ii. 397–414), Tarn, *Hellenistic Military and Naval Developments*,
and Grundy, *Thucydides*, cc. 9–14, also the works by Kromayer–Veith (*Heerwesen*)
and Adcock cited in the Bibliography.

[3] Cf. the second sentence in vii. 21. 1, also the opening words of the catalogue in
61 ff. On the sources of the catalogue cf. Macan, ii. 182; it should probably be
regarded rather as a description of all the peoples in the Persian Empire than
as an accurate list of those who supplied troops to the host that crossed the Hellespont with Xerxes.

[4] On the assumption that the Sagartioi of vii. 85 count as native Persians
(cf. i. 125. 4 and HW on iii. 93. 2) and that καὶ Σάκαι is read for καὶ Κάσπιοι at the
end of vii. 86. 1 (see HW ad loc.).

supplemented by levies from the rest of the empire. Meyer maintained[1] that though the Persians incorporated in their cavalry horsemen from the kindred peoples in their eastern provinces they refrained from making much use of the infantry of their other subjects. Delbrück went much farther and argued that the army was composed almost exclusively of native Persians, from whom were drawn the forces stationed usually in the heart of the empire and also the bulk of the garrisons maintained by the satraps who governed the various provinces.[2] He admitted that additional troops would have been needed for such an undertaking as the invasion of Greece, but claimed that they could have been raised from the most warlike of the shepherds and farmers of Persis alone.[3]

No evidence is cited by Delbrück for many of his assertions. The existence of a central army in close attendance on the king is demonstrable;[4] it presumably included the 10,000 men of the Guard, the famous Immortals, but need not have been very large. There were also permanent garrisons in distant provinces of doubtful allegiance, such as Egypt, where a Persian force occupied a strong position near Memphis, the White Castle;[5] in most provinces, however, Darius seems to have been reluctant to allow his satraps to maintain large permanent forces.[6] Each satrap doubtless had his bodyguard, perhaps composed mainly of soldiers from the ruling race, but this was apparently small; it was regarded as abnormal for a satrap to have a bodyguard of 1,000 native Persians.[7] When the permanent forces in most provinces were so limited, it would have been dangerous to draw heavily on them for a war beyond the frontiers of the empire. Finally, Delbrück disregards the evidence of Herodotus, who asserts[8] that liability to military service was one of the

---

[1] *G.d.A.* iii. 77, also 69.   [2] *Kriegskunst*, 47 ff.

[3] Op. cit. 50. Delbrück does not explain why these additional levies should have been more 'professional' than the citizen soldiers of the Greek states.

[4] Cf. Isokrates iv. 145 and Meyer, 70 n. Meyer calls this central army the *Präsenzarmee*; it is ˙apparently the στρατιή of Hdt. i. 192. 1, which seems to be a permanent force.

[5] iii. 91. 3 (cf. Thuc. i. 104. 2). The corn which the Egyptians had to provide for these Persians 'and their mercenaries' amounted to 120,000 medimnoi a year; if the allowance for each man was the usual one choinix a day (vii. 187. 2), the garrison of Egypt would have been about 16,000 men.

[6] Cf. Grundy (*G.P.W.*), 49.

[7] iii. 127. 1.

[8] Notably in the last sentence of iii. 67. 3; cf. Wells, *Studies*, 147.

obligations imposed by the Persians on their subjects, and presupposes that those which did not provide ships were frequently
called on to supply troops. Delbrück argues[1] that Herodotus'
narrative is inconsistent, for after describing Xerxes' army as
composed of large unwarlike masses he stressed the strength
and bravery of the Persian warriors, but Delbrück is here misled by the ambiguity of the term Persian, which in a military
context may signify either the natives of Persis or the soldiers
of the empire as a whole.[2]

It is possible that Herodotus himself was not always on his
guard against this ambiguity, and that some of his statements
about the army in general apply in fact only to the Persians in
the narrower sense, such as his references to their method of
fighting in tens or in larger units.[3] He attributes to the whole
army an elaborate decimal organization in groups of 10,000
(myriads), subdivided into thousands, hundreds, and tens, with
a corresponding hierarchy of officers from the myriarch to the
dekarch,[4] far superior to anything on the Greek side, but it is
impossible to be sure that the contingents of the subject peoples,
mobilized for a particular campaign only, were organized in
the same fashion. Anyhow, the fact that the Guards were called
the Immortals because they were always kept at full strength[5]
indicates that the decimal organization was merely nominal in
the rest of the infantry, at least for the larger units. The Persians
of the homeland were undoubtedly the best of the infantry and
were accordingly used for the most important tasks;[6] the majority of them, if not all, were probably regular and professional
troops. Next to them came the Medes, who were so closely
associated with the Persians that their nobles shared the high
administrative posts with the Persian aristocracy. The Elamites,
called Kissians by Herodotus, also ranked high;[7] they seem to
have been included in Cyrus' original kingdom, and it has been
inferred from the monuments that Elamites as well as Medes

---

[1] Op. cit. 49, with reference to Hdt. ix. 62. 3.

[2] As pointed out by Obst, 76.

[3] In tens, ix. 62. 3; in larger units (called τέλεα; cf. HW on vii. 81), vii. 211. 3,
&c.

[4] vii. 81.   [5] vii. 83. 1; cf. Obst, 85.

[6] e.g. in iii. 155. 6. In viii. 113. 3 the Medes are said to be inferior in bodily
strength (ῥώμη) to the Persians; on their share in the administration of the empire see below, p. 78.

[7] Cf. vii. 210. 1, also HW i. 283 (on iii. 91. 4) and 386 f.

were admitted to serve in the Guards with the native Persians.[1]
Xerxes' army in 480 almost certainly contained infantry from
other peoples of the empire, but the military value of these
levies was low; most of them were naturally unwarlike, and they
fought unwillingly for their Persian masters.

In his catalogue Herodotus describes the characteristic dress
and arms of the various contingents in the Persian host, but his
account is demonstrably eclectic and incomplete, so that no
argument can safely be based on his omissions. There are only
occasional references to footwear, but this does not prove that
the rest of the army, including the Persians and Medes, went
unshod;[2] the monuments prove that the Persian Guard at least
wore boots. Herodotus' references to shields are no less selective,
and Macan argues[3] that in spite of his silence some of the
peoples of Inner Asia, particularly the Bactrians, must have been
armed with a light shield or target. A further difficulty is that
in his description of the cavalry contingents[4] Herodotus gives
no details except on the Sagartian nomads, whose principal
weapon was the lasso; for the rest he merely says of each people
that its cavalry was armed in the same way as its infantry,
though he notes that some of the Persian cavalry also wore
metal helmets. It is doubtful, however, whether the native
Persian foot-soldier was armed, apart from the helmet, in precisely the same way as the cavalry, and in particular whether
he wore the padded linen corslet, covered with metal scales,
which the Persians are said elsewhere to have copied from the
Egyptians.[5] This was certainly worn by some at least of the
cavalry, but on grounds of expense it is unlikely that it was also
worn by the infantry; moreover, in their struggle with the
Spartan hoplites at Plataia they are described as unarmed,[6]

[1] Cf. Olmstead, 238.   [2] Macan, ii. 180 f. and 168.
[3] Op. cit. 180. Meyer, 78 points out that the Assyrians on the monuments are
armed with bows (which are not mentioned in vii. 63).
[4] vii. 84 ff. (helmets of Persian cavalry in 84).
[5] i. 135 (cf. vii. 89. 3). Masistios the leader of the Persian cavalry at Plataia is
said to have worn such a corslet, and it seems to be attributed to the native Persian
infantry as well in vii. 61, though the words καὶ θώρηκας have dropped out of the
text. On the linen corslet cf. Page, *Sappho and Alcaeus*, 215 f.
[6] ix. 63. 2. See Delbrück, 46 f. and Meyer, 76 (he points out that an equipment
like that of a Greek hoplite would have impaired the mobility and speed in
attack required for a corps of archers). The words τῶν ἄλλων Περσέων τοὺς θωρη-
κοφόρους in viii. 113. 2 are puzzling; Powell (tr. ii. 718 ad loc.) proposes to read
αἰχμοφόρους (possibly those of vii. 40. 2 and 41. 1).

which in this connexion seems to mean that they had no protection for their bodies.

Greeks were amazed that Orientals should go into battle with only caps on their heads and trews on their legs.[1] Most of the infantry contingents from the eastern part of the empire had no defensive armour (except perhaps a shield), no greaves, corslets, or helmets. The Mesopotamians (called Assyrians by Herodotus)[2] form the main exception to this rule for the land force; various maritime peoples, especially the Egyptians, supplied heavy infantry as marines for the fleet. The Persian regulars carried a wicker shield (*gerrhon*), which could be set up in the ground so that the archer could discharge his arrows from behind it.[3] Their offensive weapons included a dagger and a short spear,[4] but they relied mainly, like other contingents from the eastern provinces, on long-distance weapons such as the bow, which was the national weapon of the Persians, borne by their king on his coins. There is little evidence available for the range of ancient bows.[5] Strabo says that Mithridates of Pontus shot an arrow from the roof of a temple for a distance of over 200 yards, but the effective range of a Persian archer was probably not more than 120 yards.[6]

The cavalry of the Persian homeland was perhaps provided by the great landowners and their retainers.[7] Some of them wore metal helmets and probably corslets of the Egyptian type, but otherwise they were armed in the same way as the Persian regular infantry. This native cavalry could be supplemented not only by Medes and Elamites but by the excellent horsemen of the Bactrians and the Sakai, the latter of whom were armed

---

[1] So Aristagoras in v. 49. 3; it is curious that in v. 97. 1 he is made to assert that the Persians carried neither shields nor spears.

[2] vii. 63; on the Egyptians cf. vii. 89. 3 and Macan, ii. 174.

[3] ix. 61. 3 (Plataia) and 102. 2–3 (Mykale).

[4] The αἰχμὴ βραχέα is associated with the bow as the characteristic weapon of the Persians in v. 49. 3; cf. vii. 61. 1. Meyer, 76 thinks the spear was an innovation, taken over by the Medes (and from them by the Persians; cf. vii. 62. 1) from the Assyrians.

[5] For a discussion see the long note in Delbrück, 60 f., with a reference to Strabo xiv. 1. 23 (p. 641); cf. Kromayer, *Abh. d. Sächs. Akad.* xxxiv, 10, n. 2.

[6] 100 to 150 paces according to Delbrück (foot of p. 60). In HW's note on vi. 112. 1 'bowshot' seems to be regarded as 200 yards, but the fire of the Persian archers could not have been effective at this range.

[7] Tarn, 51; he does not quote any evidence for this statement, which may be an inference from the later Parthian system (e.g. Plut. *Crassus* 21. 7).

with axes as well;[1] all these peoples, some of whom were akin to
the Persians in race and religion, could be relied on to fight
bravely for their Persian rulers. Xenophon says[2] that each
Persian horseman carried two light spears (παλτά), one to be
thrown like a javelin and the other for thrusting in hand-to-
hand fighting, and both seem to have been used by the Persian
cavalry in their first encounter with Alexander the Great at the
Granikos;[3] but although some at least of the Persian foot, for
example the Guard, were certainly armed with the thrusting
spear by 480, it may not have been taken over by the cavalry
till later.

Herodotus[4] compares the Persian cavalry with mounted
archers, saying that they discharged their arrows and javelins
from a safe distance and avoided close combat. Similar tactics
were employed by a Greek cavalry force over a hundred years
later, except that the missiles on which they relied were javelins only.[5] The history of the Persian Wars shows that an unbroken phalanx of Greek spearmen could not be successfully
charged by cavalry.[6] After Persian archers had failed to break
the ranks of the Spartan phalanx at Plataia, nothing more is
heard of the Persian cavalry until the retreat, when they helped
to protect their own fugitives and hamper the pursuers.[7] It is
impossible to say whether they could have operated effectively
against a Greek phalanx on an open plain by shooting arrows
into it without coming to close quarters until it was completely
demoralized, as the Romans were by the mounted archers of the
Parthians at Carrhae; perhaps their supply of arrows would
have been inadequate for such tactics.[8] Actually they were never
able to force the Greeks to fight on an open plain; being the
aggressors they had to fight on ground chosen by the defenders.

---

[1] vii. 64. 2; the Sakai fought well at Plataia (ix. 71. 1).

[2] *Cyrop.* i. 2. 9.

[3] Arrian, *Anabasis* i. 15. 2 and 5; the second passage implies the use of the
παλτόν as a thrusting spear, but Tarn (54 and 71 f.) maintains that in the war with
Alexander the Persian cavalry was armed with daggers and javelins at first, and did
not have spears till Gaugamela.

[4] ix. 49. 2.   [5] Xen. *Hell.* vii. 1. 21.

[6] This is the usual view; cf. Grundy, *Thucydides*, 278 f. and Tarn, 53. It is disputed (on insufficient grounds) by Kromayer–Veith, 93.

[7] Hdt. ix. 68; cf. Thuc. v. 73. 1 and Kromayer–Veith, 92.

[8] This was the problem so brilliantly solved by the Parthian commander at
Carrhae; cf. Plut. *Crassus* 25. 1 (with 21. 7) and Tarn, 89 ff.

In arms, and consequently in tactics, the infantry contingents of the patriotic Greeks differed profoundly from those of the native Persians and their eastern subjects. The Greek states in the Peloponnese and in part of Central Greece relied almost exclusively for success in war on their heavy-armed footmen, the hoplites. Although hoplites could only operate effectively on level ground, this limitation had not hitherto proved a disadvantage, for the typical offensive strategy in Greece was to invade the territory of another state and by beginning to ravage the crops on which it depended for sustenance force it to accept battle in the plain or submit without fighting.[1] The hoplites had adequate defensive armour, a rather heavy metal helmet[2] with a shield some 3 feet in diameter and greaves as well, with a spear about 8 feet long and a short sword for attack. They were drawn up for battle in close formation, which perhaps allowed no more than a space of 3 feet square to each man;[3] this formation, the phalanx, was usually eight deep in the fifth century.

A Greek state would if possible avoid the risk of combat unless approximately equal in hoplite strength to the enemy.[4] Hence the numbers would be nearly the same on both sides in a pitched battle, and any general who was tempted to snatch an advantage by deepening part of his phalanx might find himself outflanked by the hoplites of the enemy; Greek generals always dreaded a flank attack although they apparently never used it.[5] At Marathon Miltiades reconciled the conflicting claims of depth and length by making his front equal to that of the Persians, but the centre of his phalanx shallower than the rest; he was thereby enabled to defeat the Persians on both wings and then turn inwards to deal with the victorious Persian centre. But in a normal Greek battle a general would put his best troops on the right wing and his second-best on the left wing, hoping that

---

[1] See Grundy, *Thucydides*, c. 9, also Thuc. v. 14. 3 and vii. 28. 3. Even in the early fourth century this strategy was effective against the Akarnanians because their towns were all situated away from the sea (Xen. *Hell*. iv. 7. 1).

[2] Grundy, 244, n. 1; on Greek armour in general cf. the discussion in Page, *Sappho and Alcaeus*, 211 ff.

[3] This is the usual view, based on Polybius xviii. 29. 2, but attacked in Kromayer–Veith, 79 on the ground that in the Greek phalanx the men must have been less closely packed than in the Macedonian. On the depth of the phalanx cf. HW[2] 402 f.

[4] Adcock, 14.

[5] Instances in Grundy, 271. For Miltiades cf. Hdt. vi. 111. 3.

the left would be able to hold the enemy troops facing them until he had won the battle with his right.[1]

Victory in a pitched battle depended on two factors, the amount of weight brought to bear by the phalanx on its opponents, and the extent to which it was successful in maintaining its formation intact while charging.[2] The importance of weight helps to explain why Greek armies did not develop a reserve;[3] it was essential to bring as many men as possible to bear in the first charge. To heighten the shock of its impact the Greek phalanx often completed the last part of its advance at the double; Xenophon states[4] that the Thebans at the battle of Koroneia in 394 broke into a run when they were still 200 yards from the enemy, whereas the mercenaries and Asiatic Greeks in the army of Agesilaos waited until they were only a hundred yards away before they followed their example. This practice was adopted by the Athenians at Marathon for another purpose; by advancing at the double when they came within range of the Persian archers they suffered fewer casualties, and this was later the recognized method of dealing with archers.[5]

There was always a danger that if a phalanx advanced rapidly for even a short distance it might lose the close formation on which success partly depended. It was from fear of this danger, according to Thucydides,[6] that the Spartans preferred to advance steadily and slowly; they sacrificed the additional impetus gained by the final run, relying on the firm cohesion of their phalanx to break the first shock of the enemy charge, and knowing that the superiority of their own hoplites in the use of their weapons would decide the issue at close quarters.[7] Thucydides adds that the Spartans had pipers in their ranks to keep them in step; this certainly suggests that other Greek armies did not march in step, which if correct would throw light on the amazing confusion which accompanied the nocturnal retreat of the Greek army at Plataia.[8]

---

[1] Grundy, 270 f.   [2] Grundy, 267 ff.

[3] Grundy, 270 and Tarn, 4. For the use of a reserve by Nikias in his first battle at Syracuse cf. Thuc. vi. 67. 1. See also Xen. *Anab.* vi. 5. 9.

[4] *Hell.* iv. 3. 17.

[5] Diod., xiv. 23. 1; cf. How in *C.Q.* xiii, 1919, 42 (and in HW[2] 405).

[6] v. 70.

[7] Kromayer–Veith, 84 f. and Adcock, 8.

[8] See below, p. 327. The Persians seem to have learnt to march in step; cf. Xen. *Anab.* i. 8. 11 (on Kunaxa).

Greek armies at the time of the Peloponnesian War included both cavalry and light-armed troops, but there was no cavalry at all in the army with which Pausanias faced the Persians at Plataia, and the military value of his light-armed troops was probably small. Cavalry had been the principal part of a Greek army in the period when Greece was ruled by aristocracies,[1] but it had declined with the rise of the hoplite phalanx, probably because the phalanx while it kept its formation was invulnerable to cavalry attack; hence cavalry plays little part in the pitched battles of the fifth century. It was, however, useful in other ways,[2] on reconnaissance, and generally to dominate the open country, so that it could protect the foragers of its own army and disperse those of the enemy;[3] also it could defend retreating troops against pursuit.[4] The only Greek cavalry which was of any importance in the early fifth century, the Thessalian and Boiotian, eventually joined Xerxes, but their defection from the Greek cause mattered little, as there was not much ground south of the Kithairon–Parnes range that was suitable for the operations of cavalry.[5]

Every Greek hoplite at Plataia was accompanied by an attendant except the full citizens of Sparta, the Spartiatai, who are said to have had not less than seven attendants each, drawn from the Helot class.[6] Herodotus regards all the attendants, including the Helots, as light-armed troops, but their effectiveness was limited.[7] They were not entirely unarmed; Delbrück thinks that they carried at least a dagger or a hatchet and possibly a light spear,[8] and they might from the rear of the phalanx throw stones over the heads of the hoplites at an advancing

[1] Arist. *Politics* 1297[b]16 ff.

[2] Cf. Grundy, 277 f. (quoting Thuc. ii. 100. 5 for its effectiveness against light-armed troops) and Kromayer–Veith, 92 f.

[3] e.g. Thuc. vii. 4. 6.

[4] As at Plataia (Hdt. ix. 68). Cf. the Athenian cavalry at Mantineia in Thuc. v. 73. 1–3.

[5] On the unsuitableness of Attica for cavalry cf. Hdt. ix. 13. 3 and Thuc. vii. 27. 5. Adcock, 48 suggests that horses were apt to go lame on stony ground because horseshoes had not yet been invented.

[6] ix. 29 and 61. 2.

[7] Grundy, 274 remarks that the part played by light-armed troops 'was so inferior that it is very difficult to say what it actually was'.

[8] Op. cit. 36. Tyrtaios (Diehl, fr. 8, ll. 35 ff.) describes the γυμνῆτες in the Spartan army of his day as fighting with stones and javelins. Their ineffectiveness at Plataia is inferred from Pausanias' appeal to the Athenians (Hdt. ix. 60).

enemy, but they seem to have been useless against the Persian archers. The more backward Greek states, such as the Akarnanians and the Aitolians, having no hoplites in their armies, had improved the quality of their light-armed troops,[1] to such an extent indeed that they could attack even hoplites with success in broken country, but these states were not represented in the Greek army at Plataia. The only light-armed troops in it worthy of the name were a body of 800 archers supplied by Athens.

It has been argued[2] that Herodotus by his references to the part played by these archers in the campaign of 479 intended to stress the foresight shown by Athens in providing herself beforehand with specialist troops of this type, but the contention is hardly borne out by his narrative. He never says directly how many archers there were, and though one of them indirectly brought about the death of Masistios, the leader of the Persian cavalry, by shooting his horse, they failed to beat off the subsequent cavalry attack, which was only repulsed by the intervention of the rest of the Greek army. It is true that Pausanias later, when hard pressed by the Persian cavalry, appealed to the Athenians to send their archers to his aid, but they never arrived and he won the battle without them. Anyhow, it was always difficult to employ archers or other light-armed troops in conjunction with the phalanx.[3]

The Greek army was composed, like the Persian, of contingents from a number of different states, but they were united by the ties of race and religion and common institutions, and their soldiers were citizens of free republics, not subjects of an absolute monarch, to be driven into battle by their officers with whips.[4] Although the Spartans alone were professional soldiers, the Athenians, who included in their ranks many of the veterans of Marathon, were doubtless much better troops now than in

---

[1] Grundy, 275 and Kromayer–Veith 87. On the effectiveness of the Akarnanian slingers cf. Thuc. ii. 81. 8.

[2] By Wardman (see Bibliography), especially pp. 57–60, citing Hdt. ix. 22. 1 and 60. 3. That the Athenian archers numbered 800 was inferred by Meyer (408 n.) from the total in ix. 29. 2.

[3] Cf. Delbrück, 34 f. The various possibilities are enumerated (with examples) by Kromayer–Veith, 88 f. On the reasons why most Greek states were slow to develop the use of properly trained light-armed troops (Thuc. iv. 94. 1 notes that Athens had none in 424) cf. Grundy, 260 ff. and Gomme, *Thucydides*, i. 14 f.

[4] Hdt. vii. 223. 2 (*bis*); cf. HW 134 on vii. 22. 1.

431,[1] and the hoplites in all the contingents must have had some military training, to enable them to play their part in the phalanx. On their own ground Greek hoplites were formidable opponents, and those who served under Pausanias should not be despised as mere citizen militias, but on the other hand their possibilities should not be exaggerated. The organization of most of the contingents in Pausanias' army was rudimentary. That of the Spartans, consisting of five grades of officers, is regarded by Thucydides[2] as exceptional; the Athenians had only three grades. Moreover, the powers of the Spartan commander-in-chief were ill-defined, and he had to secure for his plans the approval of a council of war, apparently composed of the leaders of the various contingents. His position was in fact not unlike that of the leader of a Highland army, as described by Macaulay.[3]

The general found himself merely the president of a congress of petty kings. He was perpetually called upon to hear and to compose disputes about pedigrees, about precedence, about the division of spoil. His decision, be it what it might, must offend somebody. At any moment he might hear that his right wing had fired on his centre in pursuance of some quarrel two hundred years old, or that a whole battalion had marched back to its native glen, because another battalion had been put in the place of honour.

On paper the organization of the Persian army was superior to the Greek,[4] and its competence on the technical side is attested by the careful preparations for the invasion. Xerxes' supremacy over the six generals of the army and the four admirals of the fleet must have ensured at least a nominal unity of command for the whole expedition. These facts are beyond dispute, but there is no need to rate highly the strategic ability of the Persian generals or the efficiency of their troops. When Xerxes retired to Asia the rivalries of the Persian grandees had

[1] [Xen.] *Ath. Pol.* 2. 1. On hoplite training cf. Grundy, 269 and on the military value of a hoplite force Grundy, 255 and Gomme, op. cit. 14.

[2] v. 67. 3–4.

[3] *History of England*, c. 13 (iii. 338 in edition of 1855). Even the contingents from the Peloponnesian states in Sparta's league could not always be relied on to obey the orders of a Spartan general; cf. v. 75. 1 (possibly at Thermopylai also; vii. 220.4).

[4] See above, p. 42, and on the preparations for the invasion see below, p. 94 and HW² 401. The provision of medical supplies for the wounded, at least in the fleet, is attested by vii. 181. 2.

more scope, as is shown by the friction between the two generals left behind by him in Greece, Mardonios and Artabazos. As for their armies, the Persians of the homeland may all have been regulars, but it is unlikely that the rest were also professional troops. Moreover, the Persians in their invasion of Greece were faced on land with military problems unlike any which they had met before. When they conquered their empire they probably used their archers to disorganize the ranks of the enemy infantry, which could then be charged and routed by their cavalry.[1] These tactics had been very successful on the wide plains of Asia, but the Persian superiority in cavalry would be of little use to them in a country so mountainous as Old Greece, especially as the Greek army, being on the defensive, could choose its own positions for battle. Persian archers had already been routed by Greek hoplites at Marathon, and Thermopylai was to prove that Persian spearmen could make no impression on a Greek phalanx,[2] while in hand-to-hand fighting the daggers of the Oriental infantry were no match for the swords of the Greeks.[3] The Persian high command could obtain abundant information from its Greek subjects about the armament and tactics of the free Greeks, and it might also have learnt something from its experiences at Marathon, but apparently no attempt was made to adapt the Persian war machine to changed conditions. Perhaps the Persian leaders, in spite of the glorious record of their army in the past, realized that in this war they would have to depend for victory on their fleet.

Little need be said about the navies of the two sides, for both were composed of the same type of warship, the trireme, though the triremes of the Greeks seem to have been heavier in build[4] than those of the subject peoples which supplied ships to the Persian navy. During most of the archaic period the fifty-oared ship with twenty-five rowers on each side, the pentekonter, had been the normal type of warship in Greece; the problem of constructing a ship not much longer than a pentekonter[5] but capable of holding three times as many rowers was

---

[1] Meyer, 76 and Tarn, 51. Possibly the skirmish in vi. 29 was decided in this way.
[2] vii. 211. 2; see below, p. 144.
[3] Cf. Macan, ii. 178f.   [4] viii. 60 a (βαρυτέρας).
[5] Adcock, 31 says that to build it much longer would have put too much strain on the keel. On the sea-room needed by a trireme see below, p. 227, n. 2, also Hammond in *J.H.S.* lxxvi, 1956, 50 and nn.

solved, probably in Phoenicia, by the invention of the trireme.
Herodotus in his account of Polykrates the tyrant of Samos
indicates that he began his reign with a fleet of 100 pentekonters but that before his death he had at least 40 triremes;[1]
he made Samos the leading Greek sea-power in the Aegean, and
presumably had been quick to realize the possibilities of the new
type of warship. If it was introduced to the Greek world in his
lifetime there is no need to doubt that the fleet of the Ionian
states at Lade thirty years later was composed, as Herodotus
says,[2] entirely of triremes, or that this type of ship was being
built in Old Greece twenty years before Lade.[3] The building
of 150 or more triremes by the Athenians in the years 483–
480 would have been an impossible achievement if their ship-
wrights had not already been familiar with the construction of
such ships.[4]

In 480 the normal complement of a trireme, whether Persian
or Greek, was 200, including marines as well as rowers.[5] The
Athenian naval records show that in the fourth century the
rowers numbered 174,[6] but by this date the number of marines
on board had been considerably reduced. Plutarch indeed says
that the fighting-men on board each Athenian ship at Salamis
numbered only fourteen hoplites and four archers, but the
Chian ships which fought so brilliantly at Lade had forty
marines to each ship;[7] it is hardly conceivable that the Greeks
in 480 had less than thirty; possibly Plutarch's source transferred to Salamis evidence relating to the Athenian navy of
a later date. Herodotus alleges[8] that each ship in the Persian
navy had in addition to its own marines thirty fighting-men who

---

[1] Hdt. iii. 39. 3 and 44. 2; the significance of these two passages was pointed out
by Davison in *C.Q.* xli, 1947, 18–24 (see also Labarbe, *Loi navale*, 124 ff., especially
128, n. 3). The summary of naval history in Thuc. i. 13. 6–14. 3 is condensed and
obscure; if he meant to correct Herodotus he was wrong. On the 'thalassocracy' of
Polykrates, cf. Hdt. iii. 122. 2.

[2] vi. 8. 2. The Persian ships at Lade are called νῆες, but in a naval context this
is for Hdt. equivalent to τριήρεες (examples in Labarbe, 126, n. 1), and the Persian
fleet was composed of triremes in 490 (vi. 95. 2).   [3] vi. 39. 1.

[4] Labarbe, 125. It may be noted here that in the fourth century the average
life of a trireme was twenty years (Labarbe, 127 and n. 4).

[5] vii. 184. 1 (Persian); viii. 17 (Athenian).   [6] Labarbe, 175 ff.

[7] vi. 15. 1. On the passage in Plutarch (*Them.* 14. 2) see above, p. 21.

[8] vii. 184. 2; cf. Macan and HW ad loc., also vii. 96. 1. Persian marines on an
unnamed ship (possibly Phoenician) are mentioned in vii. 181. 2. The speculations
of Tarn (*J.H.S.* xxviii. 208 and n. 27) are unconvincing.

were either native Persians, Medes, or Sakans, but this statement is difficult to accept, and it is more likely that thirty was
the total number of marines on each ship, Greek as well as
Persian. Presumably the number of rowers was lower in ships
of this period; Meyer reasonably estimates them at about 150.[1]
How so many rowers were seated in a ship not much longer than
a pentekonter is a problem to which no agreed solution has been
found.

As an instrument of war the trireme was as much superior to
the pentekonter as the British dreadnoughts were to their predecessors,[2] and only a few poor or backward Greek states in the
Greek fleet of 480 had pentekonters. The trireme depended
essentially on oar-power; sails were carried and occasionally
used, but their function was subsidiary and they were left ashore
before a big battle.[3] Nevertheless, in the new type of warship
so much had been sacrificed to speed and mobility that the trireme suffered from serious disadvantages. Köster believes[4] that
it lacked sufficient stability and was liable to capsize, so that
it was only suited for voyages in good weather and on calm
seas. For whatever reason, triremes were unseaworthy in stormy
weather, and there are several instances of whole fleets of them
being wrecked in gales.[5] Moreover, owing to the number of men
on a trireme there was so little available space that the supplies of food and water it could carry were strictly limited and
there were no facilities for cooking meals or sleeping on board.
Hence it was desirable that the crew should be able to go ashore
every night to prepare a meal and get some sleep, and this in
turn meant that the shore on which they were compelled to
land should be friendly or at least neutral.[6]

[1] Meyer, 359 n.

[2] The comparison is due to Davison, op. cit. 18, n. 1. In 480 the Eastern
Lokrians supplied 7 pentekonters and Keos 2 (viii. 1. 2); for other small states
cf. viii. 46. 4 and 48.

[3] Xen. *Hell.* ii. 1. 29, also Thuc. vii. 24. 2. There were a few 'able seamen' on
board each trireme; cf. Labarbe, 176 f.

[4] p. 182 of his chapter on *Seekriegswesen* in Kromayer–Veith (c. 4). Köster's
conclusions were reinforced by Gomme in an admirable paper (*J.H.S.* liii, 1933,
16–24), reprinted in his *Essays*, c. 10.

[5] Köster, 182; cf. Tarn, 129. A Peloponnesian fleet suffered heavy losses off
Mount Athos in the autumn of 411 (Diod. xiii. 41. 2–3). Probably the Persian
fleet destroyed off Athos in 492 (Hdt. vi. 44. 3) was also composed of triremes, in
spite of Tarn (*J.H.S.* xxviii, 209).

[6] [Demosthenes] l. 22; cf. Gomme, op. cit. 18.

Herodotus understood that the Persians in their invasion of Greece were anxious to maintain close co-operation between their sea and land forces.[1] This strategy was due, at least in part, to the dependence of triremes on a friendly shore; in fact the Persian army after crossing the frontier into Greece had to advance ahead of the fleet in order to secure the necessary harbours beforehand.[2] The Greek fleet was subject to the same limitation, so that it had to evacuate its advanced position in North Euboia when Central Greece was thrown open to the Persian army by the Greek defeat at Thermopylai.[3] But on the whole the invading fleet was more affected by this handicap than the defenders, for if the Persian advance was held up on land Xerxes would have no option but to call on his fleet to overcome the deadlock, and this could only be achieved by an attack on the Greek fleet in a position of its own choice. The Persian fleet could not simply sail past the Greek fleet, for not only would it be unable to land on the hostile shores beyond it but it could not leave its communications exposed to attack by an unbeaten enemy fleet.[4]

The Persian ships are said to have been better sailers than those of the Greeks,[5] and as the Phoenicians were the best of all, their superiority in this respect was probably due as much to the greater experience of their crews as to the lighter build of their ships. Themistokles knew that the Greek ships were tactically inferior to those of the enemy, and that they must therefore avoid an engagement in open waters where the enemy skill in manœuvre would have free scope.[6] Probably he was also aware that if the advance of the Persians was held up on land they would be forced to attack the Greek fleet wherever it chose to offer battle, even in narrow waters where they would have no room to manœuvre and would be more liable to be rammed by the Greek ships; the heavier build of their ships would then be an asset to the Greeks, and they would be able to turn a naval engagement into a land battle on sea, which would suit better their tactically inferior fleet.[7] It was perhaps because the Persians foresaw that they might have to depend largely for victory

---

[1] vii. 236. 2; cf. Gomme, 21.   [2] See below, p. 193.
[3] Gomme, 19 f.   [4] See below, p. 207.
[5] viii. 10. 1; cf. vii. 96. 1 (Phoenicians) and viii. 60 a (heavier build of Greek ships).   [6] viii. 60 a.
[7] On this type of naval battle cf. Thuc. i. 49. 1–3.

at sea on their marines that they carried as many as thirty on each ship. Anyhow, it is clear that on sea as well as on land the Greeks were in a position to force the aggressors, unless they were prepared to acquiesce in a stalemate, to fight the decisive battles under conditions which gave an advantage to the defenders.

Illustration: the campaign of Marathon[1]

The Persian invasion of Attica in 490[2] which was repulsed by the Athenian victory at Marathon lies outside the main subject of this book, but it is instructive to re-examine Herodotus' account of the invasion and the objections brought against it by its critics, for these objections provide the best possible illustration of the weaknesses of much modern criticism as applied to the historical content of Herodotus' work.

Herodotus' narrative of the Marathon campaign,[3] after elimination of the digressions and the supernatural incidents, may be briefly summarized; additions to or comments on his narrative will be enclosed in brackets. The Persians waited for a few days after the capture of Eretria, then sailed to Attica, confident of success. They were led to Marathon by Hippias because it was the most convenient place for horsemen in Attica and the nearest to Eretria. As soon as the Athenians heard the news they marched out to Marathon, led by the ten strategoi, of whom Miltiades was the tenth.[4] They had previously (apparently after they had heard of the fall of Eretria[5] but

---

[1] My debt to Mr. Whatley is especially great in this section; references to him by pages are to his published lecture on Marathon (see Preface and Bibliography). The following works are cited by the author's name only: Macan, *Herodotus iv–vi* (London, 1895); Munro, *J.H.S.* xix, 1899, 185–97; Kromayer, *Abh. d. Sächs. Akad.* xxxiv, 1921, 3–27. Munro's final version (in *C.A.H.* iv. 234 ff.) is so extravagant that it needs no refutation (cf. HW² 417).

[2] This, the accepted date, challenged by Munro in *C.A.H.* iv. 232 f., is successfully defended by Cadoux in *J.H.S.* lxviii, 1948, 117, n. 253.

[3] vi. 102–20. On the supernatural element cf. Macan, ii. 152 ff.; he concludes that it 'is after all slight compared with what might have been expected'.

[4] vi. 103. 1; the passage naturally suggests the phrase δέκατος αὐτός used twice of Perikles by Thucydides, apparently with the implication that he was commander-in-chief on both occasions; cf. Hignett, *A History of the Athenian Constitution*, 353.

[5] So Philippides in vi. 106. 2. As he does not report the Persian landing at Marathon it had presumably not yet occurred when he set out (Grundy, 173); also the generals were still in Athens when he left (105. 1) on the 7th or 8th of the lunar month. Munro, 189, n. 2 strangely dates the arrival of the Athenians at Marathon to the 6th.

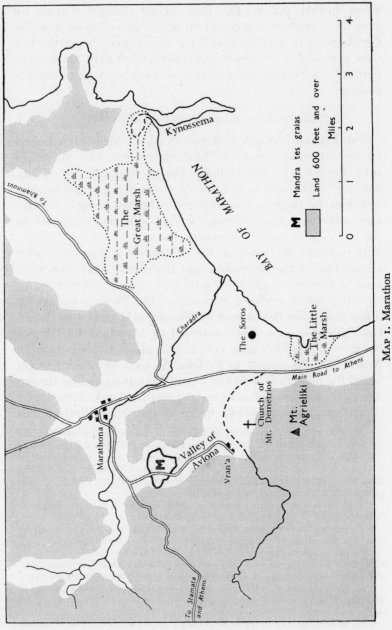

MAP 1. Marathon

before the Persians landed at Marathon) sent a courier Philippides to Sparta to ask for support. He arrived at Sparta on the ninth day of the (lunar) month, but the Spartans explained that they were forbidden by law to march out until the moon was full.

Meanwhile the Athenians had reached Marathon and had encamped there near a precinct of Herakles, where they were joined by a full levy of the troops of their Boiotian ally Plataia. A dispute then ensued between the ten generals; some, including Miltiades, urged that they should bring on a battle with the Persian army, but the rest (perhaps five in number)[1] opposed, on the ground that the Athenian army was too small. Miltiades overcame the deadlock by an appeal to the polemarch, Kallimachos, who at that time still had an equal vote on the board of generals, and persuaded him that attack was the only way to overcome the spread of Medism among the Athenians. After the decision had been taken to attack, each of the generals who supported it surrendered his *prytaneia* (presidency) to Miltiades, but though he accepted their offers he did not attack until the day of his own *prytaneia* came round. (Whatever *prytaneia* may really have meant, Herodotus seems to have interpreted it as the supreme command of the Athenian army, held by each general in turn for one day.[2])

On the day of the battle the polemarch, as was then the rule, commanded the right wing (presumably at the head of the regiment composed of the men of his own tribe);[3] to the left of him were drawn up the other tribal contingents in order,[4] with the Plataian contingent on the extreme left of the line. In order to make the front of the Athenian army equal in length to that of the enemy, the centre was made shallower (i.e. than the usual depth of eight men), in contrast to the two wings, which

---

[1] But the phrase ἐνίκα ἡ χείρων τῶν γνωμέων in 109. 2 suggests that the dissidents outnumbered their opponents. If this is correct, Kallimachos must have been able to override a majority vote of the board of generals; cf. Hignett, op. cit. 171, also Baillie Reynolds in *J.H.S.* xlix, 1929, 105.

[2] This was the interpretation put on vi. 110 by the source of Plut. *Aristeides* 5. 2; for another suggestion cf. Baillie Reynolds, 105.

[3] That Kallimachos' tribe, Aiantis, was posted on the right wing in the battle is asserted on the evidence of ταῖς Αἰσχύλου εἰς τὴν μεθορίαν ἐλεγείαις by Plut. *Quaest. Conv.* i. 10. 3 (*Moralia* 628 E).

[4] ὡς ἀριθμέοντο (111. 1), apparently not in the official order of the tribes as fixed by Kleisthenes but in one determined for the occasion by lot; cf. HW 111 ad loc.

were stronger.[1] When the omens proved favourable the Athenians charged at the double over the space, 8 stades, which
separated them from the enemy. The ensuing battle lasted for
a considerable time. The picked troops in the Persian centre,
the Persians of the homeland and the Sakai, broke through
the weak Athenian centre and pursued it inland,[2] but the two
wings of the Greek army, after routing their opponents, combined to defeat the victorious Persian centre. When the Persians
fled the Greeks pursued them to the sea and tried to seize their
ships. There was another struggle on the shore in which Kallimachos and Stesileos, one of the generals, were killed, but the
barbarians got all their ships safely away except seven, and proceeded to sail round Sounion in an attempt to surprise Athens
before the Athenians returned; it was later alleged that the
Persians had made this plan by agreement with their supporters
in Athens, the Alkmeonidai, and that after the Persians had
embarked on their ships they had received a signal flashed from
an upraised shield.[3] However, the Athenian army returned with
all haste to the city, and when the Persian fleet arrived off
Phaleron its commanders did not attempt to land, but after a
pause sailed back to Asia. A Spartan force of 2,000 men, which
is said to have marched from Sparta to Attica in three days,
arrived in Athens after the full moon, and proceeding to Marathon was in time to see the enemy dead on the field of battle;[4]
after praising the Athenians and their achievement they returned home.

There are some obvious omissions in the above narrative.

---

[1] But presumably not more than eight deep (despite the words ἔρρωτο πλήθεϊ)
in view of the reason given by Hdt. in III. 3 for this arrangement.

[2] ἐς τὴν μεσόγαιαν (113. 1); these words are used by Macan (ad loc.; cf. Grundy,
187 n.) to prove that the Persian troops were drawn up with their backs to the
sea, but his inference is really based on a false view of the Athenian position
before the battle. The Persian line must have been not only south of the Charadra
but roughly parallel to it, facing south-west; so Hauvette and Kromayer.

[3] vi. 115; cf. 124. 2. On the position of the Alkmeonidai at this time cf. Hignett,
op. cit. 180 ff.

[4] vi. 120. They must therefore have arrived at Marathon soon after the battle
(cf. HW ad loc.). As they reached Attica in less than three days after the full moon,
and so on the 18th, the battle was probably fought on the 17th day of a lunar
month; this would be 12 Sept. 490, on Boeckh's assumption that the month in
question was Metageitnion (Macan ii. 221 and n. 2; HW 109 confuses the date of
the full moon with that of the battle). Cf. also Jacoby in J.H.S. lxiv, 1944, 62 and
n. 121.

Herodotus nowhere gives any estimate for the total forces engaged on either side, though he reports[1] that the Athenians lost
192 men and the Persians about 6,400 in the battle. The Persian
infantry force which started from Cilicia with the expedition is
said to have been large and well equipped,[2] and elsewhere it is
implied that the Athenian army was small in comparison with
that of its opponents,[3] but there is no trace in Herodotus of the
fantastic figures given for the Persian host in other sources. On
the assumption[4] that the Persian centre was roughly one-third
of the whole army and that the 6,400 dead were mainly men
from the centre, which was almost annihilated, the total Persian
force which took part in the battle may be fixed at not more
than 20,000, and there is no convincing reason for doubting the
plain implication of the Herodotean narrative that the whole
of the expeditionary force was present at the battle. Later
writers fix the strength of the Athenian army at 10,000 men, but
disagree whether the Plataian levy, which they overestimate at
1,000 men, is to be included in this total.[5] As the members of
the richest classes at Athens, who in the aristocratic state and
also under the radical democracy served in the cavalry, seem
during the Persian Wars to have dismounted and fought on
foot, 9,000 is perhaps not an excessive estimate for the Athenian
hoplites who fought at Marathon, exclusive of the Plataians,
who may have numbered 600.[6] Each hoplite was probably
accompanied by an attendant, but though such attendants are
sometimes reckoned as light-armed troops,[7] their military value
was probably slight.

[1] 117. 1; the explanation of the figure 6,400 offered by Labarbe, *Loi navale*, 166
is unconvincing.

[2] 95. 1; it is said to have been augmented later by contingents from the Ionians
and Aiolians and from the Cyclades reduced to submission en route (98. 1 and
99. 1).

[3] 109. 1; 111. 3 also suggests that the Greek army was inferior in numbers to the
Persian.   [4] Grundy, third n. on p. 160; cf. Munro, 189, n. 1.

[5] Cf. HW. 114 (on 117. 1). Ephoros seems to have estimated the Athenians
(without the Plataians) at 9,000 (cf. Nepos, *Miltiades* 5. 1), an estimate which
dominated the later tradition (apart from Justin, ii. 9. 9); this estimate is valued
too highly by Labarbe (op. cit. 162 ff.).

[6] ix. 28. 6 with HW ad loc.

[7] ix. 29. 2; on the Athenian ψιλοί at Marathon cf. Hauvette, 247 and n. 5.
Perhaps some of these attendants at Marathon were slaves; so Delbrück (65, n. 3)
would explain the reference in Pausanias i. 32. 3 to the grave of the slaves who fell
in the battle. But the assertion of Paus. vii. 15. 7 that Miltiades liberated the slaves
before the battle arouses suspicion.

In the second place, although Herodotus knows that there is
a plain at Marathon enclosed on one side by the sea, he makes
no reference to the mountains that enclose the plain on the land
side or to the marshes at either end that limit its extent, the great
marsh, covering a large part of the north-eastern half of the
plain, and the little marsh, between its southern exit and the sea.
Above all, he does not mention the Charadra, the torrent which
flows down from the mountains past the modern village of
Marathona to the sea, cutting the plain in two; whatever its
precise course was in 490, it must always have been a feature of
the landscape.[1] As Herodotus never alludes to the Soros, the
mound in which the Athenian dead were buried, which is still
a conspicuous object in the south-western half of the plain, it is
a reasonable inference that he had never visited the site of the
battle.[2]

Modern scholars have naturally tried to supplement his
account by a detailed study of the topography of Marathon,
including the routes leading out of the plain, but unfortunately
they have disagreed about the precise site of the ancient
Marathon (not necessarily identical with that of the modern
Marathona) and that of the shrine of Herakles by which the
Athenian army encamped on its arrival. Moreover, Lolling's
over-hasty identification[3] of the Herakleion with the so-called
Mandra tes graias (the sheepfold of the old woman) in the valley
of Avlona was disastrous, for it entailed the conclusion that the
Athenians must have been posted a little way up the valley,
a position from which they could maintain only an indirect
control over the main road to Athens, by threatening the flank
of the enemy if they attempted to advance along this road.
A further consequence of Lolling's view was that the Athenians
must have marched out to Marathon by the more difficult
route[4] which, after passing through Kephisia and Stamata,
comes down into the plain either by the Avlona valley or by
that to the north-east of it in which Marathona is situated. It is,
however, more probable that the Athenian leaders took their
men to Marathon along the main road, by which the Persians

---

[1] Macan, ii. 238 and n. 4. On the topography in general cf. Grundy, 163 ff.,
also Veith in *A.S.* iv. 18–20.

[2] Grundy, 163 f.   [3] *Ath. Mit.* i, 1876, 67–94.

[4] On this cf. Grundy, 164 f. (on pp. 173 f. he assumes that it was the road taken
by the Athenians; cf. Hauvette, 251 and Bury in *C.R.* x, 1896, 97).

might be expected to advance, and that on their arrival they
halted near the southern exit from the plain on the northern
slopes of Mount Agrieliki,[1] a position directly commanding the
main road to Athens. The Persians dared not attempt to march
on Athens by one of the other routes, for if they began to move
up into the hills the Athenians were near enough to fall on the
residue of their army before it could get out of the plain.[2]

Macan has collected all the references to the campaign in
ancient writers other than Herodotus,[3] but the new items in
them which can be regarded as trustworthy are few. Plutarch
refers to Aeschylus for proof that the regiment of the tribe
Aiantis was posted on the right of the Greek line in the battle.[4]
Fourth-century orators refer to the decree of Miltiades as a
well-known fact,[5] from which it is reasonably deduced that the
Athenian decision to meet the invaders wherever they might
land was taken by the popular assembly on a proposal moved
by Miltiades. The author of the *Athenaion Politeia*[6] says that in
this period the ten generals were elected one from each tribe but
the polemarch was commander-in-chief of the whole army; this
may be no more than a rationalization of the confused account
given by Herodotus of the relations between the generals and
the polemarch, but it is probably correct. Plutarch's assertion[7]
that the tribal regiments of Themistokles and Aristeides, namely
Leontis and Antiochis, were posted together in the centre may
possibly be true but does not inspire confidence. Pausanias
has a careful description[8] of the topography, traditions, and

---

[1] Agrieliki (accent on the penultimate) means 'the wild-olive mountain'. Finlay
located the Herakleion here; cf. Macan, ii. 236, n. 2. This was the site for the
Athenian position advocated by Meyer, 329 n. and defended at length by Kromayer, 13 ff. That the ancient Marathon was situated near the southern exit of
the plain has been maintained by Cary (*J.H.S.* xxxi, 1911, 100 ff.) and Soteriades
(see report in *J.H.S.* xlvii, 1927, 253 f.).

[2] Cf. Delbrück, 59.

[3] ii. 174–234 (cf. HW 355 f.). The epigraphic evidence (Tod 13 and 14 and the
Marathon epigrams in *S.E.G.* x. 404; for a discussion cf. Bowra, *Greek Lyric Poetry*[2],
340 ff.) is interesting but contributes nothing to the history of the campaign.

[4] See above, p. 57, n. 3.

[5] So Kephisodotos in 357 according to Arist. *Rhetoric* 1411^{a}10 (on which see
the edition by Cope and Sandys, iii. 113 f.); Demosthenes xix. 303 says that
Aischines read in public the text of the decree. On the decree cf. How in *J.H.S.*
xxxix, 1919, 53; Hauvette, 250 had pointed out that Spartan help must have
depended on Athenian readiness to take the field.

[6] 20. 2; cf. Hignett, op. cit. 170–2.   [7] *Aristeides*, 5. 4.

[8] i. 32; cf. § 7 for the marsh and the mangers of Artaphernes' horses.

monuments of Marathon; local tradition suggests that the Persian cavalry at least were stationed in the northern part of the plain, and the painting of the battle in the Stoa Poikile represented some of the Persian fugitives as perishing in a marsh.[1]

In addition to the statements in the ancient sources which can safely be used to supplement Herodotus' account of the campaign there are others, like that just cited from the *Athenaion Politeia*, which contradict his testimony directly or indirectly. Before these can be examined it is necessary to establish what statements in Herodotus must be rejected as beyond dispute unhistorical, derived from an inaccurate tradition. An obvious example is the famous passage[2] in which he says that the Athenians charged for 8 stades at the double, a feat which no phalanx of citizen militia could have performed; presumably the truth underlying the exaggeration was that the Athenians advanced at a quick march to the attack but did not break into the double until they came within range of the Persian archers.[3] Herodotus was also certainly wrong when he said that the polemarch Kallimachos had been appointed by lot;[4] the *Athenaion Politeia* established the fact, probable on other grounds, that the archons in this period were directly elected by the people. This particular error may have been due to Herodotus himself, but the oral traditions of the campaign which he reproduced were certainly inconsistent in their references to the supreme command, although there are indications of the true view that it was still retained by the polemarch. Herodotus seems to assume in one passage[5] that Miltiades was commander-in-chief, and in another that this position was held by each of the generals in turn.

Herodotus' statement that the *prytaneia*, which he obviously took to mean the supreme command, was held by each general in rotation for a day at a time,[6] occurs in a very suspicious context. The council of war which decided in favour of an attack

---

[1] Paus. i. 15. 3; almost certainly the greater marsh is meant.

[2] vi. 112. 1. The argument used by Hauvette (261, n. 2) to defend this statement was refuted at length by Delbrück, 67 ff.

[3] This is given as an alternative explanation by Grundy, 188, n. 1, though he himself believed that δρόμῳ, misunderstood by Hdt., was a technical term for 'at the quick step'. This view, attacked by How in *C.Q.* xiii, 1919, 40–42, has been revived by Kromayer (*A.S.* 11 and n. 1); cf. also Gomme, *Thucydides*, iii. 544 f. on Thuc. iv. 78. 5.   [4] vi. 109. 2, contradicted by *A.P.* 22. 5; cf. Hignett, op. cit. 322.

[5] vi. 103. 1; see above, p. 55, n. 4.   [6] vi. 110; cf. Plut. *Arist.* 5. 2.

on the Persians is apparently dated soon after the arrival at Marathon of the Athenians (and Plataians). Yet, although Miltiades had persuaded Kallimachos by the argument that delay might be followed by the spread of Medism among the Athenians, and although the generals favourable to the offensive had surrendered to Miltiades the days of their *prytaneia*, he insists on waiting until the day of his own *prytaneia* comes round. In other words, the date of the Athenian attack is made to depend on the accident of Miltiades' *prytaneia* falling on a particular day.[1] This tradition, which may have been intended to stress the constitutional correctness of Miltiades' behaviour,[2] cannot possibly be true. Nevertheless, the delay of several days which it postulates between the arrival of the Athenian army at Marathon and the battle must be accepted as a fact, in preference to the later rhetorical version which reduced to a minimum the interval between the two events.[3]

The delay is presupposed also in Herodotus' references to the Spartans. It must be admitted that the conduct he ascribes to them[4] is peculiar. If, as is usually supposed, they were celebrating the Karneia, why does he not say so? Moreover, although they had scruples about making war on other Dorians during the Karneia, it is doubtful whether these scruples applied to war against barbarians; Leonidas took a force of Spartiates to Thermopylai in 480 about the time of the Karneia.[5] The excuse given in Herodotus for their failure to arrive in time for the battle of Marathon must have seemed unconvincing to the fourth-century apologist who explained it by the assumption that they had been delayed by a Helot revolt.[6] Anyhow, the need for these explanations could never have arisen unless the dates of Philippides' report in Sparta and of the arrival of the 2,000 Spartans in Attica were both historical,[7]

[1] For this objection cf. Munro, 192f.
[2] Cf. Hignett, op. cit. 171 (citing Berve, *Miltiades*, 81).
[3] *Postero die* in Nepos (*Milt.* 5. 3). Isokrates iv. 87 repeats a tradition (φασίν) that the battle was fought on the same day as that on which the Persians landed at Marathon.   [4] vi. 106. 3; cf. Thuc. v. 54. 2–4 and 75. 2.
[5] vii. 206. 1; see below, p. 126. Schachermeyr's attempt (*Hist. Zeitschr.* clxxii, 1951, 10f.) to grapple with this problem is inadequate.
[6] Accepted by Plato, *Laws* 698 E (also 692 D); on the possible genesis of this assumption cf. Jacoby, *F.G.H.* iii A, commentary on Rhianos, p. 116.
[7] Philippides reached Sparta on the 9th of the lunar month (vi. 106. 3) and the Spartan troops arrived in Attica on the 17th or more probably on the 18th (see

and these dates again point to an interval of several days between the Persian landing at Marathon and the battle.

When these errors have been eliminated, the narrative of
Herodotus gives an account of the campaign which is acceptable
as far as it goes, though it needs to be cautiously supplemented
in detail. His statement[1] that the Athenians advanced 8 stades
to meet the enemy proves that the Persian army on the morning
of the battle was drawn up south of the Charadra, a conclusion
which does not depend on the position of the Soros.[2] The local
traditions cited by Pausanias indicate that part at least of the
Persian army was originally encamped north of the Charadra,[3]
and it is probable that the fleet anchored in the north part of the
bay where it would be protected by the projecting promontory
of Kynosoura. Many scholars, however, have claimed that these
chapters of Herodotus, if critically examined, suggest objections
which are fatal to his version as it stands, and on these objections they have based reconstructions of the campaign which
differ from his in essential respects.[4] Their main arguments
are that the reasons given by him for the Persian landing at
Marathon are unconvincing, that the Athenian decision to attack is on military grounds inexplicable, that Herodotus, after
indicating that cavalry and horse-transports accompanied the
expedition, says nothing of any part played by the Persian
cavalry in the battle, and finally that although the Persians were
decisively beaten they re-embarked their forces with the loss of
only seven ships, and were apparently successful in getting all
their horses away.

Delbrück in his reconstruction[5] relied on the evidence of a
'secondary authority', Cornelius Nepos, supposing correctly
that the account in Nepos, apart from certain minor additions

above, p. 58, n. 4). Meyer, who rejects the excuse alleged by Hdt., suggests
(n. on p. 330) that the delay was partly due to the slowness of the Spartan mobilization. Possibly Hdt. vi. 120 underestimates the time needed for the march of the
2,000 from Sparta to Athens. It is curious that no levies from the other states of the
Peloponnesian League are mentioned (cf. Macan, i. 376 A).   [1] vi. 112. 1.

[2] Maurice (*J.H.S.* lii, 1932, 23 f.) believes that the Soros existed before the
battle, and that no inference about the battle can be based on its position. His
assumption that the Persian army was drawn up to the north of the Charadra
on the day of the battle must be wrong; see above, p. 58, n. 2.

[3] Paus. i. 32. 7.

[4] Kromayer (in *A.S.* 9, n. 1) has stated clearly the difference between the conservative and the radical type of reconstruction; cf. Hauvette, 249, ll. 18 ff.

[5] *Kriegskunst*[3], 52 ff. (accepted by Beloch, *G.G.* ii[2]. 1. 22, n. 3).

obviously due to Nepos himself, was copied from that of Ephoros.[1] The essential features in Nepos are that the delay of several days between the Persian landing at Marathon and the battle disappears, that the Athenian army, posted in a strong position, waits to be attacked by the Persians on the day after its arrival, and that it was defended from the enemy cavalry, clearly assumed by Ephoros to have been present at the battle, by trees, apparently cut down for the purpose.[2] Delbrück rightly retains, in defiance of Nepos, the long delay before the battle presupposed in Herodotus, and finds in it the reason why the Persians finally decided to attack the Athenian position; they could not afford to wait longer as the Spartan troops were expected to arrive soon.[3] The Athenians, assumed to have been drawn up in the valley of Avlona, did not move until the Persian infantry advanced within bowshot, and then charged at the double;[4] the 8 stades in Herodotus must therefore represent the distance over which the Athenians pursued the retreating Persians, up to the site of the Soros.

Ephoros' account has doubtless been much condensed by Nepos, who gives no details of the actual battle except the flight to the ships with which it ended. Yet enough remains to show that Ephoros contradicted Herodotus point-blank when he said that the battle began with a Persian attack on the Greek position. It is not likely that this assertion was derived from an authentic tradition; it is more probable that the Ephorean account of the campaign was a critical reconstruction based on the narrative in Herodotus but designed to provide solutions of the difficulties which seemed to Ephoros to be raised by that narrative. Hence Nepos' version of the campaign is no more entitled to rank as independent evidence than the hypothesis of a modern scholar.[5]

The same verdict may be pronounced more emphatically on

---

[1] This view, wrongly attacked by Meyer (332 n.), was convincingly reaffirmed by How in *J.H.S.* xxxix, 1919, 48 ff. The account of Nepos is in his *Life of Miltiades*, cc. 4–5.

[2] The text in Nepos 5. 3 is uncertain. In the parenthesis the manuscripts read *namque arbores multis locis erant rarae*. Even if the correction *stratae* (for *rarae*) is uncertain (AS 8 f., n. 1), the implication that the trees were felled is supported by *arborum tractu* in the next line. [3] Op. cit. 60.

[4] Op. cit. 60 f.; cf. 57 f. for his explanation of the 8 stades.

[5] See below, p. 221 and n. 5, and cf. How's criticism of Nepos' account of Marathon in *J.H.S.* xxxix, 48 ff. (also HW 355 f.)

the passage in 'Suidas'[1] which contains the following explanation for the supposed absence of the Persian cavalry from the
battle: 'when Datis invaded Attica, they say that the Ionians on
his withdrawal climbed trees and signalled to the Athenians that
the horsemen were away, whereupon Miltiades, being informed
of Datis' withdrawal, charged and won the battle.' This story
cannot have been derived from a trustworthy source of the
fifth or fourth century; if it was, why was it never noticed by
any of the numerous ancient writers on Marathon from Ephoros
to Plutarch? If Macan was right in asserting[2] that there is no
test of the tradition in Suidas external to the passage itself, the
tradition would be refuted by its own absurdity; what system of
signalling could have been used by the Ionians and how could
their signals be read by the Greeks (without being noticed by
the Persians) at a distance of nearly a mile?[3] But there is in fact
an external test which proves the falsity of this tradition, the
passage of Herodotus in which the Persians are said to have been
astonished to see the Greeks advancing to the attack without
either archers or cavalry;[4] obviously Herodotus believed the
Persians themselves had both, as did Ephoros also. Moreover,
Suidas does not say more than that the Persian cavalry were
absent from the battlefield; it is illegitimate to cite him[5] as
evidence for the modern view that the cavalry had been re-
embarked on the ships.

Some of the objections brought against Herodotus by the
modern critics of his account of Marathon owe their plausibility
to analogies from modern warfare, analogies which are refuted
by a careful consideration of the methods of fighting practised
by Greeks and Persians in the early fifth century. Munro argued[6]
that as the Persians failed to occupy the passes leading out of
the plain in the time at their disposal, perhaps twenty-four

---

[1] Under the heading χωρὶς ἱππεῖς, 'the horsemen are away'; on 'Suidas',
otherwise 'the Suda', see above, p. 12 and n. 6.   [2] ii. 231.

[3] Hammond (*History of Greece*, 215; also 216, n. 2 ad fin.) makes it more difficult
by dating the message one night before dawn, and so has to say that the news was
brought by the Ionians to the Athenian lines. For a similar suggestion, but in a
form nearer to Suidas, cf. Schachermeyr, 23.

[4] vi. 112. 2; Nepos, *Milt.* 5. 4 says that the Persian cavalry, 10,000 in number
(cf. 4. 1), were present at the battle. The assertion in the first Marathon epigram
(*S.E.G.* x. 404, no. 1, l. 3) that the Athenians had faced Persian cavalry is not on
the stone, but the restoration is perhaps supported by the emphasis on πεζοὶ earlier
in the line.   [5] As is done by HW 362.   [6] Op. cit. 188.

hours, between their disembarkation and the arrival of the
Athenians, they cannot have intended to advance on Athens,
and therefore their object must have been to lure the Athenian
army away from Athens to Marathon. But the occupation of
passes to bar the advance of an enemy was seldom attempted in
antiquity, unless the conditions were exceptional, as at Thermopylai,[1] for it presupposes the use of modern weapons and was
unsuited to an age when men fought with bows or spears.
Moreover, there were several passes out of the plain, three at
least practicable for an army, and the Persian commanders,
even if the idea had occurred to them, might have been reluctant to detach troops in sufficient numbers to hold them all
effectively; it must be remembered that their total force probably did not exceed 20,000 men. Munro never considered the
possibility that they may simply have made a mistake through
carelessness. Datis may not have expected the Athenians to
march out to meet him at Marathon;[2] they had not done so
against Peisistratos. Herodotus' reasons for the choice of Marathon by the Persians are plausible if not exhaustive.[3] Munro
himself pointed out[4] that Marathon is one of the few places in
Attica where there is pasture to be found in the autumn, and
though there are other places in Attica nearer to Eretria,
Marathon is the nearest which possesses useful road communications with Athens.[5] Anyhow, there was no practicable alternative to Marathon except Phaleron, and in spite of Munro[6]

---

[1] 'There is no Thermopylae between Athens and Marathon' (Whatley).

[2] Whatley, 72 thinks that 'the Persians probably had the shock of their lives
when the Athenians turned up'; on p. 71 he notes that the decision to meet the
enemy at a distance from the city was most unusual, and adds 'it is this more than
anything else which makes Marathon outstanding in the history of Greek warfare'.
Munro, 188 has to suppose that Miltiades' decree was already known to Hippias
before he landed at Marathon.

[3] vi. 102. He says that the Persians were guided to Marathon by Hippias; probably his family's partisans, the Hyperakrioi (for a probable explanation of the
name cf. Munro, 187, n. 1), were numerous in this part of Attica and could facilitate
communications with the rest of his supporters.

[4] Op. cit. 194, n. 1.; cf. Whatley, 71: 'it was a good place for feeding horses.'

[5] In vi. 101. 1 the Persians land at three different places in the territory
of Eretria. One of these was 15 miles from the city if Valckenaer's emendation
(usually accepted) of ταμύνας for the manuscript τέμενος is correct, but cf. Geyer,
Euboia (Berlin, 1903), 75 f.

[6] Op. cit. 187 (stated less cautiously in HW 358). For the opposite view, supported by such passages as Thuc. iv. 10. 5 and vi. 64. 1, cf. Hammond, History, 213,
also in J.H.S. lxxvi, 1956, 52, n. 84.

there can be no doubt that an attempt to land so near to Athens would have been very dangerous and might easily have failed.

The problem of the cavalry is more difficult. Various passages in Herodotus[1] show that a cavalry force was included in the army of invasion, and one of these presupposes its presence in the field when the battle was fought. Some have brushed aside this evidence on the ground that Herodotus could not imagine a Persian army without cavalry,[2] and have supposed that Datis and Artaphernes had no horses at all with them or very few, only enough for the higher officers and dispatch riders.[3] It was certainly difficult to transport horses by sea in ancient times. The Athenians prided themselves on the feat of shipping 300 across the Saronic Gulf in 430 and 200 in 425; when they made their great expedition to Sicily in 415 they took only thirty horses with them.[4] Curtius, relying on the untrustworthy notice in 'Suidas', supposed that the Persian cavalry had all been re-embarked before the battle,[5] but the advocates of this hypothesis have never explained why the Persian leaders, having decided to divide their forces, should have re-embarked the whole of the cavalry.[6] If the Athenians tried to counter the Persian move by an immediate return to Athens, Persian cavalry would have been better able than Persian infantry to follow close on their heels and delay their march.[7]

[1] vi. 48. 2 and 95. 1 for the horse-transports; cf. also 101. 1, 102, and especially 112. 2.   [2] Beloch, ii². 2. 80 f.

[3] The latter view is that of Beloch (loc. cit.), the former that of Wilamowitz (*A.A.* ii. 85).

[4] Thuc. ii. 56. 2 (made out of old ships), iv. 42. 1 (cf. Ar. *Knights*, 595 ff.), and vi. 43 ad fin. (note that all the thirty horses are carried in the single ἱππαγωγὸς ναῦς).

[5] Cf. Curtius, *G.G.* ii⁶ (1888), 24 f. and 812 f., n. 14, followed by Munro, Grundy (*G.P.W.* 183 f.), and HW 361 f. For recent accounts which are based on the evidence of 'Suidas' cf. Schachermeyr in *Hist. Zeitschr.* clxxii, 1951, 1–35 and Gomme in *Phoenix* vi, 1952, 77–83.

[6] The arguments suggested by Grundy (op. cit. 186) are ludicrously inadequate. Munro, 195 criticizes Bury's astounding statement that on the march to Athens the cavalry 'would have been a useless encumbrance' (cf. HW 362), but is apparently unconscious that his own theory is open to the same objection. He and Grundy both assume that the Athenians would have returned to Athens by the Stamata route.

[7] So rightly Kromayer in *A.S.* 18. Gomme evades this difficulty by his supposition that the Persians, having decided to re-embark their whole army (starting with the cavalry) during the night before the battle, still had part of the infantry ashore at dawn, but fails to explain why the infantry were still drawn up south of the Charadra.

Herodotus' repeated assertions that Datis' army included cavalry can only have been derived from the oral traditions of the campaign which he had collected. Moreover, it is likely that cavalry formed an appreciable part of the Persian force, in view of the fact that the Persians owed their previous successes in war to a combination of archers and cavalry, but transport difficulties may have kept down the cavalrymen in 490 to 800 at most.[1] Herodotus clearly implies that they were present when the Athenians attacked, but he does not say where they were stationed in the Persian line. Kromayer has argued elaborately[2] that they were in the centre, but the analogy of Plataia makes it more probable that they were on the wings; if the Greek army faced north-east with its right close to the shore it could only have been attacked in flank on its left wing. Delbrück assumes[3] that if the Athenians had advanced across the open plain they must have been attacked in flank by the enemy cavalry, but the timing and speed of their advance may have taken the Persians by surprise. It must be remembered that the Persians had never before faced an army of Greek hoplites in a pitched battle, and that their cavalry were only mounted archers who avoided coming to grips with enemy infantry;[4] once the hoplites came to close quarters, this cavalry would be of no use.[5] In the campaign of Plataia the Persian cavalry, who had harried the Greeks in their second position, similarly disappear from the scene as soon as the battle is joined, not to be mentioned again until it is over, when they do what they can to delay the Greek pursuit.[6] Presumably the Persian leaders, misled by their previous experience, had relied unduly on their

---

[1] Delbrück, 52 gives 500–800 cavalry, but characteristically underestimates the total Persian force at 4,000–6,000 men. Schachermeyr (op. cit. 24) argues that the Persians must have had cavalry to attack Eretria, which was strong in cavalry.

[2] Op. cit. 15–19 (cf. *A.S.* 13–16), but the Πέρσαι τε αὐτοὶ καὶ Σάκαι in the Persian centre (Hdt. vi. 113. 1) need not be and probably were not cavalry. Whatley, 73 says cautiously 'we do not know how Persians drew up'.

[3] Op. cit. 53; cf. 73 for his reply to Meyer, who evaded the problem too easily in his text (p. 331; he comes nearer to the correct solution in his n. on p. 333).

[4] ix. 49. 2; cf. the story in ix. 18.

[5] So Strahan, p. 216 of his school edition of Book VI (Macmillan, 1891); his appendix on Marathon, apparently based on a paper by Swoboda, is still worth reading.

[6] I owe this point to Mr. Whatley, who points out that the only certain reference to cavalry in Hdt's. account of the actual battle of Plataia is Mardonios' white horse in ix. 63. 1, though the 1,000 picked Persians with him *may* have been cavalry.

archers to throw the enemy ranks into confusion, but Marathon and Plataia were to prove that Persian archers were ineffective against Greek hoplites at close quarters.[1]

Why did the Athenians decide to attack? The military arguments against their decision seem overwhelming: they had probably disorganized the Persian plans by marching out to Marathon, occupied a good defensive position, and had a weighty reason for delay in the approach of the Spartan reinforcements. Herodotus says that the decision was made by Kallimachos on Miltiades' advice after a council of war. Nepos transposes the council to Athens before the army set out,[2] but this is a guess of no independent value, as his source clearly confused two quite different things, the decision adopted in Athens, probably by the assembly, to take the field rather than trust to the walls,[3] and the decision of Kallimachos at Marathon to leave his strong position and advance into the plain against the Persians. There need be no doubt that there was an interval of several days between the arrival of the Athenians at Marathon and their decision to engage the enemy,[4] but the explanation of this delay given by Herodotus, that Miltiades was waiting for the day of his *prytaneia* to come round, is untenable; the only possible solution is that the council of war and the decision to attack must be dated to the day before the battle.[5] As the Persian army was already in position when the Athenians advanced, its leaders must have brought it across the Charadra earlier in an attempt to end the deadlock by offering battle in the southern half of the plain about 8 stades from the Athenian position.[6]

It has often been maintained that in spite of Herodotus Kallimachos' decision must have been precipitated by some move

---

[1] The Athenian charge δρόμῳ (vi. 112. 2) 'was Miltiades' triumphant solution of the problem of *comminus versus eminus*' (Whatley, 74). Cf. Tarn, *Developments*, 52 f.; he claims that 'Plataea definitely killed the Persian archer as the main infantry force'.   [2] *Miltiades* 4. 4–5. 2.

[3] In view of Thuc. i. 89. 3 and 93. 2 there can be no doubt that Athens really was encircled by walls at this time; cf. Beloch, ii². 1. 21, n. 2.

[4] See above, p. 63, n. 7, and cf. Whatley, 73; he draws an interesting parallel between this campaign and that of Dunbar in 1650.

[5] The attempt of Hauvette (op. cit. 254) to defend the account in Hdt. vi. 110 is unconvincing.

[6] Kromayer, 25. Hdt. vi. 111. 3 shows that the Persian army was already drawn up for battle before the Athenians arranged their forces.

on the part of the enemy which caused the Athenians to act quickly.[1] The favourite hypothesis has been that the Persians were beginning to divide their forces and to re-embark half their army (including all the cavalry) in order to land it at Phaleron, while leaving the other half behind at Marathon to watch the Athenian army and engage it if it tried to march back to Athens. This reconstruction, so flagrantly at variance with the implications of Herodotus' narrative,[2] rests on no ancient evidence worthy of the name.[3] Moreover, if the Persian army which fought in the battle numbered 20,000, the total of the expeditionary force must on this view have been 40,000, but no convincing argument has been produced in support of this figure.[4] Lastly, if the function of the troops left behind was merely to keep the Athenian army in check, why did it not withdraw behind the north bank of the Charadra, especially as it had now been deprived of all its cavalry?[5]

Herodotus has provided a sufficient explanation for the Athenian decision in his statement[6] that Miltiades' main argument was not military but political, the danger that the activities of Hippias' Athenian partisans might soon produce a pro-Persian revolution. Delbrück's claim that politics played no part in this campaign is contrary to our best evidence and improbable in itself.[7] Treason had been active at Eretria; it would indeed be strange if there were no traitors in Attica. The deadlock before Marathon recalls the deadlock before Lade, and the parallel makes it likely that now, as then, the Persian leaders, when disconcerted by unexpectedly strong resistance, proceeded to organize a fifth column in the ranks of their

---

[1] e.g. Munro, 189 ff., followed by HW 361.

[2] Kromayer (op. cit. 8) remarks that Curtius virtually scrapped our only trustworthy account and produced a *tabula rasa* on which anyone can paint whatever picture he pleases.

[3] On 'Suidas' see above. Nepos indeed says (4. 1 and 5. 4) that the Persian army included 200,000 infantry and that 100,000 fought in the battle, but as he makes no reference to any division of the Persian forces before the battle the second figure looks like a belated product of rationalism; it is to be noted that the cavalry (estimated at 10,000 in both passages) are assumed to have been present at the battle.

[4] The speculations of Grundy (160 and n. 3) are inconclusive. Whatley, 71 rightly considers 20,000 a maximum for the *total* expeditionary force.

[5] Cf. Kromayer, 8, also his criticism of Lehmann-Haupt in *A.S.* 17 f.

[6] vi. 109. 5.

[7] Hauvette, 252 and n. 1; cf. Kromayer, 7 (also in *A.S.* 11–13).

opponents;[1] as they were on Attic soil it need not have been difficult to get in touch with Hippias' partisans, both those in the Athenian lines and those left behind in the city. Perhaps also the long period of waiting proved a severe strain on the steadfastness of a citizen militia face to face with the enemy.[2] Anyhow, Miltiades was sufficiently alarmed by the activities of the pro-Persians to call for an immediate offensive. Their preparations were in fact nearly complete, if any inference can safely be based on the shield signal said to have been displayed by the traitors to the Persians on the following day.

Finally, as the Persian army certainly got away after the battle with the loss of only seven ships, it must somehow have obtained enough time to re-embark without sustaining heavy casualties in the re-embarkation.[3] The Athenian wings after their initial victory would probably have refrained from pursuing the fleeing enemy wings but would instead have regrouped their forces to defeat the Persian centre, and there is something to be said for Delbrück's suggestion[4] that even after the destruction of the Persian centre a fresh pause occurred, during which the weary troops were induced to make a fresh effort and advance across the Charadra for an attack on the Persian naval camp, which was stoutly defended. The Persian cavalry probably retreated ahead of the infantry as soon as the Persian wings had been defeated, and anyhow the re-embarkation of horses must have been an easier matter in ancient than in modern times.[5]

A minor problem is raised by Herodotus' reference to the shield signal. He says[6] that it was shown to the Persians 'when they were already on board their ships'; in its context this can only mean 'after the battle was over'. Followers of Curtius maintain that this timing of the signal originally referred to the embarkation of the first half of the Persian force,[7] which on their view was to sail round to Phaleron while the other half

---

[1] Hdt. vi. 9. 2–4 and 13. 1.   [2] Cf. Kromayer in *A.S.* 12.

[3] Kromayer (op. cit. 22) agrees with Delbrück that the assumption of a long interval between the main battle and the Athenian attack on the Persian ships is practically a necessity, but his own explanation is unduly complicated.

[4] Delbrück, 62 and 64f. (criticized rather captiously by Kromayer, 20ff.).

[5] Cf. Kromayer, 7.   [6] vi. 115 *ad fin.*

[7] e.g. Macan, ii. 166f., also Munro, 193 and n. 1; but Munro admits that the Persians did not wait for the signal to divide their forces. HW 361 after some hesitation accept the evidence of Hdt.

remained at Marathon. But if the first half started before the battle, how could the Athenian army have got back to Athens before the Persian fleet reached Phaleron? Plutarch's statement[1] that the Athenians returned to Athens on the same day as the battle is not derived from Herodotus and is improbable in itself; it seems to be derived from the rhetorical tradition. It is also to be noted that even on this view the real difficulty remains, that the embarkation had begun before the showing of the signal, which therefore cannot have been the cause of the embarkation. Some have rejected the incident of the shield signal as a fiction,[2] perhaps one which became current soon after the battle, but Herodotus is curiously emphatic in his insistence that the shield really was shown.[3] There is no evidence for the modern view that the signal was sent from the summit of Mount Pentelikon, a view which perhaps rests on the assumption that it must have been visible from Athens as well as from Marathon. Perhaps the conspirators who arranged the signal did not know that by the time it could be sent the issue would be already decided.[4]

In Herodotus the signal is used to explain why the Persians decided after the battle to sail round Sounion in an attempt to forestall the return of the Athenian army to Athens; hence he must have believed that the signal was sent by the traitors to show that their preparations were complete.[5] It is strange that the Persians should have ventured on such a bold stroke after a defeat in which they had lost nearly one-third of their army, but the tradition recorded by Herodotus said explicitly that the Persian fleet arrived off Phaleron and lay off the shore there for some time before returning to Asia.[6] Perhaps Datis had received

---

[1] *Aristeides* 5. 5 (αὐθημερόν), treated with too much respect by Hammond, *History*, 216, n. 2; Whatley, 75 is sceptical (cf. Hauvette, 266). Hdt. vi. 116 merely says 'as quickly as they could.' Grundy's estimate of 'nine or ten hours' (op. cit. 191) for the voyage of the Persian fleet from Marathon to Phaleron is far too small for a voyage of 90 miles (cf. HW 211).

[2] e.g. Delbrück, 73, end of n. 9 and Maurice in *J.H.S.* lii, 1932, 17 f.

[3] vi. 124. 2. A shield signal was certainly used by Lysandros before Aigospotamoi (Xen. *Hell.* ii. 1. 27).

[4] Hauvette, 267 and Macan ii. 166 (end of § 1; he suggests that the signal may possibly have been sent from the summit of Agrieliki). For the spelling Πεντελικὸν (sc. ὄρος) cf. Paus. i. 32. 1 and Wrede in *R.-E.* xix. 1. 534.

[5] vi. 115. This seems to rule out the suggestion of Baillie Reynolds (*J.H.S.* xlix. 1929, 100 ff.) that the message conveyed by the signal was negative: 'the plot has failed.'

[6] vi. 116. The statement in Plutarch (*Arist.* 5. 5) that the Persians were making

information from the traitors, by the shield signal or otherwise, which led him to think that even after his defeat it was still worth while to attempt a landing at Phaleron,[1] but the Athenian victory and the prompt return of the army had put an end to all hopes of a pro-Persian rising in Athens.

for the islands but were driven back by the wind and current to the coast of Attica seems to be an Ephorean 'explanation'.

[1] The tradition in vi. 116 was accepted by the usually sceptical Beloch (ii². 1. 23). It is curious that neither Datis nor Artaphernes is mentioned by name in Herodotus after their departure from Delos for Eretria until their return voyage to Asia (vi. 118. 1, 119. 1).

PART II

THE INVASION

I

THE ANTECEDENTS OF THE INVASION

Relations between Persians and Greeks to the death of Darius

IN the seventh century before Christ the Medes and Persians were living on the Iranian plateau, in the western part of the modern kingdom of Persia. At first the Medes, under kings who had made their capital at Ecbatana (Hamadan), took the lead, and are said[1] to have begun their expansion by reducing to subjection the Persians, who had occupied the lands to the south-east of Media. Towards the end of the century the Medes, in the reign of their greatest king Kyaxares, turned westwards to invade the valley of the Tigris, and overthrew the decadent kingdom of the Assyrians, capturing its capital Nineveh in 612. In this enterprise they were assisted by the Babylonians, who had previously thrown off the supremacy of Assyria, and under their new king Nebuchadnezzar successfully asserted their claim to the southern part of the old Assyrian Empire by a victory over the Egyptian ruler Necho. But in the new coalition of Media and Babylonia Media was certainly the more important partner, and Kyaxares proceeded to extend his dominions westwards through the northern part of Nearer Asia until on the Halys river he clashed with the Lydians under their king Alyattes. This must have been about 590, for the ensuing war is said to have been terminated in its sixth year by an eclipse[2] which can be dated to 28 May 585. A reconciliation was brought about by the secondary powers, the kings of Cilicia and Babylonia; Alyattes' daughter was given in marriage to Kyaxares' son, and the Halys seems to have been accepted as the boundary between the Median and the Lydian Empires.

Soon after the settlement Kyaxares died[3] and was succeeded by his son Astyages. After a long reign, of which no details are

---

[1] By Hdt. i. 102. 1; cf. HW i ad loc.
[2] Hdt. i. 74. 2 with the note in HW, also HW² i. 450, note E.
[3] Cf. HW i, top of p. 94, also 383, n. 5.

known, he was overthrown in 550[1] by a rising of the Persians under their young ruler Cyrus, who had become king of the Persians a few years earlier in succession to his father Kambyses. Astyages had probably become unpopular with his Median subjects, for the Babylonian records show that his own troops revolted against him during his struggle with Cyrus. In spite of his appropriation of the treasures found in Ecbatana, the supremacy of Cyrus seems to have been accepted by the Medes, who were so closely akin to the Persians that they were often identified with them by the Greeks and the Jews,[2] and although in the new Persian Empire the Medes were called upon to pay tribute,[3] they were recognized as one of the two master-races of the empire and their nobles were early employed in high positions.[4]

Cyrus must have been occupied at first in the years after 550 with the consolidation and reorganization of his new territories. But his sudden rise to power had alarmed Croesus, who had succeeded his father Alyattes as king of Lydia, and eventually Croesus formed a coalition with the other kings menaced by the expansion of Persia, Amasis of Egypt and Nabonidus of Babylonia.[5] Herodotus says that Croesus was the aggressor, crossing the Halys and occupying Pteria in Cappadocia, but Cyrus soon advanced to meet him. The battle which followed was indecisive, and Croesus retired to winter in his capital, Sardis. Cyrus was not deterred by the lateness of the season, and the rapidity of his movements enabled him to catch the enemy off their guard. His own forerunner, as Herodotus says,[6] he arrived unexpectedly outside Sardis, defeated the Lydian army in the plain outside the town, and before long succeeded in capturing the almost impregnable citadel. What happened to Croesus is uncertain,[7] but his kingdom was incorporated in the Persian Empire.

This event, which probably happened in 541,[8] first brought

---

[1] The date is derived from the Babylonian annals of Nabonidus; cf. HW i. 385.

[2] HW i. 383, n. 3.

[3] Medes pay tribute, Persians are exempt (iii. 92. 1 and 97. 1).

[4] Mazares (left by Cyrus to conquer the Lydian revolt) and also his successor Harpagos; cf. i. 156. 2 and 162. 1.   [5] i. 77. 2.

[6] i. 79. 2 (αὐτὸς ἄγγελος); the translation is that of Myres, *The Dawn of History* (1911), 131.

[7] The various ancient traditions are discussed by HW i. 98 f.

[8] HW i. 98; see below, p. 286, n. 1.

the Persians into contact with the Greeks. Croesus had subjugated the Greek states on the mainland of Asia Minor, thereby securing access to the seaports on the west coast of his realm, but though they had been compelled to pay tribute[1] they had apparently been excused the burden of military service. It was natural that Cyrus, when he had conquered Croesus, should expect to take over the Ionian states as well, but he was irritated by their previous refusal to revolt from Croesus at his bidding,[2] and refused to renew the treaties which they had made with Croesus. Miletos alone obtained from him an agreement on the old conditions;[3] the rest, faced with a new and more disagreeable form of subjection, decided to take up arms in their own defence, although their appeal for help to Sparta, by now the leading state in European Greece, failed to produce any effective aid. Cyrus departed almost at once for Ecbatana, but his generals Mazares and Harpagos speedily overcame the resistance of the Greek states on the Asiatic mainland;[4] the Ionian states alone are mentioned, but presumably those of Aiolian and Dorian stock were also forced to submit.[5]

Herodotus asserts[6] that when the Persians were about to conquer Ionia, those of the Ionians who were islanders had no cause for fear because the Persians themselves were not a maritime people and the Phoenicians had not yet become their subjects, and a little later he says[7] that the Aiolians who lived on the islands, the inhabitants of Lesbos and Tenedos, also felt secure. But after describing the conquest of the Ionians on the mainland he adds[8] that the Ionians on the islands were so alarmed that they submitted to Harpagos. This last statement cannot refer to the Cyclades, as even forty years later none of them was subject to Persia,[9] and Herodotus is presumably thinking here of the great islands near the Asiatic coast, Samos and Chios, and possibly Lesbos as well, since the mainland

---

[1] i. 27. 1; for the conquest cf. i. 26, and on the position of the Ionians under Croesus see HW on i. 141. 1.

[2] i. 141. 3; cf. 76. 3.   [3] i. 141. 4 (cf. 141. 1).

[4] Harpagos successfully used the technique of the siege mound, copied from the Assyrians (i. 162. 2 and HW ad loc.).

[5] Resistance by the Dorians would be useless after Karia and Lykia had been reduced by Harpagos, who had Aiolians as well as Ionians in his army (i. 171. 1). On the submission of the Dorians of Knidos cf. i. 174.

[6] i. 143. 1.   [7] i. 151. 3.   [8] i. 169. 2; cf. HW ad loc.

[9] v. 30. 6 (where Hude brackets τῶν Κυκλάδων).

Aiolians had made common cause with the Ionians against Cyrus.[1] Chios had received a grant of land on the mainland from the Persians[2] and was perhaps thereby committed to a policy of subservience to Persia; the Lesbians, who certainly held territories on the mainland later, may have been in a similar position.[3] When Polykrates seized the tyranny of Samos he certainly defied Persia and allied himself with Amasis king of Egypt, but he may in this respect have reversed the policy of the oligarchy which he had overthrown.

Whatever may have been the reaction of the Greeks in the adjacent islands to the Persian conquest of the mainland, the career of Polykrates proves that during the lifetime of Cyrus they had no reason to fear a Persian attack by sea. The acquisition of sea-power by the Persians is apparently connected by Herodotus[4] with the inclusion of the Phoenician states in their empire. When did this event occur? After his conquest of Lydia Cyrus had turned his arms successfully against the Babylonian kingdom and added it to his dominions, but though he was expected to attack Egypt next he preferred to campaign on his eastern frontiers,[5] where he finally died in battle; the Phoenicians on the conquest of Babylonia may have sent gifts to the new lord of the Near East,[6] but their definitive incorporation in the Persian Empire probably did not take place until after Cyrus' death. Herodotus makes the Persian councillors praise Cyrus' son Kambyses as a better man than his father because he had added 'Egypt and the sea' to the realm bequeathed to him by Cyrus.[7] The adhesion of Phoenicia was apparently followed closely by that of Cyprus, which threw off its former allegiance to Egypt.[8] Cilicia seems to have entered the empire while Cyrus was alive on favourable terms which allowed it to retain its hereditary rulers. The acquisition of Phoenicia and Cyprus gave Kambyses naval supremacy in the eastern Mediterranean

---

[1] i. 151. 3.   [2] The territory of Atarneus (i. 160. 4).

[3] A ship of Lesbian Mytilene was with Kambyses in Egypt (iii. 13. 1), but the Lesbians might have submitted, like Polykrates, after Kambyses' accession.

[4] i. 143. 1.

[5] Hdt. says (i. 153. 4) that Cyrus left Sardis soon after the conquest of Lydia because he still had to deal with Babylon, the people of Baktria, the Sakai, and the Egyptians; cf. HW ad loc.

[6] Cf. Olmstead, *History of the Persian Empire*, 56.

[7] iii. 34. 4; cf. iii. 19. 3 and HW ad loc.

[8] iii. 19. 3; cf. ii. 182. 2.

and explains why Polykrates now decided to submit to the Persians before they invaded Egypt.[1]

Amasis, who had ruled Egypt for forty-four years, died in the year before the Persian invasion, and the resistance offered by his son Psamtek III was soon overcome by Kambyses' troops, whereupon the Libyans west of Egypt and the Greek kingdom of Kyrene promptly submitted without resistance (525).[2] For whatever reason, Kambyses lingered in Egypt for nearly three years, during which Herodotus records expeditions of his army against the oasis of Ammon and the Ethiopians, both alleged to have ended in disaster; finally, in 522 he was recalled by alarming news from the Persian homeland. A revolt had been started there by a man who claimed to be Kambyses' younger brother Bardiya, whom the Greeks called Smerdis. According to the official story, published later by Darius in the famous inscription at Behistun and accepted by Herodotus, he was really a Magian called Gaumata, trading on the fact that the real Smerdis had been secretly assassinated on Kambyses' orders before the conquest of Egypt, but some modern historians[3] doubt Darius' veracity and believe that the leader of the revolt really was Cyrus' son Bardiya. Kambyses died in Syria on his way back, either by his own hand or as the result of an accident, and Smerdis reigned unchallenged for seven months[4] until Darius son of Hystaspes, member of a collateral branch of the royal family, formed a conspiracy with six other Persian nobles. The conspirators sought out and slew Smerdis in a castle in Media,[5] whereupon Darius with their consent proclaimed himself king.

His accession was followed by a series of revolts in the central part of the empire, even in the Persian homeland, the course and suppression of which are fully described in the Behistun inscription. They seem to have been successfully crushed within two years, and Darius then had leisure to reorganize his empire.[6] Herodotus claims for him the credit for dividing the whole empire into twenty provinces (exclusive of the homeland); these

---

[1] iii. 44. 1.

[2] iii. 13. 3; cf. iv. 165. 2. On the date cf. HW i. 394, n. 2.

[3] e.g. Beloch, ii[2]. 1. 4, n. 1 and Olmstead, 108 f.   [4] iii. 67. 2.

[5] HW i. 275 on Hdt. iii. 68. 2; the date of the assassination is equated with 29 Sept. 522 (Olmstead, 108).

[6] And also to start building a new capital in the homeland (to replace Pasargadai) later known as Persepolis; cf. Olmstead, 172 ff.

were called satrapies and each had a single satrap (governor).[1] There is some dispute whether the provincial divisions described by Herodotus reflect correctly the organization established by Darius early in his reign or correspond to some later reorganization, on the ground that they do not tally exactly with any of the three lists given by Darius;[2] it is, however, possible that Darius intended his lists to be catalogues of the principal peoples of his empire, not of the satrapies which he had created.[3]

In spite of Herodotus' assertion here, it is certain from what he says elsewhere that the satrapal organization of the empire was not originated by Darius. The government of large areas by a noble of high rank must go back to Cyrus, for it was Cyrus who had made the Persian Oroites 'governor of Sardis', as the satrap of the province of Lydia–Ionia was called, and under Kambyses, if not earlier, the satrapy of Hellespontine Phrygia, with its centre at Daskyleion, was governed by another Persian, Mitrobates.[4] Even the division of powers designed to curtail the satrap's authority can be traced back beyond Darius. When Cyrus conquered Lydia he left a Persian, Tabalos, in charge of the acropolis at Sardis, entrusted the collection of the wealth of Lydia to a native Lydian, Paktyas, and appointed the Mede Mazares to command the field army.[5] Moreover, each satrap had at his side a 'royal secretary', directly responsible to the king, who kept a close watch on the satrap's actions and helped on occasion to bring about his downfall.[6]

Darius probably deserves the credit for the second innovation attributed to him by Herodotus, the regulation of the tribute which was henceforward to be paid by each satrapy to the central government. Although Herodotus here alleges[7] that under

---

[1] iii. 89. 1.

[2] At Behistun, Persepolis, and Nakhsh-i-Rustam; cf. HW i. 405 f., and for a full discussion Ehtécham, *L'Iran sous les Achéménides*, 132–59.

[3] This is the conclusion of Ehtécham, 158; note the warning given by Meyer, 97 n.

[4] iii. 120. 1–2. On the Lydian satrapy (called Sparda by Darius) cf. HW ii. 9 (on v. 25. 1).

[5] i. 153. 3 (cf. HW ad loc.) and 156. 2. The acropolis at Sardis had its own governor in 334 (Arrian, *Anabasis* i. 17. 3); cf. Huart, *La Perse antique*, 90.

[6] iii. 128. 3–5 (especially the parenthesis in 3); the story shows that the institution was prior to Darius' accession.

[7] iii. 89. 3.

Cyrus and Kambyses the subject peoples merely offered gifts because as yet there were no fixed arrangements for the payment of tribute, it is clear from other passages[1] that the 'gifts' were merely tribute in another form. Ehtécham concludes[2] that the reforms introduced by Darius in this part of the administration were the replacement of gifts (except those from certain peoples on the frontiers of the empire)[3] by a fixed tribute, the payment of this in precious metals and not in kind, and the assessment of the contribution of each satrapy at a round sum, calculated in Babylonian talents. Herodotus gives details of[4] the amounts due from nineteen of the twenty satrapies, which make a total of 7,600 Babylonian or 9,800 Euboïc talents; he adds another 4,680 Euboïc talents as the value of the gold dust annually contributed by the Indians of the twentieth satrapy, but this item seems more open to question than the rest.[5] The economic prosperity of the empire was fostered by the restoration of peace, the construction of great trunk roads, the encouragement of agriculture, and the introduction of a standard gold coinage.[6]

When the task of internal pacification and consolidation had been completed, the empire was ready for further expansion. In the far east Cyrus had stopped at the frontiers of India, but Persian troops now invaded the Indus valley and added it to the empire as the satrapy of Hindush, apparently before 513.[7] It was more important for the future of the Greeks that Darius was equally active in the west. Samos, which after Polykrates' death had become independent, was recovered when a Persian army established Polykrates' brother Syloson there as tyrant.[8] The Battiad rulers of Kyrene, who had submitted to Persia in 525 and had later been forced by their subjects to flee, were

[1] Notably iii. 67. 3; cf. iii. 13. 3 and iv. 165. 2.

[2] Op. cit. 94 ff.

[3] Ethiopians, Arabians, and Colchians (iii. 97); Ehtécham, 96 thinks Darius established a fixed tariff for these as well.

[4] iii. 90–94 (total in 95; cf. HW i. 287 ad loc., also the second note on iii. 89. 2).

[5] Cf. Beloch, ii². 1, p. 2, n. 3; Meyer, 85 thinks the figure fluctuated, but that given by Hdt. seems too high even for a maximum.

[6] For these measures cf. Ehtécham, 102 ff. (also HW on iii. 89. 3).

[7] On the conquest and the famous voyage of Skylax which preceded it cf. Hdt. iv. 44, and on the date Olmstead, 145, n. 42.

[8] iii. 139–49. As 139. 1 dates the conquest near the beginning of Darius' reign it may be as early as 518.

restored by Aryandes the satrap of Egypt.[1] Darius' interest in
the far west is shown by the dispatch early in his reign of two
triremes which under the guidance of his Greek physician,
Demokedes of Kroton, got as far as South Italy.[2] Finally, in
513 or 512, Darius in person led a great army across the Bos-
poros into Europe[3] and marched northwards. He certainly
crossed the lower Danube a little above the head of its delta,[4]
but the traditions repeated by Herodotus on the subsequent
course of the campaign which take him as far as the Volga are
fantastic and incredible.[5] It is possible that Darius intended to
fix his frontier at the Danube, and that his expedition beyond
the river was merely intended to strike terror into the peoples on
the north bank.[6] But the trans-Danubian barbarians, called
Skythai by the Greeks, wasted the country before his advance
and avoided battle, so that in the end the Persians were forced
by shortage of supplies to retreat. The result of the campaign
was clearly regarded as a failure, all the more damaging to
Persian prestige because Darius himself had been in command;
it is significant that Byzantion, Kalchedon, and Perinthos
promptly disowned their recent submission to Persia,[7] and that
Darius made his way back to Asia across the Hellespont.

Some have supposed[8] that the main objective of the expedi-
tion had been to conquer Thrace, but Darius had merely re-
duced the coastal tribes between Byzantion and the Danube.
Herodotus says that on his return Darius ordered his general
Megabazos to subdue Thrace,[9] but the conquests made by
Megabazos seem to have been confined to the parts of Thrace
near the Aegean. They were, however, sufficient to give the
Persians control of the important coast road to the Strymon

---

[1] iv. 165–7 and 200 ff.   [2] iii. 135–8.

[3] iv. 87 ff.; on the figure 700,000 for his army see below, p. 351. *I.G.* xiv. 1297
(= no. 252 in Jacoby, *F.G.H.*; the so-called Capitoline chronicle of A.D. 15–16)
dates the expedition to the year 513–512, and though its authority is not high (it
ascribes to the same year the murder of Hipparchos, which certainly occurred in
the summer of 514) the date is not unlikely; cf. HW i. 429. Wade-Gery in *J.H.S.*
lxxi, 1951, 215 prefers 514.   [4] iv. 89. 2.

[5] Cf. HW i. 432 f.; the implication of Strabo (p. 305) that Darius did not get
beyond the Dniester is probably inference rather than independent tradition
(Meyer, 115 n.).

[6] So Beloch, ii². 1. 5–6 and p. 6, n. 1.

[7] v. 1 and 26; cf. iv. 143. 1. Perhaps Abydos also revolted (Strabo, 591).

[8] e.g. Grundy and Macan; for criticism of this view cf. HW i. 431.

[9] v. 2. 2; cf. v. 10 (last sentence).

and to bring about the submission of Amyntas king of Mace-donia;[1] Persian influence in Europe was thereby extended to the borders of Thessaly, the northern frontier of Old Greece. On Darius' inscription at Nakhsh-i-Rustam there appears a new category of Ionians,[2] possibly the Greeks of Europe, and an entry, Skudra, usually identified with Thrace and Macedonia.[3] Persia under Darius had become a factor to reckon with in the politics of the Greek homeland. There, and even farther west, states menaced in war by their neighbours, statesmen driven into exile by their opponents, began to look to Persia for help, just as three centuries later Greek states and statesmen appealed to the rising power of Rome. Whether Darius was bent on further conquest in Europe or not, this proximity and growing inter-relation of the Persians and those Greeks who were still inde-pendent increased the risk of a collision between them.[4]

For twelve years or more after Megabazos' campaign the Persian Empire remained stationary in the west, but it is not safe to infer from this fact that Darius had no intention to extend his dominions farther in this direction, for in the winter of 500 he gave his approval to a plan for the conquest of Naxos and probably of other islands in the Cyclades as well.[5] But the Naxians withstood a four months' siege, and the previous mobil-ization of the naval contingents from the Asiatic Greek states facilitated their revolt when the expedition returned unsuccess-ful to Asia in the autumn of 499. As the satraps were not allowed to maintain large armies in peacetime,[6] the governor of Lydia–Ionia, Darius' half-brother Artaphernes, could do nothing to check the rising in its early stages, and the rebels had ample time to make their preparations and appeal to their kinsmen in Old Greece. It is strange that Meyer, after insisting that a conflict between the free Greeks and the Persians could not be

---

[1] v. 17–21, where the truth is distorted by a later tradition invented to glorify Amyntas' son, Alexander I; see below, p. 273.

[2] *Yaunā takabarā*; *taka* is apparently a kind of coiffure (Ehtécham, 148, n. 3 and Meyer, 297 n.).

[3] The identification, accepted by Olmstead, 157 f., is queried by Ehtécham, 152.

[4] Cf. Meyer, 297 f.

[5] v. 32 (cf. 31. 2–3). The chronology of the revolt in the text is based on that given by Macan, *Herodotus iv–vi*, ii. 62 ff.

[6] Cf. Grundy, 49. This fact is sufficient to refute the assertion of Lysanias of Mallos (Plutarch, *H.M.* 24) that already at the time of the Ionian expedition to Sardis a Persian army was besieging Miletos. On Artaphernes cf. v. 25. 1.

long delayed, should have condemned the Ionian Revolt as a movement foredoomed to failure.[1] Although the rebels got little support from the homeland they won over Cyprus, and in 497 defeated the Phoenician ships off Cyprian Salamis; even after they lost Cyprus it was not till 494 that they were overcome by the reconstituted Persian navy at Lade, and even then the victory was only achieved by Persian exploitation of treachery among their opponents.

The Persian Empire had begun to constitute a serious threat to the states of Old Greece when it acquired a great navy under Kambyses. Those states ought to have realized that the rising of the Asiatic Greeks offered them a valuable opportunity to restore the balance of power at sea;[2] the history of the revolt shows that the Ionians with even moderate support from the homeland could have maintained their maritime supremacy. The refusal of Sparta to give the rebels any help is sufficient to refute the theory[3] that the guiding principle of her foreign policy for the last fifty years had been one of inflexible hostility to Persia. Even if she was now menaced herself near home by the threat of a resurgent Argos, her statesmen could have encouraged the maritime states of Sparta's Peloponnesian League to give naval support to the Ionians. Herodotus' view,[4] that the Athenians and Eretrians, by sending ships to Ionia in 498 and by joining in the march on Sardis, were directly responsible for bringing about Persian intervention in European Greece, only shows his weak grasp of historical causation. The clash between Persia and the Greeks of Europe was bound to come soon, and if the latter had been wise they would have hastened to the support of their kinsmen in Asia; even if they could not make head against the Persians on the mainland they could have preserved the independence of the three great islands, Lesbos, Chios, and Samos, which contributed 230 out of the 353 Greek ships at Lade, and could have cut off the Persians from Europe. The opportunity was thrown away, and the states of Old Greece might have been finally ruined by their short-sighted selfishness.

After the suppression of the revolt, Darius sent his nephew

---

[1] Meyer, 300 ff., answered by Beloch, ii². 1. 8.
[2] Cf. the admirable analysis in Beloch, ii². 1. 9 (also n. 1).
[3] For a recent version of this theory cf. Hammond, *History of Greece*, 194.
[4] v. 97 (last sentence); cf. vi. 98. 2.

Mardonios to the west in 492 to restore Persian rule in Thrace and Macedonia.[1] Although Mardonios was successful on land, the fleet which accompanied him suffered heavy losses in a storm off Mount Athos. This reverse may explain why Darius, who had determined to take vengeance on Athens and Eretria for the support they had given to the Ionians, was not ready for the attempt till 490, but it cannot be the reason why the punitive expedition went by sea.[2] If Darius had wished to reach Eretria and Athens by the land route he would have been forced to secure first the submission of Northern and Central Greece, and though Herodotus alleges[3] that in 491 Darius sent envoys to various states in the islands and Old Greece demanding the tokens of submission, earth and water, this tradition is probably unhistorical.

It is unlikely that Darius at this stage proposed to do more than conquer Eretria and Athens; if Attica was conquered and placed under the rule of a pro-Persian tyrant it would provide the Persians with a bridgehead which would be useful when they decided to extend their dominions on the mainland. In the summer of 490 the expeditionary force, probably about 20,000 strong, sailed westwards from Samos[4] across the Aegean, landed in Naxos and destroyed the town, then received the submission of several other islands in the Cyclades before it landed in Euboia. Eretria was attacked, and after a brief siege betrayed by two of its leading citizens; in accordance with Darius' instructions[5] its temples were sacked and burnt and its inhabitants enslaved. The Persian army then crossed to the north-east corner of Attica, where it landed at Marathon, but the Athenians marched out to block the road to Athens.[6] A deadlock ensued

---

[1] vi. 44. 1; cf. vii. 108. 1. The assertion in vi. 43. 4 that Eretria and Athens were the ultimate objectives of this expedition is untenable, in spite of Grundy, 151 f.; cf. Beloch, ii[2]. 2. 84 ff. and Macan, op. cit. ii. 74.

[2] As suggested by Olmstead, 159; but see Beloch, loc. cit. (p. 85).

[3] vi. 48–49, criticized by Beloch (loc. cit., p. 86, also 1. 40 f., n. 6); the evident bias of the story against Aigina may explain its origin. The murder of a Persian herald at Sparta (vii. 133), authenticated by the curious story of the Wrath of Talthybios, must belong to 481.

[4] vi. 95. 2; on the numbers see above, p. 59.

[5] vi. 101. 3. This frightfulness was doubtless deliberate (Hdt. says it was in revenge for the burning of Sardis), but it was a grave error of policy, for it showed the Athenians clearly what they had to expect if defeated; cf. Olmstead, 160 f.

[6] On the problems raised by Herodotus' account of the campaign of Marathon see above, pp. 64 ff.

until the Athenians, prompted by Miltiades, attacked and defeated the Persian troops, who are said to have lost 6,400 men;[1] after this reverse the Persian expedition returned to Asia.

Herodotus asserts[2] that the Athenians at Marathon were the first Greeks to stand their ground against a Persian army; they were certainly the first to inflict a decisive defeat in fair fight on the hitherto unconquered Persian infantry. Their victory encouraged the patriotic Greeks by showing them that resistance was not hopeless, and also dealt a severe blow to the prestige of Persia, a blow which before long had repercussions in the western half of the empire. Darius, after such a setback, could no longer afford to abandon his policy of western expansion. He was so deeply committed that nothing short of the reduction of European Greece would now serve his purpose, but with no base on the Greek mainland he had no choice but to take up again the plan of an advance by land. The route was in Persian hands up to the borders of Thessaly, but after that the Greek states, if they combined, could put up a formidable resistance. Darius determined to make sure of success by elaborate preparations,[3] but they were not yet complete when the Egyptians rose in revolt, and soon after, in November 486,[4] Darius died.

The Persian preparations for the invasion

When Darius became king he had connected himself with the family of Cyrus by marrying two of his daughters, Atossa and Artystone, as well as a daughter of his son Smerdis.[5] Atossa bore Darius four sons,[6] of whom the eldest, Xerxes, became king in

---

[1] vi. 117. 1.

[2] vi. 112. 3; cf. HW ad loc. A Persian army had been destroyed in an ambush by night in Karia six or seven years earlier (v. 121).

[3] For three years (vii. 1. 2–3); on this long delay cf. Grundy, 200. Tarn's explanation (*J.H.S.* xxviii, 1908, 209) that Darius was replacing pentekonters in his fleet by triremes is based on a doubtful inference from Thuc. i. 14. 2 (on which see above, p. 52, n. 1). Busolt, 632 believes that the three years of preparation are a fiction of Greek tradition to account for a delay which was perhaps due to Darius' failing health.

[4] On the date cf. Olmstead, 228 and n. 45, also HW ii. 125 (on Hdt. vii. 4). The chronological data in Hdt. vii. 1, 4, 7, and 20. 1 are perplexing; see HW ii. 133 for a reconstruction which places the revolt of Egypt in 487 (others date it to 486; so Olmstead, 228).

[5] iii. 88. 2–3. Artystone was Darius' favourite wife (vii. 69. 2).

[6] vii. 2. 2.; cf. HW i. 265 on iii. 31. 6.

preference to Artobarzanes, the eldest of the sons born to Darius by another wife before his accession. In Herodotus the choice of Xerxes to succeed his father on the throne is not assured until shortly before Darius' death, but in fact he seems to have been recognized as heir apparent much earlier.[1] Xerxes was tall and handsome[2] and must have had some kingly traits, including an occasional magnanimity illustrated in the stories told about him, and some charges against him, notably the ascription to cowardice of his hasty retreat from Greece after his defeat at Salamis, are unfounded; but when every allowance has been made for the hostile bias of our sources it is clear that he was not equal to his high position, which he owed to his birth and not to his merits. Brought up as a king's son and in the unwholesome atmosphere of harem intrigues, he was lecherous and cruel,[3] and in consequence of his inability to control his entourage firmly he ended his inglorious reign as the victim of a palace conspiracy.[4] He cannot, however, be blamed for the failure of the long-delayed invasion of Greece; the expedition was well planned and carefully prepared, and Xerxes had the wisdom to entrust its execution to the generals he had inherited from Darius.

First of all it was necessary to crush the rebellion in Egypt, and here Xerxes acted promptly. In the year after Darius' death Egypt was reconquered and reduced to a greater degree of subjection than before;[5] the old Persian policy of respectful homage to the native deities was now given up. Babylon also rose in revolt before long; its rebellion is dated by Ktesias before, by Arrian after, Xerxes' invasion of Greece,[6] but the evidence of Babylonian documents seems to fix it to 482. In his description of Babylon Herodotus speaks of the temple of Zeus (otherwise Bel-Marduk) with its statue of the god in solid gold

---

[1] Olmstead, 214 ff., especially 215, n. 3.

[2] vii. 187 (last sentence); for Xerxes' magnanimity cf. vii. 146 and 147.

[3] As shown by the story in ix. 108–13.

[4] Ktesias, *Persika* 29; cf. Aristotle, *Politics* 1311ᵇ38.

[5] vii. 7 (cf. Olmstead, 235). Egypt, not Bactria, must surely be the restless land in the inscription of Xerxes cited by Olmstead, 231.

[6] Ktesias, *Persika* 22 (he attributes the suppression of the revolt to Megabyzos son of Zopyros); Arrian, *Anabasis* vii. 17. 2 (also iii. 16. 4). On the date cf. Olmstead, 236 f. and the paper by Cameron cited in n. 22. Obst (211 ff.) follows Lehmann-Haupt in dating the revolt to 479. Meyer (in a supplementary note, introduction, p. xiv) suggested that there might have been two revolts.

12 cubits high; he adds a note that it was removed from its
temple by Xerxes and that he killed a priest who tried to stop
him.[1] Herodotus nowhere mentions a Babylonian revolt under
Xerxes, and his reference to the statue is too brief to show
whether its removal by Xerxes was the cause or the sequel of
the rising; Arrian says that Xerxes on his return from Greece
demolished the temple of Bel and other shrines in Babylon.
Cyrus had sought the favour of Bel to legitimize his rule in
Babylonia,[2] but the removal of the statue was a demonstration
that here too, as in Egypt, the attempt at conciliation of a
subject people by deference to its gods had been abandoned as
a failure.

Aeschylus in the *Persai* represents Xerxes as a ruler intoxi-
cated by power, whose rash invasion of Greece brought to ruin
the great empire built up by the wisdom and self-restraint of
Darius. The contrast is dramatically effective, but it ignores the
fact that the Greek expedition was a legacy to Xerxes from his
father. Darius by his invasion of Europe had initiated a policy
of further expansion in the west, and though he may have intended to defer the conquest of the Greek mainland until the
time seemed ripe, his hand was forced by the participation of
Athens and Eretria in the Ionian revolt and the subsequent
defeat of the Persian punitive expedition at Marathon. After
this blow to the prestige of the Persian army it was difficult for
Xerxes to reverse his father's policy and to refrain from further
conquests beyond the present frontiers of the empire in the west.
Herodotus' account[3] of the council held by Xerxes before he
made his final decision is doubtless unhistorical in its present
form, but it may contain a substratum of truth, learnt by Herodotus from some of his Persian informants; Xerxes himself,
being no general, may have been reluctant to venture on a
major expedition in which success was uncertain,[4] and may

---

[1] i. 183. 2–3. Meyer, 130 puts the removal of the statue before the rising; for
the other view cf. Olmstead, 237. Hdt. says that Darius had thought of removing
the statue; if this is correct it suggests that the conciliation policy was proving
a failure before his death.   [2] Olmstead, 51 ff.; HW i. 386.

[3] vii. 8–11. Xerxes himself is made to state the principle that military empires
must continue to expand till they meet with a check. For scepticism about the part
played in these chapters by Mardonios cf. Busolt, 634, n. 1.

[4] Cf. Olmstead, 248, Artabanos is assigned the typical Herodotean role of 'the
warner', the wise counsellor who cautions his master (usually in vain) against the
temptations of excessive prosperity.

have been supported in his reluctance by his father's brother
Artabanos, but he was in the end persuaded by the war-party,
perhaps led by his cousin Mardonios,[1] who could claim to be
well acquainted with the problems to be solved.

Confronted with an empire which stretched from Macedonia
to the Indus, with resources in money and manpower to match
its extent, the Greek states, small and disunited, might to a
superficial observer seem destined to certain destruction if they
attempted to resist; such was the conclusion reached by the
priests at Delphi, who through Apollo's oracle warned the faithful to save themselves from ruin by timely submission to their
inevitable destiny.[2] But those who judged more carefully could
see many weaknesses in the Persian colossus. Most serious of all
was that the empire owed its creation to brute force and was
only held together by brute force.[3] The Persians and Medes and
some of the Iranian peoples to the east of them were genuinely
attached to the Achaimenid dynasty, but most of the peoples in
the western half of the empire felt little loyalty to rulers whose
rule remained alien to the end, and had no zeal for wars of
conquest in which they had to serve against their will.

Persia's apologists claim that her conquests had brought
peace to western Asia and that Persian administration was a
great improvement on any imperial system that had preceded
it, notably in the tolerance shown by it to the religions and
customs of its subjects. These claims are not unfounded, but
there is something to be said on the other side. The satraps had
too much power, and the checks imposed on its abuse by Cyrus
and Darius tended in practice to be ineffective; Grundy rightly
doubts[4] whether they 'could guarantee the provincial from acts
of oppression on the part of officials who had a mind to act in
arbitrary fashion'. The fixed taxes in money imposed by Darius
on the provinces of the empire were perhaps not excessive, but
in addition every province had to make its contribution to the
feeding of the king's court and army, Babylonia being responsible
for this during four months of every year.[5] Further, the expenses

---

[1] Son of Gobryas. His mother was a sister of Darius (vii. 5. 1) and he had
married a daughter of Darius in 492 (vi. 43. 1).

[2] See below, p. 444.

[3] The weaknesses of the empire are well expounded by Beloch ii². 1. 3–4.

[4] *G.P.W.* 43.

[5] i. 192. 1; on what follows cf. HW i. 404, Meyer 86 ff. Particular areas inside

of local administration were not defrayed from the tribute; each province had to bear the burden of maintaining the satrap and his staff, and some at least of those which had a garrison were expected to contribute to its cost.[1] As only a small proportion of the direct taxes paid in money to the king ever found its way back to the provinces, the result was an ever-growing accumulation of precious metal in the central treasuries which soon brought on a financial crisis.[2] Hence the richer provinces of the empire had by now good reasons for discontent with Persian rule.

Unwilling subjects would not make good soldiers or good sailors. This did not matter so much in the army, for on a distant expedition the size of the army would be restricted by the difficulties of routes and commissariat, so that a large proportion of the total force could be supplied by the loyal and warlike troops of the Iranian plateau. But in the conquest of Greece the role of the navy would probably prove to be more important than that of the army, and it was a handicap to the Persian Empire under Kambyses and his successors that its position as a sea power depended on fleets supplied entirely by the subject peoples of the eastern Mediterranean. The Persians of the homeland had no fleet and no experience of maritime affairs,[3] and though some of them served as marines on some of the ships in the navy,[4] they must have felt uncomfortable on an element alien to them. Of the peoples which supplied contingents to the Persian navy, all except the Phoenicians (and perhaps the Cilicians) had little enthusiasm for a Persian victory, and the Egyptians, Cyprians, and Ionians had all been in revolt from Persia on one occasion or another within the last twenty years. The history of the Persian navy since its creation by Kambyses had been inglorious; it had been beaten off Cyprus by the Greeks

a province might be ordered to contribute regularly to the expenses of a member of the royal family or even a private person honoured by the king; cf. ii. 98. 1, also Thuc. i. 138. 5, Xen. *Anab.* i. 4. 9 and ii. 4. 27.

[1] In Egypt the contribution was in kind and additional to the tribute (iii. 91. 2) but in Cilicia a sum of 140 talents was deducted from the tribute for this purpose (iii. 90. 3) and so is not included in the grand total of all the provincial tributes in iii. 95. 1.

[2] Olmstead, 298 f.   [3] i. 143. 1.

[4] vii. 181. 2 (Persian marines on a ship probably Phoenician). The statement in 184. 2 that there were thirty additional marines, Persians, Medes, or Sakans, on *every* trireme in the Persian fleet is difficult to accept.

of Asia and Cyprus in 497, and its one recorded victory, that of Lade in 494, had only been won with the aid of treachery. Xerxes and his advisers decided to ensure success on sea against Greece by collecting a fleet larger than any previously raised by the empire; the total of ships mustered for the invasion in the spring of 480 may have been 600 triremes.[1]

Even on land the Persians could not feel sure of victory. The Iranian stocks in the empire provided excellent cavalry, and with these, backed by the famous Persian archers, Cyrus had been able to conquer western Asia fairly easily, but the geographical conditions in the peninsula of Old Greece were ill-suited to the methods of fighting which until now had brought Persia success, except in Scythia. Of the Persian infantry, the archers had proved ineffective at Marathon, for the Athenian phalanx when it came within bowshot had closed so quickly that their arrows had had little effect, and in hand-to-hand combat their lack of defensive armour had put them at a serious disadvantage against Greek hoplites. There were, indeed, some spearmen in the army which the Persians brought against Greece in 480, including the 10,000 Immortals, but on the one occasion on which they appear in action against Greek hoplites, at Thermopylai, they had no success because, as Herodotus points out,[2] their spears were shorter than those of the Greeks, and in the campaign of 479 nothing more is heard of them.

Above all, the moral factor must not be forgotten. Herodotus has given noble expression[3] to the Greek political ideal of a number of independent city states, uniting in a free association to defend their culture and their way of life, states in which citizens enjoyed equality and freedom under no other rule than that of a self-imposed law administered by magistrates of their own choice. The Persians too had their ideals, derived from a monotheistic religion purer and loftier than the polytheism of the Greeks, and their sons, at least those of the nobility, were taught to ride and shoot and tell the truth,[4] but their political system was the rigid absolutism of all oriental monarchies under

---

[1] On this estimate see below, pp. 346 ff.   [2] vii. 211. 2.

[3] Especially in vii. 103. 4–5; it is noteworthy that this eloquent passage is put in the mouth of an exiled Spartan king. Cf. the remarks of an Athenian exile in Andokides ii. 10.   [4] i. 136. 2.

which the king alone was supreme and all his subjects, even the noblest of his own Persians, were no more than his slaves.[1] As the Persian royal judges told Kambyses when he wanted to marry his sister, they did not know of any law which commanded a brother to marry his sister, but they had found one which authorized the king of Persia to do whatever he pleased.[2] In such a monarchy the ruling peoples, Persians and Medes, were prepared to fight bravely to maintain their privileged position, but most of the subject peoples were at best apathetic and had no zeal for the cause of an alien despotism.

When Xerxes had announced his decision to invade Greece, elaborate preparations were made to ensure the success of the expedition. The figures given by Herodotus for the army of invasion are incredible, and even the more moderate estimates of fourth-century writers cannot be accepted;[3] possibly the Asiatic troops who crossed the Hellespont with Xerxes were composed of six infantry divisions of 10,000 men each, exclusive of the 10,000 Immortals under their commander Hydarnes and about 9,000 to 10,000 cavalry. An army of this size with such a large cavalry force could not be transported by sea across the Aegean but must advance to its goal by the long land route through Thrace and Macedonia.[4] To facilitate the achievement of the army in this part of its march, two pontoon bridges were thrown across the Hellespont at Abydos and another bridge was constructed over the river Strymon near its mouth,[5] the coastal road through Thrace was constructed or improved, and at certain places on it magazines of provisions were collected.[6] As in the last stages of the Ionian revolt, the fleet was intended to maintain the closest possible contact with the army, and because Mardonios' fleet in 492 had been wrecked off Mount Athos, a canal was dug through the neck of land which joins the Athos peninsula to the mainland of Chalkidike; three years were needed for the completion of this work,[7] which aroused the admiration and incredulity of later ages.

---

[1] Cf. Huart, *La Perse antique*, 88 f.; the story in Hdt. viii. 118. 3–4, though probably unhistorical, is a good illustration.   [2] iii. 31. 4.

[3] On these estimates and on the one suggested in the text see below, Appendix I, pp. 350 ff.

[4] Beloch, ii². 1. 38.   [5] vii. 33–36 and 24.

[6] vii. 25. 2; cf. 115. 3 for the road (later called the *vetus via regia*; cf. HW ad loc.).

[7] vii. 22. 1; see the first note on vii. 23 in HW.

The Persian preparations are said to have taken four full years, from the end of the Egyptian revolt until Xerxes set out from Sardis to Greece in the spring of 480.[1] According to Herodotus' account all the land forces from Asia had been ordered to meet Xerxes earlier, at Kritalla in Cappadocia,[2] apparently towards the end of the summer of 481, but the contingents from the western parts of Asia Minor may have joined him later, at Sardis or even at Abydos.[3] Xerxes is said to have led against Greece contingents from all the peoples in his empire,[4] and Herodotus gives a description of the dress and arms of each, but it is unlikely that the more unwarlike peoples were included in the army,[5] which had to be kept down to a manageable size.

It seems to have been in autumn 481 that Xerxes reached Sardis,[6] which was to be his base for the invasion. The ensuing winter was probably spent in final preparations for the coming campaign; these included the sending of heralds to all states of Greece (except Athens)[7] to ask for earth and water as evidence of submission. Xerxes had perhaps learnt from Darius[8] the value of diplomacy as a means of producing breaches in a hostile coalition, and the ability of the Greeks to resist him in the field would be diminished if he could previously induce as many Greek states as possible to stand aloof from the patriotic league which had recently been created to resist the invasion. Ephoros[9] even supposed that Xerxes, afraid that the League might obtain valuable reinforcements from Gelon, the powerful tyrant of Syracuse, had already ordered or persuaded Carthage to invade Sicily in the coming year to keep the Sicilian Greeks fully occupied at home, but this speculation is refuted by the silence

---

[1] vii. 20. 1 (with note in HW). Perhaps the Babylonian revolt had caused further delay.

[2] vii. 26. 1. Kritalla cannot be identified with certainty; for some modern speculations cf. HW ad loc., also the additional note in HW[2] 416.

[3] Cf. Grundy, 213 n.

[4] As Darius had done against Scythia (iv. 87. 1). For the 'army list' of Xerxes cf. vii. 61–88.

[5] Cf. Beloch, ii[2]. 1. 38, n. 4.

[6] This seems to follow from the statement that he wintered there (vii. 37. 1).

[7] vii. 32, where Hdt. excepts Sparta as well as Athens, but see above, p. 87, n. 3. On the return of the envoys cf. vii. 131, and on the states that medized see above, p. 18.

[8] vi. 9. 3–4.

[9] Fr. 111 in Müller, *F.H.G.* i. 264 (= fr. 186 in Jacoby, *F.G.H.*); see above, p. 17.

of Herodotus.[1] Nevertheless, it is obvious that the Greek prospects would be more hopeful if all the doubtful and lukewarm states could be induced to give their whole-hearted support to the National League.

The Greek states on the eve of the invasion

Athens and Sparta had become reconciled in the years just before Marathon and had arranged to combine in resistance to the menace of a Persian invasion of Old Greece. Whether their union was cemented by a defensive alliance against Persia or based on an informal understanding,[2] the relations between the two powers seem to have been less cordial in the first half of the decade after Marathon.[3] The defeat inflicted on the Persians by the Athenians and the prolonged pause that followed it apparently induced a false sense of security in the Greeks; the old internecine wars between one Greek state and another were resumed,[4] and the threat from the East was forgotten. In the end, however, the long delay was responsible for the salvation of Greece, thanks to the far-sighted genius of one man, the Athenian Themistokles. Clearly conscious throughout his career that the result of the coming struggle would be decided on the sea,[5] he made good use of the respite after Marathon, first of all to introduce constitutional reforms designed to adapt the government of Athens to changed conditions and above all to ensure continuity of command in war, and later, when a new vein of silver was discovered in the state-owned mines at Laureion, he persuaded his fellow citizens, previously

[1] The evidence of Ephoros is accepted by Meyer, 355 f. (with a suggestion that Ephoros may have got it from Antiochos of Syracuse!) and by Grundy, 254 ff., but is rejected by Beloch, ii[2]. 1. 72, n. 2, and by Macan, *Herodotus vii–ix*, ii. 186.

[2] The first view is that of Busolt (579, n. 3) and Macan (op. cit. ii. 195), the second that of Berve, *Miltiades*, 74 and n. 1. Berve reacts too strongly against the erroneous view that Athens entered the Peloponnesian League after 510; there must have been at least some interchange of oaths ἐπὶ τῷ Πέρσῃ between Athens and Sparta before 490.

[3] Macan, ii. 196.

[4] Hdt. vii. 145. 1 shows that the war between Athens and Aigina was not the only such war in progress in 481.

[5] Already in 493–492 (Thuc. i. 93. 3) Themistokles had made a beginning on the fortifications of the Piraeus. On his genius cf. Thuc. i. 138. 3, and on the part played by him in Athenian politics after 490 see Hignett, *A History of the Athenian Constitution*, 183 ff. (especially 188).

accustomed to share out the surplus profits from the mines, to use the money to build warships enough to raise the total Athenian fleet to 200 triremes.[1] Most of the usual sources of ship-timber, including Macedonia, were now controlled by Persia; perhaps that used for the new Athenian ships came from the forests of South Italy.[2]

Themistokles must have drawn closer again the old ties between Athens and Sparta, and his outstanding abilities seem to have impressed the Spartan government,[3] always inclined to be suspicious of the new-fangled Athenian democracy. Sparta, faced with the prospect of losing her hegemony in Peloponnese to her old enemy Argos, was determined to offer a desperate resistance to the invaders,[4] and she could count on the support of the league of states which she had built up during the course of the last eighty years and which now included all Peloponnese except Argos and the small states of Achaia, bordering the southern shore of the Corinthian Gulf. The army of the Peloponnesian League, composed of the 5,000 professional soldiers contributed by the full citizens of Sparta (the Spartiatai),[5] an equal number of Sparta's subjects, the Perioikoi, and the yeoman farmers who provided most of the heavy infantry in the other states of the League, was a formidable force, and the squadrons raised by the maritime states would be a valuable supplement to the new Athenian navy.

Although the Peloponnesian League and Athens were the two main supports of the national resistance to Persia, Sparta, perhaps prompted by Themistokles,[6] decided to attempt the creation of a wider Hellenic League directed primarily against

---

[1] Hdt. vii. 144. 1–2 and *A.P.* 22. 7; Hdt. implies that the 200 triremes (*A.P.* speaks of 100) were additional to the ships already possessed by Athens, but this cannot be right, in spite of the arguments of Labarbe, *B.C.H.* lxxvi, 1952, 407 ff. (especially 419–421).

[2] Themistokles' interest in the west is indicated by the story in viii. 62. 2 (cf. HW 256 ad loc.) and the fact that he gave the names Sybaris and Italia to two of his daughters (Plut. *Them.* 32. 2).

[3] He seems to have convinced them that the issue of the war depended on success at sea and that the main Greek effort must be made with the fleet; cf. Meyer, 373.

[4] Her determination was shown by the murder of Xerxes' envoys at Sparta; this murder, which is to be dated to 481–480 (see above, p. 87 and n. 3) may have been deliberate and intended to show Sparta's allies that she would fight to the end (Beloch, ii². 1. 40 and n. 6).   [5] On the numbers see below, p. 436.

[6] vii. 139. 5 (a polemical passage) stresses the activity of the Athenians in raising the other Greeks to resist Xerxes.

Persia; invitations were issued, probably to all states on the Greek mainland, to send delegates to a congress which was to be held in the temple of Poseidon at the Isthmus[1] of Corinth, a convenient centre for the states of mainland Greece. It is curious that this step was not taken until late in the summer of 481, but the Spartans and Themistokles perhaps calculated that the imminence of the danger would introduce a sense of greater urgency into the deliberations of the Probouloi, as the delegates to the Congress were called.[2] While the first meeting of the Congress, which was presumably presided over by a Spartan chairman, was still in session, news arrived that Xerxes had reached Sardis with his army;[3] the invasion could therefore be expected next summer.

Herodotus describes the states which sent delegates to the Congress as 'those who were of the better way of thinking about Greece'[4] and in a later context as 'those Greeks who had sworn together against the Persian'.[5] The oath implied in the second description must have been taken during the first meeting of the Congress; the Probouloi present swore in the name of their states to wage war in concert against the invader and not to desert the common cause.[6] It has been assumed that the pledges which they exchanged went beyond these immediate objectives, but the evidence is too scanty to establish any wider purpose. It was agreed that the supreme command of the forces of the new league on both land and sea should be in the hands of the Spartans; the Athenians had put in a claim to the naval command, but wisely withdrew it when it was opposed by the other allies.[7]

---

[1] So Busolt, 654 and Macan, ii. 219 (on the temple cf. viii. 123. 2). The tradition in Pausanias iii. 12. 6 that the first meeting of the Congress was held in the Hellenion at Sparta is probably a later invention.

[2] vii. 172. 1; on all questions relating to the League cf. the careful examination by Brunt in *Historia*, ii, 1953, 135–63.

[3] vii. 145. 2 (first sentence); this is the evidence for dating the first Congress to autumn 481.

[4] vii. 145. 1 (Brunt's translation); cf. 172. 1.

[5] vii. 148. 1 (after the sending of the spies and before the mission to Argos).

[6] Cf. the oath sworn by the islanders in ix. 106. 4.

[7] viii. 2. 2 and 3. 1 (where the claim is clearly dated to autumn 481). Hdt.'s comment in 3. 2 on the abandonment of the claim by the Athenians (during the present emergency only!) is cynical. Presumably it was Themistokles who persuaded them to give way, but the testimony of Plutarch (*Them.* 7. 3–4) to this effect is worthless.

When the National League had been duly constituted and the question of the hegemony decided, the first business before the Probouloi[1] was to put an end to the wars still in progress between some of the member states, especially the war between Athens and Aigina. It was also resolved to send three spies to Sardis; on their arrival they were promptly detected by the enemy, but Xerxes ordered that they were to be given facilities for obtaining full information about his forces and then sent home unharmed. He calculated, says Herodotus, that if the Greeks received an accurate report on the strength of his army they would realize the futility of resistance. Finally, the Probouloi decided to send envoys to four states which had not been represented at the Congress, Argos, Crete, Corcyra, and Syracuse.

Elsewhere Herodotus mentions[2] another oath sworn by the patriotic Greeks, that they would if victorious take a tithe for the god at Delphi from all Greeks who submitted to Persia unless they had done so under compulsion. This oath is quoted in connexion with a list of states in Northern and Central Greece (including the Thessalians, Lokrians, and most of the Boiotians) which gave earth and water to Xerxes, but it is unlikely that the Central Greeks openly medized until after the fighting at Thermopylai, and the oath must be earlier than that. If it was originally drafted in general terms and did not name any particular offender, there is no reason why it should not have been sworn by the Probouloi at their first meeting.[3] This second oath may have been in part a bid for the support of the Delphic priesthood;[4] its main purpose, however, seems to have been to warn the uncommitted states not to be over-hasty in making their peace with the invader but to wait until the pressure of events left them no choice.

There were special reasons for the decision to send envoys to four states which had not yet joined the League; it does not prove that all the states of mainland Greece (except Argos and Achaia) had sent delegates to the first congress. Subsequent events show that the Thessalians (and probably the mountain tribes living round the Thessalian plain) were not represented

---

[1] On the decisions taken by the Probouloi cf. vii. 145, and on the spies vii. 146–7.
[2] vii. 132. 2; on the list of medizing states in 132. 1 see above, p. 18.
[3] Brunt, op. cit. 136 f.   [4] Macan, ii. 220.

there. In Central Greece the Akarnanians and Aitolians were too remote and politically undeveloped to play any part yet in Greek history, but the Phokians and Lokrians, both of whom sent troops to Thermopylai later,[1] as well as the small Boiotian states of Thespiai and Plataia, had doubtless obeyed the summons to attend the Congress. Herodotus remarks[2] that the Phokians sided with the National League only because their enemies the Thessalians had gone over to the Persians, and that they would have sided with the Persians if the Thessalians had supported the Greeks; this sensible observation, indignantly challenged by Plutarch, recalls Macaulay's verdict[3] that the Highland tribes which rallied to the cause of Charles the First in Scotland only did so because the hated Campbells of Argyll had joined the other side.

The motive which induced the Phokians to enter the patriotic alliance must have influenced other states in favour of the invader; a National League headed by Sparta and Athens was not likely to attract the support of their bitterest enemies, Argos and Thebes. It has often been supposed[4] that all the Boiotian states, including Thebes, sent delegates to the first congress because Plutarch says that in the next spring the Thebans contributed a force of 500 men to the League army which was sent to Thessaly, but this evidence, suspicious in itself, comes from a tainted source, and no inference can safely be drawn from it. A more probable view is that Thebes and the other pro-Persian states genuinely desired a Persian victory from the start, but were careful not to commit themselves to either side until they could make contact with the Persian land forces. Herodotus, who usually condones the malevolent neutrality of Argos, at times admits[5] that she was frankly pro-Persian. Her position inside the Peloponnese, the inner citadel of Greek resistance, and menacing Sparta's communications with the Isthmus, made her ambiguous attitude a cause of great anxiety to the patriotic Greeks; this explains why the Congress decided to invite the Argives to join the alliance, and why the Spartans offered them

---

[1] vii. 203. 1; the Lokrians also supplied seven pentekonters to the fleet at Artemision (viii. 1. 2).

[2] viii. 30. 1, censured by Plutarch, *H.M.* 35; cf. Hauvette, 111.

[3] *History of England*, c. 13 (iii. 317 in the edition of 1855).

[4] e.g. by Brunt, 143. On the evidence of Plut. *H.M.* 31 see above, p. 23.

[5] viii. 73. 3 (last sentence); on the story in ix. 12 see below, p. 279.

large concessions.[1] The Argives, however, had no intention of entering the League, and by making exorbitant demands as the price of their adhesion ensured the failure of the negotiations.

It is strange that the Probouloi should have appealed to Crete, as its numerous city-states had few contacts with the politics of the Greek mainland.[2] The Cretans refused to give any aid, and claimed later that their conduct had been dictated by an oracle from Delphi.[3] The sending of envoys to Corcyra and Syracuse is more intelligible, as both had large navies.[4] If the Probouloi knew by now that Xerxes' fleet numbered 600 triremes, they must have been seriously alarmed by their own great inferiority at sea. The figures in Herodotus for the contingents of the loyal states at Salamis more probably represent the number of ships manned by each state in the course of the war;[5] the total, if twelve are added for the ships then guarding Aigina,[6] comes to 378. The gap between this and the Persian total could be wiped out or much reduced if Corcyra and Syracuse could be induced to send a large proportion of their fleets.

The Corcyraeans gave a favourable reception to the envoys and promised assistance, but though they manned sixty ships next year, these ships, which would have been a valuable reinforcement to the Greek fleet, got no farther than the south coast of Peloponnese. Herodotus, who is very hostile to the Corcyraeans, says that they deliberately held aloof, expecting the Persians to win.[7] Syracuse was now ruled by a military dictator, Gelon. He had greatly developed the resources of his state, but Herodotus must be exaggerating when he makes Gelon say[8] that he was prepared to help the Greeks with 200 triremes, as well as a large land force. Herodotus' version of the speeches exchanged by the envoys and Gelon cannot be trusted in detail,

[1] vii. 148–9; note the remark attributed to the Argives in 149. 3 that 'they chose rather to be ruled by the barbarians than to yield to the Lakedaimonians in anything'.

[2] The Cretans were later famous for their archers, and it may have been thought that a body of these would be a valuable supplement to the Greek forces (cf. Macan, ii. 225). In view of Herodotus' silence the allegation of Ktesias (*Persika* 26) that Cretan archers were present at Salamis (by invitation of Themistokles and Aristeides!) must be rejected.

[3] vii. 169. On the attitude of the Cretans cf. Macan, loc. cit., and Grundy, 240 f.
[4] Cf. Thuc. i. 14. 2.   [5] See below, p. 210.
[6] HW 249 (on viii. 46. 1).
[7] vii. 168; they made the excuse (168. 4) that they had been prevented by the Etesian winds from rounding Cape Malea.   [8] vii. 158. 4.

but he must be right on the two essential points, that a mission was sent to Gelon by the Probouloi and that the negotiations broke down when Gelon's claim to the supreme command on either land or sea was firmly rejected by the envoys.[1] In the long run Gelon's attitude made no difference, for even if he had agreed to send help[2] he would have been prevented by the Carthaginians, who seized the opportunity presented by the Persian attack on Old Greece to invade Sicily on their own account next year. Perhaps the free Greek republics would have been embarrassed by the presence of a strong naval contingent led by Gelon, whose government represented the antithesis of all that they were fighting for, but at the time his refusal must have been felt by the leaders of the National League as a grave disappointment.

After the first session of the Congress the Probouloi probably returned home for the winter, but they were back at the Isthmus in the spring of 480, when envoys arrived from Thessaly asking them to send a force to occupy the pass of Tempe,[3] through which ran the main road into Thessaly from the north. The powerful family of the Aleuadai, who controlled the chief city, Larisa, had for some time been intriguing with Persia; Thorax, the head of the family, had obtained the position of Tagos, the temporary leader appointed by the Thessalian Confederation in times of crisis, and doubtless hoped to make his leadership permanent with Persian support.[4] His policy would naturally be opposed by the local dynasts who controlled the other cities in the Thessalian plain, such as the Echekratidai of Pharsalos, and some of these dynasts must have been responsible for the appeal made in the name of the Thessalians to the Greeks at the Isthmus.[5] A force of 10,000 hoplites was sent by the Probouloi

---

[1] On these points the arguments of Brunt (op. cit. 158–62) are decisive.

[2] The Sicilian tradition (which incidentally accepted the Greek embassy as a fact) said that though Gelon had rebuffed the envoys he would have sent help if he had not been prevented by the Carthaginian invasion (vii. 165).

[3] vii. 172 (especially § 1) and also 174 (on the date).

[4] Macan, ii. 251–5 and Westlake in *J.H.S.* lvi, 1936, 12–24 should be consulted for Thessalian politics in this period. For Thorax and his brothers cf. ix. 58. 1, also ix. 1 and vii. 130. 3. The opening sentence of vii. 172, when compared with the second sentence of 174, proves (cf. Westlake 16) that Thessaly, or at least the Aleuadai in the name of Thessaly, had already medized before the expedition to Tempe (Westlake thinks the Aleuadai had entered into relations with Persia as early as 492).   [5] Macan, 252 f.; Westlake, 16 f. (on the Echekratidai).

to Thessaly in May 480 under a Spartan general Euainetos; it included an Athenian contingent led by Themistokles and was joined at Tempe by a body of Thessalian cavalry, but after a few days there the League army retired, and in consequence the Thessalians decided to side with the Persians.[1]

Herodotus attributes the retirement of the army to the discovery that Tempe could be turned by another pass;[2] there were in fact four passes in all from Macedonia into Thessaly, including the two noted by Herodotus. The rapid abandonment of an undertaking of such magnitude seems to call for a more convincing explanation than that offered by Herodotus; de Sanctis went so far as to maintain[3] that there never was a large-scale expedition to Thessaly but merely a reconnaissance by a small group of envoys and officers headed by Euainetos and Themistokles. This scepticism is excessive, but the timing of the expedition is certainly peculiar. Why should the Probouloi have sent a large army to Thessaly at least two months before Xerxes' troops could arrive on its northern frontier?[4] It would be characteristic of Herodotus to be well informed on the facts of the expedition but mistaken about its purpose. Perhaps this demonstration in force, asked for by Thessalian loyalists, was intended to encourage the anti-Persian elements in Thessaly to come out into the open, but when the response proved disappointing the Greek leaders decided that without the support of a united Thessaly they could not hope to defend all the passes against the superior numbers of the Persian army.[5]

The loss of Northern Greece without a blow was not necessarily a disaster for the patriotic Greeks; in view of the known attitude of the Aleuadai they cannot have expected Thessaly's support at the outset,[6] especially if it had sent no delegates to the

---

[1] vii. 173–4. It is curious that the expedition went by sea as far as Halos in Phthiotid Achaia and returned by the same route (173. 1 and 4); the suggestion that the Probouloi mistrusted the attitude of the Boiotians is a reasonable one (in spite of Grundy, 228).   [2] vii. 173. 4; on the passes see below, p. 107.

[3] *Riv. fil.* lviii, 1930, 339–42. He points out on p. 339 that an army of 10,000 hoplites implies the presence of an equal number of light-armed attendants (cf. ix. 29. 2).

[4] De Sanctis, op. cit. 340; cf. Hdt. vii. 174. Westlake (op. cit. 18, n. 28) argues unconvincingly that the expedition was merely planned when Xerxes was at Abydos and that it did not arrive in Thessaly until Xerxes was already in Thrace.

[5] Macan, 252 f.; Westlake, 19 (Westlake perhaps underestimates the strength of the pro-Persians in Thessaly at this time).   [6] Westlake, 16.

first Congress, and if they intended to stand on the defensive on land there were farther south stronger positions available for their army than the long northern frontier of Thessaly. They had much greater cause for despondency when they heard the report of the embassy to Gelon, especially if they had reason to doubt the sincerity of the promises made by the Corcyraeans. The two discouraging responses given to Athens by Delphi before this time[1] were based on a forecast of the coming campaign which might have been made by observers less deeply interested in the result than those who controlled Apollo's oracle, for even if the Greeks might hope to achieve a stalemate on land they must have seemed incapable of avoiding defeat at sea in the long run.[2] If the Persians succeeded in bringing their huge fleet intact from the Hellespont to the waters of Central Greece they were apparently bound to win the war, for although, being the aggressors, they would have to attack the Greek navy in whatever position it chose to occupy, they ought to be able, in virtue of a superiority of at least three to two, to wear down its resistance by sheer weight of numbers. If the Greek cause was to be saved at sea it could only be by a miracle but to anticipate the deliverance of Greece by a miracle required greater faith than was to be found in the priests of Delphi.

[1] vii. 140 and 141; on the date see below, pp. 442 f.

[2] Hdt. in vii. 138. 2 has correctly stressed the two grounds for the despondency felt by the Greeks on the eve of the invasion, the failure of many Greek states to rally to the National League and the numerical inferiority of the Greek fleet. Macan, ii. 239 curiously minimizes these handicaps when he credits Themistokles with an optimistic forecast of the outcome.

II

THERMOPYLAI

The Persian invasion of Northern Greece

Xerxes, after spending the preceding winter in Sardis, set out from there in the spring of 480[1] with the army of invasion and marched to the Hellespont, where he crossed into Europe opposite Abydos. He had now been joined by the fleet, which accompanied the army as it continued its advance through the Persian province of Thrace. Fleet and army parted company at Akanthos,[2] but were reunited again at Therma, the port at the head of the Thermaic gulf; here they were in the kingdom of Macedonia, which had been a vassal of the Persian Empire since 492.[3] Xerxes seems to have left the Hellespont in the first half of June and to have arrived at Therma early in August.[4]

So far the Persians had been advancing through lands and seas under their direct or indirect control, but at Therma they were confronted by the mountain barrier which stretches eastward from the central chain of Pindus and marked the northern frontier of the Greek homeland, the Cambunian and other ranges, ending in the great peak of Olympus near the Aegean coast. All possibility of Greek military opposition to the invasion at this frontier had been removed over three months earlier, when the Thessalians and the other peoples of Northern Greece finally decided to join the Persian side,[5] but the difficulties of the terrain by themselves constituted a problem for the Persian high command.[6] In particular, the divergence of the main land route from the neighbourhood of the coast meant the temporary suspension of that close co-operation between the army and the fleet on which the Persian plan of campaign was based. After passing the mouth of the river Peneios, south of

---

[1] vii. 37. 1. [2] vii. 121. 1. [3] vi. 44. 1; cf. HW 80.
[4] See below, Appendix XIV, p. 453. [5] See above, pp. 102 f.
[6] Cf. the discussion in Grundy, 221–3.

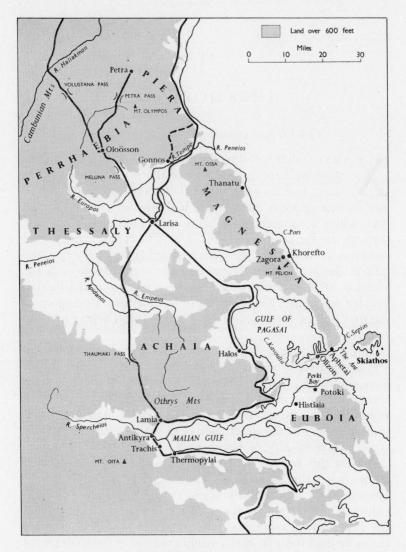

MAP 2. North-eastern Greece

Mount Olympus, the fleet must make its way along a dangerous stretch of rocky coast before it could recover contact with the main road to the south at the entrance to the Gulf of Pagasai. In view of the perils of navigation along this coast the Persian admirals needed to complete this part of their voyage in the shortest possible time. The land force had no such reason for haste, and as its rate of progress was bound to be slower anyhow it started southwards from Therma several days ahead of the fleet.

Herodotus has little to relate about the advance of the Persian army from Therma to Thermopylai, and even this brief account raises many problems. It is true that the advance was unopposed, but this is not an adequate explanation of his brevity, for he had given a detailed description of the march, far less essential to his story, from the Hellespont to Therma. He seems to have temporarily lost interest at this point.[1] Although he had apparently visited Thessaly and had been impressed by the girdle of mountains which completely surrounds the central plain, except at the point where the Peneios makes its way into the Aegean through the gorge of Tempe between Olympus and Ossa,[2] he knew little about the routes leading into Thessaly from the north. He had perhaps travelled along the most frequented, the road which turns inland from the coast through the Tempe gorge and on to Larisa, and he had also heard of a route from the sea across the mountains on the north side of Tempe which came out at the city of Gonnos, near the western exit from Tempe, but he shows no knowledge of the two roads which lead from Macedonia across the mountain ranges to the west of Olympus and come out into what was then the territory of the Perrhaiboi, a people dependent on the Thessalians and living in the mountainous country to the north of the central plain.[3] Of these two routes the westernmost ascends from the upper valley of the Haliakmon and crosses what is now called the pass of Volustăna, while the other, starting from Petra, crosses the mountains farther east, near the western slopes of Olympus; by this route, the Petra pass, Aemilius Paulus invaded Macedonia from Thessaly in 168. This route finally meets

---

[1] Like Diodoros, who brings Xerxes from Akanthos to the Malian Gulf in a single sentence (xi. 5. 1–2).

[2] vii. 128. 2–130.   [3] Macan, i. 164.

the road from the Volustăna Pass at Oloösson, in Perrhaibia,
but unlike the Tempe and Gonnos routes, which lead directly
into the Thessalian plain, the two westernmost routes, now combined in one, must cross the mountains in the south-east of
Perrhaibia by the Meluna Pass before descending into Thessaly
proper.[1]

Herodotus begins this section of his narrative with the statement that Xerxes, after his arrival at Therma, having seen the
Thessalian mountains, Olympus and Ossa, and having heard
of the Tempe gorge between them through which the Peneios
flows, decided to take ship and inspect the river where it flows
into the sea. The reason given for this decision is that Xerxes
intended to invade Thessaly 'by the upper road through the
land of the Macedonians who dwell inland, until he came to the
Perrhaibians, passing by the city of Gonnos; for by this way he
was informed that it was safest to go'.[2] In a later section Herodotus says that the Greek forces which had been sent earlier
in 480 to block the pass of Tempe[3] were informed on their
arrival that there was another pass into Thessaly 'by Upper
Macedonia through the Perrhaibians and by the city of Gonnos',
and he adds that this was 'the way by which the army of Xerxes
did in fact make its entrance'.[4]

The story of Xerxes' excursion by sea to the outfall of the
Peneios[5] is in itself somewhat suspicious, since it serves Herodotus as an excuse for a disquisition on the geography of
Thessaly and an improbable story about Xerxes' comment, but
the sequel is still more peculiar. We are first told that Xerxes
after his trip returned by sea to Therma, but in the next sentence Herodotus continues as follows: 'he then was staying in
the region of Pieria many days, for the road over the mountains
of Macedonia was being cut meanwhile by a third part of his
army, that all the host might pass over by this way into the
land of the Perrhaibians.'[6] Pieria, once the home of the Pierians

---

[1] Macan, i. 165 A; cf. HW 174 f. Grundy apparently never fulfilled his promise
(p. 231) to discuss these routes later.

[2] vii. 128. 1 (Macaulay's translation).   [3] See above, p. 102.

[4] vii. 173. 4 (Macaulay's translation).

[5] In his favourite Sidonian gallery, but accompanied by some if not all of his
fleet; cf. vii. 128. 2 and Macan, i. 163. The view of Legrand, vii. 125 f., that the
voyage was really a military reconnaissance, is unconvincing.

[6] vii. 131 (Macaulay's translation).

but by 480 part of Macedonia, included the northern and eastern slopes of Mount Olympus and the coastlands as far as the
mouth of the Haliakmon.[1] If Xerxes was in Pieria he could not
be in Therma.[2] Herodotus does not say that Xerxes after returning to Therma by sea then made his way by land to Pieria to
inspect the work of his pioneers, and this solution is anyhow
incompatible with the later passage from the Diary[3] in which
the Persian fleet is said to have sailed from Therma eleven days
after Xerxes had left it on his southward march; hence the fleet
sailed on the twelfth day of the Diary. Xerxes probably reached
Trachis two days later, on the fourteenth day, but if he had
spent several days in Pieria on the way he cannot have made the
journey from Therma to Thermopylai in thirteen days. Nor
can the march of the army have preceded his, for Herodotus
states clearly that his pioneers were working on the road while
he himself was in Pieria. Herodotus, here combining bits of information from different sources, has failed to work out their
various implications or to combine them in a consistent whole.

The statement that Xerxes waited for some days in Pieria
while a third part of his army was improving the road southwards through the mountains looks like a piece of authentic
tradition, but Herodotus' belief that this road was the route
through Gonnos cannot be accepted, still less his assertion that it
was the route actually followed by the invading army in 480.
The Gonnos route was important as the shortest detour by
which the main route through Tempe could be turned, and like
the main route it led directly into the Thessalian plain, but it
was rough and difficult[4] and would only be used by an army
if no other was available. Herodotus' description of it[5] as 'the
safest way' for Xerxes into Thessaly is ludicrous under the circumstances; the way through Tempe is narrow but quite suitable for an army which, like that of Xerxes, could count on a
friendly reception by the inhabitants. Why should Xerxes have
troubled to use the Gonnos route at all when Tempe was available?[6] Herodotus seems to have been impressed by what he had

[1] Cf. Macan, i. 170 A, HW 176 f.

[2] Macan, i. 270 B notes the inconsistency, but his explanation is inadequate.
Grundy, 221 ignores the difficulty.

[3] vii. 183. 2; see below, Appendix V.

[4] Cf. Livy xliv. 3. 3 and 5. 1 ff. (cited by HW 175).

[5] vii. 128. 1 (last sentence).   [6] Cf. Macan, i. 164 f.

heard, perhaps at Tempe, about the Gonnos route, and somehow picked up the mistaken idea that it was the route followed
by Xerxes and his army.

Gonnos is indeed in Perrhaibia,[1] but other references in Herodotus do not fit his account of the route. The Macedonians on
the northern slopes of Olympus through whom it passed in the
first part of its course can hardly be described as 'the Macedonians who dwell inland' or their territory as 'Upper Macedonia'.[2] These passages suggest that Herodotus, obsessed with
the Gonnos route, failed to understand clearly what his informants told him, and that they were really referring to one if not
both of the other two routes from Macedonia into Perrhaibia,
those of Petra and the Volustăna Pass. This conclusion is supported by Herodotus' observation[3] that the invasion was preceded by work on a mountain road undertaken by one third of
the Persian army. If this report is correct (and there seems no
sufficient reason for doubting it) then Xerxes must have intended to use one if not both of the two westernmost routes, as
the Gonnos route must certainly be ruled out. At an earlier
stage on the march the Persian army had been divided into
three columns,[4] and the existence of three main routes into
Thessaly may have prompted a similar division of the army for
the advance from Therme to Larisa, where the three routes
again converged, especially as in this part of the advance the
army must lose contact with the fleet. But the indications of
such an arrangement in Herodotus are too slight to permit of
certainty on this point.

Herodotus' account of the march of the Persian army from
Therma to Thermopylai is even briefer than his description of
its preparations for the march. After dealing with the adven-
tures of the fleet on its voyage from Therma and its arrival at
Aphetai he says that Xerxes and the land forces after making
their way through Thessaly and Achaia had invaded the land
of the Malians 'two days before';[5] in its context this can only
mean 'two days before the day on which the fleet reached
Aphetai'. He adds that in Thessaly Xerxes held a contest between the Persian and the Thessalian horses, in which the latter

---

[1] vii. 173. 4; cf. Strabo 440 (end).   [2] vii. 128. 1 and 173. 4.
[3] vii. 131.   [4] vii. 121. 2; cf. HW 171 f.
[5] vii. 196; see below, Appendix V, pp. 379 f.

were left far behind, and that of all the rivers in Thessaly the
Onochonos was the only one to be drunk dry by the Persian
hordes. In Achaia he mentions the river Apidanos as one on
the army's line of march,[1] but he is mainly concerned here
with Xerxes' visit to Halos, near the west shore of the Gulf of
Pagasai, since this enables him to introduce[2] a detailed account
of a legend connected with the locality. There is no need to
doubt[3] that Xerxes really passed through Halos, which is
situated on the easier road from Thessaly to Malis. This road
avoids the chain of Othrys, which bounds the Thessalian plain
on the south, by keeping fairly close to the coast. The other
follows a more direct line to the south from Larisa to Krannon
and over the pass of Thaumaki until it eventually joins the other
at Lamia.[4] Herodotus' reference to the Apidanos suggests that
part at least of the army advanced by this route, while Xerxes,
accompanied by another part of the army, took the eastern
route through Halos.[5]

Myres has claimed that the Greek defence of Thermopylai
was ruined by the rapid advance of Xerxes' striking force,[6] but
the passage in Herodotus to which he refers does not really
support his interpretation;[7] if the Greek leaders did not expect
Thermopylai to fall so quickly, the reason suggested by this remark in its setting is that they thought they had sent a force
sufficient for the immediate needs of the defence,[8] not that the
Persians reached Thermopylai earlier than they had anticipated. Herodotus does indeed say that Xerxes left Therma
eleven days before the fleet set sail,[9] and indicates that he

---

[1] vii. 196.

[2] vii. 197; the connexion of the local legend in our texts of 197. 1 with the
temple of Laphystian Zeus is suspect, and the clause which gives it is bracketed by
Macan, i. 206 (followed by Powell in his translation).

[3] In spite of Macan, i. 292 A.

[4] It is disputed whether Lamia formed part of Malis in 480. That it did is
maintained by L. and F. Harmening in *A.S.* 27; for the opposite view cf. the
authorities cited by them (p. 27, n. 1), also Macan, i. 297 B.

[5] Grundy, 258 f.

[6] *Herodotus*, 252 (citing Hdt. vii. 206. 2); his assumption on p. 255 that Xerxes
arrived in Malis on Day 12 of the Diary is unfounded, and seems to be an unjustifiable inference from Hdt. vii. 210. 1.

[7] Nor does vii. 206. 2 support the words used by Grundy, 292: 'the alleged mis-
calculation made by the Spartans as to the time at which the Persians would
arrive before the pass'.

[8] See below, pp. 125 ff.   [9] vii. 183. 2.

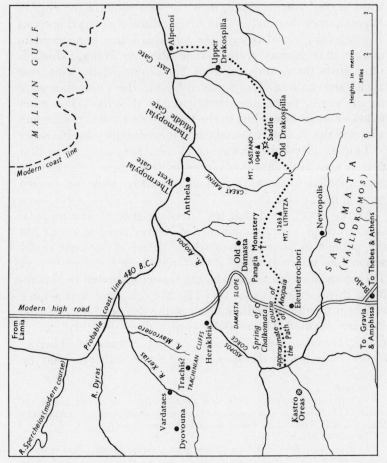

MAP 3. Thermopylai and surrounding country

Labels on map:

MALIAN GULF

Modern coast line

Alpenoi

East Gate

Upper Drakospilia

Heights in metres

Miles 0 1 2 3

Thermopylai Middle Gate

Saddle

Old Drakospilia

MT. SASTANO 1048

Thermopylai West Gate

GREAT RAVINE

Anthela

R. Asopos

MT. LITHITZA 1263

Nevropolis

SAROMATA (KALLIDROMOS)

To Thebes & Athens

Brálo

Old Damasta

Panagia Monastery

Eleutherochori

Anopaia

DAMASTA SLOPE

Modern high road

Probable coast line 480 B.C.

From Lamia

Spring of Chalkomata

approximate course of the Path of

ASOPOS GORGE

To Gravia & Amphissa

R. Mavronero

Herakleia

TRACHINIAN CLIFFS

Trachis?

Vardataes

Dyovouna

R. Xerias

R. Dyras

R. Spercheios (modern course)

Kastro Oreas

reached Thermopylai thirteen days later, on the fourteenth day of the Diary, but this chronology is at variance with other indications in Herodotus, and even if Xerxes himself covered the 140 miles in less than fourteen days it is extremely unlikely that his army advanced so rapidly.[1] There is nothing in Herodotus to suggest such frantic haste. Xerxes has leisure enough on the way to spare a day in Thessaly for a horse-racing contest, and when he reaches the Malian plain he pauses for four days before beginning the attack. The Greek army under Leonidas had already taken up its position at Thermopylai by the time Xerxes arrived in the territory of Trachis, to the west of the pass; we are told earlier[2] that, like the fleet, it had set out from the Isthmus of Corinth 'when they heard that the Persian was in Pieria'. This is clearly a reference back to the chapter,[3] already discussed, in which Xerxes is said to have spent several days in Pieria while part of his army was preparing the road for the invasion of Thessaly. Hence the Greek forces had ample time[4] to reach their appointed positions on land and sea before the Persian army reached the gateway to Central Greece, the pass of Thermopylai.

The Greek decision to defend Thermopylai

The expedition to Thessaly had been an afterthought, but Herodotus may be right when he says[5] that the decision of the patriotic Greeks to stand on a new line of defence farther south was not finally adopted until the expeditionary force had returned from Tempe to Corinth. His narrative has been taken to mean[6] that the choice of the new line was made by a council composed of the leaders of the various contingents in the army, but it is more probable that the decision, which had important political as well as military implications, was referred to the Probouloi.[7] Although they are not mentioned here by Herodotus

---

[1] Even though Grundy, 223 speaks of 'the rapid march through Thessaly'.
[2] vii. 177. [3] vii. 131.
[4] Macan (i. 264 B) says that the Greeks 'had no time to lose if Xerxes was now in Pieria', but this is based on the mistaken assumption that the Persian fleet could have advanced to seize the Euboian channel without the co-operation of the army on land. [5] vii. 175. 1.
[6] By Busolt, 667; see also Busolt, *Die Lakedaimonier*, i. 407 and n. 125.
[7] Cf. the discussion in Macan, i. 255 f. Ephoros ascribed the decision to the σύνεδροι of the Greeks (Diod. xi. 4. 1), but his use of this term was perhaps loose (so Busolt, referring to Diod. xi. 55. 6 and 29. 1).

they had certainly been in session at Corinth less than two months earlier, when the appeal for help had been received from the pro-Greek parties in Thessaly.[1] It was decided to send the fleet to Artemision in North Euboia and to occupy with an army the pass of Thermopylai. If the decision was reached soon after the evacuation of Thessaly the plan must have been fixed early in May 480; naturally its execution was deferred until the Persian forces were approaching the northern frontiers of Thessaly.[2]

Herodotus gives the following reasons for the decision of the Greeks to defend the pass at Thermopylai: it was narrower than the pass at Tempe and nearer to their own country, and also (if the usual text is correct)[3] it was the only pass in the neighbourhood, for at the time when they made their decision they did not know of the Anopaia path, which was later used by Xerxes to turn the Greek position. There is no sufficient reason to doubt Herodotus' assertion[4] that the Greeks had no knowledge of the existence of this path until they heard of it from the Trachinians on their arrival at Thermopylai. Most of the Probouloi had no personal experience of fighting in this region, and those who had, the Phokians and possibly the Lokrians, would not be anxious to point out the weaknesses of a position which they wanted their allies to occupy.

On the evidence available to the Probouloi Thermopylai could be successfully defended by a comparatively small army, unlike the line of Kithairon farther south, and this consideration must have helped to influence their decision. During the campaign of 480 they had to keep the fleet at full strength to meet the menace of the Persian navy; even Herodotus realized[5] that if the Greeks were decisively beaten at sea their positions on land, however impregnable by direct assault, could easily be turned by the enemy. The fleet sent to Artemision, according to Herodotus,[6] included 271 triremes, later reinforced by 53 more, and if we accept his figure of 200 men for each trireme the total complement would be 64,800, of whom perhaps 6,800 were

---

[1] vii. 172. 1; on the chronology see below, Appendix XIV, p. 453.
[2] vii. 177; Grundy, 271 f. finds something sinister in this interval.
[3] vii. 175. 1. Cf. Macan's footnote on l. 5 of his text; some manuscripts omit μία.
[4] vii. 175. 2, questioned by Macan (ad loc.).   [5] vii. 139. 2–4.
[6] viii. 1 and 13. 1; 17 gives 200 men to the trireme of Kleinias (cf. vii. 183. 1 ad fin.).

hoplites. This was a serious deduction from the scanty manpower of the confederates, and it is a significant fact that most of the states which sent contingents to the land army destined for Thermopylai were not represented in the fleet at Artemision; the only exceptions were the Spartans themselves, the Corinthians, and the Northern Lokrians, whose contribution to the fleet was only seven pentekonters.[1] However, the pass of Thermopylai, if guarded by an adequate force, was believed to be impregnable by direct attack, and so long as the Greek fleet maintained its position the Persians would be unable to turn the defences of the Greek army by landing troops in its rear.

Herodotus[2] describes the choice of the Thermopylai line as 'the opinion which prevailed', thereby suggesting that it was not adopted without opposition from some of the Probouloi. These may have been delegates from Peloponnesian states, suspicious of a plan which involved sending their contingents so far north. It is, however, extremely unlikely that the Spartans originally shared this view and only yielded to the vigorous protests of the Central Greeks, especially the Athenians.[3] There was no line defensible by the limited land forces at the disposal of the Probouloi in 480 between Thermopylai and the Isthmus of Corinth, and though some of Sparta's allies may have preferred from the start to retire to the Isthmus the Spartans themselves could never have countenanced such folly. The pass of Thermopylai was often regarded as the gateway into Greece Proper,[4] and Herodotus here says that the Greeks resolved to guard it and 'not let the barbarian pass by into Hellas'.[5] To abandon the whole of Central Greece, including the large island of Euboia, to the enemy without striking a blow in its defence would have betrayed a want of self-confidence which would have had the worst possible effect on the spirits of the patriotic Greeks.[6] Moreover, the loyal states in this area, especially Athens, had a right to expect that some attempt would be made to protect their territories from invasion.

[1] viii. 1. 2.   [2] vii. 175. 1; cf. Last in *C.R.* lvii, 1943, 64 B.
[3] Grundy, 270 f. assumes that the Spartans yielded under pressure from the Athenians, who threatened to secede.
[4] vii. 176. 2, viii. 4. 1.
[5] vii. 175. 2, expanded in Diod. xi. 4. 1.
[6] Cf. Delbrück, 79: 'the defence of Thermopylai was a moral postulate.'

It must be admitted, however, that when the time for action arrived the land forces sent to Thermopylai by Sparta and her Peloponnesian allies were surprisingly small. The troops who marched north from the Isthmus under Leonidas,[1] one of the two Spartan kings, were composed of 500 hoplites from Tegea, 500 from Mantineia, 120 from Orchomenos and 1,000 from the rest of the Arcadian states, 400 from Corinth, 200 from Phleious, and 80 from Mykenai, while Sparta was represented by 300 of her full citizens, the Spartiatai. These are the figures given by Herodotus, but their total, 3,100, does not agree with the evidence of the poet Simonides, who in an epigram probably written soon after the battle described how the Persian host of three millions was withstood by 4,000 men from Peloponnese.[2] As Simonides' total for the Peloponnesians is not likely to be an overestimate, the enumeration in Herodotus must be incomplete. Perhaps Herodotus forgot the Eleians, the only important Peloponnesian ally absent from his list (apart from those serving in the fleet), but they may have delayed to send their contingent until the Olympic festival was over. Diodoros adds 1,000 Lakedaimonioi,[3] apparently distinct from the 300 Spartiatai and so presumably of perioikic status, but it is unlikely that his source, Ephoros, had any grounds for this statement except general probability and the discrepancy between Herodotus and Simonides.[4] As perioikoi fought side by side with Spartiatai in the Spartan contingent at Plataia next year it was natural to suppose that they must have done so at Thermopylai. But at Plataia, according to Herodotus,[5] the perioikoi were equal in number to the Spartiatai; why should they have been more than three times as many at Thermopylai? Moreover, in 480 many perioikoi would be needed to supply the marines and possibly some at least of the rowers on the Spartan fleet. Finally, Herodotus' account of the last day's fighting at Thermopylai leaves no room for the presence of a perioikic contingent; if

---

[1] 'Leonides' in Hdt.; the true Spartan form of the name was perhaps 'Lanidas' (Macan, i. 304 B and HW 223).

[2] vii. 228. 1.

[3] Diod. xi. 4. 5. Ktesias (*Persika* 25) gives 300 Spartiates and 1,000 perioikoi as the Lakedaimonian forces present *at Plataia*.

[4] Possibly the 1,000 in the speech of Demaratos (vii. 102. 3) helped to suggest it; cf. Munro in *J.H.S.* xxii, 1902, 307, n. 22.

[5] ix. 10. 1 and 11. 3; cf. 28. 2.

perioikoi had formed part of the original force, when and under what circumstances had they left it?[1]

Even if Simonides' figure is correct, the total for the Peloponnesians in Leonidas' army is still low. Why did not Sparta send more? It is true that the Central Greeks were those who would be exposed to immediate invasion if Thermopylai fell, but how could Sparta expect them to rally in full strength to its defence unless a considerable army was sent by the Southern Greeks? The political situation in Central Greece was very complex. In the western half of the area Akarnania and Aitolia were neutral, but they were culturally and politically undeveloped, and though there were routes from the upper Spercheios valley into Aitolia which turned Thermopylai, they were much too circuitous to be of any use to the Persians, who would anyhow have been ill-advised to provoke the vigorous Aitolian mountaineers by an attempt to penetrate their country. Farther east the Dorians of the upper Kephisos valley had perhaps already medized, probably under Thessalian influence,[2] but their neighbours the Phokians, old foes of the Thessalians, supported the patriotic cause, as did the Lokrians of Opous. The vital question for Leonidas was the attitude of the Boiotian states, led by Thebes. Their response was disappointing; patriotism towards Hellas counted for little against hatred of Athens. Of the two states situated on the southern edge of Boiotia, and therefore more inclined to take an independent line, the Plataians were with the Athenians in the fleet, and the Thespians contributed to Leonidas' army 700 hoplites, probably their total hoplite force,[3] but the Thebans sent only 400 and the other states of Boiotia none at all. As the Lokrians joined Leonidas with all their available forces (reasonably estimated at 1,000 by Ephoros),[4] and the Phokians also provided 1,000 hoplites,[5] the contingents which Leonidas received from the Central Greeks amounted to 3,100; Ephoros' attempt to swell the total by the

---

[1] Grundy (p. 276, ll. 10–12) denies that Leonidas had any perioikic troops. Their presence is not proved by the word Λακεδαιμόνιοι in vii. 208. 2 in spite of Macan, ad loc.

[2] viii. 31.

[3] vii. 202 (end); the 1,800 Thespians at Plataia were not hoplites (ix. 30).

[4] In Diod. xi. 4. 7; Pausanias x. 20. 2 absurdly estimates them at 'not more than 6,000'. Hdt. vii. 203. 1 says πανστρατιῇ, but some Lokrians were serving in the fleet. [5] vii. 203. 1.

addition of 1,000 Malians is unconvincing on geographical and other grounds.[1] Thus Leonidas' force numbered not much more than 7,000 hoplites in all. To this we must add the camp-followers; there seems to have been a fair number of Helots in attendance on the Spartans, but it would be rash to assume that there must have been seven Helots to each Spartiate, as at Plataia.[2]

This total compares unfavourably with the 10,000 hoplites sent to Tempe earlier under Euainetos and Themistokles, but unfortunately Herodotus gives no detailed figures for the contingents in the Thessalian expedition. The presence of Themistokles suggests that a fairly large force from Athens was included in the land army on that occasion, and this makes it all the more surprising that the Athenians, so vitally concerned in the defence of Central Greece, sent no hoplites at all to Thermopylai.[3] It is not a sufficient answer that they were now making their main effort on sea; if the Corinthians, with forty ships at Artemision, could find 400 hoplites for Thermopylai, surely the Athenians, who needed only 6,000 at most as marines, could have sent some of the 8,000 hoplites who represented them next year at Plataia.[4] Perhaps the Probouloi hoped to rally the Boiotians to the patriotic cause and calculated that they would achieve their object more easily if there were no Athenians or Plataians in the force sent; if so, their calculation was unduly optimistic, for most of the Boiotian states were hoping for a Persian victory. The Thebans might under pressure send 400 men with Leonidas, but, as Herodotus says,[5] when they sent them they had other thoughts in their hearts.

Yet Herodotus' account of Thermopylai, taken as a whole, does not support the contention that the Greek resistance collapsed because the Spartans had not sent enough troops. Their original calculation may indeed have been upset by the need to detach 1,000 hoplites to guard the Anopaia, but Herodotus does not suggest that this force was too small for its task,

---

[1] Diod. xi. 4. 7, criticized by Busolt, 675, n. 2.

[2] The assumption is made by Grundy, 273, but HW (n. on vii. 229. 1) seem to hold that at Thermopylai there was only one Helot to each Spartiate. For Plataia cf. ix. 28. 2.

[3] The problem is noted by Gomme in *J.H.S.* liii, 1933, 22 (= *Essays*, 199) but his answer to it is unsatisfactory.   [4] ix. 28. 6.

[5] vii. 205. 3 (end); the size of the contingent is given in vii. 202 (end).

or that the men retained by Leonidas were too few for the
defence of the main pass. In one chapter, however, he seems to
agree with Sparta's modern critics; there he alleges[1] that the
Greeks were seized with panic on the approach of Xerxes' army
and that Sparta's Peloponnesian allies wished to withdraw to
the Isthmus, but Leonidas, yielding to the vigorous protests of
the Phokians and Lokrians, decided to remain, and sent messengers 'to the cities' bidding them send help, since his present
numbers were not enough to withstand the Persian hosts.

The tradition in this chapter, manifestly hostile to the Peloponnesians, is unacceptable. Whatever the rank and file might
think, the Greek leaders on both land and sea knew that the
defence of the positions of Thermopylai and Artemision was
inextricably linked, and that one could not be abandoned without exposing the defenders of the other to grave peril. In its
ignorance of strategic realities this chapter closely resembles
those which attribute timidity and irresolution to all the Greeks
at Artemision (not, as some assert, to the Peloponnesians alone)[2]
and is equally unhistorical, as one item in it clearly reveals.
What were 'the cities' to which Leonidas sent for reinforcements? If he had sent to headquarters at Corinth, he could not
expect to receive them from there in time to face the first
Persian attack, even if he had known that it was to be delayed
for four days, and it is not to be supposed that he appealed for
troops to the states of Boiotia; apart from the loyal Thespians
they had supplied only the contingent of 400 Thebans, more or
less under compulsion from Leonidas, and it was not likely that
they would send more now that the danger was imminent and
Leonidas not present to enforce his demands in person. As the
tradition in this chapter is obviously fictitious, it is unnecessary
to assume that it has some foundation in fact, to conjecture that
the alleged panic was either caused by a temporary retirement
of the fleet from its station[3] or confined to the ordinary soldiers,
not shared by the leaders.[4]

[1] vii. 207. It is true that in 208. 1 he speaks of a report received by Xerxes while
still in Thessaly that 'a small army' was waiting at the pass, but this is merely the
conventional contrast between Greek and Persian numbers which has an exact
parallel in viii. 6. 1 for the fleet at Artemision (see below, p. 179 f.).

[2] See below, pp. 190 f.

[3] Cf. Macan, i. 309 f. (though he doubts the truth of the story in vii. 207).

[4] So HW 223 (ad loc.).

There are two other passages in Herodotus which must be examined in this connexion. In the first[1] he describes the arrival at Thermopylai of the Phokian and Opountian Lokrian contingents and says that they came by invitation, 'for the Greeks themselves invited them, sending them a message that they themselves had come merely as the forerunners of the army, and that the arrival of the rest of the allies was to be expected any day'. It is natural to infer from this that 'the Greeks' who are the subject of the sentence are Leonidas and the commanders of the contingents at Thermopylai, and on this view the story presupposes[2] that the Phokians and Lokrians had not been represented at the Isthmus and were now for the first time called upon for help by the patriotic Greeks. Legrand[3] would stress the word αὐτοί (they themselves) to mean that Leonidas took it upon himself to appeal to the two peoples for support without having received explicit authority to do so, but the recurrence of the word later in the same sentence is clumsy, and possibly the first αὐτοί is corrupt.[4] Whoever was responsible for the invitation, the tradition plainly asserts that some persons in authority gave an assurance to the Central Greeks that the troops sent with Leonidas were only the forerunners (πρόδρομοι) of a larger force.

This tradition is repeated and developed three chapters later.[5] There Herodotus explains that the men under Leonidas' command were sent off first (i.e. before the rest) by the Spartiatai to encourage 'the rest of the allies' (clearly the states of Central Greece are meant)[6] for they were afraid that these allies might go over to Persia if they saw the Spartans slow to act. At this time, Herodotus continues, the Spartans were busy with the celebration of the Karneian festival, 'but they intended as soon as the festival was over to leave a garrison in Sparta and come to help in full strength with all speed'. The rest of the allies (here the term refers to the Peloponnesians alone) were similarly circumstanced, for they were busy with the Olympic festival (which coincided with the last days of the Karneia) and so they

[1] vii. 203. 1.   [2] So Macan, ad loc.
[3] vii. 213 A, n. 2.
[4] Macan reads αὐτόθεν (with Stein).
[5] vii. 206.
[6] Cf. Macan, ad loc. Hence these states are here presumed to be in alliance with the Peloponnesians.

merely sent a portion of their available forces as 'forerunners'[1]
of the rest, since they never expected the fighting at Thermopylai to be over so quickly.

The core of the tradition in this chapter is not quite the same
as in the other. In the first we have an official pronouncement
made to Central Greek states to account for the comparatively
small size of the army sent to their aid by the Peloponnesians,
in the second we have an explanation of the reasons by which
the Spartans and other Peloponnesian states were influenced
when they failed to send more troops with Leonidas. Macan
has called attention[2] to 'the decidedly apologetic ring' of the
tradition in this chapter, but he insists that both the apology
and the real reason (by which he presumably means that the
allies never expected Thermopylai to fall so soon) show that the
defence of the double position at Artemision and Thermopylai
was seriously intended by the Spartans and that they believed
at the time that they had made adequate provision for it on land
as well as on sea.[3] If the tradition is accepted at its face value
Macan's inferences from it are sound, but the historian must
always be on his guard when confronted with a statement about
an intention which was never carried out.

Obst rejects the tradition altogether, for he maintains that the
Spartans believed at the time that they had sent enough troops,
and that this fact, stated by the written source which Obst
presumes to have been used by Herodotus, was preserved in
Ephoros' assertion[4] that the Greek synhedroi sent a sufficient
force of hoplites. This is unconvincing; Ephoros may have meant
no more than what is normally implied in the Herodotean
narrative, that Leonidas' army was sufficient for its immediate
purpose. Obst sees in the tradition under examination an implicit avowal that the troops sent north from Peloponnese were
inadequate, and as he believes that the Spartans could never
have held this opinion before Leonidas' defeat he regards the
whole account in both chapters as an invention of Central
Greek states which felt that they had been betrayed by the

[1] προδρόμους; the same word is used in vii. 203. 1.
[2] i. 309 B. Giannelli, *La spedizione di Serse*, 26 regards this as 'indubitably the
official Spartan version'.
[3] Macan argues elsewhere (ii. 269) that 'the defence of Thermopylai was intended to be serious and thorough'.
[4] In Diod. xi. 4. 1; cf. Obst, 102f.

Peloponnesians.[1] This explanation would be very convenient if it could be accepted, but there are two serious objections to it. A tradition invented after the war by the Central Greeks to exculpate themselves and transfer the blame to Sparta would certainly have been less oblique in its approach; it would have alleged boldly that though the Spartans had promised speedy reinforcements they had in fact had no intention of sending any. Moreover, Obst failed to notice the difference between the two forms of the tradition. The later chapter may represent a more elaborate version produced by Sparta and her Peloponnesian allies after the war, but in the earlier chapter Herodotus reports what claims to be an official pronouncement made in public at the time by Greek leaders.

Some eminent scholars have seen that the pronouncement must be accepted as an historical fact, but they proceed to nullify its implications by the claim that it was insincere. Meyer[2] says cautiously: 'the anxious peoples of Central Greece may have been encouraged by a statement that a larger army was on the way.' Munro once supposed[3] that the Greek leaders did send such a message but did not seriously intend to keep their promise; in the statement that a larger army was to follow he saw a mere pretence which it was convenient to maintain. In a later version[4] he said that the military chiefs emphasized their intention of bringing up the main army in support after the Olympic and Karneian festivals without dwelling on the proviso that the fleet should first have won its victory. Grundy believes[5] that the Spartans doubtless hoped the Central Greeks 'would accept this instalment as surety for the discharge of the whole obligation and would contribute their share in full without delay'; this hope, he admits, was disappointed, and he suggests that the Central Greeks, notably the Phokians and Boiotians, saw through the pretence and were distrustful of the Peloponnesian good faith. He supports his view by the chapter in Herodotus[6] in which Leonidas himself is represented as convinced of the inadequacy of his forces and sending out appeals

---

[1] Obst refers in a footnote (103, n. 1) to Meyer iii[1], § 219 (note), but Meyer in his text (p. 379) seems to believe that a promise may have been made by the Spartans to the Central Greeks.

[2] iii[1], § 219 (p. 379). [3] *J.H.S.* xxii, 1902, 307.

[4] *C.A.H.* iv. 284. [5] Grundy, 275 f.

[6] vii. 207.

for reinforcements, but it has been shown above that this part of the tradition is not to be trusted.

Giannelli,[1] like Grundy, maintains that the Spartan leaders were convinced of serious military risks in the defence of a position so far from their base as Thermopylai and would have preferred to defend the Isthmus lines, but that they had to undertake the minimum necessary to pacify their Central Greek allies, particularly the Athenians, since they feared that if they refused to do anything they would lose the indispensable help of the Athenian fleet. There were faint hopes that the Central Greeks, including the Boiotians, would rally to the defence, or that the fleet at Artemision would win a decisive victory, but the Spartans had little confidence in either of these hopes, and when they dispatched one of their kings and the flower of their troops to Thermopylai they must have thought that they were sending them to almost certain death. If forced to act, they would do the minimum. Conscious of being on a bad road and yet committed to go on by it, they were determined to limit their concessions to the inevitable as much as possible. Giannelli insists[2] that it is wrong to attribute double-dealing to the Spartan government, and that its irresolution was due to the fact that in a war conducted by a coalition strategical considerations tend to be subordinated to political necessities; he finds an illuminating parallel[3] in the Franco-British expedition to the Dardanelles, undertaken on political grounds to relieve the pressure on Russia, but strongly disapproved by the British high command, especially Lord Kitchener. Yet Giannelli believes that the Spartans really promised to send the reinforcements and that when they did so they had no intention of fulfilling their promise; he cannot reasonably complain if others who share these beliefs draw the obvious conclusion from them that the Spartans acted in bad faith to their allies.

Why have scholars supposed that the Spartan promise was not seriously meant? Those who hold this view can be divided into two groups. One group apparently infers from the catastrophe which befell the defenders of Thermopylai that with such a small force the defence was destined to end in failure, and that its disastrous conclusion must have been predictable by

---

[1] Op. cit. 26 ff., especially 32–33.   [2] Op. cit. 31–33.
[3] Op. cit. 35–36.

such experts in military affairs as the Spartans. In this form the
view presupposes that what actually happened was bound to
happen; it is not limited to the contention of more cautious
critics,[1] that the defenders of a pass through a range of mountains are bound to find their position turned in the long run.
The Herodotean narrative does not support the view that the
fall of Thermopylai was inevitable in the way in which it ultimately occurred; it represents the defenders of the main pass
as performing their task successfully on the first two days with
comparatively slight losses, and attributes the final disaster to
the incompetence of the Phokian contingent which had been
detailed to guard the Anopaia.

For these reasons the scholars in the second group[2] maintain
that Leonidas' army was adequate for the end in view, to hold
up the Persian army while the Greek fleet attempted to secure
a decision at Artemision. Munro holds[3] that the Greek forces
at Thermopylai were enough to defend so strong a position for
a few days. Delbrück says[4] that quite a small army was sufficient to block the actual pass, and that the Greek defences were
turned in the end not because the army was too small but because the defenders of the Anopaia allowed themselves to be
caught off their guard. Delbrück and Munro seem to draw a
distinction between the strength of Thermopylai against direct
attack and its vulnerability to a more elaborate and circuitous
turning movement than one following the Anopaia; this view
raises topographical questions which must be examined later.

It is possible that some critics in the first group are affected
subconsciously by the story that Leonidas sacrificed himself as
the result of an oracle. According to the report circulated later
by the Spartan government, the oracle had been received from
Delphi at the very beginning of the war,[5] and foretold that one
of two things would happen: either Sparta would be conquered
and sacked by the Persians or one of her two kings would die in
battle. Herodotus does not mention the oracle until the eve of
the final struggle, and then uses it to explain why Leonidas and

---

[1] Critics such as Delbrück, 75 ff.   [2] e.g. Meyer, iii¹, § 219 (p. 379).
[3] *J.H.S.* xxii, 1902, 307.   [4] Delbrück, 79.
[5] vii. 220. 3; hence the oracle was known to Leonidas (220. 4). Legrand, vii. 190
points out the connexion between this oracle and the story told in vii. 239 (the
authenticity of c. 239 is rightly defended by Legrand, 185 and Myres, *Herodotus*,
254 f.).

his 300 Spartiates fought to the end; in this version Leonidas, knowing the oracle, sacrificed his own life and the lives of his Spartiates as an act of *devotio*, to preserve Sparta from the fulfilment of the alternative doom predicted by the oracle. This story is an unhistorical legend first circulated after the battle,[1] but it became the prevailing version and so naturally influenced other parts of the tradition. Ephoros explains[2] that Leonidas took such a small force with him from Sparta because he knew that they were foredoomed to die. Herodotus does not go so far, but he may have been under the influence of the legend when he wrote that Leonidas set out from Sparta 'having chosen the three hundred who were appointed by law and men who chanced to have sons'. Macan[3] has pointed out the difficulties of this statement. The reference to those 'appointed by law' suggests the normal royal bodyguard composed of 300 picked Spartiates, called the Hippeis, and though it is conceivable that, as members of the corps were bound if necessary to fight to the death in defence of their king, they should have been chosen only from married men who had sons to succeed them, this is inconsistent with Herodotus' assertion that on this occasion they were specially chosen by Leonidas. Powell omits the first article in the notice and translates 'men of ripe years who possessed sons'; Legrand[4] by ruthless emendation produces the statement that Leonidas arrived with men chosen from the Corps of the Three Hundred and also from those who were fathers of families. It seems better to keep the manuscript text, and to see in the reference to 'fathers of families' the influence of the legend, suggesting that those who chose the force knew from the beginning that it would be sacrificed.

If the legend is rejected as unhistorical, and if the rest of Herodotus' narrative points to the conclusion that Thermopylai fell not from lack of men to hold it but 'because some of the men defending it were the wrong kind of men',[5] why do Munro and others who accept both these premises still maintain that the Spartans never seriously intended to send a larger army later? Some critics question the grounds for delay alleged by the

---

[1] See below, Appendix IV.
[2] In Diod. xi. 4. 3–4 (but without any mention of the oracle).
[3] i. 307, closely followed by Giannelli, 30 and n. 1.
[4] vii. 214, n. 4.   [5] Quoted from Last, *C.R.* lvii, 1943, 64 A.

Spartans and their Peloponnesian allies, the celebration of the
Karneia and the Olympia. It has been argued[1] that the Karneia
cannot have constituted a religious objection to a military expedition as such, since one was in fact sent before the Karneia
was over, and as there was no objection to it in principle its
size was simply a matter for decision by the Spartan government. Herodotus, however, merely says[2] that the Karneia was
'in the way', and that the Spartans thought that they had made
adequate provision for the immediate needs of the defence (as
indeed they had, on a reasonable calculation). Perhaps, in the
mood of our own Francis Drake, they felt that they had time
enough to finish their games and beat the Persian too. Legrand
notes[3] that in the next book a similar nonchalance is represented
as a magnificent disdain before the barbarian menace.

When all this has been pointed out, it must be remembered
that the Spartans can never have intended to send to Thermopylai the whole expeditionary force of their League (composed
of two-thirds of the available hoplites from each member state)
whatever they may have said later.[4] The Isthmus position was
their last line of defence, nearer to their base and with a better
claim than Thermopylai to be regarded as impregnable, provided that the Greek fleet was able to hold its own against the
enemy. The Spartan high command had to ensure that a sufficient force was held in reserve to defend this position, especially
as so much of the available manpower in the maritime states
had to be assigned to the fleet.

It has been suggested that the Spartans at the outset did not
feel much confidence in the prospect of a Greek naval victory,
but this argument has been carried too far by its author.[5] If the
Greek fleet at Artemision was beaten so decisively that the
Persian fleet could continue its advance without opposition,
further Greek resistance on land at the Isthmus of Corinth would
be useless and the Spartans must have known it. On the other
hand, when the Probouloi made their plans for the defence of
Central Greece, the Persian fleet outnumbered the Greek by
more than three to two, and the position which the Probouloi

---

[1] By Giannelli, 26 f.
[2] vii. 206. 1; Powell (tr. p. 714) brackets ἐμποδών.
[3] vii. 215, n. 2, referring to Hdt. viii. 26.
[4] On vii. 206. 1 see above, p. 120.
[5] H. M. Last in *C.R.* lvii, 1943, 64 f.

had to choose for the Greek ships, Artemision, was less well suited to their favourite tactics than the later position in the straits of Salamis. If the Greek fleet found its position at Artemision untenable against superior numbers and was compelled to retreat, the army also would have to retire from Thermopylai.

It is significant that Grundy, who accuses the Spartans of double-dealing an account of the smallness of the force sent by them with Leonidas, minimizes the difficulties of a Greek retreat by land in face of the enemy.[1] Even if Leonidas could have got his men from the neighbourhood of the pass by the route across the mountains through Mendenitza to Elateia in Phokis,[2] he would have been compelled eventually to rejoin the main road to the south, and once on it he would be exposed to pursuit by the Persian cavalry. Moreover, the Boiotians must have caused the Spartans much uneasiness by their ambiguous attitude; there was a strong probability that they would declare in favour of the Persians as soon as the Greek forces were in retreat from Central Greece on land and sea. With all these grounds for anxiety the Spartan leaders, though believing that the troops under Leonidas were sufficient to hold the pass for the present, may perhaps have welcomed the occurrence of the Olympia and Karneia at this juncture as an excuse for withholding their main army for a few days until the situation in Central Greece became clearer, both on land and sea. So much surmise about their attitude is permissible, but the tradition as it has come down to us does not support the view that they never seriously intended to fulfil their promise to send more men later and that they deliberately abandoned Leonidas and his men to destruction.

Topographical

The division between Northern and Central Greece may be regarded as a line running almost due east from the Ionian Sea to the Aegean, extending from the Gulf of Ambrakia (modern Gulf of Arta) to the Gulf of Malis. In the eastern sector of this division the line is formed by the river Spercheios, flowing eventually into the Malian Gulf, which here penetrates deeply

---

[1] Grundy, 276.
[2] On this route cf. Grundy, 265, also Macan, i. 2. 399 B.

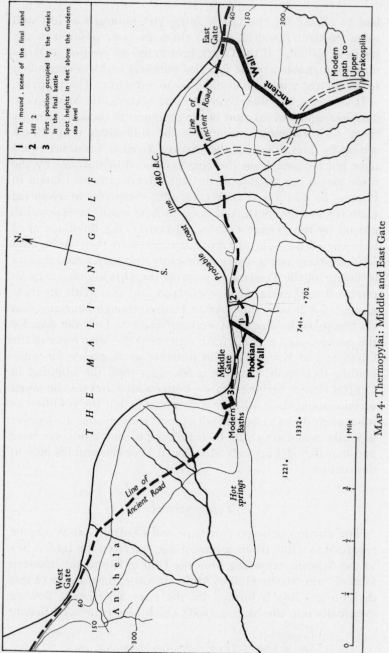

MAP 4. Thermopylai: Middle and East Gate

into the land. The appearance of the gulf and of the shore to the south of its western extremity has been much altered during the last twenty-four centuries by the masses of debris brought down by the Spercheios, which in 480 must have entered the gulf several miles above its present mouth.[1] In Herodotus' time the main road from the north crossed the Spercheios near its mouth, at the town of Antikyra.[2] South of the river and along the southern shore of the gulf stretched a narrow plain, bounded on the south by the great mountain barrier of Oite, divided roughly into two parts by a depression near the middle of the chain.[3] At this point, the modern pass of Pournaraki, it sinks to less than 2,200 feet,[4] and it is near here that the river Asopos has eaten its way through a great cleft in the mountains to enter the Malian Plain. The Asopos Gorge is a conspicuous feature of the landscape in the view of the plain from the north, and so are the Trachinian cliffs, to the west of the gorge, where the mountain chain descends steeply into the plain; both were duly noted by Herodotus,[5] and although his orientation is here ninety degrees out, his detailed description should leave no doubt that he had personally visited the region and carefully noted its salient characteristics.[6]

To the east of the Asopos Gorge the chain of Oite rises again, to a height of nearly 5,000 feet, the summit being known later in antiquity as Kallidromos[7] (now Saromata). In this sector the mountains approach close to the sea, and the coast road, which here ran almost due east, was in 480 hemmed in between the mountain cliffs on the south and the waters of the Malian Gulf on the north. According to Herodotus[8] the narrowest part of the pass began at the river Phoinix, then a small tributary of the Asopos running into it due east (Herodotus says south) of the Gorge; he adds that at this point there was only room for

---

[1] Grundy, 279.

[2] vii. 198. 2; Grundy, 281 dislikes the view that Antikyra was actually at the mouth of the Spercheios.

[3] Cf. the admirable description in Grundy, 259 ff.

[4] The modern high road is 2,165 feet above sea level at its highest point (*Handbook of Greece*, 229).

[5] vii. 199; on his faulty orientation cf. Grundy, 277, and see below, p. 358.

[6] Grundy, 279 and 267. Bury (in *B.S.A.* ii. 83) absurdly claimed that Hdt. had not seen Thermopylai or even a plan of it.

[7] Cf. Livy xxxvi. 15. 10 and Strabo 428.

[8] vii. 200. 1. The river Phoinix can still be identified (Grundy, 284).

a carriage-road, and uses a word[1] which implies that the road-
way here had been artificially constructed. Elsewhere the main
pass, called Pylai or Thermopylai, is described by Herodotus as
50 feet wide,[2] though he notes that the narrowest parts of the
road are in front of (i.e. west of)[3] the pass proper, by the river
Phoinix, and behind it (to the east of it) near the town of Alpenoi, and that in both places there is only room for a carriage-
way. Since his time the appearance of Thermopylai has been
much changed by the silting-up of the Malian Gulf. Grundy,
whose thorough survey of the region first provided the solution
of many problems,[4] decided that the 5-yard contour represents
fairly closely the course of the coastline in 480, except at some
points where mountain streams have pushed masses of debris
forward into the plain; at these points he took the 10-yard
contour as his guide.[5] His reconstruction of the 480 coastline,
based on these criteria, produced a result which tallied with
the data given by Herodotus. Grundy gave to the pass proper
the name of the Middle Gate; the narrower passages, near the
Phoinix and near Alpenoi, he called the West Gate and the
East Gate.

Herodotus' description[6] leaves no doubt that the main pass,
Thermopylai in the narrower sense, fortified earlier with a wall
by the Phokians as a defence against Thessalian invasions, was
at the Middle Gate, near to the hot springs, the water of which
had been deflected across the approaches by the Phokians to
make attack more difficult.[7] The reason why defence was concentrated at the Middle Gate rather than at one of the much
narrower western and eastern gates is to be found in the character of the mountains to the south. Herodotus describes the
mountain 'west' (really south) of the Middle Gate as 'impass-
able and precipitous, rising up to a great height and extending

---

[1] δέδμηται; cf. Grundy, 285. [2] ἡμιπλεθρον (vii. 176. 2).

[3] ἔμπροσθε and ὄπισθε represent the point of view of a traveller coming from the
north; see below, p. 356.

[4] Stählin (article on Thermopylai in R.-E. v A. 2. 2405) says justly that 'Grundy
first brought order out of chaos'; cf. Béquignon, La Vallée du Spercheios, 43 f.

[5] Grundy, 287.

[6] vii. 176. 3–4; cf. Grundy, 288. On the two names cf. vii. 201; πύλαι may refer
to the gate in the Phokian wall (L. and F. Harmening in A.S. 33 and n. 1). The
pass of Thermopylai must be meant by the words ἡ διὰ Τρηχῖνος ἔσοδος ἐς τὴν
Ἑλλάδα (vii. 176. 2) in spite of Macan, ad loc.; cf. A.S. 32, n. 2.

[7] On this cf. Grundy, 289.

towards the range of Oite'.[1] There are also steep hills or cliffs to
the south of the West Gate, but the total height of the spur
which here projects from the mountains is only between 300 and
400 feet, and above it there is a wide and fairly easy passage by
which the West Gate could be turned.[2] The East Gate seems to
have been the position held by Antiochos III of Syria against
the Romans in 191, perhaps because the silting-up of the gulf
had by then made the Middle Gate less defensible,[3] but the hills
above it were vulnerable to attack, and had to be occupied with
light troops and artillery. At some uncertain date, possibly in
191 or perhaps later,[4] a wall was built up the hill from the East
Gate for half a mile to the south-west, and then in a direction
slightly east of south, following the line of the ridge. Grundy,
who describes the wall, observes that as there is a steep fall in
the ground to the west of the wall it must have been built
against the possibility of attack from the west. Before it was
built, the ridge on which it stands must have been occupied in
force by any army defending the East Gate. Grundy concludes
that the East Gate was not a position defensible by a small army,
like that of Leonidas, against an enemy greatly superior in
numbers.

On military grounds, therefore, Leonidas must have occupied
the position at the Middle Gate, as clearly indicated by Herodotus. Later on he says incidentally[5] that Leonidas' men on
their arrival had reconstructed the Phokian Wall, and that the
Greek army was posted behind it (i.e. to the east of it) except
when they sallied out into the narrow part of the pass to attack
the Persians. For their last stand they retreated behind the wall
to a mound, later marked by a stone lion, while some of the
Persians attacking in front pulled down the wall.[6] Grundy
rightly identifies the mound with a hill about 150 feet high,
slightly to the east of the narrowest part of the Middle Gate,
protected in the rear by a small but deep valley between it and

---

[1] vii. 176. 3 (Macaulay's translation).   [2] Grundy, 285; cf. *A.S.* 41.
[3] Kromayer in *A.S.* vol. ii. 146 f. thinks the East Gate was a better position
for an army larger than that of Leonidas; for the troops on the hills above the
East Gate cf. Livy xxxvi. 18. 3.
[4] Grundy, 291 describes the wall and calls it pre-medieval; it is dated by
Béquignon (in *Rev. Arch.* iv, 1934, 20) to 191 B.C. Some attribute it to Justinian
(on whose fortifications in this area cf. Stählin, 2422 f.).
[5] vii. 208. 2, 223. 2; cf. also 176. 5.   [6] vii. 225. 3.

a second mound farther east; south of the first mound and
separating it almost completely from the main mountain is a
second small deep valley which is a branch of the first.[1] Grundy's
view that the main road in 480 passed over the neck of land
which connected his first mound with the mountain, and not to
the north of this mound, has been confirmed by the arguments
of Stählin.[2] It is more doubtful whether the existing remains of
walls on this neck of land are to be regarded as identical in site
with the old Phokian wall, as Grundy supposed,[3] but the solution of this problem is of minor importance if his identifications
for the mound and the course of the ancient road are correct.

Leonidas on his arrival in the territory of Trachis (in which
Thermopylai was situated[4]) heard for the first time of the existence of the Anopaia Path, and assigned its defence to the
Phokian contingent of 1,000 hoplites, who volunteered for this
service.[5] The Anopaia must have passed somewhere to the
north of the summit of Kallidromos, for the Persian force under
Hydarnes, which used it to turn the Greek position, completed
the circuit from the Persian camp, in the plain west of the
Asopos, to a point east of the East Gate in not more than
eighteen hours, including the hours of darkness.[6] Above the
southern entrance to the Asopos Gorge lies the junction of the
two mountain streams which form the Asopos. The one which
comes in from an easterly direction flows in the early part of
its course along the bottom of a remarkable upland valley, the
valley of Nevropolis, at a height of about 3,000 feet, north of
the main ridge of Kallidromos. This valley is bounded along its
northern side by another ridge rising to a height of 1,263 metres
in the peak of Lithitza, which Grundy named the Great Gable,[7]
almost due south of the West Gate. To the east of Lithitza

---

[1] Grundy, 288 ff., also second n. on p. 312.

[2] Grundy, 289 and Stählin, 2411 f. (attacking *A.S.* 39 f.).

[3] Grundy, 288. Marinatos, who excavated the site after Stählin wrote his
article, is said to have proved that the wall was built before 480 and that it faced
south, but if this is correct what can have been its purpose? Cf. Pritchett in
A.J. Arch. lxii, 1958, 212.

[4] So *A.S.* 28 (against Macan, i. 300 f.). Alpenoi was the first town in Lokris
where it joins Malis (vii. 216). 'Trachis' when used in Hdt. of the Greek position
must mean the territory of Trachis, not the town; see below, p. 141, n. 6.

[5] vii. 217. 2; cf. 212. 2.

[6] On the details in the following account see below, Appendix III.

[7] Cf. Kromayer in *A.S.* ii. 141, n. 1.

a deep gorge, the Great Ravine of Grundy's description, bends back almost to the main ridge of the mountain, and to the north-east of the gorge rises the peak of Sástano,[1] whose precipitous slopes on their north side overhang the Middle Gate. Sástano, the height of which is given as 1,048 metres, is connected on its south side by a saddle with the main mass of Kallidromos. There has been much controversy about the precise line followed by the Anopaia, but the problem is of topographical rather than historical interest,[2] since, whatever route is assumed for the earlier part of the path, the wayfarer must in the end have reached the same point at the head of the Great Ravine and have crossed the saddle of Sástano near the site of the derelict modern village of Old Drakospilia before beginning the descent to the site of Alpenoi.[3] The saddle was almost certainly the position chosen by the Phokians sent to guard the Anopaia, as it agrees best with the data bearing on that position in Herodotus.

The Anopaia was important because it was the shortest possible route by which the main pass of Thermopylai could be turned, just as the way through Gonnos was the shortest route to turn the defile of Tempe.[4] Delbrück maintains that there is always more than one route through any chain of mountains, even mountains so formidable as the range of Oite, and that the defenders, unless they have large forces at their disposal, cannot guard them all adequately.[5] Some of the routes into Central Greece were too circuitous to be considered by the Persian generals,[6] who could not afford to lose contact with the fleet for long. East of Thermopylai the range of Oite is continued under the name of Knemis, and the main road must therefore hug the coast of Lokris until a gap in the mountains enables it to turn inland past the Phokian towns of Hyampolis and Abai into the valley of the Kephisos. This valley, lying south of the Oite–Knemis chain, is roughly parallel to the coast, and the head of it[7] is not

---

[1] Usually called Sastáni; on the name cf. Stählin, 2402, ll. 11–13.

[2] So Delbrück, op. cit. 82.

[3] Kromayer in *A.S.* ii. 143 (cf. his *Schlachtenatlas*, iv. 1, text col. 8) and Stählin, 2402. Note Munro's admission (*C.A.H.* iv. 295) that invaders 'must inevitably pass that point on their way towards Alpeni'.

[4] See above, p. 109.   [5] Op. cit. 75.   [6] See above, p. 117.

[7] At this point the stream flowing through it is the Pindos, a tributary of the Kephisos.

far from the depression between the two parts of the Oite
range, that depression near which the Asopos makes its way to
the Malian Gulf and which is now traversed by the modern highway from Lamia to Bralo (situated near the head of the Kephisos valley) and so on to Thebes and Athens. Did a route (or
routes) cross the mountains in 480 from the west of Thermopylai
to the head of the Kephisos valley, and if it did why was it not
used to turn the Greek position?

Herodotus does not mention any such route in his seventh
book, which contains his main account of Thermopylai and the
fighting there, but later on, after the Greek resistance had been
overcome and the Persians were free to resume their advance,
he says[1] that their army, guided by the Thessalians, advanced
from the land of Trachis into Doris; 'for a narrow strip of the
Dorian territory stretches down in this quarter, about thirty
stadia in breadth, lying between Malis and Phokis.' The word
translated as 'a narrow strip' means originally the leg-piece or
neck of a wineskin according to Powell,[2] who compares the
'Maestricht appendix' of Holland. He and other commentators have rightly inferred from this chapter that all the Persian
army, or at least the greater part of it, was supposed by Herodotus to have followed this route, but such a route, wherever it
may have crossed the Oite depression, must have offered serious
difficulty to the transit of a large army, and it would be wasted
labour when the defeat of Leonidas had thrown open the easier
coast road. There are indications elsewhere in Herodotus that
part at least of the Persian army marched along the coast road,
which has been described[3] as 'the only route suitable for a force
of cavalry and a large baggage train'; we must suppose that at
the same time a detachment[4] was sent across the mountains by
the alternative route into Doris.

The description of the Doris route given by Herodotus is not
precise enough to identify its modern equivalent beyond all
doubt, and his reference to the Dorian 'appendix' further com-
plicates the problem. What does he mean when he ascribes to
it a breadth of thirty stades? Powell suggests[5] that he is referring

---

[1] viii. 31. Kirsten (followed by Pritchett, *A.J. Arch.* lxii, 1958, 207, n. 39)
strangely supposes that this refers to the Mendenitza route.

[2] Cf. his note (ad loc.) in his edition of Herodotus, Book viii.

[3] Cf. HW 243 f.   [4] Probably more lightly equipped (Macan, i. 2. 399 B).

[5] In his first note on viii. 31.

to the width of the upper Kephisos valley, to which Doris
'stretches down in this quarter', but it is also possible that thirty
stades was the breadth of the Dorian appendix in the part where
it was crossed by the route.[1] Anyhow, the reference to Doris
would be pointless unless the route passed through the appendix,
and this consideration has been held to rule out all the modern
routes from the north into the upper Kephisos valley except
two.[2] One of these, a route starting from the Malian Plain at
a point to the east of the northern exit of the Asopos gorge,
followed a line over the Pass of Pournaraki to Bralo which was
roughly identical with the modern highway. This route existed
in the last century, before the construction of the highway, as
the shortest route from Lamia to Phokis, and was described by
several travellers;[3] was it available in 480? The other is the
route which goes up from the plain through the Asopos Gorge
itself for a distance of about $3\frac{1}{2}$ miles, emerging at the southern
exit of the gorge into an upland valley behind the main ridge of
Oite, from which valley there is a passage to the Dorian plain;
this passage is described as long but not difficult by Grundy,[4]
who thinks that it nowhere attains a height much over 1,000
feet.

Munro, while believing that the Asopos Gorge was the route
referred to by Herodotus in the eighth book, maintains that the
other, the equivalent of the modern highway, was also in use in
480, and that both were occupied by the Greeks.[5] He argues that
Leonidas covered the first route by placing the Lokrian contingent as a garrison in the citadel of Trachis, which on his view
was identical with the citadel of the later Herakleia, the modern
hill of Sideroporto, situated on the left or western bank of the
Asopos at its northern exit from the gorge,[6] and that the second
was guarded by the Phokians, whom he supposes to have been
stationed at or near the point where it was crossed by the
Anopaia, so that the Phokians effectively controlled both the
Anopaia and the north–south route across the Pournaraki Pass.
There are, however, serious objections to a location so far west
for the Phokian detachment,[7] and Munro's identification of

[1] A.S. 55. [2] Ibid.
[3] A.S. 54 and n. 2; cf. Pritchett, 211 B, ll. 1–3.
[4] Grundy, 261 and n. 2.
[5] J.H.S. xxii, 1902, 312–14; cf. C.A.H. iv. 292 f. and 295 f.
[6] See below, p. 357. [7] See below, Appendix III.

Trachis with Herakleia, though accepted by many, is improbable.[1] We hear nothing of the Lokrians after they are alleged, in a tradition almost certainly unhistorical, to have joined with the Phokians in a protest to Leonidas against a Peloponnesian plan to withdraw to the Isthmus,[2] but it is to be noted that no other Greek contingents are mentioned by name in the rest of the narrative except those who played a special part in the fighting on the last day, the Phokians, Spartans, Thespians, and Thebans; hence the subsequent silence of Herodotus about the Lokrians is no justification for the supposition that they had been detached on some special service.

Others have argued that only one of the two routes was practicable in 480. That at least one of them existed then is not only proved by the testimony of Herodotus but rendered probable by the need of the Delphic sanctuary for some way of communication with the northern members of its Amphictyony more direct than the long circuit to the south of Mount Parnassos and through Phokis to the coast road.[3] Such a way would be provided as far as Doris by the road through Amphissa and the pass of Graviá (between Parnassos and the mountains of Aitolia to the west) to Bralo; Grundy assumes that it went on through the Asopos Gorge to Malis and Thessaly. The obvious objection to this assumption is suggested by Grundy himself;[4] he says that as in some places the chasm is only 12 feet wide between high precipitous cliffs on either side, the route is liable to interruption by even a slight rise in the Asopos, and that such an interruption is likely to occur frequently because the Malian Plain is visited by frequent storms, even in summer. A recent visitor, Pritchett, has emphasized the difficulties of the route.[5] He tells how a first attempt to get through, made in the month of April, had to be abandoned because the water was too high, and even in July, on a later visit, he had to proceed cautiously because at times the water was up to his knees. It has been suggested[6] that in antiquity the depth of the Asopos in the gorge would have been greater, since the mountains from which it flows were more thickly wooded than they are now. Pritchett is primarily arguing against the

---

[1] See below, Appendix II.   [2] vii. 207; see above, pp. 119 ff.
[3] Grundy, 262; cf. Macan, ii. 270.   [4] Op. cit. 262.
[5] Pritchett, 204 B.   [6] By the Harmenings in *A.S.* 56 (ll. 4–7).

view of Leake and Grundy that the Anopaia began by ascending the gorge, but his argument, if valid, would also prove that
Herodotus' direct route into Doris cannot have passed through
the gorge; it must be remembered that Herodotus nowhere
explicitly says that it did.

Pritchett was informed by a goatherd that very few now use
the route through the gorge and that most of those who do so
ride on animals, whereas Grundy notes[1] that when he was in
this region there was considerable mule traffic through the
gorge, even after the making of the new road. Grundy identifies
Herodotus' way into Doris with the Asopos Gorge route, and
denies that a practicable north–south route on the line of the
Pournaraki Pass existed in 480.[2] His arguments are of unequal
value; for example, he asks why Hydarnes did not begin his
march by an ascent of the road up to the point where the Anopaia path turns off to the east, but this objection does not hold
against those who do not accept Grundy's account of the
Anopaia. He is on firmer ground when he stresses the importance of the part played by Herakleia in later operations in this
region, especially in and after 279. This is intelligible if the
alternative route from Trachis into Central Greece passed
through the Asopos Gorge, because the entrance to the gorge
was effectively controlled by the citadel of Herakleia; but if the
route left the Malian Plain at a place some distance to the east
of the gorge and went over the Pournaraki Pass, those who
wished to use it could have ignored the garrison of Herakleia,
which would have been cut off from the supposed road by the
gorge.

Cary argued[3] that as early as the first decade of the fourth
century the occupation of Herakleia was important to the
Spartans because they wished to control the alternative route
from the Kephisos valley to the north, but there is no direct
evidence to support this view. The Spartans founded Herakleia
in 426, but a desire to control this route is not included among
the motives for the foundation given by Thucydides,[4] nor does

---

[1] Cf. his first note on p. 261 (also p. 302, ll. 11–17).

[2] Cf. his long and important note on pp. 267–9, and observe his stress on the condition 'practicable from a military point of view'.

[3] *C.Q.* xvi, 1922, 98–99.

[4] But note that the Spartans thought Herakleia τῆς ἐπὶ Θρᾴκης παρόδου χρησίμως
ἕξειν (Thuc. iii. 92. 4). See below, p. 356.

he say that Brasidas used it when he passed through Herakleia
on his way to Thessaly and Macedonia.[1] When Philip II of
Macedon was trying to penetrate into Central Greece late in
the year 339 and was unable to use the direct route because the
fortified post of Nikaia, built to control the coast road through
Thermopylai, had been occupied by the Thebans, he is said to
have effected a surprise by getting his army through to Kytinion
in Doris, but no details of his march have been preserved.[2]
Thirteen years earlier, when his adversaries had mustered in
strength for the defence of Thermopylai, he had made no attempt to force a passage.[3]

The defences of Thermopylai were turned on three famous
occasions, by the Persians in 480, by the Gauls in 279, and by
the Romans in 191, and on each of these the attackers achieved
their objective by making use of the Anopaia path and taking
by surprise the troops posted to guard it. On the last two occasions the defenders had closed the route through the Asopos
Gorge by placing a strong garrison in Herakleia. The topographical indications in Pausanias, the main source for the
Gallic attack, are far from clear and have been variously interpreted,[4] but a more detailed account of the Roman operations
of 191 has been preserved in Livy and in Plutarch's *Life of Marcus Cato*,[5] the leader of the Roman force which surprised and
defeated the Aitolian troops guarding the Anopaia. There is no
suggestion in either of these writers that there was any other
route which turned Thermopylai except the Anopaia; they
naturally ignore the Asopos Gorge route because it was blocked
by the occupation of Herakleia. Grundy argues[6] that there
cannot have been a north–south route on the line of the modern
highway in and after 480, because if it had existed it must have
been used at some time to turn Thermopylai, and he rightly
calls attention to the occasions on which strong armies, confronted with opposition at the pass, made no attempt to force

---

[1] Thuc. iv. 78. 1.

[2] Philochoros, fr. 135 in Müller, *F.H.G.* i. 406f. (frr. 56 A and B in Jacoby,
F.G.H., no. 328); cf. Beloch, *G.G.* iii². 1. 563 and n. 2. On the date (Nov.–Dec. 339)
cf. Beloch iii². 297f.

[3] Diod. xvi. 38. 1–2; cf. Dem. xix. 83–84. On the date (352) cf. Hammond's
article in *J.H.S.* lvii, 1937, 44–78.

[4] See below, p. 362.   [5] c. 13. Cf. Livy xxxvi. 17–19.

[6] Op. cit., n. on pp. 267 f.

the passage.[1] In 224 Antigonos Doson, king of Macedonia, solved the problem by taking his army south from Thessaly to the Isthmus of Corinth through the friendly island of Euboia;[2] this shows that a defence of Thermopylai against penetration from the north depended on the possession of Euboia by the defenders.

In modern times the deforestation of the mountains above Thermopylai has been extensive,[3] and it is a reasonable assumption that the ridge now crossed by the Pournaraki Pass was so thickly wooded in antiquity that no route over the mountains existed at this point.[4] This is on the whole more probable than the alternative assumption, that in 480 the route through the Asopos Gorge was unusable.[5] Anyhow, the testimony of Herodotus proves that one of these two routes existed in 480, and if there was a route starting from west of the Thermopylai pass which went through to Doris, why was no use made of it by Persian troops until the Greek defenders of the main pass had been overwhelmed?

Any answer to this problem must be hypothetical.[6] Grundy's suggestion, that the Persians did not know of its existence until Hydarnes and his men were led up it by Ephialtes on their way to the Anopaia, is not impressive; the Thessalians in the Persian army must have been well informed about it since they afterwards guided a Persian force into Doris by this route.[7] Grundy's second suggestion is better, that no considerable force could make its way through the gorge with an adequate commissariat train because the huge boulders in the bed of the gorge only leave room enough for mule transport, and so no vehicles can pass this way. Munro, in an attempt to answer this objection,[8] urges that Grundy has exaggerated the transport difficulty by his supposition that the Persian commissariat was entirely wheeled, and that in fact, as Herodotus shows, it was largely

---

[1] Cf. his valuable long note on pp. 262–4.

[2] Polybius ii. 52. 7–8.

[3] Pritchett, op. cit. 205 A; Kromayer in *A.S.* ii. 142, n. 2 assumes some deforestation between 480 and 191.

[4] Kromayer (in *Schlachtenatlas*, iv. i, col. 6) tacitly presupposes that no route suitable for troops existed here in 480; cf. also *A.S.* iv. 55.

[5] The Harmenings (*A.S.* 55–56) refuse to decide between them.

[6] Cf. Grundy, 268 f. [7] viii. 31; see above, p. 134.

[8] *J.H.S.* xxii, 1902, 313, n. 30, with references to Hdt. vii. 125 and 187. 1 (cf. ix. 39. 2 for the Greek transport system).

composed of pack animals and camels. Grundy's third suggestion is that the Persian army, which had now been out of touch
with the fleet for several days, was running short of supplies,
and that it was therefore urgently necessary to restore communications with the fleet,[1] but he strangely supposes that
Xerxes hoped to achieve this by a speedy victory with the fleet;
it is far more likely that the unexpected losses of his fleet in the
storm compelled him to aim at a rapid decision on land.

The history of this region shows that the surprise march of
Philip of Macedon to Kytinion late in 339 is the only known
example of a successful penetration in ancient times from the
north into Doris by an invader who did not control Thermopylai;
it was a bold move which entailed considerable risk and illustrates the new spirit introduced into Greek warfare by the great
Macedonians.[2] The leaders of the Persian army in 480 were far
too cautious to incur the hazards inseparable from any attempt
to use this route (although they must have heard of it from the
Thessalians) so long as the main road to the south was controlled
by the Greeks. It has been pointed out[3] that a force venturing
into Central Greece by the Doris route would be separated
from the main Persian army for several days, as it would have
to make a long detour through Phokis before it could take the
Greek army in the rear, and during these days it would be in
the heart of a hostile country and in great danger itself of encirclement by an enemy force superior in numbers. It was quite
a different matter to send a detachment southwards by this
route when the main road to Phokis and Boiotia was safely in
Persian hands and the Greek resistance on land in Central
Greece had collapsed.

On topographical grounds, therefore, Leonidas was justified
in thinking that if he could hold the main pass and the Anopaia as well he could hold up indefinitely the Persian advance
on land into Central Greece. It is not unreasonable to argue
that the forces at his disposal were sufficient for this task, provided that losses in fighting were made good by reinforcements;
anyhow, the Greek losses in the battles of the first two days

---

[1] Grundy, 269. This view is defended by Caspari in *J.H.S* xxxi, 1911, 106 f.;
he finds confirmation of it in viii. 25.

[2] Cf. Tarn, *Hellenistic Military and Naval Developments* (1930), 43 ff.

[3] In *A.S.* 56.

were apparently not heavy.[1] Many scholars have supposed that
Leonidas was only expected by the Greek high command to
hold the pass for a few days, just long enough to enable the
fleet to force a battle with the Persian navy, but this view is
unsatisfactory. It will be argued later[2] that, though the Greeks
in 480 were making their main effort on the sea, their admirals
realized that they must force the Persian fleet to take the offensive and attack the Greek ships in their chosen position, and
they could only hope to achieve this result if the Persians were
reduced to a stalemate on land by the inability of their army
to force Thermopylai. Hence the Greek plan of campaign de-
manded that Leonidas' defence of the pass should be indefinitely prolonged, and there was no ground to anticipate that
he would be unsuccessful in maintaining his position if the high
command kept him provided with adequate supplies and reinforcements. If Thermopylai fell, it fell because Leonidas made
a serious mistake when he left the defence of the all-important
Anopaia path entirely in the hands of the Phokians.[3] It is true
that they had volunteered for this service[4] and had special local
knowledge, but Leonidas should have stiffened their ranks with
more trustworthy troops and in particular should have sent
some Spartiate officers with them to ensure that a vigilant defence was maintained, and above all that due precautions were
taken against the danger of a surprise attack.

The fighting at Thermopylai

When the Greeks heard that Xerxes was in Pieria they sent
their fleet to Artemision, while the army under Leonidas occupied the pass of Thermopylai.[5] Herodotus says that the Phokians
and Lokrians joined them at Trachis, but by this he means not
the town but the territory of Trachis,[6] which probably stretched
across the Asopos to the East Gate of Thermopylai and so included the whole of the pass. The Greek position is located
'within the pass'[7] and was evidently in the Middle Gate. On

---

[1] vii. 211. 3, wrongly questioned by Obst, 111, who relies on the worthless
evidence of Diod. xi. 9. 2 (inconsistent with xi. 7. 4!).

[2] See below, pp. 181 f.   [3] Cf. Beloch ii². 2. 101.

[4] vii. 217. 2 (not inconsistent with 212. 2).   [5] vii. 177.

[6] vii. 203 (end). viii. 21. 1 is conclusive. Cf. Legrand, vii. 212 A, n. 4, also *A.S.*
28 and n. 4.

[7] vii. 201; cf. Grundy, 293 and see above, p. 131.

their arrival the Greeks had rebuilt the old Phokian wall and held it with part of their troops, but they also had outposts stationed some distance in front of the wall, though still in the Middle Gate.[1] Leonidas knew nothing about the existence of the Anopaia path until he reached Thermopylai; when he heard of it he assigned the duty of guarding it to the Phokian contingent, 1,000 hoplites.[2] Much earlier the path had been used by the Thessalians in a war with the Phokians to turn the Phokian position in the pass,[3] so that it must have been well known to the Phokians, but the Lokrians surely ought to have been better acquainted than the Phokians with the country behind Thermopylai. Perhaps Leonidas chose the Phokians because they volunteered for the task[4] and because his Peloponnesian hoplites were unused to mountain warfare. The path was difficult for an army and ought to have been easy to guard.

Xerxes and his troops, after crossing the Spercheios, encamped in the territory of Trachis.[5] The camp must have been pitched in that part of the territory which was situated to the west of the Asopos, and so west of the West Gate of the Pass,[6] but the Persians may, like the Greeks, have pushed forward outposts in front of their main positions; it has been suggested that these had advanced through the West Gate to occupy the village of Anthele.[7] Xerxes is said to have sent a mounted scout to reconnoitre the Greek positions;[8] the main force was hidden from view as it was posted behind the Phokian Wall, but the Spartans, according to the story, were then taking their turn on outpost duty, and the scout found them exercising themselves or combing their hair. Their behaviour, as the exiled Spartan king Demaratos duly explained to the astonished Xerxes, exhibited the confidence of Spartan soldiers in the face of danger, so this part of the story perhaps belongs to the legend,[9] but the scout's reconnaissance may be authentic.

Four days elapsed between the arrival of the Persian army at

---

[1] vii. 208. 2. [2] vii. 212. 2 and 217. 2.

[3] vii. 215 (Thessalians guided along the path by the Malians).

[4] vii. 217. 2. [5] vii. 201.

[6] Grundy, 293, also 296 and n. 1 (arguing from the story in vii. 208); cf. *A.S.* 26 f. and 57. [7] Macan, i. 301 A and *A.S.* 57.

[8] The story is in vii. 208 (Demaratos' commentary follows in 209).

[9] Macan, i. 311 A; cf. Obst, 105 (who stresses the connexion between the two chapters 208 and 209). Grundy (second note on p. 296) remarks on the accuracy of the topographical detail in the story.

Trachis and its first attack on Thermopylai. Herodotus' explanation for this delay,[1] that Xerxes was waiting for the Greeks to
run away, is absurd, but the delay and its duration must be
accepted. The Greek position was so strong that Xerxes may
have hesitated to risk a frontal attack, and he may have decided
to rely on his navy to end the deadlock; if it could defeat the
Greek fleet and compel it to retreat, the Greek army would be
forced to abandon its position without a battle. It was probably
on the fourth day[2] of his sojourn in Trachis that Xerxes received
bad news: the Persian navy had reached Aphetai the previous
afternoon but had suffered so severely from storms that it was
in no condition to undertake an immediate offensive. The
Persian army, which had been out of touch with the fleet for
several days, was probably running short of supplies,[3] and on
the next day, four days after it had reached Trachis, Xerxes
began his attempt to force the passage.[4]

The first attack was made by the Medians and Kissians, of
whom the Kissians came from the region of Sousiane, the ancient
Elam;[5] the infantry of these two contingents ranked among the
best in the army, inferior only to the Persians themselves. When
these were roughly handled by the Greeks, Xerxes withdrew
them and sent in some of his best troops, taken from the corps of
the ten thousand Immortals, all Persians of the homeland and
commanded by a Persian noble of the highest rank, Hydarnes,[6]
but they had no better success, and although the fighting went
on all day the barbarians made no progress and must have
sustained heavy losses.[7] There are clear indications in Herodotus
that during this day and the next the Greeks occupied a position
which was indeed some distance in front of the Phokian wall
but still inside the Middle Gate.[8] In this narrow passage the
Persians could derive no advantage from their superiority in

---

[1] vii. 210. 1; cf. Grundy, 296 f. Ephoros here inserts a Persian peace-offer,
suitably answered by Leonidas! (Diod. xi. 5. 4–5); cf. Macan, i. 311 B.

[2] Day 17 of the Diary; see below, Appendix V.   [3] See above, p. 140, n. 1.

[4] Day 18 of the Diary. For the fighting on this day cf. vii. 210–11 (valueless
rehash of this in Diod. xi. 7).

[5] iii. 91. 4; cf. vii. 62. 2 with Macan's note.

[6] Son of the Hydarnes who was one of the Six who helped Darius to the throne
(iii. 70. 2); cf. HW 120.

[7] There is no reason to doubt this, though Hdt. exaggerates in vii. 211. 3.

[8] This follows from a combination of the Spartan tactics in vii. 211. 3 with the
important evidence in 223. 1 (last sentence) and 223. 2 (first sentence).

numbers, and their armament was less suitable than the Greek for hand-to-hand fighting. Ephoros, having noted that else-where Herodotus had pointed out the inadequacy of their defensive arms, asserted that the Persians were handicapped at Thermopylai by the smallness of their shields,[1] but in this battle Herodotus stresses the fact that the spears of the Persian pike-men were shorter than those of the Greeks as a main reason for their defeat.[2]

In his account of the second day's fighting Herodotus re-marks that the various Greek contingents took part in the battle, relieving each other by turns,[3] and presumably they had also fought in rotation on the day before, but Herodotus does not mention any by name in the first battle except the Spartans; perhaps it was the Spartans who beat off the attack of the Per-sian Immortals. Herodotus specially notices the virtuosity of the Spartans in this type of fighting, describing how they would draw on the barbarians by a pretended retreat and suddenly at a suitable moment turn about and attack; these tactics could only be used under such conditions by a highly-trained and well-disciplined infantry. Grundy suggests[4] that their object was to keep the enemy at close quarters. They were thus able to inflict heavy losses on the Persians while their own casualties were slight, as those of the victors usually were in a hoplite battle; the evidence of Herodotus on this point[5] is to be pre-ferred to that of Ephoros, who says that the Spartans and Thespians together numbered only 500 (out of an original 1,000) at the beginning of the final battle.

The battle on the first day is said to have lasted all day;[6] the Persians resumed the attack on the next day, but Herodotus has little to say about the fighting except that the enemy fared no better than on the previous day.[7] It has been argued that by

---

[1] Hdt. ix. 62. 3, Diod. xi. 7. 3; cf. Grundy, 299.

[2] vii. 211. 2. Hence the Persian soldiers did not deserve Hdt.'s harsh verdict in vii. 210. 2 (equally unsuitable if moved to the end of 212 with HW 224).

[3] vii. 212. 2.   [4] Op. cit. 297; cf. A.S. 59.

[5] vii. 211. 3, followed in Diod. xi. 7. 4; contrast xi. 9. 2, wrongly preferred by Obst, 111, who by including the hypothetical perioikoi makes their losses on the first two days 1,500 out of an original 2,000.

[6] In the last sentence of vii. 210, which is oddly placed in the narrative; it has been proposed to remove it to the end of 211 (A.S. 59, n. 2).

[7] vii. 212. 1, also 212. 2 (end). Note that the Persians hoped the small Greek army would be weakened by its losses.

the morning of the second day Xerxes must have taken the
decision to send some of his picked troops, the Immortals, by
night along the Anopaia route to turn the Greek position, for as
this force set out on its march soon after sunset, it must have
made its preparations earlier in the day.[1] This argument is
sound, but it does not justify the conclusion that the Persian
attempts to break through on the second day were only a feint
to mislead the Greeks. The Thessalians, who had used the path
against the Phokians once in their history, must have reported
its existence to Xerxes, and it was only necessary to find a
Malian to act as a guide, the Trachinian Ephialtes, son of
Eurydemos,[2] but it must not be forgotten that when the Thessalians used it they had met with no resistance. It was not
likely that it would be left unguarded now. Herodotus indeed
says that the troops under Hydarnes were surprised when they
encountered the Phokians, as they were not expecting any opposition,[3] but the Persian leaders cannot have counted on this,
and they must have realized that if Hydarnes' men on their
march up the narrow and difficult path found it barred by a
body of well-armed and vigilant defenders their chance of success would be very slender. The turning movement by the
Anopaia must have seemed to them a desperate gamble which
would be disastrous if it failed and was only to be tried when
all hope of a break-through along the coast road had been
abandoned.

After two days of unsuccessful fighting in the pass Xerxes
decided that the turning movement must be tried. If it was to
have any chance of success it would obviously have to be carried
out at night, and the force detailed for the operation set out
from the Persian camp, situated on the left or western bank of
the Asopos, 'about the time when lamps are lit',[4] an hour or less
after sunset. Herodotus says that the force was composed of
Hydarnes and the men under his command, but it is unnecessary to conclude from this that all the 10,000 Immortals were
sent.[5] After crossing the Asopos they marched all through the
night;[6] their precise route is disputed, but whichever way they

---

[1] Cf. *A.S.* 60.

[2] vii. 213. 1; 214. 2 adds that he was a Trachinian. See also Ktesias (*Persika* 24),
who notes the presence of the Thessalian Thorax in Xerxes' army; cf. Busolt, 684 f.,
also HW on vii. 214.   [3] vii. 218. 2.

[4] vii. 215; cf. Macan ad loc.   [5] See below, p. 363.   [6] vii. 217. 1.

went they had to arrive eventually at the saddle which joins
Mount Sástano to the main ridge of Kallidromos.[1] This saddle
was almost certainly the position of the 1,000 Phokians who were
guarding the path for Leonidas, and the Persians, guided by
Ephialtes, reached it just as day was dawning. The Phokians,
according to their own account, did not hear the enemy approaching until they were close at hand;[2] they had allowed
themselves to be caught unprepared and were still putting on
their arms. As the path runs over open ground at this point,
the Persians were able to discharge volleys of arrows against
their opponents. The Phokians fell into a panic. Grundy maintains that if they had fallen back into the thick forest through
which the path runs east of the saddle, they could have prevented the Persians from getting through. Instead they fled to
the heights, presumably those to the south of the saddle, and
left the passage free for the Persians, who now began the descent with all speed. But they had still a long way to go, and
several hours would elapse before they could reach the coast
road by a path coming down to the sea just to the east of the
East Gate.

At this point the true tradition is lost in the mist of legend.[3]
When the mist clears again, Leonidas and his Spartiates are
still in the Middle Gate, together with the Thespians and
Thebans; it is not known whether any light-armed troops or
camp-followers (apart from Helots) remained with them.[4] All
the Peloponnesian troops except the Spartiatai have disappeared,[5] as well as the Lokrians. The three contingents which
remained had originally totalled 1,400 hoplites, and it is unlikely that they had suffered heavy losses in the fighting of the
two previous days. Acting under Ephialtes' advice, the main
Persian army deferred its attack 'until the time when the market

---

[1] See above, p. 133, and below, p. 364.

[2] On what follows cf. Grundy, 304, and on the descent his second note on p. 310,
but his view that the Phokians had deposited their arms in the φρούριον half a mile
to the north of the saddle (304; cf. 303) is unsupported by evidence, unless he
thinks this is meant by the κόρυμβος of vii. 218. 3.

[3] On this question see below, Appendix IV.

[4] Grundy's total of 3,500 for the whole force (op. cit. 306) apparently includes
2,100 Helots, seven for each Spartiate as at Plataia (ix. 28. 2); cf. Grundy, 273
and see above, p. 118, n. 2.

[5] The reference to the contingent from Mykenai in Pausanias ii. 16. 5 does not
mean that its 80 men (Hdt. vii. 202) stayed with Leonidas to the end.

begins to fill',[1] which is between nine and ten in the morning. By this time the leaders of the Greeks still left in the pass knew that Hydarnes' turning movement had succeeded and that they would soon be surrounded. Leonidas had determined not to surrender but to fight on till the end. He and those with him marched out to meet the enemy 'as men who knew that they were going out to their deaths',[2] and as they were resolved to sell their lives dearly they advanced beyond their former position to a place where the Middle Gate becomes wider.

Here they maintained a desperate struggle for some time. Many of them had their spears broken in the conflict but they fought on with their swords; some of the Persians were driven into the sea and so met their end. In this battle two half-brothers of Xerxes, sons of Darius and his niece Phratagoune, were killed, and several Spartans fell, including Leonidas. An epic contest developed for possession of his body, a contest finally won by the Greeks, who presented an unbroken front to the enemy and even drove them back four times. In the end, however, they were forced to retreat by the news that Hydarnes' force was approaching. The Thebans now decided to abandon the hopeless struggle,[3] but the rest withdrew eastwards, crossed the Phokian wall, and for their last stand occupied a hill just behind it,[4] which was afterwards marked by a lion sculptured in stone as a memorial to Leonidas. Here the survivors defended themselves with their swords[5] and even with their hands and teeth until they were finally overwhelmed in a shower of missiles.

Thanks to the incompetence or treachery of the Phokians the desperate hazard of Hydarnes' turning movement had succeeded, and the gateway by land into Central Greece lay open

---

[1] vii. 223. 1; cf. iv. 181. 3. The evidence of iii. 104. 2 would make the ἀγορᾶς διάλυσις some appreciable time before noon (HW i. 290 in their note ad loc. fix it at about 10 a.m., whereas in their note on ii. 173. 1 they put it at 11 a.m.).

[2] vii. 223. 2. The position occupied by them is identified by Grundy with that marked '2' on his map opposite p. 310.

[3] vii. 233. 1; Hdt. here reproduces the bitterness of his anti-Theban sources.

[4] Undoubtedly Grundy's 'Hill 1'; see above, p. 131, also Stählin, 2414. Some wrongly locate the final stand on 'Hill 2' (so the authors of A.S. 63 and Kromayer in Schlachtenatlas, iv. 1, text, end of col. 6); this view is based on a misconception about the course of the road at this point (see above, p. 132 and n. 2). The speculations of Munro in J.H.S. xxii, 1902, 318, n. 37 are to be rejected.

[5] μαχαίρῃσι in 225. 3 is presumably identical with ξίφεσι in 224. 1 (but see Macan's note on 225. 3).

to the Persians. At the time the news of this disaster, which
entailed the withdrawal of the Greek fleet from its advanced
position at Artemision, must have been most disheartening to
the patriotic Greeks. It is not surprising that the Spartans tried
to reassure them by an official announcement that Leonidas had
met his death in fulfilment of an Apolline oracle and that all
had proceeded according to plan.[1] Whether this fiction did
much at the time to encourage the despondent may be doubted,
but the memory of the reverse on land was speedily offset by
the decisive triumph on sea at Salamis, and after the war the
official Spartan version of the last stand at Thermopylai
steadily gained ground at the expense of any relics of an authentic tradition that had survived. Greek imaginations were fired
by the story of the last desperate battle in the pass and the
noble sacrifice of those who gave their lives there. Sparta gained
more than the obscure Thespiai from the legend,[2] and Leonidas
most of all; he might have been blamed for his failure to hold
the pass, but instead he was lauded for the heroism of his end.[3]

[1] Munro, op. cit. 316. This is preferable to the suggestion of Legrand (vii. 189 f.)
that the oracle was invented to defend Leonidas against the charge of a useless
sacrifice of lives.

[2] The curiously shadowy part played by the Thespians in the final drama is to
be explained by the Legend, which found their presence embarrassing.

[3] So Simonides in his poem on those who fell at Thermopylai (preserved in Diod.
xi. 11. 6) ; on it cf. Bowra in *C.P.* xxviii, 1933, 277–81. On the later transference of
Leonidas' bones to Sparta cf. Pausanias iii. 14. 1 (where he mentions the stele
commemorating the 300 Spartiatai who fell with Leonidas). The date indicated
for the transference by our texts of Pausanias (440) is perplexing, cf. Macan i. 351 f.
Hdt. in vii. 224. 1 says that he had ascertained the names of all the 300; some have
supposed that he had read them on the stele, but his language suggests that he had
learnt them from oral tradition.

III

ARTEMISION

The site of the Greek naval station and its implications

HERODOTUS says[1] that when the Greeks resolved to block the Persian advance on land at Thermopylai they decided at the same time that the fleet should sail to Artemision in the territory of Histiaia; the reason he gives for this decision is that the two places were near to one another and so communication would be easy between the army and the fleet. He then describes[2] the topography of the two positions, beginning with Artemision, which he dismisses briefly: 'leading out of the broad waters of the Thracian Sea there is a narrow channel lying between the island of Skiathos and the mainland of Magnesia, and next after this strait there follows in Euboia the sea beach called Artemision, upon which there is a temple of Artemis.' There is some difficulty about the construction of this sentence, reflected in different methods of punctuation,[3] but the meaning is clear and it is not necessary to delete either of the two references to Artemision as a gloss;[4] if they are retained it is clear that for Herodotus Artemision meant a beach identified by a temple of Artemis.

Plutarch also[5] describes Artemision as a beach in Euboia, but adds that it was beyond Histiaia and facing north, opposite Olizon in the territory of Philoktetes (i.e. Magnesia). He gives an account of the small temple of Artemis, here worshipped as Artemis Proseoia,[6] which was apparently still standing in his own day, surrounded by a grove of trees, and of the marble stelai near it, one of which was once inscribed with an epigram[7] on the Athenians who defeated the Persians in the neighbouring waters; there was even a place on the beach where the darkness

---

[1] vii. 175. 2. [2] vii. 176. 1.

[3] It seems best to put a colon after Ἀρτεμίσιον in l. 1 (Stein and Macan).

[4] Powell in his translation omits both; Stein deleted the second only.

[5] *Them.* 8. 3–6; Homer, *Iliad* ii. 716–18. [6] Προσηῴα in Greek.

[7] *Them.* 8. 5 (= Simonides, no. 109 in Diehl, ii². 127).

of the sand below the surface was said to mark the place where the corpses and the wreckage of the ships had been burnt. An epigram[1] (as restored by Bergk) on the Megarians who fought here indicated that the temple stood on a hill, but the rediscovery of the inscription which contains the epigram points to a different restoration of the relevant line.

Lolling[2] fixed the site of the temple by discovering on a hill in North Euboia, a little to the east of the modern village of Potoki, a slab of marble giving the names of those who contributed to the restoration of the temple of Artemis Proseoia; the inscription was dated by him between 146 and 75 B.C. He rightly inferred from his discovery that the beach mentioned by Herodotus and Plutarch must be that of the adjacent bay of Pevki (or Peuke) on which Potoki stands; he noted that in his time sailing ships overtaken by storm in the sound north of Euboia which could not reach the roadstead of Oreos or the Gulf of Volo usually took refuge in Pevki Bay, and claimed that the bay was roomy enough to shelter the largest fleets.[3] Hence Kromayer[4] concluded that the Greek fleet was drawn up across the mouth of the bay to face the Persian offensive on the last day of the fighting at Artemision. But the distance, according to his map, is not more than 4 kilometres, and would therefore not hold more than 200 triremes in line abreast (on the assumption[5] that 20 metres of front are to be allowed for each trireme). If the Greek fleet was really drawn up across the mouth of Pevki Bay on the last day, when it numbered over 300 triremes, part of it must have been drawn up in two lines;[6] the alternative is to suppose that part of the fleet was stationed in a position or positions on the Euboian coast farther west.

The description of Artemision as a promontory in some ancient writers[7] is probably erroneous. Herodotus and Plutarch both say explicitly that it was a beach, and their testimony also

---

[1] Simonides 96. Bergk's reading was still kept by Diehl, ii[2]. 119, but Wilhelm had rediscovered the relevant inscription and published it in 1898; cf. Tod, *GHI*. no. 20, l. 7.

[2] *Ath. Mittheilungen*, viii, 1883, 7–23.　　　　　　　　[3] Op. cit. 16.

[4] *Schlachtenatlas*, iv. 1, col. 3.

[5] Cf. Rados, 326 (20 metres is over 65 feet), and Tarn in *J.H.S.* xxviii, 1908, 219; see below, p. 227, n. 2.

[6] As Tarn (op. cit. 219) supposes the Persian fleet to have been; see below p. 189.

[7] Scholiast on Ar. *Lysistrata* 1251 and 'Suidas' s.v.; cf. Lolling, 8, n. 4.

disproves the modern suggestion[1] that the name could be
used for the waters between North Euboia and Magnesia.
Lolling's discovery proved that the beach to which they referred
was that of Pevki Bay, but some scholars are still unwilling to
admit that the Greek fleet had its station there. Köster argues[2]
that the correct location of the temple by Lolling did not settle
the question, in view of the fact that the temple gave its name
to the neighbourhood; actually Herodotus limits the name to
the beach situated near the temple, and gives no support to the
supposition (which Köster professes to extract from Herodotus'
words) that by Artemision we must understand the whole coast
up to Oreos. Grundy, who does not refer to Lolling's paper,
says dogmatically[3] that the station of the Greek fleet must have
been 'well within the strait, at a point west of the mouth of the
Pagasaetic Gulf where the fair way is much narrower than in
the outer part of the channel', but though he alleges that the
name 'Artemisian shore' was apparently applicable to this part
of the coast of Euboia he does not cite any ancient evidence
in support. Presumably he would have agreed with Macan's
contention[4] that the name Artemision 'must be applied to a
considerable extent of shore on the NW coast of Euboia in
order to harmonize the scene with the story of the fighting'.
Prentice[5] follows Grundy's view that the station of the Greek
fleet was west of the entrance to the Bay of Pagasai and tries
to clinch it by the argument that otherwise the Persian fleet
could not have reached Aphetai without a battle, but as this
fact can be explained in other ways the argument is invalid,
and anyhow the location of Aphetai inside the entrance to the
Gulf of Pagasai, accepted by Grundy and Prentice, is probably
wrong.[6]

Grundy, Macan, and Köster are in fact rejecting the evidence
of Herodotus and Plutarch when they insist that the Greek fleet
must have occupied a station farther west than Pevki Bay and
nearer to the point where the channel narrows (at Argyronisi,
about 4 miles north of Oreos). Their insistence apparently de-
rives from the assumption that the Greeks must have controlled

---

[1] Cf. the authors cited by Macan, i. 257 B.   [2] Köster, 66.
[3] Grundy, 322; cf. the map opposite p. 268.   [4] ii. 264.
[5] *T.A.P.A.* li, 1920, 9 f.
[6] See below, pp. 176 f., and on the evidence of Strabo 436, p. 177, n. 2.

the entrance to the Oreos channel from a station as near to it as possible; perhaps they believed that if the Greeks had been stationed at Pevki Bay the Persians might have sent part of their fleet through the Oreos channel and so cut the line of the Greek retreat. Macan[1] thinks that the tactical aim of the Greek fleet (which he describes as 'perfectly simple and obvious') was to prevent the passage of Xerxes' ships through the channel, and that the Greek admirals achieved this by taking up their station along the Euboian strand, from which they could attack the Persian ships in flank if their admirals attempted to force their way along the channel. Macan has here anticipated Custance[2] in pointing out the value of a Greek position flanking the line of a possible Persian advance, but he fails to realize that a station at Pevki Bay was just as effective for this purpose and perhaps served as well some other purpose which was no less important to the Greeks.

According to Herodotus[3] the Greeks chose Artemision as the position for their fleet because it was near to Thermopylai and so close contact could be maintained with the army. Towards the end of his narrative of the operations at Artemision he describes[4] the rather primitive method by which this contact was maintained. There was a man of Antikyra[5] waiting at Artemision in a boat furnished with oars, prepared to carry a message to the land force if the fleet was hard pressed, and his opposite number, an Athenian, was waiting with a thirty-oared boat at Thermopylai, in readiness to report to the fleet if the army was defeated. From this it would appear that the two messengers were only to be used if either arm of the Greek forces met with a serious reverse, and were not intended to provide a regular channel of communication between army and fleet. This is not surprising, as Artemision is separated from Thermopylai by nearly 40 miles of sea.[6] If the Greeks planned to hold up the double advance on land and sea of the Persian forces in a defensive position which would permit close co-operation between their army and navy, why did they station their fleet so far from their land force? It is true that as their enemy had a strong fleet they could not do what the Greeks did

---

[1] ii. 280.   [2] See below, pp. 208 f.   [3] vii. 175. 2.
[4] viii. 21. 1.   [5] Presumably the Malian Antikyra (vii. 198. 2).
[6] Cf. Macan, ii. 264.

against Philip of Macedon in 352 or against the Gauls in 279, post their fleet in close proximity to Thermopylai, as their ships could then have been attacked from the east by a Persian fleet advancing through the channel between north-west Euboia and the mainland, a channel which opens into the Malian Gulf 20 miles or more to the east of Thermopylai, but surely they could have found a suitable station on the Euboian shore just inside the southern entrance to the channel? Such a station would have made the fleet's communications with the army much easier and quicker, and would have been equally effective if the only object of the Greek admirals was to bar the advance of the Persian navy into the waters that lie between Euboia and Central Greece.

If Artemision is identical with the beach of Pevki Bay, its choice by the Greeks as the station for their fleet must have had a purpose additional to that mentioned by Herodotus, and a glance at the map shows that this purpose can only have been to guard against a Persian landing in North Euboia.[1] The island of Euboia stretches alongside the greater part of the eastern coast of Central Greece, separated from it merely by the strait called the Euripos, and in one place, at Chalkis, this strait narrows to a breadth of only 40 yards. Whatever may have been the size of the Persian army, there can be no doubt that it was far superior in numbers to the land forces which the Probouloi at Corinth were prepared to spare for the defence of Central Greece. If the Persians had been allowed to land part of their army in North Euboia they could have advanced to Chalkis without much opposition,[2] and once there they would have found means to block the Greek fleet's line of retreat through the Euripos bottleneck and to land troops on the opposite shore, thereby cutting the communications of Leonidas' army.

It is tempting to conjecture[3] that the genius of Themistokles was responsible for the choice of Artemision, a position which combined so many advantages. Not only did it cover Euboia effectively, but as it lay on the east side of the waterway into the Malian Gulf it ensured that the enemy would not dare to

---

[1] Grundy, 265 makes this point but does not stress its importance.
[2] So when the Aitolians held Thermopylai in 224 to bar the southward march of the Macedonian Antigonos Doson, he got his army to Corinth by taking it through Euboia; cf. Polybius ii. 52. 7–8.   [3] With Grundy, 269–70.

attempt an advance into the Gulf until they had eliminated the danger of a Greek flank attack, and this they could only do by a frontal assault on the Greek ships in their chosen position. It is true that this position was separated by nearly 40 miles from that of the army under Leonidas, but it does not appear in the sequel that any grave disadvantage resulted from this handicap. Possibly some rudimentary form of intercommunication between army and fleet was arranged, perhaps by means of smoke signals exchanged between the heights above the two positions;[1] in some such way Leonidas could have notified the admiral Eurybiadas that the Persian frontal attack on land had begun. The two special messengers seem to have been held in reserve, so that in the event of a serious crisis on land or sea they could convey the detailed information of an oral report.

Herodotus was aware that the Persian plan of campaign necessitated close co-operation between the naval and land forces; in a speech which he puts into the mouth of a Persian admiral[2] he makes the point that if the Persian army and fleet advance together each can support the other, whereas if they are separated neither will be of any use. He also knew[3] that a resolute defence of a strong position on land would be useless if an enemy controlled the sea and could thereby turn the position by landing troops in its rear. Yet he failed to draw the necessary conclusions from these presuppositions. If the Persian invasion of Greece was to be a double attack delivered simultaneously on land and on sea, the Greek defence would have to be adapted to meet it, with the army and fleet acting in close co-operation throughout. Above all, the interdependence of the Greek forces on land and sea was so great that a defeat entailing the retreat of either force from its station must have as a necessary and inevitable consequence the immediate withdrawal of the other.[4] Herodotus notes that the two Greek positions were near together, and refers belatedly to the provision which had been made for communication between them; in his description of the final battle at Artemision he even says[5] that the whole aim of the Greeks was to defend the channel of Euripos and not

---

[1] Cf. Grundy, 265 f.   [2] Achaimenes (vii. 236. 2).
[3] vii. 139. 2–3 (in what may well be a 'late' passage).
[4] Cf. Grundy, 263 f., Macan, ii. 260 ff.
[5] viii. 15. 2. ('Hellas' is here used for Greece south of Thermopylai; cf. vii. 175. 2, viii. 4. 1).

to let the barbarians penetrate into 'Hellas' (i.e. Central Greece). These statements are not enough to prove that he clearly understood the fundamental principle governing the strategy of the Greek high command at this stage. For him the connexion between the two positions is, as Bury[1] has well said, 'a superficial connection determined by an accident of vicinity, instead of the vicinity being determined by an essential connection in strategy'. Herodotus apparently understood[2] that Artemision could not continue to be held by the Greek fleet if Thermopylai was forced by the Persian army; he failed to keep in mind the fact that Thermopylai would be untenable if the Greek fleet retired through the Euripos, and when he is repeating thoughtlessly what he had heard from his informants he can assert that the Greek admirals at Artemision seriously contemplated and on one occasion even carried out a withdrawal as far as Chalkis. It is in such passages as these that he betrays his inability to grasp the essential principles of a sound strategy.

The Greek fleet at Artemision

The account given by Herodotus of the naval operations in the waters of Northern Greece down to the retirement of the Greeks from Artemision is contained in two blocks of narrative,[3] separated by the continuous story of the fighting at Thermopylai. The second block takes up the tale again at the point where the first left off, the arrival of the Persian fleet at Aphetai in Magnesia, and opens[4] with a list of states which sent contingents to the Greek fleet; the numbers are given for the ships in each contingent, making a total of 271 triremes and 9 pentekonters. It is not certain whether the detailed figures in Herodotus for the various contingents are to be referred to the precise point in his narrative where they occur; if they are, the 3 guardships (1 each from Athens, Aigina, and Troizen) which had been captured some days earlier are not included in them.[5] Moreover, the figure for the Athenian contingent presumably does not include the 53 Attic ships which joined the fleet on

---

[1] *B.S.A.* ii. 1895–6, 85.   [2] viii. 21. 2.   [3] vii. 179–95 and viii. 1–25.
[4] viii. 1.
[5] This is the view of Labarbe (in *B.C.H.* lxxvi, 1952, 387 f.). Macan inclined to the opposite view; cf. his notes on vii. 180 (l. 1) and viii. 1 (l. 7).

the day after the first naval engagement. Even so, more than half of the original fleet of 271 triremes was supplied by the Athenians, for in addition to the 127 manned by their own population and the Plataians they had provided the 20 triremes which were manned by the Chalkidians of Euboia (and possibly also by the Athenian cleruchs settled in the territory of Chalkis).[1] Of the other Euboian states Eretria sent 5 and Styra 2 triremes; of the Cyclades Keos alone was represented at Artemision, by 2 triremes and 2 pentekonters (the other 7 pentekonters belonged to the Opountian Lokrians). The 113 triremes contributed by states belonging to the Peloponnesian League were composed of the following contingents: Corinth 40, Megara 20, Aigina 18, Sikyon 12, Sparta 10, Epidauros 8, Troizen 5. The dispute about the leadership of the fleet had been settled earlier in favour of Sparta,[2] whose admiral Eurybiadas was commander-in-chief of the Greek navy throughout the campaign of 480.

Various explanations have been suggested for the absence of the fifty-three Attic ships from the first battle at Artemision; the most popular is that they had been posted earlier to Chalkis to guard the rear of the main Greek navy against a possible circumnavigation of Euboia by a Persian fleet.[3] Obst suggested[4] that this was one of three reserve squadrons, the other two being stationed at Aigina and at Pogon (in the territory of Troizen, the modern harbour of Poros). The last is supposed by Obst to have been intended to prevent a Persian landing in the Argolid, but in the passage cited by him from Herodotus[5] Pogon seems to be merely the rendezvous of those Greek ships which had not been ready in time to fight at Artemision. A better case can be made for the existence of a reserve squadron at Aigina, and Obst's view on this has been re-argued by Labarbe.[6] It is remarkable that Aigina had only eighteen ships at Artemision, for among the states of Old Greece she had been the leading naval power until the rise of Athens to first place. Even at Salamis, where a Greek defeat would have been promptly

---

[1] See Macan's note ad loc.

[2] viii. 3. Eurybiadas is called ναύαρχος in viii. 42. 2. Herodotus is not necessarily thinking there of the Spartan ναυαρχία (normally tenable for a single year only) though Eurybiadas may have held this office in 480 (so Beloch, ii². 2. 271 f.).

[3] See below, p. 187.   [4] Obst, 119.   [5] viii. 42. 1.

[6] B.C.H. lxxvi, 389 f.

followed by a Persian occupation of Aigina, the Aiginetans supplied only thirty ships, the best in their fleet. Herodotus notes[1] that they had other ships manned as well, but that they were held in reserve for the defence of Aigina itself. Such a reserve is more intelligible at that stage, for by then the whole of the Persian fleet had reached Phaleron and the threat to Aigina was close at hand. When the Persian navy was still north of Artemision it was unlikely that its admirals would have ventured to detach a squadron for a raid into the Saronic Gulf, where it would be cut off from its base and might at any moment be intercepted and destroyed, and the same objection applies to Labarbe's suggestion[2] that the Persians might have sent ships into the Gulf 'from their reserves in Asia Minor'. Nevertheless, the smallness of the Aiginetan contingent at Artemision is a real problem; it is possible that when the Peloponnesians agreed to meet the Persian navy so far north they insisted that a reserve fleet (twenty-five ships or more) should be left to cover Aigina and with it the approaches to the Isthmus and the Argolid.

The affair of the scout-ships and the temporary withdrawal from Artemision of the Greek fleet

The advance of the Persian fleet from its stations at and near Therma in Macedonia to the harbour of Aphetai in Magnesia was probably completed before the fighting at Thermopylai began, and this may be one of the reasons that prompted Herodotus to describe the voyage before he turned to the operations on land. His narrative of the voyage[3] is preceded by his version of a Delphic story which told how Apollo's oracle had warned the men of Delphi to pray to the winds;[4] the story ends with the words 'and even to this day the Delphians in accordance with the oracle propitiate the winds'. Thereby Herodotus implies that the prayer to the winds was crowned with success, and so prepares the minds of his readers for the disastrous storm sent by the gods of Greece to cripple the Persian armament during its voyage along the dangerous Thessalian coast.

---

[1] viii. 46. 1.   [2] Op. cit. 389 (were there in fact any such reserves?).

[3] Legrand, vii. 181 concludes that Hdt. vii. 179–95 'est surtout le récit d'une navigation'.

[4] vii. 178. The story is not necessarily false, but even if it is its falsity would not affect the argument.

After this introductory chapter[1] Herodotus begins his main
narrative with a sentence which in its opening words seems to
refer to the main Persian navy setting out on its voyage southwards from Therma, but abruptly focuses its attention on a
small section of the fleet, a reconnaissance squadron of ten of
the swiftest ships sent on ahead of the main fleet.[2] This squadron
is said to have sailed straight to Skiathos, where it surprised
three Greek ships, one each from Troizen, Aigina, and Athens,
posted at Skiathos in front of the Greek navy (which Herodotus
presumes to be by now in its station at Artemision)[3] to keep
watch. When the three Greek ships saw the enemy approaching,
they fled. The enemy pursued them, and quickly captured the
Troizenian ship. The handsomest man of her crew, a marine
called Leon, was taken by his captors to the prow of the ship
and slaughtered there; Herodotus' reference to the purpose of
this proceeding is hard to interpret, but possibly the sacrifice was
simply an offering to the gods of the first-fruits of victory, such
as Procopius[4] attributes to the Thulitai of Scandinavia.

The Aiginetan ship offered a more stubborn resistance, led
by one of its marines, Pytheas son of Ischenoös, who after the
capture of the ship fought on valiantly 'until he was hacked all
to pieces'.[5] His bravery made such an impression on the
Persian marines that they exerted themselves to save his life,
applying myrrh to heal his wounds then wrapping them in fine
linen bandages; the presence of such medical stores on board
the ship is evidence of efficient organization. Pytheas survived
and was well treated by the Persian marines, who made much of
him and later displayed him to the rest of the fleet. The sequel to
his story is told later by Herodotus;[6] he remained on board the
ship which had captured him, a Sidonian vessel, until it was
in turn captured by the Greeks in the battle of Salamis, whereupon Pytheas returned safe home to Aigina. His story shows

[1] Which may well have been included in Herodotus' first draft, in spite of
Macan (notes ad loc.).
[2] vii. 179; cf. Macan's first note on this chapter.
[3] This has been denied, but on inadequate grounds; see below, p. 161, n. 4.
In προφυλάσσουσαι, the προ is local (Macan).
[4] De bello Gothico, ii. 15. 24 f., cited by Blakesley (cf. HW 210). Was Leon's
fate commemorated later at Troizen, as Bergk supposed, by a poem of Simonides
(141 in Diehl, ii². 137; cf. J. M. Edmonds, Lyra Graeca, ii. 365 and n. 1)?
[5] κατεκρεουργήθη ἅπας in vii. 181. 1 (Macaulay's translation).
[6] viii. 92. 1. Did Hdt. hear the story in Aigina from Pytheas himself?

that the marines on board Phoenician ships were supplied by
Persians, and that one at least of the ten reconnaissance ships
was supplied by the Sidonians; perhaps all were, as the Sidonian triremes are elsewhere[1] said to have been the best sailers
in the fleet.

Phormos, the captain of the Athenian ship, somehow contrived to escape from the initial attack, but he was closely pursued by part of the Persian squadron, until finally he ran his
trireme aground at the mouth of the river Peneios in the north-
east corner of Thessaly. Although he had to abandon his ship,
which was captured by the enemy, he landed his crew and
managed to bring them all safely back by land to Athens.[2] The
story, which Herodotus presumably heard later in Athens,
raises two difficulties. If the Persians surprised the three Greek
guardships off Skiathos, why did Phormos flee with his trireme
to the north, and why so far north as the mouth of the Peneios,
which is about 70 miles from Skiathos? Secondly, how could he
and his men make their way safely through Thessaly to Athens
if Thessaly was already occupied by Persian troops, as it must
have been if the Persian reconnaissance squadron had only a few
hours start of the main fleet?[3]

Hauvette and others[4] have tried to solve the first difficulty by
the supposition that the three guardships were in fact cruising
a long distance north of Skiathos, not very far from the mouth of
the Peneios, but this solution does too much violence to Herodotus. It flatly contradicts his statements that the guardships
were posted at Skiathos,[5] and it does not explain what purpose
would be served by making them cruise so far ahead of the
main fleet; in view of the superiority of Persian to Greek ships
in speed it would have been dangerous to post the three ships
so far north, for they would probably be intercepted by the
enemy before they could get back to Skiathos to give the alarm.
The alternative is to suppose that the guardships were for some
reason unaware of the oncoming Persian squadron until too
late, until their direct line of retreat from Skiathos to Artemision was blocked. Blakesley[6] suggested that the ten Persian ships

---

[1] viii. 96. 1.   [2] vii. 182; Hdt. tells the story in five lines.
[3] Which sailed from Therma eleven days after Xerxes' departure (cf. vii. 183. 2).
[4] Hauvette, 347 f. and Köster, 55 f.; cf. Macan, i. 269 A.
[5] vii. 179 and viii. 92. 1.   [6] ii. 289, n. 493 (on Hdt. vii. 182).

surprised the Greeks at Skiathos by approaching from the open sea to the east. Munro's first hypothesis,[1] that the Persians may have touched at Skyros on their way and then have approached Skiathos from the south-east, seems improbable, and is not proved by the presence on board the Persian ships of a Skyrian pilot named Pammon. More attractive is his later view,[2] that the Persians approached Skiathos under cover of night and perhaps surprised the Greek ships in the harbour at dawn, so that they were forced to flee northwards. Some such explanation must be adopted if Herodotus' account is correct, but it is surprising that an Athenian trireme could keep ahead of its pursuers, the swiftest ships in Xerxes' navy, during a chase of 70 miles which may have lasted eight hours or more.[3]

The story of Phormos has been reported by Herodotus with tantalizing brevity; after stating where he and his crew landed from their ship he merely adds that 'they passed through Thessaly and made their way to Athens', as though the journey presented nò difficulty. Yet only eight chapters earlier[4] he himself has described how the Thessalians had finally decided to side with the Persians, more than three months before the event recorded here. How could 200 Athenians, citizens of a state notoriously hostile to Xerxes, have traversed Thessaly in safety from the north-east corner of the country to its southern border, unless they had been helped by the connivance of the pro-Greek elements in Thessaly? If they returned to Athens by the main road to the south, they must clearly have done so before it was blocked by the advance of Xerxes' troops,[5] but if they made their way home by a devious route to the west they might have escaped from Thessaly at any time after the main Persian army had passed through it into Achaia and Malis.

It is, however, probable on other grounds that the ten swiftest Persian ships left Therma several days before the main fleet started its southward voyage. After a brief digression describing the impression made on the Greeks at Artemision by the fate of their three guardships Herodotus returns to the ten Persian

---

[1] In *J.H.S.* xxii, 1902, 308. For Pammon cf. Hdt. vii. 183. 3.

[2] *C.A.H.* iv. 285.

[3] On the speed of a single trireme see below, p. 168.

[4] vii. 174; see above, p. 103.

[5] This is the view of Macan (ii. 277); cf. Legrand, vii. 201, n. 3 and Labarbe 394, n. 2.

ships, saying that three of them sailed up to[1] a reef called
Myrmex (the Ant) situated in mid-channel between Skiathos
and Magnesia, about which they had received information
from Pammon of Skyros, and proceeded to mark it by a stone
pillar which they had brought with them for the purpose;[2]
this fact shows that they had intended all along to proceed
as far as Skiathos. But even while Herodotus is describing the
fixing of the pillar on the 'Ant', the barbarians engaged in this
task suddenly, before the main verb in the sentence is reached,
turn into the main body starting from Therma, just as at the
beginning of the story the main fleet of Xerxes had in the course
of a single sentence contracted into the ten scouting vessels.

Herodotus' tendency to confuse the advance of these ten ships
with that of the main fleet has led many to conclude that they
started from Therma on the same day, but after describing
the marking of the 'Ant' Herodotus goes on to say that the main
body[3] set sail from Therma 'now that the difficulties of the passage had been cleared away'. The natural inference from these
words is that the Persian navy did not start from Therma until
the ten scout ships had returned from Skiathos to headquarters
to report. Köster, calculating the distance from Therma to
Skiathos at 110 nautical miles, reasonably allows a total of
seven days for the mission of the ten ships, three days for their
journey each way and one day for the marking of the Myrmex.[4]
From this it follows that the original departure of the ten ships
from Therma must have been at least seven days before the
main fleet started. In the combined diary of the Persian army
and fleet, reconstructed by modern scholars from the indications
in Herodotus, the day on which the main fleet started from
Therma is Day 12, eleven days after Xerxes set out from Therma (Day 1); hence the sending of the ten ships from Therma
cannot have been later than Day 5 and may even be as early as
Day 1.[5]

[1] So Macaulay rightly translates ἐπήλασαν in vii. 183. 2; cf. Legrand, vii. 201,
n. 5. Macan changed his mind between i. 270 and ii. 276!

[2] κομίσαντες; cf. Legrand, 201, n. 6.

[3] This seems to be the meaning of αὐτοί in vii. 183. 2 (so Macaulay).

[4] Köster, 56 f. It is curious that the Greeks at Artemision did not interfere with
this operation (but this must not be used to prove that the Greek fleet had not
yet reached its station). Munro suggested that the Greeks mistook the three Persian vessels for their own guardships (*J.H.S.* xxii, 1902, 308).

[5] Cf. Munro, loc. cit.

This piece of evidence has to be ignored by those[1] who hold that the ten ships started at the same time as the main fleet. They seem to have been misled partly by the sentences with which Herodotus introduces and concludes his narrative of their exploits, in which he seems to confuse their voyage with that of the fleet as a whole, partly by his curious description of the effect which their capture of the three Greek guardships had on the Greeks stationed at Artemision.[2] In the digression already mentioned Herodotus tells how the news about the guardships was transmitted to Artemision by fire-signals from Skiathos, whereupon the Greeks in the fleet are said to have been so alarmed that they moved their anchorage from Artemision to Chalkis, intending to guard the Euripos, although they left some men behind to keep watch by day on the heights of Euboia. Consistently with this narrative Herodotus reports later[3] that the Athenians were at Chalkis at the time of the great storm which blew up after the start of the main Persian navy from Therma.

The capture of the three guardships is clearly quite inadequate as a cause for the panic which the signals from Skiathos are said to have produced in the Greek fleet. Köster ingeniously supposes[4] that the fire-signals were somehow misunderstood by the Greeks at Artemision, or that the scouts on Skiathos assumed overhastily that the main enemy fleet was approaching and sent out the wrong signals. Although the second suggestion seems far-fetched, the first is perhaps not impossible, for the communication of news by fire-signals was still in a very elementary stage.[5] But Köster's hypothesis requires him to maintain that the Greek fleet returned to Artemision as soon as its leaders discovered their mistake, some days before the storm, whereas Herodotus says later[6] that it did not return to Artemision until after the storm began. The beacons on Skiathos must have been prepared for use in a particular emergency, and it can hardly be doubted that the event of which early warning was to be given in this manner was the approach of the main Persian fleet. As Herodotus shows elsewhere a tendency to confuse the movements of the ten scout-ships with those of the main fleet, it is reasonable to assume that he has been guilty of the same

[1] e.g. Grundy, 322.   [2] vii. 183. 1.   [3] vii. 189. 2.
[4] Köster, 58 f.   [5] Labarbe, 393, n. 2, cf. HW 287.   [6] vii. 192.

confusion here, and that the news which was signalled from Skiathos was the advent of the great Persian armada;[1] if this assumption is correct, the alarm in the Greek fleet on the arrival of the news is sufficiently explained.

There is nothing in Herodotus to suggest that the panic was confined to the sailors and not shared by those in command.[2] He ascribes to the Greeks at Artemision an anxiety to retreat southwards on two other occasions,[3] after the arrival of the Persian fleet at Aphetai and after the third day of fighting on sea, but on the latter occasion the fleet does not begin to retire until it has received the news of Leonidas' defeat and death on land, and on the former occasion the admirals finally decide to stay where they are. Whatever truth there may be in the allegation that they contemplated flight on these two occasions, the fact remains that in both Herodotus describes unfulfilled intentions, unlike the withdrawal of the Greek fleet to Chalkis, which in his account is not an abortive proposal but a movement actually carried through to its conclusion;[4] the use of the imperfect tense of the verb to describe the movement is not to be interpreted as meaning merely that the Greeks intended to or began to change their anchorage, for Herodotus believes that the Athenian ships at least were present in the harbour of Chalkis while the storm was raging.[5]

Herodotus makes three distinct statements here, that panic caused the Greeks at Artemision to retire, that the whole fleet abandoned its station, and that it retired as far as Chalkis. Some have rejected all three statements as manifestly unhistorical,[6] and most scholars would probably agree that at least two of the three must be inaccurate. Even if Herodotus' motive for the retirement is dropped, what remains cannot be accepted as it stands. The obvious objection to it is that Herodotus here ignores the necessary connexion between the Greek positions on land and sea; while Leonidas and his army remained at Thermopylai the Greek admirals could not have imperilled his force by a retirement with their whole fleet as far as Chalkis.

---

[1] The meaning of ταῦτα (first word in vii. 183) is astonishingly vague.
[2] The explanation of Grote, criticized by Bury, *B.S.A.* ii, 1895-6, 86.
[3] viii. 4. 1 and viii. 18.   [4] Cf. Bury, 87 f.
[5] vii. 189. 2; on μετορμίζοντο (vii. 183. 1) see Macan, ad loc.
[6] e.g. Obst, 96 ff. and Macan, i. 269 B (but in ii. 276 ff. he adopted Grundy's explanation; see below, p. 165).

Kromayer[1] tries to defend Herodotus; while admitting that the retirement as described by him was contrary to sound reason he pleads that panic is essentially unreasonable. But however great the panic may have been it is hard to believe that a Spartan admiral in supreme command of the confederate fleet would have ventured to leave the position assigned to him when by retirement he would expose to almost certain destruction an army commanded by a Spartan king and made up for the most part of contingents from Peloponnese. Hence those who agree with Herodotus that some movement of ships from Artemision took place at this juncture usually correct his account by adopting one of two alternative assumptions: on the first, the whole fleet was withdrawn from Artemision but did not retire far enough to uncover Leonidas' position; on the second, most of the fleet remained at Artemision but part of it was sent back to Chalkis after and in consequence of the message received from Skiathos.

The second view was persuasively argued by Bury. He insisted that some actual movement of ships was presupposed by the Herodotean narrative, and found a clue to it in the unexplained arrival of fifty-three Athenian ships at Artemision on the morning after the first sea-fight.[2] On Bury's hypothesis these ships had been with the main fleet at the start, but had later been sent to Chalkis to guard the Euripos at its narrowest point against a possible enemy attack from the south; they had been detached for this service on receipt of the fire-signals from Skiathos, which must have been sent not to report the approach of the Persian main fleet but (so Bury supposed) to warn the Greeks that the enemy had detached a squadron to circumnavigate Euboia and so attack the Greek fleet from the rear.

At first sight this hypothesis seems to clear up tidily a number of loose ends, but like so many modern reconstructions of this type it leaves other loose ends still in the air. The alleged Persian circumnavigation of Euboia is far from certain, although Herodotus records it without misgivings,[3] but even if it is accepted other difficulties remain. Why did Herodotus say that the whole Greek fleet left Artemision if in reality only fifty-three

---

[1] *Schlachtenatlas*, iv, col. 5.   [2] viii. 14. 1. Cf. Bury, 88 f.
[3] See below, Appendix VI.

ships did so? The suggestion[1] that his information about the
Greek fleet was derived exclusively from Athenians who had
been aboard one or more of the fifty-three ships is unconvincing;
not only does it presume in Herodotus a serious lapse from his
usual practice of collecting information from several sources, but
it fails to account for his statement[2] that the fleet returned to
Artemision on the day after the storm began. This cannot have
been derived from an informant on one of the fifty-three ships,
for on Bury's view these ships were still at Chalkis after the day
in question. And if the object of the Greek admiral in sending
them to Chalkis was to hold up the Persian squadron at the
Euripos, why did he think it necessary to send so many ships,
practically one-sixth of his entire fleet? As the Euripos at Chalkis
is only 40 yards wide,[3] surely a much smaller force would have
sufficed to block the Persian advance there. When Herodotus
reports the arrival of the fifty-three ships at Artemision he gives
no hint that they had previously been watching the Euripos at
Chalkis; this is an extraordinary omission if he had obtained his
information from one or more Athenians who had been with the
fifty-three ships throughout the campaign.

On the alternative view, maintained by Grundy[4] and others,
Herodotus is right in making the whole Greek fleet retire from
Artemision for a time, but wrong in attributing its retirement to
panic; the true explanation of this withdrawal is to be found in
the approach of the gale from the north-east, which decided the
Greeks to move to a less exposed position until the gale had
blown itself out. The defenders of this view also disagree with
Herodotus' statement that the fleet retreated as far as Chalkis.
Grundy thinks[5] that it may have retired to 'the shelter of the
great cliffs of Mount Kandili, in the neighbourhood of the
modern Limni'; in this position it would be far to the east of
Thermopylai, and Grundy has to make the further assumption[6]
that Leonidas had been duly informed of the fleet's intention to
return as soon as the gale dropped. Macan, who after rejecting
Herodotus' account as unhistorical in his first volume gave a
cautious assent in his second to Grundy's hypothesis, denies

---

[1] Made by Munro in *C.A.H.* iv. 284.   [2] vii. 192. 1–2.
[3] See above, p. 153.
[4] Grundy, 323 ff.; cf. Giannelli, 10 ff., especially 12 and note.
[5] Op. cit., note on p. 325.   [6] Op. cit. 324.

bluntly[1] that Thermopylai could have been left exposed on the sea side, and will only admit that the Greek fleet may have moved down the channel at Oreos to gain shelter from the storm.

Herodotus cannot be right in his assertion that the whole fleet retired all the way to Chalkis, and Grundy's suggestion that it withdrew as far as Limni is almost as difficult; if Herodotus has blundered in attributing to the Greeks a withdrawal so far as Chalkis from their original position, nothing is gained by attempts to minimize his error. The fundamental weakness of Grundy's view, promptly pointed out by those who preferred Bury's, is that he never explains why the Greek fleet needed to be afloat when the storm burst, or why, even if it was, it needed to retire so far. Grundy[2] insisted on the 'astonishing suddenness' with which north-easterly gales spring up in the North Aegean, giving 'little or no warning of their approach', but if the Greek admirals had time enough to run before the storm into the inner strait they ought to have had time to beach their ships on the shores of Pevki Bay.[3] As Munro urged,[4] even if the Greek ships were afloat, there was fair shelter on Artemision beach and complete safety in the harbour of Histiaia (Oreos).

Herodotus says definitely that the whole Greek fleet retired from Artemision for a time, and also that it retired all the way to Chalkis. Of these two statements the second must be false, but the first is not necessarily impossible, in spite of the difficulties raised by Grundy's attempt to explain it. Obst asserts that it must be unhistorical but makes no serious effort to justify his assertion;[5] in particular he ignores the fact that Herodotus here attributes a definite retreat to the Greeks, whereas in the two parallel passages he speaks merely of an unfulfilled intention to do so. If the fleet did retire, could it have withdrawn merely to the harbour of Histiaia? The position at Artemision,

---

[1] Macan, ii. 277; on the next page he approaches more nearly to Grundy's view in the suggestion that the Greek fleet may have shifted its moorings 'perhaps round the cape *Lithada* into the channel of *Atalanti*'.

[2] Op. cit. 324.   [3] Macan, i. 285 B; cf. Obst, 96 f.

[4] In *J.H.S.* xxii, 1902, 309, n. 25 (so editors of Grote in abridged ed., n. 1. on p. 199). This objection is valid (in spite of Macan, ii. 278) even if the gale was blowing straight up the Oreos channel.

[5] He merely refers (97, n. 4) to Grundy, 332 f., but Grundy is there concerned with Hdt. viii. 4 and viii. 18. Obst is, however, justified in his criticism of Grundy's 'explanation' of Hdt. vii. 183. 1.

essential for the defence of North Euboia, was inconveniently
remote from any centre of population. While the storm was
raging and for a day after the Persians would be in no state to
land troops in Euboia, and the Greek admirals perhaps decided
on a temporary withdrawal to a station where anchorage would
be safer and supplies more abundant, so that the sailors could
be refreshed and heartened for the impending struggle. If this
explanation is correct, the Greek fleet presumably returned to
its station after the storm abated, probably on the day before
the Persian fleet arrived at Aphetai. Herodotus' narrative clearly
implies that the Greek navy had returned to Artemision before
the Persians reached Aphetai, and the grounds on which this
implication has been challenged are insufficient to disprove it.[1]

The advance of the Persian navy from Therma and the great storm

The narrative given by Herodotus[2] of the voyage and the
storm is interrupted near the start by a long digression, in which
he endeavours to estimate the size of the Persian forces on land
and sea before the fighting began, and by minor digressions
later; if these are omitted the essential elements in his account
can be stated briefly. Eleven days after Xerxes' departure the
fleet set out from Therma, and after sailing all day reached
Sepias and the beach lying between the town of Kasthanaia
and the promontory of Sepias;[3] the ships that arrived first were
moored to the land, but as the beach was small the rest were
anchored farther out towards the sea in eight rows. Early on
the next morning a gale from the east began to blow with great
force. Some of the Persians were able to beach their ships in
time, but those ships which were caught on the open sea by the
storm were driven ashore at various places with heavy loss, not
less than 400 warships[4] on the lowest estimate, in addition to a
vast number of provision ships and other craft. The storm raged
for three days but stopped on the fourth. Meanwhile the Greek
fleet had returned to its station at Artemision.

There are three indications of time in this narrative, but the

---

[1] See below, pp. 179 f.   [2] vii. 183. 2–195.   [3] vii. 183. 3; cf. 188. 1.
[4] The νέας in the first line of vii. 190 are clearly warships; see below, p. 172.

first,[1] though precise, is unhelpful in this context, and the other two both raise difficulties. In particular the statement that the Persian fleet traversed the distance from Therma to Sepias in a single day[2] cannot be accepted. The voyage by the shortest distance across the open sea would be between 90 and 100 miles,[3] and Tarn has proved conclusively by an examination of the available evidence on the speeds of ancient warships and fleets that although a single warship might under favourable conditions average 8 miles an hour the maximum speed achieved by an ancient fleet was not more than 5 miles an hour.[4] Ephoros was perhaps conscious of this difficulty when he made Pydna the starting-point of the voyage,[5] thereby shortening to about 70 miles the distance covered in one day, but Herodotus says explicitly[6] that the fleet started from Therma, thereby agreeing with his previous observation that it was stationed at Therma and the towns between Therma and the Axios.

Herodotus may, however, be wrong in his assumption that the whole Persian navy sailed in a body from Therma. Even if it numbered only 600 vessels it must have been divided into smaller and more manageable units,[7] and some of these may have been moved forward earlier to advanced bases in the harbours on the peninsula of Pallene, from which the voyage to the Magnesian coast would be appreciably shorter than from Therma. Provided that the various squadrons of the Persian fleet arrived simultaneously at their goal it was not necessary that all should start at the same time. It is a possible hypothesis[8] that one or more squadrons sailing from Skione and neighbouring ports started early on the day before the storm, whereas the squadrons that had to come from Therma or near it set sail

---

[1] vii. 183. 2, that the fleet began its voyage eleven days after Xerxes set out from Therma.

[2] vii. 183. 3.   [3] Cf. HW 210.

[4] *C.R.* xxiii, 1909, 184–6 (the volume is incorrectly dated 1910 on the title-page). For a useful summary of Tarn's arguments see HW 210 f. A special problem is posed by the voyage of Aemilius Paulus described in Livy xlv. 41. 3.

[5] Diod. xi. 12. 3. Labarbe in *B.C.H.* lxxvi, 1952, 395, n. 2 thinks Pydna may have been a stage on the voyage, but it is dangerous to attach importance to the evidence of Ephoros on such a point.

[6] vii. 179 (l. 1) and 183. 2; cf. vii. 124.

[7] Cf. Tarn in *J.H.S.* xxviii, 1908, 206. Such subdivision of the fleet would be facilitated by its territorial organization.

[8] So Munro in *C.A.H.* iv. 284 f. (but it is unnecessary to assume that the famous diver Skyllias must have embarked on the Persian fleet at his native Skione).

a day or two before, and that Herodotus mistakenly conflated
these two facts into a single statement. Recent writers,[1] reacting
vigorously against his assertion that the voyage from Therma to
Sepias was accomplished by the whole fleet in a single day, have
claimed that it could not have taken less than three days. This
is a reasonable estimate for the whole fleet, but if only part of it
had to cover the full distance from the head of the Thermaic
Gulf it is just possible that it did so in two days. The Persian
admirals must have realized that this was the most difficult
stretch of their journey and may have instructed the squadrons
concerned to exert themselves to the utmost in order to cover it
as quickly as possible.

Herodotus says[2] that the ships wrecked by the storm were
driven ashore at five places, the Ipnoi (Ovens) at Pelion, the
beach where the fleet was stationed, Sepias itself, the city of
Meliboia, and Kasthanaia. These places are not mentioned in
geographical order, for the northernmost is Meliboia and the
southernmost Sepias, by which Herodotus apparently means
the promontory of Sepias which he has mentioned earlier. A
passage in Livy[3] indicates that Meliboia lay at the foot of the
southern slopes of Mount Ossa, and an inscription has fixed its
position at the modern Thanátu. The 'Ovens' are usually taken
to be the cliffs of Cape Pori, which is formed by a projecting
spur of Mount Pelion. There has been disagreement about the
site of Kasthanaia, but since Strabo[4] describes it as a village
lying under Pelion it must be either Zagorá, which lies close
under the highest summit of Pelion, or its port Khoreftó; the
identification with Zagorá has been supported by the existence
of numerous chestnut-trees (κάστανοι) in the neighbourhood.[5]
Cape Sepias is most probably the rather blunt headland on the
mainland opposite Skiathos, just before the coast of Magnesia
begins to turn towards the south-west, the point now known as
Kato Georgi; Wace's proposal[6] to identify Sepias with Cape
Pori cannot be accepted.

The fifth place mentioned by Herodotus is the beach at or off

---

[1] e.g. Tarn (op. cit.), 213 f., also Köster, 61 and 56; Labarbe, 395, n. 2 speaks of
'2 or 3' days.

[2] vii. 188. 3; cf. the valuable discussion in Tarn (op. cit.), 210 ff. (with map).

[3] xliv. 13. 1–3; cf. Macan, i. 279 A.   [4] ix. 5. 22 (p. 443).

[5] So the local tradition heard by Tozer at Zagorá (Tarn, op. cit. 210, n. 37).

[6] *J.H.S.* xxvi, 1906, 145 ff.

which, according to his account, the whole Persian fleet anchored on the night before the great storm. This beach is twice
described[1] as lying between the city of Kasthanaia and the
Sepiad promontory, but this description cannot be assumed
to mean that the beach extended all along the shore from
Kasthanaia to Sepias;[2] not only is there no such beach in existence now but Herodotus insists that the beach was small, so
small that the greater part of the Persian fleet had to be moored
out to sea in eight rows. In this sentence he says that the Persian
ships were anchored πρόκροσσαι; the word echoes a passage in
the *Iliad*[3] where Homer is explaining the arrangement of the
Greek ships in the naval camp before Troy. According to the
most probable interpretation of the Homeric passage[4] the ships
of the Achaian chieftains were drawn up on the shore, and
therefore farthest from the battle, whereas the rampart round
the naval camp was built close to the sterns of these ships which
were drawn farthest to the plain; although the beach was large
it was not large enough to contain all the ships (presumably
not large enough to contain them all if they were drawn up in
a single line along the shore) and so the Achaians had drawn
up their ships πρόκρόσσας. The reason given by Homer for this
arrangement strongly supports the meaning 'in rows' for the
word; it could not have been used by him to mean 'with their
prows facing the sea' and there is no need to suppose that
Herodotus read this meaning into it.[5] The translation 'ranged
in regular intervals' (and so in a row) suits his use of the word
here and in the other passage in Herodotus where it occurs,[6]
describing the heads of griffins 'set at regular intervals' round
a cup.

Herodotus clearly had the Homeric passage in mind when he
described the anchorage of the Persian fleet, but the circumstances were different, for whereas the Achaian ships were
drawn up on dry land the Persian ships were afloat, anchored in

---

[1] vii. 183. 3 and 188. 1.

[2] In spite of Macan's note on αἰγιαλός (n. on vii. 188, l. 15).

[3] xiv. 30–36.

[4] That of D. B. Monro in his school edition of the *Iliad* (3rd ed., revised, 1893),
Books xiii–xxiv (note that he read πρύμνῃσιν in l. 32, not πρυμνῇσιν).

[5] See Monro's note on *Iliad* xiv. 35. It is significant that Herodotus here makes
πρόκροσσος an adjective of three terminations, as in the Homeric passage, whereas
in Hdt. iv. 152. 4 it has only two.

[6] iv. 152. 4.

eight rows off the shore, and the number of rows is a detail not found in Homer. Also the beach in Homer is wide, though not wide enough to hold all the Achaian fleet, but in Herodotus the beach is 'not large'. The supreme difficulty, emphasized by Tarn, is that there is no single beach on the rocky shores between Khoreftó and Kato Georgi which satisfies Herodotus' description of the strand at which the Persian fleet is said to have anchored. Instead there are on this coast a few small beaches, starting with that at Khoreftó,[1] and it has been suggested that the Persian fleet was in reality strung out along all these beaches; if this was so, Herodotus misunderstood his informants. Another hypothesis is that the level of the Mediterranean has risen since 480 and that there may then have been a beach, now submerged by the sea, such as that presupposed by Herodotus.[2]

These explanations, as Tarn pointed out, are inconsistent with the fact that some of the wreckage was driven ashore as far north as Thanátu. The 'Hellespontine' wind which brought the storm, though identified by Herodotus[3] with the Apeliotes or east wind, should rather be equated with a north-east or east-north-east wind, and if the Persian fleet had been anchored at sea off the coast between Khoreftó and Kato Georgi such a wind ought to have driven every ship that was wrecked straight on to the adjacent shore;[4] if some of the wrecked ships were driven ashore as far north as Thanátu it could only have been because they had not yet passed that point on their voyage. If the Persian admirals knew that the squadrons sailing from Therma could not on that particular day (whether it was the second or third day out from Therma[5]) hope to reach the strait between Magnesia and Euboia before nightfall, they must surely have arranged for their ships to anchor at a number of different stations along the Magnesian coast, since the few beaches were each too small to contain a large number of ships, and on the other hand it was desirable that as many as possible of the crews of the triremes should be able to land in order to

[1] It seems hypercritical to exclude this beach from those 'between Kasthanaia and Cape Sepias' with Tarn (op. cit.), 212.

[2] Cf. Tarn, 212. The hypothesis reappears in modern discussions of the topography of Salamis; see below, p. 398.

[3] vii. 188. 2. Cf. Macan (ad loc.) and Grundy, 325.

[4] Tarn, 213.

[5] See above, p. 169.

prepare a meal and get a proper sleep,[1] especially as they might have to fight the main Greek fleet on the next day.

So far the Herodotean account seems vulnerable to criticism. It must also be admitted that there are clear traces of exaggeration in the duration attributed to the storm and in the losses which it is said to have inflicted on the Persian ships. The storm, which came from the north-east quarter, is alleged to have lasted three days and three nights, but according to a proverb quoted by Aristotle in the *Problemata*[2], even in the winter a gale from the north never lasted for more than two days. It is therefore likely that the storm blew itself out on the day after it started,[3] and that the Persians were able to resume their voyage on the second day after that on which the storm began, not, as Herodotus says, on the third.

Herodotus[4] gives 400 as the lowest estimate known to him for the ships lost by the Persians in the storm; he had therefore heard other accounts which gave a higher total. He interrupts his narrative at this point by a digression[5] on Ameinokles of Magnesia and the wealth he had gained from precious objects washed ashore, and when the story is resumed Herodotus says that no estimate existed for the shipwrecked provision-ships and other vessels. Hence the 400 ships of the first passage must be warships, and this interpretation is confirmed by a later passage[6] which represents the loss of 400 ships wrecked in the storm as a deduction from the original strength of the Persian navy. As Herodotus believed that its strength at Therma was 1,207 (or perhaps 1,327)[7] triremes, he naturally found no difficulty in the report that it had lost 400 of them in the great storm (as well as a further 200 off Euboia in a later storm), but modern writers have usually been more sceptical.[8] The extreme hypothesis, propounded by Munro,[9] is that the great majority of the Persian warships got safely round the heel of Magnesia before the storm

---

[1] There were no facilities for either on board ancient triremes; cf. Gomme, *Essays*, 193.

[2] xxvi. 9 (= 941ᵃ20); cf. Macan, i. 282 and HW 216. Köster accepts the evidence of Herodotus on the duration of the storm.

[3] Munro (in *C.A.H.* iv. 287) allows only twenty-four hours for the storm.

[4] vii. 190 (first sentence).

[5] It is hardly necessary to suppose (with Macan, i. 282 B and HW 215) that this digression is later than the original draft.

[6] vii. 236. 2.   [7] Cf. Tarn, 203 f.

[8] Köster, 63 is an exception.   [9] In *C.A.H.* iv. 287.

began, although the rearguard may have been caught too far
north.

Macan and Tarn had already minimized the damage done
by the storm to the Persian warships off the Magnesian coast.[1]
Macan suggested that the principal losses were sustained by the
merchant ships, which were presumably moving up behind the
squadrons of the fleet and were caught by the gale in the open
sea when the storm began. Tarn believed that a considerable
part of the Persian fleet was wrecked by the storm, but he held
that the main loss was sustained by the ships sent to circumnavigate Euboia; these he estimated at 120, one-fifth of his
total for the whole Persian navy, and like Bury he assumed that
they had been detached from the rest before the gale began.
The fact that the Persian admirals numbered their ships after
their arrival at Aphetai[2] was accepted by Tarn as evidence
that the main fleet must have suffered some loss in triremes off
Magnesia during the storm, but he ascribed to a poetical
source the exaggerated figure given for these losses by Herodotus. He argued that as the triremes had been anchored close
to the land during the night it would have been possible to
draw them to safety on shore before the full force of the storm
broke, since the storm gave a warning of its imminence which
many of the captains in the Persian fleet must have understood.
Herodotus, however, in the passage on which Tarn's argument
seems to be based,[3] merely says that at dawn, after a period of
cloudless and windless weather, the sea began to boil and the
tempest fell on the Persians, and Grundy, who was well acquainted with summer conditions in this part of Greece, speaks
of the astonishing suddenness with which such storms spring up
in these seas, giving little or no warning of their approach.[4]
If this is correct, many of the Persian warships may have been
struck by the gale before there had been time to drag them
ashore.

Tarn took over from Herodotus, as most English scholars
have done, the tradition that the Persians tried to attack the
Greek fleet from the rear by sending a large squadron to sail
round Euboia, though, like many of his predecessors, he found
himself compelled to reject Herodotus' statements concerning

---

[1] Macan, i. 282 ; Tarn, 213 and 215.
[2] viii. 7. 2 (last sentence) ; cf. Tarn, 215.   [3] vii. 188. 2.   [4] Grundy, 324.

the time and place at which this squadron was detached from
the main fleet. But the alleged Persian circumnavigation of Euboia, although repeated in good faith by Herodotus, is almost
certainly false,[1] and any hypothesis which is based on it must
break down somewhere. Tarn's estimate of 600 triremes for
the original Persian fleet may well be correct, but it follows
that if 120 of them were lost round Euboia there could not have
been many wrecked off the Magnesian coast, on Tarn's calculation that before the fighting began at Artemision the reorganized
Persian fleet numbered not more than 450 triremes and possibly
less. In the end Tarn estimated the losses of the main fleet in
the storm at between 20 and 30 triremes.[2]

Four hundred is a more probable figure than 450 for the
Persian triremes which survived the storm, a figure which does
not include the 15 intercepted on their way to Aphetai by
the Greeks.[3] If the original fleet was composed of 600 triremes,
and if the tradition of heavy losses in an attempted circumnavigation of Euboia is rejected as a baseless invention, the
conclusion must be that over 180 Persian warships, nearly one-
third of their whole fleet, were wrecked off the Magnesian coast
by the gale. Perhaps the real content of the report which Herodotus regarded as the most credible of those he had heard was
precisely that one-third of the warships had perished in the
storm; as he believed that the original fleet numbered 1,207
he reproduced this in the form that the Persians lost 400 ships.
If the exaggerated estimates in Herodotus are ignored, it may
well be true that the losses sustained by the Persians in the great
storm amounted to nearly one-third of their fleet.[4] Herodotus,
in the chapter which describes the capture of the fifteen Persian
ships left behind by the rest on the last stage of the voyage to
Aphetai, notes that one of the captives was Penthylos, the commander of the twelve ships sent by Paphos in Cyprus, and that
the ship on which he was sailing was the sole survivor of the
Paphian squadron, the other eleven having been wrecked in the
storm.[5] Tarn dismisses this account on the assumption that it
was derived from the poetical source which on his view was

---

[1] See below, Appendix VI.   [2] Tarn, 216.   [3] vii. 194.
[4] Cf. Grundy, 325 ('the loss relatively to the size of the fleet seems to have been
very considerable').
[5] The significance of this evidence was pointed out by Hauvette, 349.

responsible for the other errors detected by him in this part of
Herodotus' narrative,[1] but the report is not suspicious on internal grounds, and the detail about the Paphian losses could
have been part of the information which the Greeks obtained
from their prisoners before they sent them off to Corinth.[2]

There are other indications that the storm must have inflicted heavy losses on the Persian fleet. The story that the Delphians had been commanded by Apollo to pray to the winds,[3]
even if it is a fiction invented after the event by the Delphic
priests, proves that the winds had given powerful aid to the
Greek cause. The same conclusion is to be drawn from the
similar story that the Athenians, on the bidding of an oracle
urging them to call for help on their son-in-law, had prayed to
Boreas,[4] who according to the legend had taken for his bride
Oreithyia, daughter of the Athenian king Erechtheus. After the
war the Athenians built a temple to Boreas on the banks of the
Ilissos, while the Delphians set up an altar to the winds and
offered sacrifice to them. There were doubtless ancient cults of
the winds in both places, but their revival after the war must be
significant of the part played by the winds in the Greek victory.
If the Persian admirals had been able to bring the whole of
their original fleet safely to Aphetai they might have overwhelmed the Greek resistance by mere weight of numbers. The
heavy losses which they sustained in the gale so reduced their
strength that they no longer had a crushing superiority over the
Greek fleet; in the words of Herodotus,[5] 'all this was brought
about by God in order that the Persian fleet might be made
more equal to that of the Greeks and might not be very much
the larger.' Natives of the British Isles will be reminded of the
fate of the Spanish Armada and the inscription on the medal
struck to commemorate its dispersal: FLAVIT ET DISSIPATI SVNT.[6]

The arrival of the Persian fleet at Aphetai and the battles off Artemision

If the storm blew itself out on the day after it started, it is
possible that the Persian fleet was able to resume its voyage on

---

[1] Tarn, 215 f.   [2] vii. 195 (last sentence).   [3] vii. 178; see above, p. 157.
[4] vii. 189; cf. HW 215.   [5] viii. 13 (last sentence).
[6] Modern works give other forms of this inscription; that in the text is taken from
a medal (struck at Middelburg, Holland) in the Ashmolean Museum, Oxford.

the early morning of the next day,[1] about forty-eight hours after
the storm began. Sailing close to the shore it rounded the heel
of Magnesia and anchored at Aphetai,[2] apparently arriving
there early on the afternoon of the same day. Aphetai is described by Herodotus as a place in Magnesia,[3] the last port at
which the Argonauts touched before beginning their voyage
across the open sea, and is probably to be identified with some
point on the south coast of the Magnesian peninsula. Herodotus
has complicated the problem by his statement[4] that the Persian fleet after rounding the promontory of Magnesia sailed
straight into the gulf which leads towards Pagasai, which ought
to mean that Aphetai was at some point in Magnesia just inside
the Gulf of Pagasai (the modern Gulf of Volo) and beyond the
Aiantian promontory.[5] It is true that to reach this point the
Persians would have had to pass the Greek position at a distance of only 5 or 6 miles, but there was no reason why the
Greek admirals should have been unwilling to allow them to do
so;[6] the Gulf of Pagasai was a cul-de-sac, and if the Persians
wished to outflank the Greek land force with their fleet they
would have to sail out of the gulf again southwards, whereupon the Greeks could have attacked them in flank near the
entrance, a little north of Histiaia, to the narrow strait which
here separates Euboia from the mainland to the west. The
identification of Aphetai with a site inside the Gulf of Pagasai
is nevertheless ruled out by the rest of the evidence, and the
passage which suggests it can perhaps be explained in some
other way. It can hardly have been intended by Herodotus to
mean 'the gulf that leads to the Gulf of Pagasai', but perhaps
he regarded the channel north of Euboia and the Gulf of
Pagasai as one continuous gulf. The alternative is to suppose
that Herodotus here misunderstood what his informants told him.

Herodotus elsewhere indicates for Aphetai a site on the south
coast of Magnesia. He remarks incidentally, much later in his
narrative,[7] that Aphetai was about 80 stades from Artemision.

---

[1] Day 16 of the 'Diary'; see above, p. 172.

[2] vii. 193; on the time of its arrival at Aphetai cf. viii. 6. 1.

[3] In the first clause of vii. 193. 2, on the assumption that τῆς Μαγνησίας goes
closely with χῶρος.   [4] vii. 193. 1.   [5] Now Cape Kavoulia.

[6] In spite of Wace (*J.H.S.* xxiv, 1906, 146). The objection made to Wace's view
by Gomme (*J.H.S.* liii, 1933, 22 = *Essays*, 197) misses the real difficulty.

[7] viii. 8. 2.

If the latter is correctly located at Pevki Bay, Aphetai must be one of the harbours in the southern part of Magnesia facing the Greek position, and Herodotus clearly implies[1] that the Persian fleet at Aphetai and the Greek at Artemision were in full view of each other. There are only two sizeable harbours in this stretch of the Magnesian coast, that of Plataniá, a little way past Cape Sepias to the south-west, and that of Olizon, farther to the west, at the narrowest point of the peninsula; Plataniá is the better harbour and has a good water supply (which Olizon has not) and has been identified with Aphetai by modern scholars who have studied the question on the spot.[2] Kromayer[3] points out that the Gulf of Olizon has only a limited sandy beach which could not have contained the whole Persian fleet and that this is also true of the Bay of Plataniá. There are indications that the Persian fleet was strung out in several positions along the coast; it has been suggested that Aphetai was the headquarters of the Persian admirals and the centre for repairs.[4]

Fifteen of the Persian ships failed to reach their new anchorage. They had put out to sea much later than the rest,[5] and when they saw the Greek ships at Artemision they mistook them for their own fleet and sailed towards them, whereupon the Greeks, realizing what had happened, put out to meet them and captured them all. This squadron included the Paphian ship of Penthylos already mentioned[6] and another supplied by the tyrant of Alabanda in Karia, and may have been composed of ships which had not been ready to start with the rest. It was under the command, perhaps only temporary, of Sandokes, a Persian of high rank who as governor of Aiolis seems to have been subordinate to the satrap of Hellespontine Phrygia.[7]

The story of the capture of this squadron is perplexing, especially if it sailed close to the shore, as the rest of the fleet had done; those who make it put out to the open sea[8] have simply mistranslated Herodotus. Grundy supposes that the main

---

[1] viii. 4. 1 and 6. 1 ; cf. Wace , 146.

[2] Wace, 146 and Fabricius in *Gnomon*, ii, 1926, 13 ff. cf. *A.S.* iv. 582. Fabricius, 13 dismisses as an 'interpolated passage' the description of Aphetai as near Pagasai (or Iolkos) in Strabo 436.

[3] *Schlachtenatlas*, iv. 1, col. 4 and n. 1.

[4] Köster, 65; on the positions of the Persian fleet see below, p. 185.

[5] vii. 194. 1 (first sentence) correctly translated by Macaulay.

[6] See above, p. 174.   [7] Cf. Macan, i. 288.

[8] Baehr, followed by Macan (ad loc.), refuted by Giannelli, 11, n. 2.

Persian fleet must have already entered the Gulf of Pagasai and so have been out of sight when the fifteen ships entered the channel,[1] but this explanation is based on his erroneous identification of Aphetai with a site inside the Gulf. It is possible that the rest of the Persian ships had already reached their stations and been hauled ashore, but even if night was approaching when the fifteen ships came in sight[2] their mistake remains mysterious; if they were hugging the Magnesian coast how could they suppose that a fleet stationed some miles away across the open strait was their own? Herodotus' account here is too condensed to be completely intelligible, but it affords no justification for the extraordinary hypothesis, based on a faulty chronology, that would identify the capture of these fifteen ships with the first sea-fight off Artemision, which was really fought two days later.[3]

If Herodotus' account of the incident of the fifteen ships is correct, the Greeks must have been back at Artemision by late afternoon of the day on which the Persian fleet reached Aphetai. Some have maintained that they did not arrive until after midday of that day, Day 16 of the Diary;[4] this contention is not only unnecessary but also at variance with the indications in Herodotus. In the crucial passage[5] he says that the day-watchers ran down from the heights of Euboia (presumably the heights above Artemision), where they had been posted by the Greek admirals on their earlier withdrawal, on the day after the storm began,[6] and reported the shipwreck of the Persian fleet, whereupon the Greeks returned to Artemision. Herodotus supposes them to have been at Chalkis when they received the report, but if they had merely retired to Histiaia[7] they could have returned to their original station on the afternoon of the same day, or they may have started at dawn on the following day, the day on which the Persians resumed their voyage. Anyhow, Herodotus certainly implies[8] that they were back in time to see the Persians arriving at Aphetai and that the

---

[1] Grundy, 327; cf. the location of Aphetai on his map (facing p. 266). The evidence in Strabo 436 ('near Pagasai') is worthless.

[2] As supposed by Giannelli, 11.   [3] See below, Appendix V.

[4] e.g. Giannelli, 11; cf. Kromayer, *Schlachtenatlas*, iv. 1, col. 4.

[5] vii. 192. 1; cf. 183. 1 for the posting of the ἡμεροσκόποι.

[6] This must be the meaning of the relevant sentence in vii. 192. 1, but the text may be corrupt; cf. Macan's note (ad loc.) for the difficulties.

[7] See above, pp. 166 f.   [8] viii. 4. 1 and 6. 1.

Persians on their arrival found the Greeks already at Artemision.

Three notes of time given incidentally by Herodotus in three
different and widely separated contexts[1] presuppose, when
combined, that the Persian army arrived at Thermopylai two
days before the fleet anchored at Aphetai, and that the first
sea-fight, which coincided with the first day's fighting on land,
was fought two days after the day on which the fleet reached
Aphetai. Several scholars have been unable to understand why
the Greeks should have allowed the battered Persian fleet two
whole days in which to rest and recover from the damage sustained in the storm, but they diverge in their explanations of the
supposed crux. Some have rejected one or more of the chronological notices in Herodotus and have assumed that the late
afternoon when the Greeks made their first attack[2] and the early
afternoon when the Persians arrived at Aphetai[3] belong to the
same day. Those who hold this view, including Bury, naturally
find no difficulty in Herodotus' plain implication that the Greek
fleet was already back at Artemision when the Persian appeared
off the southern coast of Magnesia; Bury indeed believes that
the bulk of the Greek fleet had never left Artemision and that
the account in Herodotus introduced to explain its return is
for the most part pure fiction.[4] Others, who accept the chronology indicated by Herodotus, conclude that the Greek fleet lost
the precious opportunity to attack the Persians on their voyage
to Aphetai because it had not yet returned to Artemision. Giannelli tries to extract this conclusion from the passage in Herodotus[5] when he says that the Persians had previously heard of
of the presence at Artemision of 'a few Greek ships' and that
when they saw the ships for themselves on their arrival they
were eager to attack. What they saw, says Giannelli, was only a
small vanguard, for the main body of the Greek fleet was at the
time just emerging from the Malian Gulf. But other passages
in Herodotus prove that the whole Greek fleet had already
returned to its station,[6] and the reference to the 'few Greek
ships' in the passage cited by Giannelli is simply a product of

---

[1] vii. 196, vii. 210. 1, and viii. 15. 1; see below, Appendix V.
[2] viii. 9 (δείλη ὀψίη).   [3] viii. 6. 1. (δείλη πρωίη).
[4] B.S.A. ii, 1895–6, 94.   [5] viii. 6. 1; cf. Giannelli, 15, n. 3.
[6] vii. 192, viii. 4. 1.

Herodotus' conviction that the Persian ships were vastly superior in number to the Greek, and therefore likely to despise the
smaller forces of their opponents.[1]

A passage in the eighth book of Herodotus[2] has been interpreted by Kromayer and others to mean that the Greeks on their
return to Artemision found the Persians already installed at
Aphetai; but ἀπικόμενοι must there be translated 'those who
had come to Artemision',[3] as described in the seventh book,
where Herodotus has indicated with sufficient clarity, by the
order in which he has narrated the events, that the Greeks were
back at Artemision before the Persians appeared in sight.
Kromayer[4] argues that this cannot be right, for if the Greeks had
already returned to Artemision the Persian fleet after its heavy
losses would never have dared to continue its voyage to Aphetai
in face of the Greek fleet, while the Greeks would never have let
slip such a favourable opportunity to attack. Yet a few lines
later Kromayer himself, describing the character of the fighting
at Artemision during the first two days, explains it by the statement that the Greeks 'still did not feel themselves a match for
the enemy in open waters'. Even after its losses the Persian fleet
outnumbered the Greek by more than four to three,[5] and its
ships were tactically far superior to those of the Greeks; if the
Greek fleet had wished to dispute the passage of the Persian
fleet through the strait between Skiathos and the mainland of
Magnesia they would have had to fight in open waters where
the enemy would have had plenty of sea-room and could take
full advantage of their greater speed and skill in manœuvre.

These considerations, however, do not explain why the Greeks
allowed two days to pass before they ventured on their first
attack; if that attack was directed, as seems probable,[6] only
against an isolated section of the enemy fleet, why was it not
made two days earlier, when the Persians had not fully recovered from their experiences in the storm? Any answer to
this question must necessarily be conjectural, but Herodotus

---

[1] Cf. the parallel passage about the land forces in vii. 208. 1 (above, p. 119, n. 1).
[2] viii. 4. 1.
[3] So Macaulay. The καί in this sentence is perplexing (see the notes of Macan
and Legrand ad loc.) but its precise meaning is irrelevant here; the second explanation in HW 236 (first note on c. 4) is as good as any.
[4] *Schlachtenatlas*, iv, col. 5.   [5] On the lowest estimate, 415 to 271.
[6] See below, p. 185.

may be correct in his assertion[1] that the Greeks were much
disappointed when they realized how many Persian ships had
survived the storm, even though his next statement, that they
thereupon contemplated an immediate retreat southwards, is
a fabrication, invented to introduce the story that Themistokles was bribed by the Euboians to keep the fleet at Artemision.
In view of the decisive advantage in numbers still possessed by
the Persians, the Greek admirals may have decided to wait until
they were reinforced by an additional fleet of fifty-three ships
from Athens, which was expected to join them soon.

Many modern scholars,[2] dominated by the idea that the defence of Thermopylai was foredoomed to speedy failure, have
supposed that the admirals of the Greek fleet shared this conviction, and must therefore have based their plans on the firm
belief that they had only a short respite in which to secure the
desired decision by sea. But Themistokles at least must have
known that if the Greeks wished to force the enemy to fight they
could not employ the method of a frontal attack on his fleet as
a whole, for they would then be compelled to fight in the comparatively open waters of the channel north of Euboia, waters
favourable to the Persian tactics and disadvantageous to the
Greeks. The Persian navy must somehow be forced to take the
initiative, to attack the Greeks in their chosen position off
the shores of Pevki Bay, where their flanks would be protected by
the land at either extremity of the bay. It was, however, to be
anticipated that the Persian high command would in the first
place rely on its hitherto invincible army to overcome the Greek
defence on land. The Greeks for their part had no reason to
doubt that the enemy advance on land would be held up indefinitely at Thermopylai, and if it was, Xerxes would have no
option but to order his admirals to take the offensive, even if
that meant attacking the Greek fleet in a position which offered
little scope for their tactical skill. On this calculation the battles
at Artemision ought to have followed the fighting at Thermopylai; Ephoros supposed that they did![3] The calculation was falsified by the rapid collapse of the Greek resistance on land, but
to say that this result was inevitable is to be wise after the event;
there is no evidence that its inevitability was foreseen by the

---

[1] viii. 4. 1.
[2] Notably Munro in *J.H.S.* xxii, 1902, 307 and 318.
[3] Diod. xi. 12. 1.

Greek admirals at Artemision and was the supreme factor in their decisions. On the contrary, the pause after the arrival of the Persian fleet shows that the Greeks did not feel pressed for time and were prepared to wait for the enemy to make the first move.

Why did they change their minds? It was probably on the day after their arrival at Aphetai that the Persians, who at present had no intention of attacking the Greeks, decided to number their ships,[1] presumably to check the losses they had suffered in the storm. During the course of this review, according to Herodotus[2], the famous diver Skyllias of Skione made his escape from the Persians across the strait to Artemision; Herodotus adds[3] that on his arrival Skyllias made known to the Greek leaders the Persian losses in the storm and also the dispatch of a Persian squadron to sail round Euboia. It is unlikely that both parts of this message are historical. Some have objected to the first, on the ground that the Greeks knew all about the Persian losses already,[4] others to the second, either because the circumnavigating squadron had been sent off before the storm and its departure observed by Greek watchers on Skiathos or Euboia,[5] or because the whole story of the dispatch of this squadron is to be rejected.[6] If the sending of a squadron round Euboia, apparently dated by Herodotus to the same day as the naval review,[7] is struck out as a later accretion to the tradition, the message of Skyllias must have been confined to the information about the storm. The objections to this view have been decisively answered by Bury (who believes in the 'Euboian' squadron but holds that it was detached from the main fleet before the storm) in the following passage:

The Greeks cannot have been so wonderfully well informed during the storm as to the Persian losses, and when the storm had abated it was a matter of great consequence to them to learn the details. If

---

[1] viii. 7. 2; cf. Tarn, 215, HW 237 (ad loc.). On the date of the naval review (probably Day 17 of the Diary) see below, Appendix V, p. 384.

[2] viii. 8. 1.   [3] viii. 8. 3.

[4] Cf. Macan, i. 2. 369 B. Munro in *C.A.H.* iv. 288 seems to accept both parts, though previously (in *J.H.S.* xxii, 1902, 312) he had agreed with Bury in rejecting the second half of the message.

[5] So Bury (op. cit. 95). Macan (ii. 278) toys with this view but refuses to commit himself to any.   [6] See below, Appendix VI.

[7] This is the natural implication of viii. 7 and especially of the parataxis of the two clauses in the last sentence.

Skyllias brought this information, his arrival was an event. . . . His coming was remembered, and so he was the obvious person to be utilized when other news had to be carried according to the exigencies of the story.

When they had heard from Skyllias the details of the Persian losses the Greek leaders held a council of war on the morning of the next day,[1] but Herodotus' account of their deliberations is vitiated by his acceptance as fact of the second part of the message attributed to Skyllias. He asserts[2] that the Greeks decided to stay where they were for the rest of that day, to encamp on shore for the first part of the night, and to set sail after midnight in order to meet the enemy squadron that was sailing round Euboia. The last of these alleged decisions was never carried out, and all probability is against it. Even those who regard the dispatch, either earlier or now, of a Persian squadron round Euboia as a fact have been unable to accept it.[3] A few ships would have been sufficient to hold up the Persian squadron opposite Chalkis; why send the whole fleet? And how could the Greek fleet retire in a body to Chalkis, when its retirement would open to the Persians the strait between North Euboia and Lokris and so enable them to land troops behind the Greek position at Thermopylai? The alleged resolution is not attributed by Herodotus to cowardice, and it is not easy to see how it got into the story, but it must be discarded as incredible in itself and as closely connected in the tradition with the fictitious circumnavigation of Euboia by the Persians.

After reporting the alleged decision of the Greeks Herodotus goes on,[4] apparently with no feeling of incongruity, to inform his readers that late in the afternoon of the same day the Greeks sailed out to attack the enemy, desiring to make trial of his method of fighting and of the *diekplous*. This is followed by a very unconvincing chapter[5] which starts with a conventional opening on the amazement of the Persian admirals and sailors at the mad folly of the Greeks in presuming to attack with their few ships a fleet so superior in numbers and speed.[6] Herodotus

---

[1] Day 18 of the Diary; see below, Appendix V, p. 384.   [2] viii. 9.

[3] e.g. Grundy, 328f. Macan (ii. 281) refuses to face the problem.

[4] viii. 9 (last sentence).   [5] viii. 10.

[6] ἄμεινον πλεούσας (viii. 10. 1); this incidental admission is of the utmost importance. Cf. the statement of Themistokles later (viii. 60 a) that the Greek ships were βαρυτέρας.

then proceeds to describe the reactions of the Ionians in the
Persian navy; some sympathized with their fellow Greeks and
deplored their inevitable destruction, but others were delighted
and competed with one another to win the prize offered by
Xerxes to the ship which should be first to capture an Athenian
ship.[1] Having incidentally mentioned that the Persians, hoping
to capture the entire Greek fleet, had tried to surround it,[2]
Herodotus then narrates the course of the battle from the Greek
side.[3] When the first signal was given the Greeks arranged their
ships with their prows towards the enemy and with their sterns
drawn together in the middle, and when the second signal was
given they joined battle, although in a small place and prow
against prow. In spite of these handicaps they took thirty
enemy ships, including that of Philaon, brother of the ruler of
Cyprian Salamis; the first enemy ship was captured by an
Athenian, Lykomedes, who received the prize for valour.[4]
During the fight Antidoros of Lemnos went over with his ship
to the Greeks, the only captain on the Persian side to do so. The
battle, in which the Greeks got the best of it,[5] was broken off by
the approach of night.

There may be some truth in the motive alleged by Herodotus
for the assumption of the offensive by the Greeks, although it is
hardly consistent with his previous picture of their alarm when
confronted by the Persian fleet at Aphetai.[6] The *diekplous* which
the Greeks wished to test must be, as the run of the sentence
shows, a manœuvre practised by the Persians, even if a fragment of Sosylos which would have supported this interpretation
has been proved to refer not to this battle but to one fought at
another Artemision;[7] the Greeks wished to discover how the
Persian manœuvre of the *diekplous* worked in action. If Herodotus by his use of the term here meant the manœuvre famous

---

[1] The alleged reward may be a fact; cf. Macan, ad loc.
[2] This may be the meaning of the imperfect ἐκυκλοῦντο (viii. 10. 1).
[3] viii. 11.
[4] Lykomedes' exploit is transferred to Salamis in Plutarch (*Them.* 15. 3) but
in spite of Munro (*C.A.H.* iv. 289) Herodotus' version is more likely to be the true
one; cf. HW 238.
[5] On the assumption that ἑτεραλκέως (in viii. 11. 3) was used here and in ix.
103. 2 by Herodotus in its Homeric sense; cf. the notes of Macan and Powell
here, also Aeschylus, *Persai*, 952. It was apparently misunderstood by Ephoros
(cf. Diod. xi. 12. 6). See below, p. 257, n. 5.
[6] viii. 4. 1.   [7] See below, Appendix VII.

under the same name in the Peloponnesian War he was probably
guilty of an anachronism, for in Thucydides it seems to be a
fairly recent Athenian invention,[1] but here and in his account
of the sea-fight at Lade Herodotus may have used the word as
a general term for naval manœuvres.[2] It is curious that he has
not mentioned why the Greeks waited until the late afternoon
to launch their attack, especially as they followed precisely the
same plan on the next day. Diodoros[3] explains that the Greek
plan, attributed by him to Themistokles, was to take advantage
of the fact that the Persian fleet occupied several harbours on the
opposite coast and so was scattered; this idea was presumably
taken by Diodoros from Ephoros. There is no need to suppose
that Ephoros was here drawing on an independent tradition,
for with this one exception his account of Artemision is a pitiable
re-hash of Herodotus;[4] he seems to have made an intelligent
deduction from Herodotus at this point, but was hampered in
following out its full implications because they did not agree
with the general picture of the battle as given by Herodotus.

If the Greeks decided to attack after hearing Skyllias' report,
his detailed information about the Persian losses may have
been the stimulus that encouraged them to make the attempt.
Possibly they heard during the morning from Thermopylai
that the Persian attack on land had begun, but it is unlikely that
this contributed to their decision. On the other hand, they did
not intend to be involved in a pitched battle in the open strait
with the whole Persian fleet; they planned to concentrate their
ships in an attack against one of the Persian squadrons strung
out along the opposite coast, hoping to inflict serious losses on it
before the rest of the Persian fleet could arrive on the scene.
By attacking in the late afternoon the Greek admirals ensured
that if the other Persian squadrons sailed out to succour the one
attacked the Greeks would be able, protected by the approach
of night, to break off the engagement and retire in safety to their
own station.[5]

The obvious difficulty of this reconstruction is that, while it
explains how the Persians came to have thirty ships captured by

---

[1] Cf. Grundy, 333 n. On Lade cf. Hdt. vi. 12. 1 and HW 68 (ad loc.).
[2] So Powell on viii. 9.   [3] xi. 12. 5–6.
[4] Munro in *C.A.H.* iv. 284; cf. Prentice in *T.A.P.A.* li, 1920, 6.
[5] Kromayer in *Schlachtenatlas*, iv. 1, col. 5, section 2.

the Greeks, it differs widely in many respects from Herodotus'
narrative of the battle. Modern accounts tend to conform to the
following pattern:[1] the thirty ships were captured by a surprise attack on an isolated Persian squadron before the other
squadrons arrived; when they did, the Greeks managed to resist
their assault until nightfall by retreating in convex line with
their prows towards the enemy ships and occasionally charging
them. Contrast now the account in Herodotus.[2] When the Persians see the Greeks approaching they decide to surround them
and are apparently successful, for Herodotus seems to regard
the Greek fleet as having been arranged in a huge circle with
the sterns inwards and bows outwards, like the formation of the
Peloponnesian fleet before its fight with Phormion in the Corinthian Gulf,[3] but on that occasion the Athenians were sailing
round and round the outside of the circle. If the Persians at
Artemision were doing the same thing, how could the Greeks
charge their ships prow to prow? And how could a fleet so inferior to its opponents in tactical skill maintain a vast circle of
271 ships in unbroken formation?[4] Some have supposed that
they were really drawn up in a crescent or an arc,[5] but the picture in Herodotus' mind was quite different and, preposterous
though it was, it is in harmony with his statement that the
Persians were trying to surround the Greeks. He clearly supposed that it was in the ensuing engagement that the Greeks
captured the thirty ships and had had the better of the fighting
when night fell,[6] but it is incredible that a hand-fought battle
between the full forces of the two navies in the comparatively
open waters between their positions should have had a result
so unfavourable to the Persians.

Although Herodotus' report on the first sea-fight raises such
difficulties, the main item in it, that the Greeks captured thirty
Persian ships, is probably correct; his statement that the Greeks
attacked in the late afternoon also seems reliable, and supports
the view that their object was to take a Persian squadron by

---

[1] e.g. Tarn in *J.H.S.* xxviii, 1908, 217.
[2] viii. 10. 1 (last sentence) and viii. 11.   [3] Thuc. ii. 83. 5.
[4] These questions are rightly raised by Macan (i. 2. 372 f.).
[5] Macan (loc. cit.); cf. Tarn, 217 ('retreating in convex line').
[6] This interpretation of ἑτεραλκέως in viii. 11. 3 is supported by the statement,
two lines below, that the Persians after the battle returned to Aphetai πολλὸν
παρὰ δόξαν ἀγωνισάμενοι.

surprise and win a quick triumph before the rest of the enemy
fleet had time to intervene. The Greek admirals followed the
same plan on the late afternoon of the next day, although they
had been reinforced meanwhile by fifty-three Athenian ships.
Herodotus merely says[1] that they attacked some Cilician ships
and destroyed them, then returned to Artemision at nightfall.
The previous absence and opportune arrival of the fifty-three
ships have been variously explained,[2] but there is nothing in
Herodotus to contradict the common-sense view[3] that they had
arrived late because they represented the final instalment of
the gigantic shipbuilding programme which the Athenians had
been carrying out during the last three years, and that they had
not been ready in time to sail to Artemision with the rest; perhaps also the Athenians had found difficulty in collecting enough
men to provide their crews. There is a suggestion of anti-climax
in Herodotus' account of the second day's fighting, and its
meagreness has been compared with that of his description of the
fighting on the second day at Thermopylai.[4] The fact that the
fighting on the second day is not mentioned by Diodoros cannot
be regarded as a proof that it was not mentioned by Ephoros,
still less that it never occurred at all or should be transferred to
another time and place;[5] the omission may reflect merely the
carelessness with which Diodoros condensed his source.[6]

These two battles are separated in Herodotus by two chapters[7]
in which he relates the course and results of a second storm in
the night following the first battle. The second of these chapters
deals with a storm and heavy rain which fell on the Persian

---

[1] viii. 14. 2. Powell (edition, p. 80 ad fin.) would make the number of the
Kilikian ships twenty by inserting κ'.

[2] The most popular hypothesis is that they had been sent to Chalkis to protect
the rear of the Greek fleet from the Persian circumnavigating squadron; so Bury
in B.S.A. ii, 1895–6, 88 f.

[3] Köster, 76, anticipated by Duncker, vii. 242.

[4] Cf. Legrand, vii. 197–8; he cuts down the fighting at Artemision to two days,
coinciding with the first two days of the fighting at Thermopylai.

[5] The favourite suggestion is that the Cilician ships were the survivors of the
Persian circumnavigating squadron wrecked in the storm, but the scene of the
encounter is variously placed, either off south-west Euboia near Chalkis (so Bury
and his followers) or off north-east Euboia (Köster, 70–71).

[6] Tarn, 217 f. accepts the story of the second day's fighting as told by Herodotus,
but suggests that Ephoros had got hold of a genuine bit of the lost Phoenician
tradition which made Artemision a two-day fight (so it was for the Phoenicians!).

[7] viii. 12–13.

squadron sent to sail round Euboia and conveniently destroyed
it; the contents of this chapter are naturally rejected by those
who regard the circumnavigating squadron as fictitious or attribute its destruction to an earlier storm. In the first chapter
Herodotus describes a thunderstorm coming down from Mount
Pelion on the same night with heavy rain and causing much
distress to the main Persian fleet; at the end of the chapter he
sums it up as heavy rain and loud thunder with swollen tor-
rents rushing to the sea. In spite of its close association with
the mythical storm in the next chapter there is no need to
doubt[1] that there was such a storm at Aphetai, though Herodotus may have exaggerated its effect on the morale of the
Persians.[2] His assertion that the corpses and wrecks from the
first sea-fight were carried to the prows and oars of the Persian
ships at Aphetai is feasible on the assumption[3] that they were
blown ashore by a wind coming up from the south in the opposite direction to the thunderstorm, and the reference to the
prows and oars of the Persian ships indicates that some of them
at least were anchored in the harbours, not drawn up on the
beaches. Köster[4] ingeniously supposes that the Persians were
rowing gently forward while their ships were at anchor, to
relieve the strain on the anchors from the wind blowing in from
the sea; even if the chains gave way they would be ready to row
out. If there was a wind, it plays no part in Herodotus' account
of the thunderstorm, and though the storm may have alarmed
and distressed the Persians at Aphetai Herodotus does not claim
that they suffered any material damage from it.

Although the Greeks had taken the offensive in the fighting on
the first two days they were obviously still determined to avoid
a general engagement with the enemy fleet in open waters.
By their attacks on isolated enemy squadrons late in the day
they reduced the slight margin of superiority in numbers still
possessed by the Persian fleet and at the same time gave useful
practice to their own crews; the morale of the Greek marines

---

[1] As some do, e.g. Legrand, viii. 16, n. 2. Munro is sceptical about the wind in
J.H.S. xxii. 310 and n. 28.

[2] οἱ στρατιῶται οἱ ταύτῃ in viii. 12. 2 may include marines as well as sailors;
cf. HW. ad loc. (p. 239) and Powell (edition of Book VIII).

[3] Macan, i. 2. 374 B (followed by HW 239).

[4] Köster, 73 f.; he compared the behaviour of Menodoros in Appian, *Bell. Civ.*
v. 89. 370.

and sailors was thereby improved, whereas it might have been
undermined if they had waited passively in their station until
the enemy decided to attack. Perhaps their leaders also hoped
that the damage which they had inflicted with comparative
impunity on the Persians in these two engagements would provoke them to pass to the offensive and attack the Greek fleet in
its chosen position. Herodotus may be right in producing this as
one of the two reasons why the Persian admirals moved out at
midday on the next day with their whole fleet to attack the
Greeks;[1] it is also possible that Xerxes after the failure of his
first attempts to force Thermopylai had sent them a message
commanding them to attack as soon as possible. Herodotus
says[2] that the Greeks waited quietly at Artemision for the enemy
onset, and that the Persians formed their ships into a crescent
to surround them, whereupon the Greeks sailed out to meet
them and joined battle. It is unlikely, however, that they ventured far from their position in Pevki Bay, where the projecting
points of land at either end of the bay protected them from flank
attacks; the statement that the Persians were hampered by their
superior numbers may reflect the fact that the mouth of the bay
was too narrow to allow them to engage more than half their
fleet at once.[3]

The engagement which followed, the third battle of Artemision, was the most important sea-fight that had ever been
fought in the Mediterranean, in view of the number of ships
and men engaged in it,[4] and it is to be regretted that Herodotus
dealt with it so briefly;[5] perhaps he was unable to get any clear
picture of the battle as a whole from his informants. He does,
however, report that it was contested with desperate energy by
both Greeks and Persians and that the two sides were evenly
matched; it is clear that the battle was indecisive, for although the Persian fleet had to withdraw before nightfall to
its anchorages and thereby leave the Greeks in control of the
corpses and wreckage, yet the Greek fleet, as Herodotus admits,
had been roughly handled, especially the Athenian contingent,
in which half the ships had been damaged.[6] The Greeks had
sustained heavy losses in men and ships, but according to

---

[1] The other motive was fear of Xerxes (viii. 15. 1).   [2] viii. 16. 1.
[3] See above, p. 150.   [4] Cf. Tarn, 219.   [5] viii. 16–18.
[6] viii. 18.

Herodotus[1] the Persian losses in both were far heavier. On the
Greek side the Athenians fought best; of the Athenian captains
the bravest was Kleinias son of Alkibiades, who had provided
a trireme for the Athenian fleet at his own expense.[2] The best
fighters on the Persian side were the Egyptians; they had an
advantage in boarding tactics because their marines were more
heavily armed than most of those in the Persian fleet.[3] Herodotus backs up his verdict on the Egyptians by the information
that they captured five Greek ships with their crews as well.[4]

The composite fleet of the Greek confederates had no cause
to be ashamed of the part it had played in its first great battle
with Xerxes' navy, but its heroism was robbed of its reward
by the sudden collapse of the Greek resistance on land. Herodotus[5] indeed alleges that after their experiences in this sea-
fight the Greeks again contemplated flight to the south, but his
assertion here is as worthless as his ascription of this intention to
the Greeks at an earlier stage, and he himself implies later that
they deferred their withdrawal until they heard the bad news
from Thermopylai.[6] Herodotus claims that on three separate
occasions the Greek fleet or its leaders had carried out or contemplated a retreat from their appointed position covering
Euboia and the waters behind it. The first of these statements[7]
may be due to a misunderstanding, the second and third[8] seem
to be pure inventions. Between them they are responsible for
the paradox in Herodotus' narrative of the first clashes on land
and sea between Greeks and Persians, the paradox so well
brought out by Macan:[9] the picture of the army as a band of
heroes fighting heroically, of the fleet as a mob of poltroons
repeatedly retreating or meditating retreat from its post, contrasted with the historical facts that it was the army which was
beaten and by its defeat let the Persian invader into Central
Greece, while the Greek fleet had held its own until the disaster
at Thermopylai made withdrawal inevitable.

[1] viii. 16. 3.
[2] viii. 17. Macan, ad loc. (cf. HW 239) wrongly makes this Kleinias identical
with the Kleinias killed at Koroneia in 447/6; he was probably his uncle, and
brother to the Alkibiades who was the grandfather of the famous Alkibiades (cf.
Dittenberger in *Hermes*, xxxvii, 1902, 1 ff.).
[3] Cf. vii. 89. 3, also HW 376 (ll. 1–4).
[4] viii. 17.   [5] viii. 18.   [6] viii. 21. 2.
[7] vii. 183. 1; see above, pp. 165 ff.   [8] viii. 4. 1 and 18.
[9] Macan, ii. 261.

Many have sought the answer to the paradox in the hypothesis that, apart from some slight contributions made by informants (Greeks and others) who had fought on the Persian side, Herodotus drew his materials for his account of Artemision wholly from Athenian sources. In view of what we know about his methods this hypothesis is very unlikely; moreover, it does not really explain the paradox. When Herodotus later describes the mood of the Greek fleet after it had taken up its station at Salamis, he contrasts the attitude of the Peloponnesians, anxious to retire from their advanced position to the Isthmus of Corinth, with that of the Athenians, then identical with that of the Megarians and Aiginetans.[1] Such a contrast between the temper of the Athenians and that of the rest has been imported by modern scholars into the operations near Artemision,[2] but no trace of it is to be found anywhere in Herodotus' version of these events. In the legend relating the bribery of Themistokles by the Euboians[3] it is presupposed that he was as eager to retreat as the other admirals; if Themistokles had opposed the retreat his influence would have prevailed and the Euboians could have saved their money. In the other two relevant passages it is the whole fleet that withdraws or plans withdrawal; so far are the Athenians from resisting the proposal to retreat that in the second passage[4] they are closely associated with it. Whatever Plutarch might think, there is no bias in Herodotus' statement[5] that when the withdrawal began the Corinthians led the way and the Athenians brought up the rear. Herodotus certainly had Athenians, as well as others, among his informants on Artemision, but in view of the size of the Athenian contingent there is nothing surprising about the prominence of the Athenians in his narratives of the first and last sea-fights, while his ascription to them of the *aristeia* in the final battle[6] is strikingly confirmed by Pindar's verdict that at Artemision 'the sons of Athens laid the bright foundations of Freedom'.[7]

[1] This identity of interest is expressed somewhat belatedly in viii. 74. 2; earlier Themistokles is represented as standing alone against the Peloponnesians.

[2] Notably by Grundy, c. viii (especially item 6 at the top of p. 324, which is a statement without any foundation whatever in Herodotus' narrative; cf. also pp. 340 f.). Cf. the valuable observations of Macan, ii. 267 f.

[3] viii. 4. 2 and 5. 1–3. The story has rightly been rejected by most scholars; cf. Grundy, 328 f. and HW 236 f.   [4] viii. 18.

[5] viii. 21. 2, criticized by Plut. *de Malign. Her.* 34 (last sentence).

[6] viii. 17.   [7] Pindar, fr. 77 Schröder (65 Bowra) quoted in Plut. *Them.* 8. 2.

Pindar was right; the untried Greek navy had acquitted itself brilliantly in its first encounter with the barbarians. Some have supposed that the third battle of Artemision was a Greek defeat,[1] but this is an error based on false presuppositions. The battle ended without decisive result, but the Persian fleet had been badly mauled, and was doubtless glad to retire to lick its wounds. When its leaders heard next day that their opponents had withdrawn, they were slow to credit the news,[2] and even when it was confirmed they were in no hurry to pursue. If the Greek army had held out a few days longer at Thermopylai, the Greek fleet might have fought again with greater success,[3] for they were better placed to repair their losses than the enemy.[4] As it was, they retired to a new position where, given the inevitable stalemate on land at the Isthmus of Corinth, the enemy fleet would be bound to attack them sooner or later under conditions even more unsuited to their special methods of fighting than they had been at Artemision and even more favourable to the tactics of the Greeks.

[1] Notably Tarn (op. cit. 218); cf. also Prentice in *T.A.P.A.* li, 1920, 14–15.
[2] viii. 23. 1.   [3] Cf. Macan, ii. 261, § 2 (*a*).   [4] Cf. Delbrück, 86.

IV

SALAMIS

The Persian conquest of Central Greece

THE retirement of the Greek navy from Artemision was promptly reported to the Persian admirals, who were at first unable to credit the news. When it had been confirmed by their own scout-ships, they crossed to Euboia with their fleet soon after dawn on the day after the battle, occupied the town of Histiaia, and proceeded to plunder the villages on the coast.[1] It was apparently not on this day but on the day after it[2] that parties from the fleet went across the straits on Xerxes' invitation to visit the battlefield of Thermopylai. These visitors did not return to the fleet until the next day, the third day after the last battle at Artemision and the twenty-third of the Diary; this was the day on which, according to Herodotus, the army resumed its march on Athens.[3] While the invaders had been marching through friendly territory the Persian army and fleet had been able to advance together, but it was now necessary for the army to hurry on ahead of the fleet in order to occupy Attica and secure the harbour of Phaleron before the fleet could proceed on its voyage.[4] This was evidently the reason why the fleet waited at Histiaia for three more days after the departure of the army,[5] then sailed southwards through the channel between Euboia and the mainland, arriving at Phaleron three days later (Day 29 of the Diary); we must suppose that their voyage had been so calculated as to allow the army time to reach Phaleron first.[6]

[1] viii. 23.   [2] viii. 24–25; cf. Macan's note on 25. 3.   [3] viii. 25. 3.

[4] This important point is emphasized by Macan, ii. 292; cf. Gomme, *Essays*, 199.

[5] viii. 66. 1 with Macan's note (summarized by HW 257). Giannelli, 38 and n. 2, by accepting Beloch's assumption that the three days of waiting included the day on which the fleet returned to Histiaia, curtailed still further the time available for the advance of the army.

[6] Grundy, 374 strangely thinks it probable that the fleet arrived at Phaleron shortly before the army reached Attic territory (so Keil in *A.S.* 99). Hdt. viii. 67. 1 implies the opposite, but (in spite of Giannelli, 40) his account here is not above suspicion; see below, p. 206.

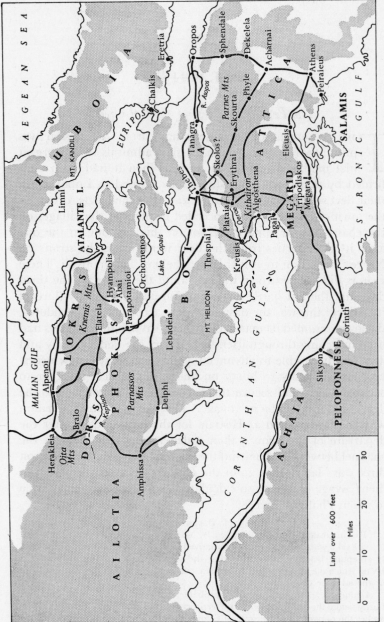

MAP 5. Part of Central Greece

This time-scheme, based on the indications in Herodotus, allows only five days[1] for the march of the army from Thermopylai to Athens. If it followed the main road through Atalante to Thebes and over Kithairon by way of the Dryoskephalai Pass to Eleusis and Athens, the distance would be over 140 miles.[2] This could be shortened by taking one of the cross-country routes into the valley of the Kephisos, but Beloch's estimate of 160–170 kilometres[3] (at most 106 miles) seems too low. Even so, scholars who have accepted it, including Beloch himself, find it hard to believe that the Persian army could have averaged over 30 kilometres a day for five days in this part of their advance. Beloch assumes that the notes of time given here by Herodotus were not derived by him from authentic tradition but represent his own calculations; Meyer[4] simply ignores Herodotus and allows fourteen days for the march to Athens.

Obst, however, argues[5] from the evidence of Xenophon in the first book of the *Anabasis* that the army of the younger Cyrus marched at the rate of from five to eight parasangs a day, and that on one stretch of its advance it marched sixty-five parasangs in twelve days; as the parasang is estimated by Herodotus[6] at 30 stades (a little under $3\frac{1}{2}$ miles), Obst concludes that the Persian troops in their advance on Athens averaged 150 stadia a day, which he equates with $26\frac{1}{2}$ kilometres (under 17 miles). Nevertheless, it seems improbable that the army as a whole advanced with such haste, as some time must have been spent in the devastation of Phokis and of the patriotic states in Boiotia. If the time-indications in Herodotus are correct, it is necessary to assume[7] that the Persians, anxious to exploit their success on land with all possible speed, sent on ahead their best troops, including their cavalry, to advance rapidly on Athens, and

[1] Or at most six. But it seems unlikely that the Persians would not arrange to reach Phaleron by land at least twenty-four hours before the fleet was due.

[2] *Handbook of Greece*, 230–3. Macan, ii. 293 (cf. i. 2. 436 A) makes Xerxes proceed from Thebes to Athens by way of Tanagra, but the distance is about the same as by the other route.

[3] ii². 2. 51; on the cross-roads cf. Macan, i. 2. 399f. (HW, top of p. 244). The distance from Athens to the Malian Plain by the modern road over the Pournaraki Pass is about 126 miles.

[4] Beloch, loc. cit.; Meyer, 376 (note on chronology). Busolt (673 f., note) would allow 9 or 10 days.

[5] Obst, 132f. quoting Xenophon, *Anabasis*, i. 2. 5–4. 11 (especially 4. 9–11).

[6] v. 53; cf. HW, ad loc., also vol. i, top of p. 243.

[7] With Giannelli, 43 (in continuation of long note starting on p. 42).

followed with the rest of their troops at a slower pace; perhaps picked troops had set out from Thermopylai on the day after its capture,[1] and the date given by Herodotus for the departure of the land force was really that on which Xerxes himself and the rest of the army resumed their march.

Herodotus supplies few details about the advance of the Persian army through Central Greece to Athens, apart from a Delphic temple-legend[2] describing a Persian attack on Delphi, an attack said to have been repulsed by a handful of Delphians with supernatural aid, and two chapters on the devastation of Phokis,[3] preceded by a digression of two chapters on previous relations between Phokis and Thessaly. The Thessalians were now in high favour with the Persians,[4] and were therefore in a good position to pay off old scores against the Phokians, who in the late sixth century had foiled their renewed attempt to extend their control in Central Greece.[5] The Lokrians had presumably joined the Persian side after Thermopylai,[6] but the Phokians, when offered protection by the Thessalians in return for a payment of 50 talents, rejected the offer with scorn, and as a result their country was exposed to the full force of Persian vengeance. Herodotus says that the Thessalians, acting as guides, led the whole Persian army by the route from the territory of Trachis into Doris and the upper Kephisos valley.[7] It is more likely that the majority of the troops, including the cavalry, followed the main road along the coast of Lokris before turning inland past Hyampolis and Abai, but the column led by the Thessalians, advancing down the Kephisos valley, seems to have been mainly responsible for the devastation of the Phokian towns and country-side.[8]

Most of the inhabitants of Phokis had retired safely to Am-

---

[1] Giannelli, n. on p. 42, following a hint in Macan, ii. 292.

[2] viii. 35–39; see below, Appendix XIII.

[3] viii. 32–33 (the digression on the earlier history is in cc. 27–28).

[4] Cf. viii. 31 (last sentence) where Doris is saved by their protection; also vii. 233. 2.

[5] The last Thessalian invasion is 'not many years before 480' in viii. 27. 2; cf. HW on 27. 1. The earlier attempt (c. 575) had been defeated by the Boiotians at the battle of Keressos; cf. Plut. Camillus, 19. 4 and Glotz and Cohen, Histoire grecque, i. 311.

[6] Hdt. mentions Λοκρούς in the list in viii. 66. 2.

[7] viii. 31. See above, p. 134, and also HW 243 f.

[8] viii. 32. 2 and 33.

phissa in Ozolian Lokris, but some stalwarts took refuge on the
heights of Mount Parnassos and still held their ground in the
campaign of the next year, raiding the Persian communications
from their stronghold.[1] By then some at least of the Phokians
had made their peace with Persia and even supplied a contingent of 1,000 men to Mardonios' army, but they may have been
driven to this submission when in 479 the Persians reoccupied
their country.[2] Herodotus is sometimes suspected of bias in
favour of the Phokians,[3] but they were the first Greek state to
stand firm even in defeat against the might of Xerxes, and there
is no real ground for doubting Herodotus' statement that their
lands were systematically ravaged and their towns burnt, including Abai with its famous sanctuary of Apollo.[4] Herodotus'
reference to the destruction of this temple is not refuted by the
fact that its oracle was consulted in the following winter by an
agent of Mardonios.[5] If the statues at Abai commemorating the
earlier victory over Thessaly had been dedicated before 480,
those seen by Herodotus may have been later replicas made after
the expulsion of the Persians; they could have been copied
from the similar statues set up in Delphi at the time of the
original dedication.

The main body of the Persian army, following the coast road
from Thermopylai, turned inland past Hyampolis and Abai
to the valley of the Kephisos and proceeded to march down it
through the pass of Parapotamioi into Boiotia, crossing the
south-eastern frontier of Phokis at the border town of Panopeus,
only 20 stades from Boiotian Chaironeia, which at this date was
apparently dependent on its more powerful neighbour Orchomenos.[6] Most of the Boiotian towns were known to favour the
Persian invaders, and they had an additional guarantee of
safety in the friendship of the Macedonian king Alexander;
Herodotus says that he protected them from harm by sending
men (whether garrisons or merely agents is not quite clear)
who by their presence attested the goodwill of the towns to

[1] viii. 32. 1; cf. ix. 31. 5.
[2] ix. 17. 1 (where Macan's text is peculiar); cf. Hauvette, 382.
[3] Cf. Munro in *J.H.S.* xxii, 1902, 314f.
[4] See the defence of his account in Hauvette, 381 ff.
[5] viii. 134. 1; on the statues cf. viii. 27. 5.
[6] viii. 34 (distance in Pausanias x. 4. 1). For the dependence of Chaironeia on
Orchomenos cf. Macan, i. 2. 405 B and Thuc. iv. 76. 3 (in 424).

Persia.[1] Only Thespiai and Plataia had to suffer for their obstinate attachment, unshaken by defeat, to the patriotic cause. Both towns were destroyed by fire, but the inhabitants of Thespiai (and probably of Plataia also) had made good their escape to the Peloponnese.[2] Those Plataians who had been serving with the Athenian ships at Artemision had left them at Chalkis when the Greek fleet retreated, and proceeded to their own town to help in the evacuation of the population, but they did not return afterwards to the fleet and so were not present at the battle of Salamis.[3]

Like the Thespians and Plataians, the Athenians had been compelled by the Persian advance to abandon their homes and seek refuge abroad, but for them the problem was much more difficult because the number of people to be evacuated, the population of all Attica, was much greater. The time available for the evacuation was short, not more than five or six days at most, if the Persian army really entered Athens eight days after the fall of Thermopylai, for the news of Leonidas' defeat must have taken at least two days to reach Athens. Beloch maintains[4] that the chronological indications in Herodotus must be rejected, on the ground that 100,000 people cannot have been successfully evacuated from Attica in five days, but such dogmatism is unjustifiable.[5] The second Delphic oracle to the Athenians, advising them to trust to 'a wooden wall', must have been delivered at latest soon after the failure of the Thessalian expedition,[6] and when they accepted the interpretation given to the oracle by Themistokles they must have decided in principle to evacuate Attica as soon as it was threatened with imminent invasion; it is reasonable to suppose that they proceeded to make such preparations as they could beforehand in

---

[1] viii. 34; Macan's note on this difficult passage is important.

[2] viii. 50. 2.

[3] viii. 44. 1; cf. Macan, ad loc.

[4] ii². 2. 51. Munro (*J.H.S.* xxii, 1902, 320) thinks the migration of the Athenians had already begun after the Thessalian expedition, but the passage on which he relies (viii. 142. 3) is even more difficult than Macan realized. If Xerxes did not reach Attica till the end of August, why should the Athenians have lost the corn-harvest of 480?

[5] Cf. the arguments of Giannelli, 43 f., and for mass evacuations of Attica in modern times Grote, iii. 453, n. 2 (= abridged ed., 204, n. 1).

[6] vii. 141. 3–4 (interpreted by Themistokles in vii. 143). On the date see Labarbe, *Loi navale*, 112 ff., especially 120.

order to facilitate the execution of their decision whenever the
need should arise, although they can hardly have expected
that Thermopylai would fall so quickly.[1] They must have begun
the actual evacuation as soon as the authorities received news
of the break-through at Thermopylai, and not have waited,
as Herodotus says they did,[2] until their fleet reached Phaleron.

Herodotus has little to say about the evacuation. He mentions a proclamation that every Athenian must be responsible
for the safety of his family and slaves, and adds that most of the
refugees went to Troizen, while the rest found shelter in Aigina
and Salamis.[3] Plutarch gives a fuller version of the proclamation,[4] which he describes as a decree of the people moved by
Themistokles, but if this alleged decree is authentic[5] it must have
been carried earlier with the proviso that it should not come
into force until the emergency arose.[6] The anecdotes connected
with the evacuation in Plutarch and other writers are probably later fabrications, such as the story[7] that Xanthippos' dog,
when left behind in Attica by his master, swam across the strait
to Salamis and expired on the farther shore, thereby giving
to the locality the name of Kynos Sema, the dog's tomb. In
this connexion fourth-century writers tell how the authorities
found the money to provide a subsistence allowance for the men
serving on the fleet; according to one version[8] the money was
obtained by a stratagem of Themistokles, while in the other,
preserved by the author of the *Athenaion Politeia*,[9] the hero of the
story is the Areopagus, which pays 8 drachmas to every man in
the Athenian navy. This second version is rightly suspect, for it
claims that the supremacy of the Areopagus in the years after
the Persian invasion was due to the patriotic conduct of its

---

[1] In spite of Grundy, 353.

[2] viii. 41. 1; cf. Hauvette, 397.

[3] viii. 41. 1; cf. Labarbe, *B.C.H.* lxxvi, 1952, 409, with notes 1–4.

[4] *Life of Themistokles*, 10. 4, see below, Appendix XV.

[5] It was suspected by Bauer (cited by Busolt, 691, n. 3). The proclamation as
reported by Hdt. is given an anti-democratic twist in *Ath. Pol.* 23. 1, where it is
attributed to the inability of the strategoi (including Themistokles?) to deal with
the emergency. Cf. also Bury in *C.R.* x, 1896, 415 B.

[6] This is perhaps Jacoby's view; see his 9th supplementary note on Kleidemos,
fr. 21, *F.G.H.*, no. 323 (iii (b), 2, p. 76).

[7] *Them.* 10. 10; cf. Philochoros, fr. 116 in Jacoby, *F.G.H.*, no. 328 (fr. 84 in
Müller).

[8] Kleidemos, fr. 21 (13 in Müller).

[9] *Ath. Pol.* 23. 1; cf. Plut. *Them.* 10. 6.

members on this occasion,[1] and the first may be merely the answer to it; probably neither version was known to Herodotus.

From Boiotia the Persians invaded Attica. As Herodotus says later[2] that they left Attica by the same road by which they had entered it, he must have believed that only one road was used, perhaps the main road from Thebes to Eleusis and on to Athens which crosses Kithairon a little to the south-east of Plataia by the pass of Gyphtokastro, but the route through Tanagra and over Parnes by way of Dekeleia to Athens may also have been used.[3] On their arrival in Attica the Persians ranged over the country-side, plundering and burning,[4] and occupied the lower town at Athens, for they found the Acropolis still held by an Athenian force. Its defenders, according to Herodotus,[5] were few, composed only of the temple treasurers and some 'poor men', who had defended the approaches to the citadel by a wooden barricade. Herodotus gives two reasons why these men had not joined in the exodus to Salamis; they were so poor that they had not the means to leave Attica, and they thought that they had discovered the true meaning of the oracle which had foretold that the wooden wall would be impregnable.

The wooden rampart was soon destroyed by the Persians, who shot blazing arrows into it from the position they had taken up on the Areopagus hill, but the defenders still held out, rejecting proposals for surrender made to them by the Athenian exiles in Xerxes' train, and rolling down huge stones on the attackers when they tried to storm the Acropolis by a frontal assault up the slope leading to the summit on the west. Herodotus says[6] that 'for a long time' Xerxes was unable to overcome their resistance, but in the end his troops found their way up by a difficult path which had been left unguarded and proceeded to occupy the gates; then they slew those of the garrison who had taken sanctuary in the temple and set fire to all the buildings on the Acropolis.[7] The conquest of the Attic mainland was

---

[1] Cf. Jacoby, *Atthis*, 75, also Walker in *C.A.H.* v. 472 ff.   [2] viii. 113. 1.

[3] Macan (i. 2. 436 A) would add the central, more direct, route through the modern Portaes pass to Phyle and Acharnai; but see below, p. 422.

[4] viii. 50. 1. The news was brought to the fleet by an Athenian who had presumably stayed behind in Attica or had been slow to leave; cf. Legrand, viii. 35, n. 3.

[5] viii. 51. 2; the siege is described in c. 52.   [6] viii. 52 ad fin.   [7] viii. 53.

now complete, but before Xerxes' army could attempt an invasion of the Peloponnese his admirals would have to overcome
the resistance of the still unbeaten Greek fleet.

The Greek fleet remains at Salamis

Herodotus says[1] that the Greek fleet on its retirement from
Artemision put in at Salamis on the request of the Athenians,
who wished to evacuate their wives and children from Attica.
The patriotic Greek states in the Peloponnese had apparently
had some ships in reserve; these ships, which had taken no
part in the previous fighting, had been mustering at the harbour of Pogon (now Poros) in the territory of Troizen, but on
hearing that the main fleet had halted at Salamis they proceeded to Salamis to join it there.[2] After a detailed account of
the composition of the united fleet, Herodotus introduces a
meeting of the strategoi,[3] apparently the admirals of the various
contingents, summoned by the Spartan commander-in-chief
Eurybiadas, to consider at what place in the territories still controlled by the Greeks they should stand and fight the enemy;
clearly the proximity of a friendly shore was regarded as indispensable for a fleet composed almost exclusively of triremes.[4]
Most of the strategoi argued in favour of fighting close to the
Isthmus of Corinth. The rest, who must have included the
representatives of Athens, Aigina, and Megara,[5] presumably
wished to stay at Salamis, but their view is not mentioned by
Herodotus, nor does he here give the grounds on which it was
based; he merely notes[6] the argument of its opponents that, if
the fleet stayed at Salamis to fight and was defeated there,
the Greek ships would be unable to escape to the land army
stationed behind the Isthmus lines, but would be cooped up in
Salamis and starved out there.

At this point news of the arrival of the Persian army and its
devastation of Attica is brought to the fleet,[7] and Herodotus,
leaving his account of the naval council unfinished, turns to the
activities of the enemy on land, including the siege and capture

---

[1] viii. 40. 1.   [2] viii. 42. 1.

[3] viii. 49. Legrand (viii. 57, n. 3) denies that this refers to a formal meeting of the
council, but surely Hdt. thought it was.

[4] Cf. Rados, 268.   [5] In view of their attitude in viii. 74. 2.

[6] viii. 49. 2.   [7] viii. 50. 1.

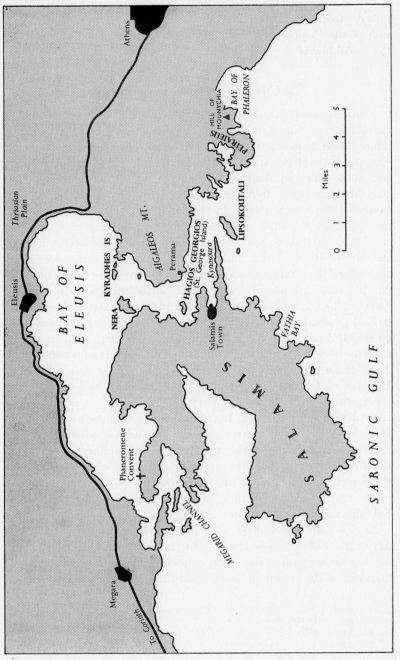

Map 6. Salamis and adjacent mainland

of the Acropolis. All the buildings on it had been burnt by the victorious Persians, but on the next day Xerxes summoned the Athenian exiles in his retinue and commanded them to offer sacrifice on the Acropolis in their traditional manner. Herodotus speculates on this reversal of policy,[1] wondering whether Xerxes had been warned in a dream or had tardily repented of his behaviour in burning the shrine. He proceeds to explain his reason for noting the incident; when the exiles went up to the citadel 'on the day after the burning' to offer sacrifice in the temple they discovered that the sacred olive-tree preserved on the Acropolis had miraculously sprouted again after the fire ('such was the story told by the exiles').

There is great diversity in modern estimates of the number of days spent by the Persians on the siege of the Acropolis,[2] but it can hardly have begun until the day after they reached Attica and must have lasted at least three days. Nevertheless, when the news that the Persians had captured the Acropolis reaches the fleet, the council of admirals appears to be still in session, and the news is said to have produced such a panic in it that several of those present left the council and promptly embarked in preparation for immediate flight, while a majority of those who remained voted in favour of a battle near the Isthmus.[3] Herodotus' narrative implies that the council now for the first time gave its answer to the question submitted to it by Eurybiadas before the arrival of the Persians in Attica, more than three days earlier. Moreover, his account of the panic produced by the fall of the Acropolis is not compatible with his earlier statement[4] that the defence had been undertaken by a handful of men in opposition to the policy advocated by Themistokles and supported by the majority of the Athenian people.

Some, accepting the panic as a fact, have conjectured that the Acropolis had been strongly garrisoned,[5] so that the news of its capture was unexpected and alarming, but it seems better to dismiss the panic as mythical, the necessary introduction to the next stage in the Herodotean story.[6] After the break-up of the council Themistokles was approached by his friend Mnesiphilos, who, on learning the decision which had been taken, is said to have pointed out to him the disastrous consequences

---

[1] viii. 54.   [2] See below, p. 212.   [3] viii. 56.   [4] viii. 51. 2.
[5] Notably Bury in *C.R.* x, 1896, 416 f.   [6] viii. 57.

which must result from a Greek withdrawal to the Isthmus, and
to have urged him to persuade Eurybiadas to summon a fresh
council, even providing Themistokles with suitable arguments.
These arguments, when reproduced by Themistokles 'with
many additions of his own',[1] convinced Eurybiadas, but in the
ensuing council Themistokles relied solely on a demonstration
of the tactical advantages which the Greeks would enjoy by
staying to fight in the straits of Salamis.[2] These must have been
evident to him all along, and the tradition of the part played
by Mnesiphilos is manifestly a spiteful invention to deprive
Themistokles of the credit for his originality and insight.[3]

In connexion with this (third) meeting of the council Herodotus relates[4] that Themistokles, when irritated by his opponents,
notably the Corinthian admiral Adeimantos, threatened to sail
away with the Athenian fleet and the civil population to southern
Italy. Some of the details in this report are suspicious and the
whole story may be a fabrication; it is perhaps significant that
Herodotus[5] regards the threat of Athenian defection as the
reason which finally decided Eurybiadas to stay and fight at
Salamis. Herodotus is at least right in describing the decision
as resting with Eurybiadas alone, the function of the council
being merely advisory.

This third council is represented by Herodotus[6] as having met
in the night which followed the day on which the previous
council had been held. As the next day dawned there was an
earthquake shock felt on both land and sea, whereupon the
Greeks decided to offer sacrifice to the gods and sent a ship to
Aigina to summon the Aiakidai to their help.[7] This ship returned

---

[1] viii. 58. 2. Hauvette, 404 makes much of this phrase, but it does little to
diminish the depreciation of Themistokles' genius implied by the story as a whole.
Cf. Grundy, 363 f.; he rightly concludes that 'this tale of Mnesiphilos . . . cannot
be regarded as reliable history'.

[2] viii. 60; in the introduction to this chapter Hdt. notes that Themistokles now
made no use of Mnesiphilos' arguments (Grundy, 366).

[3] On which see the often-quoted encomium of Thucydides, i. 138. 3.

[4] viii. 62; cf. HW, ad loc. Beloch (G.G. i². 2. 238 f. and 239, n. 1) argues against
the possibility of a mass evacuation of the whole population of Attica to the far
west at this moment. [5] viii. 63.

[6] The last sentence of viii. 56 says that the previous (second?) council had broken
up at nightfall.

[7] viii. 64. Hauvette, 406, n. 3 does not believe that the object of this mission
was to bring the actual statues of the Aiakidai from Aigina. On the return of the
ship cf. viii. 83. 2 (with HW 262 f.).

just in time for the beginning of the battle of Salamis; hence the
narrative implies that the day on which it was sent to Aigina
was the day before the battle.[1] It is not equally certain that the
vision of Dikaios, reported by Herodotus in the next chapter, is
also meant to belong to the day before the battle; it may have
been seen several days earlier.[2] Anyhow, the story enables Herodotus to return to the Persian side and relate the arrival of the
Persian fleet at Phaleron, which is said to have been followed
immediately by a council of war at Phaleron under Xerxes'
presidency.[3] After hearing various opinions Xerxes decides in
favour of a naval battle, and apparently on the same afternoon
the Persian fleet puts out to sea[4] and offers battle to the Greeks
in the waters off the south-eastern approaches to the straits of
Salamis.

Herodotus alleges that the Greeks now fell into a fresh panic,
but his explanation of its cause is unconvincing.[5] The old argument reappears that if the Greek fleet, 'staying behind at Salamis
to fight for the land of the Athenians', is defeated in its present
position its sailors and marines will be cut off in Salamis and
starved out, but Herodotus now adds to this the clause, 'thereby leaving their own land unguarded'. At this point he inter-
jects that on the same night, presumably the night before the
battle, the Persian infantry began to march towards Peloponnese;
later on he explains[6] that the fear felt by the Peloponnesian
contingents was on this occasion not on their own account but
on behalf of their fellows left in Peloponnese, although in the
intervening chapters he has described how the Isthmus was
defended by a large force posted in a strong position. The
Peloponnesians in the fleet went about the camp criticizing

---

[1] This is generally agreed and is indeed what Herodotus implies. But when the
Greeks sent the ship to Aigina they could not have known that the battle would
be fought next day, as its date depended on the date of the Persian decision to
attack.

[2] Cf. Busolt, 703 f., n. 3, followed by Hauvette, 407. Hauvette says the story is
told here as another example of the supernatural protection given by the gods to
the fleet of Athens.   [3] viii. 67. 1.

[4] viii. 70. 1. This is denied by those who (like Giannelli, 39) interpose an interval
between the council and the offer of battle by the Persian fleet.

[5] viii. 70. 2.

[6] viii. 74. 1, where ὅμως ταῦτα πυνθανόμενοι is explained by Powell (edition, 114;
cf. Giannelli, 45, n. 1) as 'in spite of news of these defences'. But HW 260 seem to
take ὅμως separately, and if this is correct ταῦτα could refer to the Persian advance
on land towards Peloponnese (viii. 71. 1).

Eurybiadas' decision, and finally a fresh council was summoned; it seems to be ascribed to the night preceding the battle.[1] Themistokles, when he sees the opposition now likely to prevail, steals out of the council and sends a messenger to Xerxes urging him to cut off the retreat of the Greek fleet; Xerxes then moves his ships into the straits after midnight. The Greeks receive information about their encirclement from Aristeides and from a Tenian trireme which had deserted from the Persian side;[2] they then make preparations to fight on the next day in their present position in the straits of Salamis.

It has been necessary to analyse in some detail the account given by Herodotus of what happened in the Greek fleet between its arrival at Salamis and the eve of the battle in order to bring out more clearly its obvious weaknesses. The most serious of them is that the precise chronology of the earlier naval operations is replaced in this section of the narrative by a tendency to telescope events; this appears in the confusion about the Greek naval councils, for the first two, apparently continuous in Herodotus, must, if historical, have been separated by an interval of some days. But it is in Herodotus' references to the Persian fleet that this foreshortening of events is seen most clearly; as soon as the fleet arrives at Phaleron Xerxes comes down to the sea to confer with his admirals, the fleet offers battle on the same afternoon, and actually fights the next day. This is obviously impossible; the usual assumption[3] is that there is a lacuna, unnoticed by Herodotus, between the Persian decision to fight and its execution, but it is equally likely that there was a long interval between the arrival of the Persian fleet at Phaleron and the council of war, as well as between the council and the battle.

In the second place, although the critics have recognized that Herodotus' account of what passed at the Persian council is untrustworthy, especially in the speech attributed to the Halikarnassian queen Artemisia,[4] they are less sceptical about his

---

[1] This is implied (but not proved) by the order of Hdt.'s narrative at this point. Grundy (379, n. 1 and 387) makes the council begin on the *morning* of the day before the battle and continue into the following night in order to fit his view on the timing of Themistokles' supposed message to Xerxes.

[2] viii. 81–82.   [3] e.g. Giannelli, 39.

[4] Macan, i. 2. 461 finds both the prominence of Mardonios and the non-appearance of the Persian admirals suspicious; Rados, 266 suggested that Mardonios

descriptions of the various councils, possibly four in number, said to have been held by the Greeks. The anxiety of the Greek admirals to escape from their station at Salamis bears a suspicious resemblance to the similar stories told of their behaviour at Artemision, though cowardice is there attributed to the Greek fleet as a whole, whereas here the attitude of the Athenians, Aiginetans, and Megarians, anxious from motives of self-interest to keep the fleet at Salamis, is contrasted with that of the rest.[1] The panic attributed to the Peloponnesian leaders at Salamis is not likely to be more historical than that of the entire fleet at Artemision; their alleged poltroonery beforehand is at variance with the courage displayed by all the Greeks in the battle.[2]

Herodotus has indeed realized[3] the advantages which a battle in the narrow waters of Salamis Strait would confer on the heavier Greek ships against their more lightly-built opponents, who needed a sea-fight in the open sea to exploit to the full their superiority in speed and manœuvre. He has also, unlike most of his commentators, grasped the fact that if the Greeks remained at Salamis the Persian fleet would be bound to attack them there. This is not disputed in the argument which he attributes to Themistokles' critics;[4] they say that in a position so exposed as Salamis a naval defeat will be calamitous, not that the Persian fleet will ignore them, and by sailing on to the Isthmus cut their communications with the main Greek force on land. Herodotus, however, simply takes the fact for granted and does not explain the grounds of his certainty. Hence some modern historians[5] have described Themistokles' plan as a strategy of despair, which could only succeed if the Persians could be lured to attack the Greek fleet in its chosen position, and maintain[6] that there was absolutely no reason why the Persian fleet should not have by-passed the Greek fleet by

---

here took the place of the court official called 'The King's Ear'. Grundy, 374 believes that Hdt.'s sources may have contained some trustworthy details about this council derived ultimately from Artemisia.

[1] viii. 74. 2 (last sentence).

[2] Grundy, 391 tries to minimize this difficulty. Munro grapples with it (*J.H.S.* xxii, 1902, 323 f.) and realizes that Hdt.'s account as it stands is incredible; cf. also Legrand, viii. 36 f. and 62, n. 1.

[3] viii. 60 (Themistokles' speech) α and β.

[4] viii. 49. 2; cf. 74. 2.

[5] Notably Grundy, 352; so too How in *J.H.S.* xliii, 1923, 131 (= HW² 413 f.).

[6] Grundy, 380 and 352.

sailing straight to the Isthmus. Anyone who pictures the situation before the battle in such terms must lean heavily on the
Herodotean version of Themistokles' message, for that alone on
their view can explain why the Persians did something which
they are supposed to have had no need to do.[1]

The story of Themistokles' message is probably mythical, part
of the legend which grew up round his name,[2] and the true
explanation of what Herodotus takes for granted has been
supplied by Custance.[3] Custance claimed that the position
taken up by the Greek fleet in Salamis Strait was justified by
sound tactical and strategical considerations. Like others before
him, he notes that the position of the Greek land force at the
Isthmus could not be turned by the Persians without their fleet,
and also insists that their army could not stay long in front of
the Isthmus lines unless they could receive supplies by sea.
Custance then states his own view in words so important that
they must be quoted in full.

> Before the King's fleet could pass to the Isthmus either the Greek
> fleet must be destroyed or a force left to neutralise its action, since
> the all-important sea-supplies might otherwise be cut off. This means
> that if the king's advance was to be continued, his fleet must divide
> or fight. To divide the fleet would probably have compromised the
> numerical superiority on which reliance was placed.[4] He decided to
> fight. . . . The principle, put into practice at Salamis, of limiting the
> movements of a hostile fleet by taking up a position flanking its
> advance, is of first-rate importance and has often been applied since.[5]

There is no difficulty[6] in the supposition that the principle of
naval warfare enunciated by Custance was understood and
acted upon by Themistokles; possibly the Ionians were acting
on the same principle when their fleet took up its position at
Lade in 494. Custance was hampered, however, by his acceptance of the view that the Persian fleet, in spite of its earlier
losses, still considerably outnumbered the Greek; he did not
realize that its margin of superiority in this respect may by now

---

[1] See How (loc. cit.), also HW 379 ff.

[2] See below, Appendix IX (a).   [3] *War at Sea*, 26 f.

[4] Custance here cites Hdt. vii. 236. 2 (in the speech attributed by Hdt. to the
Persian admiral Achaimenes).

[5] In 27, n. 1 Custance mentioned the Armada campaign of 1588, also Togo off
Port Arthur (1904) and in the straits of Tsu Sima (1905).

[6] In spite of How (HW² 413 f.).

have been very small. That this was so in fact is strongly suggested by the passage[1] in which Herodotus, after describing the
effects of the second storm, explains that 'everything was being
done by God to make the Persian force equal to the Greek or
not much larger'; it is implied in this sentence that the result
aimed at by the heavenly powers was indeed brought about.
This conclusion is not in harmony with the inflated figures
given elsewhere by Herodotus for the Persian fleet,[2] but if in
reality it originally numbered 600, then on the reasonable
assumption that it lost nearly one-third of its total in the great
storm and 70 ships in the fighting off Artemision it would have
mustered only 340 ships on its arrival at Phaleron. Such a fleet
would be only slightly larger than the Greek fleet at Salamis,
for which Aeschylus gives 310 ships, and therefore would not
be strong enough to contain the Greek fleet and at the same
time send a squadron across the Saronic Gulf to land troops in
the Argolid.

The total given by Aeschylus, although he was a contemporary who was almost certainly present at the battle,[3] is
scouted or explained away by those who put their trust in the
figures given by Herodotus for the various contingents in the
Greek fleet which mustered at Salamis before the battle, figures
which add up to 366, though Herodotus makes the answer 378.[4]
Grundy maintains[5] that the evidence of the poet on the dry
question of numbers is not likely to be exact, while Hauvette[6]
thinks that Aeschylus was influenced by a tendency of the victorious Greeks to underestimate the number of their ships in
order to heighten the merit of their triumph. Labarbe,[7] accepting the fashionable hypothesis that the Corinthian squadron of
forty ships had been detached from the Greek fleet before the
battle, concludes that these ships (and certain others which he
believes to have been associated with them)[8] were not included
by Aeschylus because they were not present in the main battle.

[1] viii. 13 (last sentence).
[2] 1207 or 1327; see Tarn in *J.H.S.* xxviii, 1908, 204.
[3] See below, p. 222, n. 4; the figure 310 is in *Persai*, 338 ff.
[4] viii. 43–48; total in 48. Hauvette, 391 notes that a total of 378 is presupposed
in viii. 82. 2.   [5] Grundy, n. on p. 354.
[6] Hauvette, 394 f.   [7] *B.C.H.* lxxvi, 1952, 432 ff.
[8] On viii. 94, see below, Appendix IX (*c*). Labarbe's attempt to support his
view by the garbled version of Lycurgus (*In Leocratem* 70) well illustrates the
dangers involved in the use of such 'secondary sources'.

This explanation shows due respect for Aeschylus' testimony, but the hypothesis on which it rests is probably false, and Labarbe's attempt to defend the figures given by Herodotus is unconvincing. The figures amount to 42 ships more than the 324 present at Artemision, and though Labarbe supposes that the losses sustained there by the Greeks were more than made good by other ships in reserve at Pogon and elsewhere, this supposition is improbable if the Greeks had lost between 50 and 70 ships at Artemision.[1]

Anyone who compares Herodotus' detailed figures for the Greek fleet before Artemision and before Salamis[2] must be disquieted by the fact that the figures for the first four contingents are the same in both lists (Athenians 180, Corinthians 40, Megarians 20, Chalkidians 20). The figures in Herodotus' second list may be explained as the totals of the ships supplied by each individual state in the list during the campaign of 480;[3] hence the figure for a state which sent all its available ships to Artemision would be the same in both lists. The total 378 in Herodotus may perhaps have been reached by inclusion of the squadron guarding Aigina, assumed to have numbered 12,[4] but the implication of Pausanias[5] that the total number of ships supplied by Aigina was larger than the 40 of the Corinthian contingent may be only a guess or a mistake.

If the Persian fleet only slightly outnumbered the Greek, it would certainly not have enough ships to contain the Greek fleet at Salamis and at the same time be able to detach a squadron to the Argolid as well; hence if it wished to advance to the Isthmus it must first attack the Greek fleet in its chosen position. Apparently the Persian admirals were reluctant to admit the necessity of such an attack, which involved the sacrifice of their tactical advantages, and waited some time for the Greeks to make the first move. The fight at Thermopylai had taken place very soon after the conclusion of the Olympic and Karneian

[1] Labarbe (*Loi navale*, 123 f.), believing that the Athenians lost 70 triremes at Artemision, has to suppose that they had had 271 by mid-July 480.

[2] See the convenient table in Grundy, 354.   [3] Tarn, 219.

[4] δυοκαίδεκα has been inserted in viii. 46. 1, after ἄλλαι by van Herwerden, after νέες by Stein; Cobet read δέκα and has been followed by Munro (op. cit. 322). Cf. HW 249, also Powell, ad loc.

[5] ii. 29. 5. As the Kerkyraian contingent of sixty ships is second only to the Athenian in Hdt. vii. 169. 3, Hdt. must have estimated the total number of ships mobilized by Aigina in 480 at less than sixty (Labarbe in *B.C.H.* lxxvi, 419).

festivals; the last day of both coincided with a day of full moon,
which in 480 was probably the 19th or 20th of August.[1] If the
Persian fleet reached Phaleron nine days after the last battle,[2]
the date of its arrival can hardly be later than 7 September,[3]
and as the battle of Salamis was fought only three or four days
before the eclipse of the sun which occurred on 2 October 480,
the interval between the arrival of the fleet and the battle must
be three weeks; for those who, like Beloch,[4] make the last day of
the Olympia coincide in 480 with the full moon of 21 July the
interval is much longer.

Herodotus' narrative of the days leading up to the battle of
Salamis is chronologically misleading. His diary of the Persian
fleet suggests that Xerxes' decision to fight the Greek fleet at
Salamis was taken on the day (Day 30 of the Diary) after his
own fleet arrived at Phaleron, and carried out on the ensuing
night; such compression of events is incredible in itself[5] and is
also irreconcilable with the other time scheme which can be
extracted from Herodotus. This, ingeniously worked out by
Giannelli,[6] is based on the cross-references from the doings of
the Greek fleet to those of the Persian land forces: the Greek
decision to remain at Salamis is dated by Herodotus to the night
which followed the day on which the Acropolis was captured,
the night which also immediately preceded the day before the
battle. Hence the Acropolis fell on the next day but one before
the battle,[7] and as its siege presumably began on the day after
the Persian army entered Attica, the interval which we are
trying to discover must on Herodotus' second time scheme be
almost exactly covered by the duration of the siege.

Giannelli's conclusion, rigorously deduced from the indications in Herodotus, is enough to discredit the second time scheme
and to show that Herodotus has deliberately or unconsciously

---

[1] Busolt, n. on 673 f.; cf. HW on vii. 206. See below, Appendix XIV.

[2] See above, p. 193.

[3] Busolt, who allows nine or ten days for the march of the army from Thermopylai to Athens (see above, p. 195, n. 4) dates its arrival to 10 Sept.

[4] ii². 2. 47–49.

[5] Though accepted by Macan, ii. 293. See above, p. 206, also Hauvette, 400
and Giannelli, 39, n. 1.

[6] Giannelli, 40 ff.; cf. his chronological table on p. 49.

[7] Thereby dating the sacrifice of viii. 54 (see above, p. 203) to the day before
the battle. Giannelli, 45 thinks that its cause may be found in the earthquake of
viii. 64. 1, which aroused superstitious terror in Xerxes.

accelerated the march of events in the three weeks before the battle. Those who attempt to evade this inference may be divided into two groups. The members of the first group all deny that the interval between the arrival of the Persian army and the battle of Salamis lasted as long as three weeks, but some of them curtail it by allowing a longer period than five or six days for Xerxes' march from Thermopylai,[1] whereas the rest shorten the interval at the other end by moving forward the date of the battle, relying for this purpose on the evidence of Plutarch, who in his Life of Camillus[2] dates the battle to 20 Boedromion (22 September). But this date seems to have been inferred by Plutarch or his source from the assumption that the vision of Dikaios must have coincided with the normal date of the procession to Eleusis (19 Boedromion) and that Herodotus ascribed the vision to the day before the battle.[3] All these suggestions defend Herodotus' second time scheme for this part of his narrative by ignoring the more precise notes of time given by him elsewhere, on which alone a sound chronology can be constructed.

The scholars in the other group minimize the discrepancy by the hypothesis that the siege of the Acropolis lasted for a fortnight or more. Herodotus says[4] that Xerxes was baffled 'for a considerable time' by the stubborn resistance of the besieged. Bury,[5] accepting from Busolt the view that the siege must have lasted for a fortnight at least, rightly concluded that if the Acropolis held out so long it must have been defended by a more efficient force than the handful of temple officials and poverty-stricken Athenians who according to Herodotus composed its whole garrison. Hence he supposed that the defence of the Acropolis was a deliberate and organized military resistance, conducted by a sizeable part of the Athenian hoplite force; he

---

[1] See above, p. 195.

[2] 19. 6; elsewhere (*Moralia* 349 F and *Life of Lysander* 15. 1) he dates it to 16 Mounychion, the day of the festival of Artemis Mounychia, on which the battle was later commemorated. This date gave rise to the fable (*Moralia* 349 F) that the battle was fought at the full moon; this has become the *traditional* full moon in HW 382, n. 1.

[3] Plut. *Them.* 15. 1 dates it to the day of the battle and is followed by Obst, 165. See the discussion in Busolt, 703 f., and cf. HW 256.

[4] viii. 52. 2; see above, p. 200.

[5] In *C.R.* x, 1896, 416 B (also 417 B). Munro (op. cit. 321) follows Bury but realizes more clearly the chronological difficulties raised by Herodotus' account.

maintained that this supposition also explained the panic which
broke out in the fleet when it heard the news that the Acropolis
had been captured by the Persians. Bury argued that, after
the victory of Salamis had proved that the 'wooden wall' of the
oracle really did mean the fleet and not the barricade on the
Acropolis, the defence of the Acropolis was represented as a
hasty improvisation carried out by a few insignificant people
and foredoomed to failure, and that this revised version passed
into the pages of Herodotus. Clearly Bury had to explain in
some way this glaring divergence between his own account and
that of Herodotus on this matter, but it is hard to see why the
Athenians should have thought it necessary to rewrite history
so drastically; why should not the gallant defenders of the Acropolis have received their due meed of praise?[1]

There is an obvious discrepancy in Herodotus between the
weakness of the garrison left to defend the Acropolis and the
panic which the news of its fall produces in the fleet, but it is
more likely that the alleged panic is exaggerated or even fictitious than that Herodotus has underestimated the strength of
the force on the Acropolis. The 'considerable time' ascribed by
him to the siege is not to be taken strictly but must be explained
as relative to the small numbers and limited resources of the defenders. Grundy rightly doubts whether the Persians could have
captured the Acropolis, even by surprise, if it had been defended
by a strong hoplite force. He also raises the question what the
Athenians could hope to gain by a successful defence of the
Acropolis, but he does not suggest an answer. Presumably he
means that the Persians had so many troops that even if they
failed to take the Acropolis they could spare a force large
enough to hold its defenders in check without unduly weaken-
ing their main army.

If the Persian fleet remained at Phaleron for three weeks before the battle, and if the delay cannot be explained by the siege
of the Acropolis, it must have been due to the hesitations of the
Persian admirals. Unable to divide their fleet after their heavy
losses in the storm and in the subsequent battles, and unwilling
to expose themselves to the danger of a flank attack by a direct
advance to the Isthmus, they could not make up their minds to
take the alternative course and deliver a frontal attack on the

[1] So rightly Grundy, 358 f. in his examination of Bury's article.

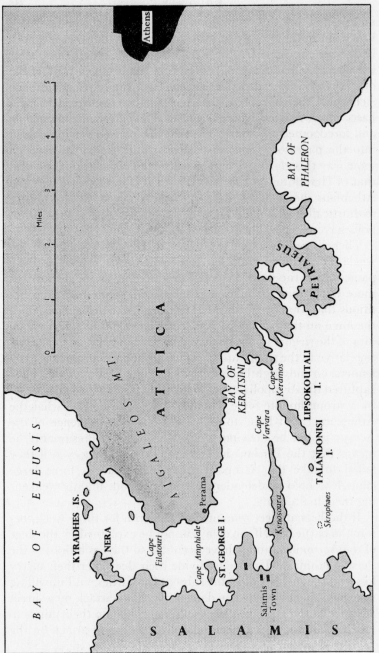

MAP 7. Salamis Strait

Greek fleet in its chosen position, so they waited for three weeks
in the hope that dissensions in the enemy fleet might bring
about its retreat to the Isthmus. Dissensions there may have
been at the outset between the Greek leaders at Salamis, and
some echoes of these may have been preserved in Herodotus, but
his narrative of the four councils cannot be accepted as it stands.[1]
Presumably Themistokles had convinced Eurybiadas that if he
kept the Greek fleet in the straits of Salamis the Persian admirals dared not sail past it and would be forced to attack it
before long, for the end of the campaigning season was not far
distant.[2] Six days after the autumnal equinox of 480 the Persians
decided to attack.

The movements of the Persian fleet before the battle

The Persian naval council at which Xerxes presided, if its
decision was to fight a battle, can hardly have been held on the
day after the fleet arrived at Phaleron.[3] There is certainly a
lacuna somewhere in Herodotus' diary of the Persian fleet after
its arrival in Attica, possibly more than one, and it is reasonable
to suppose that the Persian admirals needed a respite for their
ships and crews before attacking the enemy; there is no need,
however, to assume[4] that Xerxes could not join his fleet until the
Acropolis had fallen. Herodotus states that after Xerxes' decision had been announced to the council the Persian ships put
out to sea in the direction of Salamis and arranged themselves
undisturbed[5] in order of battle, but the day was too far advanced
for a sea-fight and night interposed, so they made their preparations for the next day. The original Persian plan, whatever it
was, is then modified by the alleged message of Themistokles,
which (on the natural interpretation of Herodotus' account)
causes the Persians to enter the straits of Salamis by night.

Herodotus undoubtedly regards the Persian decision to provoke a sea-fight as prior to and independent of the message of

---

[1] Cf. Meyer, *Forsch.* ii. 203 f. (the defence of Hdt. in Wells, *Studies*, 156 f. is unconvincing).

[2] Miltner in *Klio*, xxxi, 1938, 242. De Sanctis, *Storia dei Greci*, ii. 32 insists that the
Persian fleet could not advance farther until it had crushed the Greek fleet at
Salamis, and therefore decided to fight.

[3] See above, p. 211.   [4] As Keil does (*A.S.* 99).

[5] κατ' ἡσυχίην (viii. 70. 1).

Themistokles,[1] but as his account of the deliberations which
preceded the decision is rhetorical rather than factual he has not
explained how the Persian admirals planned to bring the Greek
fleet to battle, and so leaves in obscurity the purpose behind the
movement of the Persian fleet which followed the council, though
he gives the impression that it occurred on the same day as the
council.[2] Grundy[3] supposes that Herodotus here antedated the
forward movement of the Persian fleet, which on his view
occurred not on the afternoon before the battle but on the
following night; this explanation is very improbable and has not
found favour with later scholars. Some have supposed that when
the Persian ships had advanced to the entrance of the straits
they remained at sea all night,[4] but the description of their later
movements in Herodotus shows that he believed them to have
returned to Phaleron at nightfall.[5]

This difference between Herodotus and his critics is important, since it reflects a radical disagreement about the original
intentions of the Persian admirals. Macan holds[6] that their
first plan was to block the approaches to the straits of Salamis
at both ends, east and west, by drawing up their fleet outside
the western channel between Salamis and the Megarid (sometimes called the Minoa Channel or Trupika Bay) as well as the
eastern channel between the promontory of Kynosoura (modern
Cape Varvara)[7] and the mainland of Attica. These moves,
Macan believes, were intended to besiege the Greek fleet and
refugees in Salamis; he assumes that before long lack of food
and water would have compelled the Greek fleet to try to force
its way out and so accept battle with the Persians in the open
waters of the Saronic Gulf.[8] But even if the two ends of the
straits could have been blockaded effectively by a fleet of triremes for several days, such a policy was dangerous because

---

[1] Cf. Giannelli, 55 f. and 79.

[2] So Busolt, 697, n. 1 (attacked by Keil in *A.S.* 100, n. 2).

[3] Grundy, 377, also 382 f.   [4] e.g. Macan, i. 2. 482 B.

[5] Rados, 282 points out that ἀνάγω (viii. 76. 1) is always used of ships leaving
a harbour or a coast.

[6] Apparently following Wecklein; cf. Busolt, 698 (continuation of n. 1 on
p. 697).

[7] This identification, due to Leake, was challenged by Blakesley, ii. 403, but
cf. Macan, i. 2. 478 B.

[8] Macan, ii. 304–7 and 311 f. (cf. Giannelli, 55 f. and 79). Gomme (*Essays*,
199 f.) thinks this is what the Persians *ought* to have done.

it involved dividing the Persian fleet in face of an enemy only slightly inferior in numbers.

On the alternative hypothesis the forward movement of the Persian fleet was made by its admirals in the hope that an offer of battle outside the eastern strait might tempt the Greeks to sally forth to the attack;[1] if this is correct, the movement may belong to the day after the council, the Persian ships waiting at their stations outside the strait until the late afternoon, when on realizing that the Greeks could not be induced to come out they returned to Phaleron.[2] This explanation is attractive, for the Persian leaders would probably have tried this move before they resorted to the plan which desperation finally drove them to adopt, a plan fraught with serious dangers, of making their way into the straits by night. Yet if the original plan here attributed to the Persians is plausible in itself, the same cannot be said for the chronological scheme which attributes its execution to the afternoon before the battle, only to be superseded at once by a second and completely different plan; the coincidence is too remarkable to be accepted as fact. The forward movement of the Persian fleet must have roused the Greeks to renewed watchfulness; a further suspension of Persian naval activity had to follow before the second plan could safely be put into operation. Hence a second lacuna must be presupposed in the diary of the fleet, between the forward movement which followed closely on the Persian naval council and the night preceding the battle, unless the true explanation is that Herodotus has conflated two meetings of the council into one.[3]

Although Herodotus has not explained what on his view was the original plan of the Persian admirals, he clearly believed it to have been replaced by a new plan under the influence of the message which at this stage, according to the tradition followed by him, was sent to them by Themistokles. This message is almost certainly unhistorical,[4] but its excision from the story does not affect the credibility of the movements ascribed by Herodotus[5] to the Persian fleet on the night before the battle. Their first step was the landing of a force on the small island between

[1] This seems to be the view of Keil (*A.S.* 100).

[2] Cf. Keil, loc. cit.

[3] The decision to risk an entry into the straits by night must have been preceded by a war-council of some kind.

[4] See below, Appendix IX (*a*). [5] viii. 76.

Salamis and the Attic mainland, an island which Herodotus
later calls Psyttaleia.[1] Next, at midnight, the Persian fleet advanced; they put out to sea with their west wing, circling towards Salamis, and those posted round Keos and Kynosoura
also put out to sea. The result of this advance was the occupation by the Persians of the whole strait as far as Mounychia.
In the battle next day the western wing, occupied by the
Phoenicians, is said to have been 'towards Eleusis', while the
Ionians who formed the eastern wing were near the Piraeus.[2]
Herodotus says that the forward movement in the night before
the battle was carried out 'in silence, to prevent the enemy
noticing it'.[3] From these data Leake and Grote rightly inferred
that Herodotus conceived the Persian fleet on the morning of
the battle as drawn up in a long line stretching along the Attic
coast from a point nearly opposite the island of St. George[4] to
the eastern entrance of the straits of Salamis, and that they had
reached this position by a stealthy advance into the straits under
cover of darkness.

Herodotus' description of the forward movement of the Persian fleet is unduly condensed and therefore not free from obscurity. There is an initial awkwardness in the use of the Greek
word meaning 'to put out to sea from the shore' as both a
transitive and an intransitive verb in the same short sentence.[5]
The fact that a Keos in this neighbourhood cannot be identified
with certainty does not matter very much, for even if the explanation[6] that it is an alternative name for Kynosoura is far
from satisfactory, it must have been fairly near to Kynosoura,[7]
but what can Herodotus mean by his reference to 'those who
were posted round Keos and Kynosoura' if the Persian fleet
after its demonstration off the mouth of the straits had returned

---

[1] viii. 76. 2. Psyttaleia must be the modern Lipsokoutali; see below, Appendix
VIII.   [2] viii. 85. 1.   [3] viii. 76. 3.
[4] Hence the reference to Eleusis in 85. 1.
[5] ἀνάγω is elsewhere used by Hdt. both as a transitive and as an intransitive
verb (e.g. vi. 12. 1, iii. 41. 2); the occurrence of both uses here in the same sentence
is queried by Powell (ad loc.).
[6] Hauvette, 412 and n. 2 (following Stein); cf. HW 261. Giannelli, 58 and 60,
thinks it was a bay on the south side of Kynosoura (cf. Keil in A.S. 101, n. 3).
[7] Wilhelm (S.B. Wien, ccxi, 1929, 29–32) proposes to read Κέραμον, which he
identifies with the promontory on the Attic coast opposite Lipsokoutali. He proves
(against Beloch, ii². 2. 111 and n. 1) that Keramos really is the modern name of
this point, and assumes that it was the same in 480.

to its base at Phaleron, and how can this portion of the fleet
be contrasted with 'the west wing', since the words in which
Herodotus describes the forward movement of the west wing
definitely exclude the possibility that he was here referring to
a squadron sent to the west end of Salamis to block the alternative way of escape between Salamis and Megara?

The solution must start from a strict interpretation of the
half-sentence 'those posted round Keos and Kynosoura also put
out to sea'. As Herodotus uses the verb ἀνάγω of this movement,
the ships which carried it out cannot, as many suppose, have
been at sea already outside the entrance to the straits, and from
this it follows that Keos and Kynosoura must mark their position not at the beginning but at the completion of the movement,
the position to which they had been 'posted' in the sense that
it represented not the starting-point but the final goal of their
advance.[1] That advance had apparently been preceded by the
forward movement of the rest of the fleet, here called 'the west
wing', which Herodotus describes as 'wheeling towards Salamis';
presumably his informants meant by this the town of Salamis
inside the strait. The simplest explanation of 'the west wing' is
that by this phrase Herodotus means the ships which in the
Persian base at Phaleron were nearest to the strait; they are
naturally the first to move when the Persians decide to enter the
strait by night, and so when the Persian fleet is drawn up off
the coast of Attica facing south on the morning of the battle
they are still on the west wing[2] (now the Persian right wing)
reaching to the island of St. George, and are correctly located
by Herodotus as 'in the direction of Eleusis'.

Herodotus has described a twofold movement of the Persian
fleet; part of it was sent up the strait by night to occupy a
position along the mainland shore of the strait and to cut the
exit into the Bay of Eleusis, while the rest was instructed to
block the southern exit of the strait. Of these the first manœuvre
was far the more important and more dangerous, but Herodotus
failed to explain it clearly because he was more interested in
the other.[3] The blocking of the southern exit by the Persian fleet

---

[1] Cf. Wilhelm, op. cit. 35 ff., though in the parallel he cites from *I.G.* i². 105
(Tod, 91), ll. 9 f. the construction is made easier by the addition of πλεῖν.

[2] Cf. Hauvette, 411.

[3] See the admirable analysis in Hauvette, loc. cit.

seemed to him to provide a striking confirmation of an oracle attributed to Bakis, so striking that it evoked his most outspoken expression of his belief in oracles.[1] But if he has not sufficiently explained the nature of the first movement, he has indicated it, and has stated explicitly that the purpose of both movements combined was to deprive the Greeks of all possibility of escape.

Many have discarded Herodotus' testimony here in favour of the account give by Diodoros,[2] which he probably took from Ephoros. In this account Xerxes, hearing from Themistokles that the Greeks intend to flee from their stations in Salamis and muster at the Isthmus, decides to prevent the junction of the Greek fleet with the land forces. He sends the Egyptian squadron to block the channel between Salamis and the Megarid, and the rest of his fleet to Salamis with orders to bring the Greek ships to battle. In the main fleet the Phoenicians are said to have been on the right wing and the Greek subjects of Persia on the left; in this statement Diodoros appears to agree with Herodotus, but as he describes the position of the Greek fleet on the morning of the battle as stretching across the strait from Salamis to the Herakleion (on the Attic mainland, apparently near the modern Perama)[3] the Persian line of battle from right to left would run from north to south or even north-east to south-west, not as in Herodotus from west to east. Diodoros says[4] that the Persian ships at first preserved their formation but fell into confusion when they entered the straits; this is the only clear indication in his narrative that his source pictured the Persian fleet as entering the strait on the morning of the battle and not, as Herodotus implies, during the previous night.

The manifest discrepancies between this account and that given by Herodotus have naturally disquieted those who here prefer to follow Diodoros. Grundy, reacting violently against the very sensible dictum of an (unnamed) eminent authority that 'whenever the evidence of Herodotus and Diodoros respectively differs on any particular point, that of Herodotus is

---

[1] The oracle (quoted by Hdt. in viii. 77) has been held responsible for his reference to Mounychia (viii. 76. 1) as the eastern end of the Persian line; cf. Beloch, ii². 2. 106 and HW 261.

[2] xi. 17. 1–18. 2.

[3] The usual identification, e.g. Macan, i. 2. 500 A; cf. Hammond in *J.H.S.* lxxvi, 1956, 38.

[4] xi. 18. 4.

to be unhesitatingly preferred', tries to bring the two into
harmony by his assumption[1] that Herodotus antedated part of
his notes and so ascribed to the night before the battle that forward movement of the Persian fleet into the straits which Diodoros correctly placed on the morning of the battle; not only
is this hypothesis improbable in itself but it does not account
for Herodotus' failure to mention the sending of the Egyptian
squadron to the Megarid Channel, a remarkable omission if
the squadron really was sent. Goodwin argued[2] that Herodotus
was alluding obscurely to the sending of this squadron when he
spoke of the Persian west wing 'circling towards Salamis'; but
this will not do,[3] for 'towards' does not mean 'round' and
Herodotus was probably referring here to the town of Salamis,
not the island.

Grundy's view presupposes that Ephoros made better use of
the sources available to Herodotus, but so far as those sources
were oral they could not have been used by Ephoros, and if
Grundy meant the *Persai* of Aeschylus it must be remembered
that Herodotus contains much material which is not in Aeschylus, material which must have been mostly derived from oral
sources. A comparison of the Ephorean account of Salamis with
the *Persai* strongly suggests that the former does not rest on
independent evidence no longer extant,[4] but is a critical reconstruction of Herodotus suggested by the author's deductions
from Aeschylus. Munro, who holds this view, says[5] that the
Ephorean account 'has been built up by reflection, inference,
rationalism and conjecture'; it is essentially, like the work of a
modern historian on Salamis, 'reasoned history, not independent
historical evidence'. Ephoros' view that a squadron was sent
to block the Megarid Channel was probably based on his
misinterpretation of an obscure line in the *Persai*.[6] He assumed

[1] Grundy, 373 and 382 f.; the quotation appears on p. 370.
[2] *Papers of the American School at Athens*, i. 1882–3, 237–62.
[3] Goodwin's argument is rejected by Grundy, 385, who frankly admits that
Grote's interpretation of Herodotus was 'perfectly correct'; cf. HW 381, n. 1, and
especially Keil in *A.S.* 80 and n. 1 (as Keil observes on p. 81, if Hdt. in viii. 76. 1
was referring to the dispatch of the Egyptian squadron, why was such secrecy
necessary?).
[4] Tarn (*J.H.S.* xxviii, 1908, 232 f.) suggested that behind Ephoros' account
lies the Phoenician version of the war at sea, a version which became known
at Athens in the first decade of the fourth century!
[5] *J.H.S.* xxii, 1902, 329 f.   [6] Line 368, discussed below.

that the Egyptians were assigned to the task because they had
fought best at Artemision[1] and were not mentioned by Herodotus as playing any part in the battle of Salamis; it was an
obvious conjecture that they had been detached on a special
mission. Ephoros' assertion[2] that the left of the Greek fleet
rested on the shores of Attica when the battle began is impossible and has been abandoned by his modern followers, who
represent the Greek line as meeting the Persian obliquely.

It is, however, possible to argue, as Munro does, that although
the Ephorean account preserved in Diodoros is no more than
a critical reconstruction, it does in fact correspond more nearly
(apart from unimportant details) to what actually happened
than the reconstruction of the battle and its immediate antecedents given by Leake and Grote on the basis of the Herodotean
narrative. Many scholars,[3] while differing on the value to be
assigned to the evidence of Diodoros, have maintained that the
Persian fleet must have entered the straits on the morning of
the battle and not, as Herodotus clearly implies, during the
previous night; they defend this contention on two grounds,
that the Herodotean account contains certain manifest impossibilities, and that it is contradicted by data obtainable
from a close examination of certain passages in the *Persai*.
Aeschylus was actually present at the battle,[4] and the play in
which he describes its course and the events which led up to it
was produced less than eight years later; what then could seem
more reasonable than Goodwin's criterion[5] that 'nothing can
be accepted as historic which contradicts any plain statements
of Aeschylus about the contest'? But Aeschylus was a poet
writing a poetic drama, and the lines of the *Persai* to which
Goodwin and his followers confidently appeal may be less plain
and unambiguous than they suppose.

The relevant passages in the *Persai* are few. In the first,[6]

---

[1] viii. 17; but 100. 4 seems to show that Hdt. thought they had also fought at
Salamis (so also Aeschylus, *Persai*, 311 f.)

[2] Diod. xi. 18. 2, vigorously criticized by Rados, 320.

[3] Most English scholars have followed Goodwin in this view, which seems to
have been first popularized by Löschcke in *Neue Jahrbücher*, cxv, 1877, 25 ff.,
though he had been anticipated by Blakesley (ii. 400–19) in 1854.

[4] Cf. Ion (*F.G.H.*, no. 392), fr. 7.

[5] Op. cit. 246.

[6] Lines 366–8. Murray in the O.C.T. unjustifiably prints l. 368 before l. 367,
following Koechly.

Aeschylus, describing how Xerxes at nightfall[1] sent his ships to cut off the Greek retreat, says that he posted the main body of the fleet in three columns ($\sigma\tau o\hat{\iota}\chi o\iota$) to guard the sea-exits ($\breve{\epsilon}\kappa\pi\lambda o\iota$, also called $\pi\acute{o}\rho o\iota$ $\dot{a}\lambda\acute{\iota}\rho\rho o\theta o\iota$), and others round the island of Aias (i.e. Salamis). The verb which means 'posted' ($\tau\acute{a}\xi a\iota$), is clearly to be understood as governing the ships referred to in the last line, and so this line, as Macan pointed out,[2] cannot refer to the supposed circumnavigation of Salamis by the Egyptian squadron, whatever Ephoros may or may not have thought. It has been supposed that it refers to the posting of a cordon of cruisers round the south side of the island of Salamis,[3] but the purpose of such a precaution is not obvious. As for the three sea-exits, two are obviously the passages leading out of the strait on either side of Lipsokoutali, but the third is not necessarily to be identified with the Megarian Channel; if the Persian fleet really entered the strait by night, as Herodotus implies, it could be the channel between the Attic mainland and Salamis near the island of St. George,[4] for a Persian squadron stationed here would equally well block the alternative way of escape for the Greeks through the Bay of Eleusis.

In a later passage of the *Persai* the messenger, describing how the Greek fleet rowed forward from its stations at dawn, says that 'quickly they were all clearly visible'.[5] Those who believe that the Persian fleet did not enter the straits until the morning of the battle, notably Löschcke[6] and Goodwin, claim to infer from this line that the Greek ships were not at first visible to the Persians, and that in consequence the latter cannot have been drawn up at dawn along the Attic coast, little more than a mile away. It is impossible to extract such a precise conclusion from this line, in which the main emphasis falls on the words 'all' and 'clearly visible'. The Greek fleet had to deploy very quickly at daybreak, apparently with the right wing leading, into line of

---

[1] *Persai*, 364–5 (cf. 377 ff.). There is here a sharp disagreement with the plain statement of Hdt. (viii. 76. 1) that the main Persian fleet did not move till midnight.

[2] ii. 306, n. 1; cf. Keil in *A.S.* 82.

[3] This explanation was suggested by C. Conradt in his edition of the *Persai* (Berlin, 1888); cf. Hauvette, 416 and n. 1. It was adopted by Munro (op. cit. 327) and Beloch, ii². 2. 121.

[4] Keil (*A.S.* 85) makes it the channel between Attica and St. George; he thinks that the channel between St. George and Salamis did not matter as it is scarcely 300 metres wide and only 2 fathoms deep.

[5] Line 398.   [6] See above, p. 222, n. 3, and cf. Hauvette, 413 f.

battle, but it was not long before all the ships were clearly seen
by the enemy advancing to meet them across the strait.

Diodoros says[1] that the Persians were able at first to keep their
order as they had plenty of sea-room, but when they came into
the narrows they were compelled to withdraw some ships from
the line and fell into much confusion. This picture may have
been inferred by Ephoros from another passage in the *Persai*,[2]
but what Aeschylus says there is that, though the 'flood' of the
Persian host at first held out, at a later stage the ships fell foul
of one another because a large number of vessels had been
collected in a small space; the use of the pluperfect suggests that
Aeschylus is here referring to the manœuvres which preceded
the battle. The word for 'flood' ($\dot{\rho}\epsilon\hat{\upsilon}\mu a$) has been translated as
'stream' by some[3] who refer it to the appearance of the Persian
right wing as it entered the strait and insist that it must indicate a formation of the Persian ships in something resembling
a column, but it is a natural metaphor for a host of men, found
earlier in this same play.[4]

On the other side it has been argued that Aeschylus stresses
the nocturnal activity of the Persian fleet as a whole,[5] and that
in one passage he seems to refer to its entry into the straits by
night. Unfortunately, here too the testimony of Aeschylus is
ambiguous. He says[6] that all the sailor host was kept *diaploös*
all through the night by the captains of the ships. The word
$\delta\iota\acute{a}\pi\lambda oos$ does not occur as an adjective except in this one passage;
elsewhere it is a noun which means 'a voyage across' or 'room
to sail through, a passage', and it is argued that the adjective
must here have a similar meaning and refer to the Persian fleet
'sailing through' the strait to take up its position along the Attic
coast fronting the Greek fleet. But why should Aeschylus have
said that this movement went on all night? It is possible that
$\delta\iota\acute{a}\pi\lambda oos$ as an adjective was used by him to mean something
like 'sailing about';[7] the latest edition of Liddell and Scott

[1] xi. 18. 4.   [2] Lines 412–16.

[3] e.g. Grundy, 394 and Munro, 328.

[4] Line 88; cf. Euripides, *I.T.* 1437 and the note in Platnauer's edition.

[5] So Keil (*A.S.* 83), but his assertion that Aeschylus stresses the secrecy of the
Persian movements (cf. Hdt. viii. 76. 3) is hardly justified by the passages in the
Persai to which he refers. Blakesley (ii. 406, n. 15) inferred from *Persai*, l. 380 that
the Persians made a lot of noise.   [6] Lines 382–3.

[7] My former colleague, the late J. D. Denniston, suggested to me the parallel
of $\delta\iota a\tau\rho\acute{\epsilon}\chi\omega$, which can mean 'to run about'.

suggests the rendering 'sailing continually' and translates this
line 'kept them at the oar'.

If the testimony of Aeschylus is insufficient either to discredit
or to confirm the account given by Herodotus, an account which
was almost certainly derived from the evidence of numerous
informants who had been present at the battle, the critics of
Herodotus must base their case solely on the impossibilities of
fact which they claim to have detected in his narrative. It has
also been argued that the Herodotean account is irreconcilable
with the statement that the Persians landed troops in Psyttaleia
because they thought that Psyttaleia would be a central point
in the coming battle. But the statement is made only by
Plutarch, who asserts[1] that the chief clash of the ships was expected to take place there; no such precise assertion is to be
found in either Aeschylus or Herodotus. Aeschylus says[2] that
Xerxes sent a force to the island so that when shipwrecked
sailors sought safety on its shores the Persian troops stationed
there could slay the shipwrecked Greeks and rescue their own
men. Herodotus[3] reproduces this motivation, but adds that the
shipwrecked ships and their crews were expected, when the
battle was joined, to be cast up principally on this island, as it
lay in the path (ἐν πόρῳ) of the coming sea-fight. Herodotus has
used the phrase earlier[4] to describe the position of the Myrmex
rock 'in the fairway' of the channel between Skiathos and Magnesia, but its application here to Psyttaleia is reasonable enough.
If the Persians, advancing from the coast of Attica, planned to
drive the Greek ships down the strait into the open sea, they
would expect them to pass on either side of Psyttaleia, but
Herodotus is not committed by his use of the phrase ἐν πόρῳ to
Plutarch's view that Psyttaleia was to be the central point of
the battle.[5] Even those who claim that it was tacitly admit that
in fact Psyttaleia played no part in the battle until the end,
when its garrison was slaughtered by an Athenian force under
Aristeides.[6]

The alleged improbabilities of fact are two, that the Persians
could never have entered the straits unperceived by the Greeks,
and that they could never have allowed the Greek fleet to form

[1] *Aristeides* 9. 4.   [2] *Persai*, 450–3.   [3] viii. 76. 2.
[4] vii. 183. 3.   [5] Cf. Hauvette, 415, also Duncker, vii. 282, note.
[6] viii. 95.

in line undisturbed at daybreak on the morning of the battle
when they were separated from them by not much more than a
mile of sea.[1] Of these the first is not impressive.[2] Probably the
Persians had been at Phaleron for at least nineteen days, and
the Greeks may have relaxed their original vigilance. If the
battle was fought on 28 September the moon was in its last
quarter, and it has been calculated that it rose just under two
hours after midnight.[3] Even if the Persian fleet had been detected when it had entered the strait but before it had completed its movement, the Greeks would probably have hesitated
to risk an attack which might have had the result of throwing
their own fleet into confusion. The difficulty of detecting the
movement of enemy ships in a narrow strait has been illustrated
from an incident in the Ionian War:[4] an Athenian squadron of
eighteen ships, trying to escape through the Hellespont into the
Aegean, was not detected by a Peloponnesian squadron of sixteen ships at Abydos which had received special instructions
to intercept their flight. It is to be noted that Herodotus em-
phasizes the quietness with which the Persians made their all-
important forward movement into the strait, 'so that it might
not be observed by the enemy'.[5]

The second objection is more serious, and the attempts which
have been made to answer it[6] are not altogether satisfactory.
Herodotus' statements, if pressed, would imply an interval between the dawn of day and the embarkation of the Greek fleet,
an interval occupied by harangues addressed to a meeting of
marines by the generals, notably Themistokles, whose speech is
the only one to be recorded (in a brief summary).[7] But Herodotus
also mentions that the Persians attacked the Greeks as soon as
they put off from the shore,[8] which implies that they did not
waste much time. A Tenian trireme had deserted from the
Persian fleet during the night, bringing to the Greeks an accurate and full report of the Persian movements,[9] so that the

---

[1] The breadth of the straight part of the channel running from east to west is
given as 2,000 yards by Grundy, 396.

[2] The arguments against it are well marshalled by Keil (*A.S.* 90; cf. 100).

[3] Busolt, 702, n. 2.   [4] Thucydides viii. 102. 1-2.

[5] viii. 76. 3; this observation is fatal to Grundy's view (above, p. 216) that the
forward movement really belongs to the morning of the battle.

[6] e.g. Keil (*A.S.* 93 ff.) and Rados, 318.   [7] viii. 83.

[8] viii. 84. 1 in some texts (83. 2 in Legrand and Hude).   [9] viii. 82. 1.

Greek commanders were warned early enough to take the necessary steps; it is possible that they got their crews on board a little
before dawn in readiness for the coming attack. It has been
calculated[1] that the Greeks, if they had moved at dawn with
great speed and energy, could have completed their deployment
in fifteen minutes; the Persian fleet could certainly have rowed
across the strait in less time than this, but perhaps they were
tired after the strain of their nocturnal movement and failed to
realize the need for prompt action if they were to exploit to the
full the advantage which that movement had given them. Anyhow, if Herodotus was right in his assertion that the Persian
fleet entered the straits by night, the failure of the Persian fleet
to attack the Greeks promptly at dawn, however surprising,
must be accepted as a fact.

Defenders of Herodotus' account are at least entitled to plead
that this difficulty is trifling in comparison with that raised by
the hypothesis of Herodotus' critics, that the Persian fleet rowed
into the straits from the open sea at dawn, an hypothesis which
attributes an incredible degree of folly to the Persian high
command. On this view they enter a strait where the fairway
is not more than a mile wide, so that the maximum number of
ships in the front line would be eighty;[2] Rados rightly criticizes
those who would try to pack them more closely. Under such
conditions the scales would indeed be weighted in favour of the
heavier Greek ships, and Persian superiority in speed and tactical skill would be useless. It is therefore not surprising that
the holders of this view have had recourse to the message of
Themistokles in the form, markedly different from that in
Aeschylus, in which it is recorded by Herodotus.

In Herodotus[3] the message begins as in Aeschylus with the
statement that the Greeks are about to retreat, but to this is
added an assurance that if Xerxes attacks promptly the pro-
Persian section of the fleet (apparently the Athenians are meant)
will fight on the side of the Persians against their former allies.
Macan[4] frankly admits that this addition is 'most startling' and

---

[1] By Keil (in *A.S.* 95 f.).

[2] This problem is well discussed by Rados, 325 ff.; cf. Tarn in *J.H.S.* xxviii,
1908, 219. Grundy, 396 allows a minimum of 20 yards of front for each trireme
(surely too little; see above, p. 150). Keil's 15 metres (*A.S.* 103, n. 1) is worse still.
Custance, 13 allows 100 yards of front for each ship!

[3] viii. 75. 2–3.   [4] ii. 310. Cf. Munro (op. cit.) 331 and HW 380–1.

'hardly consistent' with the Aeschylean version of the message, but he realizes also that the message in its original form provides no explanation for the decision of the Persians to enter the strait, as he supposes they did, on the morning of the battle, and therefore concludes that only the promise of Athenian co-operation could have induced the Persian admirals to venture upon what he describes as 'a somewhat risky movement'. It would be nearer the mark to call it an act of stark lunacy, for even if the message of Themistokles belonged not to legend but to history and even if its true form has been preserved only by Herodotus it is incredible that the Persians should ever have ventured to take such a frightful risk on the bare word of a lying Greek. The Athenians had until now been their bitterest enemies; why should Xerxes credit the report that they had changed sides at such short notice? He had not, as Mardonios was to do in the next year, made any tempting offer to detach them from their allegiance.

If the message of Themistokles is rejected as unhistorical in all its forms, the hypothesis that the Persian fleet did not enter the strait until the morning of the battle is beset with serious difficulties, which become manifest in the reconstruction proposed by Giannelli. Dismissing the message as unhistorical, Giannelli has to assume that the battle began with a tactical offensive of the Greek fleet but that, as it was dangerous for it to venture into the open sea, Themistokles had instructed the ship-captains to back water after the initial advance in order to lure the enemy on into the strait.[1] This withdrawal of the Greeks is so prolonged by Giannelli that what he represents as the second stage of the battle is almost indistinguishable from Grote's view.[2] He has no real answer to the obvious objection that, if the Persians wished to confront the Greeks with the dilemma between coming out to fight or staying to be starved out, they ought to have retired into the open sea when the Greek fleet advanced, in order to draw it on after them; his attempts[3] to grapple with this problem only reveal more clearly the folly of the conduct which any view like his must attribute to the Persian admirals, a folly so astounding as to outweigh any 'impossibility of fact' which the critics of Herodotus have claimed to detect in his narrative.

---

[1] Giannelli, 65; cf. Hdt. viii. 83. 2 and 84. 1.   [2] Cf. his plan on p. 69.
[3] Giannelli, 72 f.

Ultimately the solution of this problem depends on the interpretation and the value to be placed on the various parts of
the ancient evidence. There is an antecedent probability that
the account of Herodotus, almost certainly built up from the
narratives of many who had personally participated in the
events, is substantially accurate, apart from such items in it as
are derived from the Themistokles legend. This presumption is
strengthened by the failure of Grundy's hypothesis that Herodotus misunderstood what he had been told, and by the discovery that the *Persai* of Aeschylus, if examined without any
preconceptions, contains nothing which refutes Herodotus in
any important particular. There is no ancient evidence for the
view of Löschcke and Goodwin except the account in Diodoros,
which has no independent value; their view in fact provides the
most glaring example of the frequent tendency of scholars to
prefer the speculations of the so-called secondary sources to the
evidence of our primary authorities, and on that ground alone
it must be firmly rejected. Here as elsewhere historians must
apply the principle that 'whenever the evidence of Herodotus
and Diodoros respectively differs on any particular point, that
of Herodotus is to be unhesitatingly preferred'.[1]

The results so far reached must now be summarized. Not
later than 9 September the Persian fleet reached Phaleron, but
it could not proceed farther without a battle, as the position of
the Greek fleet at Salamis flanked the line of its advance. A few
days after its arrival at Phaleron, perhaps after the fall of the
Acropolis (on the assumption that the siege lasted less than a
week) the Persian admirals offered battle outside the straits to
the east of Salamis, but the Greek fleet refused to be tempted to
fight in the Saronic Gulf. There was then a further delay of
several days until the Persians finally decided, about 27 September, to bring about a battle by a stealthy entry into the
straits during the following night, which in its earlier part would
be dark enough for their purpose. This attempt was attended
with great danger, for if it was to be successful it would have
to be carried out in the utmost secrecy, so that it could be
completed before it was noticed by the enemy. Why did
the Persians venture on this risky manœuvre? The message
of Themistokles, adduced by Herodotus to account for their

[1] See above, pp. 220 f.

decision, is a legend, but even if it was a fact it would not provide an adequate explanation for the movement described by
him. The Persian leaders were faced with a deadlock, since they
could not advance on either sea or land until they had disposed
of the threat from the Greek fleet, but in view of the lateness of
the season they could not afford to wait indefinitely. To force on
a battle by an entry into the straits in the daytime would have
been disastrous; the solution which they found for their dilemma was as ingenious as it was bold. By introducing their fleet
into the strait by night they hoped to secure adequate sea-room
for their ships, which on the morning of the battle were probably
drawn up along the north side of the strait from the island of
St. George to the vicinity of the Piraeus; in this position the
fleet could count on the support of the land forces posted along
the Attic coast.[1] In its inception this bold plan was completely
successful, but before dawn the Greek admirals had received
a full report of the manœuvre from the Tenians, so that they
were able to make timely preparations to meet it, and in the
ensuing battle they inflicted a crushing defeat on their adversaries.

The battle of Salamis

The Greek victory at Salamis was the turning-point of the
Persian War, and it is unfortunate that its course cannot be
reconstructed with any certainty. Herodotus has a few observations on the development of the battle as a whole, but in the
main he is concerned with isolated episodes which seem to belong to the later stages of the fighting when the enemy were
already defeated and beginning to seek safety in flight.[2] He is
always prone to single out the exploits of individuals in battle,
but he evidently took much trouble over his narrative of
Salamis,[3] and it compares favourably with the worthless Ephorean reconstruction in Diodoros and with the fantasies in the
sources used by Plutarch, while its defects were perhaps inevitable in any attempt to describe a naval engagement of such

---

[1] Duncker, vii. 283, n. (end of long n. on pp. 281–3) pointed out that in the
great battles fought in the Hellespont the contending fleets were always drawn up
near the two shores of the strait and at its narrowest part, each being supported by
its own land forces on the adjacent coast.
[2] Cf. Legrand, viii. 30.   [3] In spite of Macan, i. 2. 490 B.

magnitude. As Tarn[1] rightly observed on Artemision, 'even in the absence of smoke, a man at one end of the line can have had little idea of what was happening to the bulk of the fleet'. Aeschylus has a perplexing statement[2] that the Greek right wing led the way to the attack, and also notes that later on as the battle developed the Persians fell into difficulties because they had too many ships in a confined space, but otherwise he throws no light on the causes of the Greek victory. He agrees with Herodotus that the fighting began just after dawn, and adds that it went on till sunset;[3] Macan's contention[4] that it was only the weeping and wailing that continued till nightfall is refuted by the context, which shows that the weeping was coextensive with the later stages of the battle. If Aeschylus' testimony on this point is accurate, the battle must have lasted for nearly twelve hours, and the fighting must have continued with some at least of the Persian ships until the end of the day.

Herodotus' evidence on the battle order of the two fleets is unfortunately incomplete. He remarks[5] that in the Persian fleet, drawn up on the north side of the strait from west to east, the Phoenicians were on the west wing (and therefore on the Persian right) and the Ionians on the east wing towards the Piraeus, so that they would be on the extreme left of the line,[6] but he has nothing to say about the rest of the contingents in the Persian fleet. Diodoros, who agrees with Herodotus on the position of the Phoenicians and the Asiatic Greeks, also states[7] that the Cyprian ships came next in line to the Phoenicians and were followed (from right to left) by the Cilicians, Pamphylians, and Lykians, but this seems to be no more than a copy of the geographical order followed by Herodotus in his original enumeration of the Persian fleet,[8] though Ephoros here omitted the Egyptian

---

[1] In *J.H.S.* xxviii, 1908, 219.   [2] *Persai*, 399 f.; cf. 413–16.

[3] *Persai*, 386 ff. and 424–8. So Keil (in *A.S.* 105) says that the battle lasted eleven hours.

[4] i. 2. 508 A. Grundy, 402 apparently makes the battle end between 2 and 3 p.m., but gives no reasons. Hdt. viii. 96. 1 does not prove (in spite of Macan, ad loc.) that the battle finished early enough for the Greeks to anticipate a fresh attack *on the same day.*

[5] viii. 85. 1 (the only mention of the Piraeus in Hdt.).

[6] It is necessary to be precise on these details because the attempt to combine this Herodotean evidence with Goodwin's reconstruction of the battle has produced some amazing errors of orientation, e.g. Grundy, 402 and Munro in *J.H.S.* xxii, 1902, 328.

[7] xi. 19. 1; cf. 17. 3.   [8] vii. 89 ff.; cf. HW 264.

squadron because he believed that it had been sent off to block
the Megarid Channel. Herodotus has nothing to say about
the order of the Greek fleet except that the Phoenicians were
opposite the Athenians and the Ionians facing the Spartans;
from this it follows that in the tradition recorded by Herodotus
the Athenians occupied the Greek left, the Spartan contingent
the extreme right.

The right wing was the position normally occupied on land by
the contingent of the leading state, while the left was allotted to
the state which claimed the next place in importance.[1] As
Macan observes,[2] this order of battle on land was naturally
transferred to naval operations. Yet Herodotus' statement is
inadequate, for the Spartan contingent numbered only sixteen
ships at most,[3] whereas the Athenians on the lowest estimate
must have contributed over one-third of the Greek total of
310 ships. This consideration alone seems sufficient to rule out
Diodoros' assertion,[4] improbable in itself, that the Spartans
were with the Athenians on the Greek left. He alleges that the
Greek right was supplied by the Aiginetan and Megarian ships,
but this appears to be pure guesswork; it is supported by two
arguments, both unconvincing, that the contingents of these
two states, for both of which defeat would entail immediate
capture, were likely to fight desperately, and that their sailors
were the best in Greece after the Athenians, a claim which does
less than justice to the Corinthians. Many scholars[5] have been
tempted to follow Diodoros in placing the Aiginetans on the
right of the Greek line by the fact that the only contingents on
the Greek side mentioned by Herodotus in his narrative of the
battle are the Athenians and the Aiginetans. There are, however, indications in Herodotus that at least some Aiginetan
ships were close to the Athenians in the battle, and Grundy,
who here prefers Herodotus to Diodoros, argues[6] that the
Aiginetans must have been stationed next to the Athenians.

---

[1] Compare the Athenians at Plataia, where they had previously made good
their claim to this distinction against the Tegeans, ix. 26–28. 1. Rados, 303 notes
that they were also on the left at Mykale; see below, p. 256.

[2] i. 2. 491 A.

[3] Hdt. viii. 43 (on the assumption that no Spartan ships had been lost at Artemision).

[4] xi. 18. 1–2.

[5] e.g. Macan, i. 2. 490 A and Giannelli, 68 n. 1.   [6] Grundy, 393.

Aeschylus and Herodotus agree[1] that the battle began soon after
dawn. Plutarch has a story[2] that Themistokles held back the
ships (whether the Athenian ships only or the Greek fleet as a
whole is not stated) until the hour when a strong breeze sets in
from the sea and disturbs the water in the straits. Grundy[3] on
three occasions observed a morning wind which began to blow
about seven in the morning from west to east down the straight
part of the Salamis strait south of Mount Aigaleos. Hammond[4]
reports at second-hand a swell coming up the strait from the
open sea and running at right angles to the side of the channel,
dying out after the bend of the channel in the waters north of
Psyttaleia; this description is difficult to follow, as by Psyttaleia
Hammond seems to mean the island of St. George, but apparently describes a phenomenon different from that observed
by Grundy and more in harmony with Plutarch's version.

Whether Plutarch (or his source) had actually seen the wind
blowing or not, his statement of its effect on the battle is absurd;
he claims that the onset of the wind upset the enemy ships
more than the Greek because the former stood higher out of the
water with lofty prows and decks and were heavier than the
Greeks, but we know from Herodotus[5] that in fact the Greek
ships were the heavier. Moreover, as the Persians were the
attackers, it was not in Themistokles' power to delay the first
contact with the enemy until he was ready. As Tarn pointed
out,[6] here and in his account of Actium Plutarch seems to have
been dominated by the idea that 'the just cause must have the
smaller ships'. Confidence in Plutarch's accuracy is not enhanced by his reference in the same paragraph to the Persian
admiral Ariamenes, a mythical figure conflated from Xerxes'
full brother Achaimenes and his half-brother Ariabignes,[7] both
of whom were among the four admirals of the fleet at Salamis.

According to Herodotus[8] it was just after dawn, while the
Greeks were still embarking, that the ship arrived back from
Aigina which had been sent there 'to fetch the Aiakidai'; he

[1] *Persai*, 386 ff.; Hdt. viii. 83. 1.
[2] *Them.* 14. 3 (well criticized by Munro, op. cit. 330).
[3] Op. cit. 398 n.   [4] *J.H.S.* lxxvi, 1956, 46.
[5] viii. 60 a.   .   [6] Op. cit. 208, n. 28.
[7] vii. 97; in Grundy, 404 the admiral (anonymous in Diod. xi. 18. 5) has become
Ariamnes. An Ariaramnes occurs in Hdt. viii. 90. 4.
[8] viii. 83. 1–2; cf. 64. 2.

does not explain how it had been able to get through the Persian
ships which had been posted at midnight round Keos and
Kynosoura.[1] In the next chapter[2] he says that as the Greek
ships put off from the shore they were promptly attacked by the
enemy, and that the Greeks then began to back water towards
the shore they had just left, all except an Athenian, Ameinias of
Pallene, who opened the battle by ramming an enemy ship,
though in the Aiginetan tradition the feat of Ameinias was
transferred to an Aiginetan ship, the one which had brought the
Aiakidai. The initial recoil of the Greek fleet appears to be
attributed to panic by Herodotus and leads up to the appearance of a woman who, in a voice audible to the whole fleet,
urged them on to the attack after uttering the taunt 'Madmen,
how much further will you go on backing your ships?'[3] For
some of Goodwin's followers the recoil is a deliberate movement
designed to lure the Persian fleet up the strait,[4] but Grundy
wisely makes no use of it. Apart from the fact, not in itself
decisive, that it is contradicted by Aeschylus' picture of the
confident advance of the Greek fleet, it is closely linked in
Herodotus with the apparition, which is clearly meant to be
supernatural.[5]

Aeschylus reports[6] that when the Greeks advanced to meet
the Persians the Greek right wing led the way in good order,
followed by the rest of the fleet. Keil[7] has referred this statement to the deployment of the Greek fleet along the south side
of Salamis strait at dawn; he suggests that the leading ships
rowed out to take their position on the right wing and that those
next in line joined them on their left, and so on until the formation was complete. If Herodotus' general picture of the battle is
correct, the Greek right must have been held back as much as

---

[1] On the difficulties raised by Hdt.'s statement here cf. HW 262 f., also 264
(n. on 84. 2), where their misgivings in face of Hdt.'s references to this particular
ship are well founded.

[2] viii. 84.

[3] viii. 84. 2; there is no sufficient reason for suspecting πρότερον. Powell (ad loc.)
queries it, but dislikes Reiske's πικρότερον.

[4] Notably Munro, op. cit. 328; he adds in parenthesis 'if we may here draw
upon Herodotus viii. 84'. But on his view the shore to which the Greeks retire is
the *northern* shore of the strait.

[5] So Macan, ad loc.; the attempt of Myres (*Herodotus*, 280 f.) to rationalize it is
unconvincing.

[6] *Persai*, 399 ff.   [7] In *A.S.* 96.

possible to guard against the danger of an outflanking movement
by the Persian ships 'posted round Keos and Kynosoura',[1]
which presumably tried to enter the straits when the battle was
fairly joined. Rados,[2] believing that the Greek right was on the
defensive throughout the battle, concludes that Aeschylus made
a mistake here. Grundy[3] agrees that the right wing was hard
pressed by the Persians, but as he accepts Aeschylus' statement
he can only suppose that the right wing had exposed itself to
a flank attack by advancing in front of the rest of the line. It is
more likely that the Greek right had to be content with holding
its own until the battle was decided by the victory of the Greek
left over the Phoenician ships, the best part of the Persian navy.

How this victory was achieved is not clearly stated by Herodotus. If the essential part of his narrative[4] is disentangled from
the particular episodes, the conclusion emerges that the defeat
was due in the main to the Athenians and Aiginetans, of whom
the latter were awarded the prize for valour after the battle, the
Athenians being placed second.[5] Herodotus maintains that the
victory of the Greeks was inevitable, because they fought in
good order during the battle and kept their formation, whereas
the Persians fell into disorder and did nothing sensibly, although
they were encouraged by Xerxes' presence to fight far more
bravely than they had fought at Artemision. Xerxes' half-
brother Ariabignes, one of the Persian admirals, was killed,
and with him fell many other notables on the Persian side.
Among the shipwrecked Greeks the mortality was small, for
being able to swim (unlike most of the Persians[6]) they swam to
safety in Salamis. The heaviest losses were sustained by the
Persian fleet when after its defeat it began to take to flight.
Some of the Phoenicians seem to have beached their ships near
Xerxes' throne,[7] but others, attempting to make their way out
to Phaleron, were hampered by ships of their own fleet which
were still undefeated and pressing forward to take part in the
battle; presumably Herodotus means that as the Persian left
was still maintaining a vigorous struggle against the Greek right,
the line of retreat of the Phoenician ships was blocked, and this

[1] viii. 76. 1.   [2] Rados, 342.   [3] Grundy, 401.
[4] viii. 86 and 89, also 91.   [5] viii. 93. 1.   [6] viii. 89. 2.
[7] This is a natural inference from viii. 90. 1, and the statement is probable
enough even though it occurs in a suspicious context.

would fit in with the complaint made by the Phoenicians to Xerxes that their ships had been sunk by the Ionians, who might have sunk Phoenician ships if they got in the way of their own operations.[1]

The Athenians and Aiginetans were certainly acting in close co-operation during the later stages of the battle. Herodotus says that when the barbarian ships tried to escape to Phaleron the Aiginetans withstood them in the strait[2] and covered themselves with glory, for the Athenians in the conflict destroyed those ships which offered resistance and those which tried to flee, while those which were sailing out of the strait were destroyed by the Aiginetans. Scholars who accept from Diodoros the notion that the Aiginetans were on the extreme right of the Greek line proceed to picture their squadron as intercepting the retreating Persians at the exit from the strait into the open sea,[3] while others assume that the ships which had been guarding Aigina had been summoned to Salamis and had arrived in time to block the passage,[4] but the words of Herodotus do not mean more than that the Aiginetans barred the way of the fugitives while they were still in the strait and before they could reach the open sea. The anecdote about the gibe addressed by an Aiginetan ship-captain to Themistokles[5] presupposes that the Aiginetan ships were stationed in the battle next to the Athenians. Herodotus does not explain how the best Greek ships were able to defeat the best ships of the enemy, and in default of evidence speculation is useless, such as Keil's suggestion[6] that the Athenians somehow got round the west flank of the Phoenicians and then proceeded to roll up the Persian line from west to east. The Greek fleet might have been expected to do its utmost to turn the struggle into a land-battle on sea, but in the episodes from the battle recorded by Herodotus ramming plays a large part;[7] probably the heavier Greek ships could make effective use of their stronger prows against the Phoenicians

---

[1] So Hauvette, 422, referring to viii. 90. 1, but the precise meaning of the Phoenician complaint there is uncertain. The words ὡς δι' ἐκείνους ἀπολοίατο αἱ νέες might be a general charge against the Ionians that they had brought about the Persian defeat by their treachery.

[2] viii. 91 ; ὑποστάντες ἐν τῷ πορθμῷ.   [3] So Macan, i. 2. 501 f.

[4] For criticism of this suggestion cf. HW 266 (on viii. 91).   [5] viii. 92.

[6] In *A.S.* 105; he thinks the Athenians might have brought their ships through the channel between the island of St. George and Salamis.

[7] e.g. viii. 84. 1, 90. 2, 92. 1.

in the confined waters of the strait, where superior skill and speed would be useless.

Herodotus concludes his account of the fighting with the statement[1] that the enemy ships which escaped from the Greeks made for Phaleron and the protection of their land forces.[2] This is followed by three chapters,[3] the first of which is linked naturally with what precedes, as it describes the awards for valour in the battle, the Aiginetans being awarded the first and the Athenians the second place, and gives the names of the ship-captains in these two contingents who had most distinguished themselves, the Aiginetan Polykritos and two Athenians, Eumenes of Anagyrous and Ameinias of Pallene. Herodotus had previously told how Artemisia, the queen of his native city, had been hotly pursued, perhaps in the later stages of the battle, by an Athenian ship, and now reveals that its captain was this Ameinias, adding a note on the high reward which had been offered by the Athenians for the capture of Artemisia.[4] In the next chapter he introduces abruptly a curious and improbable story later current in Athens, imputing cowardly behaviour at the start of the battle to the Corinthian admiral Adeimantos and his contingent, but after repeating this discreditable legend in some detail he concludes with the remark that it was flatly denied by the Corinthians, whose claim to have played a leading part in the battle was confirmed by the testimony of 'the rest of Hellas'.[5]

The last of the three chapters deals with the destruction by a Greek force of the enemy garrison which had been placed on Psyttaleia during the night before the battle. Herodotus gives only a brief description of this exploit,[6] in which he says that Aristeides took many of the hoplites who had been drawn up

---

[1] viii. 92 (last sentence), taken up again at the end of 93.

[2] Hence not all of these can have marched westwards. The assertion in viii. 71. 1 that the Persian army began to march towards the Peloponnese on the night before the battle is very difficult; Macan (i. 2. 503 A) regards it as a misinterpretation of a movement designed to enable the land forces to co-operate with the fleet (so too Keil in *A.S.* 103 and n. 2, quoting a parallel from Diod. xx. 50. 1).

[3] viii. 93–95.

[4] viii. 93. 2; cf. 87. 2–4. The citation of the two Athenians by their deme-names suggests an official record (Macan, ad loc.).

[5] viii. 94. 4; see below, Appendix IX (c).

[6] viii. 95, dated as ἐν τῷ θορύβῳ τούτῳ. Grundy, 403 sensibly says 'when the strait was clear of the enemies' ships'.

on the shores of Salamis (presumably to help the crews of the
Greek ships during the battle[1]) and conveyed them to the island
of Psyttaleia where they destroyed the Persians stationed on the
island. He seems to assume that the action of Aristeides (which,
as Bury pointed out,[2] implies that he held an official position,
presumably that of strategos) belonged to a time when the
battle was still raging, but it is more likely that it occurred fairly
late in the day, when the sea-fight had been decided in favour
of the Greeks and the enemy ships had begun their retreat from
the straits. Aeschylus in the *Persai*[3] gives a much exaggerated
account of the affair, representing the garrison of Psyttaleia as
the flower of the Persian nobility[4] and their massacre as the
climax of the calamities which befell the Persians during the day;
perhaps he wanted the hoplites to have their share in the glory
of the Greek triumph. His assertion[5] that Xerxes witnessed the
details of this final disaster from his throne on the hill above the
straits is ignored by Herodotus and does not deserve the trust
which has sometimes been put in it. Herodotus, who must
have been familiar with the *Persai*,[6] may have been deliberately
reducing Aristeides' achievement to its proper proportions.[7]

After the flight of the enemy the Greeks proceeded to take
possession of those of the wrecked ships which were still floating
in the straits and towed them back to the shores of Salamis, but
many of the wrecks were swept by a strong westerly wind out of
the strait and past Phaleron until they came ashore on the Attic
coast at Cape Kolias;[8] possibly they were washed up at other
points also in Attica, but Herodotus mentions Kolias alone

---

[1] See above, p. 230, n. 1.

[2] In *C.R.* x, 1896, 414 ff., especially 418 A.

[3] Lines 447–71; was Aeschylus (then aged 45) one of the hoplites in Aristeides'
force?

[4] Lines 441–4; in spite of his fondness for high-sounding Persian names Aeschylus
does not give any here. The garrison is composed of 'Persians' (not necessarily
natives of Persis) in Hdt. viii. 76. 2 and 95.

[5] Lines 465 ff., stressed by Hammond in *J.H.S.* lxxvi, 1956, 38 and n. 4.

[6] A passage in Artemisia's speech (viii. 68 γ, first sentence) seems to have been
suggested by *Persai*, 728. But Hdt. only once mentions Aeschylus by name and in
a completely different context, ii. 156. 6.

[7] Hdt. gives no figure for the garrison destroyed on Psyttaleia; that in Pausanias
i. 36. 2 ('about 400') is probably one of Ephoros' inventions. For the obvious
parallel of the Spartans on Sphakteria cf. Paus. iv. 36. 6.

[8] viii. 96. 1–2; cf. Strabo 398 (§ 21). Kolias is located 20 stades beyond Phaleron
by Paus. i. 1. 5; cf. HW 268, though Honigmann in *R.-E.* xi. 1. 1077 prefers the
earlier identification with Trispyrgi, only 600 yards from (old) Phaleron.

because the women of Kolias occurred in an old oracle which had come to be connected with the battle of Salamis. Blakesley tried to argue[1] from the course taken by the wreckage that the later stages of the battle had been fought outside the straits, but this argument has wisely been discarded by his modern followers.

Herodotus reports[2] that when the Greeks had cleared the wrecks from the strait they were ready to fight again, as they expected Xerxes to use the ships in his fleet which still remained to him. This statement, which there is no reason to doubt, shows that the Greeks did not at first realize the completeness of their victory, and, if Aeschylus is approximately correct in his observation[3] that the fighting had continued till sunset, must refer to the day after the battle. But the Persian admirals and their crews were broken in spirit by their defeat and probably in no position to renew the struggle; their only desire was to make good their escape to Asia Minor unmolested. During the day after the battle the necessary arrangements were made, and the Persian navy started its flight during the ensuing night in order to outdistance any pursuit by its victorious enemies. Henceforth it never again played an effective part in this war and, although the Greeks were slow to realize it, their supremacy on sea was now complete.

[1] ii. 413, n. 39. Grundy, 403, thinks it probable that 'the pursuit was not carried far, if at all, beyond the channels on either side of Psyttaleia'.

[2] viii. 96. 1; see below, p. 245.   [3] Lines 424–8; see above, p. 231.

V

NAVAL OPERATIONS FROM SALAMIS
TO SESTOS

The two fleets after Salamis

A FEW days after the battle of Salamis the Persian land
forces left Attica and marched northwards through Boiotia
to Thessaly;[1] possibly garrisons of Macedonian and
other troops were left in the principal towns of Central Greece.[2]
The Persian fleet had apparently retired from the Attic coast
earlier. There is no need to suppose[3] that Herodotus dated its
retirement to the night after the day on which it had been defeated at Salamis; the various events which he records between
the end of the fighting and the departure of the Persian fleet may
be assigned to the day after the battle.[4] This was presumably
the day of the Persian war-council recorded by Herodotus, in
which Xerxes and his advisers took stock of the situation created
by the defeat of the fleet and reached the necessary decisions.
The fleet is said to have left Phaleron on the night following the
council,[5] and it certainly need not have waited until the army
was ready to move.

According to Herodotus[6] the Greek fleet started in pursuit of
the Persian ships as soon as they were known to have left
Phaleron and pursued them unsuccessfully as far as Andros. It
has been objected[7] that the Greeks could not have left their
stations at Salamis while the Persian troops were still in Attica,
but after the withdrawal of the Persian fleet it was not necessary
for the Greeks to retain more than a comparatively small

---

[1] viii. 113. 1.

[2] Macan, i. 2. 538 A; perhaps cf. viii. 34 (see above, p. 197).

[3] As is done by Busolt (708, n. 2) and HW 271; cf. the note on viii. 107. 1 in
Shuckburgh's edition of Book VIII.

[4] Cf. Busolt, 708 and n. 2.

[5] viii. 107. 1; Powell (ed., ad loc.) proposes to read ταῦτα μὲν τῆς ἡμέρης for
ταύτην μὲν τὴν ἡμέρην.

[6] viii. 108. 1.   [7] By Macan, i. 2. 525A.

number of ships to guard against the now remote danger of an attempted Persian landing on Salamis, and the greater part of the fleet could safely be sent in pursuit of the retreating enemy.[1] This fleet was still under the supreme command of the Spartan Eurybiadas, who was accompanied by Themistokles as admiral of the large Athenian contingent.

Unfortunately, the authentic tradition of the events that followed the arrival of the Greeks at Andros has been contaminated in Herodotus with untrustworthy items derived ultimately from the Themistokles legend. Herodotus' narrative[2] may be summarized as follows: when the Greeks arrived at Andros they held a council of war, in which Themistokles proposed that they should first pursue the Persian fleet, then sail to the Hellespont to break down the bridges. This plan was turned down by Eurybiadas, and the leaders of the other Peloponnesian squadrons agreed with him. Themistokles then used specious arguments to the Athenians to reconcile them to their disappointment, but his real object in thus speaking against his convictions was to curry favour with Xerxes, for already at the height of his glory he foresaw the possibility of a later reversal of fortune which might force him to seek refuge at the Persian court. When he had convinced the Athenians he sent his servant Sikinnos to Xerxes, who was still in Attica, to tell him that Themistokles had persuaded the Greeks not to pursue the Persian fleet or to break down the bridges over the Hellespont, and that in consequence Xerxes could retreat unhindered.

This story of Themistokles' message to Xerxes from Andros, in the form given to it by Herodotus, is incompatible, as some ancient writers[3] realized, with his earlier account of the message said to have been sent to Xerxes by Themistokles from Salamis on the eve of the battle. Thucydides, in the version which he gives[4] of the letter sent by Themistokles many years later to King Artaxerxes, assumes the historical truth of both messages, but his testimony on such a point is of no more value than his acceptance of the official Spartan denigration of Pausanias'

---

[1] Cf. Grundy, 413, followed by HW 271.   [2] viii. 108–10.

[3] Plut. *Them.* 16. 5; Polyainos i. 30. 3–4.

[4] i. 137. 4. There is surely no need to regard this letter as an historical document or to hold (with Macan, i. 532 B) that it is 'the earliest source to which the fiction can be traced'.

career after Plataia,[1] and his incidental reference to Salamis as
the place from which Themistokles' second message was sent
looks like a mere slip; it should not be used to challenge Herodotus' plain statement that Andros was the place where the
council of war was held. The story of the first message seems to
be apocryphal, even though it was repeated by Aeschylus[2] less
than eight years after the battle, and if the first message is rejected it would be easier to accept the second, provided that the
motive attributed to Themistokles by Herodotus is repudiated
as a worthless deduction from later events. His change of attitude
might be explained by his realization that it would be unwise to
provoke a split among the allies at this stage or to allow the
Athenians to persevere in their plans without support, but
Herodotus describes it in such a way as to make it appear discreditable to Themistokles.[3] If the second message really was
sent, it is not easy to find a plausible explanation for it without
altering its content,[4] or to understand how Sikinnos, starting
from Andros, could expect to find Xerxes still in Attica, for
presumably the Persian army had already begun its retreat
before 2 October, when the Spartan Kleombrotos was preparing to advance from the Isthmos lines.[5] In view of these
difficulties it seems best to abandon the story of the second
message as another fictitious item in the Themistokles legend.[6]

Some have argued that if we reject the story of Themistokles'
second message to Xerxes we must also regard with suspicion
Herodotus' account of the war council at Andros, since on their
view the council is merely the necessary prelude to the sending
of the message.[7] It is urged in support of this view that Themistokles could not have proposed an adventurous naval strategy
while the Persian army was still in Attica and when its intention
to retreat was not yet known. This objection has been met by the

---

[1] i. 128. 3–134. Herodotus was more sceptical than Thucydides in this matter;
cf. his doubts about the official story in v. 32, also Beloch in *G.G.* ii². 2. 155 ff.

[2] *Persai*, 355–60; see below, pp. 403 ff.   [3] Cf. Legrand, viii. 95–96.

[4] As Ephoros apparently saw. Diodoros xi. 19. 5–6 makes Themistokles report to
Xerxes that the Greeks were about to sail to the bridge and destroy it, whereupon
Xerxes retreated in all haste with the greater part of his forces, as Themistokles
had hoped he would do on receipt of the message (so also Plut. *Them.* 16. 5).

[5] ix. 10. 3; see below, p. 452.

[6] Meyer, 394 (end of note) is sceptical about the story, and concludes that the
message, if really sent, had no effect on the course of events.

[7] So Grundy, 415.

assumption that Herodotus has antedated the advance to Andros and that the forward movement of the fleet really followed
the beginning of the Persian retreat on land,[1] but this explanation offers too much violence to Herodotus on points of fact; he
is more likely to be right on these than in his statement of what
was said at the war council.

Herodotus gives us merely the bare bones of Themistokles'
proposal without the arguments on which it was based,[2] but we
can see what they must have been. Themistokles had realized
sooner than anyone else that the position of the Persian army in
Greece had become precarious as soon as Salamis had transferred to the Greeks maritime supremacy in the Aegean, and
that if the Greeks struck promptly at the weakest link in the
long and tenuous line of communication between the main
Persian army and its Asiatic base the army would be compelled
to retire with all haste from Europe. The squadron left behind
at Salamis would be sufficient protection against Xerxes' army
in Attica, which was in no position to attack Salamis without
its fleet, and the danger that all or part of the Persian fleet
might double back across the Aegean[3] was negligible after the
hammering it had just received. Eurybiadas is not recorded to
have mentioned this possibility; if Herodotus has reported him
correctly,[4] he maintained that the Persians would probably
withdraw from Europe soon in consequence of their naval defeat, but if they were forced to remain in Greece by the cutting
of their communications they would be driven to fight with the
courage of despair. His major assumption was clearly false, and
his objection to Themistokles' strategy seems to rest on a misunderstanding of its purpose. It is, however, possible that he and
the other Peloponnesians turned it down because they had not
yet realized the full implications of their victory at Salamis and
were not at this stage prepared to advance farther from their
base, or they may simply have thought that the season was too
late for a vigorous offensive on the other side of the Aegean.

After relating the story of the council at Andros and its
sequel Herodotus says that the Greeks, having decided to
abandon their pursuit of the Persian fleet, laid siege to Andros.[5]

---

[1] Macan, i. 2. 531 A.   [2] Cf. Legrand, viii. 95.
[3] As suggested by Grundy, 414 (end).   [4] viii. 108. 3–4.
[5] viii. 111–12; cf. 121. 1.

He insinuates that they were induced to begin the siege by Themistokles, who wished to punish the Andrians for their refusal to give him money, and he goes on to assert that while the siege was in progress Themistokles sent threatening messages to other islands demanding blackmail, which was certainly paid by two states and possibly by others as well; the digression ends with the accusation that all this money was acquired by Themistokles for his own profit and without the knowledge of the other commanders.[1] These charges against Themistokles go back to the contemporary Rhodian poet Timokreon of Ialysos,[2] but their absurdity in the Herodotean version is patent. Islanders who had had the misfortune to take the wrong side probably sought to propitiate the leaders of the victorious Greek fleet with bribes; if these were accepted, others must have had their share as well as Themistokles, but those who paid the bribes did not thereby obtain more than some diminution in the amounts expected from them. Miltiades' attack on Paros[3] had shown that a Greek campaign against pro-Persian islands in the Cyclades was a natural consequence of a Greek victory over Persia, and the presence of a large Greek navy at Andros provided a suitable occasion to levy war contributions for the upkeep of the confederate fleet from neighbouring islanders who had supported the enemy. Large sums are said to have been paid by Paros and Karystos; possibly Karystos had its lands ravaged before it consented to pay.[4] The siege of Andros was apparently unsuccessful; perhaps the Greeks were finally compelled by the lateness of the season to abandon further operations and retire to the Isthmus of Corinth, where the fleet was disbanded for the winter. The failure of the siege is less surprising than the decision of the Andrians to endure it rather than submit; they had evidently failed to realize that complete control over the Aegean had now passed to the Greeks.

The Persian fleet after its defeat at Salamis ceased to play an important part in the war. Unfortunately, Herodotus gives no estimate of the losses on either side in the battle, and the figures supplied by Diodoros,[5] presumably from Ephoros, seem

---

[1] viii. 112. 3 (mainly from Macaulay's translation).
[2] Quoted by Plut. *Them.* 21. 4.   [3] vi. 132 ff.
[4] viii. 112. 2-3.   [5] Diod. xi. 19. 3.

to rest on pure conjecture and nothing more. He alleges that whereas the Greek fleet lost only 40 ships the Persians had over 200 destroyed, in addition to those which were captured with all their crews on board. If the disparity in losses had been so great, the Greeks would surely have perceived that the Persians were in no position to continue the struggle, whereas in fact they at first expected the enemy to fight again[1] and did not grasp the full extent of their victory until they learnt that the Persian fleet had sailed back to Asia Minor.

Herodotus' appreciation of the paramount importance of naval supremacy in this war is intermittent, and he makes no serious attempt to account for the withdrawal of the enemy fleet from the main theatre of operations. As the Persian plan of campaign had been based on the close co-operation of the fleet with the army,[2] the fleet's retirement to the Asiatic coast should have entailed the removal of a considerable portion of the Persian land forces from Europe,[3] for these had largely depended on sea-borne supplies brought by merchant ships, which could no longer venture across the Aegean without naval protection. An adequate reason for these decisions of the Persian high command, so far-reaching in their effects, can be found only in the magnitude of the defeat sustained at Salamis. Ancient writers failed to understand the situation because they had over-estimated the numerical superiority of the Persians at sea on the eve of the battle; if their fleet had in reality only slightly outnumbered the Greek, the destruction of no more than one-third of their ships would have been decisive.

It has been maintained[4] that the Persian fleet was still powerful after the battle, and that the decisiveness of the Greek victory was due not to the extent of the Persian losses but to their effect on the mind of Xerxes. Herodotus tells a story[5] that during the battle Xerxes ordered the execution of some Phoenician ship-captains on a charge of cowardice. Diodoros adds[6] that Xerxes also threatened to inflict on the rest of the Phoenicians

---

[1] viii. 96. 1 and 108. 1, rightly accepted by Grundy, 412.

[2] vii. 236. 2; see above, p. 38.

[3] viii. 100. 5 (cf. 113) and Thuc. i. 73. 5 both say 'the greater part of the army', but many moderns have questioned their accuracy; cf. Busolt, 671, n. 1 and Meyer, 395 n., and see below, p. 267.

[4] By Olmstead, *History of the Persian Empire*, 255.

[5] viii. 90. 3.

[6] Diod. xi. 19. 4.

the punishment they had deserved, whereupon the Phoenician contingent, alarmed by his threats, sailed off to Asia on the night after the battle. Olmstead believes that the Phoenicians went home and that their example was followed by the Egyptians; the defection of these two important contingents was the true cause of the Persian decision to offer no further resistance in the Aegean to the Greek fleet.

Like many modern views based on the unsupported testimony of Diodoros, this hypothesis conflicts with explicit statements in Herodotus. The withdrawal of the Phoenician squadron from the Aegean is a problem which has puzzled many scholars and may have stimulated Ephoros to invent an explanation, but Herodotus says definitely[1] that the Phoenician ships were sent home by the Persian admirals. He seems to date the event not long before the battle of Mykale, but some have held that the aorist tense of the verb which records the order has the force of a pluperfect and that the Phoenicians had been dismissed earlier.[2] The departure of the Egyptians may be deduced from Herodotus' casual statement[3] that the Persian land force in Boiotia in 479 included the marines from the Egyptian ships; he notes that these men had been disembarked by Mardonios while their ships were still at Phaleron. This indication of time can only refer to the short period which elapsed between the battle of Salamis and the departure of the Persian fleet from Attica.[4] The decision to transfer the Egyptian marines to Mardonios' army proves that the Egyptian ships were not intended to play any further part in the war, and from this it follows that the Persian commanders had already on the morrow of Salamis made up their minds to send home the Egyptian ships and perhaps other squadrons as well. Possibly the Phoenician and Ionian ships were kept to cover the Hellespont crossing; as the Phoenician squadron alone is mentioned by Herodotus as having been sent home from the Asiatic coast, the Egyptian and other non-Greek ships had presumably been dismissed earlier.

The Persian fleet after its departure from Phaleron crossed to

---

[1] ix. 96. 1.
[2] Cf. Legrand, ix. 92 A, n. 1, apparently from Stein (attacked by Macan, i. 2. 791 B), also HW 329.
[3] ix. 32.
[4] See above, p. 240.

Asia, perhaps by the shortest route across the Aegean.[1] Herodotus says[2] that it proceeded with all speed to the Hellespont to protect the bridges for the crossing of Xerxes and the troops with him, and that when it found that the bridges had been broken up by stormy weather it transported the army across the strait. Thereupon part of the fleet wintered at Kyme in Aiolis, part at Samos, but early in spring 479 the whole fleet was concentrated at Samos.[3] It is said to have numbered 300 ships, including the Ionian contingent, but even if this estimate presupposes the presence of the Phoenician squadron the total is incredible. Herodotus says that the fleet took up its position at Samos to guard Ionia and prevent its revolt, but he adds[4] that the Persians did not anticipate a Greek naval offensive across the Aegean on the ground that the Greek fleet had not pursued them after Salamis. This speculation is unconvincing, but Herodotus does at least stress the decline in the morale of the Persian fleet and its anxiety for news of Mardonios' progress on land; it was obvious that only a Persian victory on land in Greece could preserve Persian domination in Ionia.

The naval campaign of 479

Herodotus has recounted the Greek naval operations during the campaigning season of 479 in two distinct sections separated by a hundred chapters. In the first[5] he describes how a fleet of 110 ships mustered at Aigina in the spring under the command of Leotychidas, one of the two Spartan kings, who is described as 'general and admiral':[6] no details are given of the composition of this fleet, but the Athenian contingent is said to have been commanded by Xanthippos. At Aigina Leotychidas was approached by six conspirators from Chios, who after the failure of an attempt to kill their tyrant Strattis had fled to Sparta and had appealed to the authorities there to liberate the

---

[1] This is a natural inference from the direction of the Greek pursuit and from the words of Themistokles in viii. 108. 2 (especially with Powell's reading οὐκέτι διώξαντας instead of the manuscript ἐπιδιώξαντας). The passages cited in the next note do not state explicitly that the Persian fleet proceeded from Salamis to the Hellespont by the shortest route.   [2] viii. 107. 1, 117. 1, 130. 1.

[3] viii. 130. 1–2.   [4] viii. 130. 3.   [5] viii. 131–2.

[6] viii. 131. 2. The term ναύαρχος suggests that Leotychidas held the Spartan office of the ναυαρχία for 479 (cf. Macan, ad loc.) but Beloch, ii[2]. 2. 272 maintains that he did not.

Ionians. The Spartan ephors must have referred these Chians to
Leotychidas, who was persuaded to venture across the Aegean
as far as Delos. Herodotus says that the Greeks were afraid to go
beyond Delos, 'since they were without experience of those
regions and everything seemed to them to be filled with armed
force, while their persuasion was that it was as long a voyage to
Samos as to the Pillars of Herakles'.[1] So for the present the
Greeks remained at Delos and the Persians at Samos, since
the leaders of both fleets were afraid to advance nearer to the
enemy.

In the second section,[2] which follows his account of the land
campaign of 479, Herodotus explains how the Greek fleet
finally took the offensive and crossed to Ionia. This section
opens with the arrival of three envoys from Samos; unlike the
Chian envoys, they seem to have had the backing of a number
of their fellow citizens, who had dispatched them to the Greek
fleet without the knowledge of the Persians or of their own
recently appointed tyrant Theomestor.[3] The Samian envoys
assured Leotychidas that the appearance of the Greek fleet off
the Asiatic coast would be sufficient to produce a general revolt
of Ionia, and that the barbarians either would not resist or
would be easily beaten, since their ships were no match for
those of the Greeks. Leotychidas is said to have been much
impressed by the discovery that the chief man in the Samian
embassy bore the auspicious name Hegesistratos, leader of the
army. He certainly accepted the assurances of the Samian envoys, and may even have given them a formal guarantee that
their state would be admitted to the Hellenic Alliance on its
liberation from Persia.[4] The envoys went on ahead, perhaps to
prepare the ground, and after a brief interval the whole fleet
advanced to Samos. The Persian fleet retired before it to a
position on the mainland, on the south side of the adjacent
promontory of Mykale, where they beached their ships under
the protection of a land force stationed there. Leotychidas, after
some hesitation, decided to attack them in their chosen position
by land, with complete success; the Persian troops were routed,
their warships and fortifications captured and burnt.

---

[1] viii. 132. 3 (Macaulay's translation).   [2] ix. 90–107.
[3] ix. 90. 1; he owed his appointment to his bravery at Salamis (viii. 85. 3).
[4] ix. 92. 1; cf. Macan's note, ad loc.

Herodotus is never at his best when describing naval operations, and was apparently not very interested in those of 479,
which he perhaps felt as an anti-climax after the great sea-
fights of the previous year. He has, however, specified clearly
the successive stages in the advance of the Greek fleet across the
Aegean. The main weakness of his account here, as elsewhere,
is that he does not elucidate fully the meaning of the movements
which he reports. This could hardly be done without some
attempt to connect the movements of the fleet with those of the
Greek land forces. Obviously there must have been some inter-
relation between these two sets of events, but for the most part
Herodotus has treated the operations on sea in complete isolation from those on land.[1] This weakness might have been to
some extent overcome by a detailed chronology, but the one
precise indication of time given by Herodotus,[2] the statement
that the battle of Mykale was fought on the afternoon of the
same day as the battle of Plataia, has not unnaturally provoked
scepticism, although the synchronism may be approximately
correct. At least we may infer from a later indication[3] that the
battle of Mykale took place towards the end of August 479,
which is the date favoured by some scholars for the victory at
Plataia.[4] The mustering of the Greek ships at Aigina is dated
to the spring, at a time when Mardonios was still in Thessaly
and the Greek land forces had not yet begun to assemble;[5]
moreover, Herodotus clearly implies in the concluding sentence
of his first section that when the Greek fleet advanced to Delos
Mardonios had not yet left his winter quarters in Thessaly.[6]

Historians have tended to dismiss this statement without
discussion, but it is perhaps not impossible if it is brought into
connexion with the size of Leotychidas' fleet. Herodotus'
estimate of 110 ships for this fleet is so peculiar that it must be
correct, but it naturally suggests a new problem; why was the
Greek fleet so much smaller than it had been in the previous
year? The difference roughly corresponds to the size of the
Athenian fleet, and it has been suggested[7] that the statesmen

---

[1] See below, pp. 319 f.   [2] ix. 90. 1, supplemented by 101. 2.
[3] ix. 117; the siege of Sestos had already started in 479 before the beginning of
the Greek autumn (18 Sept.; cf. HW 336).
[4] Beloch, ii².2.53 and Meyer, 413, but see Busolt, 725 f., n. 4, and HW 331.
[5] viii. 131. 1.   [6] viii. 133. 1.
[7] Cf. Delbrück, 96 f. and Busolt, 717 f., elaborated by Meyer, 402 f.

who now controlled Athenian policy, mistrusting Sparta's present preference for a naval strategy, deliberately crippled the offensive at sea by withholding the bulk of their fleet, sending merely a token force to Aigina. This suggestion does not accord very well with the prominent part played by the Athenians in the battle of Mykale. It is true that in Diodoros' account Leotychidas and Xanthippos, who are described as joint commanders of the navy, are said to have taken 250 triremes to Delos,[1] but this figure for the Greek fleet in 479 is as worthless as the fantastic estimates given in Diodoros for the Persian forces in Asia Minor at the same time as over 400 ships and 100,000 men.[2]

The ingenious suggestion that Leotychidas' fleet, originally only 110 ships, was later more than doubled when Athenian opposition was withdrawn,[3] ignores the basic fact that conditioned the strategy of the Greek high command in 479 as in 480, the limitations of their available manpower. In 480, when they were compelled by the formidable threat from the Persian navy to make their main effort on sea, they had to use a considerable number of their hoplites for service in the fleet as marines, possibly as rowers too, and therefore could do no more on land than occupy strong lines of defence which the Persians could not force by a frontal attack.[4] In 479, when the Greek leaders decided (for whatever reason) to pass to the offensive on land, they needed a larger army, and so were compelled to call on the services of a high proportion of the hoplites who had previously been serving with the fleet.[5] As this major effort on land was sustained until the campaign was concluded by the victory at Plataia, we must accept the implication of the Herodotean narrative that the 110 ships which mustered at Aigina under Leotychidas in the spring had not been reinforced when they advanced first to Delos and then to Samos.

If this conclusion is sound, Leotychidas' long delay at Delos becomes more intelligible. We need not accept the statement that fear of the unknown was one of the motives which halted his progress, and that the Greeks regarded Samos as no less

---

[1] Diod. xi. 34. 2.   [2] Diod. xi. 27. 1 and 34. 3.
[3] Cf. Munro in *J.H.S.* xxiv. 1904, 146 f.
[4] See above, pp. 124 f.
[5] This is true of all the states which supplied ships to the fleet, not merely of the Athenians (as implied by Delbrück, 97).

remote than the Pillars of Herakles, a gibe which perhaps reflects the impatience of Ionians, longing for a speedy deliverance from the Persian yoke, at the slowness and timidity of the Greek advance.[1] The Greek high command had probably decided that a forward movement of their navy was desirable, at least up to a point where it would cover the Cyclades and alarm the Persians by the threat of a blow at the Asiatic mainland, but Leotychidas, with a fleet not much more than one-third of that which had fought at Salamis, might reasonably be afraid to venture nearer to an enemy fleet which when last it broke contact with the Greek fleet had perhaps numbered twice as many ships as those now at his disposal.[2] He also had to remember that if he took the offensive and sought out the Persian fleet in Ionian waters he as the aggressor would have to risk a sea-fight under conditions chosen by the defenders, and perhaps in open waters, which would give full play to the tactical superiority of the Persian ships. As Herodotus says, everything beyond Delos seemed to be filled with armed forces. It has been suggested[3] that the Greek leaders were ill-informed about events in Asia Minor, since even after their victory at Mykale they did not know that the bridges over the Hellespont had been broken down in the preceding autumn.

Leotychidas' move from Delos to Samos appears in Herodotus as the result of a further and more authoritative appeal from Ionia. It has been argued that in reality the resumption of the advance was brought about by an appeal from the Greek land forces, and that the decisive factor was the desire to end the stalemate in Boiotia by bringing about a revolt in Ionia which would in turn force Mardonios to attack.[4] This explanation takes for granted the maintenance of regular contacts between the leaders of the Greek land and sea forces, but in view of the distance separating them and the difficulties of communication any interchange of messages would tend to lag behind the march of events. Herodotus has certainly ignored the possibility of such close collaboration, and it must remain no more than an interesting speculation, interesting but unnecessary,

---

[1] So Macan, i. 2. 566 A. Grundy's attempt (434 f.) to minimize the exaggeration is unconvincing.

[2] See above, p. 245. HW 279 say that fear of the enemy kept the Greeks at Delos but do not explain the grounds of the fear.

[3] By Busolt, 720, n. 1; cf. Hdt. ix. 106. 4.   [4] So Meyer, 415.

since Leotychidas' advance to Samos is in reality adequately explained by the data given in Herodotus.

What Leotychidas needed above all from the Ionians was a formal guarantee that their states were prepared to revolt as soon as he should appear with his fleet off the Asiatic coast, and that their contingents still serving in the Persian forces on sea or land would desert in the event of a battle or even join in the attack on their hated rulers. All this the Ionian envoys promised. But they were also able to inform Leotychidas that the Persian ships were in bad condition and would be no match for the Greek fleet in a pitched battle;[1] as the Ionian contingent had fought so well at Salamis, this perhaps refers to the remainder of the enemy fleet. But such a condemnation becomes unintelligible if the Phoenician ships were still with the fleet, and it is very tempting to suppose that the Samians encouraged Leotychidas by the amazing news that the Persian admirals had sent home the Phoenician contingent and had thereby revealed their lack of confidence in their prospects at sea. It is significant that they evacuated Samos as soon as the Greek fleet approached;[2] this suggests that the anti-Persian conspiracy in Samos was well organized and that the Samian envoys were able to hold out to the Greeks the prospect of a prompt defection of Samos on their arrival. Anyhow, the Persians by their retirement to the opposite mainland presented Leotychidas with an advanced base in a position which dominated the Ionian coast; the importance of a base at Samos is well illustrated by its value to the Athenians during the Ionian War of 413-404.

The further prospects of the Greeks depended largely on the extent to which discontent had spread among the Ionian subjects of Persia on the mainland. As the organization of the Persian Empire was feudal, the Persians preferred to deal with their subjects through individuals who ruled by Persian favour and were responsible for supplying to the defence of the empire the contribution of their subjects in taxes and men.[3] Hence in the Ionian city-states the Persians had instituted vassal kings, whom the Greeks called 'tyrants'. The term had originally no unfavourable connotation, but simply described a monarchical ruler whose monarchy was not based on hereditary succession

---

[1] ix. 90. 3. [2] ix. 96. 1.

[3] Cf. Schachermeyr, *Alexander der Grosse* (1949), 146.

from a 'Homeric' kingship.[1] This 'tyrannical' form of government had died out in Old Greece before the end of the sixth
century, and its retention by the Persians as an instrument of
control was bitterly resented by many of the Ionians; it was in
fact one of the most important causes of the great Ionian revolt
which began in the autumn of 499 and lasted for six years.[2]
Herodotus in his history of this revolt notes incidentally that in
Samos at least the leaders of the anti-Persian party were the
men of property;[3] the mass of the people, who in the normal
'tyranny' had little to fear from their local despot, were apparently apathetic and ready to welcome back their former
ruler Aiakes. The sequel shows that the Persians had come to
realize the true situation, and that democracies no less than
tyrannies might be docile instruments of foreign domination;
this would explain the action of Mardonios when in 492 he set
up democracies in the Ionian cities.[4] Some tyrants survived
this innovation, but they appear mostly in the island states.

In the three largest island states and in Miletos the govern-
ments set up after the second Ionian revolt in 479 were probably
oligarchic (as oligarchies are found in them later in the century)
and the same may be true of other Ionian states liberated at the
same time. Hence the anti-Persian movement in Ionia in 479
was probably led by the aristocrats, as it had been in 499. But
if the democracies to which they were opposed were radical
democracies, the patriotic parties in the various states may well
have included a majority of the middle class, the men of hoplite franchise, who might well be included among 'the men
of property'; the uprising of the Greeks of Asia Minor after
Mykale cannot have been confined to a few disgruntled aristocrats. It is also possible that the radicals too were now convinced
of the hopelessness of the Persian cause and were prepared to
rally to the aid of the winning side.

Nevertheless, the withdrawal of the Persian ships to the protection of the land force at Mykale confronted Leotychidas
with an awkward situation, similar to that which Kimon had

---

[1] Cf. Andrewes, *The Greek Tyrants*, c. 2 (especially pp. 26–28).

[2] On the chronology of the revolt cf. Macan, *Edition of Herodotus iv–vi*, ii. 62–70.
It was attributed to economic causes by Lenschau in *Klio*, xiii, 1913, 175 ff.
(followed by Cary in *C.A.H.* iv. 218 f.) but Hdt. in v. 28 stresses the prosperity of
Miletos just before the revolt.

[3] vi. 22. 1.

[4] vi. 43. 3; cf. HW 80.

to face later when the Persian ships refused battle and retired into the river Eurymedon.[1] The Greek fleet, having crossed the Aegean to engage the Persian naval forces, at first hesitated to seek them out in their refuge on the mainland. Herodotus says[2] that they considered the possibility of retiring altogether or of sailing on to the Hellespont. The former plan would have abandoned their Samian allies to the enemy, and the second would have been too adventurous while the Persian fleet was still in being. It is curious, however, that they did not simply stay where they were, secure in the possession of a strong advanced base, and the fact that they finally decided to attack the enemy fleet in its chosen position seems to show that they felt confidence in their ability to force a favourable decision. They made preparations for a sea-fight in case the Persians offered resistance,[3] but as events showed they were determined to challenge the Persian forces on land if their ships would not fight.

Their attitude makes nonsense of Herodotus' statement[4] that the land army under Tigranes numbered 60,000 men. It has been suggested[5] that he was originally a commander of 10,000 men, a myriarch, and that of his original command he retained only those who had survived the campaign in Greece and the subsequent retreat. How far this force could be supplemented from the manpower of the Persian fleet cannot be conjectured, since we do not know what contingents remained in it apart from those of the Ionian states. The Ionian marines and sailors had done well for Persia at Salamis, but circumstances had changed so much since then that the Persians dared no longer rely on their loyalty, especially as Leotychidas before the battle had sent a herald in a ship close to the shore with a proclamation urging the Ionians to revolt; the mistrust felt by the Persians for their Greek allies was so heightened by this incident that they disarmed all the Samians present in their force.[6]

On the Greek side Leotychidas possessed no land army at all and had to improvise one from the men serving in his fleet. The nucleus would be provided by the marines, but even though these probably numbered thirty to each ship[7] the total number

[1] Plut. *Kimon* 12. 5-7.　　　[2] ix. 98. 1.　　　[3] ix. 98. 2.
[4] ix. 96. 2.　　　[5] By Tarn in *J.H.S.* xxviii, 1908, 228, n. 99.
[6] ix. 98. 2–99. 1.　　　[7] See above, p. 52.

of hoplites would only be 3,300. It is, however, possible that the Greek shortage of manpower had compelled some Peloponnesian states to press hoplites into service as rowers, and if these had brought their arms with them or had obtained some from Samos they would be able to swell the total of the heavy-armed infantry. But on the most favourable computation the number of hoplites in the Greek army at Mykale cannot have exceeded 6,000, and the rest of the rowers in the Greek fleet would have been as little use in a land battle as the so-called light-armed troops in the Greek army at Plataia. The conclusion must be that the battle of Mykale was important not for the size of the forces engaged but for its result, the second revolt of Ionia from Persia.[1]

The men from the Persian fleet had landed on the southern shore of the promontory of Mykale near a temple of the Potniai, Demeter and Kore; there was also a temple of Eleusinian Demeter not far away, to give added point to the parallel between the battles of Mykale and Plataia.[2] After beaching their ships the Persians built round them a stockade of stone and wood, using the fruit-trees of the neighbourhood for timber, and crowned the rampart with stakes (*skolopes*). Herodotus defines their position by the place-names Gaison (apparently a river) and Skolopoeis; it has been reasonably conjectured[3] that the latter name became current after the battle and was derived from the Persian stockade. Skolopoeis reappears in an inscription of the fourth century,[4] but its precise location is disputed. Wiegand placed it near the village of Domatia, but Kromayer argued strongly for a site further east, near the modern Ak Bogaz.[5] Both sites have a stream flowing southwards which can be identified with the Gaison and a pass leading over Mount Mykale to the north. Kromayer's analysis of the epigraphic evidence is plausible, but he is mistaken when he dismisses Wiegand's site on the ground that it is only compatible with a Greek advance from east to west and that if Leotychidas had landed his men on the beach to the east of the Persian position

---

[1] It was Ephoros, not Herodotus, who exaggerated the scale of the battle at Mykale.

[2] ix. 97, cf. 101. 1.

[3] Cf. Grundy, 525 and Kromayer in *A.S.* 171 f., also HW 330.

[4] *Inschriften von Priene* (Berlin, 1906), number 361 (p. 183).

[5] Wiegand in Wiegand and Schrader, *Priene* (1904), 17; Kromayer in *A.S.* 172 f.

Herodotus would have been bound to mention such a daring manœuvre.[1] Arguments from Herodotus' silences are always treacherous, and Wiegand's view on this point is supported by Herodotus' assertion[2] that in the advance of the Greeks the Athenians (with the Corinthians, Sikyonians, and Troizenians next to them in that order) marched along the sea-shore and the plain, whereas the other half of the army, including the Lakedaimonians, had to make their way across a gorge and over the hills. It is natural to suppose that the Spartans occupied their normal position on the Greek right; if they did, then the Athenians must have been on the extreme left, as at Plataia, and if the Athenians were nearest to the shore the Greeks must have marched westwards after landing east of the Persian position. Leotychidas presumably felt confident of victory and wished to compel the Persians when defeated to retreat by the more difficult route over Mount Mykale.

His tactics may have been even more ambitious than this, for Herodotus describes the march of the right wing of the army by a word[3] which implies that a turning movement was intended, and it has been assumed that this plan was ruined by the impatience of the Athenians and the other contingents in the left half of the army to win the battle before the Lakedaimonians could arrive on the scene. If the two armies really were separated by a river (the Gaison) as is usually supposed, it plays no part in Herodotus' account of the advance of the Greek left. If the Persian camp was on the left bank of the stream, as Kromayer locates it on his map, Leotychidas had turned this obstacle by making his landing to the east of the Persian position. This may explain Herodotus' silence about the stream and also the decision of the Persian leaders to leave their fortified camp and meet the Greeks outside it, forming a rampart of their shields, as at Plataia.[4] When this shield wall was overthrown, the barbarians after some fierce fighting fled to their fortifications, but the Greeks followed them so closely that they were able to rush into the camp on their heels. Most of the barbarians fled after the fort was captured, but the native Persians fought to the end and inflicted heavy losses on some

---

[1] *A.S.* 173. [2] ix. 102. 1 and 3.
[3] περιήϊσαν (ix. 102. 1); cf. Grundy, 527 f.
[4] ix. 99. 3 (end) and 102. 2; on Plataia cf. 61. 3 and 62. 2.

of the Greeks, notably the Sikyonians, although the Spartans and the other contingents on the Greek right arrived in time for the final fight in the camp.[1]

The account of the battle derived by Diodoros[2] from Ephoros combines incongruously items borrowed from Herodotus with others invented by Ephoros, some of which are clearly inspired by a desire to enhance the share of the Asiatic Greeks in Leotychidas' triumph.[3] As this was the only engagement in the war in which they could claim to have contributed to the success of the national cause, Ephoros was concerned to magnify the importance of the battle; in his version the Persian land force was swelled by reinforcements from Sardis to a total of 100,000 men, of whom 40,000 were slain in the battle or the subsequent flight.[4] Herodotus was perhaps to some extent influenced by distortions of the true tradition which owed their existence to Ionian propaganda. He says that when the Samians in the Persian encampment saw that the battle was turning at the start in favour of the Greeks they did all that they could to help them;[5] as they had been disarmed it is not easy to see what they could have done, and Herodotus gives no details, though he adds that the Samians by their example encouraged the rest of the Ionians present to change sides and attack the Persians. He also states[6] that the Milesians had been sent out of the Persian camp before the battle because their loyalty was mistrusted by the Persians, but this statement also appears to be derived from later Ionian propaganda, for he has already said that the Milesians had been posted on Mount Mykale to guard the important communications to the north through the passes, and also by their special knowledge of the terrain to facilitate the withdrawal of the Persian forces in the event of their defeat. If the Milesians were detached to guard the passes it is obvious that they had hitherto given the Persians no reason to suspect their loyalty.[7] But when the Persian troops were defeated and

---

[1] ix. 102. 4–103. 1.

[2] Diod. xi. 34–36. Cf. Wells, *Studies in Herodotus*, 164.

[3] So rightly HW 332 as against Rawlinson and Macan (i. 2. 805 B and ii. 338).

[4] Diod. xi. 34. 3 and 36. 6.

[5] ix. 103. 2; ἑτεραλκής must be used here (see above, p. 184, n. 5 on ἑτεραλκέως in viii. 11. 3) in its Homeric sense (cf. Powell's edition of Bk. VIII, p. 78). The disarming of the Samians had been mentioned in ix. 99. 1.

[6] ix. 104.   [7] The inconsistency is pointed out by Macan, i. 2. 805 B.

in flight, the Milesians misled them and did all they could to ensure their destruction until they finally joined in the slaughter themselves.

Herodotus' account of the battle is clear enough within its limitations. Macan finds its precision suspicious, and claims that many of the details are simply borrowed from the authentic tradition of Plataia,[1] but the parallels between the two battles are far less close than Macan supposes, and are confined to points where parallelism was to be expected; the Spartans would naturally be on the extreme right, the Athenians on the extreme left, and the Persian infantry when on the defensive usually set up their wicker shields as a rampart so that they could shoot their arrows from behind its protection. Macan admits the one great difference between the two battles, that whereas at Plataia the Greeks were on the defensive they were the attackers at Mykale, but the Persians at Mykale did at least prefer to leave their fortified camp and meet the Greeks in a position outside it. A Persian camp fortified with a stockade appears in the accounts of both battles, but at Plataia the Greeks have to fight before they can force an entry, while at Mykale they pursue the retreating enemy so closely that they rush into the camp along with them, and the last desperate struggle takes place inside the fortifications. The main crux in Herodotus' account of Mykale is the alleged disparity in numbers of the two sides which results from his estimate of the strength of Tigranes' force,[2] but we must assume that here as elsewhere Herodotus has exaggerated the size of a Persian army; it is unnecessary to suppose that the Greek force must have been larger, or that the Ionians on the Persian side must have made a greater contribution to the Greek victory than Herodotus allows.[3]

Herodotus' observation that the battle of Mykale was fought in the afternoon may be accepted,[4] although it is connected in his narrative with the statement that Mykale was fought on the same day as Plataia, and also with the marvellous story that a herald's staff appeared mysteriously on the beach at Mykale not long before the battle and by its appearance gave rise to

---

[1] Macan, ii. 338.   [2] ix. 96. 2 (ἐξ μυριάδες).

[3] Both suppositions are entertained by Macan, ii. 338.

[4] ix. 101. 2. It is apparently rejected by Myres, *Herodotus*, 297, for he says that the Greeks, advancing from east to west (see his plan), had the light behind them.

a rumour in the Greek ranks that the army of Pausanias had just defeated Mardonios in Boiotia.[1] This is the only intervention of the supernatural in Herodotus' account of Mykale. Ephoros inevitably tried to rationalize it, by the assumption that the circulation of the rumour was due to Leotychidas, a trick which inspired the remarkable confidence shown by the Greeks.[2] Modern historians have also tried to rationalize the story, though in a subtler way; either the news of Plataia really did reach Mykale before the battle, and therefore Mykale must have been fought several days after Plataia,[3] or the Greek tradition was right in dating the two battles to the same day and the encouraging news received by Leotychidas was the report of Pausanias' earlier victory over the Persian cavalry force led by Masistios.[4] These modern attempts to explain the supernatural element in the narrative are not much better than that of Ephoros, and like his presuppose that the story of the mysterious rumour must have some foundation in fact, whereas such a tale, which appealed both to Herodotus' religious feeling and to his love of the marvellous, may have been only a pious fiction for the edification of the faithful. For those who were already convinced that the Greek victory could only be explained by the aid of the gods it was a short step to invent a story which showed their active participation in the event.

After the battle was over the Greeks burnt the whole of the Persian fortification and the ships.[5] It is not stated whether the Ionian ships in the Persian fleet were comprised in this holocaust, but as they presumably were not, the fleet beached before the battle must have included other ships as well as those of the Asiatic Greeks. Herodotus records that after the Greek fleet returned to its base at Samos a proposal was put forward to evacuate all the Greeks living in states on the mainland of Asia Minor and transplant them to some region under effective Greek control; the Spartans are said to have suggested that room might be found for them in Old Greece by expelling from the coast towns the inhabitants of those states which had sided

---

[1] ix. 100.
[2] Diod. xi. 35. 1–3.
[3] HW 331 incline to this view.
[4] So Grundy, 526.
[5] ix. 106. 1. Giannelli suggests (in *Studi in onore di Ugo Enrico Paoli*, Florence, 1955, pp. 355–8) that the Athenian leaders, including Themistokles, were responsible for the burning of the Persian fleet.

with Persia.[1] Some critics reject the report altogether as unworthy of credit,[2] while others who accept it see in it fresh
evidence of the selfishness and short-sightedness of Spartan
policy.[3] Neither attitude is justified, for later history was to show
that only the permanent protection of a strong navy could
prevent Persia from attempting to recover the Greek states on
the Asiatic seaboard,[4] and past history had provided examples
of plans for the wholesale evacuation of their populations.[5]

Herodotus declares[6] that these proposals were wrecked on
the opposition of the Athenian leaders, who claimed that
Athens as the mother-city of the Ionian colonies ought to have
the decisive voice in their fate. Perhaps the proposals in the
war council were no more than tentative suggestions, and the
part played by the Athenians in their rejection may have been
magnified by later Athenian tradition, anxious to enhance the
service rendered by Athens to Ionia on this occasion. Diodoros
says[7] that the Ionians and Aiolians were at first prepared to
agree, but this assertion is incredible;[8] they were always strongly
attached to their homes and were unlikely to fall in with such
a plan when they had just triumphantly thrown off the Persian
yoke. But as they had not been admitted to the Hellenic
Alliance they had no say in its deliberations, and the Ionians
would naturally appeal to their Athenian kinsmen to plead
their cause in the war council. If the proposals had met with
general acceptance, the next step would probably have been to
refer them to the Probouloi at the Isthmus for their approval and
the provision of means to carry out the proposals,[9] but in view
of the fierce opposition which they had aroused they were
allowed to lapse. Leotychidas, however, drew a distinction, and
limited the privilege of formal incorporation in the Alliance to
the island states which had revolted from Persia, of which only

---

[1] ix. 106. 2–3 (if τὰ ἐμπόρια ἐξαναστήσαντας is the true reading in 3. Macan reads
ἐμπολαῖα, Legrand ἔπιπλα, for ἐμπόρια).

[2] Cf. Macan, ii. 339; he makes the alternative suggestion that the debate, if it ever
occurred, took place in Old Greece before the naval campaign of 479 began. Cf.
also Meyer, Forsch. ii. 217, n. 1.

[3] Cf. Leo (cited in the Bibliography) 62f. The same view is implied by the
narrative of Grote, iii. 529 f. (abridged ed., 243).   [4] Cf. Grundy, 529.

[5] Cf. the references in Macan's note on ix. 106. 2, also HW 332 f.

[6] ix. 106. 3.   [7] Diod. xi. 37. 1–3.

[8] Cf. HW 333 (top of page).

[9] This is the obvious answer to the argument used by Macan, ii. 339.

the most important, Samos, Chios, and Lesbos, are mentioned by name;[1] the sequel suggests that contingents from some of the mainland states, though not admitted to the Alliance, were allowed to participate in the operations which followed.[2]

From Samos the Greeks sailed to the Hellespont to destroy the bridges, but when they found on their arrival that the bridges were no longer in position they again disagreed on their course of action.[3] Leotychidas considered that he had now carried out his instructions, but the Athenians wanted the fleet to stay on to besiege Sestos. It would certainly be an advantage to the Greeks to deprive the Persians of this valuable position on the European side of the straits, but its possession was not of paramount importance to the Persians so long as they maintained their hold on the vital crossing at Byzantion.[4] The Athenians, who had formerly held the Chersonese for half a century, had a special interest in Sestos, but in view of the lateness of the season Leotychidas could reasonably doubt whether he would be justified in detaining the armament on the other side of the Aegean for the prosecution of a siege which seemed likely to be protracted. In the end he and the other Peloponnesian leaders sailed home with their contingents, but the Athenians, determined to persevere in their attempt, refused to accompany them. Thucydides says[5] that they were helped by 'the allies from Ionia and the Hellespont', and though he gives no details the Hellespontine allies,[6] and probably some of the Ionians as well, must have belonged to cities on the Asiatic mainland. It has been supposed that all or some of the mainland Ionian states which had revolted from Persia had decided, when they failed to secure admission to the Hellenic League, to make separate agreements with Athens,[7] but it is possible that Thucydides here uses the term 'allies' informally to describe contingents

---

[1] ix. 106. 4.

[2] Cf. the passage from Thucydides (i. 89. 2) discussed below.

[3] ix. 114.

[4] Artabazos crossed to Asia from Byzantion with the residue of the Persian army later (ix. 89. 4).

[5] Thuc. i. 89. 2. The view of Leo, 64 (following Wilamowitz), that the word ξύμμαχοι is an interpolation, is improbable and unnecessary.

[6] Certainly Abydos, since the Athenians started from there for the attack on Sestos (ix. 114. 2).

[7] Beloch, G.G. ii². 1. 60, followed by Highby, The Erythrae Decree, 41 ff. (Klio, Beiheft 36, 1936).

which had been allowed to share in the rest of the naval campaign.[1]

The collaboration of these contingents with the Athenians in an undertaking which had been turned down by the Peloponnesians was of the utmost significance for the future relations of the three groups concerned, and it is therefore all the more remarkable that Herodotus should have said nothing about the co-operation of the Asiatic Greeks, representing the siege as a purely Athenian enterprise under the direction of the Athenian general Xanthippos; when the siege is prolonged into the winter the soldiers who grow restless at their hardships and their inability to capture the fortress are Athenians, and it is Xanthippos who refuses to abandon the siege without explicit instructions from Athens.[2] Herodotus implies that the siege had been in progress for some time when autumn started;[3] Thucydides says that it lasted into the winter.[4] Sestos had not been provisioned beforehand for a siege and was finally reduced by starvation. The Persian commander Artaÿktes tried to escape but was captured. He had by his misdeeds incurred the bitter hatred of the Greeks living in the neighbourhood, and Xanthippos surrendered him to their vengeance, which was gruesome; they crucified Artaÿktes and killed his son by stoning before his eyes.[5]

Herodotus is characteristically more interested in the fate of Artaÿktes than in the fate of Sestos. Its later history indicates that the Athenians had left it in trustworthy hands[6] before they sailed home with their booty, including the cables of the bridges, which they intended to dedicate in their temples.[7] Herodotus ends his account of the operations at Sestos with the remark that nothing more was done this year,[8] and concludes

[1] For this suggestion cf. Busolt, iii. 40, n. 1. See also the observations of H. Schaefer, *Staatsform und Politik* (Leipzig, 1932), 63 ff.   [2] ix. 117.

[3] ix. 117. The Greek φθινόπωρον began on 18 Sept.; see above, p. 249, n. 3.

[4] So Rawlinson explained ἐπιχειμάσαντες; cf. Macan, i. 2. 828 A, also Shuckburgh's n. on ix. 121.

[5] ix. 120. 4, also vii. 33. On the punishment cf. Legrand, ix. 108 A, n. 3.

[6] Possibly descendants of some of the Athenian settlers who had been taken to the Chersonese by the elder Miltiades. The inference drawn by some from the story in Plut. *Kimon* 9. 3 that Sestos later fell into the hands of Pausanias is to be rejected; cf. E. M. Walker in *C.A.H.* v. 467.

[7] ix. 121.

[8] The last sentence in ix. 121. Its authenticity is doubted, perhaps rightly, by Macan, who brackets it (i. 2. 828).

with a story about an ancestor of Artaÿktes which is intended to point the moral of his whole History.[1] There can be no serious doubt that he intended to finish his great work at this point. Thucydides rightly begins his famous sketch of the rise of Athenian power with the siege of Sestos, for the Athenian leaders by their decision to undertake the siege had taken their first important step towards emancipation of their policy from Spartan control. At the end of the next campaign they were ready for a more momentous decision, when, as Herodotus had noted earlier,[2] 'using the insolence of Pausanias as a pretext they took away the leadership from the Lakedaimonians', thereby inaugurating a development which was probably distasteful to Herodotus. It could perhaps be argued that he should either have stopped before the capture of Sestos or gone on to the capture of Byzantion, which completed the isolation of the few Persian garrisons still left in Europe, but the latter alternative would have entangled him in the sequel of Pausanias' career, while the former would have forced him to omit the final operation of the campaign of 479. By continuing his narrative beyond Mykale for a few more chapters he was able to celebrate an exploit which conferred distinction on Perikles' father[3] and gave fresh proof of the patriotism and determination of the Athenians, and which also provided a convenient excuse for the story selected by him for his final tableau.

[1] ix. 122. Cf. HW 337, also Myres, *Herodotus*, 299 f.   [2] viii. 3. 2.
[3] Xanthippos' marriage with the Alkmeonid Agariste and the birth of their son Perikles are described in vi. 131. 2, but his only other appearance before this in Hdt. (apart from the previous reference to the fate of Artaÿktes in vii. 33) is his prosecution of Miltiades the younger in vi. 136. 1.

VI

THE PAUSE ON LAND

The Persian land forces after Salamis

 AESCHYLUS and Thucydides,[1] perhaps because they were both Athenians, may have overstated the effect which the Persian defeat at Salamis had on the further course of the war, but they are nearer the truth than those German scholars[2] who deny that it made any serious difference to Persia's prospects of success on land. It is obvious that if the Greeks had vigorously followed up their victory by carrying the naval war to the coasts of Asia Minor, the Persian army would have been speedily compelled to evacuate Greece without a battle.[3] There is no exaggeration in Grundy's verdict[4] that 'after Salamis the position of the whole Persian expedition was one of extreme danger' and it is clear from the events which followed that in the decisions taken on the day after the battle the Persian leaders had proceeded on the assumption that no attempt could be made to recover the command of the sea in the near future; that they had decided to disband some if not all of their fleet is shown by the disembarkation of the marines from the Egyptian ships at Phaleron and their incorporation in the land forces,[5] and they were anxious to ensure the safe retreat of their fleet to Asia as quickly and as secretly as possible before it met with further disaster. Naturally these decisions were not known to the Greeks, but they were bound to discover sooner or later the full extent of their own triumph and the collapse of the Persian resistance at sea. The Persian high command, correctly informed of their own losses, could not afford to base their future strategy on the continued forbearance of the enemy. So Herodotus[6] rightly finds the main motive for Xerxes' retirement to Sardis in anxiety about his communications; he feared that the Greeks might be prompted by the Ionians or take it into their

---

[1] *Persai*, 728 (cf. Artemisia in Hdt. viii. 68 γ); Thuc. i. 73. 5.

[2] Notably Beloch, ii². 1. 51 and 2. 61 f. Even Meyer, 401 tends to underestimate the effects of a Greek naval offensive.

[3] Cf. Delbrück, 96 (though his view on p. 95 is nearer to Beloch's).

[4] Grundy, 408; see above, p. 243.　　　　　[5] ix. 32.　　　　　[6] viii. 97. 1.

own heads to sail to the Hellespont and destroy the bridges, and that he would then be cut off in Europe and in danger of destruction.

Xerxes' withdrawal is attributed by Herodotus[1] to cowardice, but his action was manifestly dictated by the political situation as a whole. Now that his line of retreat was threatened, he was bound to return as quickly as possible to his original base at Sardis; from there he could maintain contact with the interior of Asia and intervene promptly if any of the subject peoples should be encouraged by the news of Salamis to attempt revolt. It has been argued[2] that as the weak point in the Persian position was the untrustworthiness of the Ionian Greeks, Xerxes returned to Sardis to keep them loyal by his presence and personal authority, but as the sequel showed, even the proximity of Xerxes would not deter the Ionians from rebellion if once the Greek fleet appeared off their coasts. Anyhow, Xerxes was not in such a hurry as to return by the shorter and quicker route across the Aegean, although he sent some of his illegitimate children at once by that route to Ephesos under the care of Artemisia; it is unprofitable to speculate on the reasons for his decision to make his own way back by land.[3]

After Salamis the Persian army in Greece, entirely dependent for its communications on a long land route which might be cut by the victorious Greek fleet, was in a precarious situation. If it was to remain, it must be maintained at sufficient strength to be able to face a Greek offensive on land with fair prospects of success, but the provisioning of such a force was likely to be difficult; it could no longer count on sea-borne supplies, which might be intercepted by the Greek fleet, and must depend mainly on the resources of Thessaly and Macedonia, though these might perhaps be supplemented from Asia by the land-route through Thrace. Even if a strong army could be maintained in Greece it would be forced to remain on the defensive, for the Greek lines on the Isthmus of Corinth were by now impregnable to an attack by land alone.[4]

---

[1] viii. 103.

[2] By Delbrück, 95. A more cynical suggestion (Busolt, 713, n. 1) is that Xerxes had no temptation to remain for a campaign in which brilliant exploits and quick results were no longer to be expected.

[3] viii. 103; cf. HW, ad loc. and Hauvette, 428.

[4] Even Beloch (ii². 1. 53) admits this.

In spite of all these considerations Xerxes determined to leave a large number of his Asiatic troops in Greece, ostensibly to continue the war on land in the next year, under the supreme command of his cousin Mardonios.[1] As Mardonios was responsible for the execution of the plan he was naturally represented as its chief advocate,[2] but the arguments attributed to him by Herodotus are not likely to be authentic, and in fact the Persian leaders had no choice. However strong the strategic reasons might be for withdrawing the army in safety while its communications with Asia by land were still intact, the political arguments against such a step were overwhelming.[3] The Persian Empire had sustained a severe shock in the decisive defeat of its great armada at Salamis; the ignominious retirement of its army from Europe without any further attempt to force a battle on land with the main Greek army would have meant a loss of face that would have fatally compromised the prestige of the ruling race.

The Persian leaders, having decided to keep an army in Northern Greece, at least for the present, began to withdraw their forces from Attica three or four days after the battle of Salamis.[4] The Attic country-side had been so devastated that it was impossible to remain there for the winter, and the main body of the army of occupation retired as far north as Thessaly and Macedonia,[5] where supplies would be adequate; presumably garrisons of Persian and allied troops were left behind in Central Greece, at Thermopylai and other important places, including the cities of Boiotia.[6] It is probable, however, that the Persians, when they lost control of the sea, had to relinquish their hold on the great island of Euboia, for the Greek fleet was soon able to levy contributions without any opposition from Karystos in South Euboia, and contingents from three Euboian states, Chalkis, Eretria, and Styra, were present next year in the Greek army at Plataia.[7]

---

[1] viii. 107. 1 and 113. On the relationship cf. vii. 5. 1 and 82 (son of Dareios' sister); Mardonios had married a daughter of Dareios in 493 or 492 (vi. 43. 1).

[2] Busolt, 712, n. 1; cf. Hdt. viii. 100. 2–5 and Grundy, 409 f.

[3] Grundy, 411.

[4] viii. 113. 1, where the army is said to have returned by the same way as it had come; cf. HW, ad loc. On the chronology see below, pp. 274 and 452.

[5] Both are mentioned as winter quarters of Mardonios' army in viii. 126. 2, but elsewhere Thessaly alone (129. 3, 133, ix. 1).

[6] Macan, i. 2. 538 A; see above, p. 240.

[7] ix. 28. 5 (wrongly doubted by Meyer, 408 n.); cf. viii. 112. 2–3.

When the Persian army reached Thessaly it was reorganized, according to Herodotus,[1] who says that Mardonios there selected the 300,000 soldiers whom he had previously persuaded Xerxes to leave with him in Greece; they are said to have been composed of the full contingents of the more warlike peoples of the empire, supplemented with picked troops from the rest, including the body of Egyptian marines landed after Salamis. The troops retained by Mardonios are said to have included all the 10,000 Immortals, but these men, who had played a prominent part in the fighting at Thermopylai, are never mentioned in the campaign of the next year, and as their commander Hydarnes certainly returned to Asia with Xerxes,[2] it is probable that Herodotus was misinformed and that Hydarnes took his men with him; they would be the obvious escort for Xerxes on his return,[3] and may have remained with him at Sardis as his bodyguard.

Although some have accepted Herodotus' figure (or one near it) for the force left with Mardonios,[4] it is unlikely that the Asiatic troops in his army numbered more than 60,000, including the men under Artabazos detached to crush the revolt of the Greek states in Pallene. Herodotus, believing that the 300,000 men with Mardonios amounted to no more than one-sixth of Xerxes' original host, had to suppose that the remaining five-sixths now returned with Xerxes to Asia. Thucydides[5] accepted the tradition that Xerxes took the greater part of his army back with him, a tradition already established in Greece within eight years of the event, for Aeschylus in the *Persai*[6] represents Mardonios' army as a body of picked troops. Unfortunately there is no agreement about the original size of Xerxes' army or about the proportion between it and the army left behind with Mardonios. Modern scholars tend to believe that the number of combatants in the Asiatic contingents of Mardonios' army cannot have been much smaller than in the original army of invasion;[7] if they are right, Mardonios cannot

---

[1] viii. 113. 2–3; cf. 100. 5.   [2] viii. 113. 2 (also 118. 1 in an apocryphal story).
[3] The suggestion in the text is due to Macan (i. 2. 539 A), but he thinks that the Immortals may have returned to Greece for the campaign of 479.
[4] Grundy, 418 estimates his whole force (including Europeans) at 250,000, but see below, pp. 354 f.   [5] i. 73. 5.   [6] Lines 803 f.
[7] So Wecklein, quoted with approval by Wright, 44; cf. Beloch, ii². 2. 70 ff., also HW 273 f.

have had much freedom of choice in the composition of his force,[1] but perhaps they are wrong. Anyhow, difficulties of supply would compel him to reduce the number of non-combatants as much as possible; probably Xerxes took most of them, including his own attendants, back to Asia.[2]

Greek tradition, having magnified the number of the men who accompanied Xerxes on his return journey, drew a fancy picture of the horrors which attended their march. Already in Aeschylus[3] there is a circumstantial story telling how the Persian army began to cross the frozen Strymon on foot, only to perish miserably in the middle when the ice melted. Herodotus, who knew that the Persians had built a bridge over the Strymon before the invasion, rejected this and other fictions, but he seems to have exaggerated both the haste and the horrors of the retreat.[4] His estimate of forty-five days for the march[5] has been suspected on the ground that it is exactly half of that which he had previously given for the march from the Hellespont to Athens, but the suspicion is not justified if, as seems probable, the starting-point of the journey is reckoned from Thessaly. A march of forty-five days from Thessaly to the Hellespont would have been feasible, even though Xenophon's statement that Agesilaos in 394 marched as far in a month or less cannot be trusted. Herodotus' statement[6] that those who accompanied Xerxes were at times reduced by shortage of supplies to eating grass or the bark and leaves of trees, thereby incurring dysentery and pestilence, may reflect some partial breakdown in the Persian commissariat, but his assertion[7] that when Xerxes reached the Hellespont he brought with him next to nothing

---

[1] For the same dilemma (in different terms) cf. the end of Macan's long note, i. 2. 538 B.

[2] Busolt, 713 n. (end of long note on pp. 712 f.).

[3] *Persai*, 495 ff. On the Strymon bridge cf. Hdt. vii. 24.

[4] viii. 115–17; in 118–20 he gives and refutes the story (wrongly accepted by Grundy, 419) that Xerxes went from Eïon to Asia by sea.

[5] viii. 115. 1 (cf. Macan, i. 2. 541 B) also 51. 1. Macan believes that the forty-five days must be reckoned either from the day after Salamis or from that on which Xerxes left Attica; neither view is probable. On the march of Agesilaos cf. Xenophon *Ages*. 2. 1, a rhetorical passage; Beloch (*G.G.* iii². 2. 217) rejected Xenophon's estimate as 'quite impossible'.

[6] viii. 115. 2–3. Grundy, 418 speaks of 'a large force wholly unprovided with commissariat'; this seems improbable.

[7] viii. 115. 1 (regarded by Hauvette, 436 f. as simple exaggeration of language); cf. Beloch, ii². 2. 71.

of his army is false in its implications; if it happened to be true in fact it would be because, contrary to what Herodotus himself believed, Xerxes had not many troops with him when he left Thessaly. It must be remembered that everywhere on his route he was passing through lands subject to Persia which had not yet thrown off their allegiance; moreover, he must have reached the Hellespont not later than the middle of December, and possibly a week earlier.[1]

The two bridges of boats across the Hellespont were no longer there. Beloch, who maintains that there was never more than one bridge, insists[2] that it must have been demolished after the army had passed over it into Europe, but the traditions followed by Herodotus regarded the bridges as permanent structures and explained their disappearance as the work of a great storm which had broken them up.[3] Herodotus says that the soldiers with Xerxes were conveyed across to Asia in the ships of the fleet,[4] which had been directed to make its way to the Hellespont. After Xerxes and his men had crossed to Abydos they proceeded to Sardis, where Xerxes remained throughout the next campaigning season.[5]

Those who believe that Xerxes took hardly any troops back with him to Asia appeal to the statement of Herodotus in a later chapter[6] that Xerxes was escorted to the Hellespont by 60,000 troops under Artabazos, who then turned back to crush the revolt of Poteidaia. In the next year, after the defeat at Plataia, Artabazos brought what was left of the Persian army back to Asia,[7] and was later appointed satrap of the province of Hellespontine Phrygia, a position inherited by his descendants; the Pharnabazos who held it during the Ionian and Corinthian Wars was probably his great-grandson. As Herodotus seems to

[1] Beloch (ii². 2. 52) calculating the forty-five days from that on which Xerxes started from Thessaly, puts the date of his departure unnecessarily late, at the end of October; he assigns too much importance to Aeschylus' story of the freezing of the Strymon as evidence for the time of year.

[2] ii². 2. 90 f.

[3] viii. 117. 1; Aeschylus (Persai, 736) apparently believed the bridge was still in position when Xerxes returned.

[4] viii. 117. 1; cf. 107. 1 and 130. 1.

[5] viii. 117. 2; cf. ix. 3. 1 and 107. 3.

[6] viii. 126. 1, cited in this connexion by Busolt, 713 (n. 4 on pp. 712 f.).

[7] ix. 66 and 89, Thuc. i. 129. 1. Cf. HW 276 f.

have much information about Artabazos, it has been suggested[1]
that he derived it directly or indirectly from Artabazos' descendants, but though this may well be true it does not follow
that every statement about Artabazos in Herodotus is derived
from this source, still less that any statement which can be
traced to it must be regarded as beyond dispute. The passage
under discussion, whatever its source, can hardly be accepted
as it stands; it cannot be taken as a decisive proof that Artabazos really had 60,000 men under his command and so held
a position almost of parity with Mardonios.[2] Even if his army
numbered no more than 10,000 men, there is no reason why
a force of this size should have been needed to escort Xerxes
through territories still loyal to Persia, especially if Xerxes was
accompanied by all or a part of his bodyguard. Grundy
suggests[3] that the main purpose of Artabazos' expedition to the
Hellespont was to reorganize the line of communication along
the coast road with special reference to commissariat. It is more
likely that the connexion of his activities in this neighbourhood
with Xerxes' retreat is an afterthought, as he (unlike Hydarnes)
is nowhere mentioned in the detailed account of the retreat
given earlier by Herodotus.

Artabazos' force is described[4] as part of the army which had
been retained by Mardonios, but he may have received some
support from Macedonian troops in his attack on Poteidaia,
which had thrown off its allegiance to Persia after the flight of
the Persian fleet to Asia and the retreat of Xerxes. Poteidaia
occupied a strong position covering the whole of the narrow
isthmus which joins the peninsula of Pallene to the mainland of
Chalkidike. The revolt made Pallene virtually an island, and
as the Persians had lost command of the sea the other Greek
towns in Pallene joined the revolt; while Poteidaia held out
they would be safe from direct attack, unlike the neighbouring
Bottiaians of Olynthos, who had rashly joined the rising but
were speedily reduced by Artabazos.[5] Even Beloch admits[6] that
though the rebellion of the towns in Pallene was not of great
material significance it was all the more ominous as a symptom

---

[1] By Stein; cf. Macan, i. 2. 553, also Busolt, 713, n. 1.
[2] Wright, 46 is wisely sceptical about the details in viii. 126. 1.
[3] Grundy, 429.
[4] viii. 126. 1; on the reasons for the revolt of Poteidaia cf. 126. 3.
[5] viii. 127.   [6] ii². 1. 52.

of the moral effect which was beginning to be produced by the Persian defeat at Salamis and the withdrawal of Xerxes.

Poteidaia could only be attacked by the Persians on its nor-thern side, from Chalkidike. Artabazos seems to have had no siege train, and there is no indication that he resorted to the method, borrowed by the Persians from the Assyrians and used so effectively sixty years earlier by Harpagos against the towns of Ionia,[1] of building a mound to overtop the wall of the be-sieged city. An attempt to win Poteidaia by treachery among the besieged miscarried. The siege had dragged on inconclusively for three months when an abnormal ebb-tide suddenly laid bare the shore below the city-wall on the sea side.[2] Artabazos decided to use this opportunity to march part of his army into Pallene, but he did not act quickly enough,[3] and when the troops had completed only two-fifths of the passage they were caught by the returning tide; those who were not drowned were destroyed by some of the besieged who put out in boats. Nothing was left for Artabazos but to give up the siege and lead back what remained of his army to Thessaly, where he rejoined Mardonios.[4]

Although Mardonios and his allies still occupied all Greece north of Attica and the Megarid, he cannot have hoped to establish a new Persian frontier permanently on the Kithairon–Parnes line.[5] He must have known that it was intended to disband most of the Persian fleet[6] and that his communications with Asia might be threatened by a Greek naval offensive when the next campaigning season opened. Somehow or other the deadlock on land must be broken, and quickly. Mardonios ostentatiously consulted the principal oracles in Greece[7] (though

---

[1] i. 162. 2 (cf. HW i. 126, ad loc.).

[2] viii. 129 (the duration of the siege is given in § 1).

[3] Cf. Grundy, 430 (where 'two-thirds' is a slip for 'two-fifths'). The Poteidaians explained the disaster as the vengeance taken by Poseidon for the profanation by some Persians of his shrine outside the city wall, an explanation which naturally appealed to Hdt. (viii. 129. 3).

[4] viii. 129. 3 (last sentence), important because it refutes the theory of Munro (see below, p. 294) that Artabazos joined the main army later, in Boiotia. The fact that no further anxiety was shown by the Persians about Poteidaia suggests that they did not regard it as a serious threat to their communications; cf. Wright, 47.

[5] The hypothesis of Grundy (op. cit. 450, also 410) attacked by Macan, i. 2. 614 B and ii. 184, n. 7.

[6] See above, p. 246.

[7] viii. 133–6. On Delphi cf. Macan, i. 2. 567 B.

Delphi is not mentioned), presumably to satisfy the Greek states still loyal to Persia, but doubtless he also asked the leading men in these states, and also the Macedonian king Alexander, for their opinions on the present situation. The result of his deliberations was startling. Alexander was sent to Athens as Persian envoy extraordinary with full powers to offer the Athenian assembly very favourable terms[1] if they would abandon the Greek cause and join the Persians: the land of Attica was to be given back to the Athenians, who were to be granted full forgiveness for their former acts of hostility to Persia, and the temples which had been overthrown were to be restored; the Athenians might receive in addition to Attica any territory they wished, and they were to retain their independence in internal affairs, which meant that they would not be compelled to receive back their exiles. Herodotus explains elsewhere[2] what concessions were expected from the Athenians in return; they were to surrender control of their foreign policy by becoming allies of the Persians and helping them in their wars against all their enemies, including the Peloponnesians.

This remarkable reversal of policy can hardly have been acceptable to some of the states on the Persian side, notably the Boiotians, but Mardonios' situation was so critical that he could not afford to be swayed by sentimental considerations. It was obvious that the resistance of the enemy at the Isthmus lines could only be overcome if their position was turned by a landing in their rear, but to achieve this the Persians must first recover control of the sea. The one way in which this could be brought about without delay was by detaching the powerful Athenian contingent from the Greek navy and bringing it over to Persia. Herodotus[3] sees in this a leading motive for Mardonios' decision, but as he is here playing down the consequences which a change of sides by the Athenians would mean to their former friends, it is not until later that he explains[4] what Mardonios really sought from his bid for Athenian support, the opening of 'a wide door' into Peloponnese. After all the sufferings inflicted on the Athenians by the Persian invasion Mardonios knew that he must bid high to win them over, and the importance he attached to success is shown by the choice of

---

[1] viii. 140 a 2, cf. ix. 7 a 1.   [2] ix. 11. 2.   [3] viii. 136. 2–3.
[4] ix. 9. 2 (put in the mouth of a prominent Tegean, Chileos).

Alexander as his envoy. Herodotus was much influenced by Macedonian traditions[1] which after the war was over strove to minimize the part played in it by Alexander and to prove his fundamental good will to the Greek cause, but there is no need to doubt his statement[2] that already before 480 Alexander had had friendly relations with the Athenians and had been honoured by them with the titles of *proxenos* and *benefactor*.

The news of Alexander's mission seriously alarmed the Spartans, who feared that the Athenians might be seduced by such tempting offers, with disastrous results to their former allies, and they promptly sent an embassy to Athens; Herodotus has an odd story here[3] that they had remembered an oracle foretelling that they and the other Dorians would some day be expelled from Peloponnese by Medes and Athenians. Friction between Athens and Sparta about the strategy to be followed in the next campaign may already have arisen. Herodotus admits[4] that the Athenians, although they had no thought of accepting the Persian offer, purposely delayed their final answer until the Spartan envoys arrived. He seems to think that their sole reason for the delay was to enable the Spartans to hear the proud and resolute speech in which they dismissed Alexander and his offer, but there are indications[5] that they used the occasion of his embassy to extort from the Spartans some concession to the Athenian point of view on the future conduct of the war. As for Mardonios, his first plan had failed, but he was soon to show that he still had two in reserve.

Athens and Sparta between Salamis and Plataia

After Leonidas had fallen at Thermopylai the leadership of the Greek army was taken over, not by the other Spartan king,

---

[1] Cf. vii. 173. 3, ix. 44–45, also v. 19–21. On the golden statue of himself set up by Alexander at Delphi cf. viii. 121. 2 and [Demosthenes] xii. 21.

[2] viii. 136. 1 (cf. 140 β 1) ; on the titles see HW, ad loc. (281 f.). Macan, i. 2. 573 A suggests that there may have been some approximation between Athens and Alexander during the Ionian revolt. It is not likely that he had dared to supply the Athenians with timber and oar-spars for their new fleet (as Archelaos of Macedonia was to do later; cf. Tod, 91).

[3] viii. 141. 1; for some entertaining speculations see Macan, ad loc.

[4] viii. 141. 2. Meyer, 404 thinks that the Athenians delayed for weeks ('wochenlang') before replying to Alexander. The assertion of Plutarch (*Aristeides* 10. 6), that the Athenian answer to Alexander was spoken by Aristeides, is of no value.

[5] viii. 144. 5; a definite Spartan undertaking to advance with the army to Boiotia is alleged by the Athenians in ix. 7 β 1 (cf. 11. 1).

Leotychidas of the Eurypontid family, but by another member
of the Agiad house, Leonidas' younger brother Kleombrotos,
acting as guardian for Leonidas' young son Pleistarchos.[1]
When the battle of Salamis was fought Kleombrotos was in
command of the Peloponnesian levies engaged in building the
wall across the Isthmus of Corinth, but he died before the campaigning season of 479 opened, and was succeeded by his son
Pausanias as guardian of the young Pleistarchos and commander-in-chief of the Spartan and allied forces on land. On
the occasion of Pausanias' assumption of the command Herodotus mentions[2] that his father Kleombrotos while at the Isthmus had once been offering sacrifice before taking the offensive
against the Persians but had been deterred by an eclipse of the
sun (an eclipse which is dated to 2 October 480).[3] It is a reasonable conjecture[4] that the idea of a Greek offensive on land was
suggested by the withdrawal of the Persian army from Attica
and that the sacrifice had something to do with a plan for
harassing the enemy's retreat. How far Kleombrotos seriously
entertained this plan is doubtful; some have seen in the eclipse
an excuse rather than the true reason for his subsequent inaction, and hold that it merely confirmed his own disinclination
to advance beyond the Isthmus lines.[5] There were, indeed,
sound military reasons for such reluctance; a large proportion
of the hoplite forces of the patriotic Greeks was still on board the
fleet, and those serving with Kleombrotos were not yet numerous
enough to risk a collision with the main Persian army. Anyhow,
Herodotus says[6] that after the eclipse Kleombrotos disbanded
his army; perhaps he waited until he heard that most of the
Persian army had retired to Thessaly.

By the opening of the next campaign the Greek fleet had been
reduced to 110 ships[7] and thereby more hoplites had been
released for the army, which eventually advanced to Eleusis and
on to Boiotia. These facts suggest that the Greek leaders had

---

[1] ix. 10. 2; cf. viii. 71. 1. It is curious that Leotychidas was passed over; cf.
Beloch, ii². 2. 95.

[2] ix. 10. 3.   [3] Busolt, 715, n. 1; cf. HW, ad loc. (p. 290).

[4] Due apparently to Stein; cf. Grundy, first note on p. 443.

[5] Meyer, 394; cf. Wright, 45. The plan attributed to Kleombrotos in HW (loc.
cit.) seems foolhardy.

[6] ix. 10. 2-3.

[7] viii. 131. 1-2; see above, p. 249. On the advance of the army cf. ix. 19.

definitely discarded the strategy proposed by Themistokles in the preceding autumn, to follow up the victory at Salamis by a vigorous offensive directed against the Hellespont and Ionia in order to cut the communications of the Persian army still in Greece and so compel it to retire without fighting. When the plan was first proposed it was rejected, mainly through the opposition of the Spartan admiral Eurybiadas, but many scholars have supposed[1] that the Spartan oligarchy were converted to it in the following winter when they came to realize that the alternative to it was a land campaign in Boiotia if the Persian army was to be driven out of Greece. A proof of this change of policy is found in the enthusiastic reception given to Themistokles[2] when he visited Sparta in the course of the winter,[3] presumably to discuss with her leaders the strategy of the next campaign, for if Herodotus is to be trusted Themistokles, after the rejection of his plan by Eurybiadas, had assured the Athenians that they would resume it and carry it out the next spring.[4] Moreover, the Spartans, who had allowed a commoner, Eurybiadas, to command the allied fleet as navarch in 480, replaced him in the spring of 479 by King Leotychidas, thereby, it is argued,[5] showing the new emphasis that they now wished to give to the naval operations.

This reconstruction further assumes that before the new strategy could be put into action the Athenians had turned against its author and chief advocate, Themistokles, had either deposed him from the strategia or had failed to re-elect him in the spring of 479, and had transferred the direction of the war to his political opponents, Aristeides and Xanthippos.[6] Ephoros, who believed that Themistokles was not in office as general during the campaign of 479, supposed the Athenians to have been so incensed by his acceptance of the honours conferred on

[1] Nitzsch in *Rh. Mus.* xxvii, 1872, 226–68 (especially 258 ff.) originated this view, which was developed by Busolt, Delbrück, and others.

[2] viii. 124. 2–3; Thuc. i. 74. 1. The word καταγαγόντες in Plut. *Them.* 17. 3 has been taken to mean that Themistokles had received an official invitation to Sparta, but this may be only a conjecture by Ephoros.

[3] αὐτίκα in viii. 124. 2 would imply an earlier date, but the context does not inspire confidence in Hdt.'s accuracy here; see Macan, ad loc.

[4] viii. 109. 4.

[5] Meyer, 402. Beloch's attempt (ii.[2] 1. 52, n. 3) to minimize the significance of the appointment is unconvincing.

[6] This view is summarized by HW (389 f.), who do not accept it.

him at Sparta that they deposed him from the strategia and gave
his place on the board of generals to Xanthippos.[1] The moderns
who accept Ephoros' inference disagree with his explanation,[2]
and assume instead that Themistokles' loss of power was due to
his continued advocacy of an all-out naval offensive, which had
by now become anathema to the mass of his fellow citizens,
because they realized that it imposed a defensive role on the
Greek land forces and because they thought that the naval
offensive was not likely to affect the position of Mardonios'
army in time to deter him from a fresh invasion of Attica.[3]

Herodotus gives no direct support to this reconstruction,
apart from the fact that he nowhere mentions Themistokles in
his account of the events of 479, except in a single reference
backwards to the campaign of 480.[4] He believes that there was
serious friction between the Athenians and the Spartans in the
months preceding the march of the Greek army to Boiotia, but
he explains it by the determination of the Spartans (which he
attributes to selfish motives)[5] not to advance beyond the Isthmus position, whereas the Athenians urged them strongly to
move up to the Kithairon–Parnes line in time to cover Attica
from the danger of a second invasion.[6] On the other side it is
only fair to point out that as Herodotus usually ignores the
interrelation between the operations of the Greek army and
those of the fleet he is not likely to understand what was the real
point at issue in the tug-of-war of rival strategies which he
certainly attributes to Athens and Sparta at this juncture.

It is significant that Beloch,[7] who throughout underrates the
importance of the naval operations after Salamis, ignores the
evidence for the tug-of-war, and implies that Athens and Sparta
were of one mind in regarding the expulsion of the Persian
army from Greece as their primary task in 479 and the role of
the fleet as secondary; it was only the difficulty of providing
supplies for a large army that held up the advance on land until

[1] Diod. xi. 27. 3 (almost certainly from Ephoros).

[2] Except Hauvette, 443, who argues that Themistokles became unpopular on
account of his pride and suspicions of his honesty. But Hdt. does not regard the
attitude of Timodemos of Aphidna (viii. 125) as typical, and the reaction of the
Athenians against Themistokles described in Plutarch (*Them.* 22) appears to belong
to a later date.

[3] Meyer, 402 f.   [4] ix. 98. 4; cf. viii. 22.   [5] Notably in ix. 8.

[6] viii. 144. 5; cf. ix. 7 β 1.   [7] ii². 1. 52; cf. 2. 142 ff. on Themistokles.

the time of the harvest. In his attack on the rival theory he makes some points.[1] Aristeides' action at Psyttaleia shows that, whatever Herodotus believed,[2] he was one of the generals elected in the spring of 480 to hold office for the next archon year, and the same must be true of Xanthippos, who is in command of the Athenian contingent of the Greek fleet at Aigina in the spring of 479,[3] and therefore in the same archon year. Hence Beloch correctly concluded that the Decree of Recall,[4] which enabled Aristeides and Xanthippos to return from the exile imposed on them by ostracism, must have preceded the elections held in the spring of 480. Both certainly held the strategia in the year 479/478, for Aristeides commanded the Athenians at Plataia,[5] Xanthippos at Mykale and Sestos.[6] If both had been generals in the previous year as well, their election in the spring of 479 was a re-election, and as such cannot have had any special significance.

Beloch is less successful in dealing with Themistokles' disappearance from the narrative of Herodotus after his return from Sparta. He calls attention to the part played by Themistokles in the fortification of the Piraeus and to the invectives of Timokreon of Ialysos[7] as evidence that Themistokles was influential at Athens and in the Aegean during the period just after the Persian War, but this merely proves that if he fell from favour with the Athenians in 479 he soon recovered his former influence. Beloch argues that his predominance in the years 482–480 must have been fortified by the triumph of his strategy at Salamis, but there is no such thing as gratitude in politics. It is a real crux, as Ephoros realized, that Themistokles plays no part in the operations of 479, either on land or on sea. Beloch suggests that he did not wish to play second fiddle to Pausanias

---

[1] On the following cf. also Bury in *C.R.* x, 1896, 418.

[2] On Hdt. viii. 79 cf. HW 262 f., ad loc.

[3] viii. 131. 3; the archon year (480/479) is that of Kalliades (viii. 51. 1).

[4] *A.P.* 22. 8; cf. Hignett, *A History of the Athenian Constitution*, 189, n. 4.

[5] He is only mentioned once in Hdt.'s ninth book, in the last sentence of ix. 28; contrast the wealth of detail about his activities in 479 given by Plutarch in his *Aristeides*.

[6] Diod. xi. 36. 5, Hdt. ix. 114. 2 and 120. 4; the presence of other στρατηγοί at Sestos is implied in ix. 117.

[7] Thuc. i. 93. 3–5, Plut. *Them.* 21. 4–7. Beloch in a long note (ii². 2. 144 f.) rightly argues against Kirchhoff and Meyer that Themistokles' activity in the south Aegean, presupposed by the poem in Plut. *Them.* 21. 4, cannot be as early as 480; he would put it in 477, but perhaps 478 is also possible.

on land, but he had previously served under Euainetos when the Greek army went to Tempe.[1] In view of his interest in the naval offensive he might have preferred to serve with the Athenian contingent in the fleet in order to use his influence to press a bolder strategy on Leotychidas; Beloch is here reduced to arguing[2] that any successes the fleet might obtain would be unimportant in comparison with the glory Themistokles had won at Salamis, and that he did not wish to remain far from Athens for long at such a critical time.

In spite of the weakness of Beloch's arguments he may be right in maintaining that the argument from Herodotus' silence should not be pressed and that Themistokles really was a member of the board of generals in 479.[3] Munro once suggested that his inactivity in this year was the result of a compact made by him with Aristeides and Xanthippos on their return from exile, a compact which gave him full control of the Athenian forces in 480 in return for a promise to hand over the command to them in the next year.[4] This hypothesis is far-fetched; how could the parties to the compact know beforehand that the war would last for precisely two campaigns? Moreover, it presupposes that Aristeides and Xanthippos had before their exile been joint leaders of what Munro calls the Agrarian Party, whereas the scanty evidence suggests that in the decade after Marathon they belonged to different groups and had come into collision with Themistokles on different grounds.[5] If Themistokles was still general in 479, his inactivity may perhaps be explained by his disapproval of the strategy now in favour at Athens, the reverse of that which he had himself advocated in the previous autumn; presumably he had failed to convince the Athenians to make their main effort again on the sea, and as they had cut down the size of their contingent to the allied fleet[6] he was not prepared to undertake the responsibility of a naval offensive with inadequate forces.

There can be no doubt that the Athenians in the spring of 479

---

[1] vii. 173. 2.   [2] ii². 2. 145 f.

[3] That he was is vigorously argued by Macan, ii. 332 ff., though his conclusion (p. 334), that Themistokles approved of the policy followed in 479, seems overbold.

[4] *J.H.S.* xxii, 1902, 301 (this is the explanation favoured by HW 390).

[5] Cf. Hignett, op. cit. 184 ff.

[6] It is unfortunate (and perhaps significant) that Hdt. does not specify in viii. 131 what proportion of the allied fleet of 110 ships was supplied by Athens.

favoured an offensive movement of the Greek army into Boiotia,[1] but modern scholars disagree on the attitude of the Spartan
leaders to this strategy. Some flatly reject Herodotus' assertion
that they were unwilling to advance beyond the Isthmus and
were only forced to do so in the end by Athenian pressure, but
they disagree in their explanations of the Spartan failure to
march out in time to save Attica from a second Persian invasion.
Beloch[2] and Meyer believe that the Peloponnesians could not
move until the harvest was ready and were forestalled by the
rapidity of Mardonios' advance. Munro has suggested[3] that the
Spartans were hampered by difficulties within the Peloponnese,
as there was a serious danger that the march of their home
troops to the Isthmus would be blocked by a coalition of pro-
Persian states, Argos, Mantineia, and Elis. The contingents of
Elis and Mantineia certainly arrived too late for the battle of
Plataia,[4] and after their return home the generals in both states
were banished. Herodotus also says[5] that after the Spartan
army had marched to the Isthmus, the Argives, who had previously promised Mardonios that they would hold up the Spartan march, sent a message to him in Attica to report that they
had been unable to fulfil their promise.

The attitude of some Peloponnesian states may have been
lukewarm or ambiguous in the spring of 479, but they would
scarcely have ventured on open opposition to the patriotic
states at this stage in the war. Argos had probably hoped at the
outset for a Persian victory over her hated rival Sparta, but her
weakness compelled her statesmen to wait on events, and after
Salamis they must have been even more reluctant to commit
themselves beyond recall to the Persian side.[6] If they really gave
Mardonios the undertaking recorded in Herodotus, it was probably a kind of insurance against the faint possibility that the
Persians might win after all, as insincere as the messages of good
will sent by some Whig politicians in England to James II when
he was in exile. Sparta disliked the Mantineians and secured
their exclusion from the roll of honour on the serpent column
at Delphi after the war,[7] but their failure to arrive in time for

---

[1] viii. 144. 5; cf. ix. 7 β 1.   [2] Beloch, ii². 1. 52; cf. Meyer, 404 f.

[3] *J.H.S.* xxiv, 1904, 147 f.   [4] ix. 77; see below, p. 341.

[5] ix. 12.   [6] Cf. Macan, i. 2. 612 B.

[7] Tod, no. 19 (with his comment on p. 24); cf. Hauvette, 460 n. (end of first
paragraph of long n. on 459 f.), also HW 320 f.

Plataia, and also that of the Eleians, may have been due to nothing more than selfishness and procrastination; both had been present in the army mobilized at the Isthmus in the previous autumn.[1] The position of Sparta in the Peloponnese was more precarious than the outside world was allowed to realize, but its insecurity was mainly due to the ever-present threat from the Helots, and in the summer of 479 Sparta countered this particular menace by sending an unusually large force of Helots[2] out of Peloponnese in the army of Pausanias.

Others have admitted that Spartan statesmen were determined not to allow their army to advance beyond the Isthmus, but insist that their decision is to be explained not by the selfish motives alleged in Herodotus but by their realization of the hazards of an offensive against the enemy on a terrain so suited to the operations of his cavalry as the plains of Boiotia.[3] Those who hold this view, acknowledging that the Spartans must have been as eager as the Athenians to force the withdrawal of the Persian army to Asia, tend to suppose that the Spartans must have relied on a vigorous offensive by sea to bring this about, but found themselves baffled by the refusal of the Athenians to contribute more than a fraction of their fleet to the allied navy. They explain the tension in Herodotus between Athens and Sparta by the assumption that each of the two states was trying to force its own plan on the other; so when Athens mobilized only a few of her ships Sparta refrained from calling up the League army.[4] The strategy attributed by this view to the Spartans was undoubtedly a startling reversal of policy, but they had no alternative if they recoiled from the risks of an offensive on land; they could not hope to end the war by a strategy of complete inaction on both elements. Grundy suggested that the Spartans hoped, by delaying until the Persians entered Attica, to force the hands of the Athenians and compel them to take part in the defence of the Isthmus.[5]

[1] viii. 72 (note Ἀρκάδες πάντες).

[2] The figure is given as 35,000 in ix. 28. 2, 29. 1, 61. 2.

[3] So Nitzsch (see above, p. 275, n. 1) and Busolt; cf. Delbrück, 96 f. and Wright, 49.

[4] So Busolt, 719.

[5] Grundy, 440 f. In his second note on p. 443 he says that the Spartans had not marched their troops to the Isthmus because if they had been there earlier the Athenians would have called on them to forestall Mardonios' invasion by marching to Kithairon.

The evidence of Herodotus that the Spartans did not intend to advance beyond the Isthmus if they could help it is strongly supported by the behaviour of Mardonios. His advance from Thessaly through Central Greece into Attica, apparently in June 479, is assigned by Herodotus[1] to an overpowering desire to capture Athens for the second time, but he admits soon after[2] that Mardonios calculated the Athenians would be more inclined to accept his overtures when his troops had occupied their territory. The Athenians however, who had retired to Salamis on the news of his approach, rejected his proposals, a repetition of those previously brought by Alexander;[3] tradition reported that a member of the Council called Lykidas, who had advised their acceptance, was stoned on the spot, and that his wife and children were then killed in his home by the Athenian women.[4] Mardonios had probably not had much hope of success from these fresh overtures, but he knew that if he could not win over the Athenians to the Persian side he must somehow bring the Greek army to battle as soon as possible; he could not afford to wait on the chance of its taking the offensive.[5] He certainly did not intend to fight in Attica as it was unsuitable for cavalry,[6] and if he lingered there after the rejection of his offer the obvious explanation is that, informed by his Greek adherents about the tension between Athens and Sparta, he hoped by his occupation of Attica to induce the Athenians to put irresistible pressure on the Spartans and so resolve the deadlock on land. Herodotus says[7] that the Athenians did send envoys to Sparta as soon as they evacuated Attica, and when the ephors at Sparta still delayed, the envoys threatened that the Athenians would accept Mardonios' offer and join the Persians at once in an attack on their former allies, whereupon the ephors gave way.

Herodotus' account here may be sound in substance, but some of the details are suspicious. As Grundy says,[8] the story of the reception of the Athenian envoys at Sparta is 'one of the

---

[1] ix. 3. 1; on the chronology see below, p. 455.
[2] ix. 4. 2.   [3] ix. 5–6; on the proposals cf. ix. 4. 1.
[4] ix. 5. 2–3; other ancient writers call the victim Kyrsilos (cf. HW, ad loc., also Verrall in *C.R.* xxiii, 1909, 36–40). The story was accepted by Grote (iii. 493 and n. 1) and is defended by Hauvette, 450.
[5] See below, pp. 319 f.   [6] ix. 13. 3; cf. Thuc. vii. 27. 5.
[7] ix. 6–11 (ultimatum in 11. 1–2).   [8] Op. cit. 441.

strangest in the strange history of this time'. The Spartans are
said to have done nothing before this to help the Athenians,
partly because they were celebrating the festival of the Hyakinthia and partly because the wall across the Isthmus was nearing
completion.[1] In spite of the protests of the Athenian envoys the
ephors kept deferring their answer until at last they were warned
by a prominent Tegean, Chileos, that the Isthmus wall would
be useless if the Athenians went over to Persia; they were so
alarmed by this warning that the same night in all secrecy they
sent off 5,000 Spartiates under Pausanias.[2] When the Athenians,
who had been accompanied to Sparta by envoys from Megara
and Plataia,[3] arrived next morning to present an ultimatum,
the ephors were able to report that the 5,000 were well on their
way and that 5,000 hoplites of the Perioikoi were ready to
march.

This story is almost as discreditable to the Athenians as to the
Spartans;[4] a few weeks after their solemn assurance to the
Spartans that they would never make peace with Xerxes they
are threatening to join the Persians against the patriotic Greeks.
The details about the wall are unconvincing; it was apparently
defensible some months earlier.[5] Although Herodotus does not
say so,[6] the 35,000 Helots later associated with the 5,000
Spartiates at Plataia probably marched out with them from
Lakonia, and most critics, even Hauvette,[7] have admitted that
a force so numerous could hardly have left Sparta without the
knowledge of the Athenian envoys. It is true that we do not
know where the force was mustered,[8] but if it was ready to
march as soon as the ephors made their decision it must have
begun its mobilization several days earlier;[9] hence the ephors
must have issued the order for mobilization some time before

---

[1] ix. 7. 1.   [2] ix. 9 and 10. 1.   [3] ix. 7. 1.

[4] Macan, i. 2. 610 f.

[5] Cf. viii. 71. 2, also Macan, i. 2. 603 A. In spite of Hauvette, 452 Mardonios'
suggestion to Xerxes after Salamis that they might attack Peloponnese at once
(viii. 100. 3) is not to be taken seriously; cf. Macan, ad loc.

[6] On the assumption that the words καὶ ἑπτὰ περὶ ἕκαστον τάξαντες τῶν εἱλώτων,
omitted by some manuscripts, are a gloss. They are bracketed by many (including
Hude and Legrand) but are retained by Macan, Powell, and Shuckburgh (edition
of Hdt. ix; he notes on p. 88 that the words seem to have been read by Plutarch,
as shown by his *Aristeides* 10. 8).

[7] Op. cit. 452; cf. Legrand, ix. 15, n. 2.   [8] So Grundy, 442, n.

[9] As Grundy admits (p. 443); cf. Legrand, ix. 16, n. 2.

they are supposed to have been stirred to action by Chileos. Grundy can only suggest[1] that the content of Chileos' warning was different from the Herodotean version; the ephors knew already that the Isthmus could be turned if the Persians recovered supremacy at sea but thought they could rely on the devotion of the Athenians to the patriotic cause until Chileos, 'an able man whose opinion they valued', warned them that Athenian loyalty would not stand much longer the strain imposed on it by Spartan policy.

A further difficulty about this Athenian embassy is raised by a passage in Plutarch's *Life of Aristeides*,[2] in which, after narrating, on the evidence of Idomeneus, how Aristeides behaved on this embassy, he refutes this version by a decree, proposed by Aristeides, naming not himself but Kimon, Xanthippos, and Myronides as the envoys to be sent to Sparta. Plutarch does not cite his authority for this decree; the usual assumption that he or his source got it from Krateros is far from being established. Macan argues[3] that the embassy must have been sent to Sparta in the early spring, on the ground that when the campaigning season opened Xanthippos went off with the Athenian contingent to join the allied fleet and presumably remained away from Athens till the next winter. Macan also wished to infer from a passage of Thucydides that the Hyakinthia, dated by Hesychios to the Spartan month Hekatombeus, occurred not in May or June but earlier in the spring.[4] Thucydides, however, merely says that the Spartan–Athenian alliance of 421 contained a provision for its annual renewal by Spartan envoys in Athens at the Dionysia and by Athenian envoys in Sparta at the Hyakinthia, which merely proves that the Hyakinthia, like the Dionysia, were in the spring. Other evidence[5] points to May or June as the date of the Hyakinthia; the date probably varied between May and June in accordance with the state of the Spartan calendar, being later in a year when an extra month had been intercalated.[6] But the reference to the Hyakinthia in this section of Herodotus is not entirely above suspicion. It may be the authentic date, preserved by tradition, of an Athenian

---

[1] Op. cit. 442.   [2] 10. 10; cf. Wright, 48.
[3] 603 B and 610 A.
[4] Macan, 602 B; cf. Hesychios s.v. Ἑκατομβεύς and Thuc. v. 23. 4.
[5] Xen. *Hell.* iv. 5. 1 and 11 ff.; cf. the first note on Hdt. ix. 7 in HW 288.
[6] Busolt, 722, n. 2, followed by HW 288 (first note on ix. 7).

embassy, but it may equally well be part of an accretion which made out that the Spartans as usual were too busy keeping holiday to help their allies and supplied the name of a festival suitable to the time of year.

The argument from Plutarch's decree is also inconclusive. Even if the decree came ultimately from Krateros' collection, Plutarch supplies too little information about it to guarantee that the embassy to Sparta mentioned in it was identical with that of June 479 described by Herodotus. If it was, the Xanthippos in it cannot have been the son of Ariphron, for he was then with the fleet;[1] perhaps he was the archon for the Athenian year 479–478 who had not yet entered on his office.[2] Macan's dating of the embassy to the early spring would entail the rejection of most of Herodotus' account of it, for if the Persians had not yet invaded Attica the Spartans could not be reproached for having failed to defend it in time or for their heartlessness in preferring to celebrate the Hyakinthia, and the purpose of the embassy must rather have been to secure guarantees from Sparta or to concert measures for the coming campaign. It is conceivable that there were two embassies from Athens to Sparta in the spring of 479; if there were, how could Plutarch be sure that the decree, whether genuine or not, referred to the second and not to the first?

Herodotus' version of the embassy certainly contains some details which appear incredible, but this does not necessarily mean that his whole account is fiction, with no more foundation in fact than the memory that Athenian envoys had been sent to Sparta in June 479 on a mission, the purpose and results of which had been forgotten. Cautious historians[3] are agreed that the tradition here followed by Herodotus, though defaced by additions designed to heighten the unfavourable impression of Sparta's behaviour in this crisis, was right on the essential points, that there was serious friction between Athens and Sparta at this time, that its causes were the failure of the Spartan leaders to mobilize their army soon enough to defend Attica and their continued reluctance to take the offensive on

[1] viii. 131. 1 and 3.
[2] Busolt, 721, n. 5. The name of the archon for 479/478 is given as Xanthippos in *Marmor Parium* 52 and Diod. xi. 27. 1, as Xanthippides in Plut. *Aristeides* 5. 10.
[3] Followed for the most part even by Macan, ii. 335 f.

land, and that when the Athenians were forced to abandon their country to the invaders again and take refuge in Salamis they promptly sent envoys to Sparta with instructions to present to the ephors an ultimatum which may even have included a threat[1] that the Athenians would accept Mardonios' offer of alliance (with all its consequences) if Sparta persisted in her present policy. Whatever may have been the reasons for that policy, it must have been strongly resented by the Athenians, and the bitterness against Sparta in the tradition here recorded by Herodotus may well be contemporary,[2] even if some of the details are later embellishments.

The ephors realized that they must yield without delay, and promptly mobilized their army. Herodotus says[3] that the Spartiatai, numbering 5,000, set out first by night and were followed next day by 5,000 Perioikoi; later on he says that there were 35,000 Helots in attendance on the Spartiates, serving as light-armed troops, and implies that there were 5,000 such troops in attendance on the Perioikoi.[4] The Spartiates are said to have marched along the road which passed by Orestheion.[5] This route, which in the first part of its course went up the valley of the Eurotas, was longer than the direct road to Tegea going due north from Sparta through Sellasia, but it must have had compensating advantages, for when in 418 the Spartan army was mobilized in a hurry to prevent the imminent defection of Tegea, it advanced by way of Orestheion,[6] nor was this choice influenced by a desire to collect Sparta's South Arcadian allies on the way, for these were instructed to follow the Spartans with all haste to Tegea.

This parallel is sufficient to refute the suggestion[7] that the

---

[1] ix. 11. 1–2.

[2] It is necessary to insist on this in answer to the rather naive contention of Wright that passages in which Sparta is depreciated could only have been added to the tradition in the period after Kimon's fall from power.

[3] ix. 10. 1 and 11. 3; on the reference to the Helots in some texts of the first passage see above, p. 282, n. 6.

[4] ix. 28. 2; for the attendants on the Perioikoi cf. 29. 2 and 61. 2.

[5] ix. 11. 2; on this route cf. Loring, *J.H.S.* xv, 1895, 27 ff. and 47–52 (especially p. 52 for the reasons why this route was preferred to the direct route, which is described on pp. 57 f.), also HW 290 f.

[6] Thuc. v. 64. 1–3.

[7] Accepted by most historians, e.g. Grundy, 444; the note in HW 290 f. is misleading, especially in its implication that the longer route did not eventually go through Mantineia.

Spartans marched out by the Orestheion road in 479 because
the direct route went too near the territory of Argos. Since the
final annexation of Kynouria by Sparta in 541[1] the direct route
did not approach Argive soil until just before reaching Tegea.
As Argos was neutral in 479, the Spartan army could not
march through any part of her territory to the Isthmus but
must have taken the alternative route from Tegea through
Mantineia and Orchomenos to Sikyon.[2] Anyhow, the risk from
Argos in 479 was negligible; after Salamis the Argives were not
likely to risk a direct clash in battle with the Spartans. On their
march to Sikyon and the Isthmus the Spartans seem to have
collected the contingents of Tegea and Orchomenos; the rest of
the Arcadians were apparently left to follow later.[3]

Pausanias, son of Leonidas' brother Kleombrotos, was in
command of the Greek army which now collected at the Isthmus. Herodotus says[4] that when Pausanias left Sparta he had
chosen as his helper in the command a member of his own
family, Euryanax son of Dorieus. The only Dorieus known to
have belonged to the Agiad family in this period is the second
son of King Anaxandridas, who according to the story told
earlier by Herodotus[5] had refused to stay in Sparta on the accession of his half-brother Kleomenes and had later been killed
in Sicily. Beloch believes that this Dorieus was the father of
Euryanax, and maintains[6] that in 479 Euryanax, not Pausanias,
was the regent, but that as Pausanias was the abler general he in
fact conducted the campaign and therefore secured the chief
credit for the victory at Plataia. But Herodotus says explicitly[7]
that Pausanias on the death of his father Kleombrotos became
the guardian of his cousin Pleistarchos. It is intelligible that
when Leonidas was killed the guardianship of his infant son
should have been taken over by Leonidas' younger brother
Kleombrotos rather than by the son of his elder brother, but
why on Beloch's view should Pausanias rather than Euryanax

---

[1] Hdt. i. 82 (contemporary with the date of the fall of Sardis, on which cf.
Hignett, *A History of the Athenian Constitution*, 328).

[2] On the routes cf. Grundy, *Thucydides*, 222 and the map opposite p. 359.

[3] On the Arcadian contingents see below, pp. 437 f.

[4] ix. 10. 3; Euryanax is associated again with Pausanias in 53. 3 and 55. 1.

[5] v. 39–48.

[6] ii[2]. 2. 158 f., where he rejects as improbable the solution suggested by him in
ii[2]. 1. 53, that Euryanax and Pausanias were co-regents.

[7] ix. 10. 2; Thuc. i. 132. 1 is equally precise.

have succeeded on Kleombrotos' death to the guardianship and
with it the claim to command the army? There is also a more
fundamental objection to Beloch's view; if he is right, why had
Euryanax not succeeded to the Agiad kingship when Kleomenes
died without male heirs?[1] Beloch does not mention the improbable hypothesis[2] that Dorieus on his departure from Sparta
had forfeited or renounced his right to the succession for himself and his descendants; had he done so, his son would have
been excluded from the regency as well as from the throne.
Moreover, Herodotus, if he had known that Euryanax was
Pausanias' first cousin, would surely have said so,[3] instead of
describing him as 'a man of the same house'. On the whole it
seems best to conclude that Dorieus the father of Euryanax was
not the son of Anaxandridas but belonged to another branch of
the Agiad house.[4]

When Pausanias arrived with his army at the Isthmus he was
soon joined there by contingents from other Peloponnesian
states which had not been picked up by him on the way.[5] The
omens proved conveniently favourable for an advance, and the
combined force marched on through the Megarid into Attica,
where it was met at Eleusis by the Athenian troops under the
leadership of Aristeides.[6] The Persians had evacuated Attica on
the approach of the Greek army, which proceeded to cross the
northern frontier of Attica and took up its position at Erythrai,
on the northern slopes of Kithairon.[7] To this extent Mardonios'
second plan had been successful; by his occupation of Attica

[1] Beloch, i[2]. 1. 174 tries to meet this objection by citing the alleged Spartan
rule (probably apocryphal) in Hdt. vii. 3. 3, but though it might explain why
Pleistarchos succeeded Leonidas it is irrelevant to Leonidas' succession on the
death of Kleomenes.

[2] Mentioned by HW 290.

[3] This point was made by Rawlinson. It is challenged by Macan (i. 2. 609 B)
but he makes no attempt to meet it.

[4] When Pleistarchos died childless in 458/457 (on the date cf. Diod. xiii. 75. 1)
his successor was Pausanias' son Pleistoanax (Thuc. i. 107. 2). Beloch, i[2]. 2. 174
has to assume that Euryanax had died without issue before Pleistarchos.

[5] ix. 19. 1; Grundy, 452 points out that some troops from the patriotic Peloponnesian states must have been already present at the Isthmus to defend the wall
there if necessary. Note that Pausanias took the omens again at Eleusis; cf. ix. 19. 2
and Hauvette, 458.

[6] ix. 28 (last sentence); Leokrates and Myronides are said by Plutarch (*Arist.*
20. 1) to have been among his colleagues at Plataia. At least two generals (including Xanthippos) were with the fleet (ix. 117).

[7] ix. 19. 3; on the situation of Erythrai see below, pp. 297 and 426.

he had prevailed on the Athenians to exert pressure on the
Spartans, who had been forced thereby, against their own better
judgement, to leave their impregnable lines and advance into
Boiotia. But even there they were still in a strong defensive
position; how could Mardonios overcome the danger of a second
stalemate?

VII

THE CAMPAIGN OF PLATAIA[1]

The advance of the Greek army into Boiotia

ATTICA is separated on the north from its neighbour Boiotia
by a chain of mountains extending from the Corinthian
Gulf on the west to the Aegean Sea opposite Euboia on
the east; the western part of the chain was called Kithairon in
antiquity, the eastern part Parnes.[2] A few miles farther north
the river Asopos flows from west to east, roughly parallel to the
chain, and separated from it by a belt of territory which is for
the most part too broken by hills and ravines to be suitable for
cavalry, but north of the Asopos in the middle part of its course
is a level plain stretching to the town of Thebes, which Mardonios made his base in 479 after his advance from Thessaly.
The main road from Athens to Thebes now crosses Kithairon
by the pass of Gyphtokastro, about four miles to the east of the
site of the ancient Plataia, and as this is the lowest pass in this
part of the range[3] it must certainly have been used in the fifth
century; the road through it seems to be that called by Xenophon[4] 'the road through Eleutherai', which was probably the
normal route from Athens to Thebes in his time as now. Most
scholars identify the pass of Gyphtokastro with that known to
Herodotus and Thucydides as Dryoskephalai,[5] but as the identification has been disputed it is safer to use the modern name.

---

[1] In this chapter the following articles will be referred to by the name of the
author: Munro, *J.H.S.* xxiv, 1904, 144–65; Boucher, *Rev. Arch.*, series v, vol. ii,
1915, 257–320; Kirsten in *R.-E.* xx. 2, 1950, 2255 ff.; Pritchett, *A.J. Arch.* lxi,
1957, 9–28. For convenience the Thucydidean form 'Plataia' has been used
throughout; it occurs only once in Herodotus (viii. 50. 2) who elsewhere, like
Xenophon, prefers the plural form.

[2] Cf. the admirable description in Grundy, 445 ff., though his use of the term
'Panakton' for the upland country connecting Kithairon with Parnes is not accepted
by all scholars; see below, p. 422.

[3] 649 metres according to Ufer, 111 (references to Ufer in this chapter are to his
valuable account of the campaign in *A.S.* 107–65).

[4] *Hellenika*, v. 4. 14.

[5] Hdt. ix. 39. 1 (where the Boiotian name Τρεῖς κεφαλαί is also given) and Thuc.
iii. 24. 1; on the identification see below, p. 424.

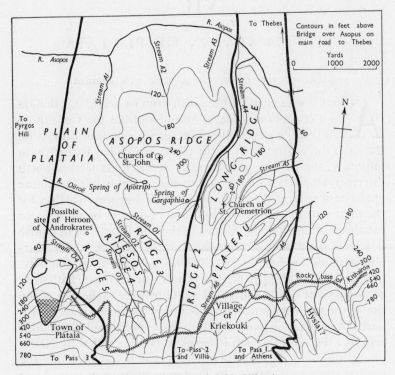

MAP 8. The battlefield of Plataia

In spite of the advantages of this route it was not the one used by Mardonios when he retired from Attica before the approach of the Greek army. Instead he took the easternmost of the three routes from Attica to Boiotia, that which goes a little east of north from Athens through Dekeleia (near the modern Tatoï) and across the Parnes range to Tanagra.[1] Herodotus has been taken to imply that Mardonios reached his bivouac at Tanagra from Athens in a single day, but his words need not be so interpreted,[2] nor is it necessary to suppose that the Persian army in its retreat made use of other routes as well as the Dekeleia–Tanagra road. Mardonios may not have had the whole of his army with him; when he decided to re-occupy Attica, a force slightly stronger than that which the Athenians could muster would have been sufficient for his purpose.[3]

Before he retreated Mardonios carried still farther the sack of Athens left incomplete by Xerxes.[4] Herodotus has a curious story[5] that when Mardonios had already begun to withdraw his troops he suddenly, on the news that a body of a thousand Lakedaimonians had occupied Megara as an advance guard, turned back and began to lead his army towards Megara, sending his cavalry on ahead to overrun the Megarid, but on the arrival of a further message that the Greeks had arrived in force at the Isthmus, he took his army back through Dekeleia. The motive given for his dash towards Megara, that he wished to capture the advance guard before the main army came up, is unconvincing; the Lakedaimonians were presumably safe behind the walls of Megara, which Mardonios could not have captured without a siege.[6] It is unlikely that he turned back with the main body of his army after he had already begun the evacuation of Attica, but the raid of his cavalry into the Megarid, which marks the furthest penetration into Greece by the Persian land forces,[7] is confirmed by Pausanias. Grundy

---

[1] ix. 15. 1.   [2] Cf. Hauvette, 454 (answering Delbrück).

[3] So Hauvette, 455; cf. Boucher, 268.

[4] ix. 13. 2. The destruction was not complete even now; cf. Thuc. i. 89. 3 and HW 291.

[5] ix. 14 and 15. 1. In the second line of c. 14 ἄλλην στρατιήν is difficult; cf. the note in Shuckburgh's edition. Legrand, ix. 17, n. 3 proposes to delete ἄλλην and to insert ἄλλη after ἀγγελίη.

[6] The explanation of Beloch (ii². 1. 54), that Mardonios hoped to destroy the detachment on its march to Megara, is improbable.

[7] So Hdt. ix. 14, with error in orientation; cf. HW, ad loc. and Pausanias i. 44. 4.

believes[1] that the raid was really a cavalry reconnaissance, to discover if possible what the Greeks were doing at the Isthmus, and that it took place several days at least before the date indicated by Herodotus. The alternative is to keep Herodotus' date for the raid while rejecting his motive, and to suppose that the cavalry were sent to the Megarid as a screen to cover the retirement of the infantry;[2] on this view the cavalry when they had completed their task may have retreated through the Gyphtokastro Pass to rejoin the main army.

Mardonios' reasons for evacuating Attica, as given by Herodotus,[3] are that the country was unsuitable for cavalry and that if he was defeated in Attica his line of retreat could easily be cut, whereas if he retired towards Thebes he would have a friendly city for his base and would be on ground where his cavalry could operate freely. Most modern historians[4] have accepted this explanation as correct. If Herodotus was rightly informed, Mardonios hoped to fight a decisive battle with the Greek army on ground which would enable him to make full use of his cavalry, and in order to gain his object he must somehow contrive to tempt the Greek forces to advance across the Asopos to the plain on its north bank. Long ago Mitford suggested[5] that Mardonios left the Kithairon passes unoccupied in order to tempt the Greeks to advance through them into the open country which he had chosen for a battle ground; this hypothesis is more attractive than Grundy's,[6] that Mardonios chose the Dekeleia route because he was afraid that the advancing enemy might cut off his retreat if he took one of the alternative routes, and thought that the route farthest from their line of advance would be the safest.

Mitford's view presupposes that Mardonios on reaching Boiotia must have crossed the Asopos and taken up a position behind the north bank. It is certain that the Persian army was north of the Asopos at a later stage in the campaign,[7] but Herodotus

---

[1] Op. cit. 448 f. Wright (*The Campaign of Plataea*), 52 also questions the timing of the raid in Hdt.

[2] Macan, i. 2. 615 f.   [3] ix. 13. 3.

[4] e.g. Busolt, 724, n. 3, Hauvette, 453, Wright, 51. The view of Grundy (op. cit. 450) that Mardonios' aim was to establish a new Persian frontier on the Kithairon–Parnes line has been discussed above, p. 271.

[5] *History of Greece* (Dublin, 1785), i. 550, quoted by Wright, 52. Cf. also Meyer, 406.   [6] Op. cit. 447 f.; cf. 445 (top of page).

[7] The Greeks are separated from the Persians by the Asopos in ix. 36.

seems to imply that it was still south of the river when the Greek
army first crossed Kithairon. He says that Mardonios after
spending a night at Tanagra marched on the next day to Skolos,
where, although he was now on territory belonging to his ally
Thebes, he proceeded to cut down the trees in order to make
a stockade as a refuge for his army if it met with a reverse;
this stockade is alleged to have measured about ten stades on each
side, which suggests that it was square.[1] The precise position
of Skolos is so uncertain that scholars still disagree whether
it was on the north or the south side of the Asopos. Anyhow,
Herodotus does not assert that the stockade was at Skolos;[2]
Hauvette, who believes that Skolos was south of the river,
thinks that the trees there were cut down by the Persians for
their stockade because Skolos was on a wooded slope whereas
there were no trees in the plain, but Herodotus seems to mean
that the trees used for the stockade included fruit-trees. Some
have tried to have it both ways[3] by the assumption that, though
the stockade was north of the river, Mardonios also constructed
a fortified post facing it on the southern side as a sort of bridgehead, but there is no evidence for the construction of two forts,
and why should Mardonios wish to defend the crossing of the
Asopos if his main object was to lure the Greek army on to the
plain north of the river?

A more serious difficulty is raised by Herodotus' description[4]
of the position taken up at this stage by the Persian army (which
is distinguished clearly by him from that occupied by the
stockade): 'Mardonios' army was drawn up by the side of the
river Asopos, stretching from Erythrai past Hysiai and reaching
to the territory of Plataia.' As all the places here mentioned were
certainly south of the Asopos, Herodotus ought to mean that
the whole Persian army was encamped at this time between
the Asopos and the range of Kithairon. Munro, accepting this
interpretation of the passage, supposes[5] that the Persian right

---

[1] ix. 15. 2–3; cf. Macan, 618 f. On the site of Skolos see below, pp. 426 f.

[2] Hauvette, 456. Pritchett, 24 A agrees with Hauvette and holds that Skolos
must have marked the southernmost limit of Mardonios' clearing of land.

[3] So Macan, i. 2. 618 B, followed by HW 292. Grundy (*Topography*, 14) says that
the Persian camp 'must have lain on both sides of the Asopus', but it is not clear
whether he is here speaking of the stockade or of what Macan (619 A) calls the
Laager, i.e. the encampment of the στρατόπεδον (cf. ix. 15. 3).

[4] ix. 15. 3.   [5] Munro, 156 f.

wing was thrown forward to Kithairon to hold the Gyphtokastro Pass and another to the west of it which led from Plataia to Megara.[1] He maintains that Mardonios must have tried to defend these passes for several reasons, to secure his own retreat from Attica, to give time for Artabazos to join him with his army, and to force Pausanias to cross the mountains at a point farther east than the Gyphtokastro Pass; Munro thinks[2] that when Mardonios sent his cavalry to the Megarid his object may have been to check any attempt by the Greeks to use either the Gyphtokastro or the Megara–Plataia Pass for their advance.

Munro's reconstruction, based on the natural interpretation of one passage in Herodotus, does violence to his narrative in several other points. Most serious of all is Munro's assumption[3] that Artabazos and the force with which he had besieged Poteidaia never rejoined Mardonios at all during the campaign of 479, whereas Herodotus states that after the failure of the siege Artabazos led the survivors back to Mardonios, who was then still in Thessaly, and later on represents Artabazos as present in the Persian camp on the Asopos a few days before the final battle.[4] This assumption is an essential part of Munro's reconstruction, as it leads up to the further assumption[5] that Pausanias was eager to force on a battle as soon as possible, before Mardonios' army could be reinforced by the troops of Artabazos. But even if Herodotus was wrong and Munro right about Artabazos, why should Mardonios have ventured so far south when he had not yet concentrated the whole of his army? Munro seems to believe[6] that Mardonios hurried southwards with such troops as were available in a desperate attempt to rush the Isthmus lines while they were still unguarded, but on reaching Thebes heard that the Spartans had already arrived in force at the Isthmus, so gave up his attempt and occupied Attica instead.

This further assumption is contrary not only to the evidence of Herodotus but to common sense as well. Even if Herodotus' story that the Spartans refused to move until after the reoccupation of Attica by Mardonios could be proved to be no more than an anti-Spartan legend, it is incredible that they

---

[1] On these passes see below, pp. 422 ff.   [2] Munro, 151 f.
[3] Op. cit. 165 and *passim*.   [4] viii. 129. 3, ix. 41.
[5] Munro, 151.   [6] Munro, 150 f.

should have made no provision at the opening of the campaigning season for the defence of the Isthmus lines against a surprise attack.[1] Mardonios could never have hoped to force the lines without the support of a fleet. The generous offer he had made to Athens through Alexander of Macedon shows how anxious he was to win Athens over to the Persian side before the opening of the new campaign, and unless Herodotus is utterly unworthy of credit Mardonios had renewed his offer in the same terms after his occupation of Athens.[2] Yet for Munro the occupation is an afterthought, and the only reason he can suggest for it[3] is that Mardonios wished to delay the Athenian navy at Salamis. This explanation hardly needs refutation. As Mardonios had no warships at all, a fleet of twenty Athenian triremes would have been amply sufficient to protect the Athenians in Salamis against any danger of a Persian landing.[4] If the Athenians did not supply a large contingent to the allied fleet this year, the reason was not that they were apprehensive about the safety of Salamis, but that they preferred to reserve most of their manpower for the land campaign which they had decided to force on a reluctant Sparta.

There is the further difficulty that Munro attributes two inconsistent strategies to Mardonios, one defensive, the other (by implication) offensive. If it was so important for the Persians to hold the line of Kithairon until Artabazos and his men could arrive, why did not Mardonios use his centre to block the direct route from Athens through Phyle to Thebes which crosses the upland plain of Skourta, a plain in which some have located the site of Panakton?[5] This is the route which Pausanias is supposed by Munro to have followed when he led the Greek army across Kithairon. Munro claims[6] that the Persian stockade checked Pausanias' advance beyond the Asopos at this point, but he had been allowed to cross Kithairon, and once established on the north side of the range he could deploy his army to the left and threaten the Persian right wing, if it really was stationed at or near the two passes which Munro believes it to have occupied. Munro's alternative strategy, that Mardonios wished by occupying the two western passes to compel the Greeks to cross the

---

[1] Cf. Grundy, 452 (ll. 13 ff.). [2] ix. 4. 1. [3] Munro, 151.
[4] See above, pp. 240 f. [5] On this route see below, pp. 422 f.
[6] Munro, 157.

mountains at a point farther from their base at the Isthmus, seems to have no sequel; although Pausanias (according to Munro) had no option but to use the Skourta route, and although his line of communication with his base was to that extent lengthened, the Persians made no attempt to cut it by advancing through one or both of the two westerly passes. The idea that Mardonios was in either sense trying to hold the line of Kithairon against the Greeks must be rejected. Although the Persian homeland was a mountainous country, its inhabitants were never skilled in mountain warfare.[1] In 479 they were well provided with excellent cavalry, while the Greeks had no cavalry at all. Why should Mardonios have stationed his forces among the rocks of Kithairon, where his own best arm would have been useless? He must have hoped, as Herodotus clearly implies,[2] to fight the decisive battle of the campaign on the plain to the north of the Asopos.

Scholars, faced with the difficulty that Herodotus seems to locate south of the Asopos the position taken up by Mardonios on his return to Boiotia, have tended to deny that the difficulty exists. The explanation which most of them have adopted[3] is that in the crucial passage Herodotus mentions Erythrai, Hysiai, and the Plataiïs not as places actually occupied by the Persians but as markers to indicate the length of the Persian line, which was drawn up opposite to them on the north bank of the Asopos. This interpretation is very artificial; if Herodotus had wished to say so, he could surely have expressed his meaning more clearly. Perhaps he misunderstood what he was told, or his informant was describing the position of the first Persian encampment after the bivouac at Tanagra; if the second suggestion is correct, Herodotus has failed to mention that the Persian army was withdrawn behind the Asopos when the stockade was completed or on the approach of the Greeks. Unfortunately Herodotus does not specify how many days elapsed between the Persian evacuation of Attica and the crossing of

---

[1] Cf. Schachermeyr, *Alexander der grosse* (Graz, 1949), 168.   [2] ix. 13. 3.
[3] e.g. Grote, iii. 496 (top of page), Hauvette, 456, Macan, i. 2. 619, HW 292 f., Kirsten, 2291. Grundy, 463 n. seems to assume that the Persians were on both sides of the Asopos at this stage. Boucher, 271 (cf. his map) supposes that the Persians south of the river were a line of outposts stretching from Erythrai to the territory of Plataia, but Hdt. ix. 15. 3 seems to be speaking of the whole Persian army.

Kithairon by the Greeks. Hauvette's hypothesis[1] that the anecdotes inserted by Herodotus between the two events indicate the lapse of several days is not entirely convincing.

It is curious that Herodotus, after describing Mardonios' route from Athens to Skolos in some detail, has nothing to say about the march of the Greeks from Eleusis over Kithairon except that its end point was the Boiotian town of Erythrai. The site of Erythrai is doubtful.[2] Grundy placed it at the northern exit of the Gyphtokastro Pass, a little to the east of the modern Kriekouki, but recent writers, while disagreeing on the precise location, have gone back to Leake's view that Erythrai was two miles or more to the east of Grundy's site; it would thus be situated between the exit of the Gyphtokastro Pass and the point (near the modern village of Darimari) where the Phyle–Thebes road emerges from the mountains. This leaves open the possibility that Pausanias crossed Kithairon by this road and then proceeded to deploy his army to the west, instead of advancing through Gyphtokastro and then deploying his army to the east.[3] There is, however, some doubt whether the Phyle–Thebes road was suitable for use by a really large force;[4] moreover, if Pausanias, who had started his march from Eleusis to Kithairon along the Eleutherai road, wished to strike into the other before it reached the northern slope of Kithairon, he would have had to diverge from the Eleutherai road and lead his army through the mountains by what would appear to be a difficult track.

If Pausanias really achieved this feat, his object must have been not, as Munro supposes,[5] to take Mardonios by surprise and turn the left flank of the Persians by crossing the Asopos, but to lead his army across the mountains by a pass which would bring him out opposite the position already occupied by Mardonios and would enable him to cover Attica effectively by interposing

[1] Op. cit. 457; so Macan, 628 B assumes that the stockade was being built before the Greeks left Eleusis.

[2] ix. 19. 3; cf. Macan, 629 A ('Herodotus takes the Greek forces over Kithairon in this chapter rather easily'). On the site of Erythrai see the discussion below, p. 426.

[3] For the second alternative cf. Hauvette, 458; this view is defended by Kirsten, 2292. Pritchett, 24 B brings the Greeks across the pass (to the west of the Gyphtokastro Pass) called the Plataia–Athens Pass by Grundy, the Middle Pass by Ufer. See below, pp. 425 f.

[4] On what follows see below, pp. 424 f. [5] Munro, 157.

his army between the Persians and the Attic frontier.[1] On the whole it is more likely that Pausanias entered Boiotia by the Gyphtokastro Pass and then led his men eastwards to Erythrai along the road which seems to have stretched along the foot-hills of Kithairon.[2] Herodotus says[3] that when the Greeks saw the Persians encamped on the Asopos they drew up their own army on the foothills of Kithairon facing the enemy position.

It is a principle of modern strategy, enunciated by Delbrück,[4] that the best way to defend a chain of mountains is not to occupy the passes, but to wait on the other side of the range and to fall on the enemy column as it emerges from the foot of the pass before the whole of it has completed the crossing. Delbrück holds that this is the principle on which Mardonios must have acted; he therefore assumes that the Persian cavalry attacked the Greeks as soon as they appeared on the northern foothills of Kithairon,[5] but though they obtained some success at first, they were compelled to break off the action when the Greeks succeeded in deploying the rest of their army to the north of the pass. This reconstruction, accepted by Munro and Macan,[6] is open to two objections. In the first place it is improbable that Mardonios should have wished to drive the Greeks back into the mountains; it suited him better to leave the passes open and tempt the Greeks to advance across the Asopos. In the second place, Delbrück's view is in flat contradiction to Herodotus, who says[7] that it was only when the Greeks made no move to descend to the plain that Mardonios sent all his cavalry against them under the leadership of Masistios.[8]

---

[1] Cf. Ufer, 123 f.

[2] This road is implied by the story in ix. 25. 1 (doubted by Wright, 54) that the body of Masistios was carried in a cart along the ranks of the Greek army; cf. Munro, 157 and HW 295 f. A road from Tanagra to Plataia is briefly described in c. 11 of a description of Greece falsely attributed to Dikaiarchos (cf. Martini in R.-E. v. 1. 562); see Müller's *Geographi Graeci Minores*, i. 102.

[3] ix. 19. 3.

[4] Op. cit. 75 ff., especially 76–77.

[5] 'As soon as (sofort als) the Greeks emerged from the Kithairon pass' (op. cit. 99 f.). [6] i. 2. 630 B; cf. Munro, 157.

[7] ix. 20; cf. HW 294 (n. on 21. 1). Shuckburgh describes κατέβαινον as the imperfect of continued action, and translates 'persisted in not descending'. Munro's method of dealing with the difficulty (p. 157, n. 20) is to deny that it exists!

[8] 'Whom the Greek call Makistios' adds Hdt. In spite of Macan (629 B) there is no reason why those Greeks who used the form Μακίστιος should not be poets, Simonides and others.

The Greek position on the foothills of Kithairon offered no scope for the normal tactics of the Persian cavalry, and forced them to make frontal attacks on the Greek spearmen. It is not clear what Mardonios hoped to gain by such attacks; perhaps he wished to discover by experiment what his cavalry could achieve under such conditions. Herodotus notes that the Megarians, who bore the brunt of the first attack, were posted on ground more exposed than that occupied by the rest of the Greek army.[1] Grundy's view of the battle, that the Persian aim was to cut the Greek army in two and seize the pass of Gyphtokastro,[2] depends on his erroneous identification of the site of Erythrai and on his assumption that the flat ground in front of his site was occupied by the Greek centre.[3]

The Megarians, when hard pressed, appealed to the generals for reinforcements. Pausanias, according to the story reproduced by Herodotus,[4] called for volunteers; when the rest of the army refused, the Athenians undertook to go with a body of 300 picked troops, led by Olympiodoros son of Lampon, who was supported by the archers serving in the Athenian forces.[5] One of these archers wounded the horse of Masistios, who was thrown to the ground, and finally killed by the Athenians. When his men discovered his death they charged in a body, and the Athenians had to call on the rest of the army for help. The Athenians were at first forced to give ground, but when the main body arrived on the scene the Persian cavalry retreated for a distance of two stades, and after discussing what they should do they decided to retire to their camp and report to Mardonios.

Lampon, the patronymic of the Olympiodoros who commanded the Athenian force on this occasion, recurs later as the name of the famous seer Lampon, one of the co-founders of the colony of Thouria in South Italy, where for a time Herodotus

---

[1] ix. 21. 1. Scholars disagree on the position of the Megarians in the Greek line. Ufer, 124 puts them on the left; cf. Munro, 157 and Kirsten, 2292. Grundy, 460 f. (followed by HW on ix. 21. 1) thinks that they were part of the Greek centre.

[2] Op. cit. 461; cf. Wright, 54.   [3] Op. cit. 460.

[4] ix. 21–24 (especially 21. 3).

[5] Meyer, 360 and n., also 408 and n. (cf. HW 295), calculated that the Athenian archers numbered 800; see below, p. 435.

made his home.[1] It is a plausible conjecture[2] that the Olympiodoros who fought against Masistios was a near relation, father
or uncle, of the seer, and that Herodotus had received his detailed account of this engagement from Lampon the younger,
either at Thouria or at Athens. Critics have complained that
these chapters show a marked pro-Athenian bias,[3] but the only
suspicious item in them is the allegation that the Athenians
alone volunteered for the post of danger when the rest of the
army (presumably including the Spartans) had refused.[4] It is
more likely that Pausanias called on the Athenians for this service because they alone had a body of archers; this is better than
the hypothesis that the duty of helping the Megarians naturally
devolved on the Athenians because they were next in line to the
Megarians,[5] for it is not certain that the Athenians were already
posted on the Greek left, the position which they occupied later
in the campaign, and even if they were, they were separated
from the Megarians by the Plataian contingent.[6]

Herodotus says that the Persian cavalry at the beginning of
the engagement charged in squadrons, presumably in succession, one squadron after another,[7] for it was not until after
the death of Masistios that they charged in a body. As they were
mounted archers they may have been content at first to discharge their arrows at the Greeks from within bowshot, but
later in the fight, when they were trying to recover the body of
their dead leader, they must have come to close quarters, for in
this stage the 300 picked Athenian hoplites are forced back from
the place where the body is lying and their archers are not mentioned.[8] When the rest of the Greek army intervened the Persians
were forced to retire; it is clear that they could not operate
effectively against an unbroken phalanx of Greek spearmen on

---

[1] For Lampon the seer cf. Tod, no. 74 (ll. 47 ff.) and p. 183. On Thouria as
the correct form of the place-name cf. Wade-Gery in *J.H.S.* lii, 1932, 217, n. 48,
and on Herodotus' residence there see HW, i. 3 and 7 f., also Strasburger in *Historia*,
iv, 1955, 23 ff.

[2] By Busolt, 727, n. 2. It is usually assumed (e.g. by Hauvette, 458, n. 1, HW
295) that Hdt.'s Olympiodoros was the seer's father, but Macan, 632 B more
cautiously suggests that he may have been his uncle.

[3] e.g. Macan, 631 B and Wright, 54 (W. strangely denies that the praise of the
Athenians is at the expense of the Spartans).

[4] ix. 21. 3. Hauvette, 459 points out that in the end the Athenians have to be
rescued by the rest of the army (ix. 23. 2).

[5] Macan, 631 B and HW 294.   [6] ix. 28. 6.

[7] ix. 22. 1, 23. 1; cf. Macan, 630 A and 634.   [8] ix. 23. 2.

the foothills of Kithairon. It is therefore not true to say[1] that the issue of the battle was decided rather by the accident of Masistios' death than by the superiority of the Greek troops, fighting in a strong defensive position. Pausanias had every reason to be satisfied with the result of this first encounter. Unfortunately for the Greeks, the enemy had learnt his lesson.[2] Mardonios, in spite of his desire to fight a pitched battle as soon as possible, was not prepared to fight again on such terms. He withdrew his cavalry to the north side of the river and waited for Pausanias to make the next move.

The movement of the Greek army to the second position

The Greeks are said to have been much encouraged by their repulse of the Persian cavalry, and after celebrating their triumph by conveying the body of Masistios in a cart along the line of their army they decided to advance to Plataia.[3] Herodotus says that they marched along the foothills of Kithairon past Hysiai to the Plataian territory, and when they got there they encamped near the spring of Gargaphia and the shrine of the hero Androkrates. If Erythrai lay two miles or more to the east of the road coming down from the Gyphtokastro Pass, a march from there to the Plataiïs would be an advance westwards, parallel to the range of Kithairon, and the verb used by Herodotus for the Greek decision indicates that the march was on the whole downhill, so that the second position of the Greeks must have been lower than the first. This new position is described as extending 'along hills of no great height and level country'.[4]

Grundy has given a lucid description[5] of the terrain between Kithairon and the Asopos which formed the theatre of the subsequent operations. Its boundary on the south is 'the limit of cultivation, where the rocky foot of Kithairon begins to rise from the rounded ridges of the plain'; this boundary is marked

---

[1] As Wright does (op. cit. 55).   [2] So Grundy, 462.

[3] The details in this paragraph are from Hdt. ix. 25. Also see above, p. 298, n. 2.

[4] διὰ ὄχθων τε οὐχ ὑψηλῶν καὶ ἀπέδου χώρου (ix. 25, end, translated by Grundy, 464). Kirsten, 2293 seems to think that the last two words mean the opposite of πεδίον. Macan, i. 2. 641 A has the Delphic pronouncement that 'it was an ἄπεδος χῶρος though not a πεδίον'.

[5] G.P.W. 453 ff.

on Grundy's map (and on others based on his) by a wavy line. North of it Grundy distinguishes four areas. (1) First come several ridges (numbered 1 to 6 from east to west by Grundy) which run from south to north, spurs of Kithairon but of no great height, and separated from each other by the valleys of streams, some of which are tributaries of the Asopos, while the others, west of Ridge 2, unite to form the river Oëroë, which eventually flows westward into the Corinthian Gulf. (2) Beyond the ridges is a depression, part of which extends from the lowest (northern) end of the modern village of Kriekouki in a north-westerly direction until it reaches the plain at a point a little to the west of the Apotripi spring; this part of the depression plays a prominent part in Grundy's reconstruction of the campaign.[1] (3) The plain just mentioned stretches from the north of Plataia without a break to the Asopos and is described by Grundy as 'the only flat land in the whole battlefield'; Grundy, however, omits to notice that the plain is separated on the west from the basin of the Oëroë by the hills of Pyrgos and Moraitiza,[2] which rise from the plain less than a mile west of the Asopos tributary called A1 on his map. (4) Between the depression and the Asopos rise three hills, which Grundy has distinguished from each other by appropriate names, the Asopos Ridge, the Long Ridge,[3] and the Plateau; he notes that the northern slope of each of these ridges is longer and more gradual than the southern slope. The first two descend to the Asopos, but the Plateau, which lies to the south-east of the Long Ridge, is separated from the Asopos by Stream A5.

In which of these four areas is the second Greek position to be sought? Local tradition identified Gargaphia with the spring usually called Apotripi, and this tradition is accepted by Wood-house,[4] but most scholars have followed Leake's view that it is to be found in a group of springs between a half and three-quarters of a mile slightly south of east from Apotripi.[5] When Herodotus wrote, Gargaphia and the Androkrateion could easily be located on the ground, but though the site of Gargaphia is reasonably certain still, that of the Androkrateion is

---

[1] Op. cit. 454.   [2] On these cf. Kirsten, 2269.
[3] Called Μακρυὰ 'Ράχη in Kirsten, 2269.
[4] In J.H.S. xviii, 1898, 37 f. Pritchett, 21 B, n. 78 calls the spring Alepotripi.
[5] Grundy, n. on pp. 465 f., followed by Munro, 159. So now Kirsten, 2270 and Pritchett, 21 B; see below, pp. 427 f.

not. The only trustworthy evidence for its position[1] seems to prove that it was less than 7 stades from Plataia, to the right of the direct road from Plataia to Thebes, but though this, the obvious interpretation of the evidence, has been accepted by Grundy and Beloch,[2] it is contested by those who wish to locate the shrine on one of the summits of the Asopos Ridge or the Long Ridge; the favourite choice is that summit of the Asopos Ridge which rises to a height of 300 feet north of Apotripi and contains the church of St. John.[3]

If the Androkrateion really was within seven stades of Plataia, the second Greek position should have been in the depression already described as lying between the ridges which come down from Kithairon and the three hills close to the Asopos. There are two objections to this conclusion. The first is that a position in the depression could hardly be described as 'along hills of no great height and level country'.[4] The level country ought to be the plain stretching north from Plataia to the Asopos, and Grundy believes that the Greek left did in fact extend into that plain, but his explanation of the hills as 'the lower ends of the ridges which come down from Kithairon'[5] does not agree with the positions assigned to the Greek right and centre on his map, where they seem to be almost at the lowest points of the depression. Secondly, when Herodotus after a digression of four chapters returns to the new position occupied by the Greeks, he describes them as 'encamped on the Asopos'.[6] In the same paragraph he reports that when the Persians discovered that the Greeks were now 'at Plataia' they moved along to 'the Asopos in this part of its course',[7] a statement which incidentally proves that the Greek move to the second position was not merely downhill and northwards, but also a lateral move towards the

[1] Thuc. iii. 24. 1–2.

[2] Grundy, long note on pp. 466 ff.; Beloch, ii[2]. 2. 124.

[3] This seems to have been the view of Hauvette (cf. his map on p. 455); it was defended by Woodhouse (op. cit. 38 f.) who was followed by Munro, 158 and Macan, 640 B. Ufer, 136 ff. identifies the site of the shrine with the church of St. Demetrion. See below, pp. 430 f. It must be remembered that *on Grundy's map the contours are calculated in feet from the level of the bridge over the Asopos on the Athens–Thebes road*; Kirsten gives the height of the church of St. John above sea level as 352 metres (about 1,150 feet).

[4] ix. 25. 3 (Grundy's translation).   [5] Op. cit. 468.

[6] ix. 31. 1 (ll. 1–2).

[7] τὸν ταύτῃ ῥέοντα (ix. 31. 1, l. 4); cf. Macan, ad loc., also Legrand, ix. 31, n. 4 (he curiously wishes to omit the τόν).

west. The implication of the whole paragraph is that the second
Greek position was near the Asopos, and this picture is confirmed
by the later notice[1] that the Spartans alone were posted near
the spring of Gargaphia, while the other Greek contingents
were far from the spring and near the Asopos; it is implied
that they were near enough to the Asopos to draw water from
it until they were prevented by the arrows of the Persian
cavalry.

Grundy's solution of this crux[2] is that the description of the
Greek second position as near Gargaphia and the Androkrateion refers only to the 'first phase' of the Greek move to
the second position, a temporary halt during which the Greek
commanders marshalled their troops before they proceeded to
lead them up the Asopos Ridge. He admits that the description
of the Greek army as encamped on the Asopos refers to this
supposed first phase, but explains it by the assumption[3] that
Herodotus (or his informant) here follows local Plataian usage,
which is supposed by Grundy to have given the name Asopos
not to the river which flows east from Thespiai but to the stream
(Grundy's A1) which starts from the spring of Apotripi and
flows north to join the Thespian Asopos. This supposition has
not found favour with later scholars.[4] Beloch pointed out[5] that
Apotripi (and therefore presumably the stream flowing from it)
ran dry in the long drought of August 1899, that Herodotus in
his sixth book regards the Asopos as the boundary between the
territories of Plataia and Thebes, where only the Thespian
Asopos can be meant, and that the same conclusion follows from
a passage in Thucydides' account of the Theban attack on
Plataia in 431.

Beloch,[6] accepting Grundy's identifications for Gargaphia and
the Androkrateion, believed that the Greeks occupied a position
between these two points. But whereas for Grundy the occupation of this position by the Greek army was 'probably of short
duration'[7] and was followed by a further advance to the crest
of the Asopos Ridge, Beloch maintains that the Greeks remained
in the depression until they were forced to retreat. He is thereby

---

[1] ix. 49. 3.

[2] Op. cit. 466 ff. and 473 f.

[3] Long note on pp. 470 f.

[4] Cf. HW 300 (on ix. 31. 1).

[5] ii². 2. 125; he quotes Grundy, 465 (note near foot of page), Hdt. vi. 108. 6,
and Thuc. ii. 5. 2.

[6] Op. cit. 124 ff.

[7] Grundy, 468.

forced to reject all the passages in Herodotus which indicate that a large part of the Greek army was posted near the Asopos before it began to retreat. Beloch argues[1] that the Greeks cannot at any stage have been stationed near to the Asopos because here in the plain Mardonios would have attacked them at once, and that Herodotus made a mistake when he brought the Asopos into the picture, a mistake into which he was led by the statement of his informants that the soothsayers on both sides had each prophesied misfortune to his own general if he led his army across the Asopos. This explanation does great violence to Herodotus' narrative, and Beloch's main argument is not valid against those who suppose that the Greek army in its advance had occupied the crest and northern slopes of the Asopos Ridge, a position which, although more exposed than its first on the foothills of Kithairon, still offered some protection against attacks by Persian cavalry.

Grundy's hypothesis,[2] that the two apparently discrepant pictures of the Greek second position in Herodotus represent two different phases of the same movement, could be accepted on the assumption that the first reference to the Asopos in this connection[3] is an anticipation, but the difficulty would remain that Herodotus never clearly described the subsequent advance of the Greek army from the depression to the ridge which rises above it to the north-east. This difficulty, which is perhaps not fatal to Grundy's view, may be the cause which has led most scholars to locate the shrine of Androkrates somewhere on the crest of the ridge, in defiance of the natural meaning of the passage in which Thucydides mentions the shrine,[4] and so to justify the conclusion that the Greek second position was throughout on the north slope of the Asopos Ridge and facing roughly north-east. This view also is open to criticism, apart from its very questionable location of the Androkrateion, for it does not explain how a position on the Asopos Ridge could have included level ground as well as low hills; it is possible for Grundy to represent the Greek army in his 'second phase' as

---

[1] Op. cit. 125.

[2] Which Wright, 57 seems inclined to accept.

[3] ix. 31. 1 (ll. 1–2).

[4] iii. 24. 1–2. So Macan, 640 B says frankly that this site 'cannot be sacrificed to an *obiter dictum* of Thucydides'. Others have preferred to 'interpret' the text of Thucydides in such a way as to obtain the desired result. See below, pp. 430 f.

occupying part of the Plataian plain,[1] but not for the holders of the view now under discussion, for the Androkrateion would then lose its value as an indication of position.[2]

It is a further objection to this view that it does not leave enough space for the Greek army. Beloch,[3] estimating the hoplites in the army at 20,000, can maintain that, with the normal depth of eight men to the phalanx and an allowance of one square metre to each man,[4] the army would have occupied a front of only 2,500 metres, but English scholars have generally accepted Herodotus' figure of 38,700 hoplites as not much in excess of the true total,[5] and even an army of 35,200 hoplites would have needed a front at least two miles long. The neat oblongs which represent the left, centre, and right of the Greek army on modern maps of the campaign are very misleading in this respect; on Grundy's map the Greeks in the second position do indeed occupy a front of two miles, but their front in the third position is apparently much shorter.[6] Grundy, having assumed that the Greek left stretched well into the plain, has then to reconcile this with Herodotus' statement[7] that the Athenians, who formed the left wing, began their part in the retreat by turning downwards into the plain, and can only suggest[8] that before the retreat the Greeks had been forced by the attacks of the enemy cavalry to retire from the plain and take refuge on the Asopos Ridge; this supposed retirement produces what Grundy calls the 'third phase' of the second position.

Munro finds an answer to these problems in his hypothesis[9] that the Greek army in its second position extended westwards from the Asopos Ridge across the Plataian plain to the hill of

---

[1] Op. cit. 474, where he adds 'though the amount of the extension in this direction must necessarily be a matter of uncertainty'.

[2] The church of St. John is so near Grundy's Gargaphia that if it is identical with the shrine of Androkrates the mention of both places can only have served to define the position of the Greek right (so Munro, 159); both would then have been derived from a Spartan source.

[3] ii². 2. 125.

[4] Beloch gives no reasons for this allowance. The normal figure is one square yard, derived from Polybius xviii. 29. 2; in xii. 19. 7 Polybius says that each man was separated in line of march from the man behind him by 6 feet of space.

[5] See below, pp. 436 ff.

[6] And also in the third phase; the map in HW is particularly open to this criticism.

[7] ix. 56. 2.   [8] Grundy, 478 and second note.

[9] Munro, 159 f.

Pyrgos, which was presumably held by the Athenians, forming the Greek left wing; this is also the view of Boucher, who supports it by a calculation of the space needed by an army of 38,700 hoplites.[1] According to the normal estimate, a phalanx of this size drawn up eight deep would occupy a front of over 4,800 yards, more than $2\frac{3}{4}$ miles, but Boucher holds that the Greeks in their second position, although encamped in battle order so as to be prepared for an immediate attack by the enemy, were not in strict battle formation, and he therefore allows a little more space between the files. On a calculation of 4 feet or $1\cdot2$ metres to each file he concludes that the Greek army would need a front of 5,800 metres.[2]

Grundy, emphasizing the fact that the Greek advance to the second position was a movement in a westerly direction as well as downhill, conjectured[3] that the object of the advance was offensive, to bring the Greek army across the Asopos at a point higher up the river than the Persian right wing, and then, before the enemy had time to recover from their surprise, to attack them on their exposed right flank. Although this conjecture was accepted by Woodhouse and Munro it has been generally rejected since.[4] Once the Greeks had crossed to the north bank of the Asopos they would have been exposed to attack by the Persian cavalry on ground especially suitable to its tactics, and Pausanias cannot have been so simple-minded as to suppose that because he had defeated it on the slopes of Kithairon he could expose his army to it without danger on an open plain. It is in this connexion significant that after he had led his army to its new position his seer Teisamenos announced that the omens were favourable to the Greeks if they remained on the defensive but not if they took the initiative by crossing the Asopos.[5] Grundy and Munro assume that Pausanias fell back on this excuse for inactivity because the plan which they attribute to him had misfired, but they differ in their explanations of its breakdown. Grundy thinks[6] that when the Greeks reached the top of the Asopos Ridge they found that the Persians had already moved upstream, whereas Munro blames

[1] Boucher, 286.
[2] Ufer (in *A.S.* iv), 125 and 145 allows about 5 kilometres.   [3] Op. cit. 473.
[4] e.g. by HW² 296 (on ix. 25. 2) and 408 f., also Ufer, 145 f.   [5] ix. 36.
[6] Op. cit. 473, cf. 474.

the miscarriage of the plan on the Athenians,[1] supposing that they were already on the left wing and therefore in the van when the movement began, and that either irresolution or downright cowardice on their part caused them to hang back at the critical moment and so prevented them from crossing the Asopos before the enemy arrived on the opposite bank. Both explanations are entirely hypothetical, and as Pausanias can never have intended to lead his army across the Asopos, both are superfluous.

Herodotus clearly implies in his narrative that the new position near the Asopos had been deliberately chosen by the Greek leaders, and this implication is now generally accepted. The reasons he gives for the advance[2] are the increased confidence felt by the Greeks after their victory over Masistios and the Persian cavalry and their desire to obtain a more suitable camping-ground, one which had a better supply of water. There is probably some truth in both reasons but obviously they are not the whole truth;[3] something more is needed to account for Pausanias' decision to advance from his strong position on the foothills of Kithairon. Wells, reacting against hypotheses which credited Pausanias with a bold and subtle strategy, doubted whether he really had any plan except somehow to get at the Persians and beat them,[4] but perhaps Wells would have agreed with the suggestion[5] that Pausanias' main object in moving his troops nearer the Asopos was to induce Mardonios to attack him with infantry as well as cavalry and so precipitate a decisive battle.

On this supposition, Herodotus' statement that the confidence of the Greeks had been strengthened by their repulse of the Persian cavalry is true to the extent that Pausanias had now learnt by experience that it could be successfully resisted on ground unsuited to its tactics. His action in taking the initiative may have been influenced by the time factor; as leader of a composite army made up of citizen militias which could not be kept in the field indefinitely he would naturally desire a speedy decision for the campaign.[6] Herodotus, so precise in his

[1] Munro, 160.   [2] ix. 25. 1–2.
[3] Grundy, 472.   [4] *Studies in Herodotus*, 162.
[5] Cf. Beloch, ii². 1. 55, Macan i. 2. 672 A (also ii. 379), HW² 392 and 409, Ufer, 154 f.
[6] Cf. HW² 408.

chronology of the subsequent events, has here omitted to mention how many days elapsed between the death of Masistios and the Greek advance from Kithairon towards the Asopos,[1] but the interval must have been at least long enough to make it clear to Pausanias that Mardonios had no intention of attacking the Greeks for a second time on the slopes of Kithairon, and that if the Greeks wished to bring about a general engagement without undue delay they had no option but to move forward to a more exposed position where Mardonios might be tempted to attack them with his whole force.

How exposed was the second position? If Pausanias never intended to lead his army across the Asopos, the position which it occupied near the Asopos must have been the position he had chosen. Unfortunately, the extent of this position cannot be conclusively defined from the topographical indications supplied by Herodotus,[2] but the view maintained by Kirsten and others,[3] that it was entirely confined to the hilly ground situated to the east of Stream A1, cannot be reconciled with Herodotus' plain statement that part of the Greek army was stationed on level ground.[4] Grundy, who refers this statement to the 'first phase' of the Greek advance,[5] believes that both in this and in the second phase the Greek left extended into the Plataian plain near the Asopos, but its presence there is for Grundy due to accident, not design, and is the result of its failure to cross the river; if the position had been chosen beforehand by Pausanias he would never have stationed his left wing on an open plain without any protection from enemy cavalry on its exposed west flank.

For this reason Munro and Boucher must be right in making the Greek line stretch westwards from the Asopos Ridge across the Plataian plain to the hill of Pyrgos beyond it, and in assuming that this hill was occupied by the Athenians on the

---

[1] Cf. HW[2] 391, n. 1; the assumption of Munro and Woodhouse that the 8 to 10 days said by Hdt. to have been spent by the Greeks in the second position really refer to the interval before their advance to that position is both arbitrary and unnecessary.

[2] ix. 25. 3; see above, pp. 303 ff., and below, pp. 427 ff.

[3] Cf. the map in HW; Kirsten, 2293 says that if necessary the Greek line should be extended eastwards to the Kriekouki–Thebes road rather than westwards to the hill of Pyrgos, but he seems to misunderstand the word ἀπέδου in ix. 25. 3.

[4] ix. 25. 3; see above, p. 301, n. 4.

[5] Op. cit. 468; cf. 474. See above, p. 304.

Greek left. This defensive position was certainly more exposed than one confined to the Asopos Ridge would have been, but it was for that reason more likely to tempt Mardonios to attack, and Pausanias may have calculated that if he posted his two wings on higher ground they would be able to repel any charge by the Persian cavalry, while the centre in the plain between them would at least be protected by its own wings against a charge on either flank.[1] Pausanias, anxious to bring the enemy to battle as soon as possible, hoped to achieve his aim by occupying a position more open to attack than the foothills of Kithairon and yet sufficiently raised above the plain to give his hoplites some advantage in defence against enemy cavalry;[2] whether this advantage was enjoyed by the whole army in the second position or by the wings alone, the idea behind his advance remains the same.

After relating the Greek movement to the second position Herodotus describes, six chapters later,[3] how Mardonios and his army, when they heard that the Greeks were at Plataia, moved along the Asopos to that part of its course, by which he presumably means the part due north of Plataia; hence the Persian army must have moved upstream along the left (north) bank of the Asopos to a new position some distance from its original position. The statement that the Persians heard of the movement of the Greek army after it had been carried out has troubled some scholars. Grundy believes that the Greeks moved first to the depression south of the ridges which rise from the south bank of the Asopos to the east of the Plataian plain, a depression where they would be able to deploy their army out of sight of the Persians,[4] but his reconstruction compels him to suppose that the Persians discovered where the Greek army had gone before it continued its advance to the top of the Asopos Ridge. Boucher, impressed by the risks of a flank march in such close proximity to the enemy, infers from the strange ignorance of the Persians that the Greek movement to the second position, like the later attempt to retreat from the second position, must have been made by night.[5] But if the army had moved by night

---

[1] Cf. Boucher, 291 (also 280).   [2] So HW[2] 403 f. and 409.
[3] ix. 31. 1; see above, p. 303, n. 7.   [4] Grundy, 468 and 470.
[5] Boucher, 288 (cf. 278); his suggestion has been followed by Ufer, 144 and Kirsten, 2292.

on the first occasion as well as on the second, Herodotus might have been expected to say so. Perhaps Mardonios, who desired nothing more than that the Greek army should cross the river, waited until his scouts informed him that it had halted north of Plataia, and then decided to move his own army upstream to face the new Greek position.

The Greek army in its second position south of the Asopos now faced the Persian army in its new position north of the river. But the Persians, having moved upstream, made no attempt to cross the Asopos, and a Greek seer in Mardonios' pay[1] announced that the omens were unfavourable to a Persian offensive, though favourable if Mardonios remained on the defensive. Herodotus' assertion that this announcement was unwelcome to Mardonios may be doubted;[2] certainly he made no attempt for the present to override the omens, but kept his army north of the river. The hope which had induced Pausanias to bring his army nearer to the Asopos seemed to have been disappointed, and as he was quite as unwilling as Mardonios to take the offensive by crossing the river, the recent movements of the two armies resulted in a stalemate.

The Greeks in their second position

The second section of Herodotus' account of this campaign[3] begins with the advance of the Greek army to the vicinity of Plataia. Before passing on to the corresponding movement of the Persian army to a new position facing the Greek second position, Herodotus has two long digressions, the first concerning the rival claims of the Athenians and Tegeans to a place of honour on the Greek left,[4] the second describing the order of battle in the Greek army and the size of the various contingents,[5] both hoplites and light-armed (including the Spartan helots). Herodotus then turns to the Persians, and after mentioning their march upstream from their first position, he specifies the places in line of the contingents which made up the Persian army, with minor digressions about the activities of Phokian patriots against Mardonios' line of communications and the presence of Egyptian marines from the fleet in his ranks. Having got the two armies into their new positions, Herodotus

---

[1] ix. 37. 1 and 38. 1.   [2] See below, p. 321.   [3] ix. 25–38.
[4] Cf. Macan's note on τὸ ἕτερον κέρας (ix. 26. 1).   [5] See below, pp. 312 f.

refers to the sacrifices offered by both on the following day, dated as the second[1] in the precise diary which he gives for the rest of the campaign; the mention of the sacrifices introduces two more digressions in which the previous and subsequent histories of the leading seers (both Eleians) on the two sides, Teisamenos on the Greek and Hegesistratos on the Persian, are told at great length. Each of these seers, after offering sacrifice, reports to his leader that the omens are favourable if the army remains on the defensive, but not if it crosses the Asopos to attack the foe. Neither side ventured to break the deadlock, and the two armies remained inactive, each facing the other across the river, for eight days.[2] This delay is represented as unwelcome to Mardonios, who was eager to fight a battle;[3] the reaction to it of the Greek leaders is not recorded.

Herodotus' history, as he himself once admitted,[4] always welcomes an opportunity for a digression, but the number and length of the digressions in this section, occupying nearly eleven chapters out of fourteen, seem designed to indicate a pause in the action, in which it is appropriate to catalogue the composition and battle order of the two armies before the deadlock is broken and events begin to move rapidly to the final decision. Moreover, the life stories of the two seers are sufficiently interesting in themselves to justify their insertion at this point, where the interpretation of the omens by the seers is regarded as the cause which held up the march of events during these eight days.

The remaining digression has been roughly handled by many critics. In itself a dispute between two contingents for a post of honour is not more unlikely in a Greek army of this period than in a Scottish Highlands army of the seventeenth or eighteenth century A.D.,[5] but the critics object that if such a dispute really happened it should have arisen when the Greek army took up its first position north of Mount Kithairon. Some even reject the story altogether,[6] but their arguments are weak. Although the Tegean contingent is found on one later occasion[7] occupying

---

[1] τῇ δευτέρῃ ἡμέρῃ (ix. 33. 1).

[2] ix. 39. 1, clearly referring back to the date in 33. 1.　　　　[3] ix. 37. 1.

[4] iv. 30. 1.　　　　[5] Cf. the quotation from Macaulay cited above, p. 50.

[6] Woodhouse in *J.H.S.* xviii, 1898, 41 f., followed by Wright, 85.

[7] Xenophon, *Hell.* iv. 2. 19. At First Mantineia (Thuc. v. 67. 1) in the original formation the Spartans were in the centre and the Tegeans on the right (with 'a few Spartans' on the extreme right).

the same position in a Peloponnesian army, next to the Spartans
on the right, as it did during the last stages of the Plataia campaign, this is not sufficient to disprove the assertion made by the
Tegean speaker in the debate[1] that down to 479 the Tegeans
had always been posted on one of the wings in the armies sent
out by the Peloponnesian League. Again, it is an assumption
rather than a fact that the Athenians were already stationed on
the left wing when Masistios and his cavalry attacked the first
Greek position.[2] On the other hand, Herodotus' implication
that the Greek order of battle was not settled until after the
army reached its second position is hard to accept; Grundy,
supposing two phases in the Greek advance, assumes that the
army was deployed for battle at the end of the first phase,[3] when
on his view it was still in the depression and had not yet climbed
to the summit of the Asopos Ridge. If the dispute is historical, as
it may well be, it must have been speedily decided in favour of
the Athenians, for they had proved their worth at Marathon
and their contingent was the second largest in the Greek army.
The two speeches in Herodotus are probably in the main free
compositions;[4] he would welcome the opportunity to dilate on
the ancient and recent glories of the Athenians and the dis-
interested patriotism with which they were prepared to waive
their claim and accept whatever position might be assigned to
them by the Spartan commander-in-chief.[5]

A more fundamental objection to this section of the Herodotean narrative is that raised by Woodhouse,[6] that its basic
presupposition, a period of complete inactivity on both sides
for eight days, is incredible at this stage in the campaign. In
order to do full justice to this objection, it is necessary to examine
first the main points in the next section of Herodotus,[7] in which
the Persians begin to display a greater activity, culminating in a
series of cavalry attacks which finally compel the Greek leaders
to abandon their second position. The situation with which this

---

[1] ix. 26. 2.   [2] See above, p. 300.

[3] Op. cit. 468. Note that in ix. 25. 2 the Greeks intended to encamp διαταχθέντας
(tr. by Legrand 'en ordre de bataille') ; cf. Macan, ad loc. and Boucher, 285. On
the depression see above, p. 302.

[4] Cf. also Grundy, 468 f.

[5] Plutarch, in his version of the Athenian speech (*Aristeides* 12. 2–3), makes
Aristeides, whom he assumes to have been the speaker, concentrate on this topic
to the exclusion of the rest.

[6] Op. cit. 43 ff. and 56 ff.   [7] ix. 38. 2–51.

section opens is that neither Mardonios' own seer Hegesistratos
nor the seer employed by the medizing Greeks, Hippomachos
of Leukas, could obtain omens favourable for a pitched battle,[1]
and that as a result a delay ensued which was more favourable to
the Greeks than to the Persians, as the Greek army was steadily
growing by the arrival of reinforcements. When the period of
inaction had reached its eighth day (counting as the first the
day on which the Greeks had arrived in their second position)
a Theban leader Timagenidas advised Mardonios to block the
pass of Kithairon, saying that more Greeks were coming in
every day and that by this move he would intercept many.
Mardonios acted on his advice, and at dusk sent the cavalry to
'the pass of Kithairon leading to Plataia',[2] by which the pass of
Gyphtokastro is presumably meant. The cavalry obtained a partial success, for although they failed to capture any soldiers they
intercepted a baggage train of 500 animals and also the men in
charge of the animals, bringing provisions for the Greeks from
Peloponnese, and after an indiscriminate slaughter of men and
animals they drove the rest back to the Persian camp and to
Mardonios.[3]

There followed two more days of inactivity, the ninth and
tenth of the Journal,[4] in which neither side was prepared to
bring on a pitched battle. But although the Persian infantry advanced only to the north bank of the Asopos, the cavalry of the
Medes and Persians, instigated by the Thebans, 'made attacks
continually and did damage to the Hellenes'.[5] This statement is
extremely vague. At the end of the previous sentence Herodotus
had said that neither side crossed the Asopos. Does he now imply
that this statement did not apply to the Persian cavalry, or did
they merely ride to the very edge of the Asopos and discharge
their arrows at any Greeks who ventured near the river? It is
indicated later[6] that they had in this way driven off Greeks who

[1] ix. 38. 2.

[2] ix. 39. 1. Here and in 38. 2 Hdt. uses the word ἐκβολαί of a single pass; Macan,
i. 2. 676 A compares the use of τὰς ἐκβολάς for the Middle Gate of Thermopylai in
vii. 176. 3 (last sentence). On the passes near Plataia see below, pp. 423 f.

[3] Clearly they did not remain in permanent occupation of the pass (as supposed
by Boucher, 292); the reference to their raid in the last sentence of ix. 50 is sufficiently explained by HW, ad loc. (p. 309).

[4] Hence the day which follows is ἑνδεκάτη (ix. 41. 1).

[5] ix. 40; the translation is Macaulay's (Powell gives 'continually pressed upon
the Greeks and vexed them').   [6] ix. 49. 3.

had been drawing water from the river. Macan believes that they were sent round the rear of the Greek army, but his suggestion[1] that the object of this manœuvre was to drive the Greeks northwards across the Asopos is far-fetched.

The eleventh day begins with a discussion between Mardonios and Artabazos, apparently in a Persian war council.[2] It is introduced by two statements, that the Greek army had been largely reinforced, and that Mardonios was chafing at the delay.[3] Artabazos is said to have urged that the army should retreat with all speed to Thebes, where abundant supplies had been accumulated of food for the men and fodder for the animals, and remain on the defensive while they used their wealth to corrupt the leading men in the Greek states. This plan is a re-hash of advice given to Mardonios earlier in the campaign by the Thebans,[4] and it is not clear from Herodotus whether Artabazos proposed that the army should take refuge inside the walls of Thebes, thereby reducing the cavalry to inactivity, or should merely take up its position outside and close to Thebes.[5] If Mardonios' plan had been to lure the Greek army to the plain north of the Asopos, it is arguable that he had made a mistake when he drew up his army so close to the north bank of the river; perhaps Artabazos suggested that the abandonment of the fort and all that it contained would be a small price to pay if a pretended retreat of the Persian army towards Thebes induced the Greek leaders to bring their army across the Asopos at last.[6]

Herodotus, after praising the foresight of Artabazos, describes the attitude of Mardonios, who is said to have favoured an immediate offensive, as 'stark, obstinate, uncompromising'.[7] Mardonios argues that his own army is much superior[8] to the Greek and that the Persians ought to attack at once before the Greeks receive further reinforcements; as for the omens, it is better to ignore them and not try to extort a favourable answer from them.[9]

[1] Macan, i. 2. 678 A (note on ix. 40, l. 2).
[2] ix. 41–43; cf. Macan, 680 A (on ix. 41, l. 4). [3] ix. 41. 1.
[4] ix. 2. [5] So HW 306 (on ix. 41. 2).
[6] Cf. Macan's discussion (i. 2. 680 f.), especially vii (b) on p. 681.
[7] ix. 41. 4 (paraphrase is by Macan, ad loc.).
[8] Presumably in numbers; cf. Macan's note.
[9] βιάζεσθαι (near the end of c. 41) is clearly the middle voice of the verb; Legrand translates 'plutôt que de vouloir les obtenir de force'.

The rest of his speech is mostly taken up with a discussion of a Delphic oracle and its relevance to the issue of the war; it is manifestly a product of Delphic propaganda, curiously inserted here, and may safely be ignored.[1] Finally, Mardonios orders all preparations to be made in readiness for a general attack on the following day.

In the night after the council[2] the Macedonian king Alexander is said to have crossed the Asopos on horseback to the Athenian outposts and obtained an audience with the Athenian generals, in which he informed them of Mardonios' decision to attack next day or soon after, and urged the Greeks to stay where they were, on the ground that the Persians could not delay their attack for long as they were running short of supplies and had only a few days' food left.[3] The Athenians after Alexander's departure report his message to Pausanias, whose reaction to it is to propose that the Spartans should move to the left wing to face the medizing Greeks while the Athenians take their place on the right wing against the Persians, of whose method of fighting they have already had experience at Marathon. This interchange of wings is carried out at dawn on the twelfth day[4] and is reported at once by the Boiotians to Mardonios, who promptly moves his Persians to the right wing to face the Spartans, whereupon Pausanias moves back again to the Greek right wing. Mardonios then leads his Persians back to the left wing of his army, where they are again opposite the Spartans, and proceeds to send a herald to the Spartans, taunting them with cowardice and challenging them to decide the issue of the war by a combat between an equal number of Spartan and Persian troops; to this challenge the Spartans make no reply.[5]

Neither of these two narratives can be accepted as sober history. Herodotus makes a dramatic story out of Alexander's nocturnal warning, but the details do not bear close examination.[6] It appears to be one of the tales put about after the war to exculpate Alexander for the support he had given to the Persian cause;[7] it is not even safe to infer from it that there had been some secret negotiations between him and the Athenians during

---

[1] See below, pp. 446 f.   [2] ix. 44. 1.
[3] ix. 45. 2 (last sentence).   [4] ix. 47.   [5] ix. 49. 1.
[6] The objections are well put by Legrand, ix. 42, n. 2; cf. HW on ix. 44. 1.
[7] Cf. v. 17 ff. (with HW, ad loc.) and vii. 173. 3.

the campaign.[1] The second narrative, in the form given to it by Herodotus,[2] is even more unworthy of credit. How could the two armies have had time to interchange their right and left wings twice in the morning of the twelfth day (to say nothing of the danger of such manœuvres within sight of the enemy's army) and leave room for all the events which are supposed to have followed during the same day? Even Hauvette insists on the flagrant improbability of the story, which provides one of the worst examples in Herodotus of his lack of understanding of military principles.[3] The anti-Spartan bias of the story is evident in the opening words, where Pausanias' motive for the interchange of wings is declared to be fear of the Persians, and in the wording of the challenge of Mardonios which forms its conclusion.[4]

It is possible that the alleged interchange of wings is based on some real or proposed movement of troops, but even if it is, the original form of it has been disfigured beyond hope of recognition. Those who attempt to extract something from it are forced to transfer the movement to an earlier stage in the campaign; some also jettison the corresponding change in the Persian wings. Meyer believes that some time after the Greeks occupied their second position the Spartans took over the left wing because it was the one most exposed to attack,[5] but he fails to explain why they should have moved back to the right wing when Mardonios moved his Persians upstream to face them. Munro's reconstruction connects the interchange of wings with the Greek advance from the first to the second position,[6] but the complicated manœuvre which he presupposes could have been more easily executed by a modern Prussian army than by that under Pausanias' command, and would have wasted valuable time when according to Munro's own view haste was essential, in order to get the Greek troops across the Asopos before the Persians realized what was happening.

---

[1] Macan, 690 A, followed by HW 307 f.   [2] ix. 46–48.

[3] Boucher, 294 says: 'Ce sont là des dispositions que seuls peuvent admettre et enregistrer ceux qui sont étrangers aux choses de la guerre.' Cf. Hauvette, 469.

[4] ix. 48. 3; cf. the last sentence of 46. 1.

[5] Meyer, 410 and n. 1 (the reference is wrongly given by HW, n. on 46. 1); he says that the movement cannot have taken place as late as the day before the battle.

[6] Munro, 159 f.

A more plausible suggestion[1] is that the story may have grown
out of the sending of some Athenian archers to help the Spartans
on the right wing against the attacks of the Persian cavalry;
but where the evidence is so unsatisfactory all speculation is unprofitable.

The eight chapters[2] dealing with the Persian war council and
the sequel down to Mardonios' challenge are thus characterized
by bias against Mardonios and the Spartans and by bias in
favour of Artabazos, Alexander, and the Athenians. Legrand[3]
has justly said of them that they only make it more difficult to
understand the course of events, and that they are 'so many
additions made successively to a tradition which was more
sober and more respectful of the reality'. There is, however, one
idea prominent in them which may be accepted because it
occurs elsewhere,[4] that Mardonios was anxious, more anxious
apparently than Pausanias, to decide the campaign by a pitched
battle as soon as possible. Here and elsewhere his anxiety is
motivated by the growing strength of the Greek army, but in
this section Herodotus introduces a fresh and more compelling
motive, that supplies were running dangerously short in the
Persian army.[5]

This motive is accepted by Beloch, who agrees with Herodotus that Mardonios was eager for a speedy decision. He
argues[6] that the supplies which Boiotia could offer him for the
provisioning of his large army must soon be exhausted, and that
he would then have no option but to fight or retreat. Grundy
is impressed by the enormous difficulties imposed on the Persians by their long line of communications, and thinks that their
supplies must have been seriously affected by the raids of the
Phokian patriots from Mount Parnassos.[7] It must be remembered, however, that the alleged shortage of Persian supplies is
mentioned in a suspicious context, the speech of Alexander to
the Athenians; it is, moreover, at variance with the assertion
attributed to Artabazos four chapters earlier,[8] that there was
abundant food for men and animals at Thebes; faced with the

---

[1] That of Wecklein, favoured by Wright, 90.   [2] ix. 41–48.
[3] Vol. viii, p. 132.
[4] ix. 41. 1; cf. 37. 1. The augmentation of the Greek army by the arrival of
reinforcements is given as a motive in 38. 2 and 41. 4.
[5] ix. 45. 2 (last sentence).   [6] ii[2]. 1. 56.
[7] ix. 31. 5; cf. Grundy, 476 f.   [8] ix. 41. 2.

glaring discrepancy between these two statements most scholars[1]
have preferred to accept that of Artabazos, and if they are right,
Mardonios' growing anxiety to end the stalemate by battle cannot be due to shortage of supplies. Boucher tries to reconcile
them by the assumption[2] that Thebes was an advanced depot
with supply for only a limited number of days, depending for
replenishment on the maintenance of a regular reprovisioning
from a remoter base, and that this reprovisioning was now
imperilled by the threat of a vigorous Greek offensive by sea.
This hypothesis does not really resolve the contradiction in
Herodotus, but at least it has the merit of bringing Mardonios'
strategy in Boiotia into connexion with the movements of the
Greek fleet in the Aegean.

It is the fundamental weakness in Herodotus' account of the
campaign of 479 that he deals with the operations of the two
armies in complete isolation from the Greek naval offensive;
the two sets of activities might seem to be happening not in
different continents but in different worlds.[3] In Herodotus, with
his imperfect grasp of strategic principles, such weakness is
pardonable, but Beloch was deliberately reacting against the
prevailing opinion when he denied that the advance of the Greek
fleet had any effect on the development of the campaign on
land. It is curious that Grundy and Hauvette should hold a
similar view. Hauvette asks[4] how Mardonios, who had hitherto
remained on the defensive, should have been induced to fight
by an empty rumour of an offensive undertaken in Ionia by
110 Greek ships against a fleet still nearly three times stronger.
This argument is worthless; whether the Persian fleet had or
had not numbered 300 ships in the spring of 479, it had certainly disintegrated before the Greek fleet of 110 ships crossed
from Delos to Samos.[5]

There is not enough evidence in Herodotus to establish a
precise interrelation between the campaign on land in 479 and
the various stages in the advance of the Greek fleet across the
Aegean, but if Mardonios had received any recent dispatches
from Asia he must have known that the Persian fleet had ceased

---

[1] e.g. Hauvette, 467, HW 306 (on ix. 41. 2).   [2] Boucher, 295.
[3] See above, p. 249.   [4] Op. cit. 468.
[5] See above, p. 246. It is unlikely that the Persian fleet after its losses at Salamis
ever reached the total of 300 given by Hdt. viii. 130. 2.

to exist as a fighting force, and that no effective resistance could
be offered to the Greek fleet if it ventured across to the coast of
Ionia. It was obvious that only a decisive Persian victory in
Greece could avert the risk of a general revolt of the Asiatic
Greeks and the consequent severance of the Persian communications by land with Europe, and that Mardonios had not much
time to spare if he was to achieve a decision before the impending catastrophe in Ionia.

Although many scholars have realized the close connexion
between the Greek naval offensive and the campaign on land,[1]
its full implications have not always been understood. To secure
the kind of victory which alone could turn the scale in favour of
Persia, Mardonios had to try to bring about a battle on ground
favourable to his strongest arm, his cavalry. Hence his first object was to induce the Greeks to cross Kithairon into Boiotia,
his second to tempt them to cross the Asopos to the plain beyond
its north bank. When Pausanias advanced from Kithairon to
the south bank of the Asopos and no farther, Mardonios was
baffled. Perhaps he did not expect a Greek army, composed of
a number of citizen militias, to show such self-restraint. Fortunately most of them had long been accustomed to serving
under the orders of Spartan leaders in the armies of the Peloponnesian League, and the Spartan high command had mastered
the art of exploiting unfavourable omens to keep in check the
impatience of their troops.[2]

The result was a deadlock, and, whatever Herodotus' critics
may say, there is nothing incredible in his statement that the
two armies remained inactive in their new positions for eight
days;[3] Meyer even supposes that the period between the Greek
advance to the Asopos and the final battle may have been considerably longer than the twelve days allowed for it in Herodotus' journal of the campaign. Nor is it necessary to account
for the delay by the theory that Mardonios, like the Persian
generals at Marathon, was waiting for the maturing of a conspiracy set on foot by a fifth column in the Athenian contingent;
the only evidence for this conspiracy is a chapter in Plutarch's

[1] The connexion was first established by Nitzsch; see his article cited in the
bibliography, especially pp. 258 ff. The version of this view given by HW 390 is not
wholly satisfactory.

[2] For the use of superstition to check restlessness cf. Wright, 60.

[3] ix. 39. 1; cf. Meyer, 410 (ll. 7–8) also 413 (near end of long note).

Life of Aristeides[1] describing a plot started by some Athenian aristocrats in the camp before Plataia, but in spite of some circumstantial detail the story seems to be an invention, due probably to the untrustworthy Idomeneus, to the greater glory of Aristeides, who detects the plot and deals tactfully with the plotters.[2] A stalemate was inevitable in the circumstances. Here were two armies, differing profoundly in composition, armament, and tactics, each posted on ground favourable to itself and separated by a river. The Asopos is not in itself a formidable obstacle, especially in August, but its bed is sufficiently deep to be difficult for an army to cross in face of resolute resistance from an enemy on the opposite bank.[3] Anyhow, Mardonios, like Pausanias, was reluctant to leave the position he had chosen and fight on ground which would nullify his tactical advantages.

These considerations explain why Hegesistratos, the seer in Mardonios' employment,[4] announced that the omens were favourable to the Persians provided they remained on the defensive. Mardonios was probably anxious for a speedy decision, but he wanted to fight a battle under conditions which would guarantee the complete defeat of the enemy. As Hauvette says,[5] he realized that his first offensive, the cavalry attack led by Masistios, had been premature, and he must have been willing to wait, at least for a time, to see if the Greeks would provide him with an opportunity for revenge. There is therefore no sufficient justification for the contention of Woodhouse[6] and others, that the eight days of inaction have been misdated by Herodotus, and that the eighth day of his Journal is really that on which the Greeks advanced from Kithairon to the Asopos. Woodhouse also supposed that the eleventh and twelfth days of the Journal are duplicates of the ninth and tenth days, and that the battle was fought on the eleventh (not the thirteenth) day

---

[1] c. 13; cf. Macan, ii. 88, item (2), and Busolt, 729, n. 4.

[2] So Hauvette, 148 and 465 (ad fin.), Wright, 107, and HW 306 (on ix. 41. 3). Busolt, who believes in the conspiracy, suggests that Idomeneus got his information from an Atthis, but it looks more like one of his own fictions.

[3] Cf. Grundy, 475.

[4] ix. 38. 1 (cf. 37. 1). Naturally his advice reflected Mardonios' own views. Hauvette, 465 suggests improbably that it had been influenced by Artabazos and the Thebans.

[5] Op. cit. 465.

[6] J.H.S. xviii, 1898, 56–58, also 43 ff.

of the revised Journal, ten days after the day on which the Greeks had crossed Kithairon.

Woodhouse and his followers cannot understand why Mardonios, if he was anxious to end the campaign quickly, should have waited for seven days before sending his cavalry to the pass of Gyphtokastro. The difficulty is unreal. What Mardonios needed was an overwhelming victory, which he could only win on ground of his own choosing, and when Pausanias came down from Kithairon Mardonios probably hoped that if he himself remained passive the Greeks might imprudently cross the river. Whether the plan which he finally adopted to break the deadlock was his own or suggested by a Theban,[1] it was only a second-best. He could not predict how the Greek leaders would react to a raid on their communications followed by a more vigorous and sustained offensive of the Persian cavalry. He can hardly have expected this offensive to drive the Greeks northwards across the Asopos;[2] it was more likely to decide them to withdraw from their exposed position to a new one on the foothills of Kithairon covering the two key passes. To reach it they had to march only three or four miles from their present position. They cannot have doubted their ability to carry out so short a retreat in safety, for if they marched by night Mardonios could not stop them. If they made good their withdrawal to a position on the foothills of Kithairon from which they could cover their communications with the Peloponnese, they could defy the Persian cavalry[3] and Mardonios would be farther off than before from the pitched battle which alone could restore the falling cause of the Persians in Greece. It is not surprising that he preferred to wait as long as he could, but because the Greek naval offensive made it impossible for him to wait indefinitely he had in the end to try Timagenidas' plan[4] in default of a better.

The Greek retreat

The Persian cavalry raid into the Gyphtokastro Pass on the night of the eighth day had serious consequences for the Greeks.

---

[1] Hdt. ix. 38. 2 attributes it to the Theban Timagenidas, but his bias against Thebes in this part of his narrative is conspicuous (cf. c. 40, etc.).

[2] As suggested by Macan (see above, p. 315, n. 1).

[3] On the advantages of this position (which the Greeks never reached) cf. Hauvette, 471 f.   [4] See above, p. 314.

Although the enemy after their success in capturing a Greek supply train had returned to the Persian camp and had apparently not repeated their attack on subsequent nights, the Greek attendants who had been sent to bring food from Peloponnese were afraid to venture down from Kithairon to the camp, and by the twelfth day the Greek army was coming to the end of the supplies which it had on the spot.[1] It was on this day that Mardonios, still attempting to end the deadlock, ordered his cavalry to make a general assault on the Greek lines. It had been harassing the Greeks with frequent charges since the ninth day, but now seems to have attacked the whole Greek army simultaneously,[2] and it achieved a solid success by getting at and choking the important spring of Gargaphia, on which part at least of the Greek army depended for water.

In this connexion Herodotus observes[3] that the Persian cavalry used long-distance weapons, javelins and arrows, being really mounted archers, and so it was difficult to get to close quarters with them. As Boucher has explained, they did not charge in the modern sense; they might ride forward at the gallop, but always halted a little way from the enemy to discharge their missile weapons from a safe distance. But though they had used these tactics with success earlier to prevent the Greek troops from coming down to the Asopos for water,[4] they ought not to have made much impression on Greek hoplites drawn up in a close phalanx, especially as the Greek wings at least were posted on ground which gave some protection against cavalry charges, and the Greek centre, even if stationed wholly or in part on the plain, should have been protected on its flanks by the wings.[5] Grundy's assumption that the Greek contingents posted on the plain were forced by the cavalry attacks on the twelfth day to retire from the plain to the Asopos Ridge (his 'Phase 3' of the Greek second position)[6] rests on what is probably

---

[1] ix. 50; cf. HW, ad loc., and see above, p. 314.

[2] ix. 49 (note especially πᾶσαν τὴν στρατιήν in § 2). For earlier attacks cf. ix. 40, and see above, p. 314.

[3] ix. 49, 2; cf. Boucher, 272 (he points out that the right technique for dealing with their assaults was the close phalanx formation said to have been adopted by the Phokians in ix. 18. 1).

[4] ix. 49. 3, where τοξευμάτων are presumably the arrows shot by the cavalry; Macaulay's translation seems to make them those of the infantry. The note of Legrand (ix. 45, n. 2) is peculiar.   [5] See above, p. 310.

[6] Grundy, 478 f.; he apparently refers to the same day as the loss of Gargaphia

a mistaken view of the positions previously held by the Greek left and centre. Anyhow, it is incredible that Gargaphia should have been well inside the Spartan lines and captured by a frontal assault of the Persian cavalry.[1] Probably it is to be identified with a spring in the depression lying south of the Asopos Ridge,[2] behind the Greek lines. If this is correct, the Persian cavalry must have made their way to it by riding up one of the tributaries of the Asopos and so reaching the rear of the Greek position;[3] the fact that they took the Greeks by surprise indicates that they were ranging more widely than on previous days.

Herodotus says that the Spartans alone were stationed near Gargaphia,[4] which must therefore have been behind the Greek right wing; he adds that since the Persian cavalry had prevented the Greeks from using the Asopos the whole Greek army had been depending for its supply of water on Gargaphia alone. This statement is improbable in itself, and the source here used by Herodotus apparently exaggerated the importance of Gargaphia;[5] certainly in the next chapter, after mentioning the shortage of water and the attacks of the cavalry as the causes which led to a Greek council of war, he admits that the lack of food was far more serious than either.[6] The war council, which clearly belongs to the same day as the loss of Gargaphia (Day 12),[7] decided that if the Persians did not make an attack before the end of the day, the Greek army should retreat in the second watch of the ensuing night to a position nearer Plataia. In this passage the word for 'attack' is equivalent to 'a general engagement',[8] and there is no need to suppose that because the cavalry attacks continued throughout the day the withdrawal had to be deferred for another day.[9] Pausanias had obviously decided that

the activity of the Persian cavalry described in the last sentence of ix. 49, but it must belong to an earlier day than Day 12.

[1] As supposed by Ufer, 132.

[2] See above, p. 304, also below, pp. 427 f.

[3] This is the usual view, e.g. Grundy, 478 f., Boucher, 294.   [4] ix. 49. 3.

[5] Cf. Ufer, 133. Some (e.g. Wright, 63; cf. HW on 49. 3) believe that the exaggeration was due to an Athenian source, wishing to blame the Spartans for the loss of a spring on which the whole army depended.

[6] ix. 50 (ll. 5 ff.)

[7] Grundy, 479 strangely assigns it to the day after (Day 13).

[8] συμβολήν (translated by Macaulay 'the battle'); cf. Macan 699 on ix. 51, l. 1.

[9] So apparently Grundy (480 n.), though on p. 489 he assigns the retreat to the night following the day on which the council was held.

if Mardonios did not follow up his cavalry attacks by crossing the Asopos with his infantry before nightfall the Greek army must be withdrawn without delay from its present exposed positions.

The new position chosen by the Greeks is described by Herodotus as a strip of land about three stades wide,[1] known locally at that time as the Nesos (Island) because it was enclosed by two branches of the river Oëroë; there are now four streams which flow down from Kithairon to unite in the Plataian plain, from which the river turns westwards (south of Pyrgos Hill which separates it from the valley of the Asopos) towards the Corinthian Gulf. Leake and Vischer supposed that the Nesos lay wholly in the plain,[2] but Grundy argued that this was impossible, for reasons which have been accepted as decisive by most scholars since,[3] and identified the Nesos with the ridge between the upper courses of two branches of the Oëroë (numbered by him O2 and O3); this ridge is Ridge 4 on his map, but he suggested that the Nesos position may have included the next ridge to the east (Ridge 3) as well, and so was in fact the whole of the hilly tract bounded by O3 and O1.[4]

Grundy's site for the Nesos is the only one that fits the two reasons given by Herodotus[5] for the choice of this position by the Greek leaders, that it possessed an abundant supply of water and would give the army immunity from the frontal attacks of the enemy cavalry,[6] but a serious difficulty remains. Even the more extensive of the two areas suggested by Grundy for the new position is not large enough to hold all the Greek army.[7] Herodotus, however, clearly implies that the whole army was to

[1] ix. 51. 2. The measurement between the two streams of the Ὠερόη seems, in spite of Macan (ad loc.), to describe the breadth rather than the length of the Nesos, and probably maximum rather than average breadth.

[2] This view has been revived by Kirsten; see below, pp. 428 f.

[3] e.g. Munro, 160, HW 309, and recently Pritchett, 26 A.

[4] Op. cit. 484; on p. 486 he points out that the valley of O1 was deeper (which would make it a better protection against cavalry) than that of O2.

[5] ix. 51. 3. The phrase ὥσπερ κατιθὺ ἐόντων is obscure (see Macan, ad loc.) and the genitive is peculiar; perhaps it includes both the Greeks and the Persians ('as when they were directly facing each other'). Powell obelizes κατιθὺ and translates 'as when they were by the Asopos'. Cf. also Grundy, 482.

[6] Herodotus has here again lost sight of the army's need to re-establish its communications with the Peloponnese (so Hauvette, 471, following Stein, says that his account is not as clear as it might be) but he adds in 51. 4 that this was to be its first task on reaching the new position.   [7] Ufer, 156.

retire to the Nesos as the first stage in Pausanias' plan, for he states[1] that only after reaching this position was the army to divide for the second stage of the operation, when half of it was to proceed to Kithairon to 'pick up'[2] the men in charge of the supply train, who at present dared not leave the heights. According to Herodotus this second movement was to be carried out on the same night as the retreat,[3] but it is hard to believe that, if half of the army had the Gyphtokastro Pass as its ultimate goal, it should have wasted time at the start by an unnecessary detour to the Nesos.

It has been suggested[4] that in the original plan the right wing was to retire more or less due south to the Pass, and that only part of the army, probably the left wing, was to proceed to the Nesos; this involves the further assumption that Herodotus was here following Athenian informants who gave him the impression that the whole army, not the left wing alone, had been directed to the Island. But the postulate[5] that Herodotus in this and some other sections of his account of this campaign relied exclusively on Athenian sources, though often made, is extremely improbable, and the resulting reconstruction departs so widely from our scanty evidence that it inspires no confidence. Ufer more cautiously suggests[6] that, as the whole army could not hope to find room on the Nesos, part of it (he suggests the right wing) was to extend beyond the Nesos in a southeasterly direction to the modern Kriekouki, and that from there the Spartans could easily send a force to open the Pass and bring the sorely needed supplies to the army.

Obviously the Greeks intended to withdraw to a new position nearer Kithairon which would be easier to defend[7] and would enable them to recover control of their line of communications

---

[1] ix. 51. 4.   [2] Or 'fetch away' (ἀναλάβοιεν); cf. Pritchett, 26 B.

[3] ix. 51. 4 (ὑπὸ τὴν νύκτα ταύτην).

[4] So Woodhouse in *J.H.S.* xviii, 1898, 52 ff. and Munro, op. cit. 161 f. See also Grundy, long note on pp. 492 f. Hauvette, 471 thinks that half the army was to retire towards the Pass; this is at least nearer to Hdt. ix. 51. 4.

[5] Stated by Woodhouse and accepted by many (notably Munro and Wright) but curtly dismissed by Grundy, 508, n. 1. See also Wells, *Studies in Herodotus*, c. 8.

[6] In *A.S.* 156.

[7] Kirsten, 2294 dislikes the view that the projected position was to be purely defensive, and so provides one suitable as a starting-point for a hoplite battle, but his site is improbable for other reasons and Pausanias was hardly contemplating a battle when he retired from the Asopos Ridge. Grundy, 488 thinks he and the other Greek generals intended to remain on the defensive thenceforth.

with the Peloponnese, but the details of their original plan for
the withdrawal cannot be recovered, not least because the plan
was never carried out. Herodotus blames its failure on the
Greek centre. He says[1] that when the time appointed for the
retreat arrived, 'the majority of the army' made no attempt
to reach their appointed station, but in their anxiety to get
away from the menace of the Persian cavalry[2] made straight for
Plataia, where they halted near the temple of Hera, outside the
town walls. As the Athenians and Spartans did not take part
in this flight, it must have been confined to the Greek centre,
and the Corinthians, Megarians, and Phleiasians appear later[3]
among the troops who had gone to the Heraion.

Modern critics complain that if these troops were as demoralized as Herodotus alleges, it is strange that they should have
halted in good order where they did.[4] Perhaps Herodotus has
exaggerated the panic of the centre, though if they had been
previously stationed on the plain they may have suffered more
than the wings from the attacks of the Persian cavalry.[5] But the
critics go too far when they claim that the centre in retiring to
the Heraion had merely occupied the position to which it had
been directed by Pausanias.[6] On this hypothesis Pausanias,
faced with the problem of conducting a withdrawal by night
with half-trained troops, had decided to make it still more difficult by ordering his centre and his left wing to change places
during the night; no compensating advantage is suggested for
this strange decision. It must be remembered that the centre
was composed of contingents from twenty different states[7] and
was therefore more likely to fall into confusion on a night march
in unfamiliar country. Herodotus may have done them an in-
justice in attributing to cowardice an error due to a more venial
cause.[8]

Nevertheless, Herodotus must be right on the main point, that

---

[1] Note οἱ πολλοί in ix. 52, l. 6 (actually 18,600 out of 38,700); see Macan, ad loc.

[2] ἔφευγον ἄσμενοι τὴν ἵππον (c. 52, l. 7).

[3] ix. 69. 1. On the Heraion see below, pp. 427 f.

[4] Woodhouse, 50 f., Munro, 161 f., Macan, i. 2. 706 A. On ἔθεντο τὰ ὅπλα (last
line of c. 52) cf. Legrand, ix. 47, n. 2.

[5] So Boucher, 296; Ufer, 156 f.

[6] This claim is dismissed as improbable by Grundy, 490. Pritchett, 27 A is tempted
by it but sees that it will not do.

[7] Ufer, 157 thinks that the composite character of the centre made it more
liable to panic; he accepts the account in Hdt.   [8] So Grundy, 490 f.

the centre failed to carry out its part of the general plan. This failure alone can explain why the Athenians on the left wing stayed where they were,[1] for if they had been instructed to make for the Nesos, the centre by retiring directly on Plataia would have been marching across the natural line of retreat from Pyrgos Hill to the Nesos.[2] This fact is obscured by Herodotus, who attributes the inactivity of the Athenians to their suspicion of the Spartans: 'they knew the mind of the Lakedaimonians, that they thought one thing and said another.'[3] So when the army (i.e. the centre) began to move they sent a horseman to the right wing to find out whether the Spartans were also on the move or not, and to ask Pausanias for further instructions. The messenger found the Spartans still in their old position.

The reason produced by Herodotus for the inactivity of the Spartans is surprising: he says that a Spartan officer named Amompharetos, commanding the lochos of the men of Pitana[4] (one of the five lochoi into which the Spartan army was divided in this period) said that he would never disgrace Sparta by retiring before the enemy,[5] and refused to listen to Pausanias and his fellow commander Euryanax when they remonstrated with him. This dispute, temporarily interrupted by the arrival of the Athenian messenger, is said to have continued till dawn,[6] when Pausanias decided to retreat with the rest of the Spartans and the Tegeans, thinking that Amompharetos would be bound to follow when he found himself left behind, as in fact he did. Herodotus says[7] that the Spartans in their retreat clung to the hills and the lower slopes of Kithairon, but the motive alleged

---

[1] Cf. Ufer, 157: 'as a result of the flight of the centre an entirely new situation had arisen.'

[2] Munro, 164 comes near to admitting this, and can only refute it by what he calls 'the Athenian version' of the retreat of the centre, a version which he himself regards as false!

[3] ix. 54. 1; Stein quotes Euripides, *Andromache* 445 ff. On the remark (which need not be 'Periklean') see HW² 397 (part 3 of the 'additional note').

[4] This was not its official name, but the objection raised by Thucydides (i. 20. 3) is pedantic; the reference in Hdt. ix. 53. 2 was explained and justified by Toynbee in *J.H.S.* xxxiii, 1913, 257, n. 43. See also Hauvette, 473 ad fin., and on the organization of the Spartan army in this period cf. Wade–Gery in *C.Q.* xxxviii, 1944, 117–21 and 125 f.

[5] ix. 53. 2; cf. 55. 2.

[6] On the rest of this paragraph cf. ix. 56–57.

[7] ix. 56. 2. It is unlikely that the Spartan army reached the ὑπωρέη τοῦ Κιθαιρῶνος in the strict sense; cf. Grundy, 494 n. and 499.

by him, fear of the Persian cavalry, is unconvincing; probably they were taking the shortest route to the position which they now desired to reach. Pausanias, after retiring for ten stades,[1] waited for Amompharetos and his lochos, but just as they rejoined the main body the whole of the Persian cavalry overtook them and forced the Greeks to halt.

This strange story has naturally been scouted by critics as merely a camp-tale,[2] but the refusal of a Spartan officer to obey orders on the eve of battle is not unparalleled later,[3] and the critics have perhaps failed to realize the conditions of Greek warfare in the archaic period. The story about 'the Pitanate lochos' and its commander may have been told to Herodotus by Archias of Pitana, whom he certainly met and talked with in Sparta.[4] Moreover, the rejection of the story leaves an historical vacuum which the critics tend to fill with improbable speculations. They do not deny that Amompharetos was well behind the main body of the Spartans when day dawned, but explain this fact by the hypothesis[5] that he and his lochos had been left behind to cover the retreat. There seems to be no reason for any such precaution in the original plan, in which the whole army was to be in its new position before dawn. If it was a later improvisation, what had made it necessary? Why in fact had the Spartans withdrawn no more than a mile from their original position when they were overtaken by the Persian cavalry?

Ufer argues[6] that it does not make any difference whether the Amompharetos story is true or not, as the half of a short summer night must have been taken up by the consultations necessitated by the breakdown of the original plan; similarly Woodhouse asserts[7] that Pausanias did not allow enough time for the retreat, and that as dawn was then between 4.30 and 5 a.m. he ought to have moved before midnight. But Herodotus[8] says that the retreat was due to begin with the second watch of

---

[1] δέκα στάδια (ix. 57. 2) would be 2,000 yards (cf. HW, vol. i, top of p. 243) but probably the measure is only a rough estimate (as we say, 'about a mile'). The emendation τέσσαρα στάδια, adopted by Hude in the O.C.T., is to be rejected with Legrand, ix. 50, n. 1; see below, p. 432.

[2] e.g. HW 311 (l. 3).   [3] Cf. Thuc. v. 71. 3–72. 1.

[4] iii. 55. 2; cf. Hauvette, 473 and Kirsten, 2295.

[5] Woodhouse, op. cit. 52 ff. The final refinement is the conjecture that Amompharetos was to cover the retreat of the Athenians as well (Munro, 164, also HW on ix. 57. 1).

[6] Op. cit. 157.   [7] Op. cit. 53.   [8] ix.51. 3; cf. 52, ll. 4–5.

the night and that the centre moved at the appointed time. The prevailing view, derived from Pollux,[1] is that the Greeks divided the night into three watches, and that the fourfold division was due to the Romans; this threefold division of the night is presumed in some passages of Homer.[2] Macan questions the usual interpretation of the relevant passage in Pollux, and tries to extract from it a fourfold division, but his citations from it are selective,[3] and the passage as a whole favours the accepted view. It makes little practical difference, for even if the Greeks had only three watches the second should have begun about 10.30 p.m., six hours before dawn. Boucher supposes[4] that the light-armed attendants on the right wing had to be sent away first in charge of the baggage, and if he is right they may have taken so long to get out of the way that the withdrawal of the hoplites had to be delayed, but there is nothing of this in Herodotus, who says explicitly[5] that when the battle began the Lakedaimonians and Tegeans, including the light-armed, numbered 53,000; he must therefore have believed that all the light-armed, composed of 35,000 Helots and 6,500 others, were present. His belief may, however, have been mistaken; it is unlikely that many Helots took part in the battle apart from those who were actually in attendance on the Spartan hoplites.[6]

Munro, who has followed Woodhouse in rationalizing the behaviour of Amompharetos, boldly inverts the fundamental statement in this part of Herodotus' narrative. He says[7] that 'the Athenians pretend' (a question-begging periphrasis for 'Herodotus affirms') 'to have waited for the Lacedaemonians to move but it may be surmised that really the Lacedaemonians waited for them'. Having thus rejected the reasons given by Herodotus for the Athenian (as well as the Spartan) dilatoriness he has to invent a new one, and produces several hypotheses, of which the most fantastic is that the Athenians were reluctant to abandon the security of their position on Pyrgos Hill. How secure could Aristeides expect it to be when the rest of the army had retired to Kithairon? Not much better is Kirsten's theory[8] that the

---

[1] i. 70; cf. Kromayer–Veith, 223.
[2] *Iliad* x. 252 f., *Odyssey* xii. 312 and xiv. 483.
[3] Macan, i. 2. 702 f.   [4] Op. cit. 299 f.   [5] ix. 61. 2.
[6] Some of these were killed in the battle (ix. 85. 2). On the number of the Helots see below, pp. 436 f.   [7] In *C.A.H.* iv. 335; cf. *J.H.S.* xxiv, 1904, 164.
[8] *Rh. Mus.* lxxxvi, 1937, 60 ff.; cf. his *R.-E.* article, 2295 f.

Athenians stayed where they were because they suspected the
Spartans of secretly planning to remain and monopolize the
glory of victory for themselves. Herodotus indeed reports that
the messenger sent by the Athenians to Pausanias was instructed
to find out 'whether the Spartans were attempting to set forth,
or whether they had in truth no design at all to retire',[1] but
the second half of the sentence can hardly be authentic in its
present form and may be a later embellishment.[2] With this possible exception Herodotus' account of the part played by the
Athenians during the night is quite reasonable, that on the
disappearance of the centre they sent for fresh instructions to
Pausanias, who requested them 'to march towards the Spartans
and to do in regard to the retreat the same as they did'.[3]

Herodotus declares that when the messenger returned the
Athenians in accordance with their instructions went 'in the direction opposite to that of the Lakedaimonians; for these were
clinging to the hills and the lower slope of Kithairon from fear
of the cavalry' while the Athenians turned downhill into the
plain.[4] Kirsten, asserting that the 'plain' can only mean the
plain of the Asopos,[5] claims that the Athenians must have
marched northwards, as is shown also by the statement that
they were going in the opposite direction to the Spartans. The
reason he gives for this astounding behaviour is that they, like
Amompharetos, regarded the withdrawal as a flight and so refused to obey Pausanias' orders; instead they decided to march
forwards to fight a pitched battle in the Asopos valley, an act of
insubordination characteristic of the self-sufficient spirit of the
Greek city-state in the archaic period.[6]

This bold reconstruction is unacceptable. Even the victors of
Marathon cannot have persuaded themselves, after their experiences during the last few days, that they could encounter
the whole Persian army without assistance. Kirsten's identification of the plain seems arbitrary; there is no valid reason why
it should not be the plain to the north of Plataia,[7] and whether
the Athenians were stationed on the Asopos Ridge or (more

---

[1] ix. 54. 2 (Macaulay's translation).   [2] Cf. Macan, 712 (ad loc.).
[3] ix. 55. 2, last sentence (Macaulay's translation). Cf. Ufer, 157 f.
[4] ix. 56. 2 (Macaulay's translation).   [5] Kirsten, 2295f.
[6] *Rh. Mus.* (loc. cit.) 65 f.
[7] See above, p. 302. Kirsten admits that the use of πεδίον in ix. 39. 2 does not fit
his explanation.

probably) on Pyrgos Hill, they would naturally begin their southward march by a descent into this plain. The words 'in the opposite direction' are undeniably awkward for those who believe that they started their march from Pyrgos Hill,[1] and the only plausible solution is Stein's, that the words take their colouring from the explanatory sentence which follows, and refer to the difference in the terrain covered by the two wings.[2] Kirsten ignores the word[3] which proves that the Athenians were carrying out Pausanias' orders, and has to explain away the later statement[4] that they were hurrying to his aid when they were attacked by the medizing Greeks. It is a reasonable assumption[5] that he had instructed the Athenians to join him somewhere near Kriekouki and that their quickest way to the rendezvous was over the Plataian plain and then along the depression which lies to the south of the Asopos Ridge;[6] possibly they had reached this depression when their further progress was halted by the enemy.

The battle of Plataia

Not long after dawn on the thirteenth day of Herodotus' Journal the whole of the Asiatic cavalry, which had apparently retired to the Persian camp at nightfall, again crossed the Asopos.[7] When they discovered that the Greek camp was empty, they rode on until they caught up with the Spartan army and promptly began to attack it. Mardonios, on hearing of the Greek withdrawal, decided to join in the pursuit with his Persian infantry on the left wing. He may have ordered the centre to

---

[1] Ufer, 157 f. does not notice the difficulty; he makes the Athenians march south-east, the Spartans south-south-east.

[2] Quoted by Macan (ad loc., 715 A) who disagrees with it. The crucial words (ἦσαν τὰ ἔμπαλιν ἢ Λακεδαιμόνιοι) are translated by Powell 'went contrariwise to the Lacedaemonians'. Cf. also Legrand, ix. 49, n. 3.

[3] ταχθέντες in ix. 56. 2; see Macan's note. HW comment: 'under orders' (from Pausanias).

[4] ix. 61. 1.   [5] Made by Ufer, 158.

[6] Grundy, 505; on the depression see above, p. 302.

[7] On this paragraph cf. Hdt. ix. 57. 3, 58. 1 and 4, and 59. 1. The cavalry is described in 57. 3 as ἡ τῶν βαρβάρων πᾶσα; this does not include the Boiotian cavalry, which is clearly distinguished from it though mentioned with it in connexion with the Persian retreat (c. 68), for the Boiotians were stationed on the Persian right wing.

follow in all haste, but he presumably realized the importance of engaging the Spartans as quickly as possible before they could reach an impregnable position on the rocky base of Kithairon. The Athenians, who were now marching across the plain, were hidden from his view by the Asopos Ridge,[1] but his scouts must have informed him that the Greek right wing was isolated and the rest nowhere in sight.

Herodotus says[2] that when the Spartans were overtaken by the Persians they had marched ten stades from their former position, and defines the position they had reached as close to the river Moloeis and a place called Argiopios, 'where also there stands a temple of the Eleusinian Demeter'. The Moloeis must be one of the tributaries which flow down to the Asopos from Kithairon, probably Grundy's A6,[3] but the site of the Argiopian Land is unknown and that of the temple is much disputed. It cannot be fixed by the measurement of distance contained in the context, for, like almost all the measurements given by Herodotus in his topography of Plataia,[4] it is manifestly intended to be only a rough estimate. But his narrative at least shows clearly that the Spartans had not completed their retirement and that the ground on which they were overtaken by the enemy was not unsuitable for cavalry fighting.[5] Plutarch, indeed, says that the temple was so close to Kithairon that the foothills of the mountain made the ground near the temple impossible for cavalry,[6] but this assertion occurs in a highly suspicious context and does not deserve serious consideration.

Scholars who rely on it have been led astray by the conviction that the Spartan encounter with the Persian infantry must have taken place somewhere south of the wavy line which on modern maps marks the rocky base of Kithairon,[7] a conviction based on the assumption that there can be no other explanation for the absence of the Persian cavalry from Herodotus' account of the

---

[1] ὑπὸ τῶν ὄχθων οὐ κατώρα (59. 1); cf. 56. 2.   [2] ix. 57. 2.

[3] Grundy, 495 (he had earlier identified the Moloeis with A5 in *Topography*, 33).

[4] With the exception in ix. 51. 2 they are all 10 or 20 stades. Grundy, 495 suggests a caution against crediting the measurement with 'a greater accuracy than perhaps it can claim'. See below, p. 432.

[5] So Legrand, ix. 50, n. 2; he points out the discrepancy between this and Hdt.'s statement in ix. 56. 2 that the Spartans retreated by way of the hills 'in fear of the cavalry'.

[6] *Aristeides* 11. 6–7.   [7] See above, pp. 301 f.

central phase of the battle.[1] This assumption is, however, unfounded, and the hypothesis built on it and propped up by the
worthless evidence of Plutarch is inconsistent with Herodotus'
plain implication that Pausanias had not completed his withdrawal when he was attacked by the Persian cavalry. Whatever
may have been his original intentions, he was by then probably
making for 'the northern end of that rocky bastion of Kithairon
whereon the modern Kriekouki stands',[2] but Herodotus shows
clearly that he had not reached a position safe from cavalry
attack when he was overtaken by the enemy.

There are two ways of dealing with this difficulty. Munro
simply postulates[3] that Herodotus was definitely wrong on this
point, misled perhaps by his informants. Ufer supposes[4] that
though Pausanias was still north of the rocky base of Kithairon
when he was attacked by the cavalry, he was not far away and
was able to retire slowly towards it, presumably with his troops
facing the enemy, so that by the time the Persian infantry came
up he was on ground unsuitable for the Persian cavalry, which
therefore disappears from Herodotus' narrative until the retreat,
when it did what it could to protect the infantry from the Greek
pursuit.[5] Herodotus, however, strongly suggests that Pausanias'
march was halted by the onset of the Persian cavalry, and it is
probable that its attacks were intended to hold up the Spartans
until the Persian infantry could arrive.

Pausanias, hard pressed by the cavalry, appealed to the
Athenians for aid, urging them if they were already engaged
with the enemy to send him their archers. The Athenians were
marching to join him when they were attacked by the medizing
Greeks on the Persian right.[6] Meanwhile the Persian infantry
had arrived on the battlefield[7] and had erected their wicker
shields to form a screen from behind which they discharged
showers of arrows against the Spartans and Tegeans.[8] Herodotus
says that the Greeks endured this passively for a time because
the omens were unfavourable, but in the end the Tegeans

---

[1] So Munro and Ufer; see below.   [2] Grundy, 498.
[3] Munro, 163.   [4] A.S. 159 f.; cf. 139.   [5] ix. 68.
[6] ix. 60–61. 1. Hdt.'s account here is rightly defended by Grundy, 501 n.
[7] Pausanias was being attacked by the cavalry when he appealed to the
Athenians (60. 1), but the Persian archers in 61. 3 must be infantry; their arrival
on the scene is presupposed by the last six words of 61. 2.
[8] For the rest of this paragraph cf. ix. 61. 3, 62–63, and 65.

charged and were promptly followed by the Spartans, as the omens had suddenly become propitious. The Persians now laid aside their bows and there was a struggle round the rampart of shields. Even when this fell, there was a hard fight near the temple of Demeter lasting for a long time.[1] The Persian troops were not inferior in physical strength or in courage to their opponents but they were handicapped in close fighting by their lack of shields and were not equal to the Spartans in military skill; the brave exploits of individual fighters or groups could achieve little against the solidity and discipline of the Spartan phalanx. Yet while Mardonios was there to inspire them with his presence, they fought on and caused many casualties to the Greeks. When he fell, and his bodyguard with him,[2] the Persian resistance collapsed and the survivors fled, some at least to the wooden fort north of the Asopos.

Two obvious problems are raised by Herodotus' account: why did the Persian cavalry apparently play no part in the crucial stage of the battle, and why did Mardonios cross the Asopos at all? The facile answer to the first is that Pausanias defeated the Persian infantry because he somehow contrived to fight them on ground unsuitable for cavalry; this solution, which had perhaps occurred to Ephoros,[3] is at variance with the natural interpretation of the evidence in Herodotus. Others have supposed that Pausanias faced the cavalry in a position which was protected against flank attacks; Boucher for example suggested[4] that the Greek left rested on the base of Kithairon while the right was protected by the steep slope of the Moloeis valley.

Such suggestions are unprofitable, as the position occupied by Pausanias cannot be precisely identified on a map with

[1] χρόνον ἐπὶ πολλόν (62. 2); this can hardly mean 'for several hours' as supposed by Hauvette, 479.

[2] Mardonios himself was on a white horse (ix. 63. 1) but it does not follow that the λογάδας Περσέων τοὺς ἀρίστους χιλίους with him were the 1,000 cavalry of viii. 113. 2 (as supposed by HW on ix. 63); Hammond, A History of Greece, 249 makes them 'the royal bodyguard of infantry, a thousand strong' (perhaps with reference to vii. 41. 1). Macan, 731 A (ad loc.) refuses to decide.

[3] It is implied by the language of Plut. Aristeides 11. 7 on the situation of the Eleusinion, and he is presumably indebted for it to one of his predecessors, of whom Ephoros is the most likely source.

[4] Op. cit. 303. Tarn (Hellenistic Military & Naval Developments, 52 f.) says that the Greek flanks were defended by the mountain and by a wall, but gives no explanation; is the wall supposed to be enclosing the precinct of the Eleusinion?

certainty;[1] they are also unnecessary. It is evident that Xerxes' cavalry could not charge in the modern sense a phalanx of spearmen;[2] they could only try to break up its cohesion by firing missile weapons at it from a safe distance, and they could only do this with success on a level plain. Sooner or later they had to stand aside for the infantry to take up the task of consummating the defeat of the enemy, and in this stage of the battle could do little or nothing.[3] Pausanias, however, had his men admirably under control, and though they suffered much from the preliminary assaults of the cavalry their rock-like solidity was maintained. The moderns are probably right in their view[4] that he manipulated the omens so as to delay his charge until the enemy infantry were fully committed to a fight at close quarters in sufficient numbers to make speedy retreat impossible. When they were routed, the Asiatic cavalry could again intervene to protect their retreat, as the Boiotian cavalry did on the Persian right.[5]

A general who loses a decisive battle by fighting at a disadvantage is always an easy target for criticism; moreover, the condemnation of Mardonios' obstinacy in Herodotus[6] may come from a Persian source which had special reasons for hostility to his memory. Even so it is strange that, after resolutely refusing for twelve days to cross the Asopos with his infantry, he should on the thirteenth day have risked a general engagement on ground which neutralized the special advantages which his army possessed over the Greeks. The explanation for his apparent rashness[7] was probably not psychological, as Herodotus supposed, but is to be found in aspects of the overall strategic situation which Herodotus has ignored; in other words, the situation of the Persians in Ionia was so critical that it could only be saved by a great victory on land in Boiotia,[8] and the time available was so short as to force Mardonios' hand, especially when Pausanias refused to cross the Asopos. The retreat of the Greeks offered him a last chance which would be

---

[1] Cf. Hauvette, 475: 'certainly all these movements [those of the retreating Greeks] cannot be traced on a map with mathematical precision.'

[2] See above, p. 45.   [3] Cf. the remarks of Hauvette, 477.

[4] e.g. Grundy, 502; cf. Wright, 68.   [5] ix. 68.

[6] ix. 41. 4. On 'the Artabazos source' see above, p. 270 and n. 1; also HW 276 f. and Grundy, 428 f.

[7] Boucher, 317 speaks of 'sa folle hardiesse'.   [8] See above, p. 247.

lost for ever if they got safely back to Kithairon, and the handicap of the hilly ground south of the river might seem to him to be compensated by the fact that the Greek wings during the withdrawal had become separated from the centre and from each other and so were more vulnerable. Even so his attack was a gamble; he must have known that it was and justified it by the pressing need for a rapid decision.

Boucher asks[1] why Mardonios did not lead his whole army simultaneously across the Asopos, and concludes that in spite of his proud boasts about his army in public he knew that in an offensive he could only count on the Persians of the homeland for success.[2] Obviously the battle would be decided if the best troops in the Persian army could defeat the best troops of the enemy, and that is probably why Mardonios placed his Persians opposite the Spartans, a technique which recalls that of Epameinondas at Leuktra.[3] Moreover, he had to advance with his left wing as quickly as possible if he was to overtake the Spartans in time. He must have instructed the rest of his army to follow with all speed,[4] but the centre may have been delayed by the need to make a longer march, as it was posted behind the great northward bend of the Asopos. Herodotus' account[5] of the part played by its commander Artabazos is perplexing, and may have been influenced by the apologetic tradition which he perhaps heard from members of Artabazos' family, but it suggests that Artabazos was slow to advance and that when he reached the crest of the Asopos Ridge[6] he saw enough to realize that the battle had been decided. The 40,000 men with whom he is said to have retreated to Phokis and beyond may have included troops from the left wing who had made good their escape and joined the centre.[7] Anyhow, there is no justification for the hypothesis[8] that Artabazos and his men were not with Mardonios at all during the campaign in Boiotia.

[1] Op. cit. 301 f. [2] Hdt. ix. 68 says much the same.
[3] Xen. *Hell.* vi. 4. 12.
[4] Hdt. ix. 59. 2 simply says that the rest of the barbarians followed the example of the Persians; it is not clear whether he is referring to the non-Persian contingents (if any) on the Persian left or whether he includes part of the centre as well. Cf. Ufer, 161.
[5] ix. 66; in viii. 126. 1 Artabazos is said to have enhanced his reputation among the Persians by the part he played at Plataia.
[6] Cf. Ufer, 161. [7] Cf. Wright, 69 (Grundy, 508 is ambiguous).
[8] Munro, 165; see above, p. 271, n. 4.

The troops of the Greek centre had little more effect on the course of the battle than those of the Persian centre.[1] Having taken up a position just outside Plataia near the temple of Hera, they remained there inactive until, when the rout of the Persians had already begun,[2] they received news that the battle had taken place and that the troops with Pausanias were victorious. The timing and contents of this message are incompatible with the view[3] that it was sent by Pausanias himself, for if he had known where they were to be found he must have appealed for help to them earlier. But it is not likely that he did know, since they had gone to the Heraion by mistake or in defiance of his orders.[4] Herodotus has stated earlier[5] that before the Spartan charge, while the omens were still adverse, Pausanias had prayed to Hera for a favourable issue, with his face turned towards the Heraion, but this does not prove that the temple was visible from where he stood.[6] When the troops at the Heraion heard the news, they proceeded to divide, apparently on their own initiative,[7] into two groups, and hurried to the battlefield 'without ranging themselves in any order'.[8] One group, composed of the Corinthians and apparently the other contingents from the right half of the Greek centre, advanced 'along the road leading straight upwards to the temple of Demeter across the lower slopes of Kithairon and the hills';[9] that they arrived in time for the final stage of the battle on the Greek right is possible but cannot be proved, as nothing more is heard of them. The other group, probably including all the contingents of the left centre, though only the Megarians and Phleiasians are mentioned,[10] descended into the plain, probably

---

[1] ix. 69, cf. 52.

[2] ix. 69. 1, where φόβῳ is used in its Homeric sense (not found elsewhere in Hdt.) of φυγῇ. Legrand, ix. 57, n. 1 reads φόνῳ.

[3] Suggested by Woodhouse, op. cit. 50 f.   [4] See above, p. 327.   [5] ix. 61. 3.

[6] As supposed by Ufer, 130 and 141. Grundy, 521 (paragraph 3) insists that the Spartans cannot have been visible during the battle from the Heraion.

[7] Woodhouse supposes that they were acting on Pausanias' orders, but there is no evidence that they had received any message from him.

[8] ix. 69. 1 (ll. 4–5), scouted by Macan (ad loc.) but perhaps confirmed by the defeat of the left centre in 69. 2.

[9] ix. 69. 1. The word ἄνω (not in some manuscripts) suggests that the temple was on a hill. There is the same difficulty about the identification of the ὑπωρέη and the κολωνοί here as in ix. 56. 1–2 (where κολωνοί are apparently identical with ὄχθοι); cf. Macan, i. 2. 715 B and 740 B.

[10] Perhaps because these two contingents occupied the two ends of the left centre

intending to help the Athenians, but they advanced in disorder and were routed by the Theban cavalry,[1] who slew 600 of them and drove the rest back to Kithairon.

Herodotus has not explained the relation in time between this encounter and the fighting which he has reported earlier in this sector of the battlefield. The Persian right, composed of the contingents from Macedonia and the pro-Persian states of Northern Greece, had crossed the Asopos and advanced until they overtook the Athenians,[2] but thereafter, according to Herodotus,[3] they all deliberately played the coward with the exception of the Boiotians, who fought the Athenians for a long time until they were defeated with the loss of 300 men and fled straight to Thebes. Ephoros absurdly embellished this Athenian success with the fiction[4] that the Athenians, Plataians, and Thespians pursued them to Thebes, and after defeating them in a second battle close to the city forced them to take refuge behind its walls. As the Theban dead are described by Herodotus as the foremost and noblest of the citizens,[5] the presumption is that they were serving in the cavalry. But it is surprising that a purely hoplite force, even if supported by the regiment of Athenian archers, should have inflicted such losses on cavalry, whether the battle was fought in the depression leading out of the Plataian plain or in the plain itself, and there is the further difficulty that cavalry which had sustained such a reverse should have been able to defeat the troops who came from the left centre of the Greeks to join in the battle. The only possible conclusion[6] is that when these troops arrived the struggle on the Greek left had not yet been decided. Possibly their intervention, though disastrous for themselves, helped to distract the Boiotians and so enabled the Athenians to defeat them,[7] or the Boiotians may have given up the struggle when they heard that the Persians had been routed.

(cf. ix. 28. 5–6) or simply because theirs were the largest contingents in this part of the army. The fight of the Megarians with the Theban cavalry is mentioned in Tod, no. 20, ll. 11–12.

[1] The Theban commander Asopodoros may have been the father of the Herodotus for whom Pindar composed his First Isthmian; cf. Macan, 741 A.

[2] ix. 61. 1.

[3] ix. 67. It is curious that the Thessalians, whose leaders had been closely associated with Mardonios (cf. ix. 1 and 58. 1), are not mentioned here.

[4] Diod. xi. 32. 1–2.   [5] ix. 67.

[6] Cf. Grundy, 507 (Ufer, 162 ignores the difficulty).   [7] So Macan, i. 2. 741.

Many of the defeated troops on the left wing of the Persian army escaped from the Spartan pursuit to the fort on the north side of the Asopos and were able to man its ramparts before the pursuers arrived. The Spartans were notoriously bad at siege-warfare and made no progress until the Athenians came up to help them.[1] Perhaps the Athenians already had a reputation for special skill in attack on fortified places,[2] a skill which they may have learnt from the Ionians, but their success at Plataia in breaching the Persian stockade is attributed to their courage and perseverance.[3] Herodotus, however, says that the Tegeans were the first to enter the fort through the breach; Hauvette suggested that the Athenians were the sappers, the Tegeans the storming party.[4] The fort was probably captured on the same day as the battle; Boucher's idea[5] that it may have held out for several days is not supported by anything in Herodotus. Its capture was followed by a general slaughter. Herodotus alleges[6] that, apart from the 40,000 with Artabazos, less than 3,000 of the Orientals in Mardonios' army survived, but it is not likely that all the fugitives from the left wing fled to the fort; some may have escaped with Artabazos. If the 40,000 with him were the survivors from the Persian left and centre combined, the non-European parts of Mardonios' army may have lost about 10,000 men altogether, in the battle and in the storming of the fort.

The figures in Herodotus for the Greek losses[7] are 91 Lakedaimonians, 16 Tegeans, and 52 Athenians, to which must be added the 600 from the left centre killed by the Theban cavalry. Plutarch's 1,360[8] for the total Greek losses looks like a mere compilation from the incomplete items in Herodotus; Plutarch's source has apparently added another 600 for the other half of

---

[1] ix. 70. 1–2. Perhaps (in spite of Macan, 742 B) τῶν Ἀθηναίων should be read in the fifth line of 70. 1; so Legrand, ix. 57, n. 3.

[2] The reputation was already established by 462 (Thuc. i. 102. 3) but Grundy (*Thucydides*[1], 245; cf. 282) thinks it was that of the one-eyed among the blind!

[3] ἀρετῇ τε καὶ λιπαρίῃ (ix. 70. 2).

[4] ix. 70. 3; cf. Hauvette, 481. [5] Op. cit. 310 f.

[6] ix. 70. 5. As there is no mention of any prisoners, Ephoros invented an order by Pausanias μηδένα ζωγρεῖν (Diod. xi. 32. 5).

[7] ix. 70. 5; cf. 69. 2.

[8] Plut. *Aristeides* 19. 5, possibly from an Atthidographer (Wright, 105 suggests Kleidemos), certainly not from Ephoros, who estimated the Greek losses at over 10,000 (Diod. xi. 33. 1).

the centre and rounded off the total. As Kleidemos[1] claimed that the 52 Athenian dead were all from the tribe Aiantis, it has been conjectured that Herodotus mistook the funeral monument of a single tribe for the complete total of the Athenian losses, but the difficulty remains that the Spartan and Tegean figures also seem to be too low. Even though Herodotus' figures are only for those who fell in the battle, it is unlikely that the Greeks should have lost so few men in a struggle which was so sternly contested on both wings.[2] Herodotus is sceptical about the funeral mounds erected later outside Plataia by states whose contingents had played no part in the last fight,[3] but these contingents may have sustained some casualties in the encounters of the previous days, or their dead may have been buried in a common grave and the separate cenotaphs erected later by the states concerned.[4]

After the battle was over the contingents of two Peloponnesian states made a late appearance, the Mantineians first, then the Eleians. Herodotus says that the Mantineians arrived immediately after the battle,[5] and though his dating has been questioned it is supported by their offer, vetoed by Pausanias, to pursue to Thessaly the fugitives who had escaped with Artabazos. As Elis and Mantineia were both members of Sparta's Peloponnesian League and therefore accustomed to send their quota of hoplites to league expeditions when called upon,[6] their dilatoriness on this occasion is remarkable, especially as the Greek army had been in Boiotia for a fortnight at least. After their contingents returned home, both states banished their generals, but this does not prove that their delay had been due to intrigues with Persia; the generals may have been punished as scapegoats for the stupidity or selfishness of the rest.[7]

---

[1] Plut. *Aristeides* 19. 6 (Kleidemos, fr. 14 in *F.H.G.* i. 362 = fr. 22 in Jacoby, *F.G.H.* iii, no. 323). The prominence of the Aiantid tribe in the post-Herodotean tradition of the Persian War is not above suspicion; did Kleidemos himself perhaps belong to this tribe? Cf. Wilamowitz, *Aristoteles und Athen*, i. 286, n. 36.

[2] Cf. the remarks of Grundy, 509 and Macan, i. 2. 745 A.

[3] ix. 85. 3.   [4] Cf. Macan, 772 A.

[5] αὐτίκα μετὰ ταῦτα (ix. 77. 1), unreasonably dismissed by Macan as 'a stock formula' (hardly proved by the instances he gives).

[6] So in the defence of the Isthmus in Sept. 480; cf. viii. 72, where the Mantineians must be included in Ἀρκάδες πάντες. There were 500 Mantineians at Thermopylai but apparently no Eleians; see above, p. 116.

[7] Cf. Grundy, 513 f. Macan, 758 B is rightly sceptical about Munro's speculations; see above, p. 279.

For nine days after the battle[1] the Greek army remained near Plataia; during this period they buried their dead and distributed the booty. It was apparently now that Pausanias, after offering solemn sacrifice to Zeus the Liberator in the market-place of the ruined town of Plataia, gave the Plataians a sworn guarantee of their territory and independence, in the presence of all the allies, who pledged themselves to defend Plataia against any aggression in the future,[2] while the Plataians undertook to honour the tombs of the fallen with the usual offerings every year.[3] Plutarch's statement that the Hellenic League was now reorganized on principles proposed by Aristeides seems to be an invention of the untrustworthy Idomeneus.[4]

One further task remained. The Athenians, Plataians, and Thespians must have pressed for the overthrow of Theban supremacy in Boiotia, and as Thebes had shown special zeal for the Persian cause Pausanias with the approval of his war council[5] led his army against it. According to the usual Greek practice he ravaged the open country, but the Peloponnesians were doubtless anxious to return home and might have been unwilling to remain for a long siege, so Pausanias wisely announced that he would be content with the surrender of the pro-Persian leaders. After a siege of nine days[6] the Thebans agreed to hand them over; Herodotus says that Pausanias after disbanding his army took the Theban leaders to Corinth and had them summarily executed, fearing that if they were admitted to trial they might secure acquittal by bribing their judges.[7] In spite of Herodotus' silence it is probable that Pausanias reorganized the cities of Boiotia; the federation under Theban leadership was dissolved and the close oligarchies in Thebes and

---

[1] They advanced on Thebes 'on the eleventh day after the battle' (ix. 86. 2); probably the reckoning is inclusive, as in the δευτέρῃ ἡμέρῃ of ix. 84. 1.

[2] Thuc. ii. 72. 2 and 4. But τὸ ξυνώμοτον in Thuc. ii. 74. 2 seems to refer to the alliance of 481; see Brunt in *Historia*, ii, 1953, 155.

[3] Plut. *Aristeides* 21. 2 (in a dubious context). The annual offerings are mentioned by Thuc. iii. 58. 4.

[4] Plut. *Aristeides* 21. 1–2. Cf. Busolt, 740 f., Hauvette, 482, HW 317, also Brunt (op. cit.) 153 and n. 2.

[5] ix. 86. 1; cf. Grundy, 516 f.

[6] ix. 87. 1; the dating here and in 86. 2 has been thought to be only approximate, ten days being the Greek equivalent of one week; cf. Busolt, 726 n. (cited by HW 305 on ix. 41. 1).

[7] ix. 88 (last sentence). The doubts of Macan (ad loc.) are not convincing, and Hdt. clearly approved of Pausanias' action.

other cities seem to have been replaced by moderate govern-
ments in which, as in the Boiotian states of the early fourth
century, political privileges were thrown open to all members of
the hoplite class.[1] The Theban oligarchy had been crippled not
only by the surrender of their leaders but by the loss of 300 of
their members on the battlefield at the hands of the Athenians.[2]

Athenian hoplites had given proofs of their fighting quality
against Thebans twenty-seven years before[3] and against the
Persians at Marathon; there is therefore no need to suppose that
they played an unworthy part in the campaign of Plataia.[4]
They may perhaps have made the most of their own achievements, but though there had been some friction in the field
between them and their Spartan allies they would presumably
have agreed with their fellow citizen Aeschylus that the great
victory at Plataia was the achievement of 'the Dorian spear'.[5]
If Herodotus, with his usual fairness towards the barbarians, is
careful to point out that their strength and bravery were un-
availing against the superior skill and armament of the victors,[6]
he does not thereby intend to depreciate the merits of the
Spartans; on the contrary he pays an enthusiastic tribute to
Pausanias, that he had won 'the most glorious victory on
record'.[7] Thucydides also says[8] that Pausanias was highly
esteemed by the Greeks for his leadership at Plataia. It is not
necessary to infer from these tributes that Pausanias lured
Mardonios into a trap by a feigned retreat and a deliberate
dispersion of his army in three separate groups;[9] it is not likely

---

[1] Cf. Busolt–Swoboda, *Griechische Staatskunde*, ii. 1413 (with notes 1 and 2),
also Diod. xi. 81. 2–3 and *Hellenica Oxyrhynchia*, 11.

[2] ix. 67. See above, p. 339.

[3] Hdt. v. 77–78; the fashionable date for the victory there recorded is 506,
but 507 is also possible.

[4] Cf. Grundy, n. on p. 508 and Wells, *Studies in Herodotus*, c. 8.

[5] *Persai*, 816 f.

[6] ix. 62. 3, 63. 2. Hauvette, 477 is not at his best on these passages.

[7] ix. 64. 1; cf. Grundy, 508. Herodotus' high estimate of Pausanias' character
is shown by the three stories he tells of his behaviour after the battle (ix. 76,
78–79, and 82. 2–3); in v. 32 he is sceptical about the official story of Pausanias'
subsequent Medism, more sceptical than Thucydides.

[8] i. 130. 1.

[9] The inference was drawn by Wright, 66 f. and 118. He is, however, wisely
suspicious (op. cit. 99) of the statement of Plato (*Laches* 191 B–C, accepted by Meyer,
411, n. 1) that the Spartans used the tactic of feigned retreat in their attack on
the Persian shield wall at Plataia; this is an obvious transference from Thermopylai
(Hdt. vii. 211. 3).

that all that happened on the day of battle was intended to happen in just that way by Pausanias. But he had at least contrived to maintain a fair measure of control over his heterogeneous army during a difficult campaign, and in the final struggle he had kept his men well in hand until the Persian infantry was irretrievably committed. Strategically the land campaign in Boiotia was a mistake forced on the Spartans by Athens, but it enabled them to justify their high military reputation and to set the seal on the Greek triumph by defeating the Persian on his favourite element. The prestige of Persia was shattered on land as well as on sea, and henceforward her troops were always haunted by the consciousness of their inferiority to Greek hoplites. When they met them again in a great battle at the end of the century, Klearchos and his mercenaries on the field of Kunaxa confirmed the verdict of Plataia.

APPENDIX I

The numbers of the Persian fleet and army

(All references in this appendix to Beloch, unless otherwise stated, are to his discussion in his *Griechische Geschichte*, ii². 2. 61 ff.)

(*a*) *The fleet*

OUR earliest authority, Aeschylus, claims to know that the Persian fleet at Salamis numbered 1,207 ships. He says (*Persai* 341 ff.)

> Ξέρξῃ δέ, καὶ γὰρ οἶδα, χιλιὰς μὲν ἦν
> ὧν ἦγε πλῆθος, αἱ δ' ὑπέρκομποι τάχει
> ἑκατὸν δὶς ἦσαν ἑπτά θ'· ὧδ' ἔχει λόγος.

It has often been suggested (e.g. by Tarn in *J.H.S.* xxviii, 1908, 203) that the 207 swift ships were included by Aeschylus in the 1,000, but this interpretation is improbable, for the particles μέν and δέ clearly imply a contrast between the chiliad and the swift ships, and in the preceding passage on the Greek fleet (ll. 338 ff.) the δεκὰς ἔκκριτος is similarly marked off from the remaining 300; so rightly Beloch, 67 and Macan, ii. 150, n. 5. Some ancient writers however, including Ktesias (*Persika*, 23) estimated the Persian fleet at 1,000 (cf. HW 365, n. 2).

The figure 1,207 reappears in Herodotus (vii. 89. 1) as the total of the Persian triremes at Doriskos, before they had sustained heavy losses by storms and in the fighting at Artemision. Hauvette (*Hérodote*, 313) conveniently supposes that the occurrence of the same figure in both authors proves its derivation from an official catalogue of the ships present in the naval review at Doriskos, but here and elsewhere he evades the question why the same figure recurs in Aeschylus for the fleet at Salamis, in spite of all the losses it had sustained in the interval. It is more likely that the 1,207 triremes of Herodotus are ultimately derived from Aeschylus, or from a *Greek* tradition followed by Aeschylus. Herodotus, referring the figure 1,207 back to Doriskos, appears to have justified its application to Salamis by the assumption that the losses of the Persian fleet in the interval had been made good by the arrival of fresh contingents (viii. 66).

This assumption is irreconcilable with two other passages, in which storms off the coast of Magnesia and off Euboia are said to

have destroyed 400 and 200 Persian warships respectively (vii. 190;
viii. 7. 1 and 13) and even if the loss of the second squadron is
mythical, it is probable that nearly one-third of the Persian warships were wrecked by the first storm (see above, pp. 174 f.); moreover, the fleet must have lost at least 70 more ships by capture and
battle at Artemision. The only new contingents which had come in
since the storm were some of the islanders (Karystos, Andros, and
Tenos are mentioned in viii. 66. 2), which cannot possibly have replaced the Persian losses. It is true that Herodotus believes that the
Persian navy was joined after Doriskos by a fleet from the Greeks of
Thrace and the adjacent islands, a fleet said to have numbered 120
(vii. 185. 1) but this is an absurd overestimate (cf. HW, ad loc. and
365, n. 1). Moreover the position of this notice proves that the fleet
in question was supposed to have joined the main navy before the
great storm, and in the passage under discussion (viii. 66. 1) Herodotus expressly says that 'the Persians on their arrival in Attica, in
my opinion, were no fewer in number, both by land and by sea,
than when they arrived at Sepias and Thermopylai' (this previous
occasion had been chosen by Herodotus for an enumeration of the
Persian forces on land and sea while the host was still $\dot{a}\pi a\theta\dot{\eta}s$ $\kappa a\kappa\hat{\omega}\nu$;
vii. 184. 1).

Tarn's attempt (op. cit. 204, n. 12) to justify the statement in viii.
66. 1 by the suggestion that Herodotus was referring not to ships or
crews but only to fighting men, including marines, is inconsistent
with the whole tendency of this chapter, which is closely connected
with the enumeration of the Persian forces in Book VII (cf. Macan,
i. 2. 459), and if the Persian fleet had lost more than one-third of its
number since it left Therma the number of marines on board must
have been diminished in the same proportion. This chapter of Herodotus must therefore be interpreted in the obvious way, and the
absurdity of his calculation can only be explained by a desire to
reconcile his account with the Aeschylean total for the Persian fleet
at Salamis; his additional 120 ships for the Greeks of Thrace should
have raised this total to 1,327, but he seems to have forgotten their
existence when he reached Book VIII.

Herodotus, after giving the total 1,207 triremes for the Persian
fleet on its arrival at Doriskos, adds the figures for the separate contingents (vii. 89 ff.) as Phoenicians 300, Egyptians 200, Cyprians 150,
Cilicians 100, Pamphylians 30, Lykians 50, Dorians of Asia 30,
Karians 70, Ionians 100, Islanders (possibly from the Cyclades) 17,
Aiolians 60, Hellespontine Greeks 100. Diodoros says (xi. 3. 7) that
the number of triremes exceeded 1,200, but the separate figures
which he proceeds to give amount to precisely 1,200; he agrees with
Herodotus on the numbers of the first three contingents and the

Ionians, but modifies the other figures, ending with 50 from the Islands, 40 from the Aiolians, and 80 from the Hellespont. Like Herodotus, Diodoros allows 3,000 for ships other than triremes, but he calls them all τριηκόντοροι, whereas Herodotus (vii. 97) also includes πεντηκόντεροι καὶ κέρκουροι καὶ ἱππαγωγὰ πλοῖα in the total.

Some modern writers (e.g. Hauvette, loc. cit. and Grundy, 219) have accepted 1,207 as the number of Persian warships at Doriskos. But there is one clear indication in Herodotus (viii. 13, last sentence; see above, p. 209) that the Persian fleet at Salamis was only slightly superior in ships to the Greek; if this is correct it can hardly have numbered more than 600 at Doriskos, and the traditional 1,207, already known to Aeschylus, must be an invention. If it is, it follows that the figures given by Herodotus for the contingents of the maritime peoples must also be fictitious; it is significant that though Ephoros accepted four of them he allowed himself a free hand in altering the rest. The traditional total may have arisen from a desire to credit Xerxes with a fleet larger than that which Agamemnon led against Troy; in our manuscripts of the second book of the *Iliad* the figures given for the separate contingents of the Greek fleet add up to 1,186, and though variants were known in antiquity for some of them they probably made no important difference to the total (1,200 ships in Thuc. i. 10. 4).

Elsewhere in Herodotus 600 is given as the total number of ships in the Persian fleet on various occasions, and Grundy (p. 219) speaks of this as 'the ordinary naval levy of 600 ships', which on his view was doubled for the special effort in 480. But this repeated appearance of fleets of 600 in Herodotus arouses suspicion, as the fleets mentioned differ profoundly in their composition. That which accompanied Darius against Scythia was composed exclusively of Asiatic Greeks, Ionians, Aiolians, and Hellespontines (iv. 87. 1 and 89. 1), whereas at Lade these states were in revolt and not included in the Persian fleet of 600, composed of Phoenician, Cyprian, Cilician, and Egyptian contingents (vi. 6 and 9. 1.). In 490 the fleet under Datis is said to have numbered 600 before it reached Ionia (vi. 95. 2), but Herodotus' implication that on this expedition no use was made of the Ionians is improbable, as they had been subdued three years before. The most incredible of these estimates is the first. Even at the crisis of their fate the Ionians and Aiolians could muster no more than 353 ships, at Lade (vi. 8), and their normal strength was perhaps 200, the size of the navy raised from them by Artaphernes in 499 (v. 32). The second 600 (vi. 9. 1) is also improbable, for the behaviour of the Persian admirals before Lade strongly suggests that they had no decisive superiority in numbers over the 353 ships of their opponents. Finally, it is unlikely that the Persians took 600 warships against Eretria and Athens in 490; 200 would have been more than sufficient to deal with any resistance they might have to face on sea (cf. Meyer, 325 and note on 326). From all this it follows that 600 in Herodotus is a stereotyped figure, as Tarn supposed (op. cit. 204), for any large Persian fleet, whatever its composition, and it is tempting to agree with Tarn that 600 was the number of warships in the largest fleet ever raised by the Persian Empire, the fleet mustered by Xerxes in 480.

Although Tarn's estimate for the fleet is reasonable and may well be correct, his attempt to deduce it from the organization of the fleet, like the attempts of others who have arrived at results different from his, rests on no solid foundation. Herodotus says (vii. 97) that the fleet was led by four admirals, Xerxes' brother Achaimenes, commanding the Egyptian contingent, his half-brother Ariabignes over the Ionians and Karians, while the rest (837 according to Herodotus) were under Prexaspes and Megabazos. Macan rather hesitatingly inferred from this the existence of four Persian fleets of 300 each. Munro originally supposed (*J.H.S.* xxii, 1902, 299) that there were four fleets of 200 each, since that was the size of the Egyptian squadron under Achaimenes (vii. 89. 2) and the fleet of Ariabignes would also number 200 if, as is probable, it included the 30 ships of the Dorians of Asia. Such juggling with the figures in Herodotus is unjustifiable. On what ground does Munro accept as trustworthy Herodotus' totals for the Egyptian, Ionian, Karian, and Dorian contingents, while cutting down all the rest by 50 per cent. (as he must do to reduce 807 to 400)? Nothing is gained by Munro's reference to the 200 ships sent round Euboia, as this fleet is probably unhistorical (viii. 7. 1; see below, Appendix VI) or to the 200 ships sent to block the Megarid Channel before Salamis. In fact the number comes from Plutarch (*Them.* 12. 5); Ephoros (in Diod. xi. 17. 2) merely says that Xerxes sent the Egyptian fleet, which Ephoros, probably following Herodotus, had numbered at the start as 200 ships (Diod. xi. 3. 7.). It is highly probable that the 200 ships of Plutarch are ultimately derived from Herodotus' figure for the Egyptian squadron; why should this be more reliable than his 300 for the Phoenician contingent?

It is therefore not surprising that Munro later abandoned this reconstruction and produced another modelled on Tarn's, with some unconvincing modifications which brought up the total of Xerxes' fleet to 730 (*C.A.H.* iv. 273 ff.). As a sample of his later method it is sufficient to quote his figure for the Phoenician fleet, 210 ships, said to be made up of three squadrons of 60 ships with 10 cruisers (to which he finds a reference in vii. 179) attached to each squadron. The Phoenician ships were the '207 swift ships' singled out by Aeschylus; they numbered 207, Munro asserts, because three had been wrecked on the Myrmex reef. This assertion is founded on a mistranslation of the relevant passage in Herodotus, vii. 183. 2 (see above, p. 161), and ignores the losses which the Phoenicians must have sustained in the two battles off Artemision.

Tarn's estimate of 600 for the fleet at Doriskos is probably correct, but his attempts to deduce it from the supposed organization of the fleet, though ingenious, rest on flimsy foundations (cf. Beloch, 70). Having shown that Carthaginian fleets were organized later in groups of sixty ships each, he concludes (*a*) that this grouping was derived from Phoenicia, (*b*) that the Phoenician contingent in the fleet of Xerxes probably numbered 120, two squadrons of sixty, and (*c*) that after the adhesion of Phoenicia to the Persian Empire this organization must have been extended to the other fleets in the Persian navy. The first two of these conclusions may perhaps be true, but hardly justify the third, which is not proved by Herodotus' statement (iii. 19. 3) that $\pi\hat{\alpha}\varsigma\ \dot{\epsilon}\kappa\ \Phi\text{οι}\nu\acute{\iota}\kappa\omega\nu\ \mathring{\eta}\rho\tau\eta\tau\text{ο}\ \dot{\text{ο}}\ \nu\alpha\upsilon\tau\iota\kappa\dot{\text{ο}}\varsigma\ \sigma\tau\rho\alpha\tau\acute{\text{ο}}\varsigma$ (on its natural interpretation). Tarn postulates five fleets on a territorial basis, each composed of 120 ships, but the figure 120, so essential for his reconstruction, occurs nowhere in Herodotus' list of the contingents at Doriskos, and the alleged 120 ships from the Greeks of Thrace, which are supposed to have joined the Persian navy later (vii. 185. 1) are generally regarded with suspicion; if there were any such, they certainly did not number 120 (HW 365, n. 1). Tarn obtains 120 for his hypothetical 'Northern Fleet' from Diodoros (xi. 3. 8) by combining his 40 ships of the Aiolians with his 80 ships of the Hellespontine Greeks, but there is no real reason why those two figures (for which Herodotus has 60 and 100) should be more trustworthy than any of the others in Diodoros (it is a wild supposition that they were derived by Ephoros from well-informed local tradition at Kyme!) and it is incredible that the contingents of these two groups combined should have amounted to one-fifth of the whole Persian navy. As Tarn has to find five admirals for his five fleets he supposes that the most important of them, the Phoenician, was commanded by Xerxes himself, but surely it would have been beneath the dignity of the Great King to hold any position below that of admiral-in-chief of the combined fleets. Tarn is doubtless right in arguing that a navy of 600 would have been unmanageable as a unit and must have been subdivided into several fleets, but it is impossible to be sure that these fleets were all of the same size; if Herodotus is right about the admirals, there may have been four fleets of 150 ships each, but how can we know?

It seems better to abandon all attempts to fix the number of ships in the separate contingents, but Tarn's total of 600 for the fleet at

Doriskos may be accepted. Although the detailed figures in Herodotus inspire no confidence, his narrative of the war makes sense only on the supposition that the Persian fleet did not greatly outnumber the Greek either at Artemision or at Salamis. Herodotus, in a passage of great importance (viii. 13, last sentence) which contradicts his usual assumption of the vast superiority in numbers of the Persian warships, says that this was the result planned by God when he sent the storm to destroy the Persian fleets. As the divine intention cannot have been frustrated, and as one-third of the Persian fleet was probably destroyed by the storm (see above, p. 174) 600 is a reasonable estimate for its strength at the beginning of the invasion.

(b) *The land forces*

From the outset the Greeks grossly exaggerated the size of the army which Xerxes led against them in 480; the poet Simonides in his epigram on the Peloponnesians who fought at Thermopylai (Hdt. vii. 228. 1) calculated the Persian host at 300 myriads (3,000,000 fighting men). Herodotus states that the foot-soldiers brought by Xerxes from Asia were first numbered after the crossing into Europe, at Doriskos, and found to be 1,700,000 (vii. 60. 1); his estimate of 300,000 for the troops later added from the European territories under Persian control, including the Macedonians and the medizing Greeks, is admittedly based on conjecture (vii. 185. 2). The Asiatic cavalry are said to have numbered 80,000 (vii. 87. 1); to these Herodotus adds bodies of charioteers supplied by the Indians and Libyans and a camel corps of Arabians, but these additional troops, later calculated at 20,000 (vii. 184. 4) are expressly said to be excluded from the figure for the cavalry (vii. 86 and first sentence of 87) and therefore bring the total number for the fighting men from Asia up to 1,800,000.

This total is manifestly unacceptable on practical grounds; as Macan puts it (ii. 157) Herodotus' final results show 'with how little critical faculty or concrete imagination he handles the problems of time and space, of movement and rest, of supply and accommodation involved'. Here, as elsewhere, the later tradition cannot be used to correct the Herodotean account. Ktesias (*Persika*, 23) gives 800,000 for the army of invasion (excluding the charioteers) and this was perhaps copied by Ephoros, as Diodoros (xi. 3. 7) says that the land forces were 'over 800,000' (perhaps including the charioteers), but Ephoros seems to have added 'nearly 200,000' for Xerxes' allies in European Greece (Diod. xi. 5. 2), bringing up the final total for the land forces to not less than 1,000,000 men. Another fourth-century estimate for Xerxes' army was 700,000 (Isocrates vi. 100, xii. 49),

which may have been ultimately derived from Herodotus' figure
(iv. 87. 1) for the army with which Darius invaded Scythia, said by
Herodotus to have been composed of all the nations in Darius'
empire. This figure reappears in Justin (ii. 10. 18) whose source
combines it with Herodotus' estimate of 300,000 for the *auxilia* to
reach the Ephorean total of 1,000,000.

In fairness to Herodotus it is important to remember that inflated
estimates of Persian armies are found elsewhere in writers with practical experience of warfare who were present at the battles which
they described. Arrian gives the army of Darius III at Issos as
600,000, at Gaugamela as 1,000,000 (*Anabasis* ii. 8. 8, iii. 8. 6); these
estimates are almost certainly derived by Arrian from Ptolemy, who
was present at both battles. It is, of course, possible that Alexander's
Court Journal, from which Ptolemy may have taken these figures,
deliberately exaggerated the numbers of the enemy (cf. Caesar,
B.G.), but Xenophon, who was present with the Greek contingent
at Kunaxa, had no such motive for estimating Artaxerxes' army on
that occasion at 900,000 men (Xen. *Anabasis* i. 7. 12). Moreover,
Herodotus' figure for the army with which Darius I invaded Scythia
may have been derived from the record of his forces which he set up
near Byzantion on two stelai, one in Greek letters and one in
cuneiform (iv. 87. 1–2). An Oxford scholar has suggested to me that
some of these estimates may have been due to a genuine misunderstanding, that the Persian unit of calculation may have been a
chiliad, misinterpreted by the Greeks as a myriad, so that all figures
derived from Persian official sources were automatically multiplied
by ten. This explanation would reduce the figures in Xenophon
and Arrian to credible proportions and would give an army of
70,000 for the Scythian expedition of Darius I, but must remain an
hypothesis only; if applied to the Herodotean figures for Xerxes' army
it produces 170,000 infantry and 8,000 cavalry. These numbers are
curiously near to Munro's total of 180,000 for the army of invasion,
though Munro makes the proportion of cavalry to infantry much
higher.

Munro claimed to derive his conclusions (*J.H.S.* xxii, 1902,
294 ff.; cf. *C.A.H.* iv. 271 ff.) from data in Herodotus, particularly his
account of the organization of the Persian infantry in vii. 61–83,
which must now be examined. After stating the total for Xerxes'
Asiatic infantry and the method by which it was ascertained (vii. 60)
Herodotus proceeds to give an Homeric catalogue of the forty-six
nations in the host; the arms and dress of each contingent are described and there are occasional notes on matters of history and
legend relating to the particular peoples named. Fourteen of these contingents had an archon of their own, but the remaining thirty-two

were grouped together under fifteen archontes, so that there were twenty-nine archontes in all. At the end of the list Herodotus observes (vii. 81) that the archontes, who are all named and were all Persians of high rank, were in charge of the army and were responsible for the organization and numbering of the host, and that it was they who appointed the chiliarchs and myriarchs (commanders of bodies of 1,000 and 10,000) while the myriarchs nominated the officers in charge of bodies of hundreds and tens, the hekatontarchs and dekarchs. In the next chapter the archontes are said to be subordinated to the supreme authority of six generals (Mardonios, Tritantaichmes, Smerdomenes, Masistes, Gergis, and Megabyzos), but in vii. 83 Herodotus notes that the division of 10,000 picked troops (the Immortals) from the homeland of Persia, commanded by Hydarnes, stood outside this organization and was not subject to the orders of the six generals; in this respect Hydarmes is clearly differentiated from the twenty-nine archontes.

Munro revived the hypothesis (apparently originated by de Gobineau; cf. Hauvette, 310 and n. 4) that the twenty-nine archontes were really identical with the myriarchs; he then suggested that the thirtieth archon was Hydarnes, the commander of the 10,000 Immortals, and so reached a total of 300,000 for the Asiatic infantry. He and Macan (ii. 162) rejected Herodotus' figure of 80,000 for the Asiatic cavalry in favour of 60,000. Munro further supposed that this represented the full levy of the Persian Empire (excluding the dominions in Europe) and that it was organized under the six generals in six armies, each containing 50,000 infantry and 10,000 cavalry, but (unlike Macan) he supposed that only half of this levy, consisting of three out of the six armies, was employed in the invasion of Greece. He argued that 60,000 was probably the normal size of a Persian army corps on the ground that this was the figure given by Herodotus for the armies commanded by Artabazos and Tigranes; Herodotus, having erroneously moved the archontes one grade higher up, proceeded to assign them 60,000 men each, and so multiplied the correct total by six.

It is not a fatal objection to this hypothesis (in spite of Hauvette, 310 and Beloch, 73) that it identifies the Herodotean archontes with the myriarchs, for Herodotus' statement that the archontes appointed the myriarchs is incredible (unless the archontes were here confused with the generals by Herodotus or his source). Less defensible is Munro's further assumption that Herodotus, having estimated the total number of the infantry at 1,800,000, proceeded to reduce them to 1,700,000 by subtracting 80,000 as the (erroneous) total for the cavalry and 20,000 as the (estimated) number of the charioteers and camel corps. Why should Herodotus have subtracted these two items from what he believed to be the correct total for the infantry? Why should he not have added them to it? Further, Herodotus insists that Hydarnes' force stood outside the army organization under the six generals and twenty-nine archontes; if he believed that the latter commanded 60,000 men each, he could not have associated Hydarnes with them, still less have assigned to him a force of 60,000. Finally, Herodotus gives his figures for the infantry and cavalry without misgivings, as though he had received them from what he believed to be a reliable tradition, whereas his 300,000 for Xerxes' European troops is clearly given as his own estimate (vii. 185. 2); so also the 20,000 for the charioteers and camel corps (vii. 184. 4).

The second cardinal postulate of Munro's reconstruction is that each Persian army corps numbered 60,000 men. This is based on the figures given by Herodotus for the commands of Artabazos and Tigranes (viii. 126. 1, ix. 96. 2), but why should these Herodotean figures be regarded as any more reliable than those which Munro rejects? Tigranes is archon of the Medes in vii. 62 and was therefore on Munro's hypothesis originally a myriarch; Herodotus' assertion that his force at Mykale numbered 60,000 is irreconcilable with his account of the battle, which shows that he cannot have had more than a nominal ten thousand; see above, p. 254. Even more hazardous is Munro's assumption (cf. *C.A.H.* iv. 272 and n. 2) that only three distinct commands can be detected in the operations on land, those of Mardonios, Artabazos, and Tigranes. Munro makes much of the tripartite division of Xerxes' infantry during the advance from Doriskos to Akanthos, but in Herodotus' description of this (vii. 121. 2–3) we meet again all the six generals who had been mentioned earlier (vii. 82). It is true that three of the six are only mentioned in these two passages, but of the other three (Mardonios, Masistes, and Tritantaichmes) Tritantaichmes occurs again in viii. 26. 2; some manuscripts there read Τιγράνης, which Munro and Macan accept, but there is good manuscript authority for the reading Τριτανταίχμης, which is preferred by Hude and Legrand and defended by Powell (edition, p. 88). Munro's final argument to show that Xerxes was accompanied to Greece by only three of the six army corps is equally unsatisfactory. Herodotus indeed mentions only three hipparchs in vii. 88, but there is no need to follow Munro in regarding them as myriarchs commanding 10,000 men each; the size of their commands was presumably decided by the size of the army of invasion.

If attempts to deduce the size of Xerxes' army from its organization are unacceptable, what is left? Some German scholars, notably Delbrück, have applied to this problem the method of criticism called *Sachkritik*, a criticism based on the 'realities' or 'facts', the facts in this sphere being considerations of time, space, and supply. This approach has been unduly discredited by the extravagances of some of its exponents, for it has real value. Its weakness is that its results are mainly negative; it can show the practical impossibilities involved in the Herodotean figures, but the estimates with which it claims to replace them are often vitiated by faulty arguments, such as Delbrück's famous contention that because a Prussian army corps of 30,000 men on the march was anything from 9 to 15 miles long, a force of 30,000 Persians on the march must have been as long (cf. Hauvette, 311 f.). The subjective element in such calculations is shown by the variations in the estimates given by Delbrück at different times for the size of the Persian army in 480 and in 479.

An interesting example of the use of *Sachkritik* to fix a maximum for Xerxes' army in 480 is provided in an article by Maurice (*J.H.S.* i, 1930, 210–35). Maurice argued that the problem of water-supply would be crucial for the army in the 134 miles of its advance, estimated by him (op. cit. 213) at not less than seven marches, from the river Skamandros to Doriskos, and after a thorough examination of the supplies of water now available in this region he calculated that the Persian host numbered not more than 210,000, of whom 60,000 were non-combatants. On practical grounds this total may be accepted as a reasonable *maximum*, although the proportion of non-combatants seems too small, but there are obvious weak links in the chain of proof. Climatic changes may have diminished the supplies of water available in this part of the route, and it is possible (cf. Macan, ii. 156) that a considerable part of the land forces may have been conveyed by sea from Asia to Doriskos. Maurice admits (op. cit. 234) that a larger force could have been moved if the march had been made by successive bodies of troops moving at sufficient intervals of time to enable the rivers Skamandros and Melas to recover from the drain put on them, but rejects this solution on the ground that 'such a movement would have taken a very long time'. He puts too much trust here in Herodotus' statement (vii. 56. 1) that the crossing of the Hellespont was completed in 'seven days and seven nights'; this estimate is not only suspicious in itself but at variance with the later statement (viii. 51. 1) made in a serious chronological context, that the Persians spent a month on the crossing into Europe (cf. Macan, i. 2. 436).

Beloch (72 f.) starts with the reasonable assumption that Mardonios' army at Plataia was not much larger than the Greek (which Beloch estimates at 25,000 hoplites and as many light-armed troops) and stresses the fact that after the battle Artabazos led 40,000 survivors back to Asia. Like Meyer (377 n.), Beloch holds that the army which crossed the Hellespont was not much larger (he suggests about

60,000 Asiatic troops), but though this supposition may indeed be correct it cannot be proved, for the ancient evidence is against it; the tradition that Xerxes took the bulk of his army back to Asia, leaving only a body of picked troops with Mardonios, was established as early as 472 (Aeschylus, *Persai* 803 f.; see above, p. 267). It might be argued in support of this tradition that the defeat at Salamis, by depriving the Persians of the command of the sea, must have made the provisioning of their troops much more difficult and so compelled them to cut down radically the size of their army, but the value of this argument depends on what the numbers of the army were at the start; if they were not excessive, then the loss of sea-borne supplies need not have made much difference.

A modern historian, unless he takes refuge in complete scepticism, can only fall back on his own estimate of probability. If the Asiatic troops of Mardonios in 479 numbered 50,000 to 60,000 men, is it conceivable that the fighting-men who crossed the Hellespont a year earlier were more than twice as many? Some English scholars estimate Xerxes' army in 480 at a minimum of 180,000 men, but to the present writer even this figure seems too high, and he would prefer Meyer's conclusion that the Asiatic troops in 480 should not be estimated at more than a maximum of 100,000 men 'together with a large body of attendants, probably more numerous than the fighting men' (Meyer, 375, ll. 2–5). Perhaps, as Tarn suggested (*J.H.S.* xxviii, 1908, p. 208, n. 27), the six generals in Herodotus had 10,000 troops each; in addition to these there would be the Immortals under Hydarnes, making a total of 70,000 Asiatic infantry, with a cavalry force which may be estimated at 9,000. This army of approximately 80,000 men, which could be supplemented by contingents from Thrace and Macedonia, would have been large enough to overcome any resistance which the Greeks could offer on land in 480 (when so many men were needed for the fleet), and the provisioning of a larger force (swollen by an equal number of non-combatants) would probably have imposed an intolerable strain on the organization of the Persian Empire.

APPENDIX II

The site of Trachis

HERODOTUS describes the approach to Thermopylai from Achaia along the shore of the Malian Gulf 'from the point of view of a traveller coming from Achaia' (vii. 198. 2) and it is a reasonable conjecture (Grundy, 279) that when he visited Thermopylai he came to it from Northern Greece across the Spercheios. He marks the first stages on the route by the rivers which it crossed; about 20 stades from the Spercheios is the Dyras, and 20 stades farther on is the Melas. Five stades beyond the Melas is Trachis (vii. 199. The town was apparently situated on or near the road; cf. Grundy, 282). Herodotus adds that here, at Trachis, is the widest part of the land between the mountains and the sea, for the plain amounts to 22,000 plethra; Rawlinson's assumption that this figure is an error for 22 plethra (2,200 Greek feet or less than half a mile) makes the breadth of the plain too narrow, but the usual explanation that by plethra Herodotus meant the square measure (10,000 square feet for each plethron) is not entirely satisfactory (Harmening in *A.S.* 29, equating Herodotus' figure in square measure with 2,167 hectares or roughly 22 square kilometres, sees in it the area of the Trachinian plain). After a reference to the mountains which surround the territory of Trachis on the land side Herodotus says that they are pierced *south of Trachis* by a gorge through which the Asopos flows, but though his hypothetical traveller seems to continue his journey across the Asopos below the mouth of the gorge to the river Phoinix, described as 15 stades from the Pass of Thermopylai (200. 1), Herodotus gives no indication of the distance from Trachis to the Asopos or of that from the Asopos to the Phoinix.

As Trachis has been identified by Leake, Munro, and others with the later Herakleia, it is necessary to cite the ancient evidence bearing on the location of Herakleia. Thucydides, relating how the Spartans in 426 founded a colony in this region at the request of the Trachinians and Dorians (both hard pressed in raids by the neighbouring Oitaioi), says that 'they set to work and built afresh the walls of the city, which received the name of Herakleia and is situated about 40 stades from Thermopylai and 20 from the sea' (iii. 92. 6; Jowett's translation, adapted). Livy, in connexion with the defence of Herakleia by the Aitolians against the Romans in 191, describes it as situated 'in radicibus Oetae montis', and continues:

'ipsa in campo, arcem imminentem loco alto et undique praecipiti
habet' (xxxvi. 22. 5). This passage shows that in 191 Herakleia was
composed of a citadel and a lower town; Munro noted (*J.H.S.* xxii,
1902, 313) that the latter was strong enough to defy the Roman
besiegers for twenty-six days (compare Livy xxxvi. 22–24, especially
23. 6). Livy's statement (xxxvi. 22. 8) that when the Romans delivered an assault one party attacked 'ab altero amniculo quem
Melana vocant' does not mean that Herakleia extended right up to
the Melas, which is here simply an indication of direction. Finally,
Strabo speaks of Herakleia as 'what was formerly called Trachis, a
Spartan foundation', and adds that it is distant about 6 stades from
the ancient Trachis (ix. 4. 13 = p. 428).

There is now general agreement that the citadel of Herakleia
was the flat-topped hill which overlooks the lower end of the Asopos
gorge on the west (photograph in Stählin, *Das hellenische Thessalien*,
Plate XII. 1, facing p. 224); this site, now called Sideroporto, is described by Grundy (note on p. 264) as 'in an exceedingly inaccessible
position, in the angle, as it were, between the Asopos ravine and the
line of the Trachinian cliffs'. In the same note Grundy observed that
in and after 279 'an effective defence of Oeta included the occupation
of Heraklea as well as of Thermopylae' and concluded that the
reason for this precaution must have been that Herakleia commanded
the way through the Asopos gorge. This suggested to Munro the
hypothesis that Sideroporto (in which he saw the citadel of Trachis)
must have been occupied by the Greeks in 480 to bar to the Persians
the route through the gorge southwards into Doris; he assumed the
existence in 480 of a lower town below this citadel situated on the
Thermopylai road (op. cit. 313 and n. 31). Although this hypothesis
stands or falls with Munro's view that the sites of Trachis and Herakleia were practically identical, it is possible to maintain their identity
while rejecting Munro's supposition that Sideroporto was held by
the Greeks in 480 (so Labarbe in *B.C.H.* lxxviii, 1954, 4–5, n. 5).
The Trachis of Béquignon (*La Vallée du Spercheios*, 244–9), whose
description is not easy to follow, seems to be in the main identical
with Munro's; it is not clear whether the ravine which he calls
Skliphoméli is identical with the Skalorema of the plan in Stählin
(*H.T.* 206). His statement on p. 257 that the distance of his site from
the Melas agrees with Herodotus' figure seems to demand more
justification than he has seen fit to give.

Two other sites suggested for Trachis can be dismissed briefly.
One is an isolated flat-topped mountain situated on the left (west)
bank of the Asopos in the valley above (i.e. south of) the gorge. This
site, called the Κάστρο ῾Ωρηᾶς or Kastro Horaias, is well described by
Béquignon (260f., with photograph on Plate XI), though he wrongly

implies that Grundy identified it with Trachis (261, n. 6; the same mistake is made by Stählin in his article on Trachis in *R.-E.* vi A. 2. 1864). This identification, quite irreconcilable with the data in Herodotus, was due to Lolling and passed from him into the pages of Baedeker (still in the English edition of 1909, p. 197). Grundy (264 n.) conjectured that the Kastro was the stronghold of the Oitaioi mentioned by Thucydides (iii. 92. 2), Stählin (*H.T.* 210 f.) that it was the site of Homilai, a place which appears in later inscriptions and in Ptolemy.

Stählin's own site for Trachis, in the plain 6 stades due north of Sideroporto (*H.T.* 208 and *R.-E.* vi A. 2. 1863 f.), is inferred from a combination of Strabo's evidence with the statement of Herodotus (199) that the Asopos gorge was *south* of Trachis. Stählin failed to observe that in the chapter (176) in which Herodotus describes the pass of Thermopylai his orientation is 90 degrees out; as Grundy says (277), Herodotus evidently wrote under the impression that the road ran through the pass from north to south. It is natural to suppose that he was still under this impression when he placed the Asopos gorge south of Trachis and that in reality it lay east of Trachis or only slightly south of east (cf. Grundy, 282: 'after passing the Melas he must have been going nearly due east'). Béquignon (op. cit. 256 f.; cf. Harmening in *A.S.* 24) also insists that Herodotus' orientation is faulty in c. 199 and that Trachis must be placed west of the gorge; he notes (244) that excavations on Stählin's site in 1932 failed to provide any support for his view.

The evidence of Strabo is not easily reconcilable with that of Herodotus, and it is far from certain that his 'ancient Trachis', six stades from Herakleia, occupied the same position as the Trachis of Herodotus. Grundy (283 f.) suggested that in 426 the population of Trachis either removed itself or was removed to the neighbourhood of Herakleia for greater protection. Munro claimed that by Strabo's time 'Herakleia had completely retreated up the hill' and that 'the ruins of the lower town, six stades below, were exclusively known as Trachis' (op. cit. 313, n. 31).

Thucydides has been assumed by Munro and others to state that Herakleia was founded in 426 on the same site as Trachis, and the first part of his account of the foundation, quoted above, might mean that new (possibly enlarged or stronger) fortifications were erected on the old site and the name changed, but as Gomme observes in his note on this passage (*Commentary on Thucydides*, ii. 395) the careful geographical details that follow suggest a change of site; moreover, Grundy's view that Herakleia must have been founded on a different site from Trachis is proved by the evidence of Herodotus, to which we can now turn.

The distances on the road given by him (vii. 198. 2 and 199)
cannot indeed be pressed rigorously, for the unit of measurement
seems to be an approximate one, 10 stades, just as we say 'about a
mile', or 5 stades, 'about half a mile'. These units can be combined
or multiplied, but as the one verifiable datum, the distance of
15 stades from the river Phoinix to Thermopylai, is said to be 'very
fairly correct' (Grundy, 280) the others also may be presumed to be
close approximations, including the 5 stades reckoned for the distance between the river Melas and Trachis (about 1,000 yards; cf.
note of HW i. 242 f. on Hdt. ii. 149. 3). As the Herodotean Dyras is
agreed to be the modern Gourgo-potamo the Melas must be one of
the streams now called Mavraneria (cf. Grundy, 278). There appear
to be two of these. One of them, named Mavropotamos by Stählin
in *H.T.* 196, was there said by him to rise near Katodyovouna and
enter the plain at Vardataes; he added that it received a tributary,
the Mavroneri (called Mavronero by some), flowing from the
Trachinian cliffs. He repeated this view in 1931 (article 'Melas
No. 14' in *R.-E.* xv. 1. 439) but three years later he argued that the
Melas, now apparently identified with the Mavroneri tributary,
reached the coast in 480 below its junction with the Xerias, which,
as his map shows, must be the stream which he had earlier named
Mavropotamos, on the ground that unless Herodotus had crossed
them below their point of union he must have mentioned the Xerias
(*R.-E.* v A. 2. 2404).

Béquignon also identifies (op. cit. 64) Stählin's Mavroneri with
the Melas; he says that it does not dry up in the summer but receives
on the north side a little torrent, the Xerias, which does run dry in the
hot weather. It is hard to believe, however, that the road from Achaia
to Thermopylai went so far out into the plain in 480 as a point below
the present junction of the Xerias and Mavronero (cf. Harmening
in *A.S.* 26), and the distance from the Dyras to the Melas given by
Herodotus appears, to judge from the maps, to show that the river
which he called the Melas must be identical with the modern Xerias
(so rightly Gomme, op. cit. ii. 396).

Grundy unfortunately became entangled in a polemic against
Leake at this point and failed to state explicitly which branch of the
Mavraneria he equated with the Melas of Herodotus, but it can be
inferred from his statements on p. 283 that it must have been the
Xerias. Leake had held (cf. Grundy, 282) that Trachis coincided
with the lower town of the later Herakleia. Grundy in reply said that
'my very strong impression is that Leake has placed the Herodotean
Trachis several miles east of its true site'. Grundy himself (p. 283)
identified the Trachis of Herodotus with 'the remains on the steep,
flat-topped hill three miles west of Sideroporto, near the hamlet of

Konvelo'. Béquignon, having carelessly mixed up Grundy's 'Konvelo' with the hamlet of Kouvelo (which is close to the Kastro Horaias) brushes aside Grundy's site without further examination. Harmening complains (*A.S.* 25 and n. 2) that he could not find Grundy's Konvelo on a modern map, and it is certainly unfortunate that Grundy did not indicate the location of his site more closely. If, however, we hold fast to the identification of Herodotus' Melas with the Xerias, it follows that the town of Trachis, situated only 1,000 yards or so farther along the road, cannot possibly be identical with the lower town of Herakleia, and so all inferences based on the supposed identity of site must be rejected.

APPENDIX III

The Anopaia path

[In this Appendix Stählin's article on Thermopylai in *R.-E.* v A. 2 is referred to as Stählin, his book *Das hellenische Thessalien* as *H.T.*]

HERODOTUS' account of the path used by Hydarnes' force in its turning movement is as follows (c. 216; *all references to Book VII unless otherwise stated*): the path begins from the Asopos river which flows through the gorge (i.e. that previously mentioned in c. 199) and is named Anopaia like the mountain across which it goes; the path stretches along the ridge of the mountain (for ῥάχις in this sense cf. iii. 54. 2) and ends at Alpenos, the first place in Lokris on the side of the Malians, and the stone called Μελάμπυγος (so the manuscripts; some emend to Μελαμπύγου) and the seats of the Kerkopes. In the preceding chapter Herodotus has explained that the path was discovered by the local inhabitants, the Malians, and that by guiding Thessalian invaders along it in an earlier war they had enabled them to turn the position of the Phokians, who were defending the main pass.

The Persians sent by Xerxes to carry out the turning movement are described (215) as 'Hydarnes and those under his command', which presumably means the Immortals, but Herodotus nowhere says explicitly that all the 10,000 Immortals accompanied Hydarnes on this occasion. The Persians left their camp 'at the time of the lighting of lamps' (215). After describing the path Herodotus says that the Persians, having crossed the Asopos, made their way along the path all through the night, having on their right hand the mountains of the Oitaioi and on their left those of the Trachinians (217. 1). At dawn they arrived 'at the summit of the mountain', where 1,000 Phokian hoplites were posted (cf. 212. 2), protecting their own land and guarding the path, having volunteered to Leonidas for this service. It is clear that by the words ἐπ' ἀκρωτηρίῳ τοῦ ὄρεος Herodotus must mean the highest point of the path, not of the mountain, since a little later he describes (218. 3) how the Phokians fled before the Persians to the peak (κόρυμβος) of the mountain. The Phokians had received warning of their approach from the rustling under their feet of the leaves which had fallen from the oak-trees covering this part of the mountain (218. 1). After routing the Phokians Hydarnes and his force began the descent κατὰ τάχος (218. 3); this descent was shorter and the distance to be covered much less than the way round and the ascent (223. 1). Xerxes, acting on the previous instructions of Ephialtes, deferred his frontal attack on the main Greek force 'until the hour when the market place fills' (see above, p. 147, n. 1) but it was not until some time had elapsed that Hydarnes and his men arrived on the scene and decided the issue of the battle.

Modern scholars who have tried to trace the line of the Anopaia have disagreed profoundly in their results, whether they have inspected the terrain for themselves or have relied on the reports of travellers; this is not surprising, for no hypothesis has succeeded in finding a place for all the data given by Herodotus, and every modern writer naturally tends to stress those bits of the ancient evidence which suit him and to dismiss the rest. Grundy (note on pp. 299 f.) supposes that when Herodotus said that the path 'began from the river Asopos which flows through the gorge' he meant that the path began with an ascent of the gorge, and Stählin claims (2416) that the careful description of the gorge in c. 199 is only explicable if it had a part to play in the story. Such arguments are decisive only for those who wish to be convinced. Herodotus, like all travellers who have visited Thermopylai, was impressed by the sight of the Asopos gorge, and if he had clearly realized that the path began by an ascent of the gorge to its southern exit on the uplands near the modern Eleutherochori, surely he could easily have conveyed this to his readers. He had certainly traversed the coastal road through the pass of Thermopylai, but his account of the Anopaia path must have been derived from others.

Attempts have been made to find a short cut to the solution of the problem. Typical of these is Munro's hypothesis (*J.H.S.* xxii, 1902, 313) that Trachis, on his view identical with the later Herakleia, was garrisoned by the Greeks and so blocked the entrance to the gorge. Munro himself used his hypothesis to prove that Hydarnes' force must have reached the southern exit of the gorge by a detour to the west, but it has also been used by Pritchett (*A.J. Arch.* lxii, 1958, 205 A) to support the view that the Persians must have crossed the Asopos in the plain, below its *northern* exit from the gorge; both arguments are invalid if the identification of Trachis with Herakleia is mistaken (see above, Appendix II). Nothing is gained by an appeal to the testimony of Pausanias, who in x. 22. 8 speaks of two paths through the mountains of Oita, the second of which, 'easier for the march of an army, led through the territory of the Ainianes, and was the path which enabled Hydarnes to attack Leonidas and the Greeks in the rear'. This passage is unworthy of the attention lavished on it and has rightly been scouted by Burn (in *Studies presented to D. M. Robinson*, i. 487; Pritchett's endeavours to make something of it are wasted labour). Although Stählin has inferred from it (*H.T.* 226) that the valley of Dyovouna belonged to Ainis in the third century B.C., it is in the highest degree unlikely that this passage preserves any independent testimony about Hydarnes' route, and it may be merely a careless inference from Herodotus' description of the line of march in 217. 1; certainly the path cannot have passed 'through' the land of the Ainianes.

Some have sought to justify their conclusions by elaborate calculations of the time taken by the Persians for the ascent, but these depend on two factors, both of which are uncertain, the size of the Persian force and the season of the year. Beloch (ii². 2. 48) places the fighting at Thermopylai in late July, and his view is accepted without discussion by Stählin (2416; so also L. and F. Harmening in A.S. 51) and Grundy (op. cit. 304), who allow 9 hours for the ascent from nightfall to dawn, from 7.30 p.m. to 4.30 a.m. Busolt's date for the march, near the end of August (see below, pp. 452 f.) is perhaps more probable and would allow another hour for the ascent. If Hydarnes really was accompanied by all the 10,000 Immortals, his rate of progress would be slowed down considerably, and those who believe that he was, if they accept the earlier date, must identify the Anopaia with one of the shorter and easier modern routes. So Pritchett, accepting the arguments of Labarbe (see below, pp. 449 f.) that the last battle at Thermopylai was fought on 3 or 4 August, insists (op. cit. 203 B) that the Anopaia must have been a broad track. But even if Herodotus is taken to imply that Hydarnes had all his Immortals with him, the implication may be part of the apologia offered later by the Phokians for their failure (that their small force had been attacked by all the élite of the Persian army) and the force actually sent with Hydarnes may have numbered not more than 2,000.

The time argument, however, may be used to rule out the route suggested by Munro (followed by Myres, *Herodotus*, 248 and 250). It is true that this route was apparently used by the Gauls under Brennus in 279, but they were able to carry out their turning movement in the daytime under cover of a mist which concealed their approach from the Greek outposts on the heights (Pausanias x. 22. 10–11). The route goes up from the plain by the valley of the river Melas past the modern villages of Vardataes (or Vardhátes; cf. Burn, op. cit. 487) and Dyovouna. Stählin (*H.T.* 204 and n. 1) judges the time from Dyovouna to Eleutherochori (which is some distance beyond the crossing of the Asopos) at four hours, which seems slower than the three hours' easy walking taken by Mr. Jerome Farrell from Mustapha Bey to the crossing of the Asopos (quoted by Munro in *C.A.H.* iv. 295, n. 1; cf. Farrell in *C.R.* xxiv, 1910, 116 f.). But though a single wayfarer might traverse this part of the route in three hours during the daytime, Hydarnes' force, even if it numbered no more than 2,000 men, must have taken at least half as long again to do it in the dark (cf. also the criticisms of Burn, 487). Hence Munro was compelled to place the scene of Hydarnes' encounter with the Phokians at the Panagia monastery, considerably to the west (about two hours' journey; cf. Stählin, loc. cit.) of the only site which agrees with Herodotus' statement that the encounter took place at the summit of the path.

Grundy, accepting Herodotus' evidence on this point, places the Phokians on the saddle (near the site of the deserted village of Old Drakospilia) which connects the outlying peak of Sástano (or Sastáni; see above, p. 133, n. 1) with the central chain of Saromata, the ancient Kallidromos. Sástano is precipitous on its north and west sides, and between it and Lithitza, the other outlying peak of Saromata to the south-west, is interposed the deep gorge called by Grundy 'the Great Ravine', which extends almost to the central chain. Hence any force desiring to turn the position of defenders in the pass below without a long circuit into Doris and Phokis is compelled to make its way to the head of this ravine and across the saddle in order to reach the easier valleys which come down to the coast east of Sástano (Stählin, 2402) and in fact the divergent versions of the Anopaia all concur at this point of the route. As every route hitherto suggested must pass this point, and as the descent to Alpenoi certainly begins here (on every view except that of Leake), it seems reasonable to conclude with Leake, Grundy, and Kromayer that the Phokian position was here. This conclusion is strongly supported by Herodotus, for the Phokians were posted at the summit of the path, and as soon as the Persians had routed them they began the descent (217. 1 and 218. 3); the second of these statements follows naturally from the first, and the description of the descent in 223. 1 is only true if it started at the saddle.

The one strong argument against this view is Herodotus' reference (218. 1) to the numerous oak-trees near the Phokian position. There are now no oak-trees near the Saddle (perhaps there never were) but oak-trees are found near the Panagia monastery (Grundy, 302, cited by Munro, 314) and in the Nevropolis valley (Pritchett, op. cit. 210A; cf. his admirable photograph of them on Plate 55, fig. 7). This is undeniably a serious difficulty, but the picturesque detail in Herodotus about the rustling of the oak-leaves seems to the present writer less dependable than the repeated assertion that the brush with the Phokians occurred at the top of the path just before the descent. Perhaps the oak-leaves are 'derived from a topographical rather than a historical source' (a phrase used by Munro in another connexion; C.A.H. iv. 296).

Munro also appealed to the passage in Herodotus (217. 2) which describes the Phokians as 'protecting their own country and guarding the path'. As he assumed the existence in 480 of a route which started from the plain at a point east of the northern exit of the Asopos gorge and crossed the mountains in a southerly direction (more or less on the line of the modern high road) to the upper Kephisos valley, he decided that it must have been protected by the Phokians against any enemy attempt to use it and that therefore the Phokians must have been posted at or near the intersection of the Anopaia with this hypothetical road. There is, however, nothing to prove the existence in 480 of this road (as distinguished from the route up the Asopos gorge; see above, pp. 135 ff.) and the words of Herodotus on which Munro relies are compatible with the interpretation that the Phokians posted to guard the Anopaia were at the same time covering Phokis, which would be exposed to immediate invasion if the main Greek force was destroyed or forced to retreat by the success of an enemy turning movement along the Anopaia (the attempt of Pritchett, 210 A to use the phrase in support of the Nevropolis route is unconvincing).

The site of the Persian encampment, the starting-point of Hydarnes' march (215), was probably on the left or western bank of the Asopos below its exit from the gorge (Grundy, 293; cf. A.S. 27). From this it follows that the Immortals must have crossed to the right bank of the Asopos either below the northern or above the southern end of the Asopos gorge in order to reach the slopes of Kallidromos. There are now several routes by which the Sástano saddle can be reached from the northern exit of the gorge, but Herodotus might be taken to suggest that there was only one in 480. Grundy, 301 pointed out that in the neighbourhood of the Panagia monastery the monks had caused new paths to be constructed; this argument was turned against Grundy by Burn (op. cit. 482), who argued that the paths used by Grundy serve mainly to connect the Panagia with the Old Drakospilia chapel and Eleutherochori and that without the monastery and chapel they would not exist, but how can such dogmatism be justified? There is evidence for steady deforestation of the northern slopes of Kallidromos (cf. Pritchett, 205, n. 22), but it is impossible to be sure that they were so thickly wooded in 480 as to rule out the existence at that date of any particular track up the slopes situated east of the Asopos gorge.

Thomas Gordon, a Scotsman who reached the rank of Major-General in the Greek army (cf. D.N.B. viii, 230 ff.), described in 1838 a route starting from what is now the village of Damasta (the former Old and New Damasta have been replaced by a single village at the foot of the Damasta spur; cf. Pritchett, 205, n. 20) up a slope just west of the Damasta spur and past the spring of Chalkomata onwards to Eleutherochori (Pritchett, 205, n. 23 points out that the modern village is situated at the place marked Palaio-Eleutherochori on most maps, about one kilometre east of the modern Lamia–Athens high road). Kromayer argued that the first part of this route was used by Marcus Cato in 191 when the force under his command was sent to turn Thermopylai. His object was to reach the route followed by Hydarnes in 480 (on which Kromayer accepts Grundy's view) but as the Aitolians had blocked the approach up the Asopos gorge by their occupation of Herakleia, the Romans had to discover a route to the east of the gorge which would strike into the path somewhere near the site of the Panagia (on Cato's probable route see Kromayer in *A.S.* ii. 142 and n. 2). Kromayer himself descended the route downhill from the Panagia to the plain and affirms that it would have offered no difficulty in 191 if the forest had already been cleared or at least had had a way made through it, but he does not believe that it was used by Ephialtes, and he explains Ephialtes' choice of the Asopos-gorge route by the hypothesis that the slopes above Damasta were still covered by impenetrable forest in 480; so also Stählin (2421), who explains that the Romans, unlike the Gauls, were not forced to go round by the Dyovouna route because since 279 the slopes above Damasta had been made more accessible.

Kromayer's argument is really circular; unless it can be proved that Ephialtes did not use the Chalkomata route there is no need to suppose that it was impracticable in 480. The advocates of the view that the Nevropolis valley was used for the middle part of the march naturally make Hydarnes' force begin by ascending the Damasta slope, for the Persians must complete the first stage, to Eleutherochori, as quickly as possible in order to have time for the long detour to the south by the Nevropolis valley. Those who suppose that the Anopaia in the first part of its course must have ascended the Damasta slope past the Chalkomata spring all agree that the words τὸν Ἀσωπὸν διαβάντες at the start of Herodotus' account of Hydarnes' march (217. 1) are conclusive proof that the Persians must have crossed the Asopos below its exit from the gorge (Pritchett, 206 A; cf. *A.S.* 51), but Herodotus' reference to the Asopos may mean (Stählin, 2417) that the Anopaia path in the strict sense began at the point, just south of the place where the river enters the gorge, where the track branched off from the north–south Asopos-gorge route which goes on into Doris.

Behind the Damasta slope rises the peak of Lithitza (1,263 metres high) separated from Sástano by the Great Ravine to the north-east and from the main chain of Saromata to the south by an

extraordinary valley (well described by Burn, 483) near the summit
of the mountains, a valley formed by a constituent stream of the
Asopos which flows from east to west, and providing a natural line
of communication from Eleutherochori to Old Drakospilia and
beyond. Gordon's hypothesis that the Anopaia went through this
valley, and therefore south of Lithitza, has recently been revived by
Burn and Pritchett. The problem whether the Persians on the eastward part of their march went along the north or the south side of
Lithitza cannot be decided by reference to Herodotus' statement that
in this stage they had the mountains of the Trachinians on their left
and those of the Oitaioi on their right, for although the territory of
Trachis must have continued to the east of the Asopos along the coast
until it met the territory of Lokrian Alpenoi (c. 216; see above, p. 132,
n. 4) we do not know how far it extended into the mountains to the
south, and although Thucydides (iii. 92. 2) mentions Oitaioi as
neighbours of the Trachinians in 426 it is little more than a convenient assumption that their territory extended beyond the east of
Eleutherochori to include the Nevropolis valley and the peak of
Lithitza which rises on the north side of the valley (an assumption
made by Harmening in *A.S.* 30 f., citing in 30, n. 3 Strabo ix. 4.
10, p. 427, who says there that the Northern Lokrians are contiguous
to 'the Ainianes who hold Oita', but the date and relevance of this
evidence are both doubtful). Herodotus would doubtless have been
surprised at the emphasis laid on this part of his testimony, which is,
perhaps wisely, ignored by Grundy; if it is to be taken strictly it
suggests that the Persian march from the crossing of the Asopos
until dawn (cf. ἐπορεύοντο πᾶσαν τὴν νύκτα in 217. 1) was predomi-
nantly in a west to east direction, but it has been twisted to suit most
of the proposed solutions.

As the Nevropolis-valley route involves a long detour to the south,
those who support it have to locate the encounter with the Phokians
at the eastern exit from the valley, on a saddle 1,200 metres high
(described by Stählin, 2415 f.) between two peaks of Lithitza; from
this point the path turns in a northerly direction to Old Drakospilia
and the Sástano saddle. The recent advocates of this route do not
describe this section of it clearly, but presumably it goes downhill for
some time before rising again to the Sástano saddle. It is therefore,
like Munro's route, open to the objection that it disregards the clear
indications in the Herodotean account placing the encounter with
the Phokians at a point which is not only the highest point on the
Anopaia but also the beginning of the descent, a descent shorter and
quicker than the ascent. The claim that Herodotus' description of
the Anopaia as κατὰ ῥάχιν τοῦ ὄρεος (216) is applicable only to the
Nevropolis route has been refuted by Myres (cf. his letter to Burn

quoted in Burn, 489), who pointed out that the first part at least of
that route was transverse to the ὄρος, not κατὰ ῥάχιν.

The further objection made by Myres to the first part of Burn's
route, that if the Persians crossed the Asopos below the gorge in the
plain they could not have escaped the notice of enemy scouts
stationed in front of the main Greek position, had been anticipated
by Stählin, who pointed out (2416) that the Persians would have
needed torches because they had started after nightfall, and if they
had gone up the Damasta slope with torches in their hands they
would have been observed by the Greeks, whereas the whole purpose
of their night march was to take the Greeks by surprise. Harmening
(A.S. 53) implies that Persians ascending by the Damasta route,
even with torches, would not have been visible from the Greek
position, but as Stählin has studied the problem on the spot his argument seems decisive, and it is curious that Pritchett makes no attempt to meet it. If it is sound, it also disposes of the hypothesis
(A.S. 49 f.) that the Persians went up the Damasta slope as far as
the site of Old Damasta and somehow contrived to keep below the
slopes of Lithitza by skirting the Great Ravine until they reached
its head and joined Grundy's path below the Sástano saddle.

This process of elimination leaves us with Grundy's route, which,
leaving the Asopos south of the place where it enters the gorge,
goes up a side valley, rough and steep, to a place where it reaches the
limestone saddle between Eleutherochori and the Panagian monastery. It then descends the depression in which the monastery lies, and
from there climbs slowly upwards through the forest along the north
side of Lithitza, and so onwards round the upper part of the Great
Ravine to the site of Old Drakospilia and the Saddle; cf. the careful
description in Grundy, 301–3. This path has since been traversed
and described by Stählin (2416 f.), who estimates the distance from
the mouth of the Asopos Gorge to the Saddle at 15·2 kilometres and
the whole distance to Platanakos, near the site of Alpenoi, at just
under 20 kilometres (less than 12½ miles), whereas Grundy, 303
reckons the total distance to Alpenoi as not much less than 17 miles.
Stählin, 2418 allows 7 hours and 20 minutes for the march from the
present Asopos bridge (at the entrance to the gorge) to the Saddle;
this looks like an underestimate for a force of at least 2,000 men, but
the Persian vanguard might just have covered the distance in the
ten hours which would have been available if the march took place
near the end of August.

There are now two ways down from the Saddle to the coast.
The easier, 5 miles or more in length from the Saddle (cf. Grundy,
303), descends to a point on the road lying east of the East Gate of
the pass, near the site of Alpenoi, and must therefore be the route

intended by Herodotus; the other is a steep path which descends into the pass about midway between the Middle and the East Gate and is probably fairly recent (Grundy, 304 f.; cf. Kromayer in *A.S.* ii. 149, n. 2). The view of Stählin (op. cit. 2415) that these were alternative routes, both of which existed in 480 and were known to Herodotus, is improbable; the mention of the Μελάμπυγος λίθος (now identified with a curiously-shaped rock still visible; cf. Pritchett, 211 A) and the Κερκώπων ἕδραι is intended to confirm the reference to Alpenoi, not to indicate an alternative route.

Grundy's version of the route has sometimes been challenged on grounds which are themselves open to criticism. No proof is available that the approach to the Asopos gorge was closed by a Greek occupation of the hill Sideroporto, the citadel of the later Herakleia (see above, pp. 135 f.), nor do the words τὸν Ἀσωπὸν διαβάντες in 217. 1 prove that Hydarnes and his men must have crossed the Asopos below its exit from the gorge. Recent critics (cf. *A.S.* 52) stress the difficulties presented by Grundy's path and its unsuitability for the march of a large body of men. Pritchett (op. cit. 204 B) says that it took him an hour and a quarter (cf. Grundy, 301) to pass through the gorge in July, and that even then he was sometimes knee-deep in water (this part of the route is described by Grundy, 261). Pritchett also claims that the small valley from above the head of the gorge to the modern high road (Grundy, 301) is really 'a slight notch in a steep mountain side with an angle of at least 25 degrees' and the track up it so steep that he cannot believe that it could have been used by a force of any considerable numbers (he supposes that Hydarnes had all his 10,000 men with him); Stählin on the other hand says (2417, ll. 23–26) that the path is indeed steep but quite tolerable. Perhaps there is a strong subjective element in both judgements.

Stählin (2416) has tried to find further confirmation for Grundy's route in Herodotus' repeated statement (214. 1 and 3) that Hydarnes' march involved some sort of detour, but surely any turning movement must do that, and it is doubtful whether we can press the description (223. 1) of the first half of the Persian march as ἡ περίοδός τε καὶ ἀνάβασις. Strictly speaking it implies a circuit before the ascent proper began (so Myres against Burn in Burn, 489) and if stressed would certainly fit Munro's path best, though it would also be compatible with Grundy's route, but perhaps Herodotus only meant that the ascent involved a detour, and if he did, then the phrase cannot be used to exclude the ascent up the Damasta slope. Can lighted torches on this path be seen at night from advanced positions in front of the Middle Gate? If they can, the Damasta route must be ruled out, but if not, it is still a possibility for the first part of the Anopaia; it must, however, join Grundy's path before the Saddle if the Phokians really were stationed there. The present writer, faced with a conflict in the evidence of modern witnesses and in default of personal inspection of the ground, can only say that he finds the combined testimony of Leake, Grundy, and Stählin more impressive than that of their opponents. Their view that the Phokian guards were stationed on the Sástano saddle, over which all the routes suggested for the Anopaia must pass, is in full accord with the weightiest items in the evidence on this point obtainable from Herodotus.

APPENDIX IV

Thermopylai: the final problem

THE official version of the final catastrophe at Thermopylai (hence-forth referred to as 'the Legend'; see above, p. 124) was that Leonidas remained behind with his bodyguard of 300 Spartans to fight and to die as an act of *devotio*, performed in fulfilment of a Delphic oracle, which had foretold that Sparta could only be saved from destruction at the hands of the Persian invaders if one of her kings perished in battle. This story was accepted by Herodotus and repro-duced in his narrative (cf. Grundy, 307). He always has a weakness for oracles, and this one provided an explanation for an awkward fact, the departure of Sparta's Peloponnesian allies (and presumably the Lokrians as well) before the final combat; they had left because they had been sent away by Leonidas, who did not wish them to be involved in a hopeless struggle. But the explanation in turn suggests a fresh difficulty; if Leonidas was so anxious to save the lives of his other allies, why did he allow the Thebans and Thespians to remain with him to the end? The Legend insisted, very improbably, that the Thebans stayed against their will and were kept by Leonidas as hostages, but it could not account convincingly for the presence of the Thespians: 'they stayed very willingly, for they said that they would not depart and leave Leonidas and those with him, but they stayed behind and died with them' (vii. 222; Macaulay's trans-lation). It must be remembered that whereas the 300 Spartans who fell with Leonidas were only a fraction of the total number of Spar-tiatai, the 700 Thespians who gave their lives at Thermopylai were practically the whole hoplite force of their little state (see above, p. 117); this consideration constitutes a serious objection not only to the Legend but to some modern hypotheses which try to provide an alternative explanation for Leonidas' last stand.

Herodotus' whole-hearted acceptance of the Legend was disas-trous; in consequence of it he has failed to do justice to any other traditions still current in his time. As Macan has observed (i. 324 A, note on l. 8) the true narrative breaks down at the point where the Legend intervenes. But if we excise the legendary elements we are not left with a complete lacuna; some vestiges of another tradition survive. Herodotus, after describing the rout of the Phokians and the beginning of the descent from the Saddle by the Persians, should logically have told us at what stage the bad news reached the Greeks in the Middle Gate. His narrative at this point (vii. 219) is curiously vague. He says that the Greeks received three warnings of what was to happen, in the following order, (1) from the seer Megistias, (2) from Persian deserters, (3) from the 'day-watchers' hurrying down from the heights. The first warning evidently precedes the second, which reached the Greeks 'while it was still night', whereas the scouts began their run down the mountain 'when day was now dawning'. The seer is said to have predicted 'the death which was to come on them at dawn', a statement presumably derived from the epigram written on him later by his friend Simonides (vii. 228. 3). The deserters brought news of the Persian turning movement, but as they had come from the Persian camp and arrived before dawn they could only report the fact that Hydarnes' men had started and the purpose of their march; they could not know that it had succeeded. What then was the message brought from the heights by the day-watchers? Herodotus presumably did not know, for nothing else could explain his astonishing failure to tell us what it was.

In the next sentence (219. 2) we read: *thereupon* the Greeks deliberated and their opinions were divided, for some urged that they should not desert their post, while others opposed them. The word ἐνθαῦτα, which begins the sentence, must be temporal, and whatever Ephoros may have made of it (see below, p. 377) Herodotus clearly uses it to date the council of war after the arrival of the day-watchers and therefore some time after daybreak. As the function of the war council was merely advisory, the final decision should have rested with the commander-in-chief, but here we have yet another inexplicable omission in the narrative; Herodotus never tells us what Leonidas' final decision was. Instead he passes at once to the dispersal of the council (μετὰ τοῦτο διακριθέντες) and continues: 'then some went away and dispersed each to their several cities, while others of them were ready to stay with Leonidas.' At this point (vii. 220. 1) Herodotus begins with the alternative version given by the Legend, and concludes with an expression of his preference for this version, saying that he prefers to believe that Leonidas himself sent the allies away rather than that they disagreed with him and departed in such disorderly fashion (if οὕτω goes closely with ἀκόσμως, as Macaulay and Macan suppose; but it might mean 'under these circumstances' or 'after this difference of opinion'. Cf. οὕτω ἀπελαύνεσκον in vii. 119. 4). The word ἀκόσμως does not necessarily describe a panic flight, but presupposes a breakdown of military discipline; the allies in this tradition were guilty of insubordination when they retreated against the orders of their commander-in-chief. So the word is rightly rendered by Powell 'without command', and better still by Legrand 'au mépris de la discipline'. This version is here flatly opposed to the assertion in the Legend that the allies went away and departed *in obedience to Leonidas' orders* (vii. 222). Yet even in the middle of the chapter which reproduces the legend Herodotus seems to be subconsciously influenced by the unfavourable tradition when he says that Leonidas sent the allies away 'because he saw that they were not eager and were unwilling to fight to the end' (vii. 220. 2).

Unfortunately Herodotus, as a result of his preference for the legend, has failed to provide sufficient material for a reconstruction of the alternative version. That version, so discreditable to the Peloponnesian contingents, cannot have been current in any of the states to which they belonged. Nor can it have found favour at Sparta, for it diminished the glory conferred on Leonidas and his Three Hundred by the Legend and, whatever Spartan statesmen may have thought in private about the behaviour of their allies on this occasion, they would realize that nothing was to be gained by keeping alive the memory of the true facts. A version so discreditable to the mass of the Peloponnesians probably originated in one of the Central Greek states and may even have been current at Athens. It presumably approximates more closely to the truth than the other, but it is uncertain whether it supplied answers to the two vital questions ignored by Herodotus, (1) the content of the report brought by the day-watchers in vii. 219. 2, and (2) the nature of the decision taken by Leonidas after he had conferred with his war council. In the absence of any authentic tradition on either question all the attempts which have been made to solve the riddle of Thermopylai were doomed to failure from the start, and each of them is exposed to fatal objections.

The most plausible is the hypothesis of Beloch (*G.G.* ii.[2] 2. 91–105) that those who fell at Thermopylai on the third day perished because Leonidas did not receive news of the success of Hydarnes' turning movement until it was too late for an orderly retreat. Beloch showed by a careful analysis of Herodotus (vii. 219) that the precise content of the message brought down from the heights by the ἡμεροσκόποι is left obscure, and argued that as they started at dawn (διαφαινούσης ἤδη ἡμέρης) they could not have reported the final defeat of the Phokians, since day was already dawning when the Phokians were first sighted by the Persians with Hydarnes (217. 1). Hydarnes' troops first became visible from the coast road when they reached the open country by the modern village of Upper Drakospilia. Beloch assumes (op. cit. 102) that at this moment a panic broke out in the Greek army, like that in Antiochos' army under similar circumstances in 191 (Livy xxxvi. 19. 2–3), whereupon the Peloponnesians rushed away in disorderly flight (οὔτω ἀκόσμως οἴχεσθαι in 220. 4), while the Spartans and Thespians stood firm, thereby ensuring the undisturbed retreat of the rest (this view was adopted with some modifications by Munro in *J.H.S.* xxii, 1902, 317–18). Beloch's reconstruction, though plausible at first sight, may be challenged on the general ground that it is not really in harmony with the alternative version of which traces survive here and there in Herodotus; his interpretation of οὕτω ἀκόσμως οἴχεσθαι in particular is unlikely, since the phrase must be interpreted with reference to the account in 219. 2. Also Beloch has been unduly influenced by the parallel of Antiochos' defeat in 191. The Syrian army was then guarding the East Gate (Kromayer in *A.S.* ii. 146) and from there could see the Roman troops under Cato as soon as they appeared at the site of Upper Drakospilia, but Hydarnes' column when it reached the same point would surely not be visible to Leonidas and his men in the Middle Gate. Finally, whatever Herodotus may have thought, it is extremely improbable that none of Leonidas' scouts waited long enough on the heights to learn the final issue of the Phokian encounter with the Persians.

Bury (*B.S.A.* ii, 1895–6, 98 ff.) with some hesitation inclines to the view that the scouts who started soon after dawn not only confirmed the report of the deserters about the Persian turning movement but perhaps also brought the news that the Phokians had fled without offering any resistance. Bury assumes (p. 102) that Leonidas then decided to use against the Persians their own stratagem by arranging an attack against Hydarnes' column on two sides; the troops who were sent away by Leonidas had really been detached to take up a position to the east of the exit from the East Gate, near Alpenoi, and attack Hydarnes in the rear when he descended to the coast, while at the same time he would have to deal with the defenders in the East Gate of the pass (who could these defenders be? Bury does not explain. Leonidas' Spartiates and the Boiotians were in the Middle Gate, 1 mile and 3 furlongs from the East Gate; see Grundy, 290). Bury believes that the troops sent away by Leonidas were engaged with Hydarnes and that they were defeated with heavy losses, which help to make up the figure of 4,000 dead given as the total losses of the Greeks at Thermopylai in viii. 25. 2 (but that figure is usually explained as a misunderstanding of the epigram in vii. 228. 1): 'to those who fell in the pass are to be added those who were slain in fighting against the troops of Hydarnes outside the pass.'

Grundy adopted Bury's hypothesis while pruning it of its more improbable details. The 2,800 Peloponnesians (Grundy ignores the question of what had happened to the Lokrians) were indeed sent off to meet Hydarnes, but Leonidas, who is supposed to have received early news of the rout of the Phokians, had instructed them to make for the tangled forest just south of the site of Upper Drakospilia in order to hold up the Persian column there before it reached the site in force; for the march from the Middle Gate to Upper Drakospilia through the East Gate Grundy (p. 309) allows an hour and forty minutes. Grundy does not believe that these Peloponnesians ever came to grips with the Persians; they may have arrived too late, when the Persians were already in strength at Upper Drakospilia, or they may never have attempted to carry out their orders, continuing their march homewards when they had passed the East Gate. Grundy thinks the latter is the more probable alternative, on the ground that 'had there been a reasonable excuse for their conduct it would have survived in history', but the argument is not cogent; the true tradition of these events had been displaced by the Legend, which provided the Peloponnesians with a far better excuse for their withdrawal by ascribing it to a definite order from Leonidas.

The obvious objection to this hypothesis is that it is a reconstruction in the void; there is no ancient evidence for it at all. It is idle to claim (as Grundy does; op. cit. 308) that a vestige of it is preserved in the statement that it was Leonidas who detached the 2,800 from the force at the Middle Gate and sent them elsewhere, for this statement is closely bound up with the Legend and finds no place in the alternative tradition. Moreover, Grundy's version of the hypothesis, though more plausible in some respects than Bury's, raises serious difficulties of timing, and his attempts to deal with them (op. cit. 309) are half-hearted and do not convince. Hydarnes must have brought up enough men to the Saddle before he was able to rout the Phokians, but Grundy's allowance of three hours for the march from the Saddle to the site of Upper Drakospilia seems excessive, and it is hard to see why 'the rate of progress' should be the same in the daytime as at night, or why Grundy should assume that 'when they had arrived there it would take much time for the long straggling column to come up'; the allowance of time needed for this depends on whether the column numbered 10,000 or only 2,000 men (see above, p. 363). Three hours would appear to be ample time for the interval between the flight of the Phokians and the arrival of the Persians in force at Upper Drakospilia, and into this interval Grundy must compress the journey of Leonidas' scouts from the Saddle to the camp (a descent of over 3,000 feet), Leonidas' consideration of their report, and the execution of the necessary measures, as well as the hour and forty minutes needed for the march of the 2,800 from the camp to Upper Drakospilia.

Finally, it is definitely stated that Xerxes deferred his attack on the Middle Gate 'until the time when the market fills' (vii. 223. 1, presumably a tradition going back to Greeks in the Persian army). The precise time indicated by the phrase is not quite certain, but if the ἀγορᾶς διάλυσις of iii. 104. 2 is about 10 a.m. (so How and Wells, ad loc., though they differ in their note on ii. 173. 1) the attack began at or soon after 9 a.m. There is no need to doubt Herodotus' statement that Leonidas knew by then that his position was hopeless, for this is confirmed by the fact of his advance into the wider part of the pass (vii. 223. 2; see above, p. 147). Grundy seems in two minds whether to discard Herodotus' testimony here or not (third note on p. 311), but seeks to reconcile it with his theory by the assumption that Leonidas and those with him heard early from Alpenoi 'that the other division of the army had not succeeded in stopping, or possibly, had not attempted to stop Hydarnes'. Here again he seems to have given insufficient attention to the problem of timing.

Hence it is not surprising that what may be called 'the rearguard explanation' of the final problem has attracted more support. It is bluntly stated by Gomme as follows: 'he [Leonidas] found his position was turned, and it was his duty to extricate his army by a quick retreat. He at once sent back his troops; but a retreat, with the enemy in pursuit, does not consist only in a quick march with your back to the enemy. Leonidas had to keep some troops, and those the most reliable, to cover the retreat, to face the enemy. He chose that duty for himself, and his Spartans, Thebans and Thespians, running the risk, an unavoidable risk, of being cut off' (*J.H.S.* liii, 1933, 21, n. 19; cf. *Essays*, 198, n. 1). Gomme is certainly right to emphasize that the bulk of the Greek army could not retreat in safety unless it was protected from the pursuit of the Persian troops, especially the cavalry, by a rearguard which could hold up the enemy long enough to give it an adequate start (cf. Harmening in *A.S.* iv. 60 f.) but why does he speak of Leonidas 'running the risk, an unavoidable risk, of being cut off'? It was not a risk but an absolute certainty, if Leonidas had heard of the defeat of the Phokians, and if it was a certainty, then the defenders of 'the rearguard theory' are faced with the same difficulty as those who try to defend the substantial accuracy of the *devotio* story; why should the whole contingent of gallant little Thespiai have been chosen for a duty which meant certain death or capture, while Sparta's Peloponnesian allies were allowed to make their way home in safety?

Delbrück boldly asserted (*Kriegskunst*, 81, n. 3) that the Thespians, being the total hoplite force of their state, cannot have remained with Leonidas to the end; he suggested that they, with the Thebans, were overtaken on the retreat, and that thereupon the Thespians were cut down, while the Thebans surrendered. So Macan supposes that the Boiotian contingents remained 'perhaps well to the rear of

Leonidas and his Lakedaimonians, and acted as further cover to the army in retreat' (ii. 284; cf. i. 328 в). These suggestions cannot be accepted in face of Herodotus' explicit testimony (vii. 222, all the more impressive because so difficult to reconcile with the Legend) that the Thespians stayed with Leonidas to the end (cf. vii. 227), but they do at least show how serious is the difficulty which they are designed to overcome. And if the truth was as simple as the up-holders of 'the rearguard theory' claim, it is curious that no trace of it survived in the alternative (Central Greek?) tradition; if the Central Greeks had been deliberately chosen by Leonidas to share with his Spartiates in the forlorn hope, why did they not proclaim this honourable title to fame instead of incriminating those who fled?

The hypothesis of an orderly retreat encounters difficulties of timing, like Grundy's view. Harmening (cf. *A.S.* 60) ascribes to the very beginning of the third day, soon after midnight, the council of war mentioned by Herodotus in vii. 219 (see also Macan, i. 323 A: 'it is impossible to suppose that the deliberations in the Greek camp were postponed until the arrival of the scouts'), but Hero-dotus quite clearly dates the council after the arrival of the ἡμεροσκόποι, and therefore after dawn on the third day. It is true that Ephoros dates the council 'about midnight' and connects it with the arrival of the deserter Tyrrhastiadas (Diod. xi. 8. 5 and 9. 1; obviously Ephoros, because this deserter is said to be a citizen of Kyme!), but this is valueless against the contrary evidence of Hero-dotus and is simply intended to lead up to the preposterous invention of the night attack on the Persian camp. Why should the deserter's report produce such desperation in the Greek army? Harmening assures us (*A.S.* 61, n. 1) that after hearing from the deserters a de-tailed report about the size and composition of Hydarnes' force Leonidas could have no doubt that the turning movement was bound to succeed, and so arranged for the retreat of the main body to begin soon after daybreak; this argument is obviously weak and throws doubt on his whole case.

Others have held that it was imperative for Leonidas to detain the Persian army before Thermopylai a little longer for the sake of the fleet, and that for this reason he stayed behind with part of his army when resistance had become hopeless. Munro, supposing that he had been misled by the Phokians into thinking that the Persians were pursuing them into the valley of the Kephisos and so would not threaten his own retreat until next day at the earliest, suggested that Leonidas decided to hang on for one day more, because he 'must have known that the decisive battle was expected on that very day' (*J.H.S.* xxii, 1902, 318). But how could Leonidas know this? The final battle at Artemision was indeed fought on that day, but it happened then because a general engagement was forced on the Greeks by the Persians. Miltner argued in defence of Leonidas' action (*Klio*, xxviii, 1935, 228 ff., especially 237–41) that Leonidas knew by 9 a.m. on the third day that the position on land was hopeless and sent a messenger at once to the Greek fleet (cf. viii. 21), but the fleet might not be able to retire before nightfall if engaged by the enemy, and in that event could not get through the bottle-neck of the Euripos at Chalkis till midday on the next day. Miltner supposes that, if Leonidas had failed to hold up the enemy for a few hours, the Persian cavalry, guided by the Thessalians, might have made a dash for the Euripos (covering 120 kilometres in 15 or 16 hours) and so have blocked the narrow channel at Chalkis before the Greek ships could get through; Leonidas foresaw this danger and so decided that he must delay the Persian advance for a few hours more. But how does Miltner know that the Greeks had not occupied the bridgehead opposite Chalkis with some troops and left some ships in the Euripos to protect the communications of their fleet with the south at this vulnerable point? Moreover, it is hard to believe that the Persians were capable of a *Blitzkrieg* advance of this type, and still harder to believe that Leonidas could have anticipated it. Finally, Miltner is no more successful than his predecessors in dealing with the problem of the Thespians; if Leonidas knew that his force was doomed to defeat and destruction, why did he choose to involve the whole of the Thespian contingent in the same fate and allow all the Peloponnesian troops to depart?

In face of the breakdown of all modern explanations, the 'final problem' of Thermopylai is best left as an unsolved riddle; agnosticism is preferable to a pretence of knowledge. Herodotus' choice of what seemed to him the most credible account (vii. 220. 2; cf. i. 214 end) has here proved disastrous, but it may be doubted whether, if he had followed his alternative method of giving more than one λόγος, he could have discovered one which reported faithfully what happened at the start of the last day at Thermopylai. We cannot even be sure whether the alternative account which has left traces in his narrative represents an authentic tradition or a sceptical reaction against the Legend. Once the Legend was fairly launched it acquired wide popularity, and when it was accepted by Herodotus and set down by him in a narrative of unsurpassable literary art its final triumph in antiquity was assured.

APPENDIX V

The diary of the Persian army and fleet

HERODOTUS says in vii. 183. 2 that the Persian warships allowed eleven days to elapse after Xerxes' departure (ἐξέλασις) from Therma before they resumed their advance. It is usually supposed, on the evidence of vii. 183. 3, that they arrived at the Sepiad Strand in the course of the same day; Herodotus goes on to say that they were held up there by a storm for three whole days, and implies that they continued their voyage on the fourth day (vii. 192. 1, 193. 1). Apparently they reached Aphetai on the same day, which the commentators accordingly identify with the sixteenth day of the Herodotean 'diary' (counting the day of Xerxes' setting out from Therma as Day 1). The difficulties raised by this account have already been discussed (see above, pp. 167 ff.); the time allowed for the voyage of the fleet from Therma to Sepias seems to be too short, and that for the duration of the storm too long. The most probable reconstruction is that the fleet arrived at the Sepiad Strand, after a voyage of two days, on the evening of Day 13, that the storm which began the next morning (Day 14) blew itself out in twenty-four hours, and that the Persians were able to continue their voyage early on the day after that on which the storm stopped and so to reach Aphetai on the same day (Day 16); the alternative is to suppose that the voyage took three days and that the fleet left Sepias for Aphetai on the day after that on which the storm started. On either reconstruction the fleet reached Aphetai on Day 16 of the Diary.

How long was the interval between its arrival at Aphetai and the first of its three encounters with the Greeks off Artemision? There are three indications of time in Herodotus which bear on this problem: (1) the three successive days of fighting on sea coincided precisely (viii. 15. 1) with the three days of Leonidas' struggle on land; (2) Xerxes waited for four days after reaching Thermopylai before he made his first attack on the Greek army, on the fifth day (vii. 210. 1), which is presumably calculated *inclusively* from the date of his arrival in Malis; (3) Herodotus in vii. 196, after describing the arrival of the Persian fleet at Aphetai, states that Xerxes with the land force, after passing through Thessaly and Achaia, ἐσβεβληκὼς ἦν καὶ δὴ τριταῖος ἐς Μηλιέας. The natural interpretation of these words in their context is that given by Macaulay (and by Powell): he 'had already entered the land of the Malians two days before'.

Two days before what? The obvious answer is that τριταῖος refers
to the event last mentioned, the arrival of the fleet at Aphetai. How
and Wells insist (p. 217) that the passage must mean that Xerxes
arrived in Malis two days *after* some other event, which they identify
with the arrival of the fleet at the Sepiad Strand, last mentioned eight
chapters earlier! This refinement is as unnecessary as it is improbable,
for on their own reconstruction of the events (p. 373) the army arrives
at Thermopylai two days before the fleet reaches Aphetai.

The normal interpretation of the datum in vii. 196 is defended
by Legrand (vii. 209, n. 3), who, however, introduces a needless
complication by reckoning τριταῖος exclusively, in defiance of
regular Greek usage (so apparently Grundy in his table on *G.P.W.*
342; contrast the other table on p. 320). Macaulay's version is to
be preferred; Herodotus must have wished to say that Xerxes entered
Malis two days before his fleet arrived at Aphetai. From this it
follows that Xerxes arrived before Thermopylai on the fourteenth
day of the Diary, from item 2 (vii. 210. 1) that he began his attack
on the eighteenth, and from item 1 (viii. 15. 1) that the first battle
at Artemision occurred on the same day. As this battle began in the
'late afternoon' (viii. 9), the afternoon there referred to, that of the
eighteenth day, must be two full days later than the 'early afternoon'
when the Persian ships came to Aphetai (viii. 6. 1), which was on the
sixteenth day. This is the only chronological reconstruction possible
if all the three data given above are accepted and interpreted in the
most natural way.

Critics who are unwilling to accept this reconstruction have on
various grounds questioned one or more of these three data. Some
have rejected the first datum, the precise synchronism between the
three days of fighting on land and sea; so Beloch, assuming that the
first battle at Artemision took place on the same day as the arrival
of the Persian fleet at Aphetai, concludes that the fighting at Thermopylai began on the day following the third and last battle at
Artemision (*G.G.* ii². 2. 49–50), thus inverting the reconstruction of
Ephoros, who made the arrival of the fleet follow the fighting at
Thermopylai (Diod. xi. 12). Giannelli (*La spedizione di Serse*, 13 ff.
and 19–21) rightly supposes that two days elapsed between the
arrival of the Persian ships at Aphetai and the first sea-fight, but as
he interprets the second datum exclusively he makes Xerxes delay
for four days in addition to the day of his arrival in Malis, so that
his first attack on the pass occurs on Day 19 of the Diary, and the
third battle off Artemision is made to coincide in time with the
second day of the fighting at Thermopylai. Legrand (vii. 196 ff.)
reaches a similar conclusion by a different route, for he decides, on
grounds which seem inconclusive, that the three days of fighting on

sea must be reduced to two, which coincided with the first two days
of the fighting on land. It is true that Diodoros (xi. 12. 4–13. 2)
describes only two days of fighting at sea, but his omission of the
fighting on the second day may be simply due to his own carelessness
in abbreviating the narrative given by Ephoros. Legrand is compelled by his theory to conflate the events of the first two sea-fights
and put them all on the eighteenth day, although Herodotus not
only distinguishes clearly between the circumstances of the two
battles but separates them by the storm on Mount Pelion, which
Legrand has to move forward to the night of the seventeenth day.

There are synchronisms elsewhere in Herodotus which arouse
legitimate suspicion (vii. 166, ix. 100. 2) but there is no sufficient
reason to doubt that engagements between the Greek and Persian
fleets took place off Artemision on three successive days, and as the
fighting at Thermopylai indubitably occupied three successive days,
the fighting at sea may well have occurred on the same three days,
in view of the close interconnexion of the two Greek positions on
land and on sea. There is therefore nothing improbable in Herodotus' precise synchronization of the three days of fighting on land
and on sea, and it has been generally accepted by English scholars.
Macan has expressed it (i. 2. 371 A) with characteristic vigour: 'the
only synchronism to which we may cling with desperate tenacity is
the coincidence of the three days' fightings at Artemision and at
Thermopylai, this being grounded, though not absolutely, in the
strategical and tactical necessities of the case.'

Bury in an important paper (B.S.A. ii, 1895–6, 83–104) accepted
the synchronism but argued that the first Greek attack on the Persian
fleet 'in the late afternoon' of a day not clearly defined in the context
by Herodotus (viii. 9) in fact occurred on the same day as the arrival
of the Persian fleet at Aphetai ('in the early afternoon'; viii. 6. 1),
and that the first sea-fight (and with it the first battle at Thermopylai) must therefore be dated to the sixteenth day of the Herodotean diary, not the eighteenth. Any such hypothesis can maintain
the synchronism in viii. 15. 1 only by sacrificing one or other of the
two remaining chronological data noted above. If it keeps the four
days' delay before the first Persian attack on Thermopylai, it must
date Xerxes' arrival in Malis to the twelfth day of the Diary; this is
the solution offered by Macan, who connects the delay with the
interruption to the advance of the Persian fleet caused by the storm.
But on this view the arrival of the army in Malis must be *four* days
earlier than that of the fleet off Aphetai. Munro evaded this consequence by cutting down the storm to one day and dating the arrival
of the main part of the Persian fleet at Aphetai to Day 14 (C.A.H.
iv. 287 f.), but this hypothesis raises fresh difficulties. Macan, after

giving the obvious interpretation of vii. 196 in his commentary on the passage, suggests in his second volume (p. 274) that τριταῖος must mean on the third day *after* the event mentioned in the first half of the sentence. We read there that Xerxes and his army had entered Malis 'having passed through Thessaly and Achaia'. But how could the uninstructed reader be expected to infer from this that τριταῖος referred to Xerxes' crossing of the border between Thessaly and Achaia and in particular to his visit to Halos in Achaia, which is not described till the following chapter? Equally improbable is the view of Köster (p. 79) that τριταῖος means 'two days after the fleet left Therma'. Xerxes did in fact enter Malis on the fourteenth day, but Köster's interpretation is designed to evade the true inference from vii. 196 that this event occurred two days before the fleet reached Aphetai and is contrary to the natural interpretation of the Greek; the use by Herodotus of the pluperfect tense instead of the aorist is decisive (Legrand, vii. 209, n. 3).

The alternative, for those who date the first sea-fight to the sixteenth day, is to keep the fourteenth as the date of Xerxes' arrival in Malis and cut down the delay between that event and the first attack on Thermopylai to two days, instead of the four given by Herodotus in vii. 210. 1 (so Bury, 96, where he dates Xerxes' arrival at Thermopylai to Day 15, the day after his entry into Malis). But on what ground can this chronological datum be rejected if the other two are to be kept? It is neither more nor less credible in itself than they are. Herodotus' explanation of the reason which induced Xerxes to remain inactive for four days before Thermopylai ('expecting all the time that the Greeks would run away') may indeed be puerile, but the delay in itself is in no way improbable, and explanations more plausible than that offered by Herodotus may easily be suggested (see above, p. 143).

Bury's treatment of this passage is intended to pave the way for a general 'reconstruction' of Herodotus' account of the naval operations off north Euboia. It must be frankly admitted that in Hdt. viii. 6–9 the spacing out of the events which elapsed between the arrival of the Persian fleet at Aphetai and the first sea-fight is far from clear, and that if we had only the narrative of Book VIII before us we might be tempted to conclude that all the events described in chapters 6–11 occurred in the course of a single afternoon. But the first section of the naval narrative, given in Book VII, ends with the capture (vii. 194 f.) of fifteen Persian vessels which had lagged behind the main body and sailed into the Greek lines, mistaking the enemy ships for their own, whereas the narrative in Book VIII (cc. 6–11) ends with an attack made by the Greek fleet, in which thirty Persian ships are captured. Bury and his followers have to assume that the events recorded in vii. 194–5 are the same as those in viii. 9–11, as described by two different sources, but unless Herodotus is utterly unworthy of credit as an historian the assumption is unjustifiable. The two accounts differ profoundly in the circumstances of the capture, in the number of ships captured, and in other respects. Fuller particulars are given in Book VII about the names and careers of three of the captured, whereas in Book VIII only one name is mentioned, that of Philaon (brother of the tyrant of Cyprian Salamis), whose name does not occur in the earlier account (cf. Kromayer, *Schlachtenatlas*, col. 5).

If the engagement in viii. 9–11 did not take place on the same day as the capture of the fifteen ships in vii. 194, there is no convincing reason why it should not be dated two days later, on the eighteenth day of the Diary, the date fixed by the combination of the three chronological indications in Herodotus. It is not so clearly fixed by him in his continuous narrative (viii. 6–9) of the operations of the two fleets between the arrival of the Persians at Aphetai in the 'early afternoon' of Day 16 (6. 1) and the first Greek attack in the 'late afternoon' of Day 18 (c. 9). Apart from these two mentions of an afternoon there are two references to 'that day': (*a*) in viii. 7. 2, the day on which a squadron is sent off by the Persians from Aphetai to sail round Euboia; (*b*) in viii. 9, the day during which the Greeks, after receiving the message of the diver Skyllias, decide to wait until nightfall before setting out to meet the circumnavigating squadron.

These two additional notes of time are of doubtful value, for both are closely connected in the narrative with the dispatch from Aphetai of the circumnavigating squadron. There are weighty reasons (see below, Appendix VI) for doubting whether this squadron was ever sent at all, and even if it was sent it is uncertain at what point in the operations it was detached from the main fleet. If we excise from the narrative of cc. 6–9 everything in it that is connected directly or indirectly with the alleged squadron, the items that remain are: (1) the Persians hold a review of their fleet after their arrival at Aphetai; (2) Skyllias deserts to the Greeks during this review; (3) the Greek leaders after hearing his report meet in council; (4) the Greeks make their first attack in the late afternoon. It is the first of these items which by itself excludes the possibility that all these events occurred on the same afternoon as that on which the Persians reached Aphetai, even if (as has been argued) the second and third may have been wrongly transferred here from an earlier date. Busolt insisted (681, n. 3) that the Persian fleet needed reorganization after all it had gone through, and as Macan rightly observed (i. 2. 370 f.), 'the arrival of the Persian fleet at Aphetai, to say nothing of the subsequent numbering, was not to be accomplished in the twinkling of an eye'. The arrival of the Persian ships, which may have numbered 400 even after their losses in the storm, must have taken up most of the afternoon of the sixteenth day; it is therefore improbable that the review and reorganization of the Persian fleet could have been carried out until the seventeenth, and Herodotus (viii. 8. 1) implies that it took some time.

Grundy (*G.P.W.* 331 and n., also first note on p. 332) dated the naval review to the morning of Day 18; presumably he inferred from the narrative in viii. 8–9 that the desertion of Skyllias (which is certainly said in 8. 1 to have occurred during the review) and the Greek council of war that followed his arrival at Artemision must have occurred on the same day as the first sea-fight. The reference to 'that day' (c. 9, l. 2) seems to fix the council to the same day as the sea-fight, but it occurs in a suspicious context (see above), and even if trustworthy does not exclude the hypothesis that Skyllias escaped to Artemision late on the preceding day (the view of Legrand, vii. 198, that he escaped on the preceding night ignores Herodotus' explicit statement that he escaped during the review). Grundy, who accepts Herodotus' account of the dispatch of the 200 ships from Aphetai as an historical fact and assigns it to the morning of the seventeenth day, has omitted to notice that in Herodotus the dispatch seems to be contemporary with the naval review, for both are related paratactically in the imperfect tense at the end of chapter 7. The reference to 'that day' ($\tau a \acute{v} \tau \eta s\ \tau \hat{\eta} s\ \mathring{\eta} \mu \acute{\epsilon} \rho \eta s$) in viii. 7. 2 occurs in a context as suspicious as that of the second reference (in c. 9, l. 2), but it was not necessarily identified by Herodotus' informant with the day on which the Persian fleet arrived at Aphetai, and though Herodotus has been thought (e.g. by Grundy, 330) to imply that it was on the same day, he does not say so explicitly.

We are now in a position to fix the sequence of the historical events recorded by Herodotus in viii. 6–9 within the limits imposed by the chronological data supplied by him elsewhere in his narrative (see above, p. 379). The arrival of the Persian fleet at Aphetai occupied the whole afternoon of the sixteenth day; the capture of the fifteen ships recorded in vii. 194 occurred on the same afternoon, probably late in the day. To the seventeenth day must be assigned the reorganization of the fleet and the naval review; some time during this day, perhaps not until the late afternoon, Skyllias escaped and came to Artemision. Possibly in consequence of the information brought by Skyllias, a council of war was held by the Greeks on the morning of the eighteenth day; it is implied by Herodotus that they waited for several hours before they launched their first attack on the Persian fleet late in the afternoon of the same day (they may already have

learnt by signals from Thermopylai that the Persian attack on land
had begun in the morning). The second and third days of fighting,
both on sea and on land, occurred on the nineteenth and twentieth
days of the Diary, and the fleet retired from Artemision in the course
of the night that followed the twentieth day.

APPENDIX VI

The alleged voyage of Persian warships round Euboia

HERODOTUS (viii. 7) declares that the Persians after the arrival of
their fleet at Aphetai detached 200 ships with orders to sail round
Euboia past the capes of Kaphereus and Geraistos to the Euripos,
where they could block the Greek line of retreat, while the rest of the
Persian navy, left behind at Aphetai, was to remain inactive until
it received the signal that the 200 ships had reached their destination; Herodotus also notes that these ships had been instructed to
sail round the island of Skiathos in the first stage of their voyage to
conceal their ultimate goal from the Greeks. The 200 ships, which
Myres has conveniently named 'the deep-sea squadron', failed to
achieve their task; Herodotus describes later (viii. 13) how they
were wrecked by a storm which got up on the night which followed
the first sea-fight at Artemision. They were caught by a wind which
drove them on the rocky coast of Euboia; Herodotus implies that
all the ships in the squadron were destroyed by the storm.

This disaster is said to have occurred off the Hollows of Euboia
(τὰ Κοῖλα τῆς Εὐβοίας). Most scholars have located the Hollows on
the south-west coast of Euboia; so Grundy, 335, n. 3 and Geiger in
R.-E. xi. 1. 1048. Valerius Maximus (i. 8. 10) says that Appius
Claudius after hearing the reply of the Delphic oracle 'in eam
regionem secessit quae inter Rhamnunta, nobilem Attici soli partem,
Carystumque Chalcidico freto vicinam interiacens Coelae Euboeae
nomen obtinet'; this would limit the Hollows to that part of the
south-west coast which lies between Karystos and a point opposite
Rhamnous. Strabo has much the same view (x. 1. 2; p. 445) but
extends the term to cover the coast from Cape Geraistos as far up the
strait as Aulis (Lucan in *Pharsalia* v. 230 ff. mentions both Rhamnus
and Aulis). The Hollows are identified, however, by an epitomator
of Strabo with the coast east of Geraistos, between it and Cape
Kaphereus, and the evidence of the geographer Ptolemy (iii. 14. 22)
is even more perplexing. He gives a description of the principal
localities on the coast of Euboia in order, the names in the relevant
passage being as follows: Karystos, harbour of Geraistos, promontory of Kaphereus, Κοῖλα Εὐβοίας, Cape Chersonesos, mouth of the
river Boudoros, Kerinthos. This shows that Ptolemy identified the
Hollows with that part of the east coast of Euboia which lies between the capes of Kaphereus and Chersonesos. His reasons for this

identification are unknown, but as it is not supported by any other source Geiger prefers, probably with justice, to follow the combined testimony of Valerius and Strabo, claiming that the south-west coast of Euboia as far as Eretria is still dreaded on account of its storms. The language of Herodotus certainly suggests (in opposition to the view of Macan, i. 2. 376) that he was referring to a definite and well-known stretch of the coast, and Grundy gives additional reasons (loc. cit.) for placing the Hollows on the south-west coast of Euboia. If this view is correct, the wind which drove the ships on the rocks must have blown from the south-west or south (cf. Giannelli, 19) and so could not have been the same as the north-easterly gale, the Hellespontias, which caught the main fleet on its voyage south-wards from Therma (vii. 188. 2).

Herodotus' whole narrative of the dispatch and the fate of the deep-sea squadron has been condemned by some German critics as an entire fabrication grafted at an early stage on the authentic tradition of the naval operations and accepted uncritically by Hero-dotus without consideration of the manifest impossibilities contained in it; see especially the detailed examination by Beloch in *G.G.* ii². 2. 87–90 (hereafter cited in this appendix by page reference only). English scholars tend to be shocked by this ruthless treatment of a story so elaborate and so circumstantial in its details; Bury for example asserts (*B.S.A.* ii. 91) that Beloch's rejection of it is a desperate solution, 'not consonant with a satisfactory historical method'. The validity of this objection depends on whether the impossibilities detected by Beloch in the story are real or imaginary; if they are real, the tradition here reproduced by Herodotus must be dismissed as historical fiction.

It must be admitted that some of Beloch's arguments are unconvincing. (1) In a Persian council of war held after the end of the fighting at Thermopylai, and therefore at least thirty hours after the supposed destruction of the deep-sea squadron, the admiral Achaimenes is made to say (vii. 236. 2) that the fleet has already lost 400 ships. As this is the minimum figure for the ships lost in the first storm (vii. 190), Beloch argues that 'the main source' (which he presumes Herodotus to be following in vii. 236) knew nothing of the deep-sea squadron or of its destruction in the second storm. There is doubtless an inconsistency here, but it is a natural consequence of the plan of Herodotus' narrative; having decided to finish off the operations at Thermopylai before describing the second part of the naval operations, he could not allow Achaimenes to be aware of a disaster which though chronologically earlier than his speech had not yet been mentioned (cf. Giannelli, 25).

(2) If the Persian admirals really wished to cut off the retreat of

the Greek fleet, as Herodotus claims (viii. 7. 1), Beloch argues
(pp. 88 f.) that they could have achieved their object much more
quickly and effectively by extending their right wing so as to en-
circle the Greek left wing, and that this manœuvre should have been
easy to carry out in view of the numerical superiority of the Persian
fleet over the Greek. As this argument has won the approval of
Kromayer (*Schlachtenatlas*, col. 4), it must be noted that it is merely
an *argumentum ad hominem*, valid only against those who believe that
the Persians after their heavy losses in the first storm still had a
hundred ships or more to spare for a turning movement round
Euboia. If in fact the Persian fleet was now not much larger than the
Greek (see above, p. 209), an attempt to advance part of it in face
of the enemy into the channel between north-west Euboia and the
mainland would have been an extremely risky operation.

Moreover, Beloch simplifies his task by assuming too easily (p. 87)
that the first sea-fight at Artemision was fought on the same afternoon
as that on which the Persian fleet reached Aphetai, an assumption
which he claims to be the only possible inference from Herodotus'
narrative; it follows that if the deep-sea squadron was sent off from
Aphetai that same afternoon it could not possibly have got to the
Hollows in the course of the ensuing night, the night following the
day of the first sea-fight, to which night Herodotus dates its destruction. The distance from Aphetai to Cape Geraistos, including
the detour round Skiathos, is estimated at 130 nautical miles (Hammond, *History of Greece*, 232; the 250 nautical miles of Beloch 88 is
apparently the length of the complete circumnavigation of Euboia);
on the assumption that the average speed of an ancient fleet was not
more than 5 miles an hour (cf. HW 211) the voyage of the deep-sea
squadron could not have taken less than twenty-six hours.

The obvious answer to Beloch here is that his chronology is wrong,
and that on the alternative scheme described above (Appendix V)
the arrival of the Persian fleet at Aphetai, on the early afternoon of
Day 16, was separated by two full days from the first sea-fight, which
is to be dated to the late afternoon of Day 18. On this view the storm
which destroyed the deep-sea squadron occurred on the night between Day 18 and Day 19, and there would be sufficient time for
the squadron to reach the Hollows by then provided that it started
from Aphetai not later than the morning of Day 17 (Grundy, 331
and 343); Busolt's supposition (last sentence of long n. 3 on 681 f.)
that it did not set out till the dawn of Day 18 is untenable.

Grundy's solution is not open to those scholars (including Bury
himself) who like Beloch date the first sea-fight to Day 16. Those of
them who maintain that a squadron really was detached from the
main fleet at some stage on the voyage from Therma to Aphetai have

to suppose that the tradition which recorded this event was nevertheless wrong on almost all the details which have been supposed to
guarantee its authenticity, the size of the squadron, the time at which
it was detached from the main fleet, and the time and place of its
destruction. They assume, reasonably enough (e.g. Bury, op. cit.
91; see also Grundy, 330), that the squadron numbered less than
200 ships, that it parted from the rest of the fleet on the voyage from
Therma to Sepias, towards evening of the day preceding the great
storm (Day 12 of the Diary on the usual view, but more probably
Day 13; see above, p. 379), and that it was wrecked next *morning* on
the *north-east* coast of Euboia by the same north-easterly gale which
inflicted so much damage on the main fleet off the Magnesian coast.
The advocates of this hypothesis, though agreeing with Herodotus
that the deep-sea squadron passed to the east of Skiathos, postulate
that it did so not for the reason given by him but because this was
the most convenient route to its objective. This reconstruction, which
defends the Herodotean story by scrapping most of its components,
is too radical for acceptance. It is perhaps significant that when
Bury published his *History of Greece* in 1900 he tacitly replaced it
by the view that the 200 ships were sent from Aphetai (op. cit.
274). Nevertheless, his original hypothesis, though discarded by its
author, was still maintained by Munro in 1902 and by Tarn in 1908
(*J.H.S.* xxii and xxviii). No support for it can be obtained from
Ephoros, who clearly followed Herodotus here (Diod. xi. 12. 3),
although he reshuffled his figures for the shipwrecked fleets, giving
300 for the ships wrecked in the first storm and 300 for those sent
round Euboia (cf. Grundy, 330, n. 1; most manuscripts of Diodoros
have τριακοσίας, but Vogel in the Teubner text prefers to read
διακοσίας with P).

A reconstruction like Grundy's, allowing sufficient time for the
voyage of the deep-sea squadron from Aphetai to the Hollows, can
find room for all the detail in the story of the squadron as given by
Herodotus, and is to this extent more plausible than the rival hypothesis. On the other hand, by dating the dispatch of the squadron
with Herodotus to a time after the arrival of the Persian fleet at
Aphetai it increases the improbability of the story as a whole, for if
Herodotus is right in his implication that approximately one-third
of the Persian fleet had been wrecked in the first storm (see above,
p. 174) it is unlikely that its admirals would have been willing to
detach a sizeable part of their fleet so soon after their arrival at
Aphetai; indeed, they could not possibly have done so if their fleet
had originally numbered no more than 600. But even if they had
had a hundred or more ships to spare, the action attributed to them
is incredible. They had not yet made trial of the Greek fleet, but so

far they had no reason to believe that they could not defeat it in a straight fight. Herodotus' statement that their object in sending the ships round Euboia was to capture the whole of the Greek fleet (viii. 6. 2 and 7. 1) cannot be taken seriously, and recalls the similar motive attributed to Xerxes before Salamis by Aeschylus (*Persai* 361–71). The Persians had already suffered severely from the Hellespontine gale off the rocky coast of Magnesia; why should they expose a squadron to the hazards of a voyage round the almost harbourless east coast of Euboia?

Herodotus' account of the alleged circumnavigation is perfunctory, as regards both its inception and its conclusion, and it can be easily excised from his text without impairing the continuity of the narrative in which it is embedded. If it is unhistorical, then the departure of the deep-sea squadron cannot have been part of the message brought by Skyllias to the Greeks. Herodotus' report of the effect of the alleged message on the Greek admirals (viii. 9), that they decided to wait that day and sail off on the ensuing night to meet the circumnavigating squadron, has been generally rejected (cf. Grundy, 332 and second note). Anyhow, why were the Greeks ignorant of the dispatch of the squadron until Skyllias reported it to them? Herodotus has said earlier (viii. 7. 1) that the ships started their voyage by a detour round Skiathos to escape detection by the enemy, and this is accepted by Grundy (p. 331); but even if they thereby concealed their ultimate destination from the Greeks stationed at Artemision, how could they be sure that the Greeks had no scouts on the Euboian mountains? Herodotus here appears to have forgotten his own earlier reference (vii. 192. 1) to 'the day-watchers running down from the heights of Euboia'. It is theoretically possible that the ships waited at Skiathos till nightfall before continuing their voyage, but there is no hint of this in the narrative. Herodotus also asserts that after the dispatch of the deep-sea squadron the main fleet was to refrain from attacking the Greeks until the squadron announced its arrival by a prearranged signal (τὸ σύνθημα in viii. 7. 2). Where was the signal to be sent from? How could the Persians be sure that the squadron would not be held up at the Euripos? And if it was, how could it get a signal through to Aphetai or even to Thermopylai? This is one of the items in the story which prove that its inventor had not thought out the details.

A further difficulty is that the story never accounts for the complete disappearance of the 200 ships. Even on Tarn's view (op. cit. 215) that those which escaped by the north-east gale were wrecked by a second storm from the south-west, a few ships might have been expected to survive. Those who believe that the deep-sea squadron experienced only one storm have to devise some explanation for the disappearance of the ships that were not wrecked. The hypothesis which has found most favour is that of Munro (*J.H.S.* xxii, 1902, 311) that those of the 200 ships which survived the first gale got round past Geraistos to the Hollows and were destroyed there by the fifty-three Athenian ships which are said to have arrived at Artemision during the morning of Day 19 (viii. 14. 1). Munro follows Bury in the assumption that these ships had been detached earlier from the Greek fleet at Artemision to intercept the deep-sea squadron at the Euripos, but he goes far beyond Bury when he identifies the supposed battle at or near the Hollows between those ships and the survivors of the deep-sea squadron with the engagement in which the Greeks destroyed some Cilician ships. Herodotus says explicitly (viii. 14. 2) that this engagement was fought by Greek ships late in the afternoon of the second day's fighting at Artemision, therefore on Day 19 of the Diary, and after the appearance (or as Bury would say, the reappearance) of the fifty-three Athenian ships at Artemision.

There were other hazards to be reckoned with besides the weather. Herodotus' estimate of 200 for the deep-sea squadron is improbable, but if it is reduced to a more plausible figure the dangers inherent in the alleged manœuvre are thereby increased. On the most optimistic estimate the squadron could not regain contact with the main fleet for at least four days (the crews would need some rest on the way) and during that period it would be exposed to the risk of attack by a Greek squadron perhaps stationed near the south of Euboia, for the Persians must have realized that the 271 ships which awaited them at Artemision were not the whole of the Greek fleet; as the eighteen Aiginetan ships there (viii. 1. 2) were far from being Aigina's total naval strength, there must have been a reserve fleet at Aigina, and there were also the fifty-three Athenian ships somewhere in the rear of the main Greek fleet. In those circumstances the Persian admirals would have been guilty of incredible folly if, after their losses in the storm, they had detached a squadron on a difficult mission which exposed it to the risk of isolation and destruction by superior forces (cf. the damaging admission in the last sentence of Grundy's second note on p. 332). Even if it outnumbered the ships which the Greeks could spare to meet it, the Greek squadron could then have retired to the narrows against Chalkis where it could easily have defied even a superior Persian fleet.

Finally, it is certain that in 480 the Persian high command was anxious to maintain the closest possible co-operation between the army and the fleet. It is usually supposed that this policy was dictated by the needs of the army, but it may also have been imposed on the Persians by the needs of the fleet. The Persian fleet in 480 was composed mainly if not exclusively of triremes, which were very dependent on the proximity of a friendly shore (see the important demonstration of this fact by Gomme in his *Essays in Greek History and Literature*, 192 ff., especially 193 f.). Is it conceivable that the Persian admirals should have sent a large squadron to make the dangerous journey round Euboia, a journey of not less than four days, if during the whole of that period they would be cut off from the rest of the fleet and would be voyaging near to coasts which were all occupied by the enemy? Perhaps the idea of such a manœuvre was suggested to someone by the Persian turning movement at Thermopylai, but the short circuit made by Hydarnes' force on land provides no real parallel to the long detour on sea said to have been undertaken by the 200 ships in the tradition transmitted to Herodotus. Whether that tradition was based on a misunderstanding of something that actually happened or was a pure fabrication, it must be rejected, although repeated in good faith by Herodotus. Delbrück's explanation of it (*Kriegskunst*, 86 f.) is as good as any, that it originated in an attempt to narrow the discrepancy between the enormous figure given for the original Persian fleet in the popular estimate and its actual numbers in the fighting off Artemision.

APPENDIX VII

A fragment of Sosylos

SOSYLOS was a Lakedaimonian who was closely associated with Hannibal and taught him Greek (Nepos, *Hannibal*, 13. 3). He wrote a history of Hannibal in seven books, according to Diod. xxvi. 4 (where he is called Σώσιλος ὁ "Ιλιος; "Ιλιος is emended by some to Ἡλεῖος, by Jacoby to Λακεδαιμόνιος). His history is attacked by Polybius (iii. 20. 5), but if Sosylos maintained that Hannibal's capture of Saguntum was followed by long debates in the Roman Senate he was probably in the right. Not much was known about his work until a new fragment of it, on papyrus, was published by Wilcken in 1906 (*Hermes*, xli. 103 ff.); this appears as fragment 1 in Jacoby, *F.G.H.* ii B, no. 176. The extract, which contains the statement that it is taken from the fourth book (end of col. iv: Σωσύλου τῶν περὶ Ἀννίβου πράξεων δ) describes a naval battle in which the Carthaginians were defeated by the men of Massalia and their Roman allies. Wilcken identified this battle with the one off the mouth of the Ebro in 217 (Polyb. iii. 95–96; cf. Livy xxii. 19), but the details given by Sosylos cannot easily be reconciled with the descriptions of Polybius and Livy (see Jacoby's commentary in iiD, 603 f.; Jacoby himself thinks that Sosylos was describing a naval battle off the African coast near Clupea in 208, recorded by Livy xxvii. 29. 7–8).

For students of the Persian Wars the relevant part of the papyrus is the third column. The Massaliots are there said to have formed some of their ships in a single line with their prows facing the enemy (μετωπηδόν), and to have posted the rest in reserve ἐν διαστή-μασιν εὐμέτροις; this arrangement was designed to deal with enemy ships which broke through the front line. Presumably the Carthaginian manœuvre which the Massaliots were trying to guard against was that known to Thucydides as the διέκπλους (cf. Grundy, *Thucydides*, 295 f.). The method employed by the Massaliots to counter it is said by Sosylos to have been copied from an historical precedent which was known to them; they drew up their ships as described προϊστορη-κότες τὴν συμβολὴν ἣν ἐπ᾿ Ἀρτεμισίῳ φασὶν Ἡρακλείδην ποιήσασθαι τὸμ Μυλασέα μὲν τῷ γένει, διαφέροντα δ᾿ἀγχινοίᾳ τῶγ καθ᾿ αὑτὸν ἀνδρῶν (col. 3, ll. 3–10). After describing the formation Sosylos adds ὅπερ ἐποίησε κἀκεῖνος ἐπὶ τῶν ἔμπροσθεν καιρῶν καὶ κατέστη τῆς νίκης αἴτιος (the text is that of Jacoby with minor alterations; the supplements in this part of the papyrus are small and reasonably certain).

Wilcken supposed that the battle of Artemision in Sosylos was identical with the first of the three battles fought off North Euboia in 480 by the Greeks and Persians, the battle described by Herodotus in viii. 10–11. This supposition might seem to be supported by the statement (Hdt. viii. 9) that the Greeks took the offensive against the Persians 'wishing to make trial of their method of fighting and their διέκπλους'. It is implied that the diekplous was a manœuvre which the Persian fleet was likely to use; Hdt. vi. 12. 1, if not anachronistic, would prove that it was known to the Ionians fourteen years earlier. A Herakleides from Mylasa in Karia had planned an ambush which had brought about the destruction of a Persian army at a critical stage in the Ionian revolt (Hdt. v. 121); possibly when the revolt was crushed he had fled from Ionia, and while in exile had been admitted to the counsels of the patriotic Greeks before Xerxes' invasion. It is, however, far from certain that the diekplous of Hdt. viii. 9 is the same manœuvre as that mentioned by Thucydides (see above, p. 184). Moreover, if Herakleides had played such an important part in the first battle at sea fought by the Greeks against Xerxes' armada, it is curious that Herodotus, with his special interest in and close contacts with Karia, should have known nothing about it (cf. Jacoby, ii D, 605). A further objection to Wilcken's view (cf. Munro in *C.A.H.* iv. 289) is that whereas in Sosylos Herakleides seems to be in supreme command of a fleet at the time of his exploit, he cannot have held this position in the Greek fleet in 480.

Jacoby favours the view of Rühl (*Rhein. Mus.* lxi, 1906, 352–9), who argued against Wilcken's hypothesis and maintained that Sosylos was referring to an otherwise unknown naval engagement fought in the course of the Ionian Revolt near the Karian Artemision (on which see Strabo xiv. 651). Rühl suggested (op. cit. 357 f.) that the Massaliot captains might have read of Herakleides' exploit either in Skylax (who is said by 'Suidas' to have written a book on 'Herakleides king of the Mylasians') or in a collection of naval 'stratagems' (στρατηγήματα); on the second hypothesis the author of the collection could have derived his knowledge of Herakleides directly or indirectly from Skylax. Gisinger (in his article on Skylax, *R.-E.* iii A. 1. 634) accepts this identification of the Herakleides of Skylax with the Mylasian of the same name in Hdt. v. 121, but follows Wilcken in connecting his exploit with the battle in Hdt. viii. 10–11. Tarn (*J.H.S.* xxviii, 1908, 216 f.) rightly pointed out that there is no certainty that the particulars about Herakleides in Sosylos came from Skylax, but goes on to say that 'Sosylos does not profess to be quoting Skylax, neither does he suggest that the Massilians knew anything about Herakleides'; the second half of this statement is contradicted by the passage of Sosylos quoted above (col. 3, ll. 3–10), which proves that the Massaliot captains were well informed about Herakleides' exploit, whether their information was derived from a written or an oral source.

Rühl's hypothesis explains how Massaliots in the late third century could have been acquainted with details of a naval battle fought in the eastern Mediterranean in the early fifth century, although it had not been recorded by Herodotos, but his explanation creates a fresh problem: if Herakleides' stratagem had already been recorded by Skylax, why did Herodotus fail to mention an item of such special interest, whether it occurred in the Ionian Revolt or in the war of 480? More serious still is the objection that a victory of the type presupposed by Sosylos cannot be fitted into Herodotus' narrative of the Ionian Revolt. If the revolt broke out in the autumn of 499, it is unlikely that Darius could have collected a fleet strong enough to face that of the rebels (which was soon joined by the contingents of the Cypriot states) until eighteen months later. This was the fleet which was beaten by the Ionians off Cyprian Salamis in the summer of 497 (Hdt. v. 112. 1) and its defeat was followed by another long pause until the Persians mustered the fleet which fought and won the battle of Lade in 494. There is therefore no need to doubt Herodotus' implication that these were the only large-scale engagements at sea during the revolt; the victory which the Eretrians (who had sent only five ships to Asia; cf. Hdt. v. 99. 1) are alleged to have won over some *Cyprian* ships (so the untrustworthy Lysanias of Mallos in Plut. *H.M.* 24; Grundy in *G.P.W.* 100 wrongly implies that the victory was won over a *Phoenician* fleet) cannot have been very important and may indeed be a fiction. (See also Wilcken's reply to Rühl in *Hermes*, xlii, 1907, 510 ff.)

In view of these difficulties Munro suggested (*C.A.H.* iv. 289) that the Artemision of Sosylos was in Spain, that Herakleides fled to the far west after the collapse of the Ionian Revolt, like Dionysios of Phokaia (Hdt. vi. 17), and there helped the Massaliots to secure a victory at sea over the Carthaginians by a device which remained famous for centuries in Massalia. Unfortunately it is doubtful whether the place in Spain to which Munro refers was ever actually called Artemision. He speaks of the victory won by the Massaliots over the Carthaginians 'off the Iberian Artemisium (Dianium) which seems to become the boundary between their respective spheres of influence in Spain'. Strabo, however, refers to the town, the most important of the three small Massaliot foundations between the river Sucro and New Carthage, by the name Hemeroskopeion (iii. 159). After saying that it had a highly-honoured temple of the Ephesian Artemis and had been used as a naval base by Sertorius, he adds καλεῖται δὲ Διάνιον οἷον Ἀρτεμίσιον. It is called Dianium by

Cicero (*In Verrem* ii. 5. 146, also ii. 1. 87) and was presumably known to the Greeks as Hemeroskopeion. Strabo's language suggests (so Hübner in *R.-E.* v. 1. 340) that his last two words are meant as a mere translation, added by Strabo or his source Poseidonios, of the name Dianium, and that the place never bore the name Artemision. This objection is not necessarily fatal to the view that the battle in which Herakleides distinguished himself was fought in Spanish waters; Sosylos may have misunderstood what his informants told him.

As all hypotheses so far suggested are vulnerable to criticism, the obvious conclusion is that Sosylos' reference to Herakleides' stratagem is insufficient to fix with precision the time or place of its occurrence, even if the identification of his Herakleides with the one in Hdt. v. 121 was absolutely certain. Nevertheless, Wilcken's view is open to more serious objections than either of the rival hypotheses, and Munro is therefore justified in his verdict that the evidence of Sosylos cannot safely be used to supplement the account given by Herodotus of the first battle off Artemision.

APPENDIX VIII

Psyttaleia

HERODOTUS says (in viii. 76. 1) that when the Persians accepted as trustworthy the message of Themistokles they (*a*) landed πολλοὺς τῶν Περσέων on the small island between Salamis and the mainland, (*b*) τοῦτο δέ, ἐπειδὴ ἐγίνοντο μέσαι νύκτες, they advanced with their main fleet; the note of time clearly indicates that the first movement took place before midnight and therefore preceded the second. The island on which the Persians landed was certainly identified by Herodotus with Psyttaleia, for though the name is bracketed by some editors where it first appears in our manuscripts (76. 1; Powell, however, retains it in his edition with a comma before μεταξύ) all doubt is removed by Herodotus' reference to it in 76. 2 as τὴν νησῖδα τὴν Ψυττάλειαν καλεομένην.

Beloch, having identified Psyttaleia with the island now called St. George (Hagios Georgios), gets into difficulties. After describing the entry of the Persian fleet into the straits by night he says (*G.G.* ii². 2. 122) that Xerxes had to reckon with the possibility that the Greeks in face of his superior numbers (which he estimates at probably 500 and anyhow not less than 400 ships) would decline to fight. If they did, then it would be necessary for the Persians to land on the island of Salamis, and the first step to this end would be the occupation of Psyttaleia, 'which must have taken place after the entry into the strait, either on the same night or early in the following morning'. This statement is made dogmatically by Beloch, who does not face the objection that it flatly contradicts the evidence of Herodotus.

Hammond (in *J.H.S.* lxxvi, 1956, 43) admits that the occupation by the Persians of Psyttaleia (which he, like Beloch, identifies with the island of St. George) preceded the movement of the main fleet, but supposes that the picked Persian troops sent to occupy Psyttaleia set out 'from the mole near Pérama in small boats, which, moving against the background of the high Attic coast, would have been hard to discern from the Salaminian shore'. This is theoretically plausible, but how could the Persians expect that an island so far up the strait and so near to Salamis would be left unguarded? If their landing was reported to the Greeks they might have been destroyed on the island before the Persian navy had entered the strait.

Beloch maintained that his identification of Psyttaleia with St. George was confirmed by the relevant passage of Strabo, if carefully

analysed, and this view has been reargued by Hammond. Obst
(pp. 144–8), writing after Beloch, challenged his interpretation of
Strabo and defended the traditional assumption that Strabo's
Psyttaleia was the same as the modern Lipsokoutáli, but he also
pointed out that the island occupied by the Persian troops is nameless in Aeschylus (*Persai* 447 ff.); Obst concluded that Aeschylus'
island really was St. George and that Herodotus made a mistake
when he called it Psyttaleia. But if Strabo's Psyttaleia really was
Lipsokoutáli, there is no reason why the same identification should
not be presumed in Herodotus.

Obst supported his interpretation of Strabo by the hypothesis of
Negris that the level of the Mediterranean has altered considerably
since 480; Negris maintained that its level now is $3\frac{1}{2}$ metres *higher*
than it was then, but others reduce the difference to $2\frac{1}{2}$ or 2 metres
(Obst, 146–7; cf. Beloch, 113 and n. 1). Hammond has revived this
hypothesis; without finally committing himself to it he thinks it
possible that the level of the sea in Salamis strait was some 5 or 6 feet
lower in antiquity than now (op. cit. 35–36 and notes). Beloch,
however, rightly insisted that the hypothesis is far from being proved;
he argued that if the sea level had been only 2 metres lower in the
fifth century the harbour of Zea, used by the Athenian fleet, would
have been for the most part dry land.

As the authority of Strabo has been invoked by both Beloch and
Obst with equal confidence, the text of the relevant passage (ix. 1.
13–14, p. 395) must be quoted in full: εἶτα τὸ Θριάσιον πεδίον καὶ
ὁμώνυμος αἰγιαλὸς καὶ δῆμος· εἶθ' ἡ ἄκρα ἡ Ἀμφιάλη καὶ τὸ ὑπερκείμενον
λατόμιον καὶ ὁ εἰς Σαλαμῖνα πορθμὸς ὅσον δισταδίος, ὃν διαχοῦν ἐπειρᾶτο
Ξέρξης, ἔφθη δὲ ἡ ναυμαχία γενομένη καὶ φυγὴ τῶν Περσῶν. ἐνταῦθα
δὲ καὶ αἱ Φαρμακοῦσσαι, δύο νησία ὧν ἐν τῷ μείζονι Κίρκης τάφος
δείκνυται. Strabo continues (§ 14): ὑπὲρ δὲ τῆς ἀκτῆς ταύτης ὄρος ἐστὶν ὃ
καλεῖται Κορυδαλλός, καὶ ὁ δῆμος οἱ Κορυδαλλεῖς· εἶθ' ὁ Φωρῶν λιμὴν
καὶ ἡ Ψυττάλεια, νησίον ἔρημον πετρῶδες ὅ τινες εἶπον λήμην τοῦ Πειραιῶς·
πλησίον δὲ καὶ ἡ Ἀταλάντη ὁμώνυμος τῇ περὶ Εὔβοιαν καὶ Λοκρούς,
καὶ ἄλλο νησίον ὅμοιον τῇ Ψυτταλείᾳ καὶ τοῦτο· εἶθ' ὁ Πειραιεύς, καὶ
αὐτὸς ἐν τοῖς δήμοις ταττόμενος, καὶ ἡ Μουνυχία.

This description falls into two sections, each corresponding to a
paragraph of the text; the natural interpretation is that in each
Strabo first describes landmarks on the coast and then mentions the
adjacent islands. So in § 13 we have the Thriasian plain followed by
Cape Amphiale and the quarry, which is defined as ὑπερκείμενον
(presumably lying *beyond* it, i.e. lower down and nearer the mouth of
the strait), and then the ferry across to Salamis; Strabo adds that
ἐνταῦθα, in this sector, are the Pharmakoussai, two islands in the
larger of which was shown the grave of Kirke. In the next paragraph

Strabo continues with the mountain called Korydallos, which is
ὑπὲρ τῆς ἀκτῆς ταύτης, followed by the Thieves' Harbour (Φωρῶν
λιμήν) and Psyttaleia, which are closely associated in the same half-
sentence of only seven words. After a brief description of Psyttaleia
Strabo adds that near it (πλησίον) is Atalante, and, *if the text is
correct*, another nameless island said to resemble Psyttaleia (by which
presumably is meant that it was a νησίον ἔρημον πετρῶδες; cf. Beloch,
112). Finally, Strabo returns to the coast with a reference to Peiraieus
and Mounychia.

Two obvious problems are raised by these two sections. First,
Strabo apparently does not mention the island of Nerá (Leros on
some maps, e.g. Hauvette, 410; the map in HW opposite p. 249
gives both names) unless for him it is one of the two Pharmakoussai.
Secondly, in the final stretch of the strait there seem to be three
islands, Psyttaleia, Atalante, and the unnamed island, whereas now,
apart from reefs, there are only two, Lipsokoutáli and the smaller
island to the west of it called Talandónisi. Obst claimed to solve
both problems by the hypothesis that the sea level in the straits was
two metres lower in 480 than it is today; so Nerá would cease to be
an island, as it would be joined to Salamis (Obst, 147; Hammond,
36 suggests this as an alternative to his own first explanation of the
difficulty), while the reef of Skróphaes (or Skrophes), west of Talandónisi, would become a third island, the nameless island in Strabo
(Hammond, 35, n. 13, maintains that with a drop of one fathom
from the present sea level Skrophes would remain 'almost the same
in size' as it is now).

Obst's explanation of Strabo's third island is rightly scouted by
Beloch (p. 113), but Beloch's own view, with which Hammond
agrees in these particulars, involves serious difficulties. He accepts
Leake's identification of the Pharmakoussai with the modern Kyra-
des (or Kyradhes, called by some Choirades) situated in the Bay
of Eleusis east-north-east of Nerá. He then assumes that Strabo
in this part of his description is returning to the islands in all that
part of the strait which stretches from St. George to the Peiraieus;
hence he reaches the desired conclusion that the remaining three
islands in Strabo are to be identified with St. George, Talandónisi,
and Lipsokoutáli. Beloch also suggested that the mysterious Keos,
mentioned by Herodotus (viii. 76. 1; see above, p. 218) in close
connexion with Κυνόσουρα, was an island, and as he kept the usual
identification of Strabo's Atalante with Talandónisi he concluded
that Keos was the ancient name of Lipsokoutáli.

On this last point Hammond disagrees with Beloch, suggesting
that the Keos of Herodotus should rather be identified with Talandónisi, and that Strabo's Atalante was really not Talandónisi (in

spite of the similarity of name) but Lipsokoutáli. He argues that whereas Talandónisi can never have been inhabited, the Ἀταλάντη of Strabo can be proved to have been inhabited in antiquity by the evidence of Stephanus Byzantinus (s.v. 'Atalante'). But what Stephanus says is: Ἀταλάντη, ἡ ὑπ' Ἀθηναίων κτισθεῖσα παρὰ Λοκροῖς. Θουκυδίδης δευτέρᾳ. ἔστι καὶ νῆσος. καὶ ἄλλη πρὸς τῷ Πειραιεῖ. ὁ νησιώτης Ἀταλανταῖος. In this article of Stephanus the words καὶ ἄλλη πρὸς τῷ Πειραιεῖ appear to be parenthetical, so that the statement about the νησιώτης must be referred to the inhabitants of the island off Euboia, which if ἔρημος before 431 (Thuc. ii. 32) was certainly inhabited later (cf. Oberhummer in R.-E. ii. 2. 1889); hence Stephanus does not indicate whether the Atalante off Salamis was inhabited or not.

The main objection to Beloch's view is that it does violence to the natural interpretation of the two paragraphs in Strabo. He argues that Strabo first described the Attic coast stretching along the east side of the straits of Salamis and then proceeded to an enumeration of the islands, 'which he describes in the order in which they appear on a voyage through the straits from west to east' (Beloch, 111). This statement is an unverifiable hypothesis, and it is open to the minor objection that on such a voyage the traveller ought to have sighted Lipsokoutáli before Talandónisi (Hammond's identification of Lipsokoutáli with Atalante, if it could be accepted, would remove this objection) and to the major difficulty that if Strabo or his source described the mainland first and the islands after, why did he mention the Pharmakoussai islands before he dealt with the Ferry and Mount Korydallos and the Thieves' Harbour?

Under criticism Beloch revised his view (op. cit. 117) and argued that Strabo first described in § 13 the approaches to the strait, the coast, and the islands off it, and then in § 14 proceeded to describe the strait itself, beginning with the main features of the Attic coast and then enumerating the islands off it. This is, indeed, the natural analysis of Strabo's description, but it is fatal to Beloch's view, for the division between the two sectors comes at the Ferry, and both Beloch and Hammond (op. cit. 34) admit that the Ferry must have started from the Attic mainland at or near the modern Pérama, appreciably nearer to the mouth of the strait than the coast opposite St. George. Beloch (op. cit. 117) complained that Obst and all other scholars who identify Strabo's Psyttaleia with Lipsokoutáli take for granted that Strabo was a conscientious researcher whose descriptions were based on personal inspection or special maps, whereas he was really a dilettante compiling a popular work based on earlier compendia. The bearing of this argument on the present problem is not clear, as Beloch presumes that Strabo has reproduced his written source here faithfully 'in the main'. If Strabo is not to be trusted, why did Beloch appeal to his testimony to justify the identification of Psyttaleia with St. George?

As Strabo seems to begin a new section of his description with Mount Korydallos, and as he defines its position as ὑπὲρ τῆς ἀκτῆς ταύτης, which presumably means 'lower down the strait than that part of the coast from which the Ferry starts for Salamis', his Korydallos can only be identified with the Aigaleos of Herodotus viii. 90. 4 (cf. Honigmann, s.v., in *R.-E.* xi. 2. 1447). Hammond (op. cit. 33) correctly defines Mount Aigaleos as the 'long ridge between Mt. Parnes and the bend in the Salamis Channel', but later on (p. 35, n. 14; cf. map on p. 32) he distinguishes Aigaleos from Strabo's Korydallos, which he limits to the part of the ridge lying north-east of Cape Filatouri. This cape, situated at the north-western end of that part of the mainland which projects westwards into the narrowest part of the strait, is identified by Beloch and Hammond with Strabo's Cape Amphiale, but others make it the south-western corner of the same projection (so Milchhöfer in *R.-E.* i. 2. 1885, following the view of Lolling). Hammond, on very questionable grounds, locates the Phoron Limen between these two points; this is surely untenable if Strabo's description of the coastline falls into two parts, of which the second (to which the mention of the Limen belongs) deals with the mainland from Perama to the sea. Even Beloch accepted the usual identification of the Limen with the Bay of Keratsini.

There remain the two difficulties noted by Obst in Strabo's account. As for Nerá, perhaps the simplest solution is that it and St. George together formed the two Pharmakoussai. The problem of the three islands in the second sector of the strait is more difficult, but if the island of St. George cannot possibly have been included by Strabo in this sector and if the sea-level in the strait has not substantially altered since 480, then there must be something wrong with Strabo's text, as Kallenberg saw, although his remedy, the excision of all the words after Λοκρούς in the penultimate sentence of § 14, was too violent (cf. Beloch, op. cit. 112). Hammond (p. 35, n. 14) notes the frequency with which καί occurs in this short passage of Strabo; perhaps it occurs once too often in our texts. If the καί after Λοκρούς was inserted by a careless scribe, the three islands of the paragraph can be reduced to two, and the statement ἄλλο νησίον ὅμοιον τῇ Ψυτταλείᾳ καὶ τοῦτο becomes a description of Atalante. This slight correction also removes the two minor difficulties of Strabo's account in § 14 as reproduced by the manuscripts, that he gives a description of Psyttaleia and also of the third island but not of Atalante, and that he mentions the names of two of the islands and not the third.

Whether this emendation is accepted or not, the attempts of
Beloch and Hammond to identify Strabo's Psyttaleia with the
modern St. George are refuted by the inadequacy of their arguments
and also by the evidence of Herodotus. There is no need to accept
Obst's extraordinary hypothesis that Herodotus was wrong when he
identified with Psyttaleia the island occupied by the Persians before
the battle; as Giannelli observes (p. 78), he could have spoken to
some of the hoplites who had landed on the island with Aristeides.
Moreover, as Herodotus clearly places its occupation before the
entry of the main Persian fleet into the straits (see above, p. 397)
his Psyttaleia can only be at the entrance to the straits, and must
therefore be identified, like Strabo's Psyttaleia, with Lipsokoutáli.

This appendix was written before the publication of the article
by W. Kendrick Pritchett in *A.J. Arch.* lxiii, 1959, 251–62. As his
general approach to the problem and his detailed criticisms of
Beloch and Hammond are much the same as mine I have left
unaltered what I have written. Pritchett also identifies St. George
with one of the Pharmakoussai, but finds the second in the reef near
Perama, assuming that the sea-level may have been three metres
lower in 480 than now (see, however, Beloch, ii². 2. 111). His suggestion (256 A) that alterations may have been brought about in this
area by its liability to earthquakes is interesting; perhaps one of the
Pharmakoussai has disappeared since Strabo's time.

APPENDIX IX

Salamis: four historical fictions

(a) The first message of Themistokles

THE story that Themistokles sent a message to Xerxes before the battle of Salamis, a message which induced the Persians to enter the straits of Salamis with their fleet, is given in its fullest form by Herodotus (viii. 75). Beloch, followed by Obst, argued that the whole story was unhistorical, a legend without foundation, but his arguments have not been accepted by English scholars. Wells, for example (*Studies*, 165), finds fault with Obst because 'the message of Themistokles to Xerxes before the battle of Salamis, which is reported by all the ancient authorities, is cut out and its truth denied on a priori grounds'. This criticism is invalid, for two reasons. (1) The two earliest authorities for the message, Aeschylus and Herodotus, though agreeing on the central point that a message was sent, differ profoundly in almost all the details, and what later writers (e.g. Diodoros and Plutarch) have to say cannot be used to support either version, as their accounts of the matter are derived from one or other of the two primary sources and have no independent value. It may be noted that Wells himself (*Studies*, 163 ff.) attacks the use made of secondary sources by Obst and others. (2) If Herodotus in good faith repeats a tradition which is manifestly impossible or absurd, it must inevitably be discarded as unhistorical. Wells presumably would not have denied that some of the reports preserved by Herodotus must be rejected on internal grounds; it is unlikely that he disagreed with the verdict passed by his collaborator How (HW 236 f.) on another Themistokles legend, the story that he was bribed by the Euboians to keep the Greek fleet at Artemision (Hdt. viii. 4. 2–5. 3). The grounds for disbelief in that story are neither more nor less *a priori* than those brought by Beloch against the story of Themistokles' first message to Xerxes.

Wells must have been acquainted with Macan's conclusion (ii. 309) that the message 'is the most highly problematic of all the antecedents of the battle'. Macan emphasized (p. 302) the discrepancies between the accounts of the message given by Aeschylus and Herodotus with reference to (a) the content of the message, (b) the time at which it was sent, and (c) Themistokles' purpose in sending it. According to Aeschylus the message was sent before sunset on the day preceding the battle (*Persai* 355 ff.; cf. 364 f.), and the messenger reported merely that the Greeks intended to embark at nightfall and seek safety in flight (ll. 357–60). Aeschylus says nothing about Themistokles' purpose in sending the message (he does not mention Themistokles by name but says that the messenger was a Greek from the Athenian forces; cf. 355) and his silence is perhaps significant. It is, indeed, implied that the result aimed at was the one which followed the receipt of the message by Xerxes, his orders to his fleet to block all the exits, but Aeschylus fails to explain clearly how these orders were carried out in detail or how they led to a pitched battle inside the strait.

In Herodotus the sending of the message is an expedient to which Themistokles is compelled to resort by a fresh panic among the Peloponnesians in the fleet. The sequence of events in the narrative is not absolutely clear, but it is suggested that the panic arose after nightfall and was connected with a movement of the Persian land forces towards the Peloponnese, a movement certainly assumed to have begun after dark (viii. 71. 1; cf. νὺξ ἐπεγένετο in 70. 1, also Macan, i. 2. 474 A and ii. 304, n. 1). Themistokles is said to have chosen as his messenger Sikinnos, a trusty member of his own household and probably a Greek (Macan, i. 2. 475 B). Plutarch's statement (*Them.* 12. 4) that he was a Persian is perhaps based on careless reading of Hdt. viii. 75. 1, but Köster (p. 110) thinks that Sikinnos' name is Phrygian and that as a cultivated Phrygian he would have known Persian. Herodotus' version of the message is far more elaborate than that in Aeschylus. It claims to have been sent without the knowledge of the other Greek generals by the Athenian commander, because he desires the Persians, not the Greeks, to be victorious. The intention of the Greeks to run away (as in Aeschylus) comes next, but Xerxes is here urged to prevent their escape and cover himself with glory. This is explained by a final paragraph which stresses the dissensions in the Greek ranks and informs Xerxes that he is likely to witness an attack by the pro-Persians on the rest of the Greek fleet (viii. 75. 2–3).

It is not surprising that those who accept the message of Themistokles have preferred Herodotus' version of its content. The obvious objection to the version given by Aeschylus is that it fails to account for Xerxes' reaction to the message. While the Greeks maintained a position at Salamis flanking his only possible line of advance by sea, he could proceed no farther without fighting. If he was informed that they were about to flee to the Isthmus, why should he try to prevent their escape? He did not need a Mnesiphilos to tell him (Hdt. viii. 57. 2) that the retirement of the Greek fleet to the Isthmus would probably be followed before long by its disintegration.

Even if this was avoided, it would have to fight in the open waters of the Saronic Gulf, which would give full scope to the tactical superiority of the Persian ships. To tempt Xerxes to advance into Salamis strait a further bait was needed, the assurance that the Athenians had been alienated from the Greek cause by the selfishness of the Peloponnesians, and were now prepared to join hands with the enemy against their former allies (cf. HW 380f.).

However convenient this addition to the Aeschylean message may be, the disagreement between our two primary sources on its content is a crux which calls for some explanation from those who believe that a message was sent. How was Herodotus in a position to give a version so much fuller than that of Aeschylus, who was less than eight years from the events when he wrote the *Persai*? Are we to suppose that Aeschylus was acquainted with the fuller version, but because he was writing for an Athenian audience deliberately suppressed all the references to the promised treachery of the Athenian contingent, even though the promise was only a trick to deceive the barbarian? This solution is improbable, for the Aeschylean version, however unconvincing, seems to be the original nucleus of the message, while the Herodotean addition reads like an awkward excrescence which has no organic connexion with the rest of the message and is hardly consistent with it. Perhaps the oral tradition received by Herodotus contained no mention of the projected flight of the Greek fleet, but was conflated by him with the Aeschylean version, either because he deferred so far to Aeschylus' authority or because, having accepted the story of a fresh panic among the Peloponnesians on the night before the battle, he thought that the message must have included some reference to their projected flight. It must be remembered that in Herodotus the message is sent by Themistokles without the knowledge or approval of the other generals and is designed not so much to lure the Persian fleet into the straits as to prevent the Greeks from leaving them.

Ephoros, if correctly reproduced by Diodoros, agreed with Herodotus on Themistokles' motive in sending the message, but reverted to the Aeschylean version of its content, and accordingly assumed that Xerxes, in order to prevent the escape of the Greeks, must have sent a squadron to block the Megarid Channel, while sending the rest of his fleet to Salamis to join battle with the enemy (Diod. xi. 17. 1-2). Like Aeschylus, Ephoros signally fails to explain why Xerxes' decision to fight a sea-battle should have resulted from the message in its Aeschylean form. Plutarch seems to have followed Ephoros for the most part, but he makes the message begin with the words 'Themistokles the general of the Athenians, because he sides with the Great King, is the first to report to him that the Greeks are about to run away' (*Them.* 12. 5); this is a paraphrase of the opening words of the message as given by Herodotus (viii. 75. 2).

Some of the above difficulties were raised by Beloch (*G.G.* ii². 2. 119 f.). He also argued that in one tradition recorded by Herodotus the Persians had already decided to attack before the arrival of the message, which is in consequence superfluous. This argument must be rejected in view of Macan's careful distinction between the alternative plans open to the Persians (op. cit. ii. 305 ff.). The first plan was perhaps to end the deadlock at sea by offering battle to the Greek fleet in the open waters outside the eastern strait (Hdt. viii. 70. 1); when the Greeks refused to respond, the Persians were eventually forced to bring them to battle by introducing their own fleet into the straits secretly at night. It has been suggested above (p. 217) that Herodotus, in dating their adoption of the second plan within a few hours of their execution of the first, may have telescoped the course of events, and that several days may have elapsed between the movement in 70. 1 and that in 76. 1. Anyhow, the later plan, as described by Herodotus (followed by Beloch), is essentially different from the original plan. Its adoption was probably forced on the Persians by the failure of the first plan and the consequent continuation of the deadlock, but it may also have been due to an extraneous cause, the alleged message; on either supposition Beloch's argument is invalid.

On the view that Herodotus has correctly described the movements made by the Persian fleet on the night before the battle (see above, pp. 217 ff.) it follows that if Themistokles' message is historical his motive can only have been that attributed to his action by Herodotus, to prevent the flight and subsequent dispersal of the Greek fleet. Nothing else could have justified him in venturing on his own sole responsibility to tempt the Persians to advance into the strait by night; his plan would then have to be regarded as a last desperate throw designed to bring about a sea-fight at once in the narrow waters best suited to the Greek fleet, rather than incur certain defeat by allowing it to disintegrate. But the Herodotean background for this explanation of the message depends on a tradition which is itself suspect. However much some of the Peloponnesians may have murmured at the occupation of a position so far in advance of their own homes, it is incredible that the council of admirals vacillated in the way described by Herodotus when once they had decided to occupy the Salamis position, and their confidence in it must have been strengthened by the long deadlock which followed the arrival of the Persian fleet at Phaleron and the evident inability of its commanders to resolve it.

Those who believe, in defiance of the traditions preserved by

Herodotus, that the Persian fleet did not enter the straits until the morning of the battle have nevertheless preferred the Herodotean account of the message to the Aeschylean (e.g. Macan, ii. 309 ff.), presumably because they realize that the Persian admirals could not have been so foolish as to lead their fleet up the straits in broad daylight unless they had reason to believe that the Greek fleet was too disunited to offer serious opposition (see above, p. 227). But if the Persians expected to triumph without much fighting, why did they occupy the island of Psyttaleia with troops (cf. Munro in *J.H.S.* xxii, 1902, 327)? The motive for the occupation given by Aeschylus (*Persai*, 450–3) and reproduced by Herodotus (viii. 76. 2) implies that they anticipated a hard struggle. Moreover, the discrepancy in the content of the message as given by the two primary sources demands an explanation. Can we be sure that Herodotus had access to a more authentic tradition of it than that repeated by Aeschylus? Is it not possible that his fuller version is the product of later reflection, concocted by someone who appreciated the inadequacy of the Aeschylean message?

There is a further objection to the Herodotean version of the message which is insuperable, the incredibility of its alleged effect on the Persians. They knew that the Athenians were their bitterest enemies and that their enmity must have been intensified by the recent devastation of their land and the destruction of their temples. There had been no recent negotiations with the Athenians, no attractive offer of reparations on a handsome scale (such as Mardonios was soon to make; see above, p. 272) to induce them to go over to the enemy. Yet we are asked to believe that the Persians accepted without question the eleventh-hour assurances brought by Sikinnos, acted on them without delay or any attempt at confirmation, and did not even trouble to detain the messenger (viii. 75, last sentence; cf. Beloch, loc. cit.). Such credulity, in marked contrast with the caution shown by the Persians when they first heard the news that the Greek fleet had withdrawn from Artemision (viii. 23. 1), is too staggering to be accepted as fact, and the story of Themistokles' message to Xerxes on the eve of Salamis must therefore be rejected as unhistorical, no less than the story of his later message to Xerxes from Andros (viii. 110. 2–3; see above, p. 241).

The truth of the story is not guaranteed by the fact that it was current (in its Aeschylean form) comparatively soon after the event. It is impossible to explain how Themistokles came to be credited with the authorship of these two fictitious messages, but the first may have grown out of a claim made by him that he had been responsible for compelling the Persians to fight in waters favourable to the Greeks. He had indeed done so by persuading the Greeks to occupy the Salamis position, thereby ensuring that when the Persian admirals were faced with a deadlock they had no choice but to retreat or to introduce their fleet by night into the straits. Athenian gossip, however, preferred a more colourful explanation, which like other legends connected by the Athenians with the battle had the further attraction that it imputed selfishness and cowardice to their Peloponnesian allies.

(b) The report of Aristeides

Herodotus implies that Themistokles, after sending Sikinnos to Xerxes, returned to the council of war, whose members were still arguing with one another, for he is again in the council when Aristeides arrives from Aigina later in the night. Aristeides sends a message in to the council asking for an interview with him, and when Themistokles comes out reports to him that the Peloponnesians can no longer escape even if they desire to do so, for the Greek fleet is now completely surrounded by the Persians (viii. 78–79). Themistokles explains to Aristeides that he himself has brought about this result, and begs him to repeat his news in person to the councillors. Aristeides then tells them that he has just come from Aigina and has with difficulty sailed unobserved through those who were blockading the Greeks (μόγις ἐκπλῶσαι λαθὼν τοὺς ἐπορμέοντας), as the Greek fleet is now surrounded by the Persian ships. Even so, a majority of the councillors refuse to believe Aristeides' report until it is confirmed by the crew of a Tenian trireme which has deserted from the enemy and tells them 'the whole truth' (viii. 80–82).

The preparations of the Greeks for the ensuing battle were the direct result of the news brought by the Tenians (viii. 83, first sentence), not of the alleged report of Aristeides, which is therefore superfluous. It is closely linked in Herodotus with the message of Themistokles and with its suspicious background, the story of the final war council which apparently goes on all night, although Themistokles' opponents must have had a decisive majority in it (cf. Macan, ii. 303 f.). Grundy has an odd suggestion (op. cit. 387 f.) that Themistokles could not be sure of the success of his plan until the Persians blocked the western channel, so deliberately kept the wrangle going to gain time. Macan realized that the anecdote about Aristeides might be no more than a fable (i. 2. 483 A). It seems to have aroused mistrust in Ephoros, who substituted for it the statement that the news of the Persian movements was brought to the Greeks by a Samian messenger (sent by pro-Greek Ionians) who got through unperceived by swimming to the Greek camp (Diod. xi. 17. 3–4; cf. also Munro in J.H.S. xxii. 330).

Herodotus never explains why Aristeides was returning from Aigina at this moment, but if his reference to Aristeides' ostracism is meant to suggest, as it seems to do, that he was now returning to Attica for the first time since his banishment, it is misleading. Aristeides must have been recalled by the famous amnesty-decree passed in the year of Hypsichides, apparently 481–480 (*Ath. Pol.* 22. 8; on the date see Cadoux in *J.H.S.* lxviii, 1948, 118 f. and Hignett, *The Athenian Constitution*, 336 f.), in time to be elected one of the ten generals for the Athenian year 480–479 (as suggested by Hdt. viii. 95; cf. Bury in *C.R.* x, 1896, 418). The hypothesis that he was in charge of the trireme (surely Aiginetan) which had been sent to Aigina for the Aiakidai (viii. 64. 2 and 83. 2) is improbable, and it is unlikely that he would have been conveying Athenian refugees to Aigina (Grundy, 390) so long after the arrival of the Persian fleet at Phaleron (on all this cf. HW 262 f.).

Even if Aristeides' journey from Aigina to Salamis on the night before the battle was a fact, how could it have enabled him to discover that the Greeks were now completely surrounded by the Persians? It is hardly conceivable that he should have chosen for his journey the roundabout route by way of the Megarid Channel, or, if he did, that he should have continued to travel by sea all the way to Salamis town through the Bay of Eleusis, but unless he had entered the eastern strait from the north he could not have known that the alternative line of escape had been blocked by Persian ships posted in the channel between the island of St. George and the mainland of Attica, an objection which is also fatal to the alternative possibility that he entered the eastern strait from the south.

Those who maintain that the Persian fleet did not come into the strait until the morning of the battle conclude (e.g. Grundy, 390, also Giannelli, 61) that the enemy ships encountered by Aristeides were the Egyptian squadron, which according to Ephoros (Diod. xi. 17. 2) had been sent to block the Megarid Channel, but this view cannot be reconciled with the time-indications in our other authorities. Herodotus says (viii. 76. 1) that the movements of the Persian fleet produced by Themistokles' message did not begin till midnight, and even Aeschylus puts them after nightfall. The language of Herodotus (τοὺς ἐπορμέοντας in viii. 81) indicates that the blockading squadron was already in position when Aristeides slipped through it. If he had met it in the course of its voyage round the south of Salamis he could not have known its destination or have been so sure that the Greeks were completely surrounded (cf. Keil in *A.S.* 80). On the supposition that he landed at Trupika Bay he had still to make his way across Salamis island in the dark; how could he have done all this before his arrival at the Greek headquarters, which cannot have been later than 4 a.m.?

It is true that neither Aeschylus nor Herodotus mentions the dispatch of the Egyptian squadron to the Megarid Channel, and it has therefore occurred to some advocates of the above hypothesis to solve the problem by the suggestion that the squadron was sent off from the main fleet during the afternoon of the day before the battle (Labarbe in *B.C.H.* lxxvi, 1952, 433, n. 3 says 'in the evening') before the execution by the main fleet (after nightfall) of the manœuvres described by Herodotus and Aeschylus. This suggestion was made independently by Tarn (*J.H.S.* xxviii. 221 ff.) and Macan, but in Macan the Persians send the Egyptian squadron to the Megarid Channel as part of their first plan, whereas in Tarn it had been sent to occupy a harbour in the Argolid and was only later diverted to the channel when the admirals received Themistokles' message. Tarn's solution is very artificial, and it may be doubted whether the Argives would have dared to welcome a Persian squadron in their harbours (even if the Persians had enough ships to spare for such a diversion) unless they had been encouraged by the presence of a Persian army. Macan's conception of the original Persian design is far from clear (ii. 305 ff.), but he seems to suppose that it was to cut the communications of the Greek fleet with its base in Peloponnese by blocking both channels, and so compel it to come out of the straits and fight in the Saronic Gulf.

This design is really based on a combination of evidence from two discordant sources, the statement of Herodotus (viii. 70. 1) that the Persians already had some plan of attack before they received Themistokles' message, and Ephoros' assertion that the Egyptian ships had been sent to the Megarid Channel before the battle began. It is extremely unlikely that this assertion was derived by Ephoros from an authentic tradition, but though he does not say precisely when Themistokles' message reached the Persians he leaves no doubt that on his view the dispatch of the Egyptian squadron was subsequent to this event and was indeed one of the two movements of the Persian fleet ordered by Xerxes as the direct consequences of the message (Diod. xi. 17. 1–2). Those who appeal to Ephoros should abide by his testimony; his account is coherent, and there seems to be no justification for the rejection by Tarn and Macan of the date given by Ephoros for the departure of the Egyptians from Phaleron in deference to an anecdote which Ephoros seems to have condemned.

Probably Ephoros was right to ignore the anecdote as unhistorical; certainly it cannot be used as an additional support for the alleged occupation of the Megarid Channel by the Egyptians. In the original version Aristeides was perhaps supposed to have come direct from

Aigina to Salamis town and to have made his way somehow under cover of darkness through the Persian squadrons which were drawn up outside the entrance to the eastern straits. This did not, indeed, justify the attribution to him of the confident announcement that the Greek fleet was completely surrounded (cf. Legrand, viii. 76, n. 4), but if this difficulty occurred to those who first circulated the story they might have replied that the western exit from the Bay of Eleusis (which could be adequately guarded by three ships; cf. Thuc. ii. 93. 4, cited by Obst, 151, with wrong reference to iii. 93 in n. 13) would not be a practicable route for a large fleet seeking to escape in a hurry to the Peloponnese. The anecdote of Aristeides' journey is certainly dramatic (Grundy, 388), but its content is unsatisfactory, and as the alleged report had no influence on the events both it and the journey which led up to it may safely be dropped out of the historical record.

(c) *The flight of the Corinthians*

In an appendix to his narrative of Salamis Herodotus repeats (viii. 94) a story to the discredit of the Corinthians which had been told to him by the Athenians. They alleged that the Corinthian admiral Adeimantos at the very beginning of the battle had hoisted sail and fled, and that the example set by him was promptly followed by the rest of the Corinthian contingent. But when they arrived in their flight at a point off the Salaminian coast opposite the temple of Athena Skiras, they were stopped by some men (apparently of supernatural origin) who approached them in a small boat and told them that the Greeks were already victorious. With some difficulty they convinced Adeimantos, who then turned his ships round and began to return, but when he and his Corinthians rejoined the fleet they found that the fighting was all over. After this detailed account of the tale (φάτις) spread abroad by the Athenians Herodotus adds not only that it was denied by the Corinthians, who 'claimed to have played a leading part in the sea-fight', but also that their version was supported by the testimony of 'the rest of Greece'.

Adeimantos was perhaps identical with the father of the Corinthian Aristeas (so vii. 137. 3, but Aristeus in Thuc. i. 60. 2) who was prominent in the events leading up to the Peloponnesian War, but this is not enough to justify the conclusion of Wecklein (accepted by many, including HW i. 39) that the above story was not invented till 432. Hauvette has shown that the friendly relations which once existed between Corinth and Athens (cf. HW ii. 99 f.) turned to hatred as soon as the Athenians became the first sea-power in Greece, between 483 and 480 (Hauvette, 363 f. and 423). The story in Hdt. viii. 94 might have been invented at any date after 480, but probably it belongs to the period of the deadly enmity (τὸ σφοδρὸν μῖσος; Thuc. i. 103. 4) which followed the Athenian alliance with Megara about twenty years later. Adeimantos seems to be attacked merely as the leader; it is against the Corinthians as a whole that the slander is really directed.

If the Greeks were informed before dawn that the enemy had blocked the channel between the island of St. George and the mainland, as Herodotus implies, the falsity of the Athenian story is certain, for whether Adeimantos fled northwards or southwards, he would soon have encountered some part of the Persian fleet. But, as Legrand remarks (viii. 84, n. 1), calumny, which by definition has no respect for truth, does not always show respect for probability either. Nevertheless, those who believe that the Persian fleet did not enter the straits until the morning of the battle have persuaded themselves that there may have been some foundation in fact for the Athenian report; the favourite hypothesis is that the Corinthians (and possibly some ships from the rest of the fleet) were indeed absent from the main battle, not in cowardly flight, but because they had been sent off to meet the Egyptian squadron. In harmony with this view attempts have been made to locate the temple of Athena Skiras at some point on the north-eastern or northern coast of Salamis.

The location of the Salaminian Skiradion is unknown. Plutarch (*Life of Solon*, c. 9) mentions it in connexion with the supposed capture of Salamis by Solon, but the text is corrupt in two places and no conclusion can be based on it. In his paraphrase of Hdt. viii. 94 Plutarch says that Adeimantos' flight was halted περὶ τὰ λήγοντα τῆς Σαλαμινίας (*H.M.* 39 = *Moralia* 870 B). Stein understood this to mean 'at the far end of the land of Salamis', and accordingly located the shrine in the extreme south of the island, seeing in this detail a fresh proof of the falsity of the Athenian story (cf. Hauvette, 423, n. 1), but Plutarch's words might indicate that the Skiradion was somewhere near the Megarian Channel (so Macan, i. 2. 505 B). Leake suggested that it was where the Phaneromene monastery now stands, on the north of Salamis facing the Bay of Eleusis, and this site, accepted by Munro (*J.H.S.* xxii. 329) has been vigorously endorsed by Wilhelm (*S.B. Ak. Wien*, ccxi, 1929, 38), but most modern scholars have followed the view of Lolling (*Ath. Mit.* i, 1876, 131; cf. Bürchner in *R.-E.* i A. 2. 1828, also HW 267) that the Skiradion is represented by some ancient remains on the promontory of Cape Arapis, near the island of Leros and the entrance to the Bay of Eleusis; τῆς Σαλαμινίας is then supposed, rather improbably, to mean the territory of the town of Salamis.

One obvious objection to Lolling's site is that the Athenian story seems to locate the shrine at a considerable distance from the Greek camp; the Corinthians flee as soon as the battle begins, but although they turn back shortly after reaching the Skiradion, by the time they rejoin the main fleet the battle is already over. For this reason the sites favoured by Leake and Macan seem more probable. Munro (loc. cit.) would explain the late return of the Corinthians by the assumption that they spent most of the day fighting, probably against heavy odds but possibly not alone. Such reconstructions are based on two very doubtful premisses, first, that Ephoros had some authority for his assertion that the Egyptian squadron had been sent before the battle to block the Megarid Channel (he does not say, as some of his modern followers say, that it had orders to proceed into the Bay of Eleusis and attack the Greek fleet from the rear), and second, that the Athenian story must have had some foundation in fact. Why must it? Why cannot it have been a complete fabrication without any foundation whatever? It claims that the Corinthians saw no fighting on the day of the battle, but in Salamis there was a tomb with an inscription (fragments of which have been found; cf. *I.G.* i². 927 = Tod, no. 16) commemorating the Corinthians who had been killed at Salamis and were buried there. No wonder that the rest of Greece bore witness to the prominent part played by the Corinthians in the victory (Hdt. viii. 94. 4).

If the unanimous voice of Greece proclaimed the falsity of the Athenian story, it is unsafe to base any hypothesis on the assumption that the Corinthians were absent from the main battle. Labarbe, accepting Herodotus' total of 380 ships for the Greek fleet (viii. 82. 2; but cf. HW 249 on viii. 46. 1) reconciles it with Aeschylus' figure of 310 ships on the morning of the battle (*Persai* 338 ff.) by the suggestion that 70 ships (including the Corinthian squadron) had been detached from the main fleet before the battle began to meet the Egyptians (*B.C.H.* lxxvi, 1952, 421 ff., followed by Hammond in *J.H.S.* lxxvi. 40). Labarbe's hypothesis is not in itself more improbable than others which try to find some residuum of fact in this Athenian fiction, but in order to reach a total of seventy for Adeimantos' squadron he appeals to the tainted evidence of the orator Lykourgos (*In Leocratem* 70) to prove that the squadron included ships from the contingents of Sparta and Aigina. Lykourgos says that 'Eteonikos the Spartan and Adeimantos the Corinthian and the Aiginetan fleet wished to secure safety for themselves by night, but our ancestors, though all the Greeks wanted to desert them, forced the rest to become free by compelling them to stay at Salamis and fight by their side against the barbarian'. This is no more than a garbled version of the account in Herodotus of the panic in the Greek fleet *on the night before the battle* (viii. 74), and includes two obvious blunders, the reference to the Aiginetans (who really, like the Megarians, supported the Athenian proposal to stay at Salamis), and the howler which substitutes Eteonikos' name for that of Eurybiadas. Labarbe's handling of this nonsense is an outstanding example of the dangers inherent in attempts to distil precious facts from secondary sources. Anyone who hopes to find historical truth in Lykourgos' references to past history may still consult with profit the third appendix to the school edition of his speech by Rehdantz (Leipzig, 1876, 165–86).

If the Corinthians had been absent from the main battle on an honourable mission, they had no reason to conceal the truth especially if they too had seen fighting and suffered casualties. This obvious fact is obscured, however, by the curious way in which Herodotus chose to deal with the conflicting versions. To a discerning reader, as Plutarch saw, the story told by the Athenians was even more discreditable to themselves than to the Corinthians; they had invented a gross calumny against their enemies which had been given the lie by the whole of Greece. Yet because Herodotus repeats their version so fully, with circumstantial details of time and place, and because the disclaimer appended to it is so general and perfunctory, it is easy to understand why many have felt that there must be something in the story after all. If Herodotus did not believe the story he was certainly not bound by his own principles to record it. There is no need to suppose, as Meyer did (*Forsch.* ii. 203) that his reason for inserting it was hostility to Corinth, and that he acted on the maxim *semper aliquid haeret*. But having decided, for whatever reason, to repeat it in detail he ought to have seen that if he himself disbelieved it he had a duty to his readers to give them the true version with equal fullness. This was particularly necessary because in his narrative of Salamis, apparently based mainly on Athenian and Aiginetan sources, he had failed to make any mention of the part played by the Corinthians or of their position in the battle-line, although their contingent was the largest in the Greek fleet after the Athenian. As the Athenians were on the Greek left (viii. 85. 1) the forty Corinthian ships would probably have been stationed on the other wing, near the Spartans; they would thus have been involved in the stern struggle which seems to have taken place on the Greek right (see above, p. 235), whose achievements in defence, though indispensable to the success of the whole, were apparently less spectacular than those of the Aiginetans and Athenians.

(d) Xerxes' mole

Herodotus asserts that Xerxes after the defeat of his fleet made up his mind to retreat, but in order to conceal his purpose from the Greeks and from his own men attempted first to construct a mole to Salamis across the strait, and began to bind together Phoenician merchant ships to serve both as a bridge and as a wall, and also made warlike preparations as though he was intending to fight again at sea (viii. 97. 1). Ktesias dates the beginning of the mole before the sea-fight. According to the relevant passage in Photius' epitome (*Persika* 26) 'Xerxes [after the capture of the Acropolis] came to the narrowest part of Attica [i.e. the narrowest part of the strait between Attica and Salamis], which is called Herakleion, and began to construct a mole towards Salamis, proposing to cross to Salamis on foot. But on the advice of Themistokles the Athenian and Aristeides archers are summoned from Crete and arrive. Then a naval battle follows between the Persians and the Greeks.' It is reasonable to infer from this abstract that in Ktesias Xerxes was forced by the Cretan archers to abandon the work and so had to fall back on his alternative plan of bringing the Greeks to battle (cf. Caspari in *J.H.S.* xxxi, 1911, 108 f.). The version of Ktesias was probably adopted by Ephoros in preference to that of Herodotus, for it reappears in Strabo (p. 395, in the passage quoted above, p. 398).

Hammond tries to reconcile our conflicting authorities by the suggestion that after the battle Xerxes reverted to his earlier plan of a mole, which he had previously begun and abandoned (*J.H.S.* lxxvi, 1956, 52; cf. his *History of Greece*, 244). But if the mole had been started before the battle and had made such progress that archers had had to be summoned from Crete to check it, is it credible that Herodotus, who duly recorded the attempt after the battle, should have heard nothing about the previous attempt, or that Ktesias should have had access on this point to a tradition unknown to Herodotus? Moreover, if this method had been tried and abandoned before the battle, how could Xerxes expect it to be more successful now that he had lost control of the sea? Perhaps it was this consideration that caused Ktesias to date the construction of the mole earlier than Herodotus had done; the alleged intervention of the Cretan archers, who are not mentioned elsewhere, looks like fiction. As Herodotus does not say at what point of the mainland Xerxes began his mole, the statement that it started from the Herakleion seems to be a mere guess; Ktesias simply assumed that the narrowest part of the strait would be the obvious choice (cf. Caspari, op. cit. 108, n. 40).

Others have argued that Ktesias must be right and Herodotus

wrong because there was not sufficient time between the battle and the retreat of the Persian fleet for even a beginning to be made on the mole, but this objection is invalid if, as seems probable, the fleet did not depart until the second night after the battle (Hauvette, 427; see above, p. 240). Again, Ktesias clearly believed that the mole was a serious attempt to solve the problem of effecting a landing in Salamis, but this view, though accepted by Beloch (*G.G.* ii². 2. 122, where the inception of the mole is dated before the battle; cf. Köster, 111), underrates the formidable difficulties of such an undertaking, far greater than those faced by Alexander the Great when he constructed his mole at Tyre (cf. HW 268). As Macan has rightly said (i. 2. 510 B), it was 'absurd and impossible without an antecedent naval victory', and 'after a naval defeat still more so' (cf. also Giannelli, 56, n. 1). It is true that the Persians could not easily have forced a landing on Salamis from their ships while the island was crowded with armed men (cf. the valuable remarks of Hammond in *J.H.S.* lxxvi, 52 and n. 84, with his reference to Thuc. iv. 10. 5) but presumably they would not have needed to attempt it if they had been victorious at sea, for they could then have cut the line of communications and supplies between the Greeks in Salamis and their base in Peloponnese, and once the Persians were defeated they had no further hope of effecting a landing on Salamis by any means.

For Herodotus the mole was merely an expedient to gain time by deceiving both the Greeks and the Persians about Xerxes' real intentions; Grundy argues (*G.P.W.* 409 n.) that if Herodotus was right, it did not matter whether the mole was begun at a possible or an impossible point. Rados has shown that the Greeks could not even after their victory attempt anything against the Attic coast so long as it was occupied in force by the Persian infantry, and so could not interfere with the beginning of the mole (op. cit. 316 and 321; cf. also 231), but as it progressed farther into the open strait it would surely have been more exposed to attack (cf. Arrian, *Anabasis* ii. 18. 5). Herodotus' description of the proposed work is so obscure that most of the commentators have left it unexplained; was it to be a mole stretching right across the strait, or was the mole merely the starting-point for a pontoon bridge? Hammond suggests (*History*, 244) that the merchant-ships were lashed together to act as a breakwater for the protection of the mole, but though this is a reasonable interpretation of Herodotus' words, how could a mole have been constructed right across a strait which is so wide and deep even at its narrowest point? Hence Munro concludes (*J.H.S.* xxii. 331 f.) that Xerxes' design to build a mole is scarcely credible even as a pretext to mask his retreat, and this conclusion may be accepted, even though none of the various explanations for the story suggested by Munro can be reconciled with the details given by Herodotus. More plausible is Macan's final suggestion (i. 2. 510 f.) that the structure was to be a wharf or pier 'for embarkation and so on, and was never intended to reach the opposite shore'.

APPENDIX X

Plutarch on the campaign of Plataia

PLUTARCH'S account of the campaign of Plataia in chapters 11–20
of his *Life of Aristeides* (henceforth cited in this appendix as PA)
well illustrates the dangers of picking out statements from 'secondary sources' without examining them in their context. Plutarch
undoubtedly drew much of the narrative part of his account from
Herodotus (whom he cites twice by name, with open or implied
criticism, in 19. 7 and 16. 1), but he adds details of doubtful authenticity (such as the statement in 19. 1 that Mardonios was killed
by a Spartan with a stone, backed up by a questionable story of
a vision seen by a Lydian in the temple of Amphiaraos), and he
manifestly had no clear grasp of the development of events. In spite
of Herodotus (ix. 19. 2) he makes the Athenians arrive at Plataia
before they are joined by Pausanias and the rest of the Greeks (PA
11. 1–2). Thereupon Teisamenos the seer warns the Greeks not to
take the offensive; this warning is plainly dated by Herodotus (ix.
33. 1 and 36) after the advance of the Greek army to the second
position, but Plutarch never mentions this advance at all. After a
series of digressions on a Delphic oracle, the claims of Athenians and
Tegeans to occupy the left wing, and an alleged conspiracy of im-
poverished Athenian aristocrats in the camp, Plutarch is back in the
first position (μετὰ ταῦτα, 14. 1) with the first attack of the Persian
cavalry led by Masistios. After this the warning against taking the
offensive occurs again (15. 1; cf. 11. 3) but is now attributed to the
seers in both armies; in the end Mardonios decides to override it.
Alexander of Macedon communicates the decision to Aristeides,
and Herodotus' story of the double interchange of wings between
the Athenians and the Spartans follows.

At the end of this story Plutarch remarks that the day (clearly
the twelfth day of Herodotus' Journal; see above, p. 316) passed
without action (διεξῆλθεν ἀργή, 16. 7). Having failed to mention the
advance of the Greek army from the first to the second position, how
can he describe its retreat to the positions occupied by it when the
battle was fought, and what explanation of it can he offer? After the
words quoted he goes on with the statement (16. 8) that the Greeks
after deliberation decided to move their camp farther from the
enemy (πορρωτέρω μεταστρατοπεδεῦσαι) and occupy a well-watered
place. But when the Greek position was last mentioned (14. 1) it

was 'at the foot of Kithairon in strong and rocky ground'; this description is an embellishment of Herodotus' statement (ix. 19. 3) that the first Greek position was on the foothills of Kithairon. The motive alleged for the Greek decision to move to a new position (PA 16. 8) is 'because the springs near them had been polluted as a result of the superiority of the enemy cavalry'. But Plutarch has made no mention of any activity of the Persian cavalry since the defeat of Masistios, not even their raid into the Dryoskephalai Pass. His account of the nocturnal march and the ensuing battle is trustworthy in the main because he has been content to base it on Herodotus, apart from a few picturesque touches which can easily be detected (e.g. the assertion in 18. 5 that the Athenians heard the noise of the κραυγή which was coming from the battlefield); the more substantial additions at the end of his narrative, the figure for the total Greek losses (19. 5) and the story that the Aristeia were finally awarded to the Plataians (20. 1–3), are guesswork or fabrication (see above, pp. 20 f.).

Plutarch's narrative of Plataia is more like the essay of a clever journalist than a serious contribution to history. It is therefore unlikely that his contributions to the topography of the battlefield should be of any independent value; how can they be, when he has failed to distinguish the first two positions occupied by the Greeks? It is an even more serious objection that the two items frequently adduced as evidence by scholars occur in a story which has all the marks of an historical fiction, the story of the oracle obtained from Delphi by Aristeides. Apollo is said to have informed the Athenians (PA 11. 3) that they would defeat their enemies if they prayed to Zeus, Hera of Kithairon, Pan, and the Sphragitides Nymphai, if they offered sacrifice to seven named heroes (headed by Androkrates), and if they fought the battle on Attic soil in the plain of Eleusinian Demeter and Kore. Plutarch says that the recipients were perplexed by the oracle, since its last part pointed clearly to the plain of Eleusis, whereas the seven heroes were all connected with Plataia and the cave of the Sphragitides was on a neighbouring peak of Kithairon. In this impasse the Plataian general Arimnestos was guided by a dream to look nearer home for the sites mentioned by the oracle, and after careful inquiry from the oldest inhabitants discovered that there was a very old shrine of Eleusinian Demeter and the Maiden near Hysiai beneath Kithairon (τῶν Ὑσιῶν πλησίον ὑπὸ τὸν Κιθαιρῶνα, 11. 6). Arimnestos then took Aristeides to the place, which was admirably suited for a battlefield, because the foothills of Kithairon, meeting the plain at this point, would prevent the Persians from using their cavalry. Moreover, here too (ταύτῃ), close at hand (ἐγγύς), was the shrine of the hero Androkrates,

surrounded by a thick grove of shady trees (11. 8). Finally, to ensure
the complete fulfilment of the oracle, the Plataians on the proposal
of Arimnestos voted to remove the boundary stones between their
territory and that of Athens, so incorporating the Plataiïs in Attica.

An authentic Delphic oracle foretelling precisely the site of the
decisive battle in this campaign would have been known to Herodotus and, if known, recorded by him. It is a suspicious fact that the
text of the alleged oracle is not quoted; it is merely reproduced in a
prose paraphrase. The apparent occasion of its delivery is preposterous, for Aristeides is supposed to have sent a messenger to consult
Apollo at Delphi after Teisamenos has warned the Greeks not to
take the offensive; this warning points to a time after the Greeks had
occupied the second position (as does the debate about the left wing
in PA 12) but three chapters later (PA 14) they are still in the first
position. It is perhaps arguable that the position of the oracle in
Plutarch's narrative is due to a misunderstanding on his part and
that it was really delivered earlier. Parke has suggested (*A History
of the Delphic Oracle*[1], 189 ff.) that Aristeides obtained the oracle
earlier in 479 to induce the Spartans to advance into Attica, under
the impression that Mardonios would stand his ground and fight on
the plain of Eleusis; those elements in the oracle which clash with
this explanation by pointing to the Plataiïs must then be accounted
for by the hypothesis that the original oracle was 'somewhat mis-
represented by a later narrative designed to show that it was a perfect prophecy of Plataia'. Parke argues his case skilfully, but the
silence of Herodotus is sufficient to disprove the delivery by Delphi
in 479 of any oracle relating to a Greek choice of the battlefield.
If the oracle is evidently a later fiction, there is no need to discuss
the motives behind its invention or to consider whether it was concocted in the interests of Delphi or of Athens; the mention of the
Sphragitides links up with Plutarch's citation from the Atthidographer Kleidemos (PA 19. 6 = Kleidemos, fr. 22 in Jacoby,
F.G.H., no. 323) which shows that the oracle was known to Kleidemos
in its 'Plataian' version. As told by Plutarch, the story suggests an
Athenian origin, but in its present form it is a clumsy fabrication, for
although the oracle is assumed to have been delivered to Athens the
victory on the site indicated by it was won not by Athens but by
Sparta.

The two topographical notices embedded in Plutarch's story do
not merit the respectful consideration which they have received from
some scholars. One of the requirements of the story was that the two
shrines connected with the campaign of Plataia should be situated
close together, in defiance of the facts, for in Herodotus the Androkrateion is near the second Greek position and the Eleusinion is near

the Spartan third position. It is unlikely that the original author of
the story reproduced by Plutarch was sufficiently well-informed to
supply precise details about the positions of the two shrines. His site
for the Eleusinion is obviously suggested by the hypothesis, refuted
by the evidence contained in Herodotus (see above, p. 333), that the
decisive encounter must have taken place on ground unsuitable for
the Persian cavalry. It is a very naïve supposition that Plutarch himself, being a Boiotian, had discovered the sites of the two shrines by his
own researches. Both shrines had probably disappeared long before
his day, and his statements about them are general and vague, as
might be expected in view of his failure to grasp clearly the three
successive positions taken up by the Greek army north of Kithairon.
As Grundy has well said (*G.P.W.*, section 3 of the note on p. 468),
'Plutarch's topography of Platæa is quite hopeless. It was evidently
not a side of historical inquiry in which he took the slightest real
interest.'

APPENDIX XI

The topography of the Plataia campaign

(a) *The passes*

THERE are now six passes through the Kithairon–Parnes range, which originally formed the southern boundary of Boiotia (cf. Grundy, 445 ff. and Ufer in *A.S.* iv. 110 ff.). The westernmost is a mountain track which goes round the western end of Kithairon from the Boiotian port of Kreusis, on the shores of the Gulf of Corinth, to the Megarian town of Aigosthena, also on the gulf; it was dangerous in stormy weather (Xenophon, *Hell.* v. 4. 17; cf. vi. 4. 25–26) and was apparently not used in 479. The easternmost went from Athens northwards through Dekeleia and over Parnes into the Asopos valley; it was the way by which Mardonios retreated from Attica (ix. 15. 1).

West of this is the direct route from Athens to Thebes; it climbs from the plain beyond Acharnai by a stiff ascent to Phyle (2,255 ft.) and on through wild country to the watershed (2,560 ft.), then goes steeply down to the upland plain of Skourta (village of Krora, 1,840 ft.) and after proceeding onwards to the north-west crosses a low pass (about 665 metres according to Ufer, 123 n.) and descends rapidly into the Asopos valley near the modern village of Darimari (cf. the *Handbook of Greece*, 214 f. and Gomme, *Essays*, 22 f.). The pass which leads into Boiotia on this route has usually been called the pass of Portaes, but Kirsten (*R.-E.*, article on Plataia, 2291 f.) apparently maintains that the application of the name to this pass is inaccurate. It is disputed whether the Athenian fort of Panakton (Thuc. v. 3. 5) was situated in the plain of Skourta, as Grundy apparently believed, since he refers to this plain as the plateau of Panakton (p. 447, cf. Miss Chandler in *J.H.S.* xlvi, 1926, 6 f.), or was identical with the ruined fort of Gyphtokastro on the Eleutherai road (cf. Gomme's edition of Thucydides, iii. 632 f.); the evidence of Thuc. v. 42. 1 seems unfavourable to this identification, which is rejected by Hammond (*B.S.A.* xlix, 1954, 121).

Pritchett denies (*A.J. Arch.* lxi, 1957, 20 A) that the Phyle–Thebes route can ever have been practicable for a large army with a baggage train, but he admits that he has not been over the route. Gomme (op. cit. 22) thinks that though it was too difficult for traders it could have been used, by an army invading Attica from the north, to avoid the Eleutherai route; he does not, however, suggest that it ever was so used. Grundy would probably have agreed with Gomme, for he says (op. cit. 447) that 'Mardonios might certainly have made use of this route in his retreat'. But even if it was suitable for an ancient Greek army, it is improbable that Pausanias crossed Kithairon by this route in 479 (as Munro and Ufer suppose), for he was advancing towards the Asopos valley from Eleusis, not from Athens, and must have started from Eleusis along the road to Thebes which crossed Kithairon at a point farther west than Darimari, so that if he wished to strike into the Phyle–Thebes road before crossing Kithairon he would have had to diverge near the top to the right through very difficult country; the cross-country route suggested by Ufer (122 and n. 2) was perhaps too difficult for an army (cf. Kirsten, 2291 f.). The motive suggested by Munro for his change of route is unconvincing, while Ufer's seems unnecessary (see above, pp. 295 ff.), and it is better to suppose that he set out from Eleusis by the normal road to Thebes.

Where did this road cross Kithairon? Grundy describes three routes over Kithairon to the west of the Phyle–Darimari route, all three near to the site of Plataia; he names them (from east to west) as the Dryoskephalai Pass, the Plataia–Athens Pass, and the Plataia–Megara Pass, but all three names beg the questions to be solved, and Grundy's solutions are not accepted by all; the passes must therefore be distinguished by numbers. The easternmost (Pass 1), now called the pass of Kasa or Gyphtokastro, is the lowest (649 metres; Ufer, 111) and in spite of the steepness of the descent on its north side (Grundy, 447) must certainly have been in use in the fifth century (as most scholars would agree; cf. Kirsten, 2292); the road leading up to it from the plain of Eleusis may therefore be identified with Xenophon's τὴν δι' Ἐλευθερῶν ὁδόν (Hell. v. 4. 14). Pass 2 (called the Middle Pass by Ufer) is used by the modern route which runs from Vilia south of Kithairon to the neighbourhood of Plataia, and is sometimes called the Vilia Pass (over 825 metres; Ufer, 113). Pass 3, the westernmost and highest of the three (900 metres), is assumed by Grundy (*Topography*, 7) to have been followed by the road from Megara to Plataia mentioned by Pausanias (ix. 2. 3) but he admits that 'it must have been always difficult, if not absolutely impracticable, for wheeled vehicles', though 'quite practicable for infantry'.

Xenophon, however (loc. cit.), contrasts his 'road through Eleutherai' with τὴν εἰς Πλαταιὰς φέρουσαν, and elsewhere strongly implies (v. 4. 59) that these were the only two passes in this sector of Kithairon. If this implication is sound, one of the three modern passes cannot have been in use in the early fourth century. Ufer insists that the pass not in use must have been Pass 2, but Munro argues (*J.H.S.* xxiv, 1904, 155) that the Thebes–Megara road went over Pass 2, and that Pass 3 was merely a short cut for pedestrians or horsemen. Munro's view seems more probable than Ufer's, especially as Hammond (*B.S.A.* xlix, 1954, 103 f.) and others have found traces of an ancient road on the line of the route north of Pass 2 (cf. Pritchett, 18 A and also 19 A, where he identifies this route with Xenophon's road leading from the Megarid to Plataia).

If Pass 3 was not traversed by a road in Herodotus' time, the road from Megara to Thebes (identical in this part of its course with the road from Megara to Plataia) must have crossed Kithairon by Pass 2. Beloch thought it possible that the road from Plataia to Athens also crossed Kithairon by Pass 2 and then diverged from the Plataia–Megara road on the south side of the mountain; as Thucydides says (iii. 24. 1) that the Plataia–Athens road went over Dryoskephalai, Beloch suggested that the pass known to Thucydides and Herodotus (ix. 39. 1) by this name would then have to be identified with Pass 2, an identification accepted by Pritchett (op. cit. 21). Munro (op. cit. 155, n. 16) asserts that Herodotus in ix. 39 seems to apply the name Dryoskephalai to the whole group of passes, but as Macan points out (i. 2. 676 A) the plural ἐκβολαί can be used of a single pass; he compares the use of ἐσβολαί in vii. 176. 3 for the Middle Gate at Thermopylai. Pritchett's view cannot be disproved, but it seems to the present writer less convincing than the alternative view, that the Athens–Plataia road crossed Kithairon by the Gyphtokastro Pass and was therefore identical so far with the Athens–Thebes road, from which it presumably diverged on the northern slopes of Kithairon, perhaps at the point where it was crossed by the east–west road from Erythrai to Plataia (see above, p. 298, n. 2). The Gyphtokastro Pass would be a more obvious route for the road from Athens to Plataia than Pass 2, because its summit was lower and it avoided Megarian territory (Xen. *Hell.* v. 4. 14 implies that the alternative to the Eleutherai road, the road leading from Megara to Plataia, did not cross Attic soil); moreover, the other route has to make a considerable detour south of Pass 2 before it can rejoin the Eleutherai road (cf. Ufer, 112 and n. 5).

Hence the Athens–Plataia road probably crossed Kithairon by the Gyphtokastro Pass, and if so this pass must be identical with the Dryoskephalai of Thucydides (and presumably of Herodotus). As Herodotus does not say by which route Pausanias led his army into Boiotia, it is uncertain whether he crossed Kithairon by the Gyphtokastro Pass, or (as Pritchett, 24 B supposes) by Pass 2, but as he was advancing on Boiotia from Eleusis the Gyphtokastro route seems the more obvious choice and is accepted by most scholars (e.g. Grundy and Macan; cf. Kirsten, 2292).

(b) The towns

In addition to Thebes and Plataia, three other Boiotian towns are mentioned by Herodotus in his account of the campaign, Erythrai, Hysiai, and Skolos; the precise sites of all three are still disputed. Erythrai was the first position north of Kithairon occupied by the Greek army (ix. 19. 3); elsewhere it is stated that Hysiai lay between it and the territory of Plataia, and the context implies that Hysiai was west of Erythrai (ix. 15. 3); this is confirmed by the fact that the Greek army on the march to its second position in the Plataiïs passed Hysiai (ix. 25. 3). In Thucydides (iii. 24. 1) the geographical order is apparently inverted, as he describes how the fugitives escaping from Plataia by night made for the road leading to Erythrai and Hysiai; this was clearly the Plataia–Erythrai road (Xen. *Hell.* v. 4. 49) running from west to east along the lower slopes of Kithairon, and Thucydides presumably mentioned Erythrai first as the more important place on it (cf. section 4 of Grundy's note on p. 459, also Munro, 154 f.).

Hysiai was on or close to the road from Eleutherai to Thebes (Paus. ix. 1. 6), which must have gone through the Gyphtokastro Pass. Grundy (long note on pp. 464 f.) located Hysiai on the slope of Kithairon just south of Kriekouki, for two reasons: (1) Pausanias (ix. 2. 1–2) says that the ruins of Hysiai and Erythrai lay a little to the right (in Spiro's text, ὀλίγον τῆς εὐθείας ἐκτραπεῖσιν ἐς δεξιά) of a road which is shown by the context to be that from Eleutherai to Plataia. Grundy, holding that this road must have gone over Pass 2, places Hysiai to the right of his road (which really was the Megara–Plataia road) below its northern exit from the pass. (2) Grundy maintains (459 n.) that Leake's site for Erythrai, at Katsoula, is 3½ miles from the nearest point in Grundy's Athens–Plataia road, and that this could not have been described by Pausanias as only a short distance from the road; he therefore located Erythrai in a valley a little to the east of Kriekouki. Perhaps he subconsciously desired to fix Erythrai, and with it the first Greek position, as near as possible to the northern exit of the Gyphtokastro Pass, but his arguments for both his sites collapse if the road from Eleutherai to Plataia really went over the pass and only diverged from the Eleutherai–Thebes road to the north of the pass near Kriekouki (cf. Munro, 154; Ufer, 112 and 117). A further objection to Grundy's sites for Erythrai and Hysiai is that they are much too near to each other (so Ufer, 118, citing Frazer's *Pausanias*, v. 4; cf. Pritchett, 23 A).

Leake, followed by Munro and others, relied on the presence of sherds of Hellenic pottery ('that surest of tests'; Munro, 154) to locate Hysiai to the east of the road going north from the Gyphtokastro

Pass to the Asopos, roughly identical with Hill 240 on the map in Grundy's *Topography* (where on his later map 'Ruins of Tower' are marked to the east of a tributary of A6 flowing north). Pritchett (op. cit. 9 f.) has revived the criterion employed by Leake, but claims (11 A) that there is a complete absence of Greek sherds of the classical period on Ufer's site for Hysiai, which is apparently identical with Leake's. He has, however, discovered several sites with numerous fragments of Hellenic sherds and tiles; the only one which can possibly be identified with Hysiai is the Pantanassa Ridge (Pritchett, 12 B; cf. 22 B). This seems to be the ridge lying south-south-west of Leake's site, still to the right of the road but nearer to it, and on the left (west) bank of the A6 tributary already mentioned; it is the ridge marked by the word 'High' in the indication 'The High Bastions' on Grundy's later map. Anyhow, the exact location of Hysiai makes little difference to our understanding of the operations before the battle (so Beloch, ii². 2. 124).

Pritchett also found suitable remains on the Agia Triada ridge (about 2½ kilometres due east of the Pantanassa Ridge), 440 metres high, which extends out into the plain and has good views over it. Pritchett, who thinks that it is probably the site of Leake's Katsoula, finally agrees with Leake that the ancient Erythrai was situated here (Pritchett, 23 A and 13 A). Ufer wants to locate Erythrai about 6 kilometres east of his Hysiai and near Darimari, because he believes (as does Munro, 157) that Pausanias and his army advanced into Boiotia by the Phyle–Thebes road, which comes out of the mountains near Darimari. It is more likely, however, that Pausanias crossed Kithairon by the Gyphtokastro Pass and advanced eastwards along the road to Erythrai. If Erythrai (which may be tentatively identified with Leake's site) was mentioned by Herodotus because it was the position occupied by Pausanias and the right wing, the rest of the army may well have extended westwards to the exit of the pass over which they had just come (so Pritchett, 24 B).

The position of Erythrai might be fixed with more certainty if that of Skolos could be identified, but as Grundy says (449 n.), 'the exact site of Skolos is very difficult to determine', and it is not even certain whether it was on the north or the south bank of the Asopos (Kirsten, 2264 and 2291 confesses that his final decision in favour of a site on the north bank disagrees with his own map). Grundy, on admittedly slender grounds, placed Skolos on the site of Leake's Erythrai (Ufer, 119 curiously renders this as 'on the site of our Erythrai'), which suits fairly well with the statement of Pausanias (ix. 4. 4) that Skolos was only 40 stades downstream from the point where the Plataia–Thebes road crossed the Asopos. But Pausanias or his manuscripts must be mistaken, for Xenophon implies that Skolos was a good day's march from Plataia for an army (Xen. *Hell.* v. 4. 49, rightly cited by Ufer; the objection of Kirsten, 2261 is frivolous, since it is clear that Agesilaos marched with all haste to breach the stockade at Skolos before the Thebans returned); moreover, Skolos must have been within an ordinary day's march of Tanagra (Hdt. ix. 15. 2). Herodotus (loc. cit.) speaks of Skolos as ἐν γῇ τῇ Θηβαίων, which Kirsten takes to prove that it was north of the Asopos, but Strabo's description of it (p. 408) as δυσοίκητος τόπος καὶ τραχύς lying ὑπὸ τῷ Κιθαιρῶνι points to the south bank. Pritchett on the evidence of sherds (13 B and 23 B) identifies Skolos with Leake's site, the μετοχή (dependency) of the monastery of Agios Meletios, about 1,150 metres to the west of Darimari. Ufer, however, holds that this was the site of Erythrai, and locates Skolos farther east (but still on the south bank of the Asopos) near the modern Kortsa (Ufer, 119f.).

(c) Particular sites in the battle area

Only four of these have much importance for the history of the campaign, the spring of Gargaphia, the Island (to which the Greek army proposed to retreat), the chapel of the hero Androkrates, and the temple of the Eleusinian Demeter. The first two have been identified with a reasonable degree of certainty (and agreement); for the two shrines various sites have been suggested, but the evidence is really insufficient for a final decision on either. As something has already been said above (c. vii) about each of these sites, only a brief summary is necessary here.

(1) *Gargaphia*. Herodotus says that it was 10 stades from the Nesos (Island) and also that it was 20 stades from the Heraion at Plataia (ix. 51. 1 and 52); both measurements appear to be rough estimates only. The Heraion is described as 'in front of' the city of Plataia; it must therefore have been outside the town walls, but its situation is uncertain, partly because the extent of the town at the date of the battle is unknown. At a later date the town walls took in the whole of the triangular plateau (Grundy's Ridge 6) to the west of stream O4, but most scholars have supposed, in view of Thucydides' account of the siege of Plataia in 429–427, that the fifth-century town occupied only a part of this area, either the north-west corner, as Grundy originally maintained (*Topography*, 55 ff.) or the higher southern end of the plateau, as supposed by the American excavators of the site, whose view was later adopted by Grundy (*G.P.W.* 489 n.).

Ufer, however, following Beloch (ii². 1. 315, n. 2) argues that the town of Plataia already by 479 covered the whole plateau (*A.S.* 127 ff.) and draws the conclusion that the Heraion must have been situated not on Ridge 6 but on Ridge 5. He then takes as exact the

measurement of 20 stades (Hdt. ix. 52) and so identifies Gargaphia
with one of two springs on the north side of the Asopos Ridge (described by Grundy, *Topography*, 17). Neither identification has found
favour with subsequent inquirers. Ufer's claim that the Heraion
must have been visible to Pausanias when he made his famous prayer
to Hera is not proved by the passage to which he refers (Hdt. ix.
61. 3; cf. Kirsten, 2271). His location of Gargaphia would put it
close behind the Spartan position on the Asopos Ridge, and whatever Ufer may say (op. cit. 131 f.) it is incredible that the Persian
cavalry should have been able by a frontal attack to drive the Spartan
phalanx back up the slope of the ridge and so capture the all-
important spring.

The alternative is to suppose that Gargaphia was one of the springs
in the depression between the Asopos Ridge and the foothills of
Kithairon (see above, p. 302 and n. 5). The traditional site, the
spring of Apotripi (also called Alepotripi; cf. Pritchett, 21 B and
n. 78), though accepted by Woodhouse, is open to two objections,
that it has been known to run dry in summer, and that it seems too
near to the usual site for the Heraion (so Grundy, 465 f., but cf.
Beloch, ii². 2. 124). Leake therefore identified Gargaphia with a
group of springs in the depression at a point where the main routes
of the area now cross (Kirsten, 2270), between 4 and 6 furlongs from
Apotripi in a direction slightly south of east. Leake's view has been
accepted by Grundy (loc. cit.) and by most scholars since. Pritchett
says that here is the main source of water in this area, being composed of two springs (called Retsi by the locals) about 25 yards
apart, and 1,000 yards south-west of the church of St. Demetrion.

(2) *The Nesos (Island)*. Herodotus explains how there could be an
island on the mainland in these words (ix. 51. 2): σχιζόμενος ὁ
ποταμὸς ἄνωθεν ἐκ τοῦ Κιθαιρῶνος ῥέει κάτω ἐς τὸ πεδίον, διέχων ἀπ᾽
ἀλλήλων τὰ ῥέεθρα ὅσον περ τρία στάδια, καὶ ἔπειτα συμμίσγει ἐς τὠυτό·
οὔνομα δέ οἱ Ὠερόη. Most editors bracket the article before ποταμός
but Legrand defends it (ix. 46, n. 2). It has been argued that
νῆσος was used by Greeks for a piece of land which was almost
though not completely surrounded by water (e.g. HW 309, following
Macan, i. 2. 701 A), but, as Macan points out, Herodotus certainly
believed that the river started as a single stream, then divided into
two branches to form the Island, and finally reunited in the plain
(see also Legrand, 46, n. 3).

Kirsten (in his article on Oëroë in *R.-E.* xvii. 2. 2031 ff.) uses this
conclusion to revive the view of Leake and Vischer that the 'island'
lay wholly in the plain. He supposes that the river divided at the
point where it entered the plain and formed two distinct streams
which reunited three stades lower down (on the assumption that the

'three stades' in Herodotus refer to the length, not to the maximum breadth of the Nesos). No such island exists in the plain today, and there is really no evidence that it ever did. The interpretation of the description in Herodotus, quoted above, is doubtful; Kirsten's view is supported by Macaulay's translation ('the river parts in two above, as it flows from Kithairon down to the plain'), but Powell's rendering ('the river is divided near its source on Kithairon and floweth down into the plain with its channels as much as three stades apart one from another') seems nearer to the order of words in the Greek, which implies that the division of the river took place on the slope of Kithairon and before the plain was reached. Probably Herodotus was mistaken in supposing that the two streams which formed the island had originally been united (cf. Macan, loc. cit.).

Grundy had argued that a site in the plain does not suit either of the two reasons given by Herodotus for the choice by the Greeks of the Nesos position. Kirsten tries to meet the first by the supposition that there was a more abundant flow of water in the Oëroë streams before the deforestation of Kithairon (op. cit. 2032 f.) but he does not provide any effective answer to Grundy's report (*G.P.W.* 482) that the watercourses of the streams where they cross the plain offer no serious obstacle to cavalry in most of their course. Kirsten's version of his own view in a later article (*R.-E.* xx. 2. 2294) is no more convincing, and his contention that the Nesos position was chosen partly as a possible starting-point for a Greek offensive is contrary to probability as well as to the explicit testimony of Herodotus (ix. 51. 3).

Pritchett (op. cit. 25 f.), writing after Kirsten's second article, rightly prefers Grundy's site for the Nesos, but raises again the old objection that it does not agree with Herodotus' statement (ix. 51. 1) that the Nesos was ἀπὸ τοῦ Ἀσωποῦ καὶ τῆς κρήνης τῆς Γαργαφίης . . . δέκα σταδίους ἀπέχουσα. Grundy's solution (*G.P.W.* 483) that in this passage the Asopos is not the Thespian Asopos but its tributary, called A1 by Grundy, has been generally rejected (see above, p. 304). The present writer has always felt that the only possible solution is to insert κʹ (i.e. εἴκοσι) before καί with Woodhouse (*J.H.S.* xviii, 1898, 57); this neat emendation, which makes the distance 20 stades from the Asopos to the Nesos, is accepted by Pritchett. Incidentally, Herodotus' estimate of the distance from Gargaphia suggests that he or his informant identified the Nesos with Ridge 4, although the position which the Greeks intended to occupy probably included Ridge 3 as well (cf. Grundy, 484, also 486, where he observes that the valley of stream O2, between the two ridges, is not as steep as that of O1, which forms the eastern boundary of Ridge 3).

(3) *The Androkrateion.* The evidence of Plutarch on this question

(*Aristeides* 11.8 and 11.6) has already been examined (above, Appendix X). It is of no independent value, but scholars have been tempted to appeal to it in order to resolve the apparent discrepancy between the reference of Herodotus to the site and the information supplied by Thucydides; as the discrepancy is non-existent the data in Plutarch may be safely ignored.

Thucydides says (iii. 24. 1–2) that the 212 men who escaped from the besieged city of Plataia in a winter night early in 427 at first ἐχώρουν ἀθρόοι τὴν ἐς Θήβας φέρουσαν ὁδόν, ἐν δεξιᾷ ἔχοντες τὸ τοῦ Ἀνδροκράτους ἡρῷον, and proceeded for 6 or 7 stades along the road to Thebes (τὴν ἐπὶ τῶν Θηβῶν), then turned aside and followed the road leading towards the mountains to Erythrai and Hysiai (see above, p. 425). The natural implication of this passage is that the Heroön was near the Plataia–Thebes road and less than seven stades from Plataia; this is the inference drawn by Grundy (op. cit., note on p. 467; he says 'within three-quarters of a mile of Thebes', but 'Thebes' is an obvious slip of the pen for 'Plataea') and accepted by Beloch (ii². 2. 124), but it has been rejected by most scholars, who find it irreconcilable with the evidence of Herodotus.

In Herodotus (ix. 25. 3) the shrine of Androkrates is associated with the spring of Gargaphia as one of the two points near (πλησίον) to the second Greek position. Grundy, holding that both were situated in the depression south of the Asopos Ridge, assumes that Herodotus is here merely describing the first stage in the Greek advance (see above, p. 304), but Herodotus' description in the context suggests that he was referring to a position on the hills overlooking the south bank of the Asopos. For this reason it has usually been supposed that the Androkrateion must have been on the Asopos Ridge, the favourite site being that of the church of St. John, at the top of the more westerly of the two crests of the ridge. The evidence of Thucydides has then to be forced into harmony with this view. There are two ways of explaining away his apparent implication that the shrine was less than seven stades from Plataia.

Woodhouse (op. cit. 38 f.) suggested that there were two roads to Thebes, one passing to the left and the other to the right of the shrine, and that Thucydides' reference to the shrine was simply to indicate that the fugitives started along the more westerly of the two; this suggestion is far-fetched (Ufer, 137 finds it unconvincing), as 'the road to Thebes' should mean the normal route which goes due north across the Plataian plain to the crossing of the Asopos (cf. also the criticisms in Grundy's long note, 467 f.).

Kromayer suggested to Ufer (*A.S.* 137 f.) that the Plataians broke out from the east side of the town, that at first they made off across country northwards in the general direction of Thebes (this being the true meaning according to Kromayer of τὴν ἐς Θήβας φέρουσαν ὁδόν), but in the dark winter night they needed a direction-point (*Richtungspunkt*) on the skyline to guide them, and for this purpose chose the Androkrateion, knowing that they must aim to the left of it. The shrine was therefore in a commanding position on one of the ridges overlooking the Asopos, and in deference to Plutarch's evidence Ufer locates it on the top of Grundy's 'Long Ridge', near the church of St. Demetrion. But it is not known from what side of the town the Plataians chose to make their escape; they may have chosen the north because the enemy would be least prepared for a break-out on that side. Moreover, if Thucydides had wished to say that they started in the general direction of Thebes he could have used a less precise phrase than τὴν ἐς Θήβας φέρουσαν ὁδόν; the parallels from Thucydides quoted by Ufer (137, n. 1) are all quite different and do not support his contention.

Why did Herodotus mention the Androkrateion as well as Gargaphia when he was defining the second position of the Greeks? Hauvette (op. cit. 459) after noting that the Spartans were posted near Gargaphia, asserts that 'at the other extremity of the Greek line was situated the shrine of the local hero Androkrates'. But his map (p. 455) locates the shrine apparently at the church of St. John, and it is hard to understand how he can suppose (as also do HW 296) that the site of the church marks the position of the Greek left wing, in view of Herodotus' indication that part at least of the Greek army was stationed in the plain. Apart from the untrustworthy evidence of Plutarch there is no reason to suppose that the shrine was situated on a hill. Gargaphia was certainly in the depression south of the Asopos Ridge, and the Androkrateion may also have been in the depression at a point farther west and near the Plataian plain. All that Herodotus need have meant was that the Greek second position was on the hills and plain lying to the north (πλησίον) of these two points (cf. Grundy, 498).

(4) *The Temple of Eleusinian Demeter.* The evidence of Plutarch (*Aristeides* 11. 6) has been examined above (Appendix X); the attempts to reconcile it with Herodotus' narrative are wasted labour. Herodotus makes it quite plain that the position near the temple, where the Spartan retreat was halted (ix. 57. 2), was on ground suitable for cavalry, and he gives no support to the hypothesis of Ufer (op. cit. 159 f.) that the Spartans must have retreated farther south in the interval between the moment when they were overtaken by the enemy cavalry and the arrival on the scene of the enemy infantry. Later passages show that when the Spartans and Tegeans broke through the Persian shield-wall a stern contest followed παρ᾽ αὐτὸ τὸ Δημήτριον (ix. 62. 2) and that though the struggle took place

παρὰ τῆς Δήμητρος τὸ ἄλσος none of the Persians entered the temenos of the goddess or died there, though many perished on the unconsecrated ground near the temple (ix. 65. 2).

Herodotus also states that the ground where the Spartans halted was near the river Moloeis and the Argiopian Land, but there is no other clue to the location of the latter (its identification with either the 'Long Ridge' or the 'Plateau' is only a guess; cf. Grundy, 495) and even though the Moloeis is probably the tributary of the Asopos named A6 by Grundy (see above, p. 335) it is not by itself sufficient to fix the site of the temple. It is therefore not surprising that much has been made of Herodotus' remark (ix. 57. 2) that the Spartans had marched 10 stades from their former position when they were attacked near the temple. This estimate is, however, manifestly no more than a rough approximation (like all those in Herodotus' topography of this campaign, except the τρία στάδια in ix. 51. 2), and it is as wrong to assume that by δέκα στάδια here he must mean precisely 2,000 yards as it is to correct his text to τέσσερα στάδια (as Hude does in O.C.T.) in order to make it fit a particular site for the temple.

Pausanias mentions the trophy set up by the Greeks for their victory at Plataia, a memorial which is presumed to have been near the scene of the decisive clash between the Spartan and Persian infantry, and consequently near the site of the temple of Demeter. He says of the trophy (ix. 2. 6) that πεντεκαίδεκα σταδίοις μάλιστα ἔστηκεν ἀπωτέρω τῆς πόλεως. If ἀπωτέρω is used in its normal comparative sense, the trophy was 15 stades farther from the town of Plataia than something just mentioned. In fact Pausanias in the preceding section (ix. 2. 5) has described the tombs of the fallen and the Altar of Zeus Eleutherios. The former are said to be near the entrance into Plataia (κατὰ τὴν ἔσοδον μάλιστα τὴν ἐς Πλάταιαν), apparently from the east, and the Altar is οὐ πόρρω ἀπὸ τοῦ κοινοῦ τῶν Ἑλλήνων (sc. τάφου). As Pausanias refers again to the Altar in ix. 2. 6, ἀπωτέρω should mean about 15 stades farther off from the town than the Altar (so Grundy, Topog. 34; cf. Kirsten in R.-E. xx. 2. 2271; Ufer, 141 strangely measures from the tombs). Grundy, however, argued later (G.P.W. 520) that Pausanias meant the trophy was 15 stades from Plataia, 'the comparative of distance being used, as elsewhere in Pausanias, in a positive sense'; the validity of this dogmatic assertion may be doubted, even though the translations of Frazer and Jones (in the Loeb series) both agree with Grundy's later version. Perhaps it does not make much difference, as the tombs were close to the gate of Plataia and the Altar near to the tombs. Moreover Pausanias' estimate for the distance, about 15 stades, seems to be as rough an approximation as the 10 stades of Herodotus.

It may be a calculation of the distance along the Plataia–Erythrai road (see above, p. 298), and if the battlefield was in a depression the trophy may have been erected not on it but on a commanding site overlooking it. Hence the evidence of Pausanias contains too many unknowns to serve as a sure guide to the precise site of the temple of Demeter.

Macan (in his note on ix. 57. 2, closely followed by HW 312 f.) confuses himself and his readers by a digression on temples of Demeter in this neighbourhood. Pausanias indeed mentions (ix. 4. 3) a temple of Eleusinian Demeter ἐν Πλαταιαῖς, but the location could cover the territory as well as the town of Plataia, so that, as Macan admits, the temple in Pausanias could be identical with that of Herodotus (cf. Ufer, 140 and n. 3). An 'Hysiatan' temple of Demeter cannot safely be inferred from the evidence of Plutarch alone; two inscribed stones from a temple of Eleusinian Demeter were certainly found in the neighbourhood of Pritchett's site for *Hysiai* (*I.G.* vii. 1670 and 1671; cf. Frazer, *Pausanias*, v. 5, also Munro, op. cit. 163 and Beloch, ii². 2. 127), but the place of their discovery was not necessarily the place where the temple stood (cf. Frazer, loc. cit., and section 3 of Grundy's note in *G.P.W.* 458 f.). If it was, this temple cannot possibly (in spite of Pritchett, 28 A) be identical with the Demeter temple of Herodotus, as it is too far from the original Spartan position and too near the rocky base of Kithairon. Although Pritchett (op. cit. 27 B) doubts the authority of the passage in Plutarch's *Aristeides*, he allows his choice to be unduly influenced by it.

Grundy's site, on the crest of the Long Ridge, marked now by the chapel of St. Demetrion (*G.P.W.* 494 ff.), has at least the merit that, unlike the sites based on the evidence of Plutarch, it makes the battle take place on ground in harmony with Herodotus' account of it, but it is little more than a guess and is open to several objections. Kirsten's declaration (op. cit. 2271), that no sanctuary of Demeter was ever built on a height, is at least doubtful, especially as ἄνω in ix. 69. 1 suggests that the way to it was uphill, but Pritchett, who refuses to guarantee its accuracy, observes (28 A) that he has himself examined the summit of this hill without discovering any sherds of the classical period. Grundy argues that his site would explain the fact (Hdt. ix. 65. 2) that none of the Persians entered the temenos of the goddess or died there, as presumably they fled northwards after their defeat down the valleys of the streams which flow on either side of the ridge (*G.P.W.* 503 and third note; cf. Wright, 67, n. 1), but this makes Herodotus' attitude to the fact so much the more surprising, and Grundy's site does not agree with Herodotus' statement that the fierce struggle which ensued on the overthrow of the

F f

shield-wall was fought close to the temple (ix. 62. 2; cf. Ufer, 140).
The only safe conclusion is that the temple was situated somewhere
to the north of the rocky base of Kithairon near ground suitable for
cavalry, not more than ten stades from the previous Spartan position,
and possibly in the neighbourhood of the depression which lies south
of the Long Ridge.

APPENDIX XII

The Greek army at Plataia

HERODOTUS, after describing the advance of the Greek army from Kithairon to the south bank of the Asopos, gives an account of its battle array (xi. 28. 2–6), in which he states the position of all the twenty-five contingents in the army from right to left (starting with the Lakedaimonians on the right wing) and the number of hoplites in each contingent. The Spartiatai are said to have numbered 5,000 and to have been attended by 35,000 Helots. The rest of the hoplites (including the 5,000 Lakedaimonian Perioikoi) total 33,700, but the number of light-armed troops in attendance on them, calculated at one to each hoplite (ix. 29. 2; cf. HW 213 on vii. 186. 1) is fixed at 34,500; it has been suggested (by Delbrück; cf. Hauvette, 461) that the extra 800 are to be found in the regiment of Athenian archers mentioned in ix. 22. 1 and 60. 3. Hoplites, light-armed, and Helots together make a total of 108,200, which Herodotus unconvincingly rounds off to 110,000 by the addition of 1,800 unarmed Thespians (ix. 30).

The names of the states which sent contingents to Plataia naturally recur in the inscription engraved on the serpent column at Delphi and commemorating the states which 'fought in the war' (Tod, 19; cf. Hdt. viii. 82. 1 and ix. 81. 1) with one exception; the men of Pale in Kephallenia, which is said to have provided 200 hoplites (ix. 28. 5) are not mentioned on the column. This does not prove that Herodotus was mistaken and that the Paleans were not represented at Plataia; the men of Kroton, who sent a trireme to Salamis, and the Seriphians, who also fought at Salamis (viii. 47–48) are both absent from the column, and the Tenians and Siphnians were only added later (cf. Hauvette, long note 4 on pp. 461 ff.). Hence there is no substance in Beloch's suggestion (ii². 2. 75) that Herodotus must have misread the name of the Eleians (given in the form Ϝαλειοι on the column) as Παλειοι, nor in his contention that the names in Herodotus of the states represented at Plataia are simply a reconstruction made by him from the entries on the column (excluding the island states Keos, Kythnos, Melos, Naxos, Siphnos, Tenos).

Beloch finds the presence of 300 hoplites from Poteidaia 'improbable'; so too does Meyer, who says that Herodotus only mentions them, and probably many others, for example the Euboians, because they were inscribed on the war-memorial at Delphi (408 n.). Actually there is no reason why the Euboians or the Poteidaians should have been absent from the Greek army in 479. The Euboians had probably shaken off the Persian yoke after Salamis (see above, p. 266) and the Poteidaians, who had also revolted, had successfully thwarted Artabazos' attempt to reduce them by siege; as the Persian fleet had withdrawn from the West Aegean there was nothing to prevent the Poteidaians from sending a contingent of 300 men by sea to swell the forces of their mother-city Corinth, and Herodotus notes (ix. 28. 3) that it obtained permission from Pausanias to take its place next to the Corinthians in the battle-line. Herodotus obtained from his oral sources a very full account of the campaign of Plataia; why should not these have supplied him with a list of the contingents present in the Greek army and their places in the line?

Herodotus' figure 38,700 for the total of the hoplites, as Delbrück at one time admitted (cf. Obst, *Der Feldzug des Xerxes*, 66) is not improbable in itself for 479, when the patriotic states had cut down their fleet and were making their main effort on land, and unlike his total for the whole army it is not a round number but obtained by adding together the figures for the separate contingents. Some of these figures, however, have been doubted by critics, especially Beloch (ii². 2. 75–78), who maintains that they were added by Herodotus himself on the basis of his own calculations. The item which has been most criticized is the 50,000 for the contingent of the Lakedaimonians (ix. 61. 2; cf. 28. 2 and 29. 2) made up of 5,000 full citizens of Sparta (the Spartiatai), all hoplites, 5,000 hoplites from the Perioikoi and their 5,000 attendants (possibly Perioikoi of the poorer class) and 35,000 Helots in attendance on the Spartiatai. As Beloch admits the possibility of a mass mobilization of the Helots in 479 (he himself cites a parallel from 418 in Thuc. v. 64. 2) and also believes that they may have outnumbered the Spartiates at Plataia by seven to one, his criticism is here directed against the figure 5,000 for the Spartiates; so Obst (op. cit. 64) assumes that 5,000 was really the figure for Spartiates and Perioikoi together at Plataia and that Herodotus wrongly duplicated it.

This dogmatism cannot be justified by appeals to figures for Spartan armies in 418 and 394, for the Spartiates seem to have suffered heavy losses in the great earthquake of 464 (Plut. *Kimon* 16. 4–5; cf. Wade-Gery in *C.Q.* xxxviii, 1944, 125 f.) and even in 418 the figure of 3,584 resulting from Thucydides' calculations (Thuc. v. 68. 3) is for Spartiates only; as Toynbee pointed out (*J.H.S.* xxxiii, 1913, 269–71) Thucydides forgot the Perioikoi. Herodotus certainly believed that Sparta had 8,000 full citizens in 480 (vii. 234. 2), and her field army, organized at that date in five

Lochoi, may well have amounted, at least on paper, to 5,000 men, 1,000 in each Lochos (cf. Wade-Gery, op. cit. 120 f. and 125). Although the Helots were perhaps less dangerous now than later, the Spartans, when they were sending such a large army to Northern Greece, may have thought it a wise precaution to send as many Helots as possible out of Peloponnese at the same time. Herodotus is probably wrong in regarding them as part of the fighting strength of the Greek army (ix. 30 and 61. 2; cf. HW 298 f. on 28. 2); those who were not serving as attendants on the Spartiates may have been used as an army service corps to bring up supplies (so Macan, i. 2. 650 B).

The contention that Herodotus' figures for the Lakedaimonians are based merely on his own calculations is improbable, but even if it was sound it would not justify Beloch's inference from it that the figures for the other contingents must have been arrived at by the same method; the Spartans traditionally concealed their military strength (Thuc. v. 68. 2) but other states had no reason to copy Sparta's secrecy in this matter. Beloch grudgingly admits that the Athenian hoplites at Plataia may have numbered 8,000 (Hdt. ix. 28. 6) and that the figures for the contingents of the smaller states cannot be checked, but he maintains that Herodotus has over-estimated the Megarians (3,000), Corinthians (5,000), and Sikyonians (3,000). He argues that in 394 Sikyon put only 1,500 men into the field, Corinth only 3,000 (Xen. *Hell.* iv. 2. 16–17; see also the references in HW 299 on Hdt. ix. 28. 6) and that Megara could never have had a population large enough to provide 3,000 men of military age of the hoplite class. Busolt's reply to these arguments, that these three states had all been more important in the sixth century and probably declined in the second half of the fifth century, is not entirely convincing. It must be remembered that these states had supplied 72 of the 113 Peloponnesian ships at Artemision and may therefore have been represented in the same proportion (roughly two-thirds) in Leotychidas' fleet in 479. Probably as many as 80 of the 110 ships in that fleet were Peloponnesian, and if the three states concerned supplied 52 of them they would have had 1,560 hoplites serving as marines in the fleet. Hence there is some justification for Munro's conclusion (*J.H.S.* xxiv, 1904, 152) that Herodotus' figures, apart from those for the Lakedaimonian and Athenian contingents, look like estimates of the hoplites which the patriotic states could have furnished if they had turned out with all their available hoplites of military age.

Beloch has not called attention to the remarkable gap in Herodotus' list of the contingents at Plataia; the Arkadian allies of Sparta are represented only by the contingents of Tegea (1,500) and

Orchomenos (600). The Mantineians arrived too late for the battle (ix. 77), but why is there no mention of those Arkadian communities which still lived in villages, such as the Mainalioi and Heraieis (Thuc. v. 67. 1)? At Thermopylai these communities had provided 1,000 men, as many as the Tegeans and Mantineians combined (vii. 202), and a little later 'all the Arkadians' were present in Kleombrotos' army at the Isthmus (viii. 72). The commentators note their absence from the list in ix. 28, but none attempt to explain it except Macan, whose suggestion (i. 2. 652 A) that they were kept at home by 'the tardy exit of the Mantineians' is unsatisfactory. Perhaps they tended to be easily forgotten; Xenophon does not mention any Arkadians in his list of Spartan allies at Sikyon in 394, although the sequel shows that the Tegeans at least were present (*Hell*. iv. 2. 16 and 19). It is curious that the Arkadian peoples absent from Herodotus' list are all, like the Mantineians, also absent from the inscription on the serpent column, and still more curious that Beloch made no use of this fact to support his hypothesis that Herodotus got the names in his list from the column. If these Arkadians sent twice as many men as Tegea to Thermopylai, they could perhaps have sent 3,000 to Plataia, but in view of Herodotus' silence it is impossible to be sure that they were there.

These uncertainties make a precise calculation difficult, but if the effective strength of the Lakedaimonian and Athenian hoplites at Plataia was between 17,000 and 18,000, the total number of hoplites in the Greek army on the eve of the battle may reasonably be fixed at not less than 35,000 (HW 364 perhaps tend to underestimate them). The attendants on these, if we include those of the Helots who were actually employed as servants to the Spartan hoplites, may have numbered another 35,000, but though Herodotus regards them as light-armed troops their military value was probably not great; the story in ix. 60. 2–3, if historical, suggests that they could do little or nothing to check the Persian cavalry (see above, p. 334). Mardonios may have had 50,000 Asiatic troops, and 15,000 to 20,000 more supplied by his Greek and Macedonian allies, but the narrative of Herodotus suggests that the only valuable troops in his army (other than the Boiotians) were the Asiatic cavalry and the contingent of Persian infantry from the homeland, and also that apart from his cavalry he had no decisive superiority over the army of Pausanias.

APPENDIX XIII

Delphi and the invasion

THE policy followed before and during the invasion by the priests who controlled the temple of Apollo at Delphi has been examined in detail by Macan (ii. 229 ff.) and Parke (*A History of the Delphic Oracle*, c. 9, which corresponds to c. 7 of *The Delphic Oracle* published by Parke and Wormell in 1956; page references to the later work are given in square brackets). Their main evidence is necessarily drawn from the oracular pronouncements uttered in this period by the Delphic priestess, the Pythia, or rather from such of them as have been preserved by Herodotus (who is usually supposed to have obtained them directly from an official source at Delphi); the probability that some of them may have been 'edited' by the priests after the events cannot be excluded (Hauvette, 324; Grundy, 232). Herodotus gives the full text of four oracles and a paraphrase of three more, but as at least two (and possibly three) of these seven are apparently not authentic and two of the remainder were issued to Athens alone, there must obviously have been many other responses from Delphi in this period which Herodotus has not recorded.

Of the seven oracles mentioned by Herodotus, three may be regarded as favourable to the prospects of the patriotic Greeks, three as unfavourable, and one (the second oracle to the Athenians) as ambivalent. The three in the first group are (1) the assurance to Sparta that she would escape destruction if one of her kings was killed, (2) an oracle advising the Spartans to demand satisfaction from Xerxes for the death of Leonidas, and (3) a command addressed to the Delphians themselves, and by them duly passed on to the Greek leaders, to pray to the winds, as they would prove valuable helpers to the Greek cause. All these three oracles are suspect, though the authenticity of the third (vii. 178. 1), said to have been delivered just before the great storm which destroyed a large part of the Persian fleet, has been defended by Parke (182 f. [168]; cf., however, Macan, 232). The second of the two oracles to Sparta (viii. 114. 1) is dated just after Salamis, when even Delphi might have foreseen the ultimate triumph of the patriotic Greeks, but both the content and the setting of this oracle are unconvincing, and it has been generally rejected as a *vaticinium post eventum*, fabricated either in Delphi or in Sparta (cf. Macan, i. 2. 540 A and Legrand, viii. 98, also HW 273 for Verrall's view that it was derived from a misunderstanding

of an inscription). The first oracle (vii. 220. 4) seems to have
been invented by the Spartan government after the disaster at
Thermopylai to reassure the Greeks and prove that the death of a
Spartan king was part of the price to be paid for victory (see above,
p. 148). Herodotus later explains that the Spartans had been moved
to consult the Delphic oracle before the invasion by an advance
report of Xerxes' intentions sent to Sparta by the exiled Spartan
king Demaratos (vii. 239). The story of his message is probably a
fiction, though the Herodotean authorship of the chapter in which
it is narrated should never have been doubted; cf. Myres, 254 f.
and notes, also Legrand, vii. 185. Both the story and the oracle are
apparently of Spartan origin (Parke[1], 182 [167 f.] agreed that the
oracle was invented in Sparta and later sponsored by Delphi, but
he and Wormell in C.Q. xliii, 1949, 139, after a discussion of the
text of this oracle, conclude that 'it may well emanate from Delphi',
and 'may have been composed immediately after the news of
Salamis had reached Delphi'; this seems to me less probable than
Parke's earlier view). Sparta must have consulted Delphi before the
invasion, but the response which she then received, whatever its
content, was suppressed later, and after the war Delphi was naturally
willing to be credited with the authorship of the fictitious substitute
which had been so brilliantly fulfilled.

Against the three Delphic oracles, bogus or suspect, which seem
favourable to the Greeks must be set the three in the second group
which, in Macan's words, were 'calculated to discourage the Greeks
in their resistance to the Persian king, to divide them, and to justify
neutrality, indifference, and medism' (ii. 230). Delphi's ironical
reply to the Cretans (vii. 169. 2) probably did little more than
provide them with a convenient excuse for inaction, as the city-
states of Crete had for many centuries past played no part in the
politics of the Greek mainland, but it is significant for Delphi's
attitude on the eve of the invasion, as is the advice given by the
oracle to Argos to observe strict neutrality in the coming conflict
(vii. 148. 3). The phrase by which Herodotus dates the Argive
embassy to Delphi (πυθέσθαι γὰρ αὐτίκα κατ' ἀρχὰς τὰ ἐκ τοῦ βαρβάρου
ἐγειρόμενα ἐπὶ τὴν Ἑλλάδα; vii. 148. 2) is almost verbally identical
with that used to date the alleged Delphic response to Sparta in
vii. 220. 3, and indicates that Herodotus believed both to have been
delivered in 482 or the first half of 481. Whether he was right or
not, the modern hypothesis (Macan, i. 201 A, followed by HW 188)
that the oracle was really given to Argos by Delphi in 491 is untenable. How observes that the oracle must be authentic, on the
ground that 'had it been an Argive fiction it would have been disowned at Delphi after the defeat of Xerxes', but this argument is

equally valid against his attempt to date it to 491; Delphi could then have pointed out that the oracle, entirely appropriate to the circumstances within three years of the crushing defeat at Sepeia, had been illegitimately transferred by the Argives to a completely different situation. Macan elsewhere (ii. 231) admitted the possibility that the story told by the Argives about the oracle was 'in substance true'.

Sparta must have been disappointed by the reply given by Delphi to Argos, but she can hardly have expected more from her old rival than a malevolent neutrality during the invasion, and in the end, according to the Argive version repeated by Herodotus, the attitude of Argos was not influenced by the response received from Delphi but was decided by considerations of power and prestige. Far more serious for its bearing on the war was the first oracle delivered by the Pythia to the Athenians (vii. 140. 2–3), in which they were exhorted to leave their homes and city and flee to the ends of the earth as the only course by which they could escape utter destruction. It is true that this oracle was presently superseded by a second, also addressed to the Athenians, but though its terms were certainly milder (ἠπιώτερα; 142. 1) than those of the first they can hardly be described as encouraging. The priestess again predicted the inevitability of a Persian conquest of Attica; only a wooden wall (ξύλινον τεῖχος) would escape capture, and so benefit the Athenians and their children. Themistokles' explanation of this sentence was that the Athenians were to trust in their fleet for victory, but it could also mean that they were to seek safety in a mass migration by sea and found a new city elsewhere; this was in fact the meaning read into it by the professional interpreters of oracles at Athens, the χρησμολόγοι (vii. 143. 3). In the next sentence the Athenians are urged to flee before the Persian cavalry and infantry, turning their backs to the foe, with a vague assurance that some day the time will come when they can face him again (l. 10). The last two lines in their present form contain a reference to Salamis as a place where many will perish 'either at seed-time or at harvest-time', but it is not revealed which side is destined to win the battle.

Herodotus clearly assigns these two oracles (henceforth called A and B) to a time before the first congress of the patriotic Greeks at the Isthmus, as shown by the pluperfect ἐγεγόνεε in vii. 145. 1 (cf. Hauvette, 323 and Legrand, vii. 131 f.), but this dating has not found favour with modern scholars, e.g. Legrand, 132, n. 1. Macan and Parke both believe that the reference to Salamis in B (ll. 11–12) was part of the original response, and it must be admitted that their belief is supported by Herodotus, for in his account of the debates in Athens which followed the arrival of the oracle he relates that the meaning of the reference to Salamis was disputed as well as that of the two lines (B, 6–7) on the wooden wall. If, however, the battle of Salamis really was predicted in B, the prediction could only have been made after the Greek fleet had abandoned its advanced position at Artemision, for only then could the decisive battle at sea have been expected to take place so far south as Salamis. But though Macan and Parke have not hesitated to date it after the fall of Thermopylai, this date for it is chronologically impossible (cf. Labarbe, *Loi navale*, 112 and n. 3); the Persians, if Herodotus can be trusted (see above, p. 195), arrived in Attica nine days after the last battle at Artemision, and the interval is far too short for all the events that on Macan's view have to be crammed into it.

If B was delivered at some date before the fighting at Artemision, the mention of Salamis cannot have appeared in the original version. Hauvette (326, n. 1) suggested that the last two lines were simply added to it later, but Labarbe (op. cit. 114 ff.) argued convincingly that, as A and B contain twelve lines each in their present form, B must from the start have contained exactly the same number of lines as A, the harsh response which Apollo was now replacing by a milder version; hence if B has been tampered with, it must have been altered by substitution rather than addition. Pointing to the astonishing contrast between the ludicrous haziness of the chronological datum in l. 12 and the geographical precision of l. 11, Labarbe insists (115 f.) that the last line must have been part of the original B (thereby meeting the argument of Parke, 185 f. [171]) and that l. 11 as first delivered contained only a vague indication of place, later removed to make room for the definite reference to Salamis. He follows Hauvette (op. cit. 327) in dating the utterance of B soon after the unsuccessful expedition to Tempe (so Munro in *J.H.S.* xxii, 306, and n. 19) and therefore in May 480, but his attempt (120 ff.) to support this dating by the wording of B is unconvincing. Moreover, unwilling to admit that his dating carries with it the rejection of Herodotus' assertion that the debate on the oracle in Athens turned partly on the reference to Salamis, Labarbe suggests (117 and n. 3) that there were in fact two debates, and that Themistokles himself produced the present version of l. 11 after the retreat from Artemision, but his hypothesis of a second debate at this juncture is as improbable as Macan's reconstruction; there was not enough time available for an important debate, apart from the objection that the able-bodied members of the ecclesia were now serving in the fleet.

There is therefore no escape from the conclusion that if the reference to Salamis is a later alteration of the original B 11, made after the battle was fought, the debate in Athens on B, if historical, must have turned on the meaning of the 'wooden wall', and Herodotus' statement that it was also concerned with the mention of

Salamis must be fiction, grafted later on to the authentic tradition of the debate and obviously suggested by the 'edited' version of B. But if the original version contained no precise indication of place in l. 11, there would seem to be no reason why Hauvette's dating of A and B should be preferred to that indicated by Herodotus. It is intrinsically more probable that if the Athenians intended to consult Delphi they should have done so in the summer of 481 (as Argos and Sparta probably did). The prospects of the Greeks were not necessarily better then on land than after the failure of the Tempe expedition, for the defection of Thessaly and her neighbours to the Persian cause seems to have been anticipated at the outset by the Greeks, and presumably by Delphi as well; the sequel was to show that the anti-Persian elements in Thessaly were not strong enough to prevail against the Aleuadai and their supporters (see above, p. 103).

Whether the two oracles were delivered to the Athenians in the summer of 481 or the spring of 480, it is probable that the first represents the forecast of the Delphic priests and that the second was a modification of it imposed on them by external pressure, applied either by Themistokles and the Athenian envoys or possibly, as Grundy supposes (p. 237), by the Spartans, alarmed at the prospect of losing the support of the Athenian fleet. Herodotus represents the second oracle as following closely on the first, but the interval between them may have been longer than he realized (Grundy, 238). Anyhow, the Delphic priests, when compelled to eat their words to some extent, produced a second response in such ambiguous (though milder) terms that though it could be represented by the patriotic Greeks as favourable to resistance it could also, if necessary later, be explained as an exhortation to the Athenians to emigrate in a body by sea to a new home.

Labarbe holds (op. cit. 118 ff.) that oracle A as well as B was prompted by Themistokles and that he wished to intimidate those Athenians who clung obstinately to the traditions of Marathon and opposed a purely maritime policy, but this hypothesis seems to rest on nothing more than a rather muddled passage in Plutarch (*Them.* 7. 1–2). According to Plutarch, 'Themistokles as soon as he entered on office tried to persuade the citizens to leave the city and go aboard the triremes, and to meet the barbarians by sea at a point as far as possible from Hellas, but when many opposed his policy he joined the Spartans in an expedition by land to Tempe. After this failed . . . the Athenians became more favourable to his maritime policy (μᾶλλον ἤδη προσεῖχον τῷ Θεμιστοκλεῖ περὶ τῆς θαλάσσης) and he was sent with a fleet to Artemision to guard the straits.' If Plutarch thought that Themistokles was absolutely opposed to any attempt to meet the Persians on land, he was mistaken. As triremes depended on the proximity of a friendly shore (see above, p. 53), the Greek fleet could only take up an advanced position at Artemision (in spite of Plutarch no position farther north than this was practicable) if the adjacent mainland was securely held by a Greek army. Nor is Plutarch correct in his belief that the manning of the fleet necessarily entailed the evacuation of Attica. Themistokles presumably saw that it would be hopeless to defend Attica if the Persian army broke through into Central Greece and must have made previous preparations for an orderly evacuation of Attica if it should prove necessary, but he cannot have based his whole policy on the assumption that the defence of Thermopylai was bound to fail, or have been so firmly convinced of the inevitability of evacuation as early as May 480 that he induced the Delphic priests to urge it on the Athenians through the mouth of the Pythia (see below, pp. 463 f.).

Why should not the Delphic priests have believed, as early as the summer of 481, that Attica was bound to be overrun by the Persian invader and that resistance was futile? Why should they not have issued oracles to uncommitted states, such as Argos and Crete, urging them to remain neutral in a conflict which could have only one conclusion? The three certainly genuine oracles delivered by the Pythia before the invasion all suggest that the priests had made up their minds that Persia was bound to win the war. It does not, however, follow that their conviction was due to selfish or corrupt motives; in view of their oracle's reputation for prescience they must have endeavoured to forecast the course of the war as accurately as they could from the facts at their disposal. They had ample sources of information; hence it is unlikely (in spite of Grundy, 233 ff.) that they were deceived for a moment by the pretence that Xerxes' expedition was directed solely against Athens (vii. 138. 1) Having reached the conclusion that Persian victory in the coming struggle was inevitable, they strove to minimize the sufferings it would bring on the Greeks by pressing the Athenians, against whom the Persians had special grounds for enmity, to leave Greece altogether, and by advising as many states as possible to remain neutral. In an instructive parallel Meyer (370 f.) has compared their attitude to that of the prophet Jeremiah in a similar situation; Jeremiah saw that resistance to the power of Babylonia was hopeless and condemned the policy of the Jewish nationalists as futile and worse, stiff-necked opposition to the will of Jehovah. The warnings of Jeremiah were proved right by the event, but the Persian War took an unexpected turn which falsified the careful calculations of Delphi.

Others have assumed that Delphi was guilty of a more blameworthy form of Medism than this, and have maintained that her rulers had made a compact with Persia by which the safety of the

temple treasures was guaranteed; even Meyer says (p. 383) that
Delphi doubtless made formal submission to Xerxes after Central
Greece had been thrown open to the Persians by their victory at
Thermopylai. The arguments for Delphi's guilty complicity with
the national enemy seem to be that nine of the twelve states in her
Amphictyony sided with Persia, and that although the Persians were
in control of Central Greece for nearly a year they left the treasures
of Delphi untouched. Neither argument is cogent. The attitude of the
nine Amphictyonic states which joined Xerxes was obviously dictated by their geographical position; there is no evidence that it was
prompted by advice from Delphi. In the second place, their adhesion to the Persian cause provides an adequate explanation for the
immunity of Delphi; Xerxes could not afford to plunder a shrine
which was sacred to so many of his Greek allies (cf. Beloch, *G.G.*
ii². 1. 46). The Persians were not waging a war of religion, and only
destroyed foreign temples when these had been associated with a
national resistance, like the temple of Apollo at Didyma (vi. 19. 3;
cf. Meyer, 383); on other occasions Darius and his generals had
shown special respect for temples of Apollo (Tod, 10; cf. Hdt. vi.
97. 2 for the assurance given to the Delians by Datis in 490). Finally,
although the patriotic Greeks must have been disappointed by the
Pythia's gloomy predictions, they do not appear to have suspected
her priests of collusion with the invader. Their vow before the invasion (vii. 132. 2; cf. Brunt, op. cit. 136 f.) to offer to Delphi a tithe
from all states which supported the enemy (except those which had
acted under compulsion) may indeed have been a bid for the support of Delphi (Macan, i. 173 B), but the offerings made by the
patriotic Greeks to the temple after their victories (viii. 122, ix.
81. 1) indicate that Delphi had not played such a part in the war as
to forfeit their respect and veneration.

Nevertheless, the Delphians, though probably guiltless of co-
operation with the Persians, had little reason to pride themselves on
their behaviour before and during the invasion. They attempted to
put their conduct in a better light by a story (repeated by Hdt.
viii. 35–39) which asserted that Xerxes on his march from Thermopylai to Athens had detached a force in Phokis to plunder the shrine;
most of the male Delphians had withdrawn either to Lokrian Amphissa or to the heights of Parnassos, leaving only sixty men to guard
the temple, but just before the barbarians reached it they fell into
a panic and fled back by the way they had come. In Herodotus the
panic is caused by various strange happenings which are attributed
to supernatural agency, whereas Ephoros sought to rationalize it
by the assumption of a great thunderstorm which dislodged some
heavy rocks from the slopes of Parnassos (Diod. xi. 14. 2–4; the

Delphic epigram quoted in § 4 is supposed by Hauvette, 386 to have been later than Herodotus' time); possibly Ephoros was also responsible for fixing the size of the Persian force at 4,000 men (Justin ii. 12. 8). In its Herodotean form the story is clearly a temple legend embellished by the priests. Some scholars reject it entirely and deny that Persian troops approached Delphi at all (so Meyer, 383 f.); others regard this solution as too radical (e.g. Parke, 187 [173]) and believe that a Persian force advanced from the east on Delphi during the summer of 480, though they disagree about its purpose and its fate.

Scholars also disagree about the relevance to this problem of another story told later by Herodotus. Mardonios is there alleged to have informed his war council (including the leaders of the medizing Greeks) of an oracle which foretold that the Persians were fated on their arrival in Greece to plunder the shrine at Delphi and after doing this to perish utterly; Mardonios then explained that the Persians, thus forewarned, would not go to the temple or attempt to plunder it, and so would prevent the fulfilment of the oracle (ix. 42). This story as told by Herodotus is perhaps not impossible (its difficulties are exaggerated by Macan, i. 2. 684 B), but it is astonishing that Herodotus should have reported it without any reference to the Persian attack on Delphi in the previous year which he had described so fully in Book VIII; when Grundy described the council of war recorded in ix. 41 ff. (*G.P.W.* 475 f.) he refrained from mentioning Mardonios' reference to the oracle. Technically no doubt the Persians had not attempted to plunder Apollo's temple at Delphi in 480 because they had turned back before they reached it, but if Herodotus was correctly informed (viii. 35. 2), they had been officially ordered to do so, and, as Macan points out, the story of Glaukos (vi. 86) shows that in such matters the Delphic Apollo took the will for the deed. Hence Macan seems to be right in his contention that the story in ix. 42 is really inconsistent with that in viii. 35–39. The story in ix. 42 may be false, and if it is it has no relevance to the credibility of the other; if it is true, the story of a Persian attack on Delphi in 480, whether authorized or not, must be rejected (this objection is not faced by Hauvette; he raises it on p. 387 but never answers it).

The oracle cited by Mardonios is described as a λόγιον but appears to have been in verse (ix. 42. 3; cf. πεποιημένον in 43. 1). Herodotus, who does not say explicitly that it was of Delphic origin, never quotes the text of it, and it is therefore impossible to check his claim that it referred not to the Persians but to a mythical invasion of the Illyrian Encheleis. This was presumably the interpretation given to Herodotus by the Delphic priests, and was accepted by Euripides

(*Bacchai*, 1330 ff.), but it may have been originally circulated in 480
with reference to the Persians. Busolt suggested (689 f., n. 3) that it
was put out by Delphi in the winter of 480–479 to deter Mardonios
from attacking the temple (cf. Hauvette, 389), but when it was unfulfilled it was transferred by the priests to the Encheleis. This explanation is no more than a plausible hypothesis, and the accuracy
of the account preserved in ix. 42 must remain doubtful. It is evidence, however, for the existence in Herodotus' day of a tradition
which apparently knew nothing of the Delphic story recorded in
Book VIII and which looks like an alternative attempt to explain
Delphi's immunity during the war.

Many have accepted Pomtow's suggestion that the attack on
Delphi was an unauthorized raid by a band of Persian marauders
(so Parke, 187 f. [173]), but if Delphi was to be rehabilitated it was
an essential item in the story that the troops who marched on Delphi
had been sent with definite instructions to plunder the shrine, as
Herodotus asserts (viii. 35. 2); so διακρινομένη in 34 implies that the
division of the army in Phokis was a deliberate act of the Persian
high command. This version, based on the presupposition, so important for the Delphians, that Xerxes' attitude to Delphi was hostile
and uncompromising, was accepted by Hauvette (op. cit. 388 f.;
cf. Grundy, 349), but his defence of it against the criticisms of Wecklein breaks down on two points; Xerxes was not a savage, blind to
the folly of alienating his Greek allies by such an act, and if he had
set his heart on seizing the temple treasures he would not have
abandoned the attempt so tamely after the first rebuff. As the statement that he himself was responsible for sending the force to plunder
the temple was an essential part of the Delphic apologia, it cannot
be regarded as above suspicion, still less be used to support the
opposite hypothesis that Xerxes' intentions were friendly to Delphi
when he sent the troops, either to protect the temple (Munro in
J.H.S. xxii. 320) or to make an inventory of its treasures (Casson in
C.R. xxviii, 1914, 145 ff.). On Pomtow's interpretation the raid was
an irresponsible act which throws no light on the attitude of the
Persian authorities to Delphi, but it is not very probable that they
should have allowed a body of their troops to stray so far from the
main line of their advance into difficult and hostile country. Certainty is impossible, but the source from which Herodotus obtained
the narrative contained in viii. 35–39 had strong motives for mis-
representing the truth, and the whole story may easily have been
invented by the Delphic priests without any foundation in fact.

APPENDIX XIV

The chronology of the invasion

XERXES' invasion of Greece coincided with a celebration of the Olympic festival (Hdt. vii. 206. 2) and must therefore have occurred in a year of the pre-Christian era divisible by four. That this year was 480 is proved by two other passages in Herodotus. (1) He says in viii. 51. 1 that the Persians reached Athens in the archonship of Kalliades; this date, the only archon-date in Herodotus, corresponds (cf., for example, Diod. xi. 1. 2) with the Athenian year 480/479. (2) In a subsequent digression (ix. 10. 2–3) Herodotus mentions that when the Spartan regent Kleombrotos was preparing to advance with the Greek army from the Isthmus against the Persians, he was deterred by an eclipse of the sun; this can only be the (partial) eclipse of 2 October 480. It is true that Herodotus records another eclipse of the sun, apparently total, alleged to have been seen by the Persians at Sardis in the spring of the same year, when they were about to begin their march to Greece (vii. 37. 1–2), but this eclipse is unknown to astronomers and may be disregarded (for a possible explanation see HW 145).

Attempts to provide a detailed chronology of the campaign depend on the precise date of the Olympic festival in 480 and on its relation to the fighting at Thermopylai. The statements in Herodotus bearing on the latter problem are rather vague (the anecdote in viii. 26, which makes the fighting coincide with the festival, must be rejected as unhistorical; cf. Macan, i. 2. 391 A and Busolt, 673, first paragraph of note 9). He implies in vii. 206. 1 that the Karneia, which in 480 began four days before the Olympia (cf. HW, ad loc. and on vi. 106. 3) were in progress or impending when Leonidas was setting out for Thermopylai; later, after describing (viii. 71. 1) how the Peloponnesian levies on the news of Leonidas' death hurried in full strength to the Isthmus to man the fortifications there, he adds a note that 'the Olympia and the Karneia were now over' (viii. 72). Busolt argued from viii. 40. 2 that if the Athenians on their return from Artemision expected to find the Peloponnesians holding the Kithairon–Parnes line in force, there must have been sufficient time since the end of the Olympia for a complete mobilization of the League army at the Isthmus, but the tradition in this section is of doubtful value (cf. Meyer, 384 and HW 247). Even if it was sound, no precise conclusion could be extracted from it. Busolt himself wavered; after quoting the relevant passages from viii. 71 and 72 he said in his first edition (145, n. 1) that in fact the Olympia and the Karneia must have ended 'about fourteen days earlier' in view of viii. 40. 2, but in his second edition (673 f., n. 9) he substituted 'about ten days earlier'. His later view is nearer to that of Beloch, who dates the last battle at Thermopylai ten days after the final day of the Olympia (ii². 2. 48); this conclusion is not likely to be far from the truth and may be accepted as an adequate working hypothesis.

In this period the Olympian festival lasted for five days, the last of which probably coincided with the full moon, but it is disputed whether in 480 this was the full moon of 21 July or that of 19 August. According to the scholia on Pindar's third Olympian ode (33 A and 35 A, pp. 114 f. in Drachmann's edition) the festival was celebrated in the eighth month of the Eleian year, which seems to have begun about the time of the winter solstice (like the Boiotian year; cf. Plut., *Life of Pelopidas* 24. 2), and in the middle of an Eleian month, either Apollonios or Parthenios; it has been suggested that the festival occurred in Apollonios in a year when a month had been intercalated earlier in the year (cf. Ziehen in *R.-E.* xviii. 1. 3). The scholia give an Egyptian equation for the two months which fixes the possible limits of the festival between 25 June and 27 September, but as Beloch has shown (i². 2. 139 f.) these extreme limits were never reached. Anyhow, a full-moon date in 480 earlier than 2 July or later than 19 August would be irreconcilable with the narrative of Herodotus.

Beloch was less successful in his attempt (op. cit. 140) to establish a general rule that the celebration of the Olympic festival alternated regularly between July and August in such a way that the uneven numbers in the series were always held in July and the even numbers in August, from which he concluded that as the festival of 480 was the 75th it must have been held in July. The evidence cited by Beloch is not sufficiently comprehensive to prove his rule; moreover, his earliest example (apart from 480) is the Olympia of 428, and there is always the possibility that the Eleian calendar had been overhauled between 480 and 428 and that a regular cycle was not introduced until some time after 480. Nor can Herodotus' reference to μέσον θέρος in viii. 12. 1 be pressed to exclude a date near the end of August for the battles at Thermopylai; when Herodotus wrote this he was not necessarily thinking of the definition of midsummer given by Hesiod (*Erga* 663 f.) as the fifty days after the summer solstice.

Labarbe has claimed (*B.C.H.* lxxviii, 1954, 1–21) that the fighting at Thermopylai can be precisely dated by the evidence of a chapter in Polyainos (i. 32). The chapter, headed ΛΕΩΝΙΔΑΣ, contains three sections, the first of which clearly refers to Thermopylai. The third, which describes a nocturnal raid by Leonidas on the territory of an unnamed city, does not correspond to anything in Herodotus and cannot be fitted into the framework of his narrative without violence; it might nevertheless be derived from a rhetorical account of the campaign which embellished the tradition with such incidents, like the story (Diod. xi. 10) of Leonidas' attack on the Persian camp during the night before the final battle. But there is another possibility, that the third item may be concerned with a different Leonidas, the one who ruled at Sparta in the third century as Leonidas II (no. 3 in *R.-E.* xii. 2018 f.) and if this is correct the middle item may also refer to Leonidas II; it is to be noted that Melber, who edited the Teubner text of Polyainos, denied that either of the last two items had anything to do with Leonidas I (cf. Labarbe, 2). Hence the relevant section can only be judged on its own merits, and to estimate these at their true value it is necessary to quote the passage in full: Λεωνίδας μάχην συνάπτειν μέλλων ὁρῶν νεφέλας χειμερίους ἁλιζομένας πρὸς τοὺς ἡγεμόνας ἔφη ὡς οὐ χρὴ θαυμάζειν ἀστραπῶν καὶ βροντῶν γιγνομένων. ἀνάγκη γὰρ αὐτὰ συμβαίνειν, ἄστρου κινουμένου. πολλῶν οὖν διοσημειῶν γιγνομένων οἱ μὲν τοῦ Λεωνίδου προϊδόντες τὸ μέλλον θαρροῦντες ἠπείγοντο. οἱ πολέμιοι δὲ ἐκπλαγέντες ἄθυμοι πρὸς τὸν κίνδυνον ἐγένοντο καὶ παρὰ τοῦτο ἡσσήθησαν.

The last word shows that if the incident is to be connected with the command of Leonidas I at Thermopylai it must be dated before the first day of the fighting there (which on Labarbe's view coincided with Day 16 of the Diary; see above, Appendix V), and in consequence the celestial phenomena must be connected with the first storm (Hdt. vii. 188 ff.), the effects of which are presumed to have extended to the neighbourhood of Thermopylai; Labarbe, however, wishes to delay the arrival there of the storm till the dawn of Day 16 (p. 12). Leonidas then explains the phenomena to the generals as natural for the time of the year, ἄστρου κινουμένου. Labarbe equates the ἄστρον as Sirius and interprets κινουμένου as a description of its reappearance after a period of invisibility. As the heliacal rising of Sirius occurred on 30 or 31 July the final battle at Thermopylai must be assigned to 2 or 3 August (14 ff., also the table on p. 20), very near to the date given by Beloch (ii². 2. 48), whose decision in favour of the earlier date for the Olympia of 480 is thus confirmed.

Although Labarbe's conclusion has been accepted by Pritchett (*A.J. Arch.* lxii, 1958, 203 A), the arguments on which it is based are open to many objections. His reconstruction of the Parallel Diary, taken over from his earlier article (*B.C.H.* lxxvi, 1952, 398 and n. 6), is very artificial. His assumption that the second and third sections in Polyainos i. 32 refer, like the first, to Leonidas I and 480 is anything but certain, but even if he is right the account in §§ 2–3 can only be regarded as rhetorical embellishments of the Herodotean narrative. In both sections the description is vague and unconvincing, with no proper names except that of Leonidas himself; even the mysterious star remains anonymous. Moreover, the second section, if referred to the situation in Hdt. vii. 200 ff., is full of improbabilities. It ascribes the tactical offensive to Leonidas, not to the Persians. It claims that the battle was immediately preceded by a violent thunderstorm with heavy clouds, but if there had been such a storm just before the first battle Herodotus' informants could not have failed to mention it. Labarbe himself admits (p. 14) that the ancients did not trace any necessary connexion between stormy weather and the rising of Sirius; he explains the connexion as a happy improvisation by Leonidas! The fundamental weakness in Labarbe's paper is his supposition that Polyainos had access (at first or second hand) to a source for Xerxes' invasion which was eminently original and better documented in its early stages than the historians 'auxquels on recourt d'habitude' (p. 6). If a tradition contemporary with the events had dated the fighting at Thermopylai with astronomical precision, why was this priceless datum ignored by Herodotus and all later writers till Polyainos? Labarbe's hypothesis here is in fact typical of his general attitude to the sources later than Herodotus (see above, p. 24 and n. 5).

Beloch's view that in 480 the last day of the Olympic festival was on 21 July postulates a very long interval between Xerxes' arrival in Attica and the battle of Salamis, for if the Greek defeat at Thermopylai occurred about ten days after the end of the festival the Persian land and sea forces should have reached Attica on 9 August. Herodotus has indeed telescoped to some extent the march of events after their arrival, but he could hardly have done so if the Persian fleet had remained inactive at Phaleron from 9 August to 28 September, the probable date of the battle of Salamis (see below); moreover, it is on general grounds incredible that the Persian high command should have allowed the stalemate to drag on so long. Beloch does what he can to narrow the gap at both ends by moving Salamis forward to 24 September (the earliest possible date compatible with our evidence) and by assuming that Xerxes' advance from Thermopylai to Athens must have taken more than the six days presupposed in Herodotus' narrative (see above, p. 195); even so he cannot allow more than a fortnight for it, and his rather lame conclusion is that 'Xerxes can hardly have entered Athens before the middle of August, or only a few days earlier at most (ii². 2. 51). Busolt (p. 694) accepts the evidence in Herodotus that the Persian fleet reached Phaleron on Day 29 of the Parallel Diary (see above, p. 193), nine days after the fall of Thermopylai, but his assumption that the army, starting from Thermopylai on Day 23, spent nine or ten days on the march to Athens (694, n. 7) is inconsistent with his conclusion that the army and the fleet reached Attica about the same time.

Beloch's date for Salamis is derived from the statement made by Plutarch in his *Life of Camillus* (19. 6) that the Athenians were victorious at Salamis about Boedromion 20, which is equated by Beloch (ii². 2. 47 f.; see below) with 24 September 480; he explains the date Mounychion 16 given by Plutarch in two other passages (*Lysandros* 15. 1 and *de gloria Ath.* 7 [*Moralia* 349 F]) as that on which the victory was annually commemorated, the festival of Artemis Mounychia (so also Busolt, 703, n. 3). But if Boedromion 20 was not the date of the commemoration, how did Plutarch's source discover that it was the date of the battle? It is now known from an inscription of about A.D. 220 (*I.G.* ii². 1078 = *S.I.G³.* 885) that the great procession in honour of Iacchos from Athens to Eleusis was on Boedromion 19th, not on the 20th, as was once supposed (e.g. by HW 257) on the evidence of such passages as Plut. *Phokion* 28. 2 (for the modern explanation, derived apparently from A. Mommsen, cf. Busolt, 359 and n. 2, and Deubner, *Attische Feste*, 72 and n. 7, also Hopfner in *R.-E.* xvi. 1228). The vision seen by the Athenian exile Dikaios near Eleusis on the anniversary of the procession (Hdt. viii. 65, especially § 4), although its place in the course of events is not precisely fixed by Herodotus, might be assumed by a careless reader to have occurred on the day before the battle. There was, however, a variant which dated the battle, and with it the vision, to the anniversary of the procession (Polyainos iii. 11. 2), and this was the version followed by Plutarch in his *Life of Themistokles* (15. 1). The existence of these two versions may explain why Plutarch in his Camillus dated the battle *about* the 20th (περὶ τὰς εἰκάδας) of Boedromion. Anyhow, it is unlikely that this date represents anything more than a hasty inference from the story in Hdt. viii. 65. Busolt argues (704, end of long n. 3 on 703 f., followed by Meyer, 392 n. and HW 256) that the battle cannot have been much earlier than the eclipse of 2 October 480, on the ground that the decision of Kleombrotos to take the offensive, a decision abandoned after the eclipse (ix. 10. 3), is only intelligible at a time when the Persian evacuation of Attica (a few days after the battle; viii. 113. 1) had already begun; hence Busolt dates the battle to 27 or 28 September, with a preference for the latter date (702, n. 2).

It is difficult to believe that the Persians can have remained inactive in Attica for even the minimum period required by Beloch's scheme, practically six weeks (14 August–23 September) and preference must therefore be given to a chronology based on the later

date for the Olympia (cf. Busolt, especially 673 f., n. 9, and also
Munro in *C.A.H.* iv. 300, n. 1). If the Olympia ended on 19 August,
the last battle at Thermopylai was presumably not later than 29
August, and as the date of this battle corresponds to the twentieth
day of the Parallel Diary (see above, Appendix V), the first day of
the Diary, on which Xerxes set out from Therma southwards (vii.
183. 2), cannot be later than 10 August. This movement seems to
have been preceded by a pause of uncertain duration throughout
which the Persian fleet and part of the army remained inactive at
Therma (so Beloch, 52 correctly infers from the narrative in vii.
127–31), while Persian advanced troops apparently moved up to the
mountains which separate Macedonia from Thessaly (vii. 131);
the approach of these troops to the northern frontier of Thessaly
may have been the subject of the report brought to the Greeks at the
Isthmus that 'the Persian was in Pieria' (vii. 177), a report which
decided them to send the army and the fleet northwards without
delay.

If the arrival of the Persian navy (and consequently of the Persian
army also) in Attica was nine days after the break-through at Thermopylai, the date of their arrival, Day 29 of the Diary, must be not
later than 7 September 480. Herodotus in viii. 51. 1 says that they
arrived in Attica three months after they had crossed the Hellespont,
and though this estimate may be only a rough approximation, the
Persians may be assumed to have begun their march from the
Hellespont between 7 June and 14 June. In this context Herodotus
allows a month for their crossing of the Hellespont; this is more
probable than his earlier statement (vii. 56. 1) that they completed
the crossing in seven days and seven nights. On Beloch's calculation
(ii[2]. 2. 52) that they spent twenty days on the march from Sardis to
the Hellespont, they must have started from Sardis towards the end
of April 480 (ἅμα τῷ ἔαρι; vii. 37. 1). The expedition of the patriotic
Greeks to Tempe was made 'when the king was about to cross from
Asia into Europe and was already at Abydos' (vii. 174); it must
therefore be dated to the first half of May, perhaps as much as two
and a half months before the Persians reached Therma (see above,
p. 103).

Events in the campaign of 479 cannot be dated with such precision
from the evidence contained in Herodotus. Plutarch, indeed, provides exact dates for Plataia and Mykale, but his date for Mykale,
Boedromion 3 (*Camillus* 19. 5) is simply identical with the date given by
him in the same context (and also in *Moralia* 349 F) for the battle of
Plataia, and takes for granted the truth of the tradition (Hdt. ix. 101.
2) that the two battles were fought on the same day. In his *Aristeides* (19. 8) Plutarch says that Plataia was fought on Boedromion 4,

on the fourth day from the end (τετράδι φθίνοντος) of the Boiotian month Panemos, and adds that this day (i.e. Panemos 26 or
27) is the day on which the Greek synhedrion still meets in Plataia
and the Plataians offer sacrifices to Zeus Eleutherios for the victory.
He ends with the comment that the discrepancy between the two
calendars need cause no surprise, as even in his own time the be-
ginnings and ends of months varied in different states. That this was
true in the fifth century is proved by some passages in Thucydides,
which show that in the Athenian year 424/423 the Attic month
Elaphebolion was two days behind the corresponding lunar month
in Sparta (iv. 118. 12 and 119. 1) whereas in 422/421 it was two
days in front (v. 19. 1). These passages have been discussed by
Gomme (*Thucydides*, iii. 713 f.), who cites the evidence of Aristophanes (*Clouds* 607–26) that in 424/423 the Athenian calendar was
out of step with the moon. To explain the discrepancies between the
Athenian and Spartan calendars he suggests (p. 714) that 'exact
calculation of the time of the new moon was perhaps not attainable
in the fifth century' and that 'visual observation was fallible and
depended on the weather'.

These considerations are unfavourable to Busolt's tacit assumption that an Attic month began on the day after the astronomical
new moon, and that as this fell on 2 September in 480 Boedromion
therefore began on the 3rd and Boedromion 20 coincided with
22 September (703 f., n. 3; cf. Obst, 165). Beloch maintains with
greater probability (ii². 2. 48) than an Attic month did not begin
until the day after the first evening on which the new moon was
visible, and that as the new moon of 2 September would not be
visible until the evening of the 4th, Boedromion 20 must have
coincided in 480 with 24 September. By the same calculation he
equates Boedromion 3 in the Athenian year 479/478 with 26 or 27
August 479 (op. cit. 53), but he points out, as others have done, that
the date of the commemoration was not necessarily identical with
the date of the battle.

Whatever may be the explanation of Plutarch's divergent Attic
dates (Boedromion 3 and 4) for the battle, the gap between the Attic
and the Boiotian date in his *Aristeides* (19. 8), at least seven days,
seems too large, even when due allowance has been made for the
vagaries of Greek lunar calendars, to permit the supposition that the
two dates coincided in 479, and the obvious inference is that in
Plataia the annual commemoration of the victory was a few days
earlier than in Athens (cf. HW 331). Panemos (or Panamos), a
summer month in several Greek calendars, fell in the Boiotian calendar in August/September (Ziehen in *R.-E.* xviii. 3. 585), and is
accordingly equated by Plutarch (*Camillus* 19. 8) with the Attic

Metageitnion. Boeckh at one time dated the battle to Panamos (Metageitnion) 26, which he equated with 19 September 479 (see Macan, ii. 347, n. 4), but Metageitnion could not have fallen so late in 479 unless there had been intercalation in the previous winter, and anyhow Plataia cannot have been fought so near the autumn equinox. Boeckh later abandoned this view (cf. Busolt, 725 f., n. 4) and it is curious that it should have been revived by Meyer (413 n.). Even 27 August 479, the date given for the battle by Munro, is too late in the month, as Munro himself half admits (*C.A.H.* iv. 339 f.; cf. 300, end of n. 1). The only safe inference from the dates in Plutarch is that the battle must have been fought in the Boiotian year which was roughly identical with 479 B.C. (see above, p. 449) on or before Panamos 26 (or 27). As the Plataian commemoration, if later than the battle, was probably not much later, Plutarch's evidence points to a date between 1 August and 20 August for the battle.

The chronological indications in Herodotus are inconclusive. In ix. 3. 2 he says ἡ δὲ βασιλέος αἵρεσις ἐς τὴν ὑστέρην τὴν Μαρδονίου ἐπιστρατηίην δεκάμηνος ἐγένετο. This statement can be interpreted in various ways (cf. Macan, ii. 346 f.), but it is a reasonable hypothesis that the ten months are reckoned inclusively and are months of the Athenian calendar; hence if Xerxes' capture of Athens is correctly dated to early Boedromion in the archonship of Kalliades (480/479) the capture by Mardonios must be assigned to Skirophorion of the same year (late May or early June 479). Beloch reaches the same conclusion, although his date for Xerxes' capture of Athens is a month earlier than Busolt's; his language suggests (ii². 2. 52) that he reckons the ten months exclusively. Mardonios may, indeed, have planned his invasion of Attica to coincide with the time of the corn harvest, but Beloch was wrong in his attempt to confirm this assumption by the evidence of viii. 142. 3, for the remark made there to the Athenians by the Spartan envoys, 'you have already been deprived of two harvests' (καρπῶν ἐστερήθητε διξῶν ἤδη), is a notorious crux. The speech in which it occurs is supposed to be delivered not later than the end of April 479, and the grain harvest of 480 must have been garnered by the Athenians before the evacuation (so Powell, edition, 153; his suggestion that the grain was still in the granaries and was destroyed by the Persians when they invaded Attica is improbable. This particular difficulty is ignored by Macan and HW in their notes on the passage).

Busolt and Beloch both cite Herodotus' statement that the Athenian envoys, sent off in haste to Sparta when Mardonios in his advance had reached Boiotia, found the Spartans celebrating the Hyakinthia (ix. 6 and 7. 1; cf. HW 288 f.). The evidence that they collected indicated that this festival normally took place before mid-summer, but all Greek festivals (including the Isthmia, which in 390 certainly preceded the Hyakinthia; cf. Xen. *Hell*. iv. 5. 1–11) varied within a month or so according to the condition of the particular local calendar which fixed their recurrence, and if Beloch is right in his belief (i². 2. 147) that the Spartan month Hyakinthios was the month in which the Hyakinthia were held, the assertion of Hesychios that this festival was held in the month Hekatombeus (see above, p. 283 and n. 4) must be derived from a source which equated the date of the festival with Hekatombaion, the first month in the Athenian year (so Beloch, loc. cit., where he practically admits that he is dating the Hyakinthia of 479 from Herodotus, not vice versa).

Herodotus produces a diary for the later stages of the Plataian campaign, but though he is probably to be followed (as against his critics; see above, p. 320) in dating the battle twelve days after the forward movement of the Greeks from their original position on the northern slopes of Kithairon, he nowhere indicates how long they had remained in their first position, or how much time had elapsed between Mardonios' capture of Athens and the final battle. Beloch (ii². 2. 53) estimates the latter at a minimum of two months but thinks it was probably longer. Busolt (725 f., n. 4), observing that the Spartan levy set out ten days after the arrival of the Athenian en-voys (ix. 8. 1 and 11. 1), dates its departure from Sparta about the end of June 479, and allowing a delay of fourteen days for the mobilization of the Peloponnesian contingents at the Isthmus he concludes that the Greek army crossed Kithairon about the middle of July and that the battle was fought early in August (cf. HW 331). There are so many uncertain items in Busolt's calculation that his result can only be regarded as a rough approximation. The battle of Plataia was certainly fought after the beginning of the Athenian year 479/478, when Xanthippos was archon (Diod. xi. 27. 1 and *Marmor Parium* 52), but it may have been nearer to the middle of August than Busolt supposed.

Busolt rejects Herodotus' assertion that Plataia was fought on the same day as Mykale (ix. 100. 2) and assumes that the two battles were separated by an interval of about ten days, Plataia being the earlier (Busolt, 742, n. 2), but his date for Mykale, about the middle of August, may also be the correct date for Plataia. Although Hero-dotus' attitude to the synchronism is complicated by his pious belief in the supernatural 'rumour' (φήμη; see above, p. 258), there is nothing incredible in the synchronism as such. Curious coincidences do occur in history, and the language of Herodotus in ix. 101. 2 indi-cates that if Plataia and Mykale were not fought on the same day they were only separated by a very short interval (so Macan, i. 2.

801 B, though his own date for both, early September, is too late).
Beloch indeed assumes (ii². 2. 54) that the Greeks could not have
taken the offensive at sea until they had been encouraged by news
of the victory at Plataia, but in fact other reasons can be found for
Leotychidas' decision to advance with the fleet from Delos to Samos
(see above, pp. 250 ff.).

That Mykale must have been fought in August 479 and not much
later than the middle of the month is proved by the sequel. After a
discussion on the future of the liberated Greeks of Asia Minor the
leaders of the Greek fleet proceeded to the Hellespont. When they
found the Persian bridges across the strait no longer in position, the
Peloponnesian contingents sailed home, but the Athenians remained
behind, and with the help of some Ionian and Hellespontine Greeks
(Thuc. i. 89. 2) began to besiege Sestos. The siege was already in
progress by the beginning of the Greek autumn (φθινόπωρον,
ix. 117). According to the Hippocratic treatise περὶ διαίτης iii. 1
(Loeb edition of the works of Hippocrates, iv. 368, l. 10) the Greek
summer was the period ἀπὸ πλειάδων μέχρι ἀρκτούρου ἐπιτολῆς;
Busolt (742, n. 2; cf. HW 336 on Hdt. ix. 117) dates the rising of
Arcturus to 18 September, Gomme (*Thucydides*, iii. 707) to about 20
September. Herodotus seems to imply that by then the Athenians
had already spent some time on the siege; hence their decision to
besiege Sestos can hardly be later than the end of August. Beloch
argues (ii². 2. 55) that Sestos must have fallen before the beginning
of winter, because Herodotus ends his account of its fall with the
words καὶ κατὰ τὸ ἔτος τοῦτο οὐδὲν ἔτι πλέον τούτων ἐγένετο (ix. 121),
but this sentence is almost certainly spurious (Macan, i. 2. 828; cf.
Powell, *The History of Herodotus*, 79 f.). Beloch's second argument,
that Sestos must have fallen before the arrival of Artabazos at Byzantion with the survivors of Mardonios' army (ix. 89. 4, probably
about the end of October 479), on the ground that Artabazos must
have made some attempt to relieve Sestos if it was still holding out,
is not decisive. Artabazos may have been anxious to get his beaten
army back to Asia as soon as possible; now that the Persians had
lost control of the sea they could not hope to retain their European
possessions for long. Nevertheless, Herodotus' narrative does not
suggest that the siege was protracted far into the winter, and if
Thucydides thought it was, he was wrong; it is, however, possible
that by his use of ἐπιχειμάσαντες (i. 89. 2) he merely wished to convey
that the siege went on into the beginning of the Thucydidean 'winter'
(cf. Rawlinson in Macan, i. 2. 828 A).

APPENDIX XV

An inscription from Troizen

THE first detailed account of this inscription to appear in England was given in *The Times* for 14 June 1960 in an article by the paper's Athens correspondent. About two months later Mr. Michael H. Jameson, of the University of Pennsylvania, published (in *Hesperia*, xxix, 1960, 198–223) an authoritative text of the inscription, together with an English translation and a detailed commentary, and also a discussion of the date and significance of the new document. These are the only published accounts which I have seen so far, but I have derived much help from discussing the inscription orally and in writing with some ancient-historians in Oxford.

This inscription purports to be a copy of a decree moved by 'Themistokles son of Neokles of the Phrearrian deme' and 'approved by the Council and People' (ll. 2–3). After this preamble the decree consists of five sections; between the second and third of these, and again between the third and the fourth, there is a space left blank on the stone. (*a*) The first section (ll. 4–18) deals with the evacuation of Attica. The city is to be entrusted to the safe-keeping of 'Athena the Queen of Athens' and the other gods, and the free inhabitants of Attica, citizens and resident aliens (i.e. the μέτοικοι), are to remove their wives and children to Troizen, their old men and possessions (possibly including slaves) to Salamis; only the sacred treasurers and the priestesses are to remain behind, guarding on the Acropolis the property of the gods. All the other citizens and metics of military age are to embark on the 200 ships which have been got ready, and to repel the barbarian invader in company with all other patriotic Greeks, including Spartans, Corinthians, and Aiginetans. (*b*) The generals are to proceed next day to the appointment of 200 trierarchs (ll. 18–23), to be chosen from men possessing property (perhaps of a specified value; the reading is uncertain here); they must have legitimate offspring living and must not be over 50 years old. (*c*) There follow (ll. 23–40) very detailed provisions for the allocation to each ship of marines, petty officers, and rowers; the most striking item is that the marines, chosen from men between 20 and 30 years old, are to consist of twenty hoplites (the figure is restored) and four archers to each ship. When the allocation is complete, the Council and the Generals are to offer 'a placatory offering' (Jameson's translation of ἀρεστήριον) to Zeus

Pankrates, Athena, Nike, and Poseidon Asphaleios before manning the ships. (*d*) When the ships are manned, 100 are to proceed to the Euboian Artemision and 100 are to lie off Salamis and the rest of Attica to protect the land (ll. 40–44). In the last section (*e*), which is incomplete (ll. 44–47), it is laid down that in order to ensure the union of all Athenians in face of the enemy 'those who have left the country for the ten-year period' (presumably a euphemism for those exiled in and after 487 under the ostracism law) are to go to Salamis and remain there until the People makes some decision about them.

Jameson (op. cit. 198 f.) dates the inscription to the late fourth century from the letter forms, and as he does not mention any other possibility his dating was presumably approved by the distinguished epigraphists with whom he discussed the document before publication. Some Oxford epigraphists prefer a later date; one of them told me that in his opinion the inscription was not earlier than the second quarter of the third century, and I am now informed that another scholar will before long advocate this dating in print. Jameson himself has called attention to the grounds for believing that the decree was copied from an Athenian original (206 and n. 20). As the inscription is merely a copy of the original document (whatever that document may have been), the precise date does not matter much, as the reasons which prompted the Troizenians to make this copy are unknown. Jameson has suggested (207 ff.) an hypothesis which suits his dating, and doubtless another can be excogitated to suit the later dating, but such speculations can be no more than guesswork. The crucial question raised by this inscription is whether it can safely be regarded as a transcript of a decree proposed by Themistokles in 480 and duly ratified by the Athenian Ekklesia.

A decree of Themistokles providing for the evacuation of Attica, a decree roughly corresponding with the first section of our inscription, is implied by a sentence in Herodotus (vii. 144. 3) and is actually recorded by some of our literary authorities (e.g. Plut. *Them.* 10. 4), but it is not certain whether the ultimate source of these post-Herodotean accounts was literary or epigraphic. A passage in Demosthenes (xix. 303) might be cited to prove that an authentic text of Themistokles' decree was still extant in the middle of the fourth century, for in a meeting of the Ekklesia, apparently in the second half of 348, Aischines is said to have tried to rouse patriotic enthusiasm by reading out 'the decree of Miltiades, the decree of Themistokles, and the oath sworn by the Epheboi in the shrine of Aglauros'. It is, however, necessary to reckon with the possibility that even the version of Themistokles' decree current in 348 was not a faithful copy of the original decree of 480 but a fictitious reconstruction of its text concocted by a fourth-century author.

A well-known example from the fourth century of such a fictitious reconstruction connected with the history of the Persian Wars is the oath alleged to have been sworn by the patriotic Greeks before the battle of Plataia. This oath was condemned as an Athenian forgery by Theopompos (O.C.T., fr. 148 = 167 in Müller, 153 in Jacoby, *F.G.H.* ii в, no. 115). One version of it was quoted in 330 by Lykourgos in the course of his speech against Leokrates (§ 81); it is to be noted that just before (§ 77) he had quoted the oath of the Epheboi. Jameson has observed (207 f.) that in this period members of the anti-Macedonian party were prone to appeal to the glorious memories of the Persian Wars and to cite texts connected with the struggle. The Plataian Oath as it appears in the manuscripts of Lykourgos begins with three clauses, of a type which may have been common form in Greece, pledging the soldiers to do their duty in battle and obey their commanders; they then swear that in the event of victory they will never take part in the destruction of any city included in the present anti-Persian alliance, but that they will tithe (δεκατεύειν) all the states which have sided with the national enemy, and finally that they will not rebuild any of the temples which have been burnt and demolished by the barbarians but leave them in ruins for all time as a memorial of Persian impiety.

Before Lykourgos, Ephoros had given an almost identical version of the Oath in his history (cf. Diod. xi. 29. 3), but more interesting than either is the copy on a stone from Acharnai published in 1932 (cf. Tod, ii, no. 204, and the discussion by L. Robert in *Études épigraphiques et philologiques*, Paris, 1938, 307–16). The stone, dedicated by Dion, priest of Ares and Athena Areia at Acharnai, contains two documents, the oath of the Epheboi and 'the oath sworn by the Athenians when they were about to fight the barbarians'. This version of the oath (ll. 21–46) gives a fuller text of the first three clauses in Lykourgos, specifying the ταξίαρχος (this is the correction suggested for ταξίλοχος by Daux in *Rev. arch.* xvii, 1941, 177) and ἐνωμοτάρχης as officers and referring to the ἡγεμόνες and στρατηγοί. The application of the tithing clause is limited to Thebes alone, whereas in the guarantee to states which have fought on the anti-Persian side in the war Athens, Sparta, and Plataia are mentioned by name, and the guarantee is strengthened by a proviso (ll. 36–39) which, though not recorded by the literary authorities for the oath, can be paralleled from an Amphictyonic oath (Aischines ii. 115); this proviso too may have been modelled on current Greek practice (cf. Daux, op. cit. 180). In the Acharnai copy the concluding clause of the oath, the veto on the rebuilding of the ruined temples, is omitted.

Lykourgos says (§ 80) that the oath was sworn at Plataia just before the battle, while Ephoros puts it a little earlier, at the Isthmos,

after the mobilization of the Greek army there; the obvious objection
to Ephoros' date is that the Athenian contingent did not join the
army till later, at Eleusis (Hdt. ix. 19. 2). There is no place on either
occasion for the alleged oath in Herodotus, and the 'tithing' clause
had already been recorded by him in an earlier context (vii. 132. 2),
where he describes the oath taken by the patriotic Greeks against
the Medizers at a date not precisely fixed in the text (cf. the discussion by Brunt in *Historia*, ii, 1953, 136 f.) but certainly before the
fighting at Thermopylai. The alleged guarantee to the anti-Persian
states contained in the Plataian Oath was not known to Thucydides
when he wrote iii. 57. 2, as pointed out by Rehdantz, whose discussion of the oath in his edition of the *In Leocratem* (Leipzig, 1876)
is still worth reading. Rehdantz also noted that the veto on the rebuilding of the temples is attributed by Isokrates in the *Panegyricus*
(§ 156) to the Ionians alone, and argued that if Isokrates had known
in 380, when he was urging the Greeks to undertake a national war
against Persia, that a similar oath had been sworn by the European
Greeks, he could not have failed to mention it.

On these grounds Rehdantz concluded (p. 173) that the Plataian
Oath, in the form given to it by Lykourgos and Diodoros, was either
a product of the schools of rhetoric (from which it was taken over by
one of the rhetorical historians such as Ephoros) or directly invented
by a fourth-century historian (so also Robert, 315). It is, however,
unlikely that the oath was first concocted by Ephoros himself; he
had studied Herodotus carefully and had duly inserted the Herodotean 'tithing' oath in its proper place (Diod. xi. 3. 3), so that he
was compelled to omit this provision from his version of the Plataian
Oath. There are indications in the Acharnian inscription that the
Oath was composed at a time when Sparta and Athens were again
united against Thebes, as in 479 (cf. Daux, 183); this was the situation during most of the years from 371 to 362. In this decade many
pamphlets, both pro-Spartan and anti-Spartan, were written in
Athens, and perhaps it was the author of one of these who in the
interests of his argument concocted the Plataian Oath. As the date
of the Acharnai inscription cannot be precisely fixed (cf. Robert, 316)
it is uncertain whether Dion got his text of the oath from such a
pamphlet or not. His version is certainly fuller, as far as it goes, than
the other two, and his omission of the clause about the temples may
have been deliberate; similarly, Ephoros and Lykourgos may have
omitted the clause given in ll. 36–39 of Dion's text (and also the
details given in the earlier provisions) in order to formulate the Oath
more concisely. What we have in the three versions of the Oath are
in fact three different excerpts from an original text, which was
certainly a fabrication.

The existence in the second half of the fourth century of one such fraudulent document connected with the Great Persian War undeniably strengthens the case for the view that the decree contained on the stone from Troizen is also a fabrication. Here is an inscription ostensibly connected with Xerxes' invasion which, whatever its precise date, was engraved on this stone in a period when the straightforward narrative of the invasion given in Herodotus had been distorted by the activities of the rhetorical historians. It is therefore a tenable hypothesis that this inscription is not a transcript made from an original text of the year 480 but is derived from a reconstruction fabricated in the fourth century or later. Such contacts as the Troizen inscription has with the literary sources are almost exclusively contacts with the post-Herodotean tradition of the Persian Wars. These contacts seem to be confined to the first eighteen lines of the inscription. Jameson (op. cit. 205) apparently infers from this that 'only the first part of the decree . . . seems to have been generally known', but if the inscription is authentic, why is no reference found in our literary sources to any of the provisions contained in ll. 19–47? Plutarch's wording (*Them.* 10. 4) is very close to the opening of the decree, τὴν μὲν πόλιν παρακαταθέσθαι τῇ Ἀθηνᾷ τῇ Ἀθηνῶν μεδεούσῃ, though in what follows the version of Aelius Aristides (speech XLVI, cited by Jameson, 202) is closer to the decree than Plutarch's. Presumably both Plutarch and Aristides got the text from Ephoros, but where did Ephoros find it? If he had before him the full text of the decree as preserved in the Troizen inscription, why did he make no use of ll. 19–47? On the alternative hypothesis, that the inscription is not authentic, the explanation is simple; the last part of it (from καταστῆσαι in l. 18 to the end) is a reconstruction grafted by the compiler on to that text of the decree which was current in the fourth century (cf. Dem. xix. 303) and must have been reproduced by Ephoros, whose version was copied more or less closely by later writers.

On internal grounds the Troizen inscription cannot be a word-for-word transcript of the decree of 480. Jameson has noted (206 and n. 22) that the patronymic and demotic of the proposer are not found in extant inscriptions from the first half of the fifth century, and his statement (p. 206) that the style throughout is consistent with an early-fifth-century original is unacceptable. The use of πόλις (which in fifth-century inscriptions normally means the Acropolis (cf. Tod, i, index iii) for the city of Athens might be explained as a minor correction for the benefit of fourth-century readers, but the elaborate provisions of ll. 23–35 are hardly credible in the Athens of 480; they are typical rather of the radical democracy, when the Ekklesia had narrowly circumscribed the executive powers of the magistrates, and claimed to dictate their conduct in detail. But the most serious objection to the authenticity of the inscription on grounds of form is the inclusion of five different enactments in a single decree. They are, indeed, all connected in one way or another with the impending invasion, but they constitute a jumble of disparate measures, what the Romans called a *lex satura*. This type of legislation was forbidden at Rome, and no true parallel to this decree can be found in the extant Athenian inscriptions from the fifth century.

As the component parts of the decree are so disparate, it is extremely difficult to believe that they were all voted on and approved in a single session of the Ekklesia. In view of this difficulty it is of crucial importance for those who defend the authenticity of the decree to fix its approximate position in the events of the year 480. Jameson has tackled this problem (203 f.), but his answer to it is unconvincing. The decision of the Greek Probouli to meet the invader at Thermopylai and Artemision is dated by Herodotus just after the failure of the Tempe expedition (vii. 175), therefore soon after the middle of May (see above, p. 453); the implication in Diodoros (xi. 3. 9 and 4. 1) that Xerxes was then at Doriskos is obviously no more than an Ephorean inference from Hdt. vii. 174. The relation between the last section of the decree (ll. 44–47) and the decree for the recall of the exiles carried before the end of the Athenian year 481/480 (cf. *A.P.* 22. 8) is far from clear; the chronological problems raised by the Troizen decree would be less serious if it had been broken off four lines earlier. Finally, Jameson, following a suggestion made by Munro (*J.H.S.* xxii, 1902, 320) has inferred from a passage in Herodotus (viii. 142. 3) that the Athenians must have begun their evacuation of Attica before the corn-harvest was ready, and therefore before mid-June 480.

Herodotus' statement in viii. 142. 3 is beset with difficulties which have already been noticed (see above, p. 455). It was perhaps characteristic of Munro that he should have used this isolated utterance of Herodotus in order to reject his detailed account of the evacuation of Attica, which in his main narrative is plainly dated after the news of the disaster at Thermopylai reached Athens (viii. 40–41). Possibly Ephoros dated the evacuation before the fighting at Thermopylai, as that is the account given by Nepos (*Themistocles* 2. 7–8 and 3. 1), but Ephoros cannot have supposed that the Athenians evacuated Attica before they had gathered in the corn-harvest of 480, at a time when Xerxes was still more than two month's march away from the Attic frontier (Hdt. viii. 51. 1). Anyhow, there can be no compromise on this point between the Herodotean and the later (presumably Ephorean) account; one or other of them must be wrong, and Herodotus' informants, aristocrats and contemporaries,

were surely in a better position to know the facts (on Obst's acceptance of Nepos' version cf. the scathing criticism of Wells, *Studies*,
164). Herodotus clearly indicates two stages, a decision in principle
made on the motion of Themistokles by the Ekklesia to evacuate
Attica if it should be in danger of invasion by the Persian army
rather than risk a battle on land (vii. 144. 3, where ἐπιόντα is significant), and a proclamation, which must have been issued on the
basis of the decree by the magistrates (i.e. the generals), that the
emergency had arisen and that the evacuation must begin at once
(viii. 41). Plutarch has confused the decree, the wording of which he
took from the fourth-century tradition, with the proclamation, and
has consequently post-dated the decree (*Them.* 9. 3–10. 4). His mistake is, however, intelligible if he had before him the version of the
decree contained in ll. 4–18 of the Troizen inscription, for in that
version there is no indication that the decree is a precautionary
measure which is not to come into force until the need arises.

There is a further ground for regarding Jameson's dating of the
decree as too early. In the fourth section (ll. 40–44) it is enacted that
as soon as the fleet is manned half of it is to take up its position at
Artemision. But in fact the Greek fleet did not proceed to Artemision
until after the beginning of August, at least six weeks (and probably
more) after Jameson's date; cf. Hdt. vii. 177 and see above, p. 453.
Why then is it not possible to overcome these difficulties by moving
the passing of the decree to a date near the end of July? The answer
is that Jameson's date for the decree, too early for some of its provisions, is too late for others. If the final section of the decree is
historical it shows that when it was passed the political status of those
who had been ostracized in the last eight years was still undecided;
they are apparently not yet in enjoyment of full political rights. But
Bury has shown (see above, p. 277, and cf. Beloch, ii². 2. 142 f.) that
both Aristeides and Xanthippos were στρατηγοί for the Athenian
year 480/479, and they were presumably elected at the ἀρχαιρεσίαι
held some time before the end of the previous year; it is incredible
that the elections should not have been held by the middle of June
480 if the new year was due to begin about 8 July. Moreover, a
date near the end of July is too late for the clause arranging for the
allocation of crews and marines to the ships of the fleet; even Jameson's date seems improbably late in this respect. The construction of
the new Athenian fleet must have proceeded apace since the spring
of 482, and as this fleet required so many more men than the old,
some measures must have been taken before June 480 to recruit
more marines and rowers and to provide them with some training
at sea. On this ground the clause regulating the appointment of
trierarchs (ll. 18–23) also seems belated. Even if the creation of the

trierarchy was a consequence of Themistokles' navy bill (cf. Hignett, *Athenian Constitution*, 22), the first trierarchs must have been appointed before June 480; were none appointed for the expedition to Tempe, which went by sea to Halos (vii. 173. 1)?

The last section of the decree preserved on the stone (ll. 44–47) ordains that those who have been banished for ten years are to go away (ἀπιέναι) to Salamis and remain there until the People decides on their position. It is difficult to reconcile this clause with our other ancient information about the decree of recall. The author of the *Athenaion Politeia* says (22. 8) that all those who had been ostracized were recalled in the archonship of Hypsichides, usually equated with the Athenian year 481/480. Plutarch (*Aristeides* 8. 1) speaks of a decree recalling 'the exiles', though he wrongly post-dates it to the time 'when Xerxes was advancing on Athens through Thessaly and Boiotia'. That some sort of general amnesty was decreed is proved by the psephism moved after Aigospotamoi by Patrokleides, which expressly refers to the precedent of 480 (Andokides i. 77). Jameson (p. 203) thinks it possible that the proviso in the Troizen decree is not identical with the final amnesty decree, and later concludes (p. 222) that 'the recall of the exiles in our decree was not considered final. It required a further decision of the people, presumably on Salamis, whither, according to Herodotus, Aristeides returned'. Elsewhere he says (p. 205) that knowledge of the amnesty may have been derived (i.e. by those authors who record it) from the final decision of the people (he refers to l. 47 for this) embodied in a specific amnesty decree. These statements need further clarification. Jameson apparently supposes that the return of those who had been ostracized was effected by the final section of the Troizen inscription, but that they were confined to Salamis with their political rights in abeyance until they were restored to their old status by a general amnesty. This reconstruction, of which there is no hint in our other authorities, is incredible in itself. No procedure can be imagined less likely to promote concord (ὁμόνοια) between those who had been ostracized and their political opponents, while if they returned to Attica under a general amnesty which expressly singled them out for separate treatment their resentment would have been even greater. It is more likely that the proviso in ll. 44–47 is unhistorical and that its author took seriously the story told about Aristeides in Hdt. viii. 79.

It is not necessary to say much about the plan contained in ll. 40–44 for Athenian participation in the war at sea. Its divergence from the Herodotean account is evident, and is not to be minimized by the excuse (Jameson, 220) that 'the decree embodies the plan before the event and is not an account of what actually happened'. Kromayer has maintained (in Kromayer–Veith, *Heerwesen*, 149) that the strategy employed by the Greeks in their occupation of the linked positions at Artemision and Thermopylai was *Rückzugsstrategie*, the strategy of retreat, and that their purpose was not to achieve a final decision of the war in these positions but merely to check the enemy advance for a time before retiring to the final defensive positions at Salamis and the Isthmus. So Jameson believes that the battles at Thermopylai and Artemision were intended to be no more than 'delaying operations to give time for the building of the Isthmus wall and the rallying of naval units' (p. 205). But Kromayer's view, which underestimates the defensibility of Thermopylai, is just one more example of the *post hoc ergo propter hoc* fallacy; he assumes that what actually happened was planned beforehand by the Greeks. Even if he was right, the Greeks, who probably had a fair idea of the size of the Persian fleet and could not have anticipated that it would sustain such heavy losses by storm, must have planned to mobilize most of their available ships for the stand at Artemision, as in fact they did.

In connexion with the sections on the fleet two further points may be briefly noted. (1) The decree presupposes (ll. 14 and 41–42) that the Athenian fleet now numbers 200 ships ready for service. No doubt the 200 ships contemplated by Themistokles in his building programme (Hdt. vii. 144. 1) must be taken to include the triremes (whether 50 or 70) that Athens already possessed in 483. But though Labarbe seems to be wrong in his assumption that the 200 were additional to the pre-existing fleet, he is probably right in holding (*Loi navale*, 123) that the Athenians were busy building ships up to the last minute; it has been suggested above (p. 187) that the fifty-three Attic ships which appeared at Artemision after the first battle (viii. 14. 1) arrived late because they could not be got ready in time.

(2) The reading adopted by Jameson in l. 24 gives twenty as the number of hoplite marines on board each ship (in addition to the four archers mentioned in l. 25). As Plutarch says (*Them.* 14. 2) that each Athenian ship at Salamis carried 18 marines, of whom 4 were archers and the rest hoplites, Jameson supposes (p. 216) that 'the initial figure (as planned) for marines was evidently reduced by six per ship after experience at Artemision'. The experience of the Greeks at Artemision, where they had suffered much from the heavy-armed Egyptian marines (Hdt. viii. 17; cf. vii. 89. 3) might have been expected to have the opposite effect. Plutarch's figures are probably worthless, but it is easier to understand how they arose if his ultimate source had spoken of fourteen marines (including four archers), which later became fourteen marines (excluding the four archers). The restoration in l. 24 of εἴκοσιν ἐπὶ τὴν ναῦν is intrinsically less probable than the alternative δέκα ἐφ' ἑκάστην ναῦν, which suits equally well the letters still legible. But if the number of hoplites

given on the Troizen stone really was ten, the inscription cannot be authentic, for the number of hoplite marines on an Athenian trireme in 480 cannot have been as few as ten or even fourteen (see above, p. 52). The four archers may have been taken over from a literary source influenced by Ktesias' report (*Persika*, 26) of Cretan archers in the Athenian fleet at Salamis.

If the above arguments are sound, the main part of the Troizen inscription (from the middle of l. 18 to the end) cannot be a copy of an authentic decree of 480 but must be an ancient forgery, possibly reproduced in good faith by the Troizenians. According to Jameson (p. 223) it is too much to suppose that an antiquarian forger could be responsible for eight points in the inscription, of which he gives a list, but the only one which need cause any difficulty is the epithet Almighty (Παγκρατὴς) given to Zeus in ll. 38–39, and this might have been derived from the annual commemoration of the victory at Salamis, which was probably modelled on the original thanksgiving. It is useless to object that we cannot imagine why any particular items were inserted in the decree if there was no ancient warrant for them; if the inscription is a forgery, the background and motives of the forger must remain unknown. Possibly the last section was designed to explain the curious story in Hdt. viii. 79 (see above). Moreover, the possibilities of fiction open to the rhetorical historians of the fourth century were limitless; Isokrates, for example, with Herodotus' detailed narrative before him, could assert (iv. 90) that the Athenians went to Artemision with only sixty triremes to face the whole Persian fleet, and has found a modern historian to take his assertion seriously (Labarbe in *B.C.H.* lxxvi, 1952, 391 f.).

The first section of the decree (ll. 4–18) might conceivably have been an authentic document used by the forger as the foundation for his reconstruction, but it too contains suspicious elements. If the view maintained above is correct, that the decree of Themistokles implicit in Hdt. vii. 144. 3 was a provisional measure, to be carried out only when an invasion of Attica was imminent, why is there no indication of this on the stone? Surely the original decree must have specified the conditions under which it was to come into operation, and must have empowered the generals to take the appropriate action to implement its provisions when the need arose. Further, the neat dichotomy between the treatment of (a) the women and children, and (b) the old men and the movable possessions, including the removal of the former to Troizen and the latter to Salamis, seems too artificial, and like the fourth-century tradition preserved in Nepos (*Them.* 2. 8) ignores the fact (Hdt. viii. 41. 1) that some of the refugees went to Aigina. Jameson assumes (p. 213) that the κτήματα, removed to Salamis in l. 10, included the slaves, but Herodotus groups together τέκνα τε καὶ οἰκέτας. It is doubtful whether πρεσβύτας (the word is restored in l. 10) could without further explanation be used as an equivalent of the military term πρεσβυτάτους (cf. Thuc. i. 105. 4 and Jameson, 213), the men aged between 50 and 60 who were still liable for garrison duty (Thuc. ii. 13. 7). Finally, although religious enthusiasts might volunteer to stay behind on the Acropolis when the city was abandoned to the enemy, it is unlikely that the People would by decree have imposed on the priests and priestesses the obligation to stay, thereby dooming them to certain death; Jameson later assumes (p. 214) that this provision of the decree was not strictly enforced and that the priestesses were allowed to escape. The frequent echoes from this section of the decree in the post-Herodotean tradition suggest that ll. 4–18 of the Troizen inscription were known to Ephoros. They may therefore be identical with the decree of Themistokles read out by Aischines, but their authenticity is no more guaranteed thereby than is that of the Plataian Oath by the fact that it was read to a Dikasterion by Lykourgos. If the first section of the Troizen inscription is a forgery it may be earlier in origin than the rest, but there is no need to suppose that any part of this inscription is derived from an authentic decree moved by Themistokles.

(The above appendix was written in January 1961. Since it was printed Mr. Sterling Dow has kindly sent me an offprint of a paper contributed by him to *The Classical World* for January 1962 (vol. lv, pp. 105–8), in which he gives a bibliography of all the articles on the Troizen inscription, including Jameson's original publication, which have so far been published, together with a short discussion of each. The conclusion reached by the majority, with which Mr. Dow concurs, is hostile to Jameson's view that the inscription is a copy of a genuine decree of the Athenian people carried in 480.).

SELECT BIBLIOGRAPHY

The works in the following list are, with few exceptions, limited to those which have been mentioned above in the text or in the notes. Those marked with a dagger were not read by the author of this book until his own work was already in the hands of the publishers, but where the views expressed in them differ from his own he has seen no reason to change his opinions.

ADCOCK, F. E. *The Greek and Macedonian Art of War* (Sather Lectures XXX). Berkeley and Los Angeles, 1957.

A Handbook of Greece, i (compiled by the Geographical Section of the Naval Intelligence Division, Naval Staff, Admiralty). London, 1920.

BELOCH, K. J. *Griechische Geschichte²*, ii. 1 and 2. Strassburg, 1914 and 1916.

BÉQUIGNON, Y. 'Recherches archéologiques dans la vallée du Spercheios', *Rev. Arch.*⁶ iv (1934), 14–33.

—— *La Vallée du Spercheios des origines au ivᵉ siècle*. Paris, 1937.

BLAKESLEY, J. W. *Herodotus* (Bibliotheca Classica) i, ii. London, 1854.

BOUCHER, A. 'La Bataille de Platées d'après Hérodote', *Rev. Arch.*⁵ ii (1915), 257–320.

BRUNT, P. A. 'The Hellenic League against Persia', *Historia*, ii (1953), 135–63.

BURN, A. R. 'Thermopylae and Callidromus', *Studies presented to David Moore Robinson*, i. 480–9. St. Louis, 1951.

BURY, J. B. 'The campaign of Artemisium and Thermopylae', *B.S.A. Annual*, ii (1895–6), 83–104.

—— 'Aristides at Salamis', *C.R.* x (1896), 414–18.

BUSOLT, G. *Griechische Geschichte²*, ii. Gotha, 1895.

CASPARI, M. O. B. 'Stray notes on the Persian Wars', *J.H.S.* xxxi (1911), 100–9.

CUSTANCE, R. *War at Sea: Modern Theory and Ancient Practice*. Edinburgh and London, 1919.

DAVISON, J. A. 'The First Greek Triremes', *C.Q.* xli (1947), 18–24.

DELBRÜCK, H. *Geschichte der Kriegskunst. i: Das Altertum³*. Berlin, 1920.

DE SANCTIS, G. *Studi di storia della storiografia greca*. Firenze, 1951.

DIEHL, E. *Anthologia Lyrica Graeca²*, ii. Leipzig, 1942.

DUNCKER, M. *Geschichte des Altertums⁵*, vii. Leipzig, 1882.

EHTÉCHAM, M. *L'Iran sous les Achéménides*. Fribourg, 1946.

GIANNELLI, G. *La spedizione di Serse da Terme a Salamina* (pubblicazioni della università cattolica del sacro cuore). Milano, 1924.

GOMME, A. W. *Essays in Greek History and Literature*. Oxford, 1937.

GOODWIN, W. 'The Battle of Salamis', *Papers of the American School of Classical Studies at Athens*, i (1882–3), 237–62.

†GRANT, J. R. 'Leonidas' Last Stand', *Phoenix*, xv (1961), 14–27.

GROTE, G. *A History of Greece*, iii (8-volume edition). London, 1862.

GRUNDY, G. B. *The Topography of the Battle of Platæa*. London, 1894.

GRUNDY, G. B. *The Great Persian War and its Preliminaries.* London, 1901.
—— *Thucydides and the History of his Age.* London, 1911 (vol. i of the two-volume edition, Oxford, 1948).

†HABICHT, C. 'Falsche Urkunden zur Geschichte Athens im Zeitalter der Perserkriege', *Hermes*, lxxxix (1961), 1–35.

HAMMOND, N. G. L. 'The Battle of Salamis', *J.H.S.* lxxvi (1956), 32–54.
—— *A History of Greece.* Oxford, 1959.

HAUVETTE, A. *Hérodote, historien des guerres médiques.* Paris, 1894.

HENRY, R. *Ctésias.* Brussels, 1947.

HIGNETT, C. *A History of the Athenian Constitution.* Oxford, 1952.

HOW, W. W. 'On the meaning of ΒΑΔΗΝ and ΔΡΟΜΩΙ in Greek Historians of the Fifth Century B.C.', *C.Q.* xiii (1919), 40–42.
—— 'Cornelius Nepos on Marathon and Paros', *J.H.S.* xxxix (1919), 48–61.
—— 'Arms, Tactics, and Strategy in the Persian Wars', *J.H.S.* xliii (1923), 117–132 [reprinted in How and Wells², ii. 397–414].
—— and WELLS, J. *A Commentary on Herodotus².* Oxford, 1928 (corrected impression, with additions, of the edition of 1912).

HUART, C. *La Perse antique.* Paris, 1925.

JACOBY, F. 'Herodotus (7)' in *R.-E.*, Supplementband ii (1913), 205–520.

JAMESON, M. H. 'A Decree of Themistokles from Troizen', *Hesperia*, xxix (1960), 198–223.

KEIL, J. 'Die Schlacht bei Salamis', *Hermes*, lxxiii (1938), 329–40.

KÖSTER, A. 'Studien zur Geschichte des antiken Seewesens', *Klio*, Beiheft xxxii (1934).

KROMAYER, J. *Antike Schlachtfelder*, ii. Berlin, 1907.
—— (editor). *Antike Schlachtfelder*, iv. Berlin, 1924–31.
—— and VEITH, G. *Schlachten-Atlas zur Antiken Kriegsgeschichte*, iv, Part I. Leipzig, 1926.
—— —— 'Heerwesen und Kriegführung der Griechen und Römer' (iv. 3. ii in Iwan Müller's *Handbuch*). Munich, 1928.

LABARBE, J. 'Chiffres et modes de répartition de la flotte grecque à l'Artemision et à Salamine', *B.C.H.* lxxvi (1952), 384–441.
—— 'Un témoignage capital de Polyen sur la bataille de Thermopyles', *B.C.H.* lxxviii (1954), 1–21.
—— La loi navale de Thémistocle. Paris, 1957.

LEGRAND, PH.-E. *Hérodote, Introduction.* Paris, 1932.
—— *Hérodote, Histoires*, vii, viii, ix. Paris, 1951.

LEO, F. 'Über die Entstehung des delisch-attischen Bundes', *Verhandlungen d.* 32 *Philol. Versammlung*, Wiesbaden, 1877, 60 ff.

LOESCHCKE, G. 'Ephoros-Studien, i: die Schlacht bei Salamis', *Neue Jahrbücher*, cxv (1877), 25–32.

LOLLING, H. G. 'Das Artemision auf Nordeuböa', *Athenische Mittheilungen*, viii (1883), 7–23.
—— 'Die Meerenge von Salamis', *Historische und Philologische Aufsätze Ernst Curtius gewidmet*, 1–10. Berlin, 1884.

MACAN, R. *Herodotus. The Fourth, Fifth, and Sixth Books.* London, 1895.
—— *Herodotus. The Seventh, Eighth, & Ninth Books.* London, 1908.

MACAULAY, G. C. *The History of Herodotus* (translation). London, 1890.

MAURICE, F. 'The Size of the Army of Xerxes in the Invasion of Greece, 480 B.C.', *J.H.S.* l (1930), 210–35.

MEYER, E. *Forschungen zur alten Geschichte.* Halle, 1892 and 1899.

—— *Geschichte des Altertums¹,* iii. 1–417. Stuttgart, 1901 (corresponds with iv. 1–394 in the second edition. Stuttgart, 1939).

MILTNER, F. 'Seewesen' and 'Seekrieg' in *R.-E.,* Supplementband v (1931), 906 ff. and 864 ff.

—— 'Pro Leonida', *Klio,* xxviii (1935), 228–41.

—— 'Des Themistokles Strategie', *Klio,* xxxi (1938), 219–43.

MOMIGLIANO, A. 'The Place of Herodotus in the History of Historiography', *History,* xliii (1958), 1–13.

MUNRO, J. A. R. 'Some Observations on the Persian Wars': '1. The Campaign of Marathon', *J.H.S.* xix (1899), 185–197. '2. The Campaign of Xerxes', *J.H.S.* xxii (1902), 294–332. '3. The Campaign of Plataea', *J.H.S.* xxiv (1904), 144–65.

—— cc. ix and x (pp. 268–346) of *The Cambridge Ancient History,* iv, Cambridge, 1926.

MYRES, J. L. *Herodotus: Father of History.* Oxford, 1953.

NITZSCH, K. W. 'Ueber Herodots Quellen für die Geschichte der Perserkriege', *Rhein. Mus.* xxvii (1872), 226–68.

OBST, E. 'Der Feldzug des Xerxes', *Klio,* Beiheft xii (1914).

OLMSTEAD, A. T. *The History of the Persian Empire.* Chicago, 1948.

POWELL, J. E. *A Lexicon to Herodotus.* Cambridge, 1938.

—— *The History of Herodotus.* Cambridge, 1939.

—— *Herodotus Book VIII.* Cambridge, 1939.

—— *Herodotus* (translation). Oxford, 1949.

PRENTICE, W. K. 'Thermopylae and Artemisium', *T.A.P.A.* li (1920), 5–18.

PRITCHETT, W. KENDRICK. 'New Light on Plataia', *A.J. Arch.* lxi (1957), 9–28.

—— 'New Light on Thermopylai', *A.J. Arch.* lxii (1958), 203–13.

—— 'Towards a Restudy of the Battle of Salamis', *A.J. Arch.* lxiii (1959), 251–62.

RADOS, C. N. *Les guerres médiques: la bataille de Salamine.* Paris, 1915.

SHUCKBURGH, E. S. *Herodotus VIII, IX* (edition in two separate volumes). Cambridge, 1893.

STÄHLIN, F. *Das hellenische Thessalien.* Stuttgart, 1924.

—— 'Thermopylen', in *R.-E.* v A, 2 (1934), 2398–423.

STRASBURGER, H. 'Herodot und das Perikleische Athen', *Historia,* iv (1955), 1–25.

TARN, W. W. 'The Fleet of Xerxes', *J.H.S.* xxviii (1908), 202–233.

—— 'Fleet-speeds: A Reply to Dr. Grundy', *C.R.* xxiii (1909), 184–186.

—— *Hellenistic Military & Naval Developments.* Cambridge, 1930.

TOD, M. N. *A Selection of Greek Historical Inscriptions,* i, ii. Oxford, 1933 and 1948 (2nd edition of vol. i in 1946).

VOLKMANN, H. 'Die Inschriften im Geschichtswerk des Herodot', *Convivium* (*Festgabe für Konrat Ziegler*), 41–65. Stuttgart, 1954.

WACE, A. J. B. 'The Topography of Pelion and Magnesia', *J.H.S.* xxvi (1906), 143–68.

WARDMAN, A. E. 'Tactics and the Tradition of the Persian Wars', *Historia*, viii (1959), 49–60.

WELLS, J. *Studies in Herodotus*. Oxford, 1923.

—— 'Herodotus and Athens', *C.P.* xxiii (1928), 317–31.

WESTLAKE, H. D. 'The Medism of Thessaly', *J.H.S.* lvi (1936), 12–24.

WHATLEY, N. 'Marathon', in *Proceedings of the Hellenic Travellers' Club* (1929), 67–75.

WILHELM, A. 'Zur Topographie der Schlacht bei Salamis', *Wiener S.B.* ccxi (1929), 3–39.

WOODHOUSE, W. J. 'The Greeks at Plataiai', *J.H.S.* xviii (1898), 33–59.

WRIGHT, H. B. *The Campaign of Plataea*. New Haven, 1904.

INDEX